Illusions of Progress

POLITICS AND CULTURE IN MODERN AMERICA

Series Editors: Keisha N. Blain, Margot Canaday,
Matthew Lassiter, Stephen Pitti, Thomas J. Sugrue

Volumes in the series narrate and analyze political and social change in the broadest dimensions from 1865 to the present, including ideas about the ways people have sought and wielded power in the public sphere and the language and institutions of politics at all levels—local, national, and transnational. The series is motivated by a desire to reverse the fragmentation of modern U.S. history and to encourage synthetic perspectives on social movements and the state, on gender, race, and labor, and on intellectual history and popular culture.

ILLUSIONS OF PROGRESS

Business, Poverty, and Liberalism
in the American Century

Brent Cebul

UNIVERSITY OF PENNSYLVANIA PRESS

PHILADELPHIA

Copyright © 2023 University of Pennsylvania Press

All rights reserved. Except for brief quotations used for purposes of review or scholarly citation, none of this book may be reproduced in any form by any means without written permission from the publisher.

Published by
University of Pennsylvania Press
Philadelphia, Pennsylvania 19104-4112
www.upenn.edu/pennpress

Printed in the United States of America on acid-free paper
10 9 8 7 6 5 4 3 2 1

Hardcover ISBN: 9781512823813
eBook ISBN: 9781512823820

A catalogue record for this book is available from the Library of Congress.

For Mom and Dad, Mary-Scott and Randy

How can we be sure, when we hand the gun to our
special servant, that he will not turn it against us?
—Charles E. Merriam, *Prologue to Politics* (1939)

CONTENTS

Introduction. Locating Supply-Side Liberalism — 1

PART I. BUILDING LIBERALISM'S SUPPLY SIDE

1. New Deal Works—for Business — 25
2. "The Best Location in the Nation" — 56
3. Rising Tides — 89
4. Insuring Renewal, Inviting Revolt — 117

PART II. LIBERALISM'S LIMITS

5. Fighting the War on Poverty — 151
6. Making Poverty Pay — 182

PART III. REINVENTING GOVERNMENT

7. Settling Liberalism's Debts — 213
8. Federalism in Crisis — 240
9. Reinventing Democrats — 267

10. Leveraging Poverty	297
Epilogue. The New Democrats and the Idea of the State	329
List of Abbreviations	343
Notes	347
Index	415
Acknowledgments	463

Introduction: Locating Supply-Side Liberalism

In the summer of 1976, Sarah Turner brought pieces of her home's crumbling banister to Washington, D.C. She and one hundred others, each carrying fragments of their deteriorating houses, barricaded themselves in the lobby of the Department of Housing and Urban Development (HUD). From the pieces of their homes, they built a shack. A resident of Cleveland, Ohio's Buckeye neighborhood, Turner was among two thousand activists who traveled to Washington for a series of demonstrations and public hearings. Turner provided for her eight children with domestic work, and under a recent federal program, she was able to purchase her own house. But HUD and the Federal Housing Administration (FHA) failed to ensure the properties were adequately inspected—many were literally falling apart. Faced with overwhelming costs to make them livable, poor and working-class Americans, disproportionately of color, were locked into utterly untenable mortgages. Though HUD set aside funds to support essential home improvements, Turner and her allies called attention to the many ways "community development" subsidies were instead underwriting elite, business-led higher-end commercial and residential developments. In their testimony before Congress and as their makeshift shack in HUD's lobby testified, these citizens pressed the federal government to support affordable, safe housing and redevelopment of poor neighborhoods as much as it did high-end commercial and residential developments.[1]

Battles like these, waged over the distribution and administration of public resources, flared across the 1970s, a decade of seismic fracturing and reformation of American politics and economics.[2] This was a time in which resurgent conservatives, corporate titans, and pro-market intellectuals championed market-oriented policies and called for hollowing out and eliminating liberal programs intended to insulate citizens from the market's vagaries and

Figure 1. Sarah Turner protests business's control of federal community development funds, June 15, 1976. *The Plain Dealer*. All rights reserved. Reprinted/used with permission.

depredations.³ Indeed, at the very moment protesters barricaded themselves in HUD's lobby, President Gerald Ford's administration was inviting local chambers of commerce—the same business elites whose command of antipoverty and development subsidies activists protested—to carry out commercial versions of "community development."⁴ Several weeks after Sarah Turner traveled to Washington, Ford's HUD secretary traveled to Cleveland, where she underscored for business leaders the kinds of partnerships they sought: "this nation's private sector and this nation's government constitute an insoluble partnership—and verifies the proposition . . . that the Federal government, working through the private sector, can have a vital role in both housing and the economy." In emphasizing the administrative authority of elite-led public-private partnerships, community development and antipoverty programs became an early battleground in conservative efforts, as Ford administration officials put it, to roll back the "ponderous federal red tape, bureaucracy, and lack of flexibility" built up over four decades of liberal governance.⁵ The New Deal "order," as scholars have described the configuration of governance and rights that liberals began constructing in the 1930s, developed unprecedentedly vigorous federal protections for individuals and families—guaranteeing labor's right to organize, delivering generous subsidies for housing, higher education, and secure retirements. The new age, then, would be one of public-private partnerships, privatization, deregulation, and devolution. For many scholars and journalists, these emergent practices signified an epochal breakpoint—the transition to a neoliberal age.⁶

To assert such a sharp break between seemingly distinct "orders" of governance, however, would be to miss the ways in which the assumptions, policy tools, and practices of the new era depended upon, reformulated, and evolved from the old. As this book argues, market-oriented approaches to social problems, public-private partnerships, financialized and fiscally frugal governance, all often held up as symbols of neoliberalism, were deeply embedded in New Deal and midcentury practices of governance. By 1976, local clashes over the private sector's role in administering *liberal* initiatives had been decades in the making. By then, those public-private, federal-local practices were being reframed and redeployed as checks not only on multiracial insurgents such as Sarah Turner but on the liberal state more broadly—and not only by conservatives but also by a rising generation of liberals. Less a sharp historical breakpoint, then, what community activists confronted in Washington, D.C., in 1976 was rather an historical hinge. Battles with the Ford administration certainly augured a more austere social contract in the making. But, as this book argues, many of that social contract's terms were first articulated in liberalism's public-private approaches to urban, economic, fiscal, and racial governance.

* * *

By tracing the emergence and proliferation of local-national, public-private governance back to the New Deal, *Illusions of Progress* recovers a history of domestic market development initiatives in which seemingly oppositional forces—the interests of liberals and business, the public and private sectors, and the local and national—proved, in practice, to be highly complementary. Beginning in the 1930s with New Deal works programs, liberals regularly empowered local political and business elites to administer an evolving array of federal initiatives. For liberals, localism, market creation, public-private partnerships, and publicly secured financing routed through federalism, chambers of commerce, real estate interests, bankers, developers, and bond markets, all of which were hallmarks of the New Deal's public works and housing agendas, promised to meet the crisis of the Great Depression and deliver an expanding range of economic and social goods. And they promised to do so without creating overly centralized state authority or durable direct expenditures.

This worldview, which this book calls "supply-side liberalism," was born in the late New Deal, when liberals situated targeted public investments in and insurance for commercial, industrial, and residential development as wellsprings of virtuous cycles of economic growth and expanding tax revenues that might also underwrite a broader progressive social agenda. These commitments characterized not only the New Deal's Works Progress Administration (WPA) and the economic planning proposals of the National Resources Planning Board (NRPB) but, following World War II, the expansive economic and social visions of the Federal Housing Administration and urban renewal. By the late 1950s, in the wake of the McCarthyite assault on the left and as Cold War anticommunism crescendoed, many supply-side liberals had even come to believe that publicly structured, business-administered developmental partnerships, credit and security instruments, and debt markets might, in John F. Kennedy's famous phrase, create "a rising tide [that] lifts all the boats."[7] Kennedy, in fact, borrowed his phrase from a New England business and civic association.[8] Far from simply the product of macroeconomic, Keynesian fiscal policy, frequently dubbed "growth liberalism," liberals' rising tide rested upon a vast but often submerged flow of targeted, localized, and structural interventions in markets.[9] Yet, by binding national visions of social progress to the local interests of capital—that is, by endowing white business elites and fiscally precarious subnational governments with broad discretion over the shape and uses of significant federal resources—supply-side liberals very often entrenched racial inequalities of democratic power and economic opportunity they imagined their policies solving.

By the mid-1960s, the illusory nature of these solutions for poverty and racial or social inequalities was increasingly clear. For a moment, progressive policy activists within Lyndon Johnson's War on Poverty sought to empower impoverished and racially marginalized citizens to administer their own federal community development and antipoverty programs. They would not simply make poverty survivable, as much of liberal antipoverty initiatives had previously intended; they would transcend it through an ethic of "self-help." A vast ecosystem of civic associations surged forth—churches, civil rights organizations, welfare rights groups, housing advocates, and community activists—undertaking economic development plans, staffing new social service and youth centers, pursuing home improvement initiatives, and starting jobs training programs.[10] The War on Poverty's famous mandate to ensure the "maximum feasible participation" of poor people ratified decades of African American grassroots organizing that sought not simply electoral enfranchisement or racial desegregation but, as this book terms it, *administrative enfranchisement* within the many federal-local programs and public-private partnerships whose white, elite leadership so often exacerbated inequalities in marginalized communities.

For those local elites, meanwhile, the prospect of poor and minority citizens administering their own programs—that is, exercising state power—was too much to bear. Faced with blowback from key constituencies including mayors, businesspeople, and members of Congress, Lyndon Johnson himself moved quickly to claw back maximum feasible participation mandates by bringing local private-sector elites back in, a process completed by the Nixon and Ford administrations' New Federalism reforms. By 1976, this brief window of opportunity had slammed shut. Federal community development funds were, once again, underwriting local elites' development agendas to the detriment of poor communities.

The seeming intractability of neoliberal policy tools and political consensus, then, owes much to the institutional arrangements, partnerships, and political-economic and political-cultural logics of liberalism's supply side, which had positioned local business elites as effective social actors, administrators, and civic leaders since the 1930s. By the tumultuous 1970s, four decades of liberal economic-qua-social governance had taught those businesspeople to frame their civic activities and profit seeking in precisely these terms. During that decade's economic, political, and fiscal crises, a new generation of Democrats reinvented liberalism's supply side, but they began applying its methods in new realms. Decentralism, public-private partnerships, and market-oriented solutions became plausible ways to reform contested social programs and entitlements, perhaps even offering means to both reinvent government and muzzle multiracial interest groups pushing for meaningful enfranchisement within the Democratic base and American democracy. That citizens like Sarah Turner were relegated to the margins of both eras, however, does not mean that they were the same. Rather, it was in the real but fleeting possibilities of the 1960s and 1970s, in the transitory chance that the New Deal's social promise might meaningfully empower impoverished, minority citizens, that new generations of liberals and conservatives repudiated the old order. With many of its tools they began building something new.

* * *

The concept of supply-side liberalism captures a set of actors, policy relationships, and orientations toward political economy that traditional political-historical categories, most often framed in terms of warring ideologies, have rendered invisible or at least highly improbable.[11] Supply-side liberals included not only economic advisers, such as the New Dealer Alvin Hansen or the New Democrat Robert Reich, but also liberal politicians often presumed to be at opposite ends of the progressive spectrum, including Franklin Roosevelt and Bill Clinton. Supply-side liberalism also describes a coherent orientation toward the political economy that incorporated many business conservatives as partners and administrators. These local business elites, whom this book calls "supply-side state builders," forged robust policy relationships with liberals' supply-side state, often becoming key actors in policy formation and reform. These relationships were bolstered by businesspeople's expansive social and political networks, through which they lobbied for liberal development initiatives even as they fought against and redirected other aspects of liberals' social, racial, or political agendas. These partnerships were also strengthened by business's historical centrality to the American fiscal state, which, at the local level especially, is bound to the vigor and dynamism of markets and market actors.[12] Together, then, supply-side liberals and supply-side state builders constructed many of the achievements and inequalities that defined twentieth-century liberalism.

Illusions of Progress traces key conceptual and structural continuities across liberal economic development initiatives as seemingly distinct as the WPA's subsidized labor programs, midcentury urban renewal, the Appalachian Regional Commission, and Jimmy Carter's Urban Development Action Grants. Across the country, local businesspeople quickly grasped the market-making potential of the New Deal's works agenda and rushed to "sponsor" and administer subsidized labor initiatives.[13] In Cleveland, Ohio, a former railroad executive led the WPA, and he hired "400 to 500 'white collar' unemployed" to plan economically useful projects. WPA labor soon widened and deepened the Cuyahoga River to enable larger ships to bring more of Cleveland's steel and manufactured goods to global markets.[14] In smaller cities like Augusta and Rome, Georgia, the WPA offered "remarkable co-operation" in levee, transportation, and tourism developments. Augusta's chamber members even joked that WPA stood for "We Protect Augusta."[15] In tiny, rural communities, too, like Welasco and Mercedes along the Texas-Mexico border, chambers deployed the WPA to expand an "experiment station" for modernizing citrus agricultural production and processing "along the lines of greatest commercial . . . promise."[16] By the 1960s, many liberals had begun to see targeted forms of market creation—and not simply aggregate growth—"in social terms," as one official put it.[17] Supply-side development initiatives could bring poor and marginalized regions into the mainstream of modern American life without creating costly new individual entitlements or federal bureaucracies. This book thus traces domestic strands of developmental ideologies more often associated with Cold War–era international development and "modernization" programs, many of which also had roots in the New Deal.[18]

At home, supply-side liberals situated market and tax-base creation as fundamental components of a modern social welfare state *and* as pragmatic or defensive alternatives to guaranteeing more fundamental rights, welfare entitlements, or democratic reforms. Their cyclical return to markets and development-qua-social policy reflected a characteristic fiscal frugality, a wariness toward direct federal expenditures when alternatives such as insuring private investments or incentivizing public and private borrowing could limit new budget line items—and thus limit political battles over federal appropriations.[19] This outlook favoring development over direct redistribution also dovetailed with and reinforced the racial and gender priorities of "breadwinner liberalism"—economic growth would create jobs for underemployed men, support family formation, and generate tax revenues that might bolster state and municipal contributions to an expanding range of basic infrastructure and services.[20] Liberals' frequent recourse to development, then, envisioned solutions for poverty that might ultimately reduce the state's fiscal outlays for entitlements like welfare by gradually bringing a broader range of Americans into the submerged and market-oriented system of social security and wages the New Deal first forged for white, male breadwinners.[21]

If New Dealers viewed public private partnerships and decentralism as ways to enhance desperately needed state capacity, however, "New Democrats" came to view those same structures as ways to insulate programs from the mass publics and democratic contestation they believed had begun sinking the party electorally. From the 1970s through the 1990s, as they grappled with government's legitimacy crises and the Reagan administration's devolution, austerity, and pitched, racialized battles over welfare and "special interests," New Democrats reinvented supply-side tools as plausible replacements for and depoliticized versions of welfare entitlements. Tracing the evolution of liberalism's supply side, then, highlights the emergence of durable ideological and structural limits to liberals' social and racial imaginations, in which high-sounding rhetoric on behalf of economic and social progress repeatedly underwrote policies that redistributed resources to private-sector partners, the fruits of which liberals imagined trickling down, precluding more substantive political action or guarantees of social and economic rights, particularly for those at the margins.[22]

By dispersing authority over the administration of significant national capacities to urban governments and their private-sector partners, liberals effectively constructed a *decentralized administrative state*, which ceded crucial questions of policy structure, rules, and enfranchisement to a multitude of governments, authorities, and nonstate partners.[23] The local officials and business elites with whom liberals partnered led governing regimes with a variety of overlapping political tendencies and traditions, liberal and illiberal, progressive and Jim Crow, pluralistic and hierarchical. Indeed, municipalities that had incorporated working-class white ethnics and immigrants often adopted Jim Crow–like practices that circumscribed the citizenship of black, brown, and Asian residents, not despite white working-class incorporation but often because of it.[24] Yet in the most influential accounts of the New Deal's "most profound imperfections," its compromise with racist, undemocratic, or "illiberal political orders," the South and southern Democratic congressmen shoulder much of the blame. In this interpretation, the South was the New Deal's racial "wild card," a political order *external* to liberals' progressive vision and with which liberals were compelled into unprincipled alliance to stave off fascistic challenges to democracy.[25] This view is not so much wrong as incomplete. It overlooks not only northern forms of Jim Crow, but also southwestern agricultural violence, northwestern racial and ethnic exclusions, and the many other ways in which hierarchies of class, race, and ethnicity suffused the local governments and markets whose capacities New Dealers harnessed and enhanced.[26]

These were realities that African Americans grasped at the very moment the New Deal began discharging new forms of power in communities across the country. To be sure, a range of predominantly white, left-labor, and progressive activists challenged liberalism's supply side. They advocated centrally planned wage and price controls; called for decommodifying health care and other social goods; advocated massive programs of public housing; and by the 1960s, even demanded democratizing the state itself.[27] But the most sustained challenges to liberals' decentralized, supply-side state came from African Americans, who bore its disproportionate and compounding costs. Indeed, as early as 1937, the National Association for the Advancement of Colored People (NAACP) argued that "capable Negroes be employed on the board and administrative and supervisory staffs of every department of the Federal Government, and in every locality of the country in which a Federal program is launched and operated for the improvement of life and conditions among the people."[28] In a 1941 letter to the NAACP's Walter White, a black resident of Cleveland described the unprecedented situation he and his neighbors faced. There, he wrote, New Deal works programs, wielded as local redevelopment and tax-boosting initiatives, were underwriting the wholesale clearance of black homes and businesses in a Jim Crow–style "program of segregation of Negroes." These initiatives "thwarted development of economic stability of this group and strike viciously at the fundamental bulwarks of our democratic state."[29] Across the country, the New Deal empowered white elites to use public authority in ways that often amplified preexisting, highly discriminatory, and profitable practices.[30] Full social and economic enfranchisement, many African Americans understood, rested on meaningful inclusion in the local administration of emerging federal policies. If scholars have traced the contours of the "long civil rights movement" focused on securing public accommodation, employment rights, and the franchise, *Illusions of Progress* highlights how the quest for administrative enfranchisement within the decentralized administrative state became a constitutive part of the black freedom movement from the very beginning.[31]

Framing twentieth-century liberalism in terms of its evolving policy relationships and attitudes about government, growth, and fiscal policy also offers a way to synthesize powerful but often episodic accounts of modern liberalism. Field-defining works capture the waxing and waning of New Deal liberalism, emphasizing contingencies inherent in the political and economic enfranchisement of, primarily, working- and middle-class white Americans.[32] These accounts capture the ways in which liberalism as a multiracial political coalition with expanding commitments to progressive governance unraveled as it crashed up against a white homeowner politics it had inadvertently birthed and the unraveling of a corporate-industrial order through which many of its public-private social protections were negotiated.[33] Yet, in terms of capturing certain enduring aspects of liberalism, particularly its blinkered visions of democratic enfranchisement and its ambivalence about the growing state, these accounts can be episodic, yielding syntheses that highlight liberalism's "protean" qualities, its plasticity.[34]

Instead, this book contends that much of twentieth-century liberalism's plasticity derived not merely from contests over its highest social commitments but also, and often especially, from the policy relationships it forged on their behalf— its recourse to market forces, its sensitivity to fiscal limitations, its deference to localism. Far from the centralized behemoth of conservatives' imagination—and in part because liberals shared certain critiques of centralized authority—a core feature of post–New Deal governance has been the "multiplication" of state authority across nested scales of authority, its "discharge" across multiple sectors, and its mutual constitution within financial markets and federalism.[35]

Perhaps the defining characteristic of post–New Deal liberalism, then, was its wariness about the clear exercise of political power, especially for citizens at the margins. At midcentury, a loose consensus formed among liberal politicians, policymakers, and social scientists that, compared to more thoroughly centralized or bureaucratized European states, it was the American state's informality, its federalism, and its regard for the pluralistic interplay of private interests that had prevented fascism or communism from taking hold.[36] In the context of Cold War anticommunism and resurgent conservatism, this reluctance to exercise centralized political power informed liberal preferences: bureaucrats and technocrats had their place, but it was far better to discharge governing authority to imagined sites of community consensus, plural interests, and market actors or to frame instances of aggrandized state power in terms of the Cold War struggle. These preferences, of course, *did* reflect the exercise of momentous forms of political power. But it was of a halting and hesitant sort, optimistic that with the proper public inducements and rudimentary social or legal protections, the markets they made would foster a good society. Ultimately, however, liberals' multiplication of political authority at once amplified local elites' capacities and, for citizens at the margins, mystified access to power within policies often ostensibly meant to benefit them and their communities. The state liberals built was simultaneously robust and porous, large and diffuse, socially and racially aspirational but overwhelmingly dependent upon the interests and outlooks of white elites.

Nor were New Dealers unaware of the racial and ethnic violence and class inequalities that often defined local governance. Instead, they pioneered a characteristic trait of twentieth-century liberalism: the mere fact that local elites were engaging with liberal policies augured a more moderate and progressive future in the offing. As FDR explained his resistance to an anti-lynching bill, "I know the South, and there is arising a new generation of leaders and we've got to be patient."[37] Many New Dealers saw local racism as tolerable relics soon to be relegated to the past. To be sure, for many African Americans, as for many working-class and poor whites, the New Deal was a watershed moment in their sense of citizenship and partisan attachment— discriminatory wage rates in public works jobs were far better than no wages, and public work was far preferable to the racist plundering of Jim Crow markets.[38] Yet it was also the case that locally directed New Deal development programs empowered local elites to exacerbate structural inequalities, and, as the opening chapters of this book argue, underwrote initiatives that reformed and resecured their political and economic positions at a moment when organized labor, poor peoples' movements, and communist-affiliated Unemployed Councils mounted sustained challenges to local hierarchies of power. Even as the New Deal democratized certain public goods and created an unprecedented sense of democratic and economic empowerment for many Americans, liberals made racist and acquisitive structures of local governance and capital integral rather than exceptional, internal rather than external, to the workings of their growing state.

The racial, class, and ethnic exclusions of the entire country, then, which were folded into the growing liberal state, are as essential if not more so than those of the South for grasping the origins of our racially stratified times.[39] These national forms of local exclusion explain how, even without overtly racially discriminatory laws, benefits continued to flow to middle-class and elite white Americans within programs meant to redress inequalities of class and race. So many of today's structural inequalities emerged through precisely these sorts of less overt and therefore more intractable practices of interpenetrated, local-national state and market forces.

* * *

This book centers the perspectives of liberals' partners in their illusions of progress, local white private-sector elites, by excavating the archives of local chambers of commerce and local and regional economic planning associations. These were local chamber professionals, bankers, lawyers, utility officers, distributors, retailers, and real estate developers whose bottom lines were rooted in local soil. Local chamber types have often been stock characters in political and urban histories, generally construed as "Babbitts" or "boosters" who fortuitously captured the frothy overflow of the Keynesian and military-industrial states.[40] An earlier generation of political historians even dismissed their civic joinerism and political-economic activity as antiquated vestiges marginal to modern, vertically integrated, bureaucratic corporations and states.[41]

Yet their civic activities well positioned them to shape the emerging decentralized state. In 1929, the U.S. Chamber of Commerce counted 1,587 dues-paying local chambers that led the way in shaping local governments toward their ends, and there were many more non-dues-paying chambers, boards of trade, and regional business associations. Their capital was more contingent and social but less mobile than industrial titans and corporate elites, whose headquarters and branch plants they worked to recruit. As one contemporary put it, their organizations constituted "the 'commercializing' of civic movements"—their public service derived from "selfish" profit motives as well as a white, paternalistic sense of "true civic loyalty." The 1940s and 1950s were boom decades not only for national government but also for the civic and voluntary associations into which members of the midcentury service and real estate economies flooded.[42]

Rather than view business conservatives' hungry pursuit of public subsidies and market interventions as evidence of ideological incoherence or hypocrisy, this book argues that supply-side state builders asserted increasingly muscular, ideological claims to the "producerist" mantle. Historians associate producerism with nineteenth-century agriculture and labor populism, in which the "producer ethic" legitimized political privileges for those who produce tangible sustenance and wealth, guaranteeing the nation's well-being.[43] Throughout American history, of course, local business elites often considered themselves their communities' paternalistic shepherds—delivering jobs, order, and tax revenues. In the twentieth century, however, nudged along by liberals' faith in the social benefits of economic progress—exemplified in programs designed to create private markets of affordable housing or solve problems of rural poverty—businesspeople came to naturalize massive federal investments along producerist lines. Ivan Allen, the office supply company executive turned mayor of Atlanta, a supply-side state builder par excellence, characterized his city's "benevolent, civic-minded patriarchs" in just such terms: "We were white, Anglo-Saxon, Protestant, Atlantan, business-oriented, nonpolitical, moderate, well-bred, well-educated, pragmatic, and dedicated to the betterment of Atlanta as much as a Boy Scout troop is dedicated to fresh milk and clean air."[44] Nor were these businesspeople simply passive recipients of federal aid. By midcentury, liberals ratified their producerist self-conceptions by soliciting their knowledge and opinions about policy structure and goals. Through their frequent congressional testimony and persistent lobbying, then, supply-side state builders also helped produce liberal development and poverty programs.

Supply-side state builders' producerist partnerships with the state contrasts with the rise of elite national business interests such as the U.S. Chamber of Commerce, the National Association of Manufacturers, and the Liberty

League, which a flourishing literature on political conservatism often frames as intrinsically anti-statist or at least anti-liberal.[45] These more vocal but less numerous nationally oriented actors garnered headlines as they sought to roll back the broader social welfare and regulatory states within which liberals' supply-side agenda was embedded. Supply-side state builders certainly joined national elites in championing "free enterprise," complaining about bureaucracy, or fighting labor laws. But their use of "free market" rhetoric is better understood as a political trope developed as they demanded state support and decried as wasteful subsidies delivered to other regions or business sectors. Local business elites often denigrated—and thus helped obscure and naturalize—the state they built.[46]

Situating local interests of capital at the root end of evolving forms of state power and political-economic policy choices also helps recast and specify the varied processes of neoliberalization. A first wave of scholarship on neoliberalism centered the emergence of an idealized free market and capital accumulation among intellectual and global elites as both the goal of politics and, increasingly, a master metaphor or model for social and political relations.[47] These interpretations, however, lend themselves to the totalizing concept of a "neoliberal order," which risks obscuring or rendering irrelevant the meaningfully different paths a wide variety of actors took toward emphasizing markets and market-oriented methods rather than democratic institutions and processes. In the context of the 1970s' economic crises and, later, Reagan's austerity, many actors—including leftists, community activists, and nonprofit philanthropies—often turned to market-based solutions in order to maintain or revive social goods and programs the state struggled or declined to deliver.[48] When some of these often-desperate market-oriented alternatives bore fruit, however meager, New Democrats made virtues of others' necessities. Specifying these distinct processes of neoliberalization, then, allows us to capture with greater precision various underlying structural, social, and political dynamics associated with the emergence of neoliberalism through democratic governance and, perhaps, to more clearly envision alternative futures.

Indeed, as Reagan's program of devolution slashed or otherwise destabilized liberal development programs, even supply-side state builders, often working in the finance, insurance, and real estate sectors boosted by liberalism's supply side, mobilized to find alternatives to federal aid. Many turned to state and local governments for alternative development subsidies that often rendered subnational budgets more precarious—through tax abatements, accelerating bonded debt loads, direct financing, and even public venture capital pools, in which state and local governments, sometimes using public pension funds, took equity positions in fledgling businesses. In the process, businesspeople learned to describe their businesses, businesslike-methods, and market expansion—and not merely the taxes they produced or the charities they supported—in terms of social responsibility, an emergent strain of business producerism that galled conservative neoliberals such as Milton Friedman.[49] In part, these were defensive stances taken as business faced insurgent claims to state power. But businesspeople also touted their efficacy as social actors, fiscal stewards, and public administrators for historical reasons: four decades of liberal policies had endorsed business producerism, and, in the 1970s, government's legitimation crises further encouraged businesspeople and many Americans to think in such increasingly neoliberalized terms.

* * *

The 1990s' bipartisan vogue for public-private partnerships—think of George H. W. Bush's "a thousand points of light" or Bill Clinton's National Partnership for Reinventing Government—represented a certain culmination and nationalization of *urban* forms of public-private state building stretching back at least to the Progressive Era. That era's associational reforms of municipal governance, often led by local chambers of commerce, provided desperately needed administrative outposts for New Dealers.[50] In the process, urban governments, rarely before targets of or partners in federal programs, became increasingly important fulcrums in the national balance of political power.

As a work of urban history, then, this book emphasizes how the local administrative structure and public-private practices pioneered in the New Deal's works programs set the dominant pattern for twentieth-century urban policy.[51] Liberals' national investments in urban development were generally designed as short bursts to restore municipal fiscal solvency and political autonomy.[52] Subsidies were often routed through private intermediaries, bond markets, and were frequently intended to be self-liquidating (meaning an initiative's returns would retire federal loans or local borrowing). And because liberals sought to avoid costly, durable commitments to city making, their approach to urban problems routinely prioritized market and tax-base creation.

New Deal works programs thus supported vigorous if sometimes ad hoc local efforts to use public resources and planning authority to remake markets, efforts that predated but were supercharged by the New Deal.[53] By empowering urban elites across a wide array of scales and regions and encouraging new economic planning capacities, liberals and supply-side state builders frequently undertook local and regional industrial policies. Such localized structural approaches to sculpting markets have been overshadowed by the New Deal's more overt efforts to restructure markets, particularly through the National Industrial Recovery Act and the National Resources Planning Board. When the NRPB was killed by Congress in 1943, the New Deal, in historian Alan Brinkley's influential phrase, had reached "the end of reform." Political liberalism "assumed its mature and lasting form," focused on macroeconomic, technocratic, Keynesian efforts to boost aggregate consumer demand and purchasing power.[54]

But liberals had not abandoned efforts to use public authority to shape markets— rather, they were often decentralized, routed through municipal governments and credit markets. As the 1937 report *Our Cities: Their Role in the National Economy* declared, "A crucial fork in the road, which promises to be significant in the future course of American government, seems to have been reached."[55] At the very moment New Dealers began championing macroeconomic Keynesianism, many of the same economists, planners, and policymakers had, in the words of the NRPB's Charles Merriam, "discovered the urban communities."[56] Initially, federal-municipal policy relationships had been "incidental"—"developed out of a simple, administrative necessity," a search for capacity.[57] By the fall of 1937, faced with mounting judicial and congressional skepticism toward aggrandized executive branch authority, liberals perceived new approaches to long-standing priorities in tapping into and enhancing existing "local and regional planning machinery."[58] Though scholars have often construed localism and private-sector interests as barriers to state building, these dynamics helped build and legitimize new forms of social and economic state capacity. And, in the context of the pitched anticommunism of the Cold War and resurgent conservatism, rather than push for national, centralized, or truly public programs of housing or industrial policy, liberals recognized in the decentralized supply-side state an "American way" of fostering economic planning, delivering social goods, and stimulating growth.[59]

By centering the dynamics of fiscal federalism—the evolving intergovernmental, fiscal, political, and administrative structure of compound and increasingly crosscutting authorities—*Illusions of Progress* also reveals the impact of federal urban policies on a vastly wider array of urban scales than urban historians have traditionally considered.[60] Beyond New Deal works programs, the federal urban programs featured in this book, including FHA financing of affordable housing, urban renewal, and the Area Redevelopment

Administration, among many others, reached into, shaped, and were shaped by actors not only in larger cities but also in tiny municipalities, developing cities, rural communities, counties, and cooperative public-private regional planning organizations. Put another way, the federal-local "growth coalitions" scholars have identified in larger cities such as Atlanta, Chicago, and Pittsburgh, also formed in smaller, developing municipalities and all had roots in the New Deal.[61] To take the example of urban renewal, a program that formalized local clearance and development initiatives undertaken with New Deal works programs, by the time its federal subsidies ended in 1974, the majority of municipalities that employed the program had populations of fifty thousand or fewer. Between 1962 and 1974, nearly three hundred southern municipalities began renewal projects, nearly half of which had populations under ten thousand. And, as supply-side state builders pulled federal funding into such varied localities, they encountered federal planning guidelines, administrative procedures, and fiscal mandates. Liberals' goal in programs such as the long-lived 701 planning grant, established in the Housing Act of 1954, was to modernize and make competent planning partners of municipal governments. Paired with the fiscal imperative to boost property values, however, another result was the spatial, fiscal, and procedural homogenization of many urban environments, in which places as distinct as Rome, Georgia, and Cleveland, Ohio, came to share modes of organizing the social, political-economic, and built environments. That reorganization also often entailed the wholesale removal of communities of color—indeed, in southern cities of fifty thousand residents or fewer, African Americans composed nearly 60 percent of the more than eighty thousand families displaced, making them nearly five times more likely than their white neighbors to have their homes and communities destroyed in the name of progress.[62]

To capture the structural logics of this flow of resources and priorities up and down the federal system, *Illusions of Progress* traces the articulation of supply-side liberalism's emphasis on stimulating private investments and innovation through contrasting modes of political-economic planning: big city *urban* planning in Cleveland, Ohio, and *regional* planning in Rome, Georgia, and the state's rural counties and small cities.[63] By holding such differing urban scales, regions, and modes of political-economic planning as mutual referents, the book emphasizes the ways in which liberal policies and the logics of fiscal federalism arranged the reorganization and structural convergence of local power dynamics, fiscal practices, and developmental priorities. The book particularly emphasizes the waxing and waning of African

American enfranchisement and local battles over democratic accountability within federal programs and related local fiscal practices.

Though scholars have emphasized how midcentury "growth coalitions" and booster politics moderated the most violent aspects of Jim Crow, shifting our analytical frame to urban governance as a site of decentralized state building and infrastructural violence suggests stark limitations to such "moderation," whether in bigger cities or smaller, rural communities.[64] To insulate their relationships with state power, local business elites learned from one another how to champion highly brokered, Jim Crow–like forms of often-tokenized racial or class inclusion, revealing deeper interregional convergences in terms of narrowing democratic participation and administrative disfranchisement. By the 1970s, local elites had even co-opted and hollowed out the War on Poverty's participatory ethos, managing community "participation" in ways that framed federal subsidies diverted from poor communities as somehow in the best interests of the poor themselves. These dynamics were structural rather than simply regional or ideological, built into and flowing from the fiscal federal local and material forces New Dealers opted to work through rather than reform.[65]

* * *

The book's first part, "Building Liberalism's Supply Side," illuminates the development of New Dealers' supply-side state. By the late 1930s, economists, including Alvin Hansen, increasingly understood the New Deal's public works agenda and even municipal bond markets as essential inducements for private investment, complementing the emerging demand-oriented Keynesian consensus. As developmental problems, New Dealers eyed with concern the northern industrial core and capital-starved, rural, southern, and Appalachian communities; these regions compose this study's local cases. Hansen especially worried that without stimulating private investment and innovation in underdeveloped or stagnant communities, demand-oriented policies alone would fail to stimulate a sustainable recovery, auguring a slide into "secular stagnation."[66]

In large cities such as Cleveland, urban planning dated to the late nineteenth century and, by the Great Depression, was often dominated by well-established business associations, which only selectively borrowed New Deal practices and resources. In smaller, rural communities such as Rome, Georgia, meanwhile, regionalism promised to amplify capital-starved small cities' voices, perhaps even enabling them to surpass the South's cheap county courthouse politics. As Chapter 1 suggests, in Georgia, the New Deal strengthened and modernized this nascent regionalism. By the early 1960s, Jimmy Carter, a young peanut distributor from Plains, Georgia, was inspired by Romans' cooperative public-private planning and development commissions. Carter built his political career through these supply-side planning and development networks, and, as Chapter 3 suggests, Georgia's development commissions also inspired new liberal antipoverty-oriented supply-side state building, most prominently in the Appalachian Regional Commission.

While New Deal planning programs fostered potent regional economic planning in Georgia, many larger, well-established cities were ringed by suburbs and dominated by suburb-residing business elites resistant to regional resource sharing or planning. A manufacturing behemoth, its population of more than nine hundred thousand made Cleveland the fifth most populous city in the country. Cleveland's were not merely local elites: chamber leaders and corporate executives, most of whom were committed Republicans, helmed national business associations such as the U.S. Chamber of Commerce. Their own history of economic strength as well as the city's overall, however, encouraged their complacency about Cleveland's economic base.[67] Most often, they lavished subsidies on legacy industries or pursued clearance and redevelopment schemes intended to jump-start real estate markets, especially, as Chapter 2 suggests, as growing ranks of African Americans were forced to live in increasingly segregated neighborhoods. Cleveland's elites' practices of Jim Crow–style slum clearance and segregated housing, as Chapter 4 explores, were also accelerated by less familiar practices of FHA multifamily mortgage insurance programs for private housing developments on urban renewal sites. The FHA's fiscally and racially conservative practices of denying mortgage insurance for new housing in or near African American or impoverished communities not only led local public officials to pursue larger clearance projects but also stymied efforts to stimulate privately developed, affordable multifamily urban housing.

Overlooking the adaptability, creativity, and political choices of elites in both regions, then, misses important sites of contingency and convergence. Though some scholars have treated the emerging Sunbelt and declining Rustbelt as the almost inevitable result of Keynesian investments, defense spending, and capital's quest for cheap wages and tax subsidies, these accounts risk overdetermining economic and political outcomes by focusing primarily on negative inducements and submerging the political organizing and state building that shaped regional economic and political developments.[68] Historical capital scarcity in small, rural, often southern communities bred a pragmatic willingness to use public capacities to make more significant structural interventions in local markets. For these elites, gains won often seemed provisional. Meanwhile, Cleveland's public-private leadership failed to pursue more structurally interventionist strategies until the 1980s, long past the peak of generous liberal spending. While much differentiated local public-private leadership and planning, these differences often derived less from ideological stances on government's role in shaping markets than in the efficacy and timing of strategies to do so.

The book's second part, "Liberalism's Limits," emphasizes the growing contestation by minority and poor activists over the discrimination, illiberalism, and democratic discontents built into the supply-side state. Whether in the industrial Midwest or the rural, developing South, the efficacy of elites' growth partnerships frequently depended upon their ability to manage or stifle the democratic participation of African Americans and working-class whites. The explosive growth in the 1960s and 1970s of marginalized citizens' movements for "community control," localism, and administrative enfranchisement were thus direct challenges to longer-lived versions of localism nurtured by liberalism's supply side.[69] In Cleveland, African Americans and community activists sought to use War on Poverty subsidies to disrupt suburb-residing elites' use of business-civic associations as a form of remote control over city politics. Though Lyndon Johnson's War on Poverty was the result of the momentary ascendance of "the structuralist critique of growth"—the notion that upping the growth rate had not and would not solve poverty—its collapse was assured as local elites and the Johnson administration moved quickly to suppress marginalized Americans' challenges to local structures of power.[70]

Though Johnson did reassert supply-side state builders' authority, as Chapter 5 emphasizes, the purported overreach and excesses of his War on Poverty and Great Society created room for Republicans such as Richard Nixon to rebrand public-private partnerships as conservative checks on an increasingly unwieldy and wasteful liberal state. Nixon's New Federalism brought the War on Poverty and urban renewal to an end by rolling their funding and developmental mandates into loosely regulated Community Development Block Grants (CDBGs). Framed as a conservative turn, Nixon essentially recreated New Deal federalism and slanted its funding formulas to woo disaffected members and partners of the New Deal coalition—working- and middle-class white suburbanites and businesspeople. But, in an important step toward more neoliberal feints to fighting poverty, the participatory ethos of the War on Poverty retained a curious half-life in New Federalism. Chapter 6 explores how local elites draped a hollow language of "participation" over increasingly sophisticated efforts to manage marginalized communities' consent in using "community development" subsidies to fund growth agendas. It was just such local battles over the uses of CDBGs that sent Sarah Turner to protest in Washington, and it was just such hollowed out and managed forms of "participation" that would become a hallmark of neoliberal democracies.

African Americans were not alone in expressing anger over the undemocratic costs of the supply-side state. In Cleveland, a potent strain of white working-class and white ethnic homeowner politics emerged, triggered by the inflationary impact on their property taxes of elites' municipal-debt-fueled development agendas. In Georgia, meanwhile, by the 1960s and 1970s, kindred working-class white, often rural, politics emerged, protesting the lack of democratic accountability within public-private economic planning and spending. In both regions, especially after the civil rights gains of the 1960s, these white politics were increasingly articulated in majoritarian terms, a racialized claim that "special interests" illegitimately exercised public authority. Describing the desegregation battles of the 1960s and 1970s, scholars dubbed this a politics of "defensive localism" and "reactionary populism."[71] But frustrations with the liberal state emerged earlier and were not only driven by desegregation. The white majoritarian politics that animated Newt Gingrich's Republicans by the 1990s was racially motivated *and* shaped by the unequally shared burdens of liberalism's local-national, public-private partnerships.

Part three, "Reinventing Government," traces the neoliberal reformulation of key practices of and ideas about American governance, many of which were advocated by a rising generation of "New Democrats," including southerners such as Bill Clinton. The legitimation crisis that shook the American state in the 1970s provides essential context for New Democrats' unique process of neoliberalization. Key causes of that legitimation crisis, as Chapters 7 and 8 emphasize, had roots in liberalism's inequitable, competitive, debt-fueled, and combustible public-private structures of fiscal federalism.[72] Younger liberals worried that the federal government had become bureaucratically calcified, overloaded by multiracial interest group demands, and fiscally exhausted. Without recognizing the deeper continuities, New Democrats reinvented the ethos and tools of liberalism's supply side. They developed initiatives to boost the financial sector in the context of high interest rates and conservative investment markets and to stimulate new high-tech, postindustrial sectors in the context of deindustrialization and globalization.

As they appealed to wealthier constituencies and new economic sectors, New Democrats increasingly rejected contentious "interest group" politics and employed supply-side policy tools to *depoliticize* debates over entitlements and social spending.[73] By emphasizing the state's role primarily as catalyzing market delivery of social goods, and by increasingly imagining market-oriented initiatives as ways to reinvent government and democracy, New Democrats sought to drain democratic politics from contentious policies that benefited marginalized citizens.[74] When President Bill Clinton moved to "end welfare as we know it," in its place he offered public-private partnerships, decentralism, and business subsidies—bolstering businesses' producerist self-conceptions with new rounds of supply-side subsidies that replaced an essential social entitlement for the poor.

By then supply-side state builders and New Democrats alike increasingly viewed government spending as "investments" or through the lens of "triage": if resources were increasingly scarce, they should be deployed where returns were likely to be greatest. As municipal governments strained under greater debt loads, devolution, and ever more precarious budgets, an ethos of urban triage abetted disinvestment from impoverished neighborhoods by policy. In order to save struggling cities and rural regions, investing scarce public resources in private-sector developments likely to boost tax yields, or even offering tax abatements to do so, seemed hard but credible choices. Local elites implemented increasingly sophisticated ways of managing poor people's "participation" in new rounds of development projects, incorporating the ethic of participation less to solicit meaningful input than to seek acquiescence in community disinvestment and extraction. As poor and minority citizens were invited to participate in tightly managed simulacra of administrative enfranchisement, their communities, once the target if also the victims of decades of supply-side initiatives, were often simply abandoned.[75]

* * *

The inequitable outcomes of liberalism's supply side were not a foregone conclusion when, in the 1940s, the New Dealer Charles Merriam attached a soaring vision of social and economic rights to an optimistic vision of public and private cooperation.[76] As he put it in 1944 in a series of lectures titled *Public and Private Government*, "lines between 'public' and 'private' are not absolutes ... there are zones of cooperation and cohesion in the common cause and on a common basis." They had the power to carry out the "common good." But could such a system ensure democratic outcomes or guarantee social and economic rights? As Merriam mused in 1939, "How can we be sure, when we hand the gun to our special servant, that he will not turn it against us?"[77]

Writing in 1941, Oberlin political scientist John D. Lewis was more skeptical. He warned of the potential imbalances and inequalities inherent in such a system: "Wealthier, better organized white" interests would be "able to use democratic mechanisms for undemocratic ends, not just in the South, but across the country." Lewis reflected the concerns of a small but prescient group of scholar-activists who urged liberals to reform and democratize the state itself. In his study of the grassroots "participation" central to the Tennessee Valley Authority's legitimacy, Philip Selznick found local elites commandeering unprecedented federal capacities. He underscored the dilemma that defined liberals' public-private, decentralized state: "if such concepts as democracy are to be more than honorific symbols which mobilize opinion, it is essential to make explicit the forces which will operate to qualify and perhaps transform the democratic process."[78]

These critiques, of course, were leveled with far greater urgency by African Americans. From the NAACP's calls in the 1930s to democratize federal administration to Sarah Turner's demands for a more democratic form of community development, black citizens understood that ensuring administrative enfranchisement was essential to guaranteeing their own security and, ultimately, that of all Americans. On such critical questions of democratic structure, however, most liberals demurred, confident in their public-private, local-national illusions of progress.

PART I

Building Liberalism's Supply Side

CHAPTER 1

New Deal Works—for Business

Campaigning in 1932, Franklin Roosevelt attempted to fashion a national political consciousness among Americans he believed shared certain local sympathies. Here was his "forgotten man"—debtors, workers, farmers, certainly, but also local bankers and businesspeople. While Roosevelt's rhetoric increasingly emphasized class divisions, his earliest invocations of the "forgotten man" or "local people" reflected an idealized vision of Americans of diverse classes bound together by ties of community and locality. These ties were threatened by national corporations, financial institutions, and agglomerations of capital—"the money changers"—that extracted local wealth and left local people and their governments destitute. Herbert Hoover's "two billion dollar fund," the Reconstruction Finance Corporation (RFC), FDR charged, was "at the disposal of the big banks, the railroads, and the corporations." The "forgotten man," meanwhile, depended on "his little local bank or local loan company." "Here should be an objective of Government itself," he said, "to provide at least as much assistance to the little fellow"—including "the small banks"—"as it is now giving to the large banks and corporations." Roosevelt stitched together the dashed fortunes of foreclosed-upon farmers and homeowners and the devastation that threatened "Main Street, Broadway, the mills, the mines." "These unhappy times," he explained, "call for the building of plans . . . from the bottom up and not from the top down, that put their faith once more in the forgotten man at the bottom of the economic pyramid."[1]

This idealized image of local democracy was handed up from Progressive Era ideas about elite, managerial expertise and "good government."[2] For progressive reformers, democracy was often less about broad-based electoral or administrative participation than it was checking the worst depredations of industrial capitalism by delivering particular democratic outcomes or public services. Governing in the "public interest" without much direct input from the public was an urban, progressive phenomenon before it became a feature of the New Deal's administrative state, whose architects similarly hoped that "politics could be separated from administration."[3] The watchword for Roosevelt as for his top planners was "cooperation": between public and private interests; between local, state, and national governments; and between local people and local elites, who would lead in the public's interest. This was optimistic stuff indeed.

Not quite a full year into FDR's first term, however, Wyatt Foster, the secretary of Rome, Georgia's chamber of commerce, was fuming. "What I am all 'hot and bothered' about," he wrote to Macon, Georgia's chamber secretary in December 1933, is "that I am given to understand . . . that Rome and Floyd County is being discriminated against in the allotment of jobs." "For a population of 50,000, Floyd County has been allotted 674" Civil Works Administration (CWA) jobs. Meanwhile, "there are counties in Georgia with possibly less than half [our population] that are being allotted 1,000 or more jobs."[4] Foster demanded greater federal investments in Rome, and his frustration reflected an escalating sense of entitlement as he observed regional rivals administering greater levels of federally subsidized labor. Though New Dealers draped the language of cooperation over their emerging programs, their actual administrative structure—based on applications and bureaucratic decision-making—also fostered a great deal of interregional competition and jealousy between and among local elites.

If the CWA was rather disappointing, the Works Progress Administration (WPA) was tailor-made for boosters like Foster. As an internal report on the WPA's operations found, it quickly became routine "for suggestions for local projects" to "come from [sponsoring] civic organizations, private citizens, or WPA officials," many of whom were hired from the private sector.[5] WPA director Harry Hopkins noted that despite never quite ridding itself in national politics of the stink of make-work boondoggling—partially fueled, no doubt, by the sort of regional jealousies Foster expressed—local enthusiasm never waned. "There is a curious thing about these operations," Hopkins wrote in 1936. "Although they are attacked constantly in newspapers . . . workers, public officials and citizens alike exhibit strong pride in them." Hopkins well understood the competitive political dynamics that spurred local elites to charge federal programs with gross waste while simultaneously expressing their own entitlement. The dynamics were mutually reinforcing and, in the context of generous federal spending, tended toward the expansion of state capacities rather than their attenuation. "Derision," Hopkins wrote, "is reserved for projects elsewhere that they have never seen."[6]

While the WPA became the New Deal's primary program for fighting unemployment—at its peak it employed some three million Americans—the roads, sewage systems, airports, public buildings, improved utilities, and economic planning it underwrote were like manna for boosters such as Foster, whose development dreams had always been shovel ready but capital scarce.[7] In smaller, rural communities, often though not exclusively in the South, local chambers historically lacked the capital and political clout to produce the improvements and infrastructure the New Deal promised. Even the Tennessee Valley Authority (TVA), then among conservatives' and national business elites' most hated liberal initiatives, was a boon to smaller-scale businesspeople, who benefited from its cheaper and more reliable electricity as well as its developmental ripple effects.[8]

In Georgia, boosters like Foster had also struggled for decades to secure public investments from the state's reactionary county courthouse political elites, arbiters of the state's racist Democratic machine, committed to cheap labor and even cheaper government.[9] Though the realities of the white, one-party South meant that members of Rome's business elite were certainly tied into this racist system, Foster heralded the emergence of a new generation of businessperson—often in white-collar service sectors, distribution and retail, or real estate development—intent on exploiting the modern possibilities of state power and economic planning. In Rome, those tools also promised boosters the chance to overcome significant geographic constraints. The city was situated at the nexus of two rivers, an advantageous location at its founding in 1834, especially once the Cherokee Indians were forced out in 1838. But its growth as a center for real estate investment and commerce, particularly in Georgia's black belt cotton trade, was blunted by the rivers' frequent flooding. For decades, boosters including Foster, whose tenure as chamber secretary dated to the early 1920s, imagined new levies and a fantastic system of canals linking Rome to world markets via the Gulf of Mexico.

New Deal and wartime projects of state-building, then, flowed not only from the top down, from the supply side ideas of modified Keynesians such as New Deal economist Alvin Hansen, but also up from the dreams of local actors. Working through interregional networks of chambers of commerce defined by spirited competition and a pragmatically forged sense of strategic collaboration, Foster would undertake a sustained project of regionally based federal lobbying. By the 1940s, these regional business alliances augured new formations of political power organized through rural and small city regionalism. Supported by national and state resources, these regional formations would, in the decades to come, rival and ultimately surpass the old, demagogic county courthouse politics. By the end of World War II, Foster and his allies shaped not only New Deal but also significant wartime preparedness and state-level development investments. Never before had parochial strivings taken on such grandiose, nationalistic pretensions or paid such significant political and economic wages. These were wages boosters believed they earned through their hard work and risked capital, their shepherding of federal programs and local communities, all of which suffused their emerging ethos of producerism, which the New Deal and World War II only ratified and inflated.

Though emerging supply-side state builders like Foster sought to surpass the cheap government of the county courthouse machine, they continued to benefit from and enforce Jim Crow, which ensured not only that African Americans—nearly 37 percent of Georgia's population in 1930—were denied the franchise and equal public accommodation, but also that they toiled in poverty, especially as cotton prices plummeted in the pre-Depression years. As New Dealers confronted the social crisis of entrenched southern poverty and "underdevelopment," which Franklin Roosevelt dubbed the "Nation's No. 1 economic problem," their solutions fundamentally elided that poverty's basis in Jim Crow.[10] New Dealers' emerging supply side emphasized developmental over democratic solutions for social and racial crises of poverty. Well-targeted works and infrastructure spending could stimulate private investments and market creation, putting underdeveloped regions on paths to self-sustaining local public and private capital. In liberalism's emerging supply-side sensibility, then, elite-shepherded local economic growth itself would be the cradle of progress—a progressive New South, FDR foretold, would blossom in the rich soil of abundance. But by framing economic growth in socially progressive terms absent democratic reform, New Dealers empowered Jim Crow's local custodians to escape their geographic, infrastructural, and political-economic limitations in ways that often worsened black citizens' economic and social opportunity.

Competing for Capital, Maintaining Jim Crow

In the foothills of the Appalachians, Rome, Georgia, sits at the center of an equilateral triangle, about 110 miles on each side, connecting Atlanta,

Birmingham, and Chattanooga—the ABCs in boosters' argot. In the late nineteenth century, decades of reconstruction and white redemption, Rome developed a diversified base of industry, distribution, and services anchored by textile-mill villages along the city's borders. By 1920, Rome's industrial payroll reached $1 million per month, and even as agricultural prices sagged in the 1920s, particularly for cotton, tenancy rates in Floyd and nearby counties in Georgia and Alabama increased, feeding a growing pool of willing, if often desperate, laborers. By 1930, Floyd County's population had reached 48,000, 17 percent of whom were African Americans, a considerably smaller percentage than their share of the state overall (37 percent).[11]

Shepherding this growth in Rome as in other urbanizing rural cities was its local chamber of commerce. Rome's chamber was established in 1910, joining a burgeoning network of professionalized voluntary businessmen's civic associations who vied for capital, infrastructure, and transportation investments. "A mighty competition between cities is resulting from the growth in influence of commercial organizations in this country," noted the author of a 1915 survey of local chambers of commerce. These associations worked hand in glove with their local governments, and, in smaller cities especially, mayors and city council members were often leading merchants, businesspeople, and chamber leaders. At the turn of the century, more than three thousand local boards of trade or chambers plugged into regional and national networks, of which the U.S. Chamber of Commerce was just one.[12]

In the late 1920s, Wyatt Foster, Rome's chamber secretary, also served as director of the Southern Commercial Secretaries Association (SCSA), an organization of southeastern chamber secretaries and managers formed in Chattanooga in 1908.[13] Foster was born in Rome in 1882. After his father's untimely death, he was raised by family in Alabama, returning to Rome as a young man where he found work as a cashier at Citizens Bank. He was soon recruited to serve as chamber secretary, becoming its full-time executive director. In consultation with a rotating set of presidents and board members from the city's leading businesses, Foster was responsible for organizing and carrying out much of the chamber's work. Throughout his long career as chamber secretary, which stretched well into the 1940s, Foster and his wife, Nita, lived in their downtown home with her three sisters and, later, a niece.[14] Foster was an enthusiastic ringmaster in the world of fraternal business associations, making the SCSA's annual meetings can't-miss affairs—at the peak of Prohibition, one friend recalled the previous year's meeting, when all enjoyed "that gallon jug of yours."[15]

At SCSA meetings and in the pages of its periodical, the *Southern Secretary*, chamber professionals bantered about economic and political developments, including the advantages of different ways of organizing local political bodies.[16] Development and politics went hand in hand, of course, and nowhere more so, as Foster put it in one letter, than in the "small communities" that sent "the majority of those who attend the Southern Association meetings."[17] Competition over resources and capital was the constant theme. One typical boosterish news report crowed that Rome's victory in a regional mineral and agricultural exposition came at the expense of "boastful Birmingham, ambitious Anniston, hopeful Gadsden [all in Alabama], and other pretentious cities and counties" of the region.[18] Even as they competed with one another, however, small-town businesspeople were forging networks that would become significant assets as the New Deal unfolded.[19]

This organizing also reflected a nascent sense of business producerism—the notion that because businesses were essential to thriving communities and because businesspeople risked their capital, they were entitled to special consideration from political authorities. Chamber leaders especially pushed governments to develop electric grids, roads, and sewer systems, which were crucial for water-intensive textile industries relocating across the piedmont South.[20] Given meager public resources and limited capacity to borrow, however, the results were wildly uneven. From 1924 to 1929, just 32 miles of "first class" roads were paved in Floyd County. Some 1,500 miles of "second class roads" were constructed of gravel or chert rock, which easily washed out.[21] Rome's chamber worried regional competitors were leaving them behind as centers for trade and distribution and formed a committee to lobby the state for better treatment, highlighting the Primrose Tapestry Company's complaint about "the condition of the road to their plant."[22] "These people," Foster complained, "have put their own money into this plant . . . and they feel they should have some consideration in the up-keep of the road."[23] This was a public service, they argued, that businesses frankly deserved after risking capital for the betterment of the region.[24] But, raising funds was a perennial obstacle, and, as Foster put it in 1931, "our people" feel the initiative "should be built by State and Federal money."[25] Public support for road building constituted the state's expression of "consideration" for the risks associated with building a business and businesses' role in producing thriving communities.

The Depression seemed to foreclose such opportunities. In November 1929, Romans rejected a bond initiative for regional road improvements. The chamber's plans for Route 1, the "Henry Grady Highway," would have linked

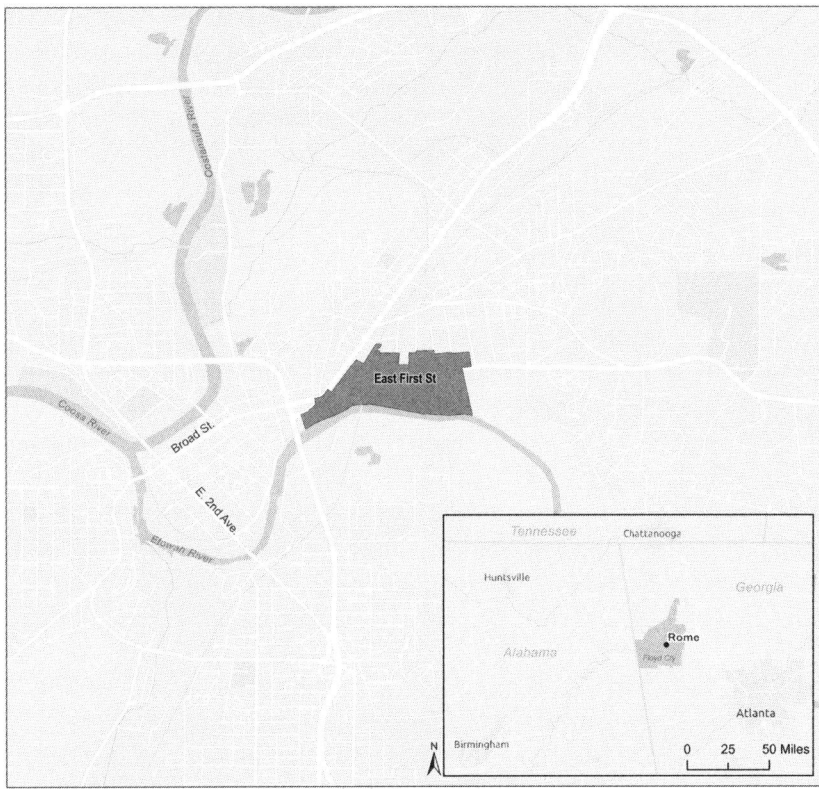

Map 1. Rome, Georgia, East First Street urban renewal project (ca. 1966–74) and environs (inset). Map by Girmaye Misgna and Justin Madron.

Rome with Columbus, 140 miles to the south and connected the city to a new road entering the state from Alabama.[26] The weeds greeting Alabama's road at the Georgia border augured a retreat from economic progress. Boosters were moving from competition over limited public and private capital to almost total scarcity.

If the Great Depression exacerbated regional capital scarcity, two other structural dynamics, one environmental, the other racial, defined more specific, longer-standing barriers to progress. Despite Rome's growth—its population rose from 13,252 in 1920 to nearly 22,000 in 1930—boosters understood that until its geographic limitations were remedied, the city would never be among Georgia's better investments. In the spring especially, melting snow inundated the city as it swept down from the Appalachians in Tennessee, roaring into the Etowah and Oostanaula Rivers that form the Coosa River at Rome. An 1886 freshet, the biggest in the city's history, washed away bridges and houses. Downtown was immersed for days when the Oostanaula crested more than forty feet above flood stage. Similar catastrophic washouts swept through in 1892 and 1916. Property values in East and South Rome remained chronically low, and the fourth ward—"the frog pond"—was essentially impervious to investment.[27]

The neighborhoods most susceptible to inundation, particularly East Rome, were home to the city's segregated black neighborhoods. Five Points, just northeast of Rome's downtown, composed the commercial heart of the community, stretching up Broad Street and out East First Street. In the 1940s, the black population in Floyd County, grew from 8,637 residents (out of 56,141 total) to 9,273 (of 62,899).[28] While black communities did contain pockets of grim poverty—tar-paper homes lacking plumbing or heat—Rome was home to a black middle class and energetic business district. In addition to barbershops and grocery stores, the district featured Graham Robinson's Drug Store, originally built for Dr. Robert Brooks's hospital, which the community called "Brook Haven." Hubert Holland's six-chair barbershop was next door, and his customers often got a trim before heading to Eli McConnell's Billiard Room. The goings-on of the community were covered by a weekly black newspaper, the *Rome Enterprise*, its title betokening community aspirations. Yet, even the "best" African Americans were excluded from Rome's political and civic associations: none were members of the chamber of commerce let alone public officials.[29]

That black residents were segregated in areas prone to flooding reflected white Romans' enforcement of Jim Crow, a racial order that African American residents resisted, enduring threats, violence, and murder. In 1900, black Romans joined others across the state in boycotting the imposition of Jim Crow streetcars.[30] Eight years later, they joined a statewide protest against convict leasing.[31] By 1919, W. T. Atwater, the *Enterprise*'s editor, helped establish a local branch of the NAACP. Faced with organizing and protest, white Romans more tightly policed the use of public space. When automobiles proliferated, the city banned black motorists from downtown streets, granting a lone exception in the case of black physicians. These boundaries were violently enforced when Dr. Brooks's wife, Anita, dared drive their car downtown. Police ripped Anita from her vehicle and arrested her.[32] Black citizens were also lynched. Accused of attempted rape in 1901, Walter Allen was seized from his jail cell by a group of unmasked men. Some four thousand white Romans watched as they hung him from an electric light pole "in the principal portion of the city." If the estimated number is credible, the crowd reflected well over half the city's population.[33] Allen was one of three black man lynched in Rome in 1900 and 1901.[34] Well into the 1930s, Rome's Ku Klux Klan, another sort of civic organization, counted leading businesspeople as members.[35]

Beyond overt acts of racial violence, Jim Crow exacted severe social, economic, and human costs. By 1930, while African Americans composed nearly 40 percent of Georgia's 2.9 million residents, decades of white terrorism, poll taxes, and fraud ensured the vast majority of black Georgians could not exercise the franchise. And, of the state's total taxable wealth ($1.05 billion in 1935), black residents held just 3.5 percent. These disparities shaped nearly every aspect of African American life, from widely divergent pay scales to considerably worse health and mortality rates.[36] As the Great Depression reached Rome, Jim Crow isolated a quarter of the city's disenfranchised population in poverty and on flood-prone property. Undercapitalization characterized much of the local political economy: a large swath of potentially valuable land was among the riskiest for investments; socially, the city's legally and extralegally segregated population lacked its own capital; and the economy as a whole relied upon underpaid black and white labor, which was frequently regional industries' most distinctive form of capital.

Such scarcity, particularly as it worsened in the Depression, presented significant challenges to the legitimacy of business leaders' dominance of local social and political life, particularly when it came to ensuring the paternalistic fealty of the city's increasingly restive white working class. Rome's 1931 Labor Day festivities offer a glimpse of these dynamics. The celebration usually included fireworks and a citywide picnic along the Coosa River.[37] The chamber organized funding, but, in the catastrophic economic climate of 1931, the Labor Day Committee's chairman lamented that their "effort to raise funds for the Labor Day Program was a flop."[38] One leader recommended considering how to address the urgent needs of the "laboring man—many of whom are hungry." Rather than sponsor fireworks displays, he suggested funds be "equitably apportioned between the whites and colored" to "give the hungry unemployed and their families 'a full tummie' with which they can fully enjoy 'Labor Day.'"[39] As opposed to some of the larger cities of the South, which had relatively better-resourced private charitable organizations and public welfare agencies, many rural communities still relied on county almshouses and fleeting voluntary acts like those of Rome's chamber.[40] These traditions were wholly swamped by the Great Depression.

Though a small episode, chamber member's anxiety about "laboring men" presaged more dramatic possibilities for how the Depression and New Deal might undermine southern paternalism.[41] Many white tenant farmers had moved to mill towns and cities like Rome, trading the prospect of autonomy for the relative security of low-wage work. But the Depression's reduced hours, pay, and furloughs made unionization increasingly attractive. By the end of 1933, unions had already formed in Rome and Dalton's peripheral textile mill towns, and the chamber's Labor Day festivities in 1934 occurred amid broad-based labor action that threatened two of the city's largest mills, Tubize Chatillon and Anchor Duck. As labor militancy rippled across the state that fall, the newly elected governor Eugene Talmadge invoked martial law, mobilizing an unprecedentedly large detachment of state troops to arrest strikers and enable mills to reopen.[42] These developments—and Talmadge's break with many white workers who supported him—directly challenged Jim Crow's social and economic compact between whites of different classes. The New Deal, however, would offer local elites new sources of capital, and with them, a new model of different sorts of business-friendly state action. These new alignments would not only bolster chamber types' places in the local social, economic, and racial hierarchy but also enable them to transcend their geographic restraints.

Boosters Greet the Early New Deal

Even prior to Franklin Roosevelt's presidency, Wyatt Foster sought guidance from the U.S. Chamber of Commerce on preparing a Reconstruction Finance Corporation (RFC) loan to provide work relief, and he made similar appeals to RFC officials in Atlanta and Washington.[43] He also reached out to the governor and future senator Richard B. Russell to inquire "what you intend to do, if anything, in securing [relief] funds for Georgia."[44] Under the Hoover administration, however, RFC funding was a risky proposition— federal loans were for "self-liquidating" projects, meaning financing would be repaid through revenues produced by the projects themselves rather than general funds. In smaller communities like Rome, the necessity of producing revenue from new infrastructure projects meant the risks of default were considerable. When, in 1932, Franklin Roosevelt said Hoover's RFC was not for the "forgotten man," small-city boosters like Foster likely nodded at their radios in quiet agreement.

And so, when Roosevelt administration officials proactively reached out to local governments, chambers, and civic organizations, they must have been thrilled. In the New Deal's opening months in 1933, Hugh Johnson, head of the National Recovery Administration, sent telegrams to local chambers, "asking for co-operation." At a chamber meeting, Foster read out Johnson's telegram, and the chamber's board of directors endorsed a "motion that the civic body take the initiative," pledging "to carry forward in every way possible the plans of President Roosevelt . . . for a rapid and complete recovery to prosperity."[45] While many businessmen, including Foster, would soon repudiate the National Recovery Administration's efforts to plan wages and prices, the New Deal's wider cultivation of local elites played out across a number of agencies.[46] Indeed, Foster received a personal letter from the TVA's David Lilienthal, soliciting "criticisms or suggestions concerning" a speech he had given on the "economic development of the South"—a matter, Lilienthal noted, that "concerns you so deeply."[47] Development did deeply concern Foster, and he considered participation in these programs a welcome expansion of his duties as chamber leader.

Johnson's and Lilienthal's missives to Wyatt Foster in his diminutive northwest Georgia city embodied Franklin Roosevelt's vision for New Deal "decentralism." By foregrounding the virtues of partnerships between the federal government and local communities, voluntary organizations, and businesses, Roosevelt depicted the New Deal as a modern version of venerable American traditions of democratic localism. Empowering councils of local or regional elites to determine the uses of work relief programs, of course, also enabled New Dealers to rapidly construct and legitimize new forms of state capacity. This vision was shaped not solely or perhaps even primarily by southern efforts to preserve the political autonomy of the Jim Crow order, but instead by Roosevelt's political pragmatism and long-standing faith in elite-led civic progress.[48] As the president explained to state representatives of the National Emergency Council, composed of cabinet members and directors of each New Deal agency, "You are the great decentralizers." Their work would make manifest the administration's "decentralization" through close coordination with "State and local governments."[49] In his second fireside chat, FDR argued that his initiatives did not augur "Government control." They were "a partnership between Government and farming and industry and transportation, not partnership in profits, for the profits still go to the citizens, but rather a partnership in planning, and a partnership to see that the plans are carried out."[50] For Roosevelt, the New Deal's burgeoning works programs would only succeed when filtered through "local knowledge" and "regional conferences" to ensure "full value ... of the final appropriations authorized in Washington." "Such machinery," he argued, "will give local communities and the nation alike new confidence in the true worth of such expenditure."[51] Works programs, especially, operated through local communities, in whose interests' local elites naturally acted.

Though scholars of the New Deal have not ignored business interests or organizations such as the U.S. Chamber of Commerce, they have missed FDR's appeal to local businesspeople like Foster, who viewed expanded developmental spending quite differently than did their ostensible national spokespersons. The result was that New Deal initiatives exposed fault lines between local business interests and more staunchly conservative national lobbying associations. The TVA and Rural Electrification Administration, for instance, relied upon local, elite administration, while Wendell Willkie, head of the energy trust Commonwealth and Southern (C&S), rode his scathing critiques of the TVA's "socialism" to the 1940 Republican nomination for president. Rural businessmen, meanwhile, viewed the TVA's competitive rates with unvarnished enthusiasm. Indeed, C&S subsidiary Georgia Power's service quality and rates generally favored Atlanta at the expense of rural regions, and frequent black- or brownouts and confounding variations in rates rankled business leaders in smaller communities who sought affordability and predictability above all else.[52] Speaking in Chattanooga, David Lilienthal touted 20–30 percent reductions in energy costs for some local businesses.[53] In light of TVA competition, a firm representing Georgia Power shareholders invited chambers of commerce to comment on the company's public relations.[54] Wyatt Foster noted that "small concerns" believed Georgia Power's "rates are too high" and that TVA competition could benefit the company. If Georgia Power would "establish rates equal to that of the Tennessee Valley Authority," few businesspeople would "advocate municipal ownership or make application to the Authority" to extend into northwest Georgia.[55] The TVA, however, only scratched the surface of potential fissures between local business interests and the wholesale anti–New Deal ideology emerging among national elites. New Deal works programs would expose many more.

Still, local frustration with the unprecedented rollout of new federal programs was almost inevitable. The CWA's program of relief was uneven—indeed, it was rumors about disparate hiring figures on CWA projects that spurred Wyatt Foster to write his irate letter to his colleague in Macon. To lead the Rome-area CWA, state officials appointed Foster's good friend E. Pierce

McGhee, a Rome chamber member, cofounder of Rome's Kiwanis Club, and proprietor of the McGhee Insurance Company. Writing McGhee, Foster was frustrated by reports that elsewhere "the Government is paying for equipment ... on the projects," while McGhee believed Rome would have to cover those costs locally. Irritated by the lack of clarity, Foster appealed to his colleague in Macon to keep him "informed on the subject."[56] Beyond airing bureaucratic frustrations, the urgency of Foster's letter underscores the reality that there was far more need for unemployment relief than the CWA was meeting.[57]

Southern chambers soon met in regional conferences to explore ways to "speed public works" since "approval of projects in the Southeastern territory is proceeding at a rate far behind that of the remainder of the country."[58] Even companies that stridently opposed the TVA were convinced of the value of public works. Georgia Power had a vested interest in economic developments that might boost energy consumption. Concerned that local governments lacked the capacity to apply for federal aid, the company "loaned" employees to assist with applications for and administration of early programs like the CWA.[59] Yet the lack of state and local matching capital was a significant hurdle, and in 1933 Georgia qualified for just 43 projects in 24 of its 159 counties. Many counties declined to apply for projects until, in 1935, the federal contribution for works projects was liberalized. The following summer 188 new projects were approved. Road construction became Georgia's top priority.[60]

In 1935, Franklin Roosevelt signed an executive order establishing the Works Progress Administration to employ greater numbers of workers and at less cost to local governments.[61] The WPA extended the organization and personnel of the Federal Emergency Relief Administration and CWA. It directly employed laborers who sought work through local public welfare agencies and offered more generous federal contributions against local costs. This was especially welcome in states such as Georgia, where the principle of self-liquidation or steep matching requirements—attempts to promote localism and efficiency by requiring local commitments—limited the New Deal's reach. Though the WPA was initially criticized as little more than a "make-work" initiative, local boosters had long backlogs of infrastructural make-work to be done. They eagerly lined up to "sponsor" projects—over the duration of the WPA, local sponsors contributed around 22 percent of total funding—reflecting the kind of decentralized interest in works programs Roosevelt had hoped to harness.[62]

By far Georgia's greatest barrier to federal resources, however, was Governor Eugene Talmadge and the racial demagoguery and federal fear-mongering he mustered to win the support of "the wool-hat boys, the dirt farmers, and the common [white] folk." Talmadge charged FDR with threatening the state's racial and moral order, disparaging federally mandated wage rates and relief that would "add on nearly every Negro of a certain age in the county to this pauper's list," threatening to "centralize all power in Washington."[63] Visiting Rome in 1934, Talmadge warned that white supremacy was in the balance: "It isn't right, it isn't fair, and it isn't honest," he said, to pay "a negro" the same as "good white men and white women" working the same jobs.[64] Talmadge's implacability ultimately led Roosevelt to federalize Georgia's work relief programs.[65] Relief continued to flow into the state, but, over time, the results were stark. In 1930, Georgia had just under 15,000 miles of paved roads; between 1935 and 1943, the state constructed 9,000 miles of new roads. Meanwhile, in neighboring Alabama, Governor Bibb Graves used New Deal resources to construct over 20,000 miles of roads, doubling the state's 1930 total.[66] Talmadge's intransigence ensured that, between 1933 and 1939, Georgia received the second lowest per capita federal spending of any state.[67]

Still, even a trickle of external capital could unleash a flood of optimism among boosters in small, rural cities like Rome. For decades, Foster and his predecessors had imagined new levees and canals that would remedy the city's penchant for flooding and connect it to larger rivers and global ports. Before the New Deal, however, their lobbying had focused on tight-fisted state officials and a fleeting campaign to recruit neighboring chambers to back a larger debt-financed waterway project. In 1936, however, Foster partnered with city commission chairman H. H. Keel, who operated a number of local businesses, to create a city levee committee composed of chamber members and city commissioners. They would seek federal support for a levee to protect the city's growing downtown from the Coosa and Oostanaula Rivers. After meeting with representatives from the Army Corps of Engineers, they drew up proposals for a levee extending two miles between the river and Rome's Second Avenue. After a year of wrangling, during which Foster and Keel secured federal funds for an additional levee on the Etowah, the Army Corps contracted with a construction firm, and, in February 1938, work was begun on the $400,000 project. By the summer of 1938, the company's payroll averaged $75,000 a month, employing as many as two hundred men at a time. Almost all were drawn from Floyd County relief rolls, a boon for the region's economy thanks to workers' restored purchasing power.

The ribbon cutting in February 1939 was made a local holiday, and thousands of Romans attended despite frigid temperatures. Airplanes buzzed overhead as chamber members christened the H. H. Keel Levee.[68] On the newly secured land, WPA laborers built a park and a new Floyd County Hospital, which, the *Rome News-Tribune* reported, consisted of beds for "sixty-five white patients, fifteen colored patients, and fifteen babies."[69] Most significantly, the project was freeing boosters from their environmental shackles.

To be sure, Rome's businesspeople greeted other aspects of the early New Deal with the sort of antagonism expressed by many other business elites. They sought to ensure that National Recovery Administration wage rates applied to as few workers as possible and decried the prospect of new direct federal social entitlements, in each case hoping to maintain the advantages of southern paternalism, Jim Crow, and regional wage imbalances. They also worked with national consultants to stymie labor organizing, blocking challenges to their political and economic authority.[70] That they disparaged parts of the New Deal, however, should not obscure the energy with which they cultivated others. As the journalist W. J. Cash noted in 1941 in *The Mind of the South*, southern elites were never "laggard in . . . denouncing the New Deal in general" even as they "grasped all possible government benefits for themselves."[71] Much more was on the way.

The No. 1 Economic Opportunity

Franklin Roosevelt made frequent trips to his retreat in Warm Springs, Georgia. During these visits, he became particularly sensitive to the region's poverty, which he increasingly believed could never be addressed so long as the South remained dependent upon external capital, public or private. FDR's rationale for federal public works spending was thus evolving from one focused on short-term purchasing power to include supply-side stimulus that could foster long-term regional fiscal independence. Throughout 1937, Roosevelt sought to make southern poverty a national political issue and a source of shame for the region's representatives, especially conservatives who threatened Roosevelt's broader agenda. He beseeched one senator, writing "I know you realize . . . the annual income of workers in the South is so low that they have little purchasing power, little to pay in the way of taxes and that therefore, education and sanitation have greatly suffered in the South."[72] The following spring, he argued that the South's feeble wages amounted to a "feudal system"—it was perhaps even "Fascist." As he put it in Warm Springs, the southern "standard of living is absolutely and totally different from what it is in the prosperous areas of the West or . . . North." Poverty wages and underdevelopment generated mutually reinforcing drag on southern growth, without which the South would never raise the taxes to deliver essential goods such as "better schools, better health, better hospitals, better highways."[73] Without an external shock to its economic system, southern poverty even threatened the sustainability of the nation's economic recovery.

Yet, the primary impediment to southern progress, FDR maintained, eliding Jim Crow entirely, did not stem from local officials' "lack of interest" in solving poverty and underdevelopment. It was due to "lack of money." He explained that "when taxes on [property] values were collected the sum received could not pay for adequate" services. "Public wealth was too low to support" sustained social improvements.[74] Yet even as FDR highlighted regional imbalances, he acceded to southern Democrats' insistence that regional and racial exceptions be carved into policies designed to put a floor under national living standards. Roosevelt's Fair Labor Standards Act (FLSA), which created a national minimum wage, excluded farm and domestic workers, positions held predominantly by African Americans and women. While FDR would attempt to purge intransigent southern Democrats in 1938, by and large he excused such clear discrimination by emphasizing the New Deal's emerging supply-side sensibility. Progress would proceed as far as the economic base and the taxes it yielded—"public wealth"—would allow.

A growing set of New Deal economists and policymakers, among them Alvin Hansen, Leon Keyserling, and John Kenneth Galbraith, nudged along FDR's thinking and helped shape the administration's emerging supply-side orientation. In distinct but complementary ways, these thinkers were coming to believe that Keynesianism, the government-subsidized aggregate purchasing-power strategy for national recovery, would be insufficient to create the kind of private-sector innovation and investments necessary for sustained growth in underdeveloped regions. This was powerfully dramatized in the fall of 1937 when, after a period of rapid economic expansion, industrial production sagged by 33 percent and unemployment spiked. In the months before the so-called "Roosevelt recession," the national economy was surging, and FDR reduced government spending to begin balancing the budget. Washington's declining contribution to public works, private contracts, materials, and purchasing power (from $4.1 billion in 1936 to less than $1 billion in 1937) rippled across industrial and consumer markets.[75] To economists, the sharp recession suggested that New Deal works programs had applied a temporary bandage to a far graver wound: industrial and private investment markets were not yet robust enough to offer sustainable employment, even in well-developed regions.

In his 1938 book *Full Recovery or Stagnation?* Hansen underlined government's growing role not only in stimulating demand but also in structuring the private investments and innovation that might restructure and jump-start a stagnating economy. Born to Danish homesteaders in Viborg, South Dakota, in 1887, Hansen perhaps had a special appreciation for the era's concerns about what the Census Bureau's 1890 statistical "closing" of the American frontier portended for the nation's internal economy—innovation, rather than mere expansion, would become a hallmark of Hansen's work. Hansen earned a bachelor's degree from Yankton College before pursuing a doctorate at the University of Wisconsin, where he absorbed the institutional analysis of John R. Commons and Richard T. Ely. He began his career at the University of Minnesota before being called east to join the New Deal and, in 1937, Harvard's faculty.[76] As Galbraith later wrote, Hansen "was a man for whom economic ideas had no standing apart from their use." By the late 1930s, Hansen's Harvard seminars were "regularly visited by the Washington policy-makers.... One felt that it was the most important thing currently happening in the country." "Often," Galbraith recalled, "students overflowed into the hall."[77]

Like Keynes, Hansen emphasized the importance of "business confidence" in shaping growth. But confidence did not magically produce innovative investment opportunities. In the absence of new technological breakthroughs and other innovations, consumer demand was ultimately a thin inducement for the kind of innovation that drove entirely new industrial and economic sectors that might demand the capital and labor inputs to push economic expansion. Even at high levels of aggregate consumption, without promising investment opportunities, capitalists might sit on their capital, invest in labor-saving, productivity-boosting innovations, or send their capital abroad. Contra Keynes, then, Hansen believed a recovery led by consumption would be fundamentally spotty. As he argued, "the problem of our generation is, above all, the problem of inadequate private investment outlets."[78]

Here was Hansen's key amendment to Keynesianism: the notion of secular (that is, long-term) economic stagnation. While John Maynard Keynes mentioned secular stagnation in his masterwork *The General Theory*, he framed it as a problem of "unemployment equilibrium" that could be corrected by demand-boosting public works spending. In Hansen's view, boosting purchasing power could smooth boom-and-bust cycles, but the economy's fundamental character reflected longer waves or cycles marked by innovation, stagnation, and regional variation. Moreover, innovation, Hansen believed, contrary to his Harvard colleague Joseph Schumpeter, was a critical but often *external* factor in capitalist development. Economic innovation was neither inevitable nor perhaps even self-generating. It was "lumpy," determined by political-economic context and history. Technology, resource development, and government policy loomed large.[79]

Hansen thus focused on the variety of ways through which government might structure private investment and innovation. His thinking coalesced in the late 1930s and early 1940s, when he became a leading consultant for the National Resources Planning Board (NRPB), where he argued that public borrowing and spending to fund infrastructure improvements, economic development, basic technological research, and public works were "utility creating"—the spending had intrinsic civic and economic value. But government investment, Hansen maintained, also shaped markets and stimulated investment decisions on the supply side. In his 1938 NRPB report *The Economic Effects of the Federal Public Works Expenditures, 1933–1938*, Galbraith gestured at the private "investment-inducing quality of . . . public works." While the study mainly argued for the importance of public works spending in providing short-term employment and purchasing power, Galbraith also included data on public works' relationship to "off-site" employment—that is, the role of public investment in stimulating private industries and employees through secondary contracts and supply chains.[80] Hansen believed government must make investments that private enterprise resisted, not only for their intrinsic value, but because they would generate private investments that would never otherwise have been created. The vast majority of the "process of production is still carried on by private enterprise," Hansen explained. "This is neither socialism in production nor even in the ownership of wealth." Rather, "the Government is becoming an investment banker."[81] Private markets needed periodic public nudges. Hansen's theory of secular stagnation had initially flowed from an inherent pessimism about the private economy—in 1936 and 1937, his pointed critique of Keynes was based on a sense that the economy had "matured," that few innovations were left to be made. But by the early 1940s and the government-fueled return to growth, he viewed public investments not as desperate stopgaps but as confident, strategic shots of adrenaline sustaining innovation in an expanding private economy.

Giving political shape to Hansen's ideas were overlapping sets of partisan, policy, and intellectual perspectives, some concerning the South. Since founding the Institute for Research in Social Science at the University of

North Carolina, Chapel Hill in 1922, Howard Odum's data-driven, "scientific" understanding of the region argued that the South constituted a distinct region whose history, problems, and culture demanded unified solutions developed through coordinated planning. Laced with statistical and spatial analysis, Odum's opus *Southern Regions of the United States* (1936) was an impassioned plea for addressing southern "poverty and social pathology." Odum inspired a young set of southern liberals who sought a federally led assault on their home states' social and economic pathologies. Clark Foreman and George S. Mitchell joined, respectively, the Interior Department and the Farm Security Administration. South Carolinian Leon Keyserling played a pivotal role in creating the National Labor Relations Act.[82] These liberals met often in Washington, and in the winter of 1937–38, the group determined to publicize their views on the problems and opportunities of the South.[83] These efforts merged with FDR's economic and partisan concerns about the region.

Roosevelt was never attuned to nor much concerned with the racial dimensions of poverty, and he hardly evinced any willingness to expend political capital on behalf of black citizens. His strategic silence about Jim Crow's inequalities defined the willful neglect at the heart of his administration's emerging solution for southern poverty. In the summer of 1938 FDR assembled a conference of twenty-two leading southern academics and businesspeople to generate economic findings on the region's plight, which Roosevelt planned to use as a cudgel in ousting intransigent southern Democrats including Senator Walter F. George of Georgia. Foreman later recalled Roosevelt arguing, "if the people understand the facts . . . they will find their own remedies"—New Deal remedies.[84] Drawing upon Odum's *Southern Regions*, conferees compiled the *Report on Economic Conditions of the South* for his National Emergency Council, his "great decentralizers."[85]

New Dealers' disinclination to address racial inequalities—whether economic or democratic—meant that any policy constructed to ameliorate poverty via development would be filtered through racist local political and economic structures. And in any event, Roosevelt was quite sanguine about the social and racial prospects of his economic approach, which would eventually pull up impoverished black and white citizens. When a woman from New York wrote to beseech him to take "a firmer hand . . . with the hardhearted South in regard to the Negro," FDR articulated his incremental, growth-based vision of social and racial reform. "We must" remember, he responded, "that for at least three generations the South was almost wholly lacking in property values and consequently in taxes, and, therefore, in the opportunity of having improved schools and roads and all the things that raised the economic level . . . if you know the South as I know it, you will realize that in three years they have made enormous strides and I am confident will continue if they are given the chance for a few years more."[86]

Touting the report as a first step toward fighting southern underdevelopment and poverty, Roosevelt set aside questions of race and history entirely. In his letter conveying the final report—in which he famously called the South "the Nation's No. 1 economic problem"—FDR framed its findings as a statement of present challenges, "without going into the long history of how this situation came to be."[87] When it came to redressing "the South's unbalance," as Roosevelt sometimes put it, economic growth would be both the cure and sign of progress. In a 1938 fireside chat, FDR explained his call for renewed federal spending on public works not in terms of meeting the unemployment emergency, as he had earlier in the New Deal. The goals had multiplied and most clearly so on the supply side: "to put idle money and idle men to work, to increase our public wealth and to build up the health and strength of the people—to help our system of private enterprise to function." "Government spending," he said, would be "a trigger to set off private activity."[88] If the Great Depression had exposed and intensified a series of social crises, by the late New Deal, led by economists like Hansen, Roosevelt settled on economic prescriptions, placing mutually reinforcing systems of private and public capital formation at the center of national narratives of social progress.

Stymied by a recalcitrant Congress, however, in his second term, Roosevelt was in no position to create bold new programs. Within his grasp, however, were existing programs, local partners, and the bully pulpit. In fireside chats, correspondence, and official statements, FDR repeatedly linked the health of southern business, especially small, local, and regional businesses, with national progress. By the summer of 1938, Roosevelt more vehemently delineated his sense of the economic preconditions essential for social progress. At the University of Georgia, he explained that "social conditions . . . were intimately dependent on economic conditions: higher wages, higher farm income and more profits for small businessmen."[89] The key to southern economic and fiscal escape velocity, then, would be the federal "investment banker," as Alvin Hansen had put it, and its local brokers: burgeoning supply-side state builders like Wyatt Foster.

New Dealers' decision to elide the issue of racial inequality and the structure of democracy itself had significant implications not only for African Americans but also for the evolution of liberalism over the next third of a century. The late

New Deal's massive, decentralized spending agenda invited local elites to pursue an expanding range of federal programs. These powers unleashed enhanced infrastructural capacities that, in local hands, built Jim Crow disparities into New Deal developments. Indeed, Atlanta's chamber oversaw the nation's first federally underwritten slum clearance and public housing project, employing the Public Works Administration (PWA) in 1935 to destroy four black neighborhoods and replace them with affordable public housing for whites.[90] Though such large-scale clearance and relocation projects were characteristic of larger cities, the New Deal authorized elites in smaller, urbanizing cities like Rome to wield the federal government's growing infrastructural power.[91] By the late 1930s, Rome's business leadership joined those in Athens, Augusta, Macon, and Savannah in studying Atlanta's slum clearance initiatives. In 1938, each city established housing authorities to win federal subsidies.

In Rome, H. H. Keel oversaw Housing Authority appointments, naming as executive director chamber leader Alfred Lee Barron, president of Rome's Coca-Cola Bottling Company. Keel also appointed Stewart A. Marshall, a Rotarian, chamber member, and president of the Marshall Manufacturing Company; Ulysses N. Howell of the Eagle Stove Works Company; attorney Wilson M. Hardy; and Osgood P. Willingham, of a leading Rome family, was named acting chairman. Under their leadership, the city's slum clearance program targeted a working-class white neighborhood of forty single-story rental homes along North Fifth Avenue and Jackson Street. They also targeted a black neighborhood in East Rome at East Thirteenth and Fourteenth Streets, the land values and tax yields of which stood to increase as New Deal levee projects were completed. Following processes of condemnation, acquisition, and clearance, the housing projects, like the neighborhoods before them, were strictly segregated and hardly equal. The white DeSoto Homes, not integrated until the 1980s, comprised 148 units and featured recreational spaces and playgrounds, including a children's spray pool. Units boasted electric refrigerators, a cutting-edge consumer technology. In all-black Altoview Terrace, by contrast, the ninety-four residences had iceboxes. Their smaller plot included a single playground.[92] Jim Crow disparities were literally built into the landscape the New Deal was remaking—whether through housing projects or by creating new white investment-worthy properties by clearing and redeveloping formerly flood-prone land once occupied by African Americans.

The local uses of New Deal spending could exacerbate other Jim Crow disparities, such as the quality of improvements to white and black schools. In Georgia, 86 percent of Civil Works Administration spending went to repairs and additions to white schools ($2.2 million versus $351,714). Federal Emergency Relief Administration spending on school improvements was even more lopsided, with 94.7 percent going to white rather than black schools ($501,656 versus just $27,932). Similar trends emerged in New Deal support for local recreational and infrastructural developments, to say nothing of the already well-documented discrimination in hiring practices, social security, and equal access to relief programs such as the WPA's National Youth Administration.[93] The local administration of federal subsidies thus underwrote the enhancement of white capital—whether public assets or private investments—while very often destroying black capital.

Fundamentally, then, the windfall of federal spending that poured into the South was based upon gradualist and, as in the *Report on Economic Conditions of the South*, willfully race-blind understandings of the fundamentally political nature of southern poverty. As federal money flowed southward, the same boosters who had instantiated or at least benefited from Jim Crow stood to gain still more from their region's poverty, this time in the form of colossal federal grants liberals believed would be the external shock that would jump-start southern economic independence and, perhaps, social progress. Poverty in general and black poverty in particular were thus linchpins for federal aid for whites and white elites—an economic windfall echoing nothing so much as the political windfall of the "three-fifths compromise."

Thanks to Roosevelt's pragmatic and partisan fusion of economic and social progress, in 1938 the federal government began pumping massive amounts of federal capital into the South, approving grants at disproportionately higher rates than for other regions. In 1940, federal grant rates to southern states reached parity with national averages, accounting for about 14 percent of state government revenues. By 1960, every state in the South (except Florida) received federal dollars at rates higher than national averages.[94] As federal funding poured into the South, "moderate" business boosters like George C. Biggers of the *Atlanta Journal* inverted Roosevelt's dictum: the South had become the "Nation's No. 1 Economic Opportunity."[95]

Naturalizing and Regionalizing Federal Aid

Alvin Hansen was confident that the emerging public investment and supply side development regime would become "natural" to the business community.[96] A 1937 Christmas wish list underscored just how right he was. "My

Dear Mister Santa Claus," it began, "let's get down to business—the business of giving." Printed in the *Southern Secretary*, the publication of Wyatt Foster's association of southeastern chamber professionals, the four-page list enumerated the wishes of seventy-six chambers of commerce from communities across southeastern states. Roanoke, Virginia's Ben Moomaw requested "a fine new municipal airport." Hod Lewis, "over in Little Rock, wants a new auditorium ready for business." In Ocala, Florida, Horace Smith, a realtor, hoped for "an athletic field, an air mail passenger line, a municipal auditorium, and a five-year agricultural program—a whale of an order, I'll grant." As John L. Morris, the *Secretary*'s editor put it, "I hope I haven't been piggish, Nick," but these businessmen "are deserving."[97] Saint Nick would not deliver these gifts. Rather, when Franklin Roosevelt secured billions in new public works spending in April 1938 in hopes of reversing the "Roosevelt recession," these wishes were that much closer to becoming reality. The number of Georgians employed on WPA projects soared to 67,203 that year, nearly tripling the number of workers in 1937.[98]

As this federally subsidized labor went to work, Hansen's ideas about private investment were vindicated. In Rome, activity on the Keel Levee, a downtown WPA-sponsored sewer project, and the federally backed housing projects touched off a resurgence in private sector investment, which in 1938 returned to pre-Depression levels and in 1939 set new records.[99] These improvements resuscitated long-standing dreams, including for a 360-mile canal project connecting the Coosa River to the Gulf of Mexico at Mobile.[100] Prior to the New Deal, a project of such magnitude, stretching across hundreds of municipalities and jurisdictions, was politically and economically fantastical. Yet, in the years before the New Deal, Wyatt Foster hoped to galvanize an interstate group of boosters behind a plan for canals and river dredging to connect landlocked communities to the Mississippi River.[101] As one supporter of Foster's Coosa-Alabama River Improvement Association (CARIA) put it in 1929, if successful, we "would then be scooping gold eagles with a shovel."[102] Foster succeeded in raising $53,000 in private seed funding from businessmen in Rome as well as Anniston, Gadsden, Montgomery, and Selma, Alabama. But the Great Depression forced boosters to focus on matters closer to home.

Inspired by the prospect of New Deal resources, however, boosters returned to regionalism and the promise of regional planning. Doing so also promised a way for this emerging class of business-civic actors to bypass retrograde county courthouse politics. The CARIA thus provided a model for amplifying small-city and rural supply-side state builders' voices in state and national politics. In 1938, Keel, Foster, and John J. "Jack" McDonough, a regional Georgia Power executive and president of Rome's chamber, revived their ambitions, focusing not only on river and canal improvements but also constructing a massive dam on the Etowah River near Cartersville. The dam would solve the region's flood problems by creating a reservoir, Lake Allatoona, also capable of providing drinking water, hydropower, recreation, and tourism opportunities (from which Georgia Power would profit handsomely). McDonough organized Washington letter-writing campaigns by regional chambers and Kiwanis and Rotary Clubs. He also called on his friend Congressman Malcolm Tarver. Initially, Tarver reported that Congress's consulting engineers and budget analysts doubted "whether [the] estimated costs of construction" were worth the "economic benefits which may be anticipated."[103] But as FDR's mandate to send federal resources southward took effect, officials reconsidered the proposal. Tarver also lobbied the White House, and in 1940 Roosevelt personally assured him the project would receive judicious consideration.[104] Within ten days, an Army Corps representative conveyed the good news: given "the recent directive of the President," the Corps would reconsider the proposals.[105] A round of hearings was scheduled for April 1941, and McDonough organized a Washington junket for CARIA members.[106] On April 28, 1941, boosters from Georgia, Alabama, and Tennessee packed into thirty rooms at Washington's Wardman Park Hotel.[107]

The CARIA's head, J. R. Hornady, publisher of the *Rome News-Tribune* and former chamber president, described his and his allies' devotion to becoming supply-side state builders. We expended "every energy to get . . . hurdles out of the way . . . to have the project" approved by Congress. Prior to the New Deal, boosters from small southern towns had primarily eyed one another as competitors. United by the prospect of winning national subsidies, they directed their competitive energies at a common target: the federal government. In explaining their work to their communities, boosters emphasized how federal administrators and bureaucrats had become the "hurdles" to regional progress.[108] A *News-Tribune* editorial typified this spirit of local struggle: "The score is tied, so to speak," but the "board of engineers in Washington . . . must be convinced of its economic importance to the state of the nation." "Teams entering this vitally important contest" from across the region "will be fully represented . . . when the chief of engineers [in Washington] calls 'Batter Up.'"[109] As they made federal subsidies a natural and deserving piece of local and regional development, the very federal bureaucrats to whom they appealed were also their chief impediments, the emerging system of intergovernmental federal transfers their new venue for political action.

Despite the funds coming from war preparedness measures, local businessmen well understood where the long-term benefits lay. The merchant Louis Loveman recalled that for "49 years . . . the main topic of discussion was the Coosa river development, and now, almost half a century later" the project was a reality.[110] When regional boosters celebrated federal funding, they rarely mentioned the war effort. I. M. Levinson, president of the Rome Retail Merchants Association, called the project "the greatest asset that Rome has ever had."[111] Even when Rome's Kiwanis president mentioned preparedness, he linked it primarily to regional economic benefits: "Not only," he wrote, "do we feel this to be essential as a defense measure but [it will also be] our greatest forward stride in the industrial development of the southeast."[112] When Congressman Tarver conveyed the news, he underscored the link between war and development: the "Blitz has hit our Uncle Sam—and our Aunt Airy Craft. They need our help. We are in the army now."[113]

Roosevelt's efforts to drape boosters' striving in patriotic bunting strengthened their emerging sense of producerism. Economic improvements constituted local expressions of the national interest. Appearing in Gainesville, Georgia, where the PWA and WPA had sponsored many developments, Roosevelt credited the city's civic spirit: federal aid, he said, "would have been wholly insufficient" without the "greater help from your own ranks."[114] Said Roosevelt on another occasion, "We are coming to realize that one extra plane or extra tank or extra gun or extra ship completed tomorrow may, in a few months, turn the tide, on some distant battlefield; it may make the difference between life and death for some of our own fighting men."[115] In managing federal programs and profitably pursuing wartime preparedness initiatives, FDR assured supply-side state builders that their work was for the good of their communities and country.

Boosters thus localized and legitimized new federal powers while nationalizing the significance of their civic contributions. Local business elites had always believed they were their community's essential stewards. But their emerging producerist ethos authorized historically unprecedented public interventions in local markets as just compensation for their civic labors. The New Deal instantiated an unprecedented sense of entitlement to federal resources on behalf of that stewardship and then raised the stakes to include victory in total war. CARIA boosters who headed to Washington to testify on behalf of defense-related river improvements, J. R. Hornady's *News-Tribune* piously explained, "are not only serving their own communities but also serving the nation."[116] Their lobbying alerted Congress to regional potentialities, and it took their dogged determination to overcome skeptical bureaucrats. Their recruitment and administration of expansive new public powers were the essential components of local and national progress.

Meanwhile, national business associations railed against further public interventions in the private sector, championing a more starkly zero-sum understanding of the relationship between public spending and private initiative.[117] At the very moment the CARIA won its federal outlays, the U.S. Chamber of Commerce mounted a campaign against federal spending, fearing greater regulatory authority and taxation. The chamber hoped to mobilize local branches behind an ideological vision of limited government and, against FDR's attacks on *big* businesses, to "bring 'American Business out of the dog house.'" Businessmen, the chamber explained, "must realize that American Business as we know it . . . is the backbone" of American life—as if local boosters needed convincing.[118] Against the more localist and pragmatic version of business producerism that was quite compatible with federal development initiatives, the U.S. Chamber touted an ideologically charged version, drawing a stark line between public-sector action and private-sector prosperity. They sought to convince local chambers that New Deal programs and the revenue they required threatened to wipe out private initiative. The synergistic relationships boosters built with the national state were rather a slippery slope to the state's takeover of the economy. In 1939, the U.S. Chamber of Commerce distributed to local chapters scripts for radio programs titled "So that you may tell the story . . ." One script explained, "For the past nine years," "the greatest of all corporations—the Government of the United States," has been going deeper into debt at the rate of $7,000,000 a day." Such deficit spending had dire consequences for business. Since 25 cents of every dollar went to "nonproductive" government spending, "only 75 cents is available for private enterprise. . . . the more government you buy, the less money you will have for business enterprise."[119] As more federal programs came online that promised to turn developmental dreams into reality, however, these ideologically charged national associations would only grow more distant from the material interests of local chapters.

In contrast, supply-side state builders' grousing about federal spending was usually about slow moving bureaucracies or regional jealousy. New Deal officials were keenly aware that bureaucratic inefficiencies risked alienating their local supplicants. "There are so many obstacles," Frederic Delano, FDR's uncle and New Deal planner, complained of the application process. Even "if a local project has a strong backing, a committee of leading citizens, including some politicians, [who are] sent to Washington to exert pressure upon the Administration or its staff," applicants become embittered "that only" by traveling to Washington "are projects reasonably certain of approval."[120] By the late 1930s, FDR was wholly familiar with the ways competitive localism within federal programs engendered such Janus-faced criticism. Speaking before the American Retail Federation in 1939, FDR narrated an account of a meeting with an ostensibly antigovernment businessperson: "In every case I find what I suspected. His local Chamber of Commerce, his local newspapers are 'yelling their heads off' to have those projects built with Federal assistance. And I say to him: 'Consistency, thy name is geography. You believe with the United States Chamber of Commerce that Federal spending on public works should cease—except in your own home town.'"[121] While local businesspeople may have agreed with complaints about regulations or the threat posed by organized labor, their understanding of federal investments in infrastructure and other assets was much more in line with Alvin Hansen's—federal spending had launched symbiotic and "natural" relationships between the public and private sectors that were fostering investments and economic expansion—so long as they flowed to the right communities and regions. Though they shared a common interest in supply-side subsidies, the fundamentally uneven and competitive nature of New Deal federalism also meant that supply-side state builders would never really cohere as a unified class or national interest group. Localism, regionalism, and competition would remain their primary organizing principles.

"Good Government Is Good Business in Georgia"

By the 1940s, Georgia's politics was slowly being remade by businesspeoples' growing sense that demagogues' extreme defense of white supremacy and rejection of the New Deal were threatening their material interests. Wyatt Foster's SCSA hosted conferences on winning federal aid and included sessions with titles such as, "Why Commercial Organizations Distrust Demagogues."[122] When it came to matters of race and poverty, Georgia's governor Ellis Arnall, a "Little New Dealer," adopted versions of Odum's economic regionalism and Roosevelt's growth-based social incrementalism. Arnall went one step further than Roosevelt, explicitly linking the region's racial progress to economic advancement. "There is no problem in the South," Arnall maintained, "that does not have its origins in the poverty and exploitation of this region. Injustices, instances of racial friction, inadequate opportunities for education and lack of opportunity for economic advancement are all attributable to the low income of the people of our section." "Wipe out poverty," Arnall argued, "and the demagogue will be robbed of his chief stock in trade."[123] He called for raising state incomes, but "gradually," and emphasized public-sector stimulus for the supply side of the economy. Arnall thus embraced the late New Deal's pursuit of private-sector growth and development as incipient social policy.

This posture worked for Arnall, who defeated Talmadge in 1942 by pledging to address "obstacles created by our own lack of vision."[124] "Georgia," he argued, "must develop an industrial-agrarian economy that will provide a high standard of living for all our citizens." In 1943, he oversaw the creation of the Agricultural and Industrial Development Board (AIDB), which would "plan [the] ordered and comprehensive development of the state and its resources." The board included representatives from government, agriculture, business, and industry, essentially becoming a local expression of New Deal economic planning championed by Alvin Hansen and the National Resources Planning Board. This was just the sort of public action Hansen had called for in a 1936 critique of Keynes's overly "mechanical" view of consumer-led growth: "it is not improbable that the continued workability of the system of private enterprise will be made possible, not by changes in prevailing economic institutions (such as those advocated by Keynes), but" in the discovery of "new outlets for profitable investment—new discoveries in technique, new ways of utilizing nature's resources, new products, and new industries."[125] The solution, he wrote, could be that the "state goes the whole way and assumes full entrepreneurial responsibility" for driving innovation.[126] This was precisely the idea taking hold in Georgia. Based at the University of Georgia, the AIDB would coordinate development efforts, steer public subsidies, and recommend growth policies across the state.[127]

The AIDB also played an important role in vertically integrating state and local development efforts. Georgia Power was one of the board's chief supporters, and its regional development experts encouraged local chamber members' attendance at the board's nine regional district meetings, an organizational structure that echoed Roosevelt's advocacy of a national system of regional planning councils.[128] Throughout 1944, two hundred communities across Georgia held "mass meetings for the purpose of organizing permanent committees on industrial development."¹²⁹ In Rome, former chamber president, CARIA veteran, and Georgia Power executive J. J. McDonough chaired the district meeting. "Georgia," the *Washington Post* wrote, "is receiving many compliments these days on the progressive policies that the state is inaugurating."¹³⁰ Like late New Deal and wartime defense contracting, Arnall's AIDB paired existing public-private partnerships with scientific and developmental expertise beneath rhetoric emphasizing the economic basis of social progress. Arnall stressed this economic approach to problems of poverty and racism: "Wipe out poverty," he explained, "and the friction will become negligible."¹³¹

By 1945, *Life* described how Arnall was moving "his state from the benightedness of Tobacco Road to" competing for "the title of 'most progressive southern state.'"¹³² "It has been charged that I am a friend of big business," said Arnall. "I admit it. I am also a friend of moderate business and little business." In 1944, the governor's words topped a full-page advertisement placed by Georgia Power in the *New York Times*, the *Chicago Tribune*, and the *Wall Street Journal*. Whereas the company's pre–New Deal advertisements almost solely emphasized the region's cheap "native-born" labor, its climate, and natural resources, by 1944, the top selling point was the state's government. "Good Government Is Good Business in Georgia," read one header. "Under the able and broad-visioned leadership of Governor Ellis Arnall," the ad continued, "Good business principles are being applied to government. . . . Far-sighted programs for the development of the state's huge industrial and agricultural resources are under way." In short, "the people of Georgia and their government believe in and cooperate with business enterprise." Only then, did the ad tout the region's "native-born" labor.¹³³

The company's emphasis on the benefits to private business of Georgia's version of "good government" reflected the quiet revolution that had occurred in the state in just under two decades. In the 1920s, Georgia's business leaders dreamed of massive infrastructure projects but competed jealously if jocularly for meager road improvements. Romans watched with frustration as floods washed away their visions of recruiting capital. Within ten years, however, Rome's white leaders had partnered with boosters from across the region, cleared portions of the black community, secured new levies to support new investments, won $60 million in federal support to open the region to the global economy through a canal to the Gulf of Mexico, and a massive new dam promised to flood the region with tourist dollars. Civic elites deserved federal support after decades of hard work, private investments, and individual initiative, which, as the nation went to war, was cast in nationalistic terms.

This did not mute criticism of the federal government when its actions threatened their bottom lines. Complaints about the regulatory and labor-related excesses of the liberal state continued to reinforce southern businesspeople's trusty antigovernment rhetoric. But the last year in which any southern state paid more in federal taxes than it received in federal spending was 1940.[134] Southern boosters had never expected or received so much from government.

* * *

In Georgia, good government still meant Jim Crow government. While the prospect of federal aid and the prerogatives of recruiting business encouraged elites to quell some of the worst expressions of Jim Crow violence, the more quotidian but no less entrenched expressions of Jim Crow remained fixed in place—and celebrated. Speaking to the Kiwanis Club of Rome on Memorial Day in 1949, Dr. E. L. Wright, the president of Rome's private Darlington School, to which leading businessmen sent their sons, delivered such a rousing defense of states' rights that the States' Rights Council of Georgia published the speech in pamphlet form. Their Confederate forefathers, he said, "fought for a *principle* that is *again* in jeopardy," the "defense of states' rights." At a moment when President Harry Truman was framing African Americans' civil rights as a domestic front in the Cold War, Wright was indignant. To those who argued "'a perfect democracy is our surest guarantee against Communism,'" Wright retorted, "we can never have a perfect democracy." Gesturing to those assembled, he closed by reassuring the city's civic leaders that "constructive forces are *already* at work" in "the civic clubs of America, composed of responsible citizens of every community."[135] The local elites to whom Franklin Roosevelt had entrusted so much of his New Deal, Wright suggested, were the proper avatars of public power and authority, not a full-fledged democracy.

White Romans' defense of the local racial order was not just rhetorical. The city gained national attention for an ugly incident of racist violence in 1942 when renowned African American lyric tenor and composer Roland Hayes, a native of nearby Curryville, visited on a shopping trip with his wife and their young daughter, Africa. On a hot July afternoon, Hayes's wife was "put out" of Rome's downtown Higgins shoe store after refusing to give up a breezy seat near the front door. Hayes came to his wife's defense, and, after departing, a police officer grabbed him from behind and dragged him by his belt back to the store. Two other officers arrived, and the three set upon Hayes, beating him to the ground. Police handcuffed Hayes and loaded him, his wife, and daughter into a patrol wagon. Africa, the *Chicago Defender* reported, "kept screaming, drowning out the sobs of the badly frightened wife."[136] He and his wife, he said, "were put in a cell, and our little girl left on the outside."[137] The family was eventually released, but newswires broadcast the story nationally. As civil rights activist Roy Wilkins put it, "There is no sense in fighting Hitler in Europe and 'deploring' Hitlerism in Georgia."[138] Writing about Hayes's beating, W. E. B. Du Bois invoked Rome to highlight the sustained violence of racism in modern American life: "What power can reach this nadir of American civilization?"[139]

A power had surely reached Rome during the New Deal and Second World War. But liberalism's supply-side forces for economic advancement were not much concerned with Jim Crow, despite rhetoric about fighting regional poverty or redressing regional underdevelopment. The emerging paradigm of public-private, local-national growth partnerships would flourish in the region and beyond, cementing ideas about the economic bases of social progress and entrenching the local business elite's role not only in driving local affairs but in building new regional and national forms of supply-side capacities in the Cold War.

In the large city, industrial North, similar logics unfolded as local elites learned to wield federal initiatives to bolster their political and economic standing. But rather than build durable, cooperative regional planning institutions and federal partnerships as small-city southern elites would, on the eve of deindustrialization, Cleveland, Ohio's business elites, most of whom shared the ideologically charged instincts and partisan affiliations of the U.S. Chamber of Commerce, developed a more halting relationship with liberals' supply-side state. One site of interregional convergence, however, was in using New Deal capacities on behalf of a Jim Crow–like effort to raze African American neighborhoods in search of new investment opportunities.

CHAPTER 2

"The Best Location in the Nation"

In 1934, *Harper's* explained the onset of the Great Depression by narrating the downfall of one of Cleveland, Ohio's most glittering fortunes, the real estate and railroad empire of the Van Sweringen brothers.[1] Oris and Mantis Van Sweringen worked their way up from newsboys to real estate moguls, buying, subdividing, and developing the land that became Shaker Heights, one of the nation's preeminent suburbs. A symbol of Cleveland's status among leading cities, in the 1920s, Shaker Heights had the highest per capita income of any municipality in the country.[2] Connecting Shaker by rail to Cleveland fed the reclusive brothers' appetites for acquiring railroads and redeveloping the city's downtown—their Terminal Tower would contain a luxury hotel and offices perched atop a massive rail terminal and retail hall. Though it was begun in 1923, the project was not dedicated until 1930, at which point the Van Sweringens' empire was collapsing. By shuttling loans and preferred and common stock offerings through holding companies, taking advantage of liberal capital markets, often without putting up any personal capital, the Vans, as locals called them, accumulated holdings valued around $3 billion: 150 corporations, twenty-three railroads with thirty thousand miles of lines, and ten real estate firms. Testifying before a Senate committee, Oris admitted that even he could not keep track of their assets and liabilities. By then, it mattered little. Like the city they had redeveloped—which defaulted on a series of municipal bonds in February 1934—the Vans were insolvent.[3]

If relative capital scarcity described the challenges facing many small-city boosters and rural governments, the inverse scenario—drowning in capital abundance—shaped the crisis for many larger industrial cities and business interests.[4] While Rome, Georgia's striving bankers and retailers might have plausibly fit Franklin Roosevelt's vision of "local people," the Van Sweringens, their bankers, and the business elites who helmed Cleveland's chamber of commerce were quite literally FDR's "money changers." Among the first to be bailed out by President Hoover's Reconstruction Finance Corporation were the Vans and Cleveland's big banks. Union Trust, which loaned more than its entire capital stock to the brothers and two other leading Clevelanders, received a $14 million federal bailout; several Van Sweringen railroads received at least $64 million in RFC financing, more than 20 percent of Hoover's total railroad bailouts.[5] Oris was unabashed: when the RFC was established, he said, "We were on the doorstep waiting for them to open."[6] It was against these sorts of cozy bailouts that Roosevelt campaigned in 1932.

But the Roosevelt administration's policy structures were often shaped less by FDR's rhetoric than by pragmatism and the exigencies of the moment. Rather than abandon the RFC, key initiatives of the New Deal, including the Public Works Administration, worked through Hoover's public corporation, which delivered federal financing not only to banks and railroads but also to state and local governments facing insolvency. The RFC and the New Deal's early works agenda, which depended upon its purchase of municipal and corporate bonds, also incorporated many of the same bankers, lawyers, corporate executives, and public officials whose 1920s debt-fueled development frenzies had helped make the Depression so great. Far from posing a threat to stability, for New Dealer Alvin Hansen restored municipal borrowing of private capital offered a vital way to revive private investments and get capital flowing toward projects with intrinsic public utility. These continuities in terms of institutions, personnel, and financial structures would prove, in practice, essential to binding Cleveland's elites, most of whom were staunch Republicans, to key aspects of the New Deal.

Roosevelt certainly would not have campaigned on such practical policy realities. But, in the context of mounting European fascism and against strident defenders of laissez-faire, others, such as the National Resources Planning Board's Charles Merriam, viewed the marriage of public purpose and private interests as a vital, moderate, path toward recovery and, over time, a more stable, cooperatively planned democratic capitalism. A University of Chicago political scientist, Merriam was also a Progressive Era municipal reformer, city council member, planner, and close ally of Chicago's business elites. As a New Dealer, Merriam championed national economic planning decentralized through local business-led public-private planning bodies that, as he knew firsthand, had matured in the teens and twenties.

Though striving businesspeople in the rural South jumped at the chance to direct federal works spending and did so on an increasingly regional basis,

Cleveland's business elites, who very often helmed nationally facing business organizations like the National Association of Manufacturers and the Chamber of Commerce of the United States, were both more confident in their abilities to manage the Depression's initial crises and more muted in their appreciation of federal support once they accepted it.[7] They were also often suburbanites and resisted regional planning initiatives that might challenge their cozy suburban autonomy. Moreover, using the chamber of commerce and other civic organizations as forms of remote control over city politics, Cleveland's business elites also faced down the mobilization of the unemployed, unhoused, and poverty stricken who threatened their hold on city affairs. These were composed primarily of first- and second-generation white ethnic immigrants but also growing ranks of African Americans emigrating from the South. As they did so, Cleveland's nascent supply-side state builders, like their small-city, rural cousins, found ways to prosper economically and politically through New Deal and wartime developments, shoring up their hold on city politics.

As Cleveland's elites took control over the local administration of New Deal works programs, those initiatives also played an unheralded role in resuscitating habits of borrowing and urban development that had contributed to the Depression's depth and breadth. Some of these new federal-local capacities—particularly to raze "slum" neighborhoods in the name of redevelopment and restored municipal fiscal solvency—were wholly new. Black residents quickly recognized that these new decentralized federal powers were underwriting Jim Crow–like practices in a city once celebrated for its relative racial tolerance. As the New Deal state emerged, then, so too did black activists' demands for administrative enfranchisement within its sprawling, public-private machinery.

Developmental Debts and the Limits of Voluntarism

As the Great Depression arrived, Cleveland's population surged past nine hundred thousand, making it the fifth largest city in the country behind New York, Chicago, Philadelphia, and Detroit. Cleveland was an epicenter of second-wave industrialization, with iron and steel powering the city's output. By the 1920s, a more diversified industrial base had developed, and a vigorous financial sector met the city's growing thirst for capital. As of 1920, thirty-eight banks, savings institutions, and trust companies held deposits of more than $800 million, and businesses also enjoyed easy access to New York City creditors. In contrast, total deposits held by banks in the entire state of Georgia in 1924 amounted to just $612 million and, thanks to this scarcity, the costs to borrow were often considerably higher. Cleveland's local wealth and its situation within elite, national networks defined "the ease with which" big city elites "could raise capital for innovative projects."[8] By the end of the 1920s, however, that easy access to capital and rippling defaults helped turn a stock market crash into the Great Depression. As *Harper's* suggested, the Depression's severity had ratcheted up as defaults ricocheted through the nation's interlocking capital markets. While many smaller, undercapitalized cities like Rome, Georgia, had been only intermittently able to tap into national flows of capital and primarily experienced the depression as budget crises, larger, well-capitalized cities like Cleveland faced staggering municipal debt burdens, corporate insolvency, and shriveling property tax revenues.

A sort of "fiscal aggressiveness"—a "buccaneering sense of political enterprise"—had driven the infrastructural expansion of larger, industrialized cities at the turn of the century.[9] By the 1920s, inflated land values and real estate speculation boosted larger cities' property tax yields, which increased the amount of debt they could carry.[10] These fiscal pressures were heightened in states such as Ohio, where rural representatives restricted local governments' ability to raise new forms of tax revenue. This only encouraged cities to more aggressively finance their needs through borrowing.[11] Servicing that debt consumed much local revenue, and, as the *Wall Street Journal* warned, new municipal outlays for infrastructure were on shaky ground precisely because of those "grossly inflated" real estate values that enabled such reckless borrowing. The 1920s' "land boom," the *Journal* explained, was the last exuberant gasp of a period "of great and extended prosperity."[12] That exuberance was underwritten with annual additions to municipal debt between 1923 and 1931 that *averaged* over $845 million (or more than $13.5 billion in 2020 dollars)—enough, one contemporary analyst explained, "to keep municipal finance in a turmoil for two decades or more."[13] And chambers of commerce were often drivers of that debt—in 1930, the *New York Times* reported that Cleveland's chamber planned to put $31.5 million in new bonds for an "improvement program . . . before the Council." By 1932, Cleveland alone held $185.5 million in gross bonded debt, or the equivalent of nearly $3.5 billion in 2020.[14]

These same dynamics threatened municipal property tax revenues, which weakened not only because real estate markets had contracted, but also because industrial firms and unrealized residential developments were increasingly delinquent on property tax payments. A study of larger cities found that tax delinquency rates doubled between 1930 and 1934. Speculators, rail tycoons, and real estate developers had helped bankrupt their cities. The Van Sweringen companies alone owed Cleveland and Cuyahoga County more than $3.5 million in back taxes.[15] Indeed, the most frequent form of defaulted municipal bonds in the opening years of the Depression—35 percent of the total—had underwritten railroad expansion.[16]

On average, then, the 151 American cities with populations above 50,000 would meet the social crises of the Depression with a quarter of their expected taxes unpaid, massive debts to service, and upward pressure on property tax rates that only produced more delinquency.[17] In 1932, the *Bond Buyer* trade publication began tracking defaulted bonds and found 678 that year alone. Defaults peaked in 1935 at 3,251.[18] The result was a rolling municipal fiscal crisis that rendered local governments especially ill-suited to delivering reliable relief or employment programs. "Cleveland," a contemporary analysis concluded, "stands as an illustration of the fact that without drastic revision of the tax system, the cities themselves are not self-supporting during a severe depression."[19]

Yet, Cleveland's elites were confident they could meet the moment without recourse to federal aid. Prior to the Depression, larger, industrial cities like Cleveland relied on a blend of public and private approaches to poverty and unemployment relief. The sheer size of Cleveland's working-class white ethnic population combined with the scale and reach of corporate, industrial, and civic organizations led Cleveland's voluntary sector, chiefly its philanthropies and chamber of commerce, to join turn-of-the-century organizational revolutions that brought scale and bureaucratic rationality to public-private relief. In smaller, less developed communities like Rome, this voluntarism functioned much more baldly as a form of businessmen's paternalism. Such intimacy was eclipsed in big cities where governments helped sustain an ethos of voluntarism (and avoided budgetary and social commitments) by contributing to private charities primarily funded and directed by elite benefactors.[20] The pioneering Cleveland Foundation, formed in 1914, was led by appointees of the Cleveland Trust Company bank and city officials, and its work-relief program met the crisis of the recession of 1914–15, when 61,000 Clevelanders lost work.[21]

If Rome's paternalistic charity was strained to the breaking point by the summer of 1931, Cleveland's elites remained confident in their professionalized philanthropic organizations. The chamber passed resolutions in

December 1931 calling for handling unemployment "on an individual basis, locally, through organization to that end," urging that relief be "provided through private contributions supplemented by state and local governments, and without any federal appropriations for such purpose."[22] Even as unemployment halved Cleveland's usual workforce, chamber president R. B. Robinette argued that the professional Associated Charities, founded in 1900, was the "proper agency" for relief. New public services "could not possibly be as efficient as the leading relief agencies now in the field."[23] Elites simply needed to bolster their commitments with a "campaign locally to bring money out of hiding."[24] The mayor, too, believed voluntary local resources would meet the challenge.[25] Mayors of other large cities concurred: local relief was both effective and preferable to federal intervention.[26] Cleveland's chamber joined the U.S. Chamber of Commerce in rejecting federal spending for relief, reflecting their confident if defensive localism and partisan leanings as well as concerns that federal spending would be "borne in great part by [taxes on] capital and industry."[27] For the moment, Cleveland's Republican-dominated chamber was aligned with its national brethren.

This confidence also reflected their faith in the statistically oriented expertise and professionalism of the voluntary organizations they led and upon which public officials often relied. Cleveland's chamber employed numerous committees composed of business elites and professional staff that studied issues of import to the city and corporate community. Committees focused on industrial development, the municipal budget, city planning, and federal matters such as taxation, all of which made Cleveland, members boasted, "the most statistically minded city in the union."[28] The committee on public finance kept detailed records on the city's fiscal health and even generated audits and budget forecasts. In the summer of 1932, the committee detailed the city's "financial problem" when it came to income, relief, and its worsening short- and long-term debt picture.[29] As the crisis worsened over the winter of 1932–33, the mayor, "unable to balance the budget," met with chamber members to detail "the difficulties of the situation" and to seek "assistance."[30]

In contrast to their striving cousins in smaller, rural, developing communities, Cleveland's elites' producerism was at once more assured and muted. The chamber's numerous committees testified to a civic outlook shaped in equal measure by a sense of privileged responsibility and self-evident authority. Chamber meeting minutes detail their patriarchal oversight of municipal affairs as they debated municipal bills and budgets and often stepped into broker solutions when political impasses or fiscal crises struck. This entitled sense of influence extended to national affairs. Whereas northwest Georgia's business boosters were comparatively late in studying federal policies, Cleveland's businesspeople weighed in on all measure of national policy, from matters with more direct impact on business, such as tax or regulatory policy, to questions concerning the efficient organization of executive branch agencies.[31]

Yet, Cleveland's government, its voluntary institutions, and its public-private systems of relief were under unprecedented strain by the winter of 1932–33. Associated Charities and the Cleveland Foundation were overwhelmed. Chamber members grappled with the "open antagonism" between the mayor and the city council, which resisted cuts to municipal services and wages.[32] The chamber's Committee on Public Finance and Taxation found that the city and county, which shared relief burdens, would see those costs rise from $13 million in 1932 to $18 million in 1933, for which they would be $11 million short. Analysts supported a new county levy to bolster welfare spending, but they acknowledged the necessity of applying to the Reconstruction Finance Corporation (RFC) "for the rest of the money needed."[33] As they faced greater unrest in white ethnic wards, turning to Washington seemed increasingly conceivable.

Demanding a New Deal

As dawn broke on the morning of July 18, 1933, sheriff's deputies arrived at a Hungarian neighborhood on Cleveland's east side. John Sparenga had been laid off in 1930 and was nearly two years and $7,200 behind on his mortgage and interest payments.[34] His bank had finally foreclosed, and deputies were dispatched to evict Sparenga, his wife, and their four children. As deputies carried away their belongings, word spread through the neighborhood. Evictions had become tragically common: by 1932, some 14,500 families had been evicted in Cleveland.[35] Once word reached members of the Small Home and Land Owners' Federation, a neighborhood "home defense" group, several thousand white ethnic Clevelanders joined an increasingly raucous protest against the Sparengas'—and their own—treatment by banks and city government. More than 160 police officers arrived, beating back the crowds with nightsticks and, as darkness fell, tear gas and fire hoses. The names of those hospitalized or detained suggest the Sparengas' support from their fellow ethnics. Louis Cseh and Joseph Szabo were detained for questioning.

Margaret Honrnyak collapsed in the crowd. Nick Scafilie suffered a broken leg. Though the Sparengas lost their home, *The Nation* reported, "This is a crowd that won't scatter, a crowd that is strangely grim and determined."[36] The city's business elites were surely appalled when the riots spurred the *New York Times*' detailed coverage of Cleveland's collapsing relief efforts.[37]

Though chamber members were wary about federal intervention in local relief efforts, far less tolerable was working-class militancy, which fueled anxieties about the city's reputation as a place to invest. Indeed, the Depression made clear that as wealthier Clevelanders decamped to suburbs such as Shaker Heights, the city had become a diverse mix of working-class and poor residents.[38] Beyond eviction riots, a national phenomenon, at least three constituencies made mounting demands for more generous relief: communist-affiliated Unemployed Councils (UC), representing interracial groups of the poor and out of work; growing ranks of African Americans who suffered overcrowded housing and disproportionately high rates of unemployment; and an increasingly aggressive labor movement. Many of these Clevelanders sought not simply relief but also greater administrative inclusion in determining the shape that relief might take.

Unemployed Councils targeted Associated Charities and its public successor, the Cuyahoga County Relief Administration. They demanded both increased spending and that recipients be brought into the administrative process "without check from the Associated Charities or any other relief body."[39] The UCs, which also protested racial discrimination, opened their first neighborhood branch office in the African American Cedar-Central neighborhood. The census tracts nearest that office sustained staggering unemployment rates: 91.5 percent, 69.9 percent, and 54.9 percent. In Ohio City and Tremont, west-side neighborhoods of Ukrainians and Poles and longer-settled Irish, unemployment rates fluctuated between 40 and 45 percent. By 1934, Unemployed Councils even emerged in the city's white Protestant neighborhoods and suburbs. Confrontations with relief agencies often elicited harsh crackdowns. The first major clash occurred in the fall of 1932 in white ethnic Collinwood when hundreds of UC members marched to Associated Charities and demanded food and clothing. Rebuffed, the crowd swarmed past police to seize what they could.[40]

African American neighborhoods faced especially intolerable conditions, though this had not always been the case. In 1900, fewer than six thousand black residents lived in the city of nearly four hundred thousand, composing just 1.6 percent of the population. Those residents were broadly diffused throughout the city. Robert Drake, an African American clerk, explained with pride in 1915, "We have no 'LITTLE AFRICA' in Cleveland.... There is not a single street in this city that is inhabited by nothing but Negroes." In the early twentieth century, then, Cleveland represented better than average opportunities for African Americans, particularly an emerging class of merchants and entrepreneurs. A robust black business district extended east from downtown along Central Avenue, and J. Walter Wills, a graduate of Antioch College, personified this enterprising generation. Wills operated a successful funeral home, the House of Wills and in 1905 established a local branch of Booker T. Washington's National Negro Business League. Wills was active in the NAACP and the Urban League and supported lawsuits targeting segregated theaters. Despite certain opportunities, discrimination, particularly in real estate and the professions, were persistent realities.[41]

This limited tolerance existed so long as African Americans occupied a statistically and electorally modest slice of Cleveland's population. As their numbers grew, so too did intolerance, segregation, and predation. By 1930, some 72,000 African Americans called Cleveland home, composing 8 percent of a city that had grown to 900,000. The majority of new black residents came from Deep South states, predominantly Alabama and Georgia, and they settled along the Central Avenue corridor west of East Fifty-Fifth Street. The poet Langston Hughes attended Central High School, and he and his mother were among the first black pioneers to push east of East Fifty-Fifth. As Hughes recalled, whites "resented the Negroes moving closer and closer," but when they yielded, "they gave way at very profitable rentals." The Urban League publicized the practice of discriminatory rents and even spurred a chamber investigation. Whites, they found, paid an average monthly rent of $13.12, while blacks paid $22.50.[42]

As the black population grew, white racial fears sped "the deterioration of the city's liberal racial climate," as one historian has described it. In 1923, when Robert R. Moton, Booker T. Washington's successor as director of the Tuskegee Institute, spoke before the chamber, a top hotel put firm limits on his accommodations: he would have to take his meals in his room. In 1928, one of the city's leading black papers, the *Call and Post,* described the "malignant fruit" of "race prejudice": "With amazing rapidity it is spreading through the very arteries of this city—once famous for its liberality to minority groups."[43] By the mid-1930s, to combat discrimination, African Americans in the Central neighborhood formed the Future Outlook League, a local "Don't Buy Where You Can't Work" campaign. In 1938, the league counted ten thousand members, operated a weekly newspaper, and, by the 1940s, pushed the NAACP to take more aggressive stances against discrimination.[44]

Cleveland also witnessed some of the Depression's most pitched battles between management and the largely segregated but increasingly militant labor movement. Labor was emboldened not only by the Wagner Act, which put the weight of the federal government behind the right to organize, but also by mounting expectations of full economic and political enfranchisement. In just a few short years, thousands of workers struck at companies including White Motor, Addressograph Multigraph, National Carbon, Electric Vacuum Cleaner, and the Industrial Rayon Corporation.[45] In the momentous winter of 1936-37, workers at Fisher Body Company in Collinwood joined a sit-down strike sweeping General Motors' affiliates across the industrial Midwest, occupying the plant for over a month. Beyond such labor action by those still employed, as the ranks of the unemployed exceeded one hundred thousand, a labor journalist described how "marching columns of unemployed became a familiar sight. Public Square saw demonstrations running into tens of thousands."[46]

While labor campaigns would win significant victories, Cleveland's CIO shops, like those in Chicago, Detroit, and Pittsburgh, continued to relegate African Americans to a narrow range of opportunities.[47] To be sure, African Americans engaged in their own activism, but their militancy lay in the future. As the city's organized business community began to recognize the explosive conditions that threatened to remake the city's political and economic order, they too began to mobilize. If Cleveland's restive population was hungry for New Deal reforms, businesspeople soon recognized that embracing their own New Deal might offer ways to maintain their authority.

Turning to Washington

Between the increasingly untenable costs of relief, violence, and national news coverage of relief riots, the chamber's City Plan Commission argued that doing nothing was "becoming more expensive than the city can bear."[48] Their concerns about violence were shared by New Dealers. As Charles Merriam left Chicago for Washington, he appended a warning to his 1934 report, "A Plan for Planning," the blueprint for the National Planning Board: "Not passive acceptance but violent explosion is the alternative if we fail to develop security and progress by rational and evolutionary methods."[49] For Merriam, forging cooperative partnerships with local business elites—an "evolutionary" rather than revolutionary vision of reform—was essential to the success of New Deal planning. Ceding such authority to local interests, however, would limit both the coherence and progressive potential of New Deal reforms.

As Cleveland's chamber debated remedies for the unemployment emergency, one 1932 report found "real agreement" in the goal of subsidizing construction employment by developing "housing" and the "elimination of slums and the improvement of blighted areas."[50] Since the teens, as labor and material costs rose, private housing developers struggled to produce affordable housing for the growing population of industrial wageworkers and emigrants, both black and white, from the deep South and Appalachia. Older housing stock was dilapidated, particularly in increasingly crowded black neighborhoods. During World War I, the federal government produced affordable housing for war workers but in the 1920s reverted to jawboning, urging developers to pursue more efficient, mass-produced methods. These efforts fell well short of the need. In the Depression, then, chamber members imagined a privately initiated housing and slum redevelopment corporation employing thousands of Clevelanders. Ideally, it would preclude federal interventions.[51]

This focus on housing and urban redevelopment was echoed in other larger, first- and second-wave industrial cities. And not simply because construction might release some of the political pressure of unemployment, but also because, in larger, older industrial cities, the Depression constituted a crisis of urban land values and property tax yields. In the 1930s, assessed land values in larger cities plummeted. Chicago's total assessed valuation plunged from $7.75 billion in 1930 to $4.7 billion in 1940.[52] In Pittsburgh, abandoned or outmoded buildings and factories meant significant swaths of the city were assessed at 30 percent below what their "sound market value" might otherwise have been. In one five-year period land values in Detroit tumbled 65 percent; up to 92 percent of properties in some areas were tax delinquent. Rather than price real estate to sell, owners overlooked substantial costs of acquiring, razing, and revitalizing properties and held to "fictitious land prices." Property owners, a contemporary analyst continued, "cling tenaciously to values that never existed or that have long since disappeared, and even jack up their prices at the very first intimation of a rehabilitation project."[53] A redevelopment initiative, then, might offer employment relief, regenerate land markets, reverse cities' "falling tax return," and yield fiscal savings since "the areas in question constitute our greatest expense in maintaining health and safety."[54]

For Cleveland's chamber, the least desirable option was a full-fledged public housing program, which, they noted derisively, was advocated by "those who look at the European countries" and admire their "practice of state building." Ideally, private enterprise would tackle the problem without public intervention. Yet, there was simply too much risk: "acquisition of land is troublesome; the cost of finance and taxation is high; the cost of building is lower than it was, but is, nevertheless, high, and rents are low." As they confronted the limitations of purely private solutions, they considered ways to recruit government subsidies that might maintain private-sector authority. The "most popular suggestion" was a form of public-private partnership, with government insulating private capital from risk by acquiring blighted land through condemnation or eminent domain and conveying it cheaply to private developers. On the supply side, this approach slashed the costs associated with clearing and assembling land, which, for outmoded industrial plants especially, could be astronomical. Chamber members concluded with pragmatism rather than dogma: public intervention might offer "medicines which are afterwards thrown away."[55]

By December 1932, however, the unemployment crisis had only worsened, and Franklin Roosevelt had won the presidency. That fall, nearly half of Cleveland's normal workforce was unemployed—some 180,000 workers. As a chamber committee argued, "any plan which offers such opportunity for the employment of labor as a building plan, should be given every encouragement." An expanded federal role now seemed inevitable, and they explored creating a publicly subsidized, privately run housing and redevelopment corporation. They could secure RFC financing, which might cover up to 65 percent of the cost of their company's slum clearance and construction projects. Many members endorsed the proposal, but the leadership vacillated, concerned that, if the corporation failed, their "'sponsorship'" of such a company linked to federal subsidies would be humiliating.[56]

As the situation worsened, however, chamber leaders warmed to the New Deal works agenda. In September 1933, Cleveland Homes Inc., led by chamber member Walter McCornack and leading bankers, received the green light from the federal government: if they could raise $2 million in local matching funds, Interior Secretary Harold Ickes guaranteed $12 million in federal subsidies for clearance and housing redevelopment. The chamber also formed an industrial mortgage loan company backed with RFC financing.[57]

While it might be tempting to view the chamber's pursuit of federal financing as an ideological breakpoint, the mechanics of policies handed from Hoover to Roosevelt assuaged concerns that they had suddenly become akin to European "state builders." The Hoover administration designed the RFC, which was effectively a discount lending branch of the Federal Reserve Bank, to jump-start capital liquidity by routing federal financing to imperiled banks and overleveraged railroads. This emphasis on the largest financial institutions explains why the Vans received such substantial RFC bailouts. The RFC also had a high degree of localism. In addition to bringing lawyers, railroad experts, and bankers to work in Washington, D.C., the RFC operated thirty-one local "loan agencies" to evaluate credit applications.[58] Cleveland's agency was led by Matthew J. Fleming, deputy governor of the Cleveland Federal Reserve Bank and a close ally of the chamber.[59] In July 1932, Hoover's RFC also began lending directly to state and local governments at 3 percent interest in order to fund relief and "self-liquidating" works projects.[60] Such self-liquidating infrastructure financing had grown in the 1920s before imploding in the Depression, because, as a contemporary analyst explained, it enabled "public services by legal means" that avoided "prevailing debt limitations and with no increase of tax burdens."[61]

Rather than reform this debt-dependent, fiscally frugal system of municipal finance that fueled so many defaults by the 1930s, the financial structure of the New Deal's public works agenda extended Hoover's reliance upon the same professional-financial-municipal networks. By the end of 1935, thousands of local governments were in some form of default. Rather than directly bail them out, New Dealers instead moved to protect bondholders and offered indirect subsidies through New Deal works programs.[62] The businesslike gloss on "self-liquidating" financing, however, elided the fact that these instruments *were* ultimately secured by a municipality's tax base, a point one analyst conceded in referencing Cleveland's waterworks, which, though financed with revenue bonds, was ultimately "guaranteed by taxing power." Yet New Dealers also worried that local governments could not borrow enough: "the borrowing capacities of municipalities," fretted one official, were at "level[s] insufficient to meet their needs under modern conditions."[63] And so they championed revenue bonds as a way to work around state limitations on borrowing and to avoid further straining local property tax burdens. And, since local revenue sources for relief and development initiatives appeared less directly dependent upon local voters' tax resources, these instruments offered the political advantage of insulating governments and their private partners from wider democratic scrutiny.[64] Through the RFC, then, the same networks of bankers, lawyers, and public officials who fueled the overheated municipal debt regimes of the 1920s became brokers of expanding forms of New Deal finance—not only for private banks and railroads but also for local governments.

The RFC's model of federal debt-financing for public works routed through private lenders and local governments also defined the structure of the early New Deal works regime. The Public Works Administration (PWA) was constructed through the RFC and similar local intermediaries, albeit with a far more generous initial appropriation of $3.3 billion. Rather than create a national works agency that conducted its own hiring and projects, much of the PWA's financing was delivered through the RFC's purchase of "self-liquidating" state and local public works bonds that provided capital for private construction contracts.[65]

The PWA was established by the National Industrial Recovery Act of 1933 (NIRA), Section 202 of which also authorized "slum-clearance" and new housing (though there was no mandate that those displaced through clearance be prioritized in new housing developments). Enticed by this federal carrot, Cleveland's elites argued that much of the city could be considered a slum, including a number of white ethnic communities and most black neighborhoods, particularly Central on the southeastern edge of downtown between East Twenty-Second and Fiftieth Streets and Woodland and Cedar Avenues. The chamber-affiliated Cleveland Homes Inc. envisioned clearing an eighty-five-block swath on the city's east side to create a massive park and high-speed parkway connecting Shaker Heights to downtown. This plan was tabled, but chamber members deemed Central the city's most pressing slum, and it was there that their private, limited-dividend corporation Cleveland Homes Inc. aimed to model private solutions for slum clearance and public housing. But chamber members failed to raise the $2 million in local matching funds, and rather than deliver $12 million in RFC financing to the chamber's corporation, by the end of 1933, the PWA simply took over the project.

In September 1934, the city issued a "declaration of taking" for the properties in Central, and, within weeks, the Cleveland Wrecking Company had begun executing its PWA contract: working west to east, laborers demolished homes in a mixed-race neighborhood before cutting a swath through predominantly black homes between East Fortieth and Fiftieth Streets. As the *Call and Post* explained, "we are now face to face with a removal problem," and officials had no solution for the hundreds of families forced to move: "Needless to say, another slum area is most likely going to be created where these families are moved to."[66] It took three years for housing to be built. Despite assurances that the complexes would not be segregated, as they sought housing in 1937, black applicants were rebuffed at the Cedar-Central Apartments and steered toward the Outhwaite Homes. Ultimately, just 9 of 650 families in Cedar-Central were black, and they were clustered at the corner farthest from downtown and closest to an increasingly crowded black neighborhood.[67]

Despite their initial distrust of federal relief and works programs, for Cleveland's chamber members, the initial hit of federal subsidies distributed through decentralized, trusted mechanisms proved habit forming. Nationally, by April 1936, the PWA, with the RFC serving as its bank, had purchased nearly $340 million in bonds to support privately contracted works programs. The agency also created a "revolving fund": a secondary, private market for this debt, the proceeds of which the government used to make new rounds of debt purchases. New Dealers hoped these initiatives would seed more expansive use of revenue bonds, which might ultimately draw down the federal government's role in subsidizing municipal debt.[68] In any event, the public seemed enthusiastic about this mechanism: in 2,613 local elections, voters approved 83 percent of local bond issuances to secure federal PWA grants and loans.[69] When the PWA came to an end, its financing had stimulated private businesses and supported a works agenda in 3,068 of the nation's 3,071 counties.[70]

Naturalizing New Deal Subsidies

Like their southern brethren, Cleveland's chamber members understood that federal financing could blunt the impact of insurgent classes, strengthen city infrastructure, and provide valuable PR messaging. Associated Charities was overstretched and soon to be dissolved, and steering public works programs could burnish elites' standing with residents. Most important, federal works spending could underwrite economic developments.

Yet, securing federal subsidies required a local matching grant. Because of the city's debt, chamber committees explored other ways to meet those requirements. They learned they could do so with other federal funds. As one report from the Committee on Public Finance and Taxation argued, "no further burden should be placed on the general taxpayer for bond interest and retirement charges at this time." Instead, the chamber "favors the financing … of necessary public works" with federal grants offered through the National Industrial Recovery Act. Since the NIRA offered direct grants before local financing was necessary, "the direct grant provisions of the [NIRA should] be exhausted" to "meet local [matching] needs."[71] Only once local needs exceeded those grant provisions should the city seek new bonded debt.

Chamber members quickly prepared an agenda of development projects. In late 1933, for instance, a rayon firm with branches in Cleveland and Virginia was considering expanding its Cleveland facility, which required new sewage infrastructure. The city could easily require the Industrial Rayon Company to pay for the improvements, and the company had already offered to cover half the costs. Yet, "as a matter of right," one chamber member argued in producerist terms, "the Industrial Rayon Company should not be called upon for any amount." Noting the company's other plant in Virginia, he observed, "It can build its expansion there or in many other cities." Members unanimously agreed to pursue "the necessary consent . . . to complete this present project."[72] Other capital recruitment and retention initiatives, grounded in businesses' expectations for public support, were soon underwritten with New Deal works spending.[73]

Still, New Dealers hewed to a narrow, fiscally cautious definition of "worthwhile" public works programs, which limited local maneuvering of federal subsidies. PWA director Harold Ickes defined "worthwhile" in terms of self-liquidation: there was to be limited redistribution of tax resources, and, as one official put it, a good project was "a first-class business proposition in which the government can't lose."[74] Fiscal moderation also meant the PWA made a much smaller dent in unemployment than FDR had hoped. To achieve greater velocity and scale of works-related unemployment relief, the Works Progress Administration (WPA) took over much of the PWA's agenda. The WPA's appropriation ($4.88 billion or nearly 7 percent of the entire gross domestic product [GDP] in 1935) and its new authority to directly hire workers and execute projects reveal how the early New Deal's fiscal conservatism was yielding to a Keynesian emphasis on deficit spending and boosting workers' purchasing power.

As in the developing South, business elites in the industrial North quickly learned to bend WPA projects toward their bottom lines. This was often enabled by chamber members' close and long-standing relationships with those hired to administer regional WPA offices. The longest tenured administrator of Northeast Ohio's WPA was Joseph H. Alexander, who worked his way up the corporate ladder at the Cleveland Railway Company, ultimately becoming its president in 1926, for which he earned over $40,000 a year, a fortune in the 1920s.[75] Like business leaders in Chicago, New York, and Philadelphia, Alexander designed WPA programs to benefit the white-collar unemployed.[76] The Cleveland Bar Association's executive committee urged him to place "indigent lawyers" on a special committee to review and recommend revisions to municipal laws. Alexander also used $500,000 in federal subsidies to employ out of work draftsmen, planners, and engineers to design economically worthwhile projects. Before a luncheon of businessmen and public officials, Alexander noted that Columbus and Philadelphia had already carried out similar white-collar planning initiatives.[77] The *Plain Dealer* editorial board, tightly allied with the chamber, trumpeted its support: "If scientifically carried out, [the program] will be of great benefit to the city." Alexander "should have little trouble in persuading Washington officials of the value of the project."[78]

By far the flashiest WPA project undertaken under Alexander was the Great Lakes Exposition, held in the summers of 1936 and 1937. A sort of mini–World's Fair, the exposition anticipated Cleveland boosters' developmental vision for much of the rest of the century: it was ostentatious, promotional, and expensive; relied on federal resources; and had little to do with addressing fundamental economic or social problems. The exposition also reflected chamber members' prideful anxieties—fears that relief riots and strikes had diminished Cleveland's reputation as a place to invest. At bottom, then, the exposition was a corporate PR scheme. Featured sponsors included General Electric, Firestone Tire and Rubber, Sherwin Williams, Standard Oil, and the White Motor Company. The upscale department store Higbee's opened a store on site.[79] Occupying more than two square miles from St. Clair Avenue north to the Public Auditorium, and along the lakefront from West Third Street to East Twentieth Street, the Exposition was visited by four million people during the summer of 1936. Extended to a second year, another three million came through. Chamber members' wives, many of whom ran the city garden club, got in on the project, commandeering WPA laborers who prepared the exposition's 3.5-acre garden site and built the massive horticultural building that hosted flower exhibitions and garden club meetings long after the exposition closed.[80] Within two years of the WPA's debut, Cleveland's business leaders—and their wives—had firmly accommodated themselves to locally administered federal development spending.[81]

Nevertheless, chamber members were aware of the growing gulf between their earlier ideological commitments to limited government and increasing enthusiasm for federal subsidies. One way they naturalized these partnerships was by turning meetings into collective grievance sessions about FDR's latest incendiary remark about big business. Minutes from one 1934 meeting note that "considerable time and thought was given to the entire lack of confidence a good portion of the people of the United States have in the future of our country due to the attitude taken by the Administration at Washington."[82] Yet the fact remained that many of the initiatives emanating from the nation's capital benefited capital, and the leading business associations—despite their ongoing rhetorical clashes with Roosevelt—also helped legitimize burgeoning partnerships with the state. Indeed, a number of Clevelanders attended the December 1934 meeting of the National Association of Manufacturers at which members debated the proper response to the New Deal's galloping pace. Upon returning home, Cleveland's representatives conceded that they had, in fact, voted to ratify the National Recovery Administration and its intricate codes. They struggled to defend the decision.[83] As one member explained, "while it may appear . . . that considerable concessions have been made to President Roosevelt . . . some very forward-looking and helpful resolutions . . . were adopted." These included a resolution "against government further encroaching upon the manufacturing business."[84] Despite the persistence of ideological instincts and rhetoric, facing the stick of local social pressure and the carrot of federal aid, strategic accommodation to and appropriation of the developmental aspects of the New Deal state was becoming the rule.

Like their southern cousins, Cleveland's businesspeople also reassured themselves of their "free enterprise" commitments through constant complaints about tangles of bureaucracy and unfair funding decisions. As the *Plain Dealer* explained, the "despair of most local WPA officials is the interminable flow of new regulations and rules of procedure from Washington and regional WPA headquarters." Many were "completely contradictory, many more of them are absurd."[85] Moreover, federal spending in other cities was simply waste, affirming the utility of federal resources at home. One chamber member's remarks underscore how the New Deal's competitive federalism enabled this outlook. Federal money, he said, "will be spent for other purposes less permanent, less useful, less worthy and the tax payers will have to pay that money back in any event. It certainly would seem to be sound business if in some way we can induce the Administration to spend this part of the money in a sensible, constructive, permanent improvement."[86]

Perhaps most important, businesspeople framed their administration of federal spending as the key to successful programs. A glowing *Plain Dealer* profile of Cleveland's WPA executive Joseph Alexander explained how, faced with Washington's vacillation and sluggish decision-making, a weaker man might have gone "on a long drunk." The article described how "a more or less continual undercurrent of friction" defined the railroad man's relationship with Washington. It took the cool-headed leadership of a man of Alexander's business pedigree to manage laggard workers, too. Alexander recounted rousting sleeping laborers during the preparation of the Great Lakes Exposition, when he spent hours "look[ing] for ... horizontal ... government employees." Most confounding, however, was the maddening relationship he was perennially renegotiating with bureaucrats. Sensibly, "Alexander's system is to disregard [rules] that no one can understand and follow to the letter those which are just absurd." When challenged by federal officials, Alexander, "sits back and smiles while they attempt to untangle the results of their own rules and regulations." He "just laughed and let Washington worry."[87]

Despite this patina of frustration, businesspeople regarded the Exposition and other WPA projects as smashing successes—and in no realm more so, perhaps, than in reviving the city's civic spirit and reestablishing their place atop it. At its peak in 1936, Cuyahoga County's WPA employed nearly 41,000 erstwhile candidates for Unemployed Council activism.[88] Many projects became sources of community pride. Thousands marched to the 1940 opening of the Ukrainian Cultural Garden. Built with WPA labor, the garden was dedicated to American democracy and freedom and featured a statue of Volodymyr the Great, the patron saint of Ukraine.[89] When the city opened the Yugoslav Cultural Garden on a rainy spring morning, one hundred thousand ethnics paraded to see Joseph Alexander christen the space dedicated to the city's Croatians, Serbs, Slovenians, and Yugoslavians.[90] Meanwhile, the most popular feature at the Great Lakes Exposition was "Streets of the World": ethnics thronged its two hundred cafes and bars late into summer nights, conversing "in their native tongues," their "eyes shining with pride as they sat at tables in outdoor gardens of buildings representing the land of their birth."[91]

Despite such fruitful partnerships with the New Deal, the *Plain Dealer* managed to register astonishment at the massive federal presence in the city. In May 1938, the paper undertook a survey on the "effect of the federal government on Greater Cleveland's economic life."[92] The WPA alone had already provided the county and city with $76 million, matched locally by the so-called "sponsors' share," just $5.4 million. Add to that financial, mortgage, and old-age insurance, not to mention RFC loans to some 1,034 Ohio companies totaling $236 million, and it was clear, as the front-page headline boomed: "CITY'S 'BIG SHOT' IS UNCLE SAM: Survey Shows Federal Government Dominates Business Life Here." Interesting, however, was the choice of the verb "dominates." Business had, in fact, played an active role in much of the city's involvement in New Deal programs, and none more so than the WPA. That same year, an incoming chamber president polled members: "What do you want your Chamber of Commerce to do?" The resounding answer was to secure public support for urban redevelopment, to make further infrastructure improvements, and to widen and deepen the Cuyahoga River to accommodate larger ships.[93] By the end of the summer, Cleveland's chamber secured another $27 million in WPA transportation improvement spending alone.[94] One chamber member described new infrastructure and the clearance and redevelopment of industrial and slum properties as "the Number One job in Cleveland."[95] Far from endangering the free market or auguring fiscal recklessness, local businesspeople, whether in capital-poor small cities of the developing South or in the nation's leading industrial cities, were learning that big federal spending was big for business.

New Deal Planning, Regionalism, and Slum Clearance

If local elites' initial use of federal subsidies was more opportunistic than planned, for liberals, promoting local and regional planning promised to both rationalize economic development and secure local fiscal capacities. Beyond merely delivering subsidies, then, New Dealers encouraged economic and fiscal planning on an unprecedented scale, and it was here that key components of supply-side liberalism coalesced.

By the second half of the 1930s, a number of New Dealers recognized that local elites were using federal subsidies to remake local markets through clearance and redevelopment schemes and by updating infrastructure to support modern production and logistical needs. A year before the United States' entry into World War II, FDR instructed the National Resources Planning Board to study "post-defense planning." The NRPB's early years were fitful, and its leaders seized on Roosevelt's mandate in hopes of forging a more coherent system of local-national planning. They aimed to broaden economic planning from "a one-time undertaking that results in a master plan," often rooted in short-term interests, to "a continuous process." Systems of "progressive planning" would be "woven together with continuously revised capital improvement programming," which works initiatives underwrote.[96] The fiscal weaknesses of local governments were central to the NRPB's thinking. As one report explained, "The sources of revenue of local units are severely limited, and the type of taxes available to them are not merely relatively inelastic but are also peculiarly susceptible to pressure from organized taxpayers."[97] Planning would enable local governments to get their fiscal houses in order.

Charles Merriam became the NRPB's most influential leader. Most often remembered as the driving force behind Franklin Roosevelt's "Four Freedoms" and the expansive postwar welfare state they envisioned, Merriam's work shaping the institutions and aims of economic planning and public private association had a profound if overlooked impact on the postwar United States. Hired as the University of Chicago's first political scientist in 1900, Merriam also served as dean of the College of Commerce and Administration (predecessor to the university's School of Business). Merriam also translated his scholarly pursuits into real-world applications. Working on city planning with the Commercial and City Clubs of Chicago, he forged ties between the university, business, philanthropies, social welfare organizations, and progressive reformers.[98] He was an enthusiastic participant in the "managerial revolution" that spurred the Chicago City Charter Convention of 1906 and, as a liberal Republican, won a seat on city council, which he held from 1909 until 1917.[99] He sat on numerous commissions that coordinated public-private initiatives, including the Harbor Commission, on which he served with the railroad executive Frederic Delano, FDR's uncle and, later, a fellow New Deal planner. Drawing upon his belief in the scientific study of political relations, Merriam developed a vision of elite-led, technocratic, progressive reform and associational governance. He was also intimately involved with efforts to solve Chicago's fiscal crisis in the Depression. As officials faced a taxpayers' strike, Merriam forged a municipal reorganization and consolidation plan to enable reentry into municipal bond markets.[100]

Refracting American political history through his experiences in Chicago, in 1920 Merriam published *American Political Ideas*, which championed the associational nature of American governance. He described how, as "the government was being centralized and while the party system was being regulated and officialized, the unofficial voluntary organizations were springing up in other and less official types of association and action. On the whole," he argued, "public opinion favored these extra-legal agencies more than it did government."[101] Nongovernment organizations provided the state with unique opportunities for enhancing its capacity by harnessing private institutions. In the vital debates of the teens and twenties, Merriam rejected both conservative and socialist alternatives and sought a moderate path that would balance, as he put it in 1922, private-sector expertise and "technical knowledge, political leadership, and popular control."[102]

As a New Dealer, his evolutionary methods married public priorities like planning with private interests and capacities, charting a path between laissez-faire and socialism. As he put it before the 1933 National Conference on Government, he anticipated the accelerating "interpenetration of industry and government."[103] Because state governments, so often captured by rural interests, remained skeptical of big cities, Merriam believed that expert-led local-national governing partnerships would be ascendant: "The city of the next generation will find itself woven more and more closely into the web of our social and economic development." By harnessing public and private initiative, emphasizing cooperation, and yoking it to democratizing acts if not forms, Merriam imagined "the saving neutrality of experts" offering a moderate path to a modern, democratic state. As he put it in 1934, "the sharp distinction between so-called 'economics' and so-called 'politics'" would "disappear, merged into . . . social engineering or management" led by experts who fused "power and responsibility."[104]

This marriage of public purpose and private initiative also described Alvin Hansen's outlook, whose fusion of demand and supply-side stimulus informed the New Deal's approach to rural underdevelopment and capital scarcity. Hansen was uniquely concerned about "inadequate private investment outlets," which he considered "the problem of our generation." To Merriam's view of regional and decentralized public-private planning, Hansen added his own spin on the value of deficit spending—not only by the federal government but also by states and municipalities. Beyond fueling rural and southern development or subsidizing useful projects like urban redevelopment, Hansen believed government borrowing itself constituted supply-side stimulus. In crises, investors pulled their money from financial markets, exacerbating downturns and producing economic stagnation. Public debt, he explained, kept private capital circulating through the financial system at moments when investors might otherwise sit on their cash.[105] Though "we hear alarmists talk about our vast public debt . . . rarely are we told about the powerful stabilizing role it plays in our economy," Hansen argued. "This vast reserve of liquid assets, constitutes a powerful line of defense against any serious recession."[106] Through its borrowing, the government as "investment banker" made public debt a useful investment opportunity for private capital in its own right and ensured capital stayed in domestic financial markets, the developmental products of that debt offering downstream private investment opportunities. Hansen even called for creating a "Board of Public Investment whose duty it is to originate novel self-liquidating public works" and which might offer direct financing to private enterprise or offer "guarantees on private loans as illustrated by the activities of the Federal Housing Administration."[107] Hansen thus situated Keynesian consumer-oriented deficit spending within a much broader vision of publicly structured supply-side investments and mechanisms for ensuring capital liquidity and innovation.

Merriam attempted to create a political structure for national economic planning that might have institutionalized Hansen's stimulative agenda. In 1936, Merriam enlisted the Social Science Research Council, of which he was a founding member, to draft proposals for a national system of regional planning bodies organized around the regional characteristics of the American economy.[108] Merriam's vision for regional planning descended well past regional councils and would integrate the "2,000 city planning boards," many of which were being "rechristened development boards or reconstruction boards" and which were often led by the local business elite.[109] Drawing upon his experience in Chicago, Merriam explained that planning "requires decentralization, functional and territorial, on many levels of government and of other private [interests] alongside the public."[110] Merriam's was a vision based upon harnessing local elite private institutions rather than imposing new forms of federal administration.[111]

Though Congress rejected Merriam's national council of regional planning bodies over fears of further aggrandizing the executive branch, local developments such as those in Georgia and in cities like Cleveland suggested broad support existed outside of Washington, D.C. Hansen's and Merriam's theories never cohered into a unified practice of national economic planning and governance, but we can trace the ways in which their ideas set in motion local and regional forms of economic planning and set the pattern for decades of liberal development policies to come. And, in any event, Hansen and Merriam were circumspect: economic planning within a democracy was never finished. Organizing the consent of voters, responding to changing market conditions, and honoring local community preferences all required cooperation, adaptability, pragmatism, and vigilance.[112] In 1938, effectively resigned to the constitutional structure of American governance, Hansen wrote: "It appears difficult, if indeed not impossible, for a complex and unwieldy democracy to do other than 'muddle through.' The twentieth century clearly does not offer any comfortable prospect of a smoothly functioning economic Utopia." But he was optimistic: "We may thus learn that there is nothing incompatible between the survival of private capitalism and a generous admixture of public investment" and planning.[113]

Yet, regionalism, which would become a key strength of southern and small-city boosters, and which was so central to the NRPB's vision, would become an Achilles' heel for larger industrial cities like Cleveland, ringed by well-established, self-interested suburban municipalities. Cleveland's quick retreat from regionalism also reflected the political preferences of its business elites who limited efforts to forge broader planning partnerships. Indeed, the Regional Association of Cleveland, formed in 1937, had the potential to be the kind of civic association that Merriam envisioned as a local hub of national economic planning. While Cleveland, like Merriam's Chicago, was an epicenter of City Beautiful–era planning, those campaigns focused on physical construction limited to discrete three- to five-year periods. In contrast, Ernest Bohn, a Republican member of Cleveland's city council and an early advocate of urban redevelopment and public housing, envisioned the Regional Association becoming an NRPB-like planning commission working continuously on regional issues of social, economic, and infrastructural development. For the Regional Association, Bohn secured a WPA-funded staff of sixty white-collar employees who implemented the NRPB's mandate: planning for the coming war as well as postwar economic reconversion.[114] On the association's board sat a number of the city's business leaders, and Bohn held regular consultations with the chamber. Bohn hired John T. Howard, a graduate of MIT's program in city planning, to serve as executive director.[115] The association also studied planning commissions from New York and London and drew upon NRPB reports and recommendations.[116]

Bohn hoped the Regional Association would generate plans, including for regional tax sharing, that might mitigate the rising costs to the city of suburbanization, which siphoned off population and property tax dollars. Under the moniker "Forward After Victory," Cleveland's mayor Frank Lausche appointed nine members to an advisory committee on planning organization, which he tasked with consulting with other cities, experts, and business leaders to develop recommendations for a more vigorous city and regional planning initiative. He named corporate attorney Walter Flory as chairman and hired Howard to serve as the committee's professional assistant.[117] Bohn saw the initiative as a launchpad for a truly regional planning body. But Flory, a suburbanite, rejected that emphasis. Rather than emphasizing the economic and fiscal interdependence of the city and its growing suburbs, "The Flory Report," issued in 1942, stressed slum clearance and redeveloping city land to create space for capital-intensive modern industry.[118] The report argued that it was "blight that has driven people out of Cleveland, seeking better living conditions." Slum clearance would "give the property owner and business man security for their investments" and, for city government, would "make secure the tax values upon which rest all local public services."[119] As capital-hungry southern boosters were transcending regional competition to win federal subsidies and create regional economic development associations, Cleveland's suburban business elites checked Bohn's aspirations for a regionalism that encompassed the entire metropolitan area. As suburbanization and population decline accelerated, the city's fiscal future hung on redevelopment.

And in any event, New Dealers also encouraged the redevelopment of slums and blight. In 1942, Hansen and his collaborator Guy Greer identified "the replanning and rebuilding of our towns and cities" as essential endeavors for public and private investment: "Manifestly they could not be undertaken by private enterprise. But they will open up large outlets for private investment."[120] As they contemplated a more comprehensive urban redevelopment agenda in the 1940s, they also recognized the ways in which the New Deal had already underwritten clearance and fiscal rehabilitation projects. Between 1932 and 1934 alone, Cleveland used federal resources to raze more than 3,000 structures. In 1938, Bohn pursued $18 million more in federal slum clearance and housing subsidies.[121] Among big cities Cleveland was typical. Real estate interests in New York City "pounced on New Deal" works programs, which underwrote a massive business-backed program of slum clearance.[122] By 1938, Mayor Fiorello La Guardia estimated the city had torn down or gutted nearly 9,000 buildings.[123] In Philadelphia, federal support for clearance underwrote the demolition of 8,328 structures, releasing land with an estimated value of $11.5 million. Boston, Detroit, and Pittsburgh also accelerated clearance after 1932.[124]

Bohn shaped Cleveland's clearance and housing agenda, and as he explained, those efforts would certainly support employment and constructing suitable housing. But they were also efficiency initiatives that would save taxpayer dollars and return land to "productive" use. He alleged that social service agencies spent $1.9 million to "maintain" the "luxury of a slum." This view of blighted areas echoed other urban reformers who fused economic and moral rationale for public or affordable housing, referring to "blighted" neighborhoods as "decadent areas" because they "receive more than they pay" in taxes.[125] As Bohn put it before a meeting of the National Association of Housing Officials, "Oh, of course we got the sob sisters, people who wanted to do something for the downtrodden masses. But I think a public housing program should be based on something sounder than that."[126] That "something" was slum clearance, redevelopment, and shoring up the local tax base.[127] Mabel Walker, an expert on urban redevelopment, explained her support in similar fiscal terms: "If our national, state, and local governments did not derive much of their revenue from the incomes and property values thus created, there would be no such thing as public education, health, sanitation, and police and fire protection as we know them to-day, not to mention recreation, relief, and other social activities carried on by governments."[128] Like Roosevelt's "public wealth" rationale for jump-starting private capital accumulation in the underdeveloped South, slum clearance dovetailed with an emerging supply-side liberalism that believed restoring "productive" land uses would offer sturdy fiscal foundations for renewed cities by creating new private investment opportunities—without having to raise local tax rates or share resources across urban-suburban boundaries. Nudged along by federal priorities, fiscal structures, and the preponderant power of its business elites, Cleveland's urban planning would focus on physical redevelopment for decades to come.

Contesting Clearance

In the 1930s, a segment of Cleveland's ethnic population came of age politically, and their interests—especially limiting property taxes—threatened to undercut business-led redevelopment plans. Eastern European ethnics supported Democrats, but they often stood at a remove from the local party, which in many cities was dominated by Irish and Italian Americans.[129] While the city's power elite worried they might become radicalized by the communist-influenced Unemployed Councils, the organization lacked significant ethnic membership precisely because so many ethnics had fled communist insurgencies in Europe.[130] No politician better captured ethnics' appreciation of American liberty and fiscal and social conservatism than Frank Lausche. One of ten children of Slovenian immigrants, Lausche's childhood home was a community institution in their St. Clair Avenue Slovenian neighborhood.[131] When he won the mayoralty in 1941, Lausche appealed in differing ways to business elites and ethnic voters. Businesspeople appreciated Lausche's law-and-order background and his willingness to buck labor leaders and party bosses. He built this reputation as a young judge during Eliot Ness's crusading days as public safety director in the 1930s.[132] With Lausche's backing, Ness cracked down on racketeering and organized crime, skirmishing with Italian and Irish labor leaders.[133] For the rest of his career, through his time as U.S. senator in the 1960s, Lausche had a standoffish relationship with Democratic regulars and organized labor. His ethnic supporters felt his values trumped partisanship.[134]

Lausche's thrifty values created a markedly different state of affairs than did the pro-business politics emerging across the South. To protect his voters' property tax rates, Lausche pledged to retire Cleveland's debt, threatening to eliminate one of business's essential subsidies. He also lowered property tax rates, reducing the average homeowner's burden by 30 percent.[135] While he pledged to support Bohn's planning efforts, when the WPA was dissolved in 1943, Lausche resisted committing new city resources. The WPA had subsidized sixty planners; Lausche funded seven.[136]

Meanwhile, the wartime housing crunch that came with emigrating Appalachian whites and southern African Americans made an already strained housing market even more so. By late 1942, the city's War Housing Service estimated that affordable housing had a vacancy rate of just 0.3 percent. In 1943, the *Cleveland Press* reported that the housing shortage for black residents was generating the city's "own 'Grapes of Wrath.'" In Cedar-Central, site of the chamber's 1934 clearance project, "nearly 80,000 Negroes are housed in homes for 30,000." "It is not a story of poverty, nor of inability to pay. . . . Many of the Negroes today are making top wages in war industries. . . . They have no place else to go, and . . . most of them are paying rents far beyond the value of the homes they must occupy."[137]

In 1941 and 1943, Bohn's Cleveland Metropolitan Housing Authority (CMHA) moved to expand the Outhwaite Homes, seizing and razing the property of black and Jewish business owners but leaving intact a white ethnic district. In a telegram to the NAACP's Walter White, one black businessman called the decision "racial economic discrimination," noting that "all the negro business[es] in this area of the new housing project . . . have been compelled to vacate."[138] The House of Wills funeral home, a pillar of the community, was slated for seizure and demolition. The NAACP rallied to its defense, seeking a federal injunction on grounds that officials were discriminating against black residents by pursuing Jim Crow–like public segregation. A federal administrator declined to intercede, noting insufficient "evidence of racial discrimination." He even justified the seizure, explaining that "private and pecuniary interests throughout the country" were "being forced to yield ground for a public project benefitting the whole community." Because the project would ostensibly "re-house Negro families who have lived in the slums . . . it is hard for me to see how it could be established that racial discrimination is involved."[139]

Yet, the implementation of Jim Crow–style segregation, the destruction of black homes, and the favoritism shown to white families only heightened the housing crisis in black neighborhoods. Cleveland's NAACP noted that middle-class black neighborhoods and businesses were disproportionately targeted for removal, dealing "a vital blow to the economic independence of the Negro group." Officials targeted "areas where Negroes dwelt in better homes, leaving the slums untouched," a strategy rumored to be pursued in other big cities, too.[140] W. O. Walker, editor of the *Call and Post*, sought meetings with Bohn and the city's elite, but these entreaties were largely ignored. Walker was clear on the costs to established "Negro businesses," which "pay high prices for property, or else they have no property at all. When they are later compelled to move from these places by right of eminent domain, they purchase their new locations at high prices again. . . . Unless these people can be relocated without suffering great losses, an effort created for the common good of the group . . . boomerang[s] and destroys the only possibility by which they can emerge from economic slavery." He concluded that the CMHA "is committed to a program of segregation of Negroes in the projects," a fact "obvious to even the most optimistic observer."[141]

The reality of such local control of federally backed programs, one NAACP report argued, made it essential that African Americans be included in the local administration and planning of the growing range of national policies.[142] Black Clevelanders trapped in crowded and dilapidated slum housing wrote letters to Franklin and Eleanor Roosevelt seeking their help in finding sanitary, perhaps public, alternatives. The letters did not reach the president and first lady. Rather, federal officials responded with form letters and routed the correspondence back to local officials whom they instructed "to help you with your problem."[143] The drive for minority administrative inclusion within the growing decentralized public-private state would persist for the remainder of the twentieth century.

"The Best Location in the Nation"

As the United States entered the Second World War, Cleveland's planners pivoted from redevelopment to managing the city's colossal war effort. This included housing and other infrastructural logistics related to the city's surging production and population. One gargantuan bomber plant alone was projected to employ 35,000 Clevelanders.[144] Between 1940 and 1943, the city added

15.5 million square feet of manufacturing space through investments totaling $321.8 million. From April 1940 to September 1944, manufacturing employment grew from 191,000 to 340,000. At the peak of wartime production in 1943, Cuyahoga County's 2,500 industrial plants devoted three-quarters of their production to the war. Cleveland's industries were among the fastest growing in the nation.[145]

Chamber members moved quickly to burnish the city's national reputation. As secretary Walter Beam put it, it "took a couple of years for us to . . . live down the . . . grossly exaggerated national publicity arising out of our relief problems." War production offered a golden opportunity for business to "influence the selection of facts about Cleveland which will cause the city to appear to our country in its best light."[146] A Cleveland Electric Illuminating (CEI) industrial recruitment advertisement announced that Cleveland was once again "the best location in the nation" for business.[147] All of this was possible, the chamber advertised in 1945, "because industry here was prepared" to lead "planning and preparation early in the pre-war national emergency program."[148] Given New Dealers' emphasis on private-sector-led planning, they were not wrong.

Chamber members worked tirelessly to win federal subsidies for infrastructure improvements essential to sustaining the city's resurgence.[149] The major impediment continued to be the city's thrifty white ethnic mayor. To win War Department funding to support river developments and transportation infrastructure, the chamber had to secure matching commitments from the city.[150] But Lausche opposed new expenditures and favored cutting municipal debt.[151] Fueled by wartime growth, by 1943, the city was on pace to reduce its debt to its lowest level in twenty years.[152] Lausche touted the interest payment savings that bond retirements offered ethnic voters, and, for business, he pledged to commit the saved funds, just $15 million, to postwar improvements. That figure was a drop in the bucket compared to the New Deal–sized spending chamber members envisioned.[153]

Stymied, the chamber invited the War Department to Cleveland for hearings that might pressure Lausche to support new bond issuances. The War Department obliged, even ordering the city to remove a bridge as a first step to federal funding for what would become one of the city's major east-west arteries, the Main Avenue Bridge. The chamber also worked closely with the Army Corps of Engineers.[154] While federal funds were ostensibly for the war effort, the chamber's aim was clear: "We must do our part . . . unless we want business to go some place else."[155] In just a decade's time, the chamber had gone from favoring localism and resisting federal interference to leveraging federal contacts to overrule local officials.

With public investments, the chamber anticipated a period of fantastic growth.[156] Flory's commission generated "a five year plan" of postwar works with "a backlog of public construction projects," recognizing "it will take more than sewer and paving projects to make up a well rounded program of the kind needed to provide post-war employment." New hospitals, bridges, shoreline improvements, and renovations to public buildings all were included. In contrast to the $15 million Lausche pledged, the chamber's 636 projects were projected to cost more than $161 million.[157] They also worked on industrial recruitment and soon landed a "whopper" of a "prize catch," as a 1946 *Time* profile put it: two General Motors plants that would employ at least 10,500. *Time* gushed: "All this had not fallen into Cleveland's lap by happenstance . . . industrialists, business leaders, bankers, Chambers of Commerce and city and county officials [got] together for postwar planning." Cleveland's burgeoning supply-side state builders must have reveled in such a glowing national ratification of their producerist commitments: "Clevelanders dote on Cleveland plans. . . . The town is the civic joiner's paradise."[158]

In 1944, Lausche was elected governor, opening a new window of opportunity for municipal debt-fueled development. Spurred along by chamber PR campaigns, Clevelanders joined voters across the country in embracing the optimistic moment, passing millions of dollars in municipal bonds.[159] It helped that the Cleveland City Planning Commission, which had proposed an astronomical $161 million works agenda (around $2.3 billion in 2020 dollars), trimmed its proposal to a more modest $68.4 million. In 1947, projecting for the period 1948 to 1953, the commission hoped to secure $94 million more to pursue improvements in transit, water, and sewage infrastructure.[160] By 1948, the total for all proposals soared to $180 million, with $124 million covered by bonds.[161]

This enthusiasm for municipally financed growth measures depended on voters' optimism about the economy. Ironically, however, as the federal Office of Price Administration (OPA) lifted wartime price controls—a move Cleveland's business leaders actively promoted—rapid inflation pushed Clevelanders and voter-consumers across the country to resist public spending and debt. Businesspeople's hunger for supply-side subsidies was compromised by their alignment with conservative critiques of liberalism's more aggressive protections of prices and purchasing power. Between 1946, when OPA's controls effectively ended, and 1948, consumer prices rose 50 percent.[162] For

Cleveland's thrifty ethnics, the value of balanced budgets and low taxes was self-evident. If they couldn't have cheap groceries, at least they could keep their property taxes manageable. Mayor Thomas Burke revived Lausche's commitment to limiting municipal debt. Despite the momentary postwar uptick, by 1949, as voters rejected more than half of new bond issues, Cleveland was once again retiring debt faster than it floated new issuances.[163] Nationally, in 1948, voters rejected 49 percent of the proposed municipal bonds.[164]

Trends favoring fiscal restraint emerged in Washington, too, where a coalition of national business associations and conservatives conflated the New Deal's economic planning agenda with its postwar social planning. Fiscal hawks had long targeted the NRPB, especially following the agency's 1942 report calling for a new and expansive slate of rights-oriented initiatives. Led by Merriam, the NRPB detailed nine new "personal rights" that included rights to work; fair pay; adequate food, clothing, shelter, and medical care; security, meaning "freedom from fear of old age, want, dependency, sickness, unemployment and accident"; and equality before the law.[165] When Roosevelt unveiled this "economic bill of rights," he drew directly upon the NRPB's work.[166] National and local business leaders, however, joined conservatives in harsh opposition to the prospect of new federal rights auguring interventions in local class, labor, and social hierarchies.[167] Challenging the very notion of "economic rights," *Plain Dealer* writer and booster William McDermott argued that the NRPB's "paganistic" report reflected "excessive expectations of what life below heaven has to offer." "Let us pray," he sneered, "the board will manage to give us" these new rights, "for what it envisions is the millennium."[168] An Ohio congressman called Merriam's designs "nothing less than the absorption of the state of all economic functions and the complete demolition of free enterprise." The head of the U.S. Chamber of Commerce considered the plan a "totalitarian scheme."[169]

Conservatives succeeded in killing the NRPB in 1943. Some opponents did display ideological hostility to planning, though there, too, the exceptions and blind spots were conspicuous. One *Plain Dealer* writer described New Deal planners' "economics [as] of the seventh grade variety and assumes borrowing money in order to have plenty of money to spend is alpha and omega."[170] The *Plain Dealer* editorial page described as "ruinous" the prospect "of the planning and spending of the pre-war period for the future of the country." "Certainly," the paper noted, "little has come from the National Resources Planning Board." Yet, spurred along by massive New Deal deficit spending and incentives to return to municipal bond markets, borrowing other people's money was once again Cleveland's chamber's favorite development tool. Another editorial reasserted fatuous distinctions between public and private initiative. "If there is a single aspect" of the NRPB's recent report "that is more disturbing than the rest, it is the heavy emphasis the committee places on public investment in private business." This "partnership between public and private enterprise," editors wrote, would result in "an economy that is half free enterprise and half state socialism." It "cannot possibly prosper."[171]

* * *

This ideologically skewed view of the New Deal informed a new history of Cleveland written by William Ganson Rose. Rose operated an advertising and PR firm that specialized in large-scale expos and fairs—his firm had directed the Great Lakes Exposition. The scions of two of Cleveland's wealthiest families commissioned him to write this history, and Rose and his assistants spent four years working on their 1,272-page tome, which was published in 1950. *Cleveland: The Making of a City* quickly became a local best seller. Part of its appeal was its inclusiveness: Rose covered the quotidian and the popular, including ethnic neighborhood profiles, the city's amusement parks, and its beloved sports franchises.

The volume was also significant for its omissions, and with them, the way it curated and refashioned Cleveland's public memory of the Depression. The 1930s was detailed over ninety-four pages. But Rose devoted fewer than five to the New Deal.[172] His assessments of "socialistic trends in government" emphasized the view that "private enterprise felt that the Government had taken from it the opportunity to make reasonable profit." Despite the WPA's fundamental role, Rose gave it no mention when he described the Great Lakes Exposition as one "of the most constructive enterprises ever undertaken by the people of Cleveland."[173] Rather than celebrate Cleveland's WPA laborers, Rose emphasized its "disheartened taxpayers" and "federal relief [that] pampered the shiftless and weakened the nation's moral structure." Without the WPA's Federal Writers Project, however, he could never have produced such a detailed work. Its series, the Annals of Cleveland, as well as WPA-conducted histories of the city's ethnic communities were almost certainly his research team's principal sources.[174]

Beneath such baldly ideological efforts to submerge government's role in Cleveland's resurgence, businesspeople continued to press for significant public subsidies. Franklin Roosevelt, like Charles Merriam, was keenly aware of the increasingly interconnected nature of the NRPB's work and planning efforts across the local, regional, and federal levels. Following the NRPB's demise, Roosevelt wrote to his planners noting their success in "building up" a peacetime "'shelf of projects.'" He credited their "instrumental" role "in keeping state, county, and city planning at work. Lots of counties and cities have their own planning commissions and we are getting a very well integrated system for almost every part of the United States."[175] Even if Cleveland's businesspeople resisted saying so out loud, federal investments in economic planning, infrastructure, and redevelopment were not simply historical exceptions to be swept under the rug—they had become part of their ongoing expectations of government, investments that ratified and reinforced their producerist positions atop the city's political hierarchy and as brokers of momentous new forms of federal-local initiatives. To these locally contingent partnerships and policies, liberals would increasingly attach soaring rhetoric about fighting poverty, generating modern housing, pursuing civil rights, and creating economic opportunity—many of the ideas, if not exactly the programs, that Roosevelt envisioned in his Second Bill of Rights.[176]

As postwar prosperity bolstered Cleveland elites' hold on local politics, their restored authority risked obscuring new challenges. Suburbanization and deindustrialization were accelerating; working-class ethnics sought meaningful influence in city politics; and African Americans, dislocated and angry with New Deal clearance and housing projects and marginalized within the industrial economy, would soon mount their own insurgencies as they faced even more ruinous postwar urban renewal clearance programs. For businesspeople, managing these interests while pursuing continued growth would necessitate expanding their partnerships with liberals' growing state. These efforts, however, were more often opportunistic, focused on physical redevelopment and clearance of black neighborhoods. In Georgia, meanwhile, small-city business elites would use federal resources to build regional public-private economic planning and development organizations to create entirely new markets.

CHAPTER 3

Rising Tides

In May 1963, President John F. Kennedy traveled to Muscle Shoals, Alabama, to mark the thirtieth anniversary of the creation of the Tennessee Valley Authority. Kennedy highlighted three decades of economic expansion throughout the valley and, with the clarity of hindsight, repudiated Franklin Roosevelt's critics. "They predicted that TVA would destroy private enterprise," Kennedy said. Instead, the "valley has never bloomed like it does today, and hundreds of thousands of jobs have been created because of the work that these men did before us." Kennedy ticked off markers of progress, citing "the tremendous economic growth of this region, its private industry, its private income." Perhaps most important, at the peak of the Cold War, Kennedy cited those who visited the TVA from "other lands"—"Kings, Prime Ministers, students, technicians, people who are uncommitted." They "come from nations whose poverty threatens to exceed their hopes," and they "compare this valley today to what it was 30 years ago, and they leave here feeling that they, too, can solve their problems in a system of freedom." The TVA, then, was anything but a sign of creeping socialism, as its most strident critics had charged. Rather, at the height of the Cold War, the valley's economic progress, its defeat of poverty through public-private, local-national means was "a fitting answer to socialism."[1]

If FDR campaigned on plans to pull the nation out of the Depression, JFK was, in some ways, more ambitious, pledging in his 1960 campaign to achieve a 5 percent rate of GDP growth. In the process, Kennedy made economic growth, once entrusted to the mysteries of the business cycle, a fundamentally political project.[2] The economic expectations voters placed on the office of the presidency would never be the same. But then Kennedy's optimism reflected the confidence that suffused the maturing fields of economics, modernization theory abroad, and the ascension of Keynesianism. By the late 1950s and the emergence of a self-consciously affluent society, liberals believed they could do more than manage market volatility, the boom-and-bust "business cycle" of classical economic theory. By blending Keynesian macroeconomic demand-side fiscal policies with targeted investments in and subsidies for the supply side, economists and their liberal patrons believed entrenched poverty was a solvable fluke of modern managed capitalism. Sustained economic growth and the social progress that growth ensured could and would reach all Americans without having to create large federal welfare bureaucracies or significant systems of redistribution.[3] These powerful ideas, so resonant at the peak of Cold War anxieties about bureaucracy, freedom, and communist infiltration, converged in the Kennedy administration, which pursued a novel synthesis of demand- and supply-side policies, local and national partnership. At Muscle Shoals, Kennedy credited the spirit of localism that drove the region's economic growth: "this has not been made to work in Washington," he said, but rather "by the people of the valley." He singled out their initiative and entrepreneurialism as clear evidence of his favored maxim borrowed from a New England business council: "a rising tide lifts all the boats." "That," Kennedy concluded, "is the lesson of the last 30 years."[4]

Rome, Georgia's supply-side state builders would not have quibbled. The city's businesses had benefited from the pressure the TVA exerted on Georgia's private utilities to lower rates and improve and expand service. And the New Deal offered the region's business leadership much more stimulus, too. Thanks to the fantastic improvements secured during the New Deal and Second World War—Kennedy had even highlighted the Coosa-Alabama River project —by the early 1950s, Rome's chamber of commerce proclaimed, Rome is "GROWING in population—GROWING culturally—GROWING industrially."[5] The full-page advertisement announced the chamber's ambitions to expand membership to one thousand by year's end. In a corresponding editorial, the paper's editors, chamber men themselves, reminded readers of the role elites played in organizing the region's growth. "Rome's present development is not just haphazard; it didn't 'just happen,'" they explained. "It has been planned, and it is still being planned. The plans are projected far into the future." They argued for the value of economic planning, touting everything from new home construction, improved infrastructure, to new schools and civic facilities. The chamber, they wrote, "is the logical leader, the necessary coordinating body, in the development of the community." "Give your support to the Chamber of Commerce," they concluded. "It is working for Rome."[6]

Their timing was good. The Kennedy administration heralded the maturation of supply-side liberalism, which placed unprecedented faith in the capacity of private-sector-led growth to ameliorate poverty and regional employment imbalances. In these years, beneath mounting tensions over liberals' gradual acceptance of the civil rights movement's agenda, the developmental alliance between liberals and local business boosters only strengthened. In Georgia, by the early 1960s, businesspeople's economic planning and development organization—multicounty regional public-private partnerships—became a primary model for and partner in the Kennedy administration's efforts to turn its "rising tide" mantra into public policy. As it developed its "Appalachian program," the Appalachian Regional Commission, the administration developed a double-barreled approach to stimulating growth. To fight poverty and unemployment, policymakers designed targeted supply-side subsidies, often in the form of direct loans and industrial development bonds to businesses as well as a raft of business-oriented infrastructure spending. In contrast to such spending on business, Kennedy's most significant demand-side policy was the twentieth century's first large-scale tax cut meant to enable consumers to keep and spend more of their earnings. Though Kennedy touted a blended approach of tax cuts and spending, these tactics would ultimately come to define the ideological poles of political debate surrounding economic growth and fighting poverty for the remainder of the century. As the 1960s dawned, however, they were two faces of a supremely confident liberalism.

Liberals' faith in economic growth also ensured that poverty continued to be immensely profitable for local elites, cementing decentralized, administrative partnerships between liberals and often conservative businesspeople. Put another way, the white poverty of Appalachia and the racialized poverty of much of the rest of the country produced the material rationale for much of the growth partnerships between liberals and local elites. The economic and institutional emergence of the postwar "New South," a ravenously developmentalist ethos that historians often equate with Sunbelt conservatism, was underwritten by supply-side liberalism. Even as small-city and rural supply-side state builders worried about the effects Jim Crow's most visible champions had on their bottom lines, Jim Crow disfranchisement and right-to-work laws together meant that, compared to their big-city cousins, they enjoyed especially tight control over the administration of federal antipoverty-oriented development subsidies. Supply-side liberalism, then, decisively boosted this new class of business and political elites as they surpassed Georgia's retrograde "wool hat" faction of race-baiting demagogues.

Partnering for Growth

As the United States emerged from World War II, a new consensus was forming among business and civic leaders, veterans, and middle-class Americans around a culturally conservative vision of economic citizenship, the value of public service, and the desirability of a positive business climate.[7] This business-led, civic ethos was thriving in northwest Georgia. In January 1945, spurred by fears that federal spending would wane, more than sixty businessmen met to discuss strategies for regional growth. Inspired, in part, by the National Resources Planning Board, civic, industry, and trade development commissions were sprouting up across the country.[8] But Georgians' emphases on multicounty regional planning and municipal cooperation was novel. At the behest of Charles Collier, the Atlanta-based vice president of Georgia Power, the group envisioned forming an organization to spur tourism and trade.[9] In Rome, the businessmen voted unanimously to create an organization to pursue a "program of development of Northwest Georgia."[10] They would educate voters on the value of public spending: "What these people must be taught is that the development of historic and scenic assets . . . is not an object in itself, but a means to an end"—economic growth.[11] These men understood that regional economic growth would proceed only so as far as its public investments allowed. Meeting in Rotary halls, country club lounges, and Kiwanis clubs, local elites began plotting ways to maximize public investments in regional development and to ensure their continued control over those resources.

Though it seemed likely that federal funding would decline thanks to the conservative turn in Congress, for a moment businesspeople looked hopefully to fresh developments in state politics. As early as 1938, in partnership with the Georgia Institute of Technology (Georgia Tech), the state's public technical university, Georgia Power sought to develop state-level versions of the New Deal's planning and infrastructure initiatives. The Industrial Development Board, an advisory committee of business interests, state officials, and university-based engineers, formed to direct Georgia Tech's research to benefit private industry.[12] In 1943, the year Congress defunded the NRPB, Georgia Tech's analysts forged their first planning partnership with a chamber of commerce, conducting for Macon's chamber a survey of its twenty-six-county trade area. The next year, Georgia Tech received Industrial Development Board funds to complete a similar report on the thirty-one counties surrounding Augusta. It soon had contracts with chambers in Albany, Rome, Valdosta, and Waycross to investigate regional labor assets, natural resources, and strategic transportation, energy, and water infrastructure improvements. The state-funded experts cataloged existing industries, utilities, and community services, and recommended best-fit industries and industry-targeted improvements for local infrastructure. Georgia Tech also offered invaluable services for modernizing local businesses. As *Georgia Progress*, a Georgia Power publication, explained, "if a community wants to set up a factory to manufacture viscose rayon"—a highly technical process—"it would be the function of [Georgia Tech's experts] to determine what are the necessary raw materials, the extent to which they are found locally, and the amount which would be required to manufacture . . . the product."[13] This service, blandly called "technical assistance," replicated a variety of New Deal industrial development efforts, particularly the NRPB's emphasis on land-use planning, natural resource assessments, and strategic, regionally tailored industrial policies.

Even more promising were potentially revolutionary changes in the state's electoral politics. In 1946, Governor Arnall, the Industrial Development Board's initial patron, was term-limited out of office, and he threw his support to businessman James V. Carmichael's candidacy. Carmichael garnered widespread acclaim through his leadership of the colossal Bell bomber plant in Atlanta's suburbanizing hinterland Cobb County.[14] The credibility of his candidacy made clear the growing support for business-oriented "good government" politics that had taken root with New Deal and wartime spending—quite literally so in Carmichael's case. As the campaign unfolded, Carmichael grew confident of receiving a significant proportion of the popular vote, possibly a majority. But the state's electoral system rendered moot the popular tally. Since Reconstruction, Georgia's elections had been conducted through evolving versions of the "county unit system," an adaptation of the Electoral College meant to keep political power in less populous, rural regions of the state. Each of Georgia's 159 counties was guaranteed one elector, with the most populous counties receiving one or two additional votes, ensuring disproportionate representation for sparsely populated, predominantly white, rural areas. Just three tiny counties could offset Atlanta's Fulton County. As one official put it, "Give me five good men in 100 rural counties and I could run the state." Political mainstay Eugene Talmadge, "Ole Gene," a master of the race-baiting stump speech, boasted that he never needed to win a county with a streetcar line.[15]

That year, an ailing Talmadge entered his final gubernatorial campaign, forcing Carmichael to more urgently appeal to rural white voters. Further complicating Carmichael's campaign, former governor E. D. Rivers, the architect of the state's first failed "little New Deal," entered the race. In a Democratic primary notable for its high turnout, Carmichael won a comfortable plurality of the vote while Talmadge won the county unit tally, taking the election. Talmadge went onto to win the general election. But Ole Gene died before his third inauguration. Pro-Talmadge forces in the legislature preposterously argued that Eugene's son Herman should inherit his father's seat since, they felt sure, Herman had received the lion's share of write-in votes (as Gene's health failed, allies organized a write-in campaign to prepare for such a fight). To their surprise, however, Carmichael received more general election write-in votes, another indication of the mounting support for the politics of economic progress. The Talmadge faction, however, discovered sufficient "misplaced" ballots in Talmadge's home county to deliver Herman the victory.[16] Though the legislature made Herman governor, the state's high court interceded, naming Lieutenant Governor M. E. Thompson acting governor until a special election could be held. In that election, Thompson, not Carmichael, ran against Herman Talmadge and lost. Talmadge won again in 1950, taking the popular vote as well.

The forces of economic progress and state-led development had been stymied by the antidemocratic county unit system and the racial fearmongering of Talmadge's rural "rustics." As the title of a 1948 feature in *Harper's* asked, "A Long Dark Night for Georgia?"[17] Carmichael blamed the county unit system for straitjacketing Georgia's progress. "Of course, I defended it" during the campaign. "I had to. But it's bad, bad, bad—the worst barrier to good government."[18] One northwest Georgia Talmadge supporter recalled businesspeople's aversion to his politics: "it was not popular to be a Talmadge-ite on Broad Street, in Rome, Georgia." "Most . . . business leaders were against us," he explained. "Our white country friends were our salvation at the polls."[19] Georgia's county unit system would persist until 1963 when the U.S. Supreme Court ruled it unconstitutional in a case brought by a Fulton County businessman, which, along with the court's decision in *Baker v. Carr* (1962), enshrined the principle of "one person, one vote."[20]

Business leaders continued organizing in other ways, and, if anything, their frustration with retrograde state politics reminded them to focus on Washington, D.C. A young, charismatic Georgia Power employee soon took charge of the northwest Georgia tourism and trade initiative. Fred F. Starr had begun his career as a salesperson and soon helmed Dalton's chamber of commerce. He played a role in lobbying for New Deal works spending and had taken at least one lobbying trip to Washington. Georgia Power promoted him to the larger Rome Area Development office where he oversaw "community development" initiatives—recruiting businesses and promoting home appliance sales to generate electricity consumption.[21] Over the next decade, Starr grew the Potentialities Committee into a multistate initiative comprising towns in southern Tennessee, northern Georgia, and western North Carolina. By 1955, Starr won state support, too, building partnerships with Georgia's Highway Department, Parks Commission, and the Chamber of Commerce along with numerous local chambers.[22] These ventures into public-private, pro-growth regionalism would be neither his last nor most significant.

Starr's efforts were bolstered by new initiatives at Georgia Tech. Dr. Kenneth Wagner was the entrepreneurial director of Georgia Tech's Atlanta-based Engineering Experiment Station (EES). Prior to World War II, Atlanta's relatively small population and a dearth of state funding hampered Georgia Tech's industrial development efforts, the principal goal of Wagner's Engineering Experiment Station. After the war, however, increased federal research and development (R&D) spending was routed to the university: in 1943–44, the station's budget was quite modest, not quite $240,000; by 1951, and the Korean War, its annual budget exceeded $1.3 million. Federal grants for military-industrial applications accounted for 80 percent of the budget.[23] Military-industrial spending enhanced the station's capabilities, and Wagner hoped to steer these assets toward R&D for the state's private civilian economy. Reflecting Georgia Tech's mandate to serve the entire state, Wagner aimed to broadly distribute the institute's influence and expertise.[24] In 1955, he secured a state grant of $50,000 to develop an "industrial development branch" within the Experiment Station. Wagner designed the branch to respond to local chambers' demands for economic base analyses as part of industrial recruitment efforts. The branch could also help guide the Experiment Station's broader research agenda by using chamber contacts to tailor research for public to private technology transfers. Between 1956 and 1960, Wagner's research team grew to a full-time staff of thirty-three that conducted industrial needs surveys for more than eight hundred manufacturing firms. Wagner soon turned his attention from data collection and analysis to supplying technical and management assistance to Georgia's businesses.

Wagner envisioned establishing branches across the state, and, in 1959, Governor Ernest Vandiver, a Talmadge-ite nevertheless convinced of the importance of economic growth, commissioned a comprehensive plan for the state's long-term industrial development. Wagner seized his opportunity.

In *A Preliminary Blueprint for Industrial Development in Georgia*, he proposed creating "industrial extension" satellite offices that would "supply needed technical assistance to local development groups, . . . expedite the collection of resource data, and . . . provide technical assistance to established business and industry."[25] Vandiver used Wagner's *Blueprint* as the basis for legislation to create Georgia Tech field offices.

The proposal's timing and emphasis on "local development groups" was no coincidence. Rome's chamber of commerce and public planning commission were among Wagner's most frequent correspondents. Since the mid-1950s, Fred Starr and two new allies in Rome explored with Wagner the possibilities of a new kind of public-private regional planning development organization. They soon allied with T. Harley Harper, a Rome furniture storeowner and chamber leader. In 1957, Harper recruited Sidney F. Thomas, a 1956 graduate of Georgia Tech's city planning program.[26] Together, they would create northwest Georgia's new regional development association.

Though Starr and Harper agreed on the promise of regional planning, their partisan leanings and personal backgrounds were quite different. Starr was a garrulous "yellow dog Democrat" with years of experience cultivating consumers and industrial clients in rural regions where voting Democratic was axiomatic.[27] Harper, meanwhile, born in 1904, was one of nine children raised in the north Georgia hills to teetotaling, hard-shell Baptists. He first aspired to become a professional church singer and enrolled in the New Orleans Seminary. During the early years of the Great Depression, he traveled with a preacher, performing in rural revivals across the South. He soon grew frustrated, however; after the preacher took his share of the earnings there was little left for the singers. He turned to the world of business, taking a job with the Baldwin Piano Company in Cincinnati, Ohio, where he trained as a salesman. Harper returned to Rome and took a position with a regional furniture chain, becoming known as an expert salesman. He and a colleague, Roy Nichols, soon opened the Harper-Nichols furniture store in 1944 on Broad Street.[28] Harper shrewdly differentiated his business by offering liberal lines of credit just as the postwar economy was taking off, and, by the late 1940s, he was becoming a civic leader. He served as a head recruiter for the 1952 chamber membership drive, was a deacon in the First Baptist Church, sat on the city building commission, and joined the board of directors of Rome's Home Federal Savings and Loan. In 1954, Harper celebrated the remodeling and grand reopening of his furniture store with a black-tie dinner and beauty contest featuring high school seniors from around the region. After the contest, the girls served as hostesses, and Harry Oldham, chamber secretary and Georgia Power official, presented the winner with a twenty-one-inch television set and sent her on to Pensacola, Florida, to compete in a five-state beauty contest. Even in the grand reopening of his furniture store, Harper thought regionally.[29]

Like Carmichael, Harper joined a new wave of business moderates who worried that one-party politics, overt racist extremism, and Georgia's rural "rustics" threatened progress, modernization, and businesses' bottom lines. Harper quietly started voting Republican, working behind the scenes to expand Georgia's party system.[30] These business boosters, whether Republican or Democrat, however, agreed with liberals on the exigencies of economic growth. Kenneth Wagner joined Starr and Harper as they hit the road to evangelize for a new public-private regional development body, which they began calling the Coosa Valley Area Planning and Development Association. Representatives of business and government from twelve counties would develop strategic plans, land use studies, and natural resource and technological R&D, and they would seek to modernize infrastructure and industrial processes. Wagner encouraged regional businessmen, at a meeting at the Calhoun Elks Country Club, to "make a complete audit of resources and assets, locally and on a region-wide basis, and to draft a program for development of these potentials." He advised the Elks to "pin down your local specific problems and assets, analyze and interpret your resources and develop a long-range comprehensive program."[31] Georgia's businesspeople were working to create a regionally based NRPB-like organization to design, fund, and implement industrial and economic planning.

Despite their enthusiasm for planning, the men understood the difficulties of funding their association solely through local taxes or state subsidies.[32] They had a federal solution in mind. Suburbanization and southern urbanization in the postwar years created challenges for once-rural municipal governments being pulled into growing metropolitan areas. While southern metropolitan areas grew rapidly during these years, as small-scale agriculture faded, half of all southern cities of 10,000 residents or more grew by more than 25 percent in the 1940s.[33] Never before faced with such demands for services, infrastructure, or land use planning, urbanizing governments struggled with new pressures and complexity. Congress offered support in the Housing Act of 1954, which, in addition to creating the federal urban renewal program, created the Section 701 planning grant program which offered two-thirds matching grants to fund strategic planning commissions in communities with populations of up to 25,000 residents. In 1957, Congress raised the population threshold to 50,000, and by 1964, Section 701 had distributed $79 million to 4,462 local governments. By 1968, the program assisted planning agencies in 65 percent of the nation's 7,609 local governments.[34] Armed with federal funds, these commissions developed infrastructure plans, shepherded economic growth, and encouraged rational development of business, industry, and housing. As local elites and an increasingly professionalized set of planners pulled these funds into every corner of the country, they at once propagated federal standards for zoning, planning, and grant writing, and injected the interests of local capital into federal programs, fostering a ubiquitous model for local and regional planning and policy administration, composed of public-private elites, professional planners, and federal subsidies. The federal government was seeding administrative partners in thousands of communities across the country.

To secure the funding, however, Harper and Starr had to win changes to state law. Well into the 1950s, Georgia's rural-skewed state legislature resisted granting local governments home rule, particularly the power to raise local revenue or set zoning standards.[35] Under pressure from the alliance of Kenneth Wagner, northwest Georgia's boosters, and the Georgia Power Company, Governor Vandiver marshaled support for the 1957 Planning Enabling Act. The act enabled adjacent groups of counties or cities to create regional planning and development commissions, which could apply for 701 funding. Like 701 grants, the act mandated a "self-help" provision: local funds were necessary to receive state or federal funds. The act also stipulated that commissions bore no responsibility to state officials, only to member communities, effectively ceding to local governments and private interests the power to invite greater federal influence on and resources for regional development. Small cities could leverage the collective power of counties to slip out of the fiscal and political straitjacket tightened over decades of Talmadge-style county courthouse rule.

All that remained was to raise seed money. Harper's "Quarters for Prosperity" campaign, based on the notion that a mere twenty-five-cent tax per person would win federal aid, galvanized the passage of new levies in each of the Coosa River watershed's twelve counties. The governor "thought he was safe" from having to deliver the $30,000 he had promised, Sidney Thomas later boasted. "No one could imagine that many counties working successfully together for the good of everyone."[36] Reflecting the terminology of the 1957 state planning law, Harper and Starr's association was redubbed the Coosa Valley Area Planning and Development Commission (CVAPDC). Sidney Thomas moved from the public planning commission to become the executive director of the publicly funded and privately led commission. The federal government soon delivered $109,000 in 701 funds, and by 1963, the CVAPDC enjoyed a $248,998 budget composed of just $62,000 in locally sourced revenue.[37] As one state official declared, the commission could "lead to the investment of public funds for needed physical developments . . . attract needed private investments, and maintain or achieve viability for each substate district—to the ultimate benefit of the State as a whole."[38]

In an era characterized by red-baiting, emphasis on the "American way," suspicion of centralized planning, and racist acrimony over the 1954 *Brown v. Board of Education* decision, northwest Georgia businessmen's embrace of federally underwritten planning and cooperative regionalism was striking. "What affects Cartersville affects the rest of the region," concluded Charles Cowan, that city's mayor. The mayor of Calhoun echoed Cowan's sentiments: "What is good for Rome is good for Calhoun, and vice versa." The *Rome News-Tribune* extolled the commission's collective vision: "Selfish motives in seeking industry, in which one town or one county vied with the others, have disappeared."[39] In another region or context, such efforts to work collectively or harness public subsidies and planning capacities might have been viewed by northwest Georgia's boosters as a threat to values of free enterprise. At home, it was government put to best use.

The elites spearheading the initiative were primarily bankers, retailers, and distributors, helming businesses whose profitability depended upon their ability to recruit bigger industries or manufacturers. And they reflected the emerging class of businessperson whose political clout was coming to rival that of the Talmadge-ite wing of state politics. Indeed, in Georgia in 1940, only one-fifth of employment was in wholesale or retail trade, finance, insurance, real estate, or other white-collar services. By 1960, those sectors accounted for well over a third of employment.[40] The elites among this set were often dedicated joiners, civic leaders, and embodiments of the midcentury associational, participatory spirit. But their perception that they represented the broader community of interests of northwest Georgia—working-class whites, unionized textile laborers, rural or urban black workers, women who took in textile piecework—relied upon a narrow reading of the community. Colonel Douglas E. "Froggy" Morrison represented Dade County and was a founding commission member. Froggy served thirty years in the U.S. Army, retiring in 1945. A Mason, a Lion, and past commander of Dade County's Foreign Legion Post, Morrison was also on the board of directors of the Bank of Dade and had served as president of both the Dade County Farm Bureau and the Soil and Water Conservation Districts of Georgia.[41] R. D. Barton Jr. was, for a time, the commission's vice-chairman. Barton owned two businesses, one of which was a furniture store in Bartow County. But he was better known for his other business, the Barton Funeral Home, which inspired his nickname: "The Friendly Undertaker." Barton was a deacon in his Baptist church, the vice-moderator of the Middle Cherokee Baptist Association, a charter member of the Adairsville Lion's Club, and an active Mason and Shriner.[42] These men were unexceptional among their peers at the Coosa commission.

At the peak of the Cold War and amid concerns about creeping socialism, publicly funded economic planning, then, gained political legitimacy largely thanks to its local private-sector stewards—their professional status and whiteness. Commission leaders, overwhelmingly white male chamber members, were referred to simply as "the planners," and planning became a ubiquitous feature of northwest Georgia's boosterism. As one front-page article glowed: "There have been 142 maps, reports, and plans completed; 46 are currently being prepared; and eight are programmed." The "planners will meet regularly with the local Planning Commissions. . . . The planners will also be working with local officials and agencies on related programs that influence the development of the community. This will involve coordinating the various Federal programs in order to most effectively serve the needs of the Community." "FUTURE PLANNING IS BEING STRESSED," boomed the headline.[43] "Progress flags are flying," began another article.[44] Another piece highlighted the noble struggle ahead: "There's an old military axiom that no plan is stronger than the men who execute it," and commissioners were "carrying on a 'war'—a war against economic blight and economic inertia. . . . It may take years. The war [is] for [the] improvement of economic, educational, industrial and business improvement in the Coosa Valley."[45] The images associated with these articles depicted middle-aged white men hunched over maps and plans, shaking hands before construction sites. Their confidence was manifest, their positions within the local and national political firmament axiomatic. Planners' position in local affairs made them uniquely suited to capitalize upon and, most important, mediate the federal role in local affairs.

In July 1960, the CVAPDC hosted its second annual meeting at Berry College under a massive tent dubbed Starr Hall, a toast to the trailblazing efforts of Georgia Power's Fred Starr. The event culminated over a decade of hard work, and nearly one thousand businesspeople and politicians attended.[46] They "lustily cheered" Kenneth Wagner when he announced that

Georgia Tech's first Industrial Development Branch would be established in Rome. A longtime resident of Rome, Georgia Power's president John J. "Jack" McDonough had been a leader of the New Deal–era Coosa-Alabama River Improvement Association, and he offered a tribute to economic planning: "High sounding phrases and long lists of objectives won't do the job. What will do it is down-to-earth, everyday planning and working in the individual cities, towns and communities where our customers live."[47] Viewed from the perspectives of business elites like McDonough, supply side liberalism's development and planning initiatives were legitimate precisely because of the decentralized, elite-led administrative authority they underwrote.

The relative invisibility, that is, the naturalization, of increasingly generous liberal development programs is grasped most clearly when contrasted with the potential for other, more contested extensions of federal authority. In an era of mounting challenges to racial, social, and political norms, Rome's business leaders, like many others across the South, sought to manage the changes in ways that would foster few challenges to their authority. A 1957 *News-Tribune* editorial reflected business's self-described moderate position on civil rights. Titled "A Time for Moderation," the piece described a speech by NAACP director Roy Wilkins in Atlanta "as extreme as anything any of the White Citizens Councils in other states have produced." Wilkins's words were like "the mouthings of the most rabid Ku Klux Klan member" and were only "causing more trouble."[48] Likewise, when they charged President Kennedy with acceding to a march on Washington, the *News-Tribune* pilloried Kennedy's "shocking display of irresponsibility." "In effect," editors argued, Kennedy "invites the intimidation of the national assembly" by "an emotion-charged mob." Congress must not be pressured by "an atmosphere of threatened violence." Rural, small-city civic leaders sought to project onto the national body politic their local practice of elite-led, racially restricted democracy: certain rights, in other words, were more alienable than others.[49] At bottom, however, *Brown* and the menace of new civil rights legislation may have threatened to unleash a range of social forces beyond their control. But, as of the early 1960s, there was little indication the federal government was interested in pursuing major structural changes to the institution business leaders cared about most—the local political economy.

Thanks to their new organizations and federal aid, the local political economy seemed to be progressing quite nicely. Georgia Tech's Rome outpost officially opened in June 1961. Reflecting the intertwined public and private interest, the Coosa commission, the public planning commission, and

Georgia Tech's branch all shared the second floor of Rome's chamber of commerce building rent-free.⁵⁰ Georgia Tech's decentralized network of development experts would help less sophisticated rural industries and businesses capitalize on new opportunities. "The preventative aspects of this program are one of its most important contributions," explained Kenneth Wagner, because businesses often "succumb for lack of guidance with distribution and sales problems. Still others urgently need information on new market opportunities, on machine design problems, and other production difficulties."⁵¹ During 1962 alone, Rome's planners undertook 103 separate "technical assistance" programs, a bland term that obscured just how actively involved public expertise was becoming in regional industry. Thirty-eight "assistance" contracts supported "product design, product packaging, product line design, . . . production contracts, public relations, materials procurement, patent application, export opportunities and many others." Another fifty-one projects supported industrial recruitment efforts through labor market analysis, zoning plans, finance arrangement, and the generation of data on transportation and infrastructure. The branch conducted mineral research that generated a new product for a tile manufacturer, and, in another instance of "technical assistance," planners developed a more efficient production method for a Coosa Valley granite quarry.⁵² By 1965, Rome's planners worked with local businesses to identify new acrylic fibers, develop better forms of "synthetic carpet backing," and identify "laminated wood members" as a good fit for the Coosa region's business base.⁵³ The publicly subsidized partnership between the Georgia Tech commission and the chamber went far beyond regional economic analyses, seeking to enhance practically every aspect of private industry.

The commission also worked with Georgia Tech engineers on industrial recruitment, designing "a system of prospect development . . . [that included] an industrial 'suspect' file" with over 150 companies. In 1962 alone, twenty-five new manufacturing operations opened in the Coosa Valley, and thirty existing plants underwent Georgia Tech–supported expansions.⁵⁴ Federal spending for defense, development, and university-led R&D had moved far beyond Atlanta and was shaping Georgia's rural economy. The rural businessmen who founded the Coosa commission were carrying forward a vision of regional economic planning and intervention most clearly articulated by the NRPB. Struck by the CVAPDC's fast success, the state partnered with Georgia Power on a promotional brochure, "Planning for an Area Development Program," to generate broader interest in the model.⁵⁵ For many businessmen, it was a revelation.

Jimmy Carter, a peanut farmer and distributor from Plains, Georgia, was particularly taken by the model of public-private development, and he traveled to Rome for a CVAPDC meeting.[56] For Carter—who relished his background in naval scientific expertise, touted his status as a rural businessman, shared postwar liberalism's faith in social progress rooted in economic growth, and whose instincts engendered skepticism toward centralization—the CVAPDC was a wonder. Carter quickly formed the eight-county West Central Georgia Area Planning and Development Commission, which soon qualified for state and federal 701 matching funds. Carter was not alone. By 1965, fourteen multicounty commissions had formed, and by 1970 every county in Georgia was a member of an Area Planning and Development Commission (APDC).[57] Most took fact-finding trips to Rome, Sidney Thomas recalled. "We were observed by people from everywhere." "Even the folks in Washington came down to see how we were doing."[58]

Supply-Side Liberalism at High Tide

John F. Kennedy did not come to the study of economics by natural inclination. At Harvard, he earned a C in his lone economics course. As he graduated from the U.S. House to the Senate, however, he worked to better understand Massachusetts's industrial decline, and he and New Deal economist Seymour Harris became frequent correspondents. As Kennedy made the final push in his 1960 presidential campaign, Harris arranged for the candidate to take another economics seminar, this time aboard Kennedy's boat the *Marlin*. On an August day in 1960, "about a hundred yards from shore," Harris recalled, he, Kennedy's close advisor Archibald Cox, and the economists John Kenneth Galbraith, Richard Lester, and Paul Samuelson gave "the senator the ABCs of modern fiscal policy. We tied to this the problem of growth which in time became the President's major economic objective." The economists worked to convince Kennedy about the value of deficit spending. It would be a long-running conversation.[59]

While Kennedy's ambivalence about deficit spending persisted into his presidency, the growth idea grabbed him immediately. Two economists, Walter Heller and Leon Keyserling, played especially important roles in defining how Kennedy aimed to solve the political problem of growth. Over his long career, Keyserling was a leading proponent of "social Keynesianism," which emphasized stimulating consumption by ensuring good wages and high rates of employment.⁶⁰ Keyserling cut his teeth in the 1930s as Senator Robert Wagner's chief legislative aide and was the primary author of Wagner's National Labor Relations Act, the New Deal's firmest support for labor.⁶¹ His longstanding commitments to demand-oriented Keynesianism also informed his work on the Full Employment Act of 1946. For social Keynesians, public investments in the supply side were legitimate if they benefited consumption by stimulating jobs with good wages. A southerner, Keyserling was also interested in the problem of poverty, and he advocated federally subsidized regional growth. Surely with southern poverty in mind, Keyserling believed "there is not meaningful stability except *a stable rate of constant growth*."⁶²

Along with his wife Mary Dublin Keyserling, who was also an influential New Deal economist, Leon Keyserling had run in leftist circles in the 1930s. Both endured painful loyalty investigations in the McCarthy-era red scare of the 1950s. He later reemerged, however, becoming an adviser to the Democratic National Committee and the AFL-CIO and the strongest voice on the Democratic Advisory Council, a group of liberal economists led by Galbraith who fused Democrats' economic and political strategies in the context of heightened concerns about communism and overly aggrandized state authority.⁶³ Though his influence waned by the 1960 elections, Keyserling led the council to emphasize sustained growth as its chief political goal.⁶⁴ The economy had entered recession in the late 1950s, and, pushed by Keyserling, the debate over stimulating growth (and risk inflation) or pursuing price stability began to take on partisan valences. President Eisenhower excused the downturn as a lesser evil in the pursuit of stable wages and prices. He would be the last successful American president to emphasize stability over growth.

Against Eisenhower's prioritizing of economic stability, Senator Kennedy joined a number of liberals who called for growth-oriented policymaking to subsidize the supply side of the economy with the ultimate goal of providing jobs and expanding purchasing power. The evolution of Senator Paul Douglas's depressed areas bill in the 1950s suggests the broad support that was coalescing behind a growth-based federal agenda that aimed to support workers and fight poverty by stimulating business and industrial growth. Douglas's relatively modest $251 million legislation offered infrastructure subsidies and direct federal loans to businesses to attract or keep industries in impoverished, deindustrializing regions, like his southern Illinois. Eisenhower twice vetoed the bill, and the National Association of Manufacturers and U.S. Chamber of Commerce fought the legislation.⁶⁵ The 1960 Democratic presidential hopefuls in the Senate—Lyndon Johnson, Kennedy, and

Stuart Symington—voted in vain to override the veto. But, the bill's emphasis on redistributing federal funds to favor impoverished or deindustrializing regions would inform the supply side of Kennedy's growth-based economic policy and would ultimately lead him to the Coosa Valley's business leaders.

In contrast to the supply side of Kennedy's economic program, the demand side was based on tax relief. The architect of Kennedy's fiscal policy honed his economic perspectives in postwar Europe. Born in 1915, Walter Heller was too young to join the New Deal at high tide. After earning his graduate degree in economics from the University of Wisconsin, he joined the staff of the Division of Tax Research of the Treasury Department where he developed tax policies to fund the war effort. Heller then helped develop the Marshall Plan and joined the Economic Cooperation Administration in Germany, leading the Mission on German Fiscal Problems.[66] Echoing New Deal economists like Alvin Hansen who focused on structuring consumer demand and private investment, Heller argued that establishing a self-sustaining German economy would require reversing "the pattern of unemployment of men and resources."[67] Two main objectives shaped his work in Germany: "(1) the creation of a million additional jobs" and "(2) stimulation of an extraordinarily high rate of capital formation." Heller filtered his New Deal sensibilities through his fiscal expertise, and he advocated slashing Germany's high wartime tax rates, which he was confident would free capital for consumers and business investment alike.

In addition to fiscal policy, Heller recognized that German federalism contained great potential for decentralizing and targeting public investments in key economic sectors, particularly through infrastructure subsidies and financing for small- and medium-sized firms.[68] Heller thus concurred with social Keynesians on the value of compensatory government spending to create jobs and stimulate growth. But he embraced a broader set of economic tools that included tax cuts and, echoing Hansen, strategic investments in the supply side to maximize innovation and productivity. Indeed, it was often when liberals set their sights on developing nations that they most fully articulated the value of supply-side approaches. As Walt Whitman Rostow, perhaps the leading advocate of Cold War–era modernization theory explained in 1964, two primary forces structured growth and development: consumer demand, based on income and population; and the "supply side," which rested "on the state of technology and the quality of entrepreneurship, as the latter determines the proportion of technically available and potentially profitable innovations." He emphasized the point in terms with which Hansen and Heller would have agreed: optimal outcomes derive "not merely from demands set up by private taste and choice, but also from social decisions and the policies of government."⁶⁹

In December 1962, in his speech before the Economic Club of New York, Kennedy outlined his administration's emerging synthesis of supply- and demand-side approaches, championing a program of deficit spending and tax cuts.⁷⁰ Echoing earlier calls by New Dealers like Hansen, Kennedy noted the critical importance of ongoing investments in "education and technical training" and "civilian research and technology" and argued that "economic growth" would depend upon overcoming "a serious shortage . . . of highly trained manpower." Yet Kennedy went considerably further than merely applying Cold War rationale to liberals' long-standing calls for such strategic investments. The speech's primary feature was his call for across-the-board tax cuts and investment credits for business. As Kennedy explained it, echoing Heller, the fiscal system developed to prosecute World War II had become "a drag on growth in peace time." The heavy levy "siphons out of the private economy too large a share of personal and business purchasing power . . . [and] reduces incentives for personal effort, investment, and risk-taking." By cutting taxes, his administration would "expand the incentives and opportunities for private expenditures." Kennedy linked the benefits of tax cuts to traditional liberal concerns, particularly the goal of "full employment" (he emphasized the point four times) and, most important, *greater* tax revenues. As Kennedy put it, "it is a paradoxical truth that tax rates are too high today and tax revenues are too low and the soundest way to raise the revenues in the long run is to cut the rates now." With more capital available to consumers, Kennedy explained, increased purchasing would enable companies to invest in innovation, which would ultimately stimulate more hiring. In the long run, "only full employment can . . . achieve the more prosperous, expanding economy which can bring a budget surplus."⁷¹

Though Kennedy's rationale for tax cuts would later be appropriated by conservatives, in the early 1960s, Kennedy's ends constituted quintessential goals of midcentury liberalism: generating tax revenues, supporting supply-side innovation, and pursuing full employment. As in the New Deal, liberals' close marriage of economic growth and social progress resulted in a policy position that was in line with much of the nation's state and local business communities. Among the reports Kennedy's Council of Economic Advisers marshaled were a series of "case histories" prepared by the Council of State Chambers of Commerce documenting the productive "economic activity" that would "offset the revenue loss caused by lower tax rates."[72] Most important, however, this alignment with business appeared to many liberals to be evidence that social progress rooted in economic growth was near at hand.[73]

Shepherded by U.S. House Ways and Means Committee chairman Wilbur Mills, the Revenue Act of 1964 signed by Lyndon Johnson was a milestone. The bill, which Heller later called "my tax cut," reduced top marginal personal income tax rates from 91 percent to 70 percent and also lowered rates at the bottom end.[74] While efforts to dramatically cut corporate rates faltered, corporations still enjoyed a reduction from 52 percent to 48 percent. The act marked a critical evolution within Keynesian economic thought, one that emphasized fiscal policy rather than merely increased or countercyclical spending as drivers of growth.[75] Indeed, Seymour Harris considered the tax cuts quintessential Keynesianism. As he put it, "This is a Keynesian technique scarcely known to Keynes because when Keynes wrote, taxes were not high, and hence a tax cut was not likely to be very effective."[76] Whether continuing to cut taxes would be an effective stimulus would remain an open question, one that conservatives would increasingly answer in the affirmative.

It would be a mistake, however, to emphasize Kennedy's newfound faith in tax *reduction* at the expense of a longer-standing commitment to targeted tax *redistribution*. Kennedy was steeped in the economic legacy of the New Deal's potent investments in infrastructure. In the Senate, he focused on resuscitating his state's flagging textile industry by similar means. Deindustrialization was a problem, which, he inquired of his economic counselor Harris in 1957, might necessitate the federal government turning "certain sources of revenue back to the states," hence his support for Douglas's depressed areas legislation.[77] As president, Kennedy focused on pockets of regional stagnation and poverty, the regions of the country, like his native Massachusetts, where he hoped to prove his "rising tide" dictum.

These "pockets" of poverty and unemployment were also drawing popular attention. John Kenneth Galbraith expressed concerns about the "insular" poor who existed on "islands" far removed from modernity.[78] Most famously, Michael Harrington's *The Other America* focused attention on the many categories of American poverty.[79] Harrington's work stimulated news reports especially focused on white, Appalachian poverty, some of which described citizens living in veritable states of nature as a rapidly modernizing American civilization left them behind.[80] After a campaign visit to Appalachia exposed him to this abject, predominantly white poverty, Kennedy began thinking of his economic development goals as powerful social policies that would benefit black and white impoverished Americans alike. Once again, Heller's New Deal values and experience in West Germany informed the administration's economic program. As Heller had argued in 1950, "carefully directed investment could help abate structural disproportions ... and could bring relief to the depressed areas" of West Germany.[81] In the postwar decades, West Germany capitalized on its system of federalism to develop nationally funded but regionally targeted industrial policies.[82] Domestically, Heller's and Kennedy's supply-side prescriptions still required institutional form and direction. They turned to federalism.

The Coosa commission's mobilization and economists' interest in targeted stimulus for business in "depressed areas" provided the administration with a model. In eastern Kentucky, a regional development commission akin to the Coosa commission was also organizing (it, too, had roots in local chambers of commerce), and it had an aggressive advocate in Kentucky's governor Bert Combs.[83] Combs joined Georgia's governor Vandiver (who was then scaling up his state's commission system) in relating to national policymakers the promise of their states' decentralized public-private commissions.[84] The federal government could use planning grant money and subsidies to help get similar commissions off the ground in depressed areas.[85] Kennedy's Area Redevelopment Administration (ARA), an updated version of Paul Douglas's depressed areas legislation, advanced the principle that local businessmen and politicians would voluntarily come together to plan regional development and administer supply-side stimulus. Kennedy would create Coosa-style commissions in "depressed areas" across the country.

Drawing upon their new partners' private-sector, local bona fides, ARA staffers touted the program's localism, "self-help," and ostensibly market-based nature. Oblivious to the history of liberalism's supply side, they believed their agency represented "a new partnership" between federal agencies, state and local governments, and the private sector. The onus was on local communities, "for unless [they] take the initiative there is little that State or Federal Governments can do for them."[86] In the context of the Cold War, they framed their program as bolstering American values of self-help, localism, and democratic capitalism. As one administrator put it, "the ARA believes in solving the unemployment problem by the free, private enterprise system."[87] Local businesspeople, not federal bureaucrats, would solve problems of poverty and structural unemployment.

The ARA suffered difficulties that led to its speedy demise. The legislation contained no seed funding to stimulate local planning. Instead, to win

ARA loans and subsidies, the nation's poorest regions were left to develop leadership and seed funding by, perhaps, securing 701 planning grants. As the CVAPDC's experience showed, this was not an uncomplicated process.[88] More vexing, many local businessmen and politicians were annoyed at being characterized as leading "depressed areas," and as one senator complained, "rightfully resent being held up before the nation as a static underdeveloped area in need of a Federal handout."[89] Most significantly, though, the ARA was underfunded and sluggish, prompting Kennedy to pen a perturbed memo to ARA administrators, demanding they "process these projects at an even faster rate."[90] In northwest Georgia, meanwhile, the ARA ran into numerous problems. In some cases, existing businesses viewed ARA support for small, new, or expanding industry as unfairly supporting competitors. Writing to an ARA staffer, a group of textile manufacturers complained about unfair "competition with private enterprise."[91] More often, however, businesspeople complained that the ARA was slow and unresponsive. One northwest Georgia textile business, Textured Products, sought an ARA loan. Their congressman complained about "bottleneck[s] . . . between officials of the Small Business Administration" and the ARA.[92] The local chamber was "embarrassed by the fact that we have told our people that this loan would be forthcoming" and angry that federal bureaucrats "neglected an area for which they were set up to serve and have offered poor excuses for such inaction."[93]

For all their complaints, however, the ARA was wholly in line with businessmen's belief that local elites were uniquely qualified to administer poverty and development programs. And, as the civil rights movement gained steam, liberal policymakers were not inclined to force local elites to embrace a more capacious understanding of administrative inclusion. A Commerce Department report written with characteristically broad language suggested the narrow boundaries to "community" participation prescribed in ARA planning. The act, staffers wrote, "requires that the widest variety of groups in a community—businessmen, labor leaders, public officials, farm group representatives, bankers, and others—participate in a community economic development plan."[94] From the start, however, the NAACP complained to ARA officials that "Negroes were not being consulted in the drawing up of these programs," and, in the right to work South, there were few labor organizations with the clout to influence planning. These realities little troubled the Kennedy administration. Assistant Attorney General Nicholas Katzenbach explained that creating a regulation "specifically requiring Negro or minority group representation in these local planning groups would probably do more harm than good."⁹⁵ National officials ratified local elites' role in administering programs designed to solve problems of deeply racialized poverty and unemployment without the input of the poor and unemployed.

With the ARA's limitations apparent, a group of Appalachian governors approached the White House in 1961 for a substantial new program. At first, ARA director William Batt recommended they develop their own programs with state or local funds. Given that a number of these officials were loudly protesting desegregation mandates, Batt quipped, "I never thought the day would come when I'd be arguing with Southern governors in favor of states' rights, states' responsibilities."⁹⁶ By the spring of 1963, however, the ARA was floundering, devastating storms in Kentucky again highlighted the depth of rural poverty, and the elections of 1964 were looming amid intensifying civil rights mobilization. Kennedy believed a vigorous federal "Appalachian program" would be politically expedient and, perhaps, effective. His advisers explicitly tied support for elite-led development to partisan triage. One staffer, evincing liberals' characteristic developmental optimism, expressed appreciation for New South business "moderates" like Rome's Harper and Starr, explaining to Kennedy that "a new South is in the making right now, but [it] is hidden mostly from view [beneath] the surface manifestations of segregation and the pratings about states rights and super-conservatism."⁹⁷ Beyond stimulating growth, subsidies might shore up the party's southern flank and even nudge the region onto a more progressive path.

In April 1963, Kennedy commissioned the President's Appalachian Regional Commission (PARC) to generate "a comprehensive program for the economic development of the Appalachian Region," shifting the rhetorical emphasis from the ARA's "depressed areas" to "economic development," a more palatable framing for businesspeople. JFK named Franklin D. Roosevelt Jr. the PARC's chairman. Through his Appalachian travels, FDR Jr. became a genuine believer in decentralized federal regional development initiatives. Roosevelt also linked delivering aid to southern states to the political strategy behind civil rights reform—though not as part of a civil rights offensive. Rather, following Kennedy's assassination, Batt recalled how Roosevelt explained to an initially skeptical President Lyndon Johnson that he "was missing a good bet" with the ARC. Here, Roosevelt argued, "was a good way for him to get into the South, a way to find common ground with Southern governors and do something ... completely outside the racial issue. Right afterwards," Batt said, "President Johnson exhibited a great interest" in the program, ensuring its ultimate passage in 1965.⁹⁸

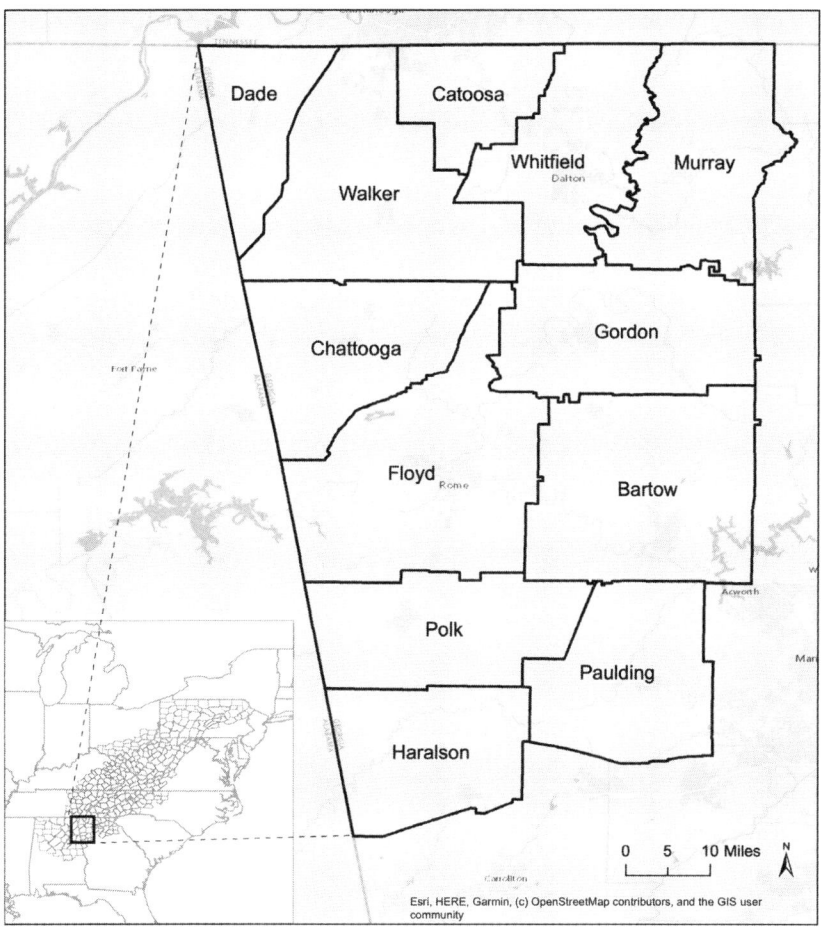

Map 2. Counties of the Coosa Valley Area Planning and Development Commission and, inset, the Appalachian Regional Commission (ca. 1960s). Map by Girmaye Misgna.

Once again, the Coosa commission served as a model, this time for the Appalachian Regional Commission (ARC). Georgia representatives touted the planning commissions, which, by 1963, had expanded to nine, including Jimmy Carter's. As Roosevelt Jr. put it during a visit to Rome, the Coosa commission would "be our guide in setting up the poverty program for the entire Appalachian area." Rome and northwest Georgia, he said, are "fortunate in having such a group which I consider a step ahead in solving the many problems that confront us."[99] The commission became a prototype for Local Development Districts (LDDs), the multicounty units that were the building blocks of the Kennedy-Johnson effort to fight rural poverty. Congress authorized nearly $1.1 billion, of which $840 million was set aside for a six-year bonanza of highway construction meant to fight poverty.[100] These astronomical budget appropriations underwrote the converging priorities of supply-side state builders and supply-side liberals who tied their goal of social progress to faith in private-sector solutions. In contrast to the ARA, which relied on local leaders to organize prior to delivering aid, the ARC sent money to governors who created a system of development districts and dispersed federal funds to local elites.[101] Georgia's moderate business-progressive governor Carl Sanders, whose 1962 election signaled the ascension of developmental politics over the "wool hat" boys, was elected cochairman of the ARC, alongside a federal executive director. In Georgia, Sanders made the APDC system the state's LDDs. Harper and Starr's commissions had become official administrative outposts in the growing supply state's efforts to solve poverty.

The ARC's passage rode a wave of increased media attention on Appalachian, largely white, poverty. *Life* magazine's issue of January 31, 1964, offered an extraordinary twelve-page report, "The Valley of Poverty," featuring photographs of white children living in squalid conditions. As the article explained, the people of Appalachia, "disease-ridden and unschooled," lived lives of "idleness" amid "a vast junkyard."[102] Despite popular attention to the *people's* plight, the bill's appropriations emphasized *place*-based solutions for private-sector growth. Indeed, ARC commissioners' description of their program would have been familiar to readers of the *Rome News-Tribune*'s coverage of the Coosa commission. As one report explained, the ARC "will formulate continuing comprehensive, coordinated plans and programs for the overall development of the region. It will help to provide the basic facilities essential to the region's growth, will help to develop its human resources, [and] will seek to encourage individual initiative and private investments."[103] Governors, boosters, and planners viewed highways as necessary for economic growth, and federal poverty planners increasingly touted modern transportation networks as critical for social progress. As one ARC official explained, the "highway system" would "break down . . . the psychological isolation" of Appalachia's poor. "I've always billed this highway system not only in economic terms, but in social terms . . . because it provides a way for linking people with contemporary America, quite literally."[104] Regional boosters got another massive hit of federal development spending and were assured that their growth plans were benefiting of the worst off. The Cold War's modernization theories had come home to Appalachia.

Not all business groups were pleased with the ARC. The National Association of Manufacturers and the U.S. Chamber of Commerce, ARA and ARC leader William Batt recalled, "were passionately opposed" to the programs, and the conservative newspaper *Human Events* made the ARA and the ARC its "whipping boy." Even *Reader's Digest*, Batt noted, "went after us."[105] But Batt pointed out the vast difference in outlook when it came to local businesspeople: "in depressed areas we worked with local Chambers hand in glove. They were the moving spirits."[106] While national business associations were leading a pro-market charge against federal overreach, allegations of centralized planning, and wasteful spending, local affiliates were becoming tightly enmeshed in the growing supply-side state.

Georgia's pioneering commissions quickly gained a reputation for winning outsized helpings of federal aid. "Keep your Confederate money," ARC staffers joked; "the South will rise again."[107] In 1965–66, the ARC delivered over $7 million to northwest Georgia counties for sewage plants, access roads to industrial sites, and, in Rome, an expanded vocational school.[108] As this funding flowed, commissioners happily reported that between 1961 and 1972, the percentage of local contributions shrank from 67 to 19 percent. "This is not to minimize the importance of local financial contribution," they noted, "but rather to emphasize the fact that cities and counties" in the Coosa region "have gotten an increase in services at no increase in costs, truly an exception by today's economic standards."[109] By 1970, Rome's CVAPDC had teamed with Georgia Tech's engineers on more than three hundred studies and worked with more than 220 new industries, which, during the 1960s, brought some 11,000 jobs to the region. The commission's work also underwrote a remarkable inventory of public projects on behalf of the "business climate" including thirty-seven new water and sewer projects, six regional airports, eight golf courses, and eight hospitals.[110] These developments augured improved fortunes for skilled workers, too. Between 1960 and 1967, Georgia saw a 1 percent uptick in manufacturing as a percentage of total employment; by contrast, in most of the commission's counties the percentage leapt upward. Bartow County saw a 9.4 percent increase; Dade, 7.7 percent; and Gordon, 8.1. (Rome's Floyd County, with a larger population and growth in the service sector, declined by 1 percent, though its total manufacturing employment increased by 6.7 percent.)[111] Between 1960 and 1967, the income per family in the commission's twelve counties experienced astonishing growth. While the state of Georgia overall reflected national trends (48 percent growth) toward rising family income (driven in part by inflation), the Coosa region enjoyed an average increase of nearly 60 percent. And its per capita increase (75.7 percent) surged passed the state average (53.2 percent).[112]

The commission had accomplished a great deal, although poverty alleviation or enfranchising marginalized communities was nowhere near the top of commissioners' priorities. By 1973, despite the efforts of then-governor Jimmy Carter to desegregate state government, across Georgia's eighteen APDCs, just 21 of the 367 board members were African Americans.[113] And, much of the CVAPDC region's income growth was concentrated among skilled and unionized workers. Nevertheless, liberals were eager to demonstrate the returns on their "antipoverty" spending. The Coosa commission became an international showpiece. In 1966, the ARC's director sent representatives from developing nations to visit the CVAPDC. In the junket were members of the Turkish Promotion and Information Center and the Nepal Industrial Development Corporation. A few weeks later, the ARC steered a Filipino community development officer to the commission. The *News-Tribune* reported that "the primary reason for his trip to the United States was to see how the U.S. is tackling some of the problems of poverty and raising the standard of living for those who need it."[114] At the height of the Cold War, the CVAPDC signified supply-side development and antipoverty efforts put to best use—business-driven, locally led, and without overweening federal involvement.[115]

As Georgia's commissions matured, between 1968 and 1973, the ratio of funding they received from local, state, and federal sources continued to shift in their favor. Local contributions dropped from 26 percent to a mere 14.5 percent; state support fell from 31 to 18.8 percent; and the federal share soared from 43 to 66.7 percent. A University of Georgia study pointed to one commission in which "each local dollar invested in the APDC program" generated $113 for "the members." This "demonstrate[s] the importance of local dues in the APDC budget."[116] It also demonstrated the generosity of supply-side liberalism and the degree to which southern and rural businessmen had become integral to liberals' efforts to grow the nation out of poverty.

* * *

In late 1961, as the APDC model was expanding, Arizona senator Barry Goldwater visited northwest Georgia to speak at Rome's Berry College. Goldwater blasted Kennedy's fiscal "irresponsibility." The "scouts of the 'New

Frontier,'" he said, "have lost their way."[117] Before his remarks, Goldwater met with Harley Harper, the retailer and early New South Republican. The senator came away impressed. "The Coosa Valley Commission," Goldwater told reporters, "is becoming nationally known because here in the Northwest Georgia area you have provided your own brains, money and technical know-how to develop the economic and development potentials of this great area." Goldwater praised the localism, self-help, and bootstrap spirit of the commissioners' work. "These dedicated men saw they had a job to do. So they got together on the regional level, raised the necessary money, and they are getting the job done. They didn't come hollering to Washington." The *News-Tribune* summed up the senator's glowing tribute, ratifying the importance of business leadership in legitimizing massive public interventions in the market: "Barry Goldwater has cited the Coosa Valley Planning and Development Commission as a perfect example of the free enterprise system functioning at the local level to solve local and state problems at home—and not looking to Washington to provide the answer."[118]

Goldwater identified self-help and localism as the antidotes to federal invasion. But, the CVAPDC's emergence also underscored the foundational role the federal government played in inspiring and organizing local initiatives and innovative forms of developmental governance—even if all involved preferred to emphasize private leadership and outcomes. Goldwater's remarks and the *News-Tribune*'s reporting suggest the fluid politics of fiscal federalism, particularly the ways in which businessmen and local elites at the peak of the Cold War had come to consider loosely regulated, locally administered federal spending a natural part of healthy, growing, and "free" markets and democratic capitalism: so long as that aid was directed to and by local elites, federal spending was wholly justified.

Boundaries existed, however, between those elites who pursued a partnership with Washington as a form of self-help and those whose social and economic development were perceived as drains on the public trust, whose exercise of state power was seen as unnatural. As a young Georgia Democrat named Zell Miller said in a 1964 campaign advertisement, Lyndon Johnson's burgeoning War on Poverty and its social planners—a very different type of planner from those cheered across Georgia—had been "educated beyond their intelligence." Miller joined a mounting chorus of whites who charged that, through Johnson's poverty war, a majority of Americans' "individual freedoms are being sacrificed away bit by bit" thanks to mandates guaranteeing the "maximum feasible empowerment" of poor and minority citizens in administering federal poverty funding.[119] Two years later, Senator Herman Talmadge—once the bête noire of economically progressive development advocates in Georgia—delivered similar remarks at the Coosa commission's 1966 annual meeting. The "community development" programs offered in the War on Poverty exposed tensions between worthy and unworthy community development programs and constituencies. "Educating and training people to earn a living is good business . . . and can do much to alleviate dependency and unemployment," he said, indicating the extent to which he now felt the need to court ostensibly moderate businesspeople. But, "if the program is subverted, as it has been in many instances, to a mere handout . . . it will not produce the desired results." In contrast, "organizations such as this commission, which concentrates on hard work, planning and development of human and natural resources, are the key to economic progress, both for the individual and the community."[120]

The racial assumptions and elite, white male consensus that undergirded liberals' booming supply-side state were suddenly under strain, making once-anodyne policy tools and delivery structures like public-private partnerships ideologically up for grabs. Definitions of the local community and the racial boundaries to administrative enfranchisement would become explosive partisan issues as poor and black Americans sought not merely a right to vote or public accommodation but also to crack open and democratize the American state itself, whether in the South or North, small city or big.

CHAPTER 4

Insuring Renewal, Inviting Revolt

If much of liberals' rural, southern development agenda emerged through direct subsidies for infrastructure and financing for market creation, their urban agenda was necessarily more complex—developed in numerous pieces of legislation, amendments, congressional committees, and in close dialogue with businesspeople. These complexities were the subject of congressional hearings held in the winter of 1955–56 to investigate private-sector solutions for a mounting crisis of urban housing. In Cleveland, a former Standard Oil of Ohio executive, Upshur Evans, introduced members of Congress to the Cleveland Development Foundation (CDF), a nonprofit organization with a privately raised endowment of $2 million devoted, he explained, to solving "America's most pressing social problem—housing."[1] Paired with Federal Housing Administration (FHA) financing for housing developments on urban renewal sites, Cleveland's supply-side state builders envisioned their $2 million purse growing into a revolving fund through which private developers would remake the city's housing and commercial real estate markets and, along with them, its tax base.

Most histories of urban renewal, the midcentury urban policy that authorized federal funds and local powers of eminent domain to raze and redevelop "blighted" urban communities, have emphasized the high modernist, megablock scale of commercial redevelopments, the disproportionate violence done to African American communities, and the failures of public housing.[2] But those dynamics also stemmed from the program's little understood initiatives to augment and obviate the need for public housing by stimulating private development of affordable, multifamily apartment housing on urban renewal sites. In the 1950s, Cleveland's elites were confident that, with supply-side financing from the FHA and renewal's direct clearance and redevelopment subsidies, they could solve the crisis of overcrowded, substandard housing in black neighborhoods—all on the basis of private profit. As Evans explained, "we believe it will pay out."³

Created in the Housing Act of 1934, the FHA secured and restructured mortgages, emphasizing longer, more sustainable terms and lower interest rates in mortgage markets ravaged by the Depression. The FHA's administrative ranks were stocked with former real estate appraisers, builders, and bankers who brought into the public agency private-sector practices of redlining: denying mortgage financing to African Americans and other ethnic and minority groups.⁴ Beyond the FHA's well-understood role in underwriting single-family, disproportionately white, suburban housing, however, in the 1940s and 1950s, Congress created an expanding range of FHA mortgage insurance programs to incentivize affordable, multifamily housing for wartime workers, veterans, and senior citizens. Between 1947 and 1951, the FHA also secured roughly 80 percent of new rental housing production, creating both new standards of living and significant profits for builder-developers.⁵ Indeed, those profits were guaranteed by FHA insurance premiums paid by mortgagers and renters, whose increased rents covered developers' mortgage insurance premiums. By then, however, Miles Colean, who helped create the FHA's more limited early agenda, had become a sharp critic of the agency's role in expanding the "welfare state," as he put it. Colean described how, by 1953, the FHA had the "power to decide who shall receive credit, how much credit shall be extended, what types of houses shall be financed, and in what locations the financing shall take place."⁶ Far from joining Colean in criticizing the FHA's expanding mandate, local elites like Upshur Evans became eager "diggers in the FHA gold mine," as *Architectural Forum* described the handsome profits to be made from the nation's expansive public-private housing system.⁷ Established in the Housing Act of 1954, then, the FHA Section 220 mortgage program would steer federal financing to new or rehabilitated housing on many formerly redlined, urban renewal sites.

There was not to be a profusion of affordable, privately developed housing associated with urban renewal. But this was not for lack of trying. Supply-side liberals and businesspeople poured a great deal of energy and resources into the expansion of one set of liberal policy tools—FHA mortgage financing—in order to transcend the sputtering public housing initiative mobilized in the Housing Act of 1949. Rather than view the Housing Act of 1954, which de-emphasized public housing, as a conservative turn toward commercial redevelopment, supply-side liberalism's tools and partnerships presented politicians with a political and fiscal middle path between conservative critics of state intervention in housing and left-progressive advocates of public housing.⁸ Even the intensified emphasis on commercial redevelopment in the 1954 act and urban renewal's fiscal structures, embedded in the federal provisioning of municipal borrowing, reflected fiscal and developmental practices rooted in the New Deal, now updated to carry out a broader social and economic vision. Such financialized forms of state building, as one scholar of the era's racial politics has put it, aimed to foster social and racial progress while avoiding "upsetting the entrenched patterns of power and privilege that had given the system its order."⁹ Yet the inequalities unleashed by supply-side liberalism's urban redevelopment and housing agendas, which exacted different but significant costs in working-class white and black communities, would, by the end of the 1960s, do just that.

The FHA's institutional conservatism and racist underwriting practices profoundly limited renewal housing and simultaneously drove up the scale of clearance projects, displacing ever-greater numbers of disproportionately black families. These biases stemmed from the fact that FHA had a substantial interest, as a contemporary analyst explained, "in avoiding any decline in prices that may directly or indirectly affect its contingent liabilities," which by 1963 included mortgage financing for more than 12,000 multifamily housing developments.¹⁰ Into the 1960s, FHA officials remained skeptical of the financial viability of housing in or adjacent to poor or minority communities. These concerns led FHA not only to reject the sorts of smaller-scale rehabilitation and renewal projects favored by residents and developers, but also to prescribe much larger clearance projects prior to approving mortgage finance. Add to those factors the more difficult, costly, and time-consuming processes of acquiring, razing, and preparing densely developed urban real estate, and urban renewal's structural bias toward megablock clearance, large-scale developments, and bigger, better capitalized institutional developers is clarified. Far from simply a vogue for large, high modernist projects, FHA norms and practices, all of which reflected supply-side liberals' fiscal frugality, assumptions about race and property values, and faith in market actors helped produce both the massive scale and paucity of housing that doomed urban renewal—and many black communities. The program's racial violence also accelerated demands for administrative enfranchisement from a rising generation of black activists who identified the liberal supply side state itself, with its decentralized and profit hungry administration, and not simply the quest for civil rights or voting rights, as an essential site for political empowerment. As Ruth Turner, a leading black activist in Cleveland argued, even as

African Americans gained more formal rights, the ravages of urban renewal eroded citizenship in fundamental ways, inspiring revolts, and, in Cleveland, ultimately spurring the election of the first African American mayor of a major American city.

The Road to Renewal

Upshur Evans was optimistic. Few people, a *Plain Dealer* profile began, have "more influence than Upshur Evans over what Cleveland is going to look like in the next decade or two." Evans's CDF was established in 1954 by one hundred of Cleveland's leading business executives to seize the initiative on the city's sputtering redevelopment and housing programs. Partially based on the example of Pittsburgh's influential public-private Allegheny Conference, the CDF would undertake "considerable public relations work" and lobbying to "cut red tape . . . and . . . provide substance, leadership, and a background of authority" in planning the federal Housing Act's redevelopment initiative, which, in 1954, was rechristened "urban renewal."[11] An executive on "loan" from Standard Oil of Ohio, Evans described the CDF's interest in slum clearance and housing not as "a matter of social consciousness—it is a matter of plain, ordinary, practical common business sense."[12]

Evans lived with his wife and their four children in Novelty, an unincorporated community on the fringe of the east-side suburbs. Reflecting his roots in rural Virginia, on their sixteen-acre property, Evans kept riding horses, sheep, chickens, and a goat the family called Satchmo. Evans had pursued a career in the petroleum industry, becoming a close associate of W. T. Holliday, board chairman of Standard Oil of Ohio (Sohio). In 1949, Holliday recruited Evans to Cleveland to become his top assistant. Reflecting the era's corporate commitments to civic improvement, Holliday agreed to pay Evans's Sohio salary while he led the CDF for a two-year term, though Evans ultimately left Sohio to helm the CDF full-time. Profit motive aside, Evans's commitment to urban renewal, which took him to Washington and federal offices in Chicago on a nearly weekly basis, stemmed, he said, from a sense of "duty to ourselves and posterity to do all within reason to save the American city, which is the fulcrum of the nation."[13]

Evans's enthusiasm also stemmed from the ways in which the Housing Act of 1954 reformed the Housing Act of 1949 (described below). The bill would expand New Deal and wartime FHA financing for private housing developments while simultaneously liberalizing local officials' ability to initiate clearance and commercial redevelopment. The CDF, in fact, was created to bring those subsidies and mortgage financing to Cleveland. The 1954 act's passage coincided with elites' increasing urgency concerning a series of interrelated problems facing Cleveland, many of which it shared with other older, northern industrial cities: suburbanization of residents and industry, class and demographic changes catalyzed by black emigration and white outmigration, and persistent, worsening fiscal constraints.[14] As early as 1941, the public-private Regional Planning Association warned "of the dangers of the present haphazard decentralization of population and business."[15] Rather than build consensus around regional or county governance, suburban annexation, or regional revenue sharing, Cleveland's business elites, most of whom lived in the suburbs, did rather the inverse: through their dominance of civic associations and the chamber of commerce, they enjoyed both suburban life and outsized influence over city affairs. Cities with less established suburban fringes, meanwhile, often in the emerging Sunbelt, managed these dynamics by annexing outlying land to ensure suburbanization occurred within city limits, preserving property and sales tax yields—Houston doubled its footprint between 1940 and 1965, adding 140 square miles in 1948 alone.[16] The entire city of Cleveland, meanwhile, covered just eighty-two densely developed square miles. Facing expensive land acquisition costs, in 1951 Ford Motor Company opted to develop a massive manufacturing complex on cheaper land in suburban Brook Park, nearer, too, to where workers were relocating. Brook Park's next-door neighbor Parma was becoming the favored destination for many white ethnic Clevelanders seeking FHA-backed mortgages. And it was also home to numerous FHA-backed multifamily apartments, two of the largest of which—totaling nearly eight hundred units—were announced the same year Ford chose Brook Park for its new plant.[17] Between 1950 and 1960, Parma's population grew from 28,890 to 82,845.[18] And between 1952 and 1969, Cleveland lost 60,000 manufacturing jobs.[19]

As cheap land and FHA mortgage insurance enticed industry and white residents to the suburbs, Cleveland's racial demographics changed significantly. In 1930, just 8 percent of the city's population was African American; by 1970, the figure was 40 percent. Southern black emigrants confronted segregated employment markets, public accommodations, and housing. In the 1940s, Cleveland's branch of the multiracial Congress of Racial Equality (CORE) undertook a series of desegregation actions, one of which targeted Euclid Beach Park. That effort resulted in the passage of a desegregation ordinance, which the park subverted by subleasing amenities to private, members-only "clubs."[20] CORE would increasingly focus its organizing energies on the high rental costs for African Americans associated with segregated slum housing markets and underfunded, overcrowded neighborhood schools. Despite the suburban boom, much of the region's housing stock remained closed to African American residents: by 1955, some 86,000 units of newly developed private housing had been constructed in the region, but, according to one community leader, fewer than 800 units were available to black residents.[21] And, as they had for much of the century, African Americans continued to pay higher monthly rents than whites for considerably inferior housing.

The other dynamic business elites monitored, and which they increasingly associated with growing slum neighborhoods, was the city's precarious budget. Though land values and tax yields momentarily stabilized during the postwar boom, by 1955 Cleveland faced a budget shortfall thanks to industrial depreciation allowances and sagging land values during the 1952–54 recession. When valuations slid nearly 10 percent, Mayor Anthony Celebrezze described the city's fiscal situation as "not too bright." The chamber-backed postwar roster of social services, new schools, and infrastructure spending were in the balance.[22] While the city could raise property tax rates, doing so only incentivized further capital flight, revealing hard limits to municipal fiscal autonomy. Meanwhile, the city's long-standing public housing advocate Ernest Bohn continued to remind city elites that slum neighborhoods were not merely underdelivering in terms of potential tax revenue, but that such "decadent" neighborhoods extracted greater-than-average costs thanks to unsanitary conditions, disease, and higher rates of policing and services.[23]

While discriminatory policing and public health expenses certainly contributed to the city's tenuous budget, at bottom, Cleveland's fiscal precarity was an artifact of the long-run development of fiscal federalism. During the quarter century following the Second World War, as state and local spending grew by over 600 percent, the failure of urban property values to grow apace meant that yawning municipal budget shortfalls became structural realities rather than fleeting phenomena. Municipal officials were trapped. Their cities were home to a majority of their region's workforce. But as the federal government taxed income at higher rates, and with many municipalities forbidden by state constitutions from levying income taxes at all, the bulk of locally produced tax dollars flew to Washington, only to flow back in the form of more contingent and less flexible federal grants and programs, many of which demanded local matching requirements. By 1952, property taxes accounted for nearly 90 percent of *locally* raised revenue but composed just half of the resources municipalities depended upon for operating expenses.[24] Though the federal government provided subsidies, cities' political autonomy waned as they grew increasingly dependent upon fiscal transfers from state and national governments, further eroding local resources through direct contributions or interest payments on bonded debt.

Liberals and urban elites alike began to read racially segregated "slum" neighborhoods as both the greatest sources of fiscal drag and as singular investment and tax-revenue-raising opportunities. As early as 1941, Alvin Hansen, whose ideas would suffuse the Housing Acts of 1949 and 1954, recognized that cities' unique fiscal fetters played an underappreciated role in stymieing redevelopment and fiscal autonomy. In a National Planning Association report, Hansen and Guy Greer argued that cities' dependence "on real estate taxation" led them to boost "assessments and rates, until they have become so high that new construction or reconstruction has been discouraged everywhere; and in the blighted areas . . . stopped altogether."[25] Hansen was concerned that these interlocking fiscal and developmental strictures would make cities feeble partners in the postwar provision of social goods.[26] Greer was attuned to the disparate revenue sources across the federal system. Short of "a nation-wide overhauling of our traditional arrangements for taxation and public expenditures," he argued, which might enable local governments to tax income at greater rates, "it seems only fair that the federal government should aid the local governments to the extent necessary to cover their urgently needed outlays."[27]

Hansen and Greer were also in close dialogue with local businesspeople and the National Association of Real Estate Boards (NAREB) and its research wing, the Urban Land Institute, a coalition of builder and business associations that hungrily pursued New Deal works programs.[28] While a housing initiative for the poor could be one positive outcome, a broader program of redevelopment, advocate Mabel Walker argued, "would be in effect a gigantic subsidy . . . handed out to property holders in these slum areas" that could make urban land "attractive enough to interest private capital." Such investment-oriented initiatives would remedy the fiscal drain of blighted slum properties that "cost the city more in services than they render in taxes."[29] Redevelopment might also entice higher-income residents who required fewer services. Pointing to the South, Hansen and Greer offered the TVA as a model that "vitalize[d] the economy of the region."[30] Targeted bursts of federal stimulus for slum clearance and housing, then, would boost private investments, ensuring long-term municipal solvency and autonomy.

For Cold War liberals, development also meant progress—that social improvement flowed from economic development was becoming axiomatic, defining Cold War international development strategies as much as domestic.[31] Urban demographic change, fiscal challenges, geopolitical Cold War competition, and the burgeoning civil rights movement were also, in differing ways, forcing white liberals to acknowledge what many called "the Negro problem," a formulation that betrayed a sense of innocence in the construction of national systems of segregation. As President Harry Truman put it in his 1949 State of the Union address, urban redevelopment and, as a component within it, a push for public housing encompassed new social and racial ambitions, chief among them raising "the standard of living" of "five million families . . . living in slums and firetraps" and three million in overcrowded housing.[32] The Swedish social scientist Gunnar Myrdal typified this strain of racial liberalism, and, in his widely read reports, he reassured white Americans that their political institutions, whatever their limitations, were poised for justice. The main problem was that "Negro people live a life almost as separate as if they were on an island with restricted communications with the mainland." "Black culture" and integration, he argued, were primarily problems of "modernization"; they were "development problem[s]."[33] "The fulfillment of this promise," Truman said, invoking his civil rights proposals, "is among the highest purposes of government."[34] Here was a similar developmental logic to that which liberals applied to economically and socially disconnected white and black poor of the Appalachian South and developing countries across the global south: a "discourse of progress" regarding broader social and civil rights was draped atop fundamentally developmental, supply-side policy structures geared toward public and private profit motives.[35]

The only major social legislation passed under President Truman, the Housing Act of 1949 was ultimately "a shotgun wedding between enemy lobbying groups."[36] Inspired by New Deal–era slum clearance initiatives, NAREB and other urban business interests sought federal subsidies to clear, assemble, and cheaply convey blighted land to private developers, the sort of sweetheart deals Cleveland's chamber had envisioned in the early 1930s. NAREB and its allies were fierce opponents of public housing, supported by a faction of left-progressive "housers," many of whom argued that slum clearance would only exacerbate the market's failure to deliver affordable, sanitary housing. The Housing Act of 1949 reflected both ends of these debates: it subsidized a clearance and redevelopment program; it liberalized FHA mortgages and created "yield insurance" to guarantee minimum profits on larger, private apartment developments; and it called for building hundreds of thousands of units of public housing in just four years.

As the legislation was implemented, however, the program's progressive aims struggled to break through its mixed emphases on public housing and redevelopment, especially in the context of dense, segregated housing markets. Under the legislation, neighborhood clearance and development could proceed only once a "workable plan" for rehousing displaced residents was established, a fact Cleveland Metropolitan Housing Authority director Ernest Bohn detailed at a 1952 chamber conference on urban redevelopment.[37] Business leaders and city officials hoped to continue New Deal–era slum clearance in Cedar-Central, which had already yielded the segregated Cedar-Central and Outhwaite public housing developments. Its proximity to the central business district and the industrial valley along the Cuyahoga River made it a promising site for commercial redevelopment and middle-income housing.[38] Those displaced by the initiative, Bohn explained, would be "primarily . . . the colored population." Though many owned their homes, most could "not [afford] a down payment" for new properties. The city, then, would turn hundreds of homeowners into renters or public housing residents.[39] There was little vacant land for a housing project that might precede displacement in black neighborhoods.[40] And white homeowners' associations and city council members had already scuttled a public housing project near a white neighborhood. For five years, then, elites failed to find a solution for rehousing one thousand black families slated to be displaced in Cedar-Central.[41] Cleveland's sputtering public housing projects reflected national trends. By 1953, the program had yielded only 260 public housing developments, and, by 1955, it had produced just 200,000 units of its 810,000-unit goal.[42] While there were some successes, the postwar experiment with public housing was brief. What made supply-side state builders such as Upshur Evans so excited about the Housing Act of 1954, then, was not simply the prospect of commercial redevelopment. The act would also enable a freer hand to use eminent domain paired with FHA mortgage insurance provisions to profitably remake urban real estate markets without having to start with housing for displaced families.

Supply-Side Solutions for Urban Housing

An intensification of federal involvement in local housing markets had not been President Dwight Eisenhower's goal when, in 1953, he established an advisory committee on housing. Eisenhower appointed Albert M. Cole, a Kansas congressman who had voted against the Housing Act of 1949, to lead the Advisory Committee on Housing Policies and Programs and the Housing and Home Finance Agency. Of twenty-three committee members, only Cole and Cleveland's Ernest Bohn, who chaired the Subcommittee on Housing for Low-Income Families, were public officials. The rest represented business.[43] Despite, or, rather, because of these personnel decisions, Eisenhower's effort to reduce municipal dependence on federal aid quickly became a tutorial in just how essential that aid was for public officials and businesses alike. As *Business Week* reported in January 1952, "Life is one long nightmare for most municipal finance officials these days." Thanks to inflation, which surged in the late 1940s and early 1950s in the mobilization for the Korean War, "municipal housekeeping costs have risen dizzily."[44] One congressional report found that, while cities with populations over 2,500 had raised revenue sources by 11 percent, in 1947 alone, costs "advanced 67 percent." Like Cleveland, many cities began retiring long-standing debts in the booming 1940s but were again borrowing to cover urgent necessities, to say nothing of supporting business's development agendas.[45] Eisenhower's committee offered a clear appraisal of cities' fiscal constraints: "Many of our cities are pressing hard on debt ceilings. Many more must function under limited taxing power . . . [and] the cost of nearly everything a city buys has risen much faster than municipal tax revenue sources could respond."[46] In his report on the status of low-income families, Bohn offered an exhibit titled, "Notes on the Cost of Slums to Local Governments"—in terms of policing, fire prevention, and more.[47] Bursts of federal investment in redevelopment and housing finance might ensure municipal fiscal independence and a lighter federal role in the future.

While the majority of the members of Eisenhower's advisory committee were opposed to public housing—the 1949 act's sputtering implementation only bolstered their case—much of the committee's work was devoted to determining how best to stimulate affordable urban housing development. Leading a subcommittee on FHA and VA housing programs was Rodney Lockwood, former president of the National Association of Home Builders. Though Lockwood was squarely against public housing, he brought to the subcommittee's work a deep appreciation for FHA mortgage financing and proposed creating an entirely new set of public-private mortgage guarantees focused on urban renewal sites. Such an initiative, he hoped, would obviate the need for public housing by further socializing the risks of private housing development.[48]

Beyond the familiar FHA Section 203 mortgage finance program—which underwrote the vast and discriminatory project of suburban single-family housing—the FHA offered numerous housing finance programs. Many builders had fond memories and fat wallets from the FHA's Section 608 multifamily wartime and veteran housing program, which expired in 1950. With Section 608, the FHA guaranteed mortgages on apartment housing up to 90 percent of the appraised cost of the project. Section 608 also covered the "reasonable replacement cost" of the development—a much more liberal form of appraisal that included the value of the structure and land as well as architects' fees and other "miscellaneous charges." Most significantly, Section 608 projects proceeded without FHA cost certification regulations—in order to expedite housing, developers were trusted to estimate their total costs, which the FHA often blindly secured.[49] Without meaningful oversight, developers inflated costs, cut corners on construction, and pocketed windfall profits when the value of their FHA-backed mortgages far exceeded expenses—a practice dubbed "mortgaging out."[50] Congress found $75.8 million in windfall profits in just 437 projects; but the FHA had secured more than 7,000 Section 608 projects; indeed, in 1950 alone, 99 percent of all new apartments were financed through Section 608. The expense to taxpayers for developers' profits was likely much higher.[51] When these windfalls garnered media coverage, a sheepish Congress was called to account. Developers, meanwhile, were unabashed: the government had invested public funds to construct thousands of housing units, which is what they delivered. Between 1941 and 1955, the Section 608 program had underwritten some 465,526 new units of housing.[52] "For all its faults the 608 program was an outstanding success in achieving the goals set by Congress," an editorial in *House & Home* complained when Congress allowed the program to lapse. "Was it necessary to burn down the whole forest to drive out a few wolves?"[53]

The Housing Act of 1954 was designed to invite the wolves back into urban renewal housing. The act's primary innovation was in its *re*marriage of private profit motives and public endeavor, targeting New Deal models of mortgage finance on precisely those neighborhoods the FHA had redlined and in which local elites had struggled to develop public housing. The 1954 act decoupled regulations mandating plans for relocation housing from approval for redevelopment plans; it set a one-time goal of just 35,000 units of public housing; and it created the FHA's Section 220 mortgage insurance program to incentivize private development of urban renewal housing. Rodney Lockwood envisioned Section 220 offering up to 100 percent financing—meaning no down payment—and forty-year terms, exceedingly liberal provisions he considered essential to recruiting capital to more costly and risky urban developments.[54] As he recognized, developers had maximized their windfall profits by building on relatively cheap undeveloped urban or suburban land, such as in New York City's outer boroughs, or in places like Parma, outside Cleveland, adjacent to Ford's new Brook Park plant.[55] Bringing them into cities would require generous incentives.

Congress, however, was skittish after the windfall controversies. As legislated in the Housing Act of 1954, the 220 program offered 90 percent mortgages on new construction and renovation mortgages. Most important, the act mandated that mortgagors submit cost certifications and that any excess proceeds of the loan be paid "to the mortgagee, for application to the reduction of the principle obligation."[56] To receive mortgage insurance, moreover, the developer was required to submit the overall renewal plan's "workable program" for eliminating and preventing slums and urban blight—that is, to protect its bottom line, the FHA weighed in on the feasibility of a local renewal project's clearance and redevelopment strategy.[57]

This level of oversight was critical, FHA officials believed, because insuring a housing development on a blighted renewal site also forced the agency to radically change its actuarial practices. Rather than use historical or demographic considerations, as the FHA continued to do in other mortgage programs, under 220, the organization would consider the projected value of the "future development of the area under the Urban Renewal plan." Section 220, then, effectively recognized that redlining had kept capital out of "blighted" communities. As one promotional brochure explained, the FHA would now "play a key role in the rebuilding and rehabilitation of blighted areas . . . similar to the role it has long played in the better and newer parts of our communities." "Urban renewal is big business," the guide explained, and the "job can never be carried out without . . . broad flow of private capital . . . into urban renewal operations."[58] Alvin Hansen could not have put it better himself. The potential to create entirely new, federally secured, private housing developments in slum neighborhoods, then, is what led Upshur Evans to leave a lucrative position with Standard Oil to become a full-time urban renewal man.

White Businessmen, Red Lines

Cleveland's business leadership quickly grasped the profit-making potential of federal mortgage insurance for investing in slum areas. They envisioned creating a $185 million revolving fund for housing and redevelopment backed by Section 220 finance.[59] Yet, working with FHA officials chastened by windfall scandals and habituated to denying mortgage insurance in blighted, predominantly minority neighborhoods presented considerable frustrations. Led by Upshur Evans, however, the CDF plunged into it work.

The CDF also believed it had a solution for the problem of where to house displaced families. Home to a shantytown in the 1930s, the Kingsbury Run creek valley ran south and east along the Cuyahoga River, gaining national notoriety after at least a dozen grisly murders and mutilations credited to the so-called "Torso Murderer." Later, the city used Kingsbury Run as an industrial dump. It was there that the CDF envisioned relocating displaced black Clevelanders. To fill in and level a portion of Kingsbury Run, the CDF bought Republic Steel's slag, the leftover stony waste from smelting ore. "This forlorn valley," exclaimed Evans, "is going to pay off . . . when its potentialities are mined and exploited by the Cleveland Development Foundation." Mayor Anthony Celebrezze matched Evans's zeal: building housing "for slum families on filled land in Kingsbury Run"—rechristened Garden Valley—"will be the greatest accomplishment in Cleveland's history."[60]

In December 1954, CDF officials, including Evans, James Lister, and James Yeilding, Cleveland's renewal administrator, visited Washington to secure a planning grant for the 105-acre project. They received conditional assurances that Garden Valley and the nearby Longwood renewal site would receive Section 220 financing. FHA backing was essential, said Evans, because it would ensure the project had "its pick of builders" who could deliver affordable housing with monthly rents between $65 and $70, figures within reach for poor and working families.[61] CDF members celebrated the "private enterprise solution to America's slum problem."[62]

Liberals' social conceptions of development were trickling down and informing the ways in which supply-side state builders understood their pursuit of federal aid as well as their producerist relationships with African Americans and the poor. "We've got to face the racial problem," one official explained to business executives. "These people are your workers and our citizens. They cannot continue to live in the lousy housing they now have." He framed the issue not only in paternalistic terms—"your workers," "our citizens"—but also by emphasizing that slum "areas . . . are a terrible liability to your pocketbooks."[63] The federal program offered business elites, the *Plain Dealer* editorialized, a way to model corporate "citizenship," and also to pursue their "self-interest" by driving up property values, limiting tax burdens,

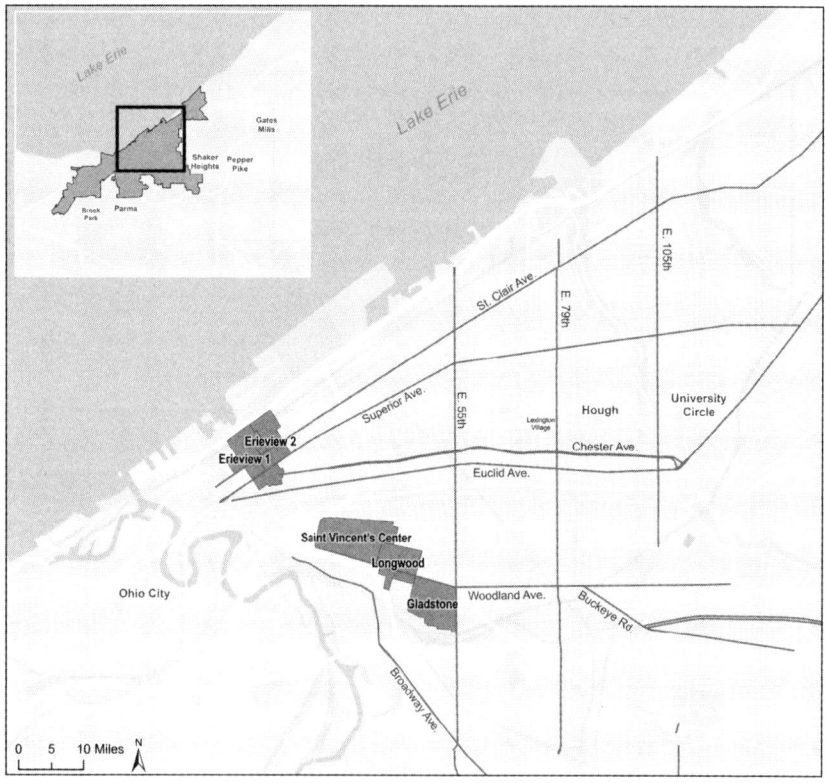

Map 3. Cleveland, Ohio, urban renewal projects (ca. 1954–74) and suburbs (inset). In seven urban renewal projects, all on the east side, Cleveland displaced an estimated 5,889 families, or perhaps some 20,000 people, 88 percent of whom were of color. Map by Girmaye Misgna and Justin Madron.

and making money.[64] But, some business elites struggled to square their pursuit of federal subsidies with their limited government instincts—many of Cleveland's chamber members remained prominent Republicans. They spent chamber meetings anticipating criticism, debating rationale for getting involved, and attempting to legitimize the initiatives. How should they respond to arguments that slums were natural aspects of urban development? A suggested reply: "there don't have to be slums if we clear out what we have." To those worried the program was too expensive, one member emphasized the fiscal bargain for local government: "the Federal Government will pay $2.00 for every $3.00 of the loss. The City will get its loss back in less than 20 years because of the five times increased tax return on the improved land."

But they were also internalizing their roles administering liberals' social agenda. While assisting those in need had never been primary reasons for pursuing New Deal works programs, their guidance of urban renewal, said one member, would "help other people."[65]

Yet, as Cleveland's business leadership planned affordable housing in impoverished communities, the FHA's instincts toward redlining died hard. In a twist of historic irony, white businessmen's efforts to secure $4 million in mortgage financing for Garden Valley proved maddening as they ran up against the FHA's ongoing actuarial and racial conservatism. FHA officials worried that the character of the neighborhoods surrounding renewal sites would jeopardize the viability of its mortgages. In February 1955, Evans made another trip to Washington to discuss financing.[66] After a three-day visit to Cleveland in April, FHA officials assured the CDF that financing was forthcoming. In May, however, FHA again expressed concern about "the extent of mortgage guarantee that can be given safely on new construction in areas surrounded by slums." While the legislation had been signed in August 1954, nationally, as of May 1955, not a single Section 220 loan guarantee had been made.[67] In September, the FHA approved financing for Garden Valley, but it continued to press the city to improve adjacent properties. Following a meeting with CDF and federal officials, Mayor Celebrezze asked the city council to give him eminent domain powers on nonrenewal sites to tell the owners to "fix up and meet our minimum standards . . . or else the city will buy you out and do the fix-up job or tear the house down."[68] Financing was finally delivered in March 1956, sixteen months after Upshur Evans's first trip to Washington. Garden Valley was among the first Section 220 programs in the country.[69] Ultimately, said FHA director Norman Mason, officials "took into account the Development Foundation's knowledge of the situation here and decided to go along." After all, the goal was to "make the land attractive to private buyers" and get capital moving through urban markets.[70] At the groundbreaking, black residents were invited to watch the city's business and political elites plunge shovels into dirt before a large billboard touting the project's public and private partners.

The CDF's experience with the FHA 220 program was typical. A congressional report on its slow rollout blamed "the negative attitude and philosophy displayed" by FHA officials. Rather than "adopting a bold and constructive approach," officials "have generally followed a negative, business-as-usual approach which just will not work in such a huge, difficult, and challenging problem as slum eliminating." In a footnote, staffers gestured at past practices of redlining, noting that FHA officers continued "to apply some of the

Figure 2. Members of the Cleveland Development Foundation break ground on the Garden Valley FHA and urban renewal housing development, May 31, 1956. Rebman Photo Studio Image from MS 351, Cleveland Development Foundation Records, container 31, Western Reserve Historical Society, Cleveland, Ohio.

standards which were previously part of the valuation procedure."[71] As part of its investigation, Congress held a series of hearings with lenders, builders, and local officials, and included a stop in Cleveland. Explaining that the city planned to displace 18,372 families—only 3,000 of which were eligible for public housing—Mayor Celebrezze urged Congress to "make [Section 220] more attractive to the investors and the builders to get into this lower economic group and build homes." As Rep, Albert Rains (D-Ala.) assured him, "that is really the meat in the coconut, and that is the problem that this committee and the Congress are wrestling with."[72]

The program's social priorities lent urgency to Upshur Evans's complaints about federal rules and delays that undermined business's affordable housing program. Speaking before Congress in 1956, Evans grumbled that ungenerous and delayed financing forced the CDF to contemplate higher monthly rents in Garden Valley, with the cheapest two-bedroom unit renting for

$79 per month, considerably above the targeted rent of $65. As a result, the project would not house the "lowest . . . income group" and might not even "accommodate the needs of the middle third."[73] The FHA's resistance to more generous terms also meant "the private developer cannot possibly realize a profit in excess of 5 percent—as compared with 15–20 percent often available in ordinary new construction," making it difficult to secure developers and builders.[74] Add to that developers' knowledge of alternative, often less regulated FHA financing available on cheaper suburban or exurban owner-occupied developments, Miles Colean explained, and no "wonder that the entrepreneurial type of builder . . . now gives [urban] rental housing a wide berth."[75] As Evans complained, 220's "present incentives to private builders" would only attract developers "whose motivations are primarily civic."[76]

Developers also complained that Section 220's cost certifications undermined the pace and profits in affordable housing starts. In his 1960 book *Our Housing Jungle—and Your Pocketbook: How to Turn Our Growing Slums into Assets*, Cleveland developer Oscar Steiner, the primary builder of the Longwood 220 project, estimated that FHA regulations—its "dictatorial rule books"—added 7 percent to his costs, causing him to fall "short of our goal of true low-cost housing." "With one hand" he argued, "the FHA recognizes the low-cost housing need; with the other it refuses to foster such housing."[77] *Plain Dealer* editors argued for loosening "FHA regulations" that "tend to defeat the purpose of the projects." If "the federal government cannot trust local institutions like the Development Foundation" to carry out "sensible, adequate solutions for pressing problems, then it can trust no one."[78] Congress and the FHA, they argued, had overlearned the lessons of the windfall scandals.

In response to supply-side state builders' lobbying, Congress again amended the Housing Act in 1956, putting "a thick sugar coating" on Section 220, as *House & Home* reported. These changes included standardizing a 10 percent profit margin for developers, which meant initial equity investments were reduced to levels closer to the 608 program. The 1956 act also created statutory wiggle room for local FHA officials to insure larger mortgages and, responding to developers' complaints, set an early date for cost certification—reopening the prospect that cutting corners and costs could reap something approaching windfalls.[79] *House & Home* celebrated the amendments, which incorporated "every incentive short of windfalls" and even expanded 220 to include luxury residential developments and "profit-laden shopping center[s]."[80]

By 1963, however, Section 220 remained markedly underutilized compared to other FHA mortgage programs. Despite the fact that 220 was paired with renewal subsidies for clearance and land preparation, on a basis of cost per unit, it was FHA's most expensive program. While average costs per unit across all of the FHA's multifamily mortgage initiatives were $17,345, Section 220's costs topped $21,000, reflecting urban renewal projects' longer time horizons and the higher construction, material, and labor costs associated with work in cities. Developers also complained that FHA's favoring of larger-scale projects meant that smaller scale builder-developers avoided renewal developments.[81] Evidence and testimony, however, suggested another reason for developers' reticence for renewal.

Because federal urban renewal powers and resources were used to prepare and cheaply convey land to private developers, compared to other FHA programs, Section 220 mortgages limited developers' ability to engineer profits by inflating land values through speculation or by using corporate shells to hide inflationary self-dealing. Indeed, even after the windfall profits scandal, a Congressional subcommittee investigation uncovered a common practice among developers of other FHA programs in which developers or sponsors of a project acquired land, which they sold at a substantial markup to a corporation, also owned or controlled by the sponsor. That corporation then secured an FHA mortgage at significantly higher values than the original purchase price. Of eighty-nine representative FHA properties, roughly half, forty-three, had a ratio of FHA valuation to the sponsors' actual costs of 150 percent, and seventy of the eighty-nine properties had mortgages that exceeded the sponsors' cost. The nineteen properties that did not see land value inflation were, "for the most part," the GAO reported, "located in urban renewal areas and insured under section 220." As of June 30, 1963, the FHA insured 12,289 multifamily housing projects at an assessed value of $10.5 billion. Only 147 of those projects were Section 220 renewal housing. Given the high costs and delays associated with urban renewal, several of the newer 220 properties were luxury projects, such as the massive Barrington Plaza project in Los Angeles.[82] Faced with red tape, higher costs, and less flexibility, developers had material incentives to pursue other FHA programs in which profits could be secured more easily and earlier—affordable rental housing projects on renewal sites were largely abandoned.

While local elites continued to work with federal policymakers, tensions with black residents came to a head. In 1958, Mayor Celebrezze brought an entourage of federal officials to tour Cleveland's projects and to celebrate the CDF as a model of public-private cooperation. Scores of picketers organized by CORE surrounded the ceremony at the Longwood renewal site, where they protested the high rents Oscar Steiner charged in his affordable housing development.[83]

Continuing its push for administrative enfranchisement within federal-local programs, Cleveland's NAACP had, as early as 1955, urged the mayor to create an urban renewal citizens advisory committee composed of black citizens "eager to lend their efforts . . . to the successful implementation of an urban renewal program which our city needs so desperately."[84] While Evans and the CDF dominated the renewal agenda, the *Call and Post* noted that "there has been little effort to place on the committee adequate representation from the ranks of the 'little people' living in the slums—the people who deserve a better fate than summary notice that they must move forthwith to make room for . . . bulldozers."[85] Squeezed by racist housing markets intensified by clearance, the remaining apartments in Longwood rented for $85 to $120 per month, far above county averages and far surpassing those the CDF had envisioned. As one critic explained, given such high rents, those displaced "have become community gypsies going from place to place in search of shelter."[86]

Meanwhile, Garden Valley opened in 1957 "with an attractive dump to the north and a field of industrial slag to the south."[87] The Garden Valley Neighborhood House, a private, voluntary agency serving the community, was formed to amplify residents' voices in the preparation, execution, and administration of the housing developments. Instead, they complained, "citizen participation" meetings were "used . . . more to sell plans than to hear citizen needs and ideas." Five years into the experiment, the organization prepared a report describing the "disaster of the private housing development." Tenants, they reported, "make their homes . . . between rubbish dumps and slag piles, amid black clouds of smoke and rodent infestation" and where the nearest service or store "is long blocks away." It was the CDF's and Cleveland Urban Renewal Authority's willful neglect of residents' perspectives, they charged, that guaranteed the program's failure. The lack of "serious development by Urban Renewal of an articulate, free citizen voice and avenues for its group expression could be one of the greatest assets to the entire renewal process," they wrote. Though "it may be easier to plan Urban Renewal without the tension of citizen involvement at every point . . . the evidence of the Garden Valley project is that because that tension has been sometimes missing, good Urban Renewal may not be taking place."[88] Greater administrative enfranchisement, they urged, would ensure a more robust and effective urban renewal program.

Prioritizing profits, developers cut corners and continually delayed plans for playgrounds and green spaces. Doomed with high rents and environmental hazards—the city continued burning trash on the dump, and residents were inundated by rats—Garden Valley's turnover rates were high. By 1963, occupancy hovered around 50 percent, and CORE worked with residents on the "unjust and unequal handling of tenant problems."[89] Like the Longwood developments, Garden Valley's private operators struggled to make mortgage payments. Pressured to protect investors, the FHA created a special amendment to the Housing Act. The so-called "Longwood amendment" authorized the FHA to secure a forty-year, $8.4 million, 3⅛ percent loan to refinance the entire suite of developments, bailing out investors.[90] Yet, Garden Valley's finances remained so precarious that Upshur Evans "saw no solution" but for FHA to take over the mortgage until it could be resold.[91] The FHA did so in December 1963, converting some units to public housing. By then, the project reflected the difficulties of creating affordable housing projects in the shadow of redlining and in search of private profit. Nationally, as of December 31, 1964, Section 220 had insured mortgages on 206 projects totaling $768.6 million, of which nearly a quarter were in "some difficulty." The situation had worsened three years later, when more than 40 percent of Section 220's $832 million in mortgages were "in difficulty" and eight projects were in foreclosure.[92] Garden Valley limped along until another foreclosure in 1973 and its subsequent demolition.[93] Despite worsening overcrowding in many black neighborhoods, redevelopment director James Lister blamed the failure on low demand for affordable housing.[94]

Yet, as a report by Cleveland's NAACP, Urban League, and Community Relations Board argued, the fatal flaw was in the Housing Act's marriage of profits—by private investors and federal mortgage backers—with the development of affordable housing, which had become a public good precisely because of market failures. "The cold economic facts of life," they charged, "must cause us to recognize that under existing Urban Renewal practice, it is impossible to build satisfactory housing at rents which those who are willing to live in this area can afford."[95] Seeking profits on slim margins, developers charged middle-income rents on freshly built slums. By the 1960s, many cities had simply given up on private development of affordable housing. Indeed, the CDF planned luxury housing developments for Cleveland's largest urban renewal project, Erieview. But there, too, the FHA's underwriting preferences would fundamentally reorient the redevelopment process.

Inviting Revolt

Testifying before Congress on November 21, 1963, President Kennedy's Urban Renewal Administration (URA) director William Slayton offered an enthusiastic and detailed overview of the Housing Act's evolution away from housing. Relying on those with closest "experience with the program," policymakers undertook "a succession of amendments over the years" that "broadened the methods and objectives" of renewal. Through their testimony, telegrams, and trips to Washington, supply-side state builders like Upshur Evans had remade urban renewal in ways intended "to revitalize the economic base and taxable resources of cities, large and small," inaugurating a phase of proactive urban economic restructuring focused on white-collar work and the suburban commuters whom planners hoped would spend more time and money in cities.[96] The 1959 amendments authorized renewal projects "located in or near a college or university area," and, in 1961, revisions enabled hospitals to receive renewal funds—providing federal stimulus for the economic transformation of deindustrializing cities into hubs of health care and research.[97] The 1961 amendments further expanded FHA mortgage insurance to include condominiums, reflecting efforts to entice higher-income residents into cities. Responding to local complaints about the blunt instrument of clearance, other revisions created new incentives for code enforcement and rehabilitating older housing stock, which was gaining cachet among an emerging set of young, white gentrifiers. By 1963, then, the Housing Act supported more subtle but no less significant means of neighborhood and market making—as well as class and racial succession.[98] Indeed, Slayton himself was something of an emissary for supply-side state builders. Before leading the URA, he worked for I. M. Pei and Associates and William Zeckendorf, leading urban renewal planning and design firms.

Slayton's testimony also revealed how smoothly supply-side sensibilities had captured and conflated social priorities like affordable housing. The pivot toward economic development, he explained, did not signal the eclipse of such progressive goals; rather, cities were preparing sturdier fiscal foundations for them. He presented aggregate figures from 403 renewal projects begun or completed that suggested a 437 percent boost in property values and, thus, municipal tax yields. He saluted efforts to remake "employment [markets] and the economic base . . . upon which the provision of housing and adequate community facilities and services is to a large extent dependent." He employed this formulation several times, highlighting the fiscal bargain for cities with data suggesting that, in 479 projects, $1.25 billion in federal financing had leveraged $7.5 billion in private spending. These investments spurred "new investment[s]" adjacent to renewal sites that would spur "higher assessed valuations and tax levies" there, too.[99] Cleveland's Erieview project was forecast to improve the area's tax harvest from $480,000 to $3 million, as the mayor testified, benefiting "public schools, parks, recreation, and public services."[100]

In light of deindustrialization and labor unrest, the chamber's consultants recommended using urban renewal powers to pursue new white-collar service sectors such as insurance—that is, they would use renewal as a sort of *post-industrial* policy, one that would consciously transform the city's economic base.[101] Proposed in the CDF-sponsored 1959 Downtown Plan and adopted three months later by the city planning commission, Erieview encompassed an area downtown between East Ninth Street and the new Innerbelt Freeway.[102] Planners imagined revitalizing the old Euclid Avenue corridor, once the main business district. "The usual citizens committee," dominated by the chamber, and "who as a rule belong to the luncheon clubs and live in the suburbs," wrote the *Plain Dealer*, "are once more devoting themselves to the cause."[103] Edward W. Sloan Jr., chairman of the CDF's board (and resident of suburban Gates Mills), cheered the twinned quest for private profit and public wealth: "urban renewal . . . has not only expanded profitable enterprise, but will strengthen the city's tax duplicate."[104] But the fact remained that these were imagined taxes harvested from incomplete developments.

Renewal's worsening racial inequities, however, were quite real. Even as African Americans gained nominal access to public space or equal employment ordinances, urban renewal destroyed black communities and turned homeowners into renters. In the early 1960s, Ruth Turner, an Oberlin- and Harvard-educated African American activist, became a leader of Cleveland CORE, and she focused on remedying root causes of inequality. Turner organized residents to highlight the Housing Authority's "unjust and unequal handling of tenant problems" in public and private housing.[105] Thanks to hypersegregation produced by displacement, by 1965, 91 percent of Cleveland's elementary school students attended 95 to 100 percent white or black schools.[106] Black schools were so overcrowded and underresourced that students attended school in three-and-a-half-hour "double shifts." Facing protests, the school board agreed to build three new schools in black neighborhoods. But each plan was plainly substandard, and CORE endeavored to block progress at one construction site. In an especially horrific tragedy, Bruce Klunder, a white CORE activist and minister, was killed when a bulldozer crushed him to death as he lay in a trench. Klunder's appalling death and the city administration's deference to the business community and white residents underscored the necessity, as Turner argued, to "begin organizing our own political machinery."[107]

By the mid-1960s, Turner identified political liberalism and, without saying so explicitly, its decentralized supply-side state as the primary impediments to full enfranchisement, highlighting the one step forward, two steps backward nature of racial progress under liberalism. "Neighborhood deterioration," Turner wrote, "is the result of federal programs supposedly designed to help. There is no better example than the ravages of urban renewal." As an ally put it, it would take "basic social and economic justice" to "make legislation meaningful."[108] Even as the era's civil rights bills were signed, Turner emphasized the necessity of enfranchising people where administrative decisions were made that degraded black citizenship: "city halls, state houses, Capitol Hill and Wall St."[109] She also rejected the idea that white CORE activists were liberals: "We think that perhaps . . . white committed" is the "more appropriate" descriptor. Said Turner, "those who concentrate on integration and ending segregation have much too narrow a goal, because . . . the basic issue here is . . . implementing . . . economic justice, social justice, political justice."[110]

Black citizens' growing alienation from the liberal state was mirrored by working-class white homeowners, albeit for very different reasons. These voters believed the fiscal burdens of urban renewal fell disproportionately on them thanks to creeping property tax levies often necessitated to retire bonded debt. In the postwar decades, a period of broadly shared if deeply contingent white prosperity, voters often approved municipal bonds for infrastructure, schools, and renewal programs. But liberal cheerleaders of municipal borrowing such as Alvin Hansen had overlooked the local costs associated with municipal borrowing, which, because of strict state and local government's limitations on prolonged deficits, were incapable of being truly countercyclical. Moreover, the costs to retire that debt were borne by homeowners, a factor that local business elites did not take for granted. As Cleveland's chamber members pushed for more borrowing to finance renewal, they tried to reassure homeowners that new bond measures "will add nothing to your tax bill if you approve them."[111] Many of the chamber's campaigns were successful. On the day Americans sent JFK to the White House, Clevelanders approved $17 million in bonds essential to securing $58 million in federal spending, including for Erieview.[112]

Cleveland's growing debt reflected national trends. During decades in which citizens constructed a "consumer's republic" of borrowers, municipalities consistently outborrowed consumers.[113] These priorities were increasingly at odds with working- and middle-class residents who understood ballooning debt and rising property tax rates as threats to homeownership. In 1962, the white ethnic city councilman Ralph Perk, a future mayor, voiced these fears in his campaign for county auditor, becoming the first city- and countywide Republican elected official since the 1930s. Twice reelected, Perk formed the Ohio Homeowners and Taxpayers Revolt, Inc. Against subsidies for businesses, he honed a small propertied populism, demanding, as he put it, to "shift the [tax] burden from the home owner to business and industry."[114] In 1962, voters twice rejected a property tax increase.[115] A 1963 bond issue, $4.5 million of which was for the city's matching share of Erieview's phase 2, became the first renewal-related bond to meet organized resistance, and, in November 1963, voters defeated it.[116]

White residents understood their property tax bills and municipal debt as rising alongside liberals' calls for racial progress, and the structural subtleties of liberalism's supply side enabled white ethnics to blame renewal's victims rather than its architects. As a social welfare expert worried, "the city has become three clenched fists ready to strike at Negroes—one Hungarian, one Polish, one Italian."[117] As a west-side councilman put it, "If my people knew that their tax dollars were being spent to [aid people]" who "neglected to care for their property until it was run-down, I'm certain [they] would never pass another Urban Renewal bond issue." The result, he said, was "a double penalty for good people who keep their properties up." Said another west-sider, "These people created the slums, why should my people pay?"[118] Through politicians like Perk, white ethnic Clevelanders increasingly construed their property taxes as being redistributed to corporate redevelopment schemes, slum clearance, and affordable housing.

Erieview, then, illustrates the ways in which liberals' fiscal ideologies and decentralized, supply-side partnerships, rather than merely conservative backlash, helped drive the splintering of the New Deal Democratic coalition by broadly undermining faith in government. The suburban-dominated chamber and CDF hoped Erieview would enable the city to retain and recruit legal and financial services firms—many of which chamber members helmed—as well as high-end residential developments. Evans even pledged to move his family from Novelty into a planned high-rise there. But, as officials sought to win mortgage insurance for the residential developments, the

FHA's actuarial conservatism played a subtle but important role in driving up Erieview's scale and bogging down its progress.

The FHA "discouraged" certain developments, particularly luxury residential towers, "unless surrounding improvements were made" since "their environments would not be conducive to their success."[119] The FHA had already rejected applications for two apartment proposals at Erieview, as city renewal director James Lister explained, "because there was no guarantee of the physical characteristics, the physical environment." Until the city developed "a large area of good, sound, physical environment . . . this was not a sound investment to underwrite."[120] The astonishing scale of Cleveland's Erieview proposal, then, initially 125 acres and later 194 acres, flowed from local elites' understanding, as Mayor Celebrezze explained in 1960, that "the FHA won't guarantee a loan on a luxury apartment with the downtown environment as it is now."[121] William Slayton later defended the emphasis on far-reaching projects: "a more limited approach . . . would, in fact, doom [certain projects] from the start" because of the "influences of obsolete and incompatible existing structures."[122] The carrot of federal financing invited the stick of FHA preferences, which sought to secure taxpayers' investments by insulating mortgages from "incompatible" neighborhoods and residents.

Erieview was soon among the largest renewal projects in the country. With an initial infusion of $10 million in federal planning funds, the city hired Slayton's former firm, I. M. Pei and Associates, to design a sprawling 163-acre campus, which, upon clearing some 237 buildings, would feature four commercial buildings as well as a high-end residential tower soaring over lawns and plazas overlooking Lake Erie.[123] News reports touted "Cleveland's chance to wipe away the wrinkles of old age."[124]

Controversies marred the project from the start. Given the amount of federal investment in Erieview, the FHA declined mortgage applications on nearby properties. Despite winning city support for a twenty-three-story apartment on Euclid Avenue, developer Albert Levin was denied FHA financing because officials believed Erieview would "fill the market for luxury downtown apartments."[125] While Levin moved on, issues of accountability continued to mark Cleveland's renewal administration. As the city conducted blight surveys and condemnations, local elites and federal officials colluded to seize properties in violation of regulations that only uninhabitable or unsound structures be razed. City inspectors had recently deemed sound the majority of the 118 buildings within Erieview's phase 1—small warehouses, shops, parking facilities, and boarding houses. With millions in

Figure 3. The I. M. Pei plan for the Erieview urban renewal site, 1961, with its sprawling geometric white buildings and towers. From *Erieview, Cleveland, Ohio: An Urban Renewal Plan for Downtown Cleveland* (New York: I. M. Pei, 1961).

federal aid on the line and with the knowledge that the FHA preferred larger tracts of clearance, city officials simply reclassified 84 buildings as "substandard."[126] Property owners appealed to the regional renewal office in Chicago. But when officials visited, shepherded by CDF leaders, they made a cursory drive through the area and rubber-stamped the city's determination.[127] Teresa Grisanti owned a well-kept, mixed-use building on the Erieview site. She appealed the loss of her property to the U.S. Supreme Court, though it was dismissed "for want of a substantial federal question."[128] Nevertheless, her suit motivated a Government Accountability Office investigation and congressional hearings. A sympathetic member of Congress read into the record the findings of a common pleas court judge, who leveled a withering critique at Cleveland's urban renewal administration: "However grandiose the government's plan," and "whether good or bad the result is tyranny."[129] Yet, federal officials made no substantive changes to Cleveland's allocations, oversight, or citizens' access to planning. And, while the seizure of a white-owned property generated a degree of outrage, the city had been razing black neighborhoods since the 1930s.

By 1964, an air of acrimony hung over Erieview, which consisted of vast acres of dirt fields between downtown and the lakefront. Cleveland's urban renewal program had spent $40 million, and, by the end of federal financing in 1974, land cleared for redevelopment comprised some 6,060 acres—one-eighth of the city's total—entirely on the heavily black east side. By 1976, nearly 30 percent of this land remained unsold and vacant, further undermining the tax base.[130]

Though Erieview was not in a predominantly black or residential area, its clearance sped the deterioration of black neighborhoods. As *Call and Post* editor W. O. Walker put it, Erieview "may build up property values in one section of the city," padding the pockets "of one or two firms at the expense of . . . the taxpayers," but the project was "lowering property values in other areas."[131] The Gladstone renewal site, near Garden Valley, had become a dumping ground for Erieview—vacant lots piled with trash that often burned with noxious smoke.[132] Most maddening for black residents were the converging housing, employment, and spatial crises, which, in Hough, where many families relocated from Cedar-Central clearance projects, produced both greater poverty and higher rents. Between 1960 and 1970, rental prices rose even as the median family income, which had been 66 percent of the county average in 1960, fell to 52 percent, with nearly 40 percent of families living below the poverty line.[133] Rent strikes, often led by CORE, rippled across the east side. In Hough, residents organized Citizens for Better Housing to win home improvement and community development funding.[134] Others just hoped to leave. As one homeowner conceded, "I'd move tonight if the city will buy my property. I'm ready to get out." Another group held out for fair compensation: as one resident put it, "I'm going to keep my property up and the city is going to give me what it's worth."[135] But later inquiries found that city officials intentionally allowed renewal-targeted properties to fall into further disrepair to ensure a lower purchase price.[136]

The city also failed to provide relocation assistance or to even keep track of where many families went. In Gladstone, at the chamber's urging, the city displaced 717 families for prospective "distribution and service industries."[137] Of 416 families who moved, 224 did so to "unknown" locations; 57 moved into other forms of "substandard" housing; and 301 still lived, as the *Call and Post* reported, "in the midst of abandoned housing."[138] City officials could not determine what had become of another 1,194 families.[139] And while white elites negotiated directly with the FHA for favorable financing, a Hough business owner described how black businesspeople struggled to secure modest loans and mortgage insurance that might save businesses operating in "urban destruction area[s]."[140] Nationally, by September 1963, some 39,339 businesses had been displaced through urban renewal, and, while the federal government did not keep demographic data on proprietors, certainly thousands of black businesses were forced to shut down and relocate.[141] A headline in the *Call and Post* reminded black Clevelanders that they had once looked optimistically to renewal: "Did We Vote for Poverty or Progress?"[142]

In April 1966, the U.S. Commission on Civil Rights (CCR) held hearings in Cleveland, much of which focused on urban renewal. The commission heard from frustrated residents, businesspeople, civil rights activists including Ruth Turner, and municipal officials. Hough had borne the heaviest burden of renewal-related crowding, and it dominated the hearings.[143] A business owner described how the area's deterioration was killing his business, forcing him to lay off four employees. As he testified, "if I seem a little nervous, it is not nervousness, it is emotion." People "are being driven out of the Hough area. I say 'driven out' because a lot of them don't want to go. . . . They are being crowded into another ghetto." The fundamental issue was that renewal was "being dictated" by elites: "We need some poor men on that board. We need . . . a man who's down with the people, . . . who suffers with them every day."[144] Mayor Ralph Locher, however, joined white ethnics in blaming black residents for the crises, citing their rural, southern roots to explain their purported inability "to conform to the rules and customs of city living."[145] Recent chamber president and corporate attorney Jack Reavis, meanwhile, described the energy he had put into the Businessmen's Interracial Committee on Community Affairs, established in 1964 to create interracial dialogue and voluntary solutions for civil rights by, for example, soliciting nondiscrimination pledges from banks and employers. He and thirty-seven white businessmen worked closely with twenty-eight black leaders, including ministers and representatives from the NAACP and CORE. The "Negroes on this committee have behaved magnificently," said Reavis, making his racial paternalism clear. Reavis also signaled his producerist outlook, noting that he had "spent over a third of [his] time on civic affairs and a good 20 percent on this endeavor." "If I were my partners," he quipped, "I would boot me out" of the firm.[146]

Attendees also heard impassioned testimony from a young African American politician, then serving his third term in the state house. Rather than urge more federal oversight, citizens committees, or spending—the usual menu of ignored neighborhood demands—Carl Stokes called on federal officials to freeze Cleveland's renewal funding until local people could get a handle on the multi-sited crisis. Two months later, the federal government did just that. Stokes especially criticized businessmen like Reavis, "the advantaged citizenry," as offering "too-little-too-late." The beginning of a solution, he said, was that "qualified Negroes" be appointed to "positions of responsibility" in government.[147]

Electing Carl Stokes

Two months after the CCR hearings, Cleveland's racial pressures finally exploded. On a hot July night in 1966, a white bar owner in Hough put out a sign: "No Water for Niggers." After two black residents were physically removed, an angry crowd formed. More than three hundred police officers arrived, and volleys of recrimination yielded to rocks, bottles, and bullets. Joyce Arnett, a twenty-six-year-old mother of three, retreated to a nearby building. Sometime after one o'clock in the morning, she called from a window, hoping to go home to her children. Caught in the crossfire, she was shot dead—it remains unclear by whom. Eight days and nights of bloody violence, fires, and National Guard patrols followed, during which three more Clevelanders lost their lives, thirty were critically injured, and more than three hundred were arrested. Some 240 fires burned broad swaths of Cleveland's east side, where renewal projects remained in rubble. In the aftermath, U.S. senator Frank Lausche, Cleveland's trailblazing ethnic Democrat, partnered with South Carolina's Strom Thurmond on a harsh anti-riot amendment to the Civil Rights Act, perhaps forgetting his generation of ethnics' Depression-era eviction and relief riots.[148]

Business elites saw that the city's reputation and their bottom lines were in the balance. They were suddenly aware of the depth of black anger—the FBI shared with the chamber a report on the likelihood of further riots.[149] In 1963, the Greater Cleveland Growth Board (GCGB) had spent $80,000 on advertisements in the *Wall Street Journal* alone, easily topping the list of *Journal* advertisers in its Midwest and Eastern editions. After Hough, however, ads could not compete with the coverage of Cleveland under national headlines such as "Racial Powder Keg."[150] Some chamber members condemned the city's white ethnics and their mayor. Cleveland Bar Association president and chamber leader James C. Davis delivered a fiery speech titled "Cleveland's White Problem" reproving ethnic "nationality groups" and proposing the ouster of Mayor Locher.[151]

Ruth Turner, meanwhile, reached out to Floyd McKissick, CORE's national director, to forge new strategies for developing political power to counter suburban business elites' domination of Cleveland. As McKissick explained, "although whites have, in many cases, moved to the suburbs from the cities, they have not given up control of the economics and the politics of these cities."[152] Part of the challenge was a generation of black politicians who felt beholden to the white Democratic machine. The "machine," Turner charged, "was used by certain individuals" for personal "benefits," but it "has not been used as the voice of the community."[153] McKissick soon secured a $225,000 grant from the Ford Foundation to fund "Target City Cleveland," a program to register and mobilize black voters and develop leaders "with the necessary competence to deal with the complex issues of institutional reconstruction"—of parties, municipal government, and administration of federal programs.[154] At a June 1967 meeting of the so-called Big Six civil rights leaders, McKissick, Martin Luther King Jr., Whitney Young (director of the National Urban League), Roy Wilkins (executive secretary of the NAACP), Bayard Rustin (leader of the A. Philip Randolph Institute of the AFL-CIO), and H. Rap Brown (chairman of the Student Nonviolent Coordinating Committee) agreed to focus on Cleveland. They would target "voter registration . . . [and] political action" in hopes of electing a black mayor.[155] King planned to spend much of the summer in Cleveland registering voters.[156] As national news outlets reported, the activists would raise "political awareness" about solutions for "housing, better employment opportunities," and "urban renewal."[157]

Carl Stokes made the failures and inequalities of urban renewal the centerpiece of his campaign. But he also sought to strike a balance between attacking business elites and decrying the programs they had dominated. He was particularly sensitive to the importance of their support in the Democratic primary, when their backing was important for beating the white ethnic incumbent, Ralph Locher. As Stokes expected, Democratic Party chairman Albert Porter refused to hold an open primary, barring him from official events. The Democratic machine's strength was confirmed by the number of black councilmen and ward leaders who refused to host Stokes. The *Call and Post* blasted councilman George White, headlining an article, "Bought and Paid For or Just Plain Stupid?" Said White, "the Locher administration has been good to me, and I'm not about to bite the hand that feeds me."[158] The paper also targeted councilman Leo Jackson: "Ducking hot issues where Negro interest is concerned is one of Leo's favorite pastimes."[159] Beyond quiet support from the chamber in the primary, Stokes deployed four thousand campaigners who won financial support from black residents.[160]

Once Stokes defeated Locher in the primary, however, business elites swung their support to the Republican, chamber leader Seth Taft, the late senator Robert Taft's nephew, the grandson of President William Howard Taft, and the CDF's chief legal counsel, who moved into the city from suburban Pepper Pike to prepare his campaign.[161] Stokes shared business elites' assumption that many white ethnics would mobilize against him, and he also worried that the Big Six civil rights figures' presence would trigger stronger countermobilization. He beseeched King, saying, "Martin . . . if you come in here with these marches . . . you're going to upset the balance we've created."[162] Stokes's concerns were justified. Ford's grant to CORE and Stokes's national support became potent campaign issues for his opponents. Locher appealed to ethnics' localist and racist fears, howling about "that wagonload of gold [that] has come . . . from the Ford Foundation for the aid of CORE. . . . Not one nickel came to the [white ethnic] Fourth Ward."[163] One white voter fumed, "I'll never buy another Ford."[164] In the general election, Republicans also employed racial fearmongering, arguing that "Taft alone can give Cleveland back to the law-abiding citizenry." Thousands of working-class white ethnics embraced racial antagonism over class or partisan loyalty. Stokes's margin of victory was 1,679 out of a quarter million votes cast. Of Cleveland's white Democrats, 70 percent voted for the Republican Taft.[165]

* * *

Their hopes for urban renewal dashed, Cleveland's black voters mobilized to make their voices heard in city politics. In the process, however, CORE's structural critiques of both liberalism and machine politics became absorbed into the mainstream success of the Stokes movement. CORE would struggle to regain its footing.[166] In part this was because black Clevelanders were optimistic about more than just a Stokes mayoralty. The Johnson administration's War on Poverty was promising to empower black communities to administer federal-local development and home improvement programs—offering the kind of participation CORE and others had long demanded. For a moment, it seemed possible to imagine the federal government cultivating participatory "community development" partnerships directly with marginalized citizens in a city led by one of their own.

Meanwhile, through their administration of urban renewal and affordable housing projects, business leaders increasingly viewed themselves as underappreciated advocates of social progress whose efforts were stymied by

FHA regulations and ungrateful residents. Those headaches, however, were nothing compared to their shock at the War on Poverty's community empowerment agenda, which elites recognized as an unprecedented threat to their relationship with the supply-side state. In meeting that threat, business elites would more muscularly articulate their producerist bona fides, expanded to include not simply their essential role in producing jobs, taxes, or affordable housing, but also their role in fighting poverty and reforming government itself. Reflecting on urban renewal's failures in Cleveland, Upshur Evans laid the blame on government's lack of businesslike management.[167] Businesspeople's rhetorical arsenal for justifying control over public subsidies grew not only through the liberal state's progressive designs but also, increasingly, through their perceptions of its inefficiencies and overreach. As the city's budget crisis simmered away, and as white ethnics undertook their own political mobilization, mastering these dynamics would be a singular challenge for Carl Stokes.

PART II

Liberalism's Limits

CHAPTER 5

Fighting the War on Poverty

Testifying before the U.S. Commission on Civil Rights (CCR) in Cleveland in April 1966, the Reverend Paul Younger, a white minister and organizer, urged federal officials to give poor people a say in programs meant to benefit their communities. "I have seen Federal program after Federal program come into Cleveland with high promises," but they are "administered to us, done for us." They end "in nothing because the money is taken" and "the work is not done." The same day, Congress of Racial Equality (CORE) leader Ruth Turner pointed out that even within Lyndon Johnson's War on Poverty, which demanded the "maximum feasible participation" of the poor, a Hough initiative organized by neighborhood people was snubbed. Eastern Hough Organized for Action was led to believe it would receive a $225,000 grant through the Community Action Program, but "they were suddenly informed of a Washington administrator's . . . change of mind [and] that the actual administration of funds would be done" by city hall's Economic Opportunities Council. Since its creation in 1964, critics had decried the council's lack of "involvement with the poor." Of the twenty-two members on the "silk-stocking" body, fifteen lived in the suburbs, and, as the *Call and Post* reported, "civil rights leaders . . . are conspicuous by their absence." Younger urged not merely "token involvement through resident participation, but integral from the ground up . . . by the residents of those poverty neighborhoods. They are able, gentlemen, they are able, only try them."[1]

The years between Turner's and Younger's 1966 testimony and Richard Nixon's New Federalism reforms in 1974, which officially ended programs including urban renewal and Community Action, saw pitched battles over the meaning of community enfranchisement in and control over federal development and antipoverty funding. For civil rights activists, poor people, and black community leaders, the War on Poverty's mandate for "maximum feasible participation" of the poor was an electric charge, an invitation to administer federal programs to benefit their neighborhoods. That commitment was based, in part, on a Ford Foundation program, Gray Areas, which, like the foundation's grant to Cleveland CORE, aimed to empower black communities to develop political leadership and work within established hierarchies and systems of democracy. These earlier efforts drew upon the experiences of international self-help "community development" initiatives and the ideas of social scientists concerned that poverty was perpetuated by cultural pathologies. Pressed by civil rights advocates, however, a set of progressive poverty advocates in the Kennedy and Johnson White Houses soon recognized that structural factors including patterns of local administration, market inequities, and bureaucratic intransigence were more obvious causes of the production and reproduction of racial poverty. These policy entrepreneurs inserted the "maximum feasible participation" principle into Community Action, raising expectations among the poor—and creating unexpected flashpoints in the politics of administration for Lyndon Johnson, local officials, and supply-side state builders.[2]

Many black activists understood Community Action as their best chance to use federal resources to break open local democracies and markets, employing protests, boycotts, and campaigns to fundamentally remake local power structures. The socialist activist Michael Harrington even viewed Community Action for the 1960s' poor as akin to the Wagner Act for 1930s' labor—the federal government was sanctioning militant efforts to radically democratize the decentralized administrative state. As federal resources and regulatory authority backed that organizing, however, rather than yield a more democratic pluralism, the latent racist assumptions among white citizens that countenanced the disinvestment, extraction, and clearance through programs such as urban renewal often became *more* explicit as black citizens gained political power—whether in Community Action or when Carl Stokes won Cleveland's mayoralty.

The Johnson administration quickly faced blowback from the sturdiest local pillars of the supply-side state, and within months LBJ attempted to tamp down Community Action's unprecedented participatory spirit—that shift may explain the denial of Eastern Hough Organized for Action's grant application. Johnson's aide Daniel Patrick Moynihan, initially supportive of maximum feasible participation, later backtracked, arguing that the principle was based upon a number of "maximum feasible misunderstandings" about local power, democracy, and citizenship. In most cities, he wrote, power was usually held "by a fairly small number of men in banks and law firms whose names are not generally known." For Moynihan, the problem was not that such supply-side state builders refused to share their authority. Rather, "it may be that the poor are never 'ready' to assume power in an advanced society: the exercise of power in an effective manner is an ability acquired through apprenticeship and seasoning."[3] The solution to entrenched, racialized poverty, Moynihan suggested, was time, not democracy.

Rather than simply signify a conservative break from a liberal poverty agenda, then, Richard Nixon's New Federalism reforms built upon Johnson's effort to suppress the "maximum feasible participation" of the poor. In differing ways, for Johnson and Nixon, the solution for the urban political crises of the late 1960s was redoubling local private-sector leadership in federal programs. Nixon's Housing and Community Development Act of 1974, the centerpiece of his New Federalism reforms, ended a set of categorical programs in favor of deregulated block grants dispersed by formula and controlled by local elites. As more local governments became recipients of federal aid, Nixon's formulas disproportionately benefited his base in suburban and Sunbelt communities. Nixon framed these initiatives as a revolutionary break from decades of liberal governance, bringing the Great Society to heel, and as a practical expression of faith in localism. But Nixon's New Federalism in fact reasserted the normatively white and elite-led vision of localism at the heart of New Deal federalism, creating new and loosely regulated resources for local governments while simultaneously supporting the diversion of resources away from poor and minority communities.

Nixon's chief innovation, however, was not simply rebranding local-national, public-private partnerships as conservative checks on the expanding liberal state; it was also in appropriating and hollowing out the participatory principle at the heart of Community Action and yoking it to a business led vision of "community development." Nixon's block grants were an early expression of the deregulatory spirit that would soon sweep Washington, D.C. But even as he stripped poverty and development programs of federal rules and urged businesspeople to take charge of block grants, Nixon continued to pay lip service to liberal values of "community development," participation, and fighting poverty—an important step toward more neoliberal public policies in which public authority and democratic accountability would be increasingly hollowed out even as ostensible social aspirations and rhetorical commitments to "participation" proliferated. While many neighborhood and poverty groups became fully fledged in fights for federal aid—and some did win important battles—their share of federal spending would remain a pittance compared to "community development" subsidies that flowed to business and gentrifying housing markets. In the process, the rhetoric of business producerism would increasingly center businesspeople and business growth not only as producers of vibrant economies but also as essential actors in projects of community uplift, while authentic community organizations became increasingly enervated and fragmented in struggles to secure even a modicum of empowerment and material support.

Fighting the War on Poverty

Lyndon Johnson's commencement speech at Howard University in June 1965, in which he made the case for his War on Poverty, was an implicit indictment of liberalism's faith that a rising tide of economic growth would lift all Americans from poverty. Without mentioning programs such as urban renewal, which was devastating black businesses and neighborhoods at the very moment he spoke, he emphasized vast and growing disparities in wages, poverty rates, infant mortality, and spatial isolation. His War on Poverty would close these gaps by making poverty's costs less extreme (Medicaid and nutrition assistance), offering support to impoverished children (Head Start), and delivering worker training (Job Corps). But the War on Poverty's primary initiative designed to "strike at poverty at its source—in the streets of our cities and . . . our countryside," as he put it a year earlier, was the Community Action Program (CAP). CAP would empower poor people to "prepare long-range plans for the attack on poverty in their own local communities." Rather than "plans prepared in Washington and imposed" on localities, poor people would call "upon all the resources available to the community—federal and state, local and private, human and material." Said Johnson, "local citizens best understand their own problems and know best how to deal with those problems." If much of the poverty war was "palliative," Community Action was an unprecedented commitment to fighting poverty by guaranteeing the expansion of administrative enfranchisement.[4] If Johnson's language was clear, however, the mixed origins and compressed deployment of "maximum feasible participation" laid the groundwork for a war over the War on Poverty.

By the late 1950s, a range of left-progressive social scientists and journalists highlighted the reality that abject poverty persisted in the postwar land of plenty. Fighting poverty at home gained increasing salience especially in the context of the Cold War contest for the allegiance of developing nations. One influential interpretation of poverty's perpetuation invoked psychological traits—cycles of attitudes among the poor reinforced growing cultural distance from societal norms favoring male breadwinning, family formation, and personal industriousness. The New Dealer Oscar Lewis, concerned with "underdevelopment," pioneered the cultures of poverty theory as he studied poverty from Tepoztlán to India to New York City. In this interpretation, structural inequalities within markets and democracy receded as explanations. These assumptions in turn informed two leading concepts among liberal philanthropies and policy advocates. The first, echoed in the Ford Foundation's grant to Cleveland CORE, emphasized "community action"—poverty groups, formerly disorganized but now guided by experts, could develop democratic and economic "competence" as they organized campaigns for improved public services. The second, "opportunity theory," contained the seeds of more fundamental structural critiques. Juvenile delinquency, Richard Cloward and Lloyd Ohlin argued, resulted from structural barriers to lower class citizens' opportunity to achieve middle-class status. Opportunity theory urged the "reorganization of slum communities," though, as historian Alice O'Connor notes, its theorists "never got much more specific about its implications for practice."[5]

In this context, the Kennedy administration took a first, cautious step toward a war on poverty with the President's Committee on Juvenile Delinquency (PCJD). The PCJD joined the Ford Foundation's Gray Areas program in seeking to become outside "change agents" in local social service delivery. While Kennedy staffers initially contemplated running poverty programs through existing agencies, department heads, including former Cleveland mayor and urban renewal champion Anthony Celebrezze, who led JFK's Department of Health, Education, and Welfare, were unenthusiastic about organizing the poor to improve service delivery.[6] As they confronted bureaucratic and interagency resistance, PCJD's director David Hackett came to believe that federal agencies and local administrations would never lead a meaningful war on poverty.[7]

An alternative vision of liberal democracy, one focused on administrative empowerment and social equity, was taking hold withing executive branch agencies. Officials were doubtlessly cognizant of demands coming not only from African American communities but also from white New Left college students, most famously in Students for a Democratic Society's "Port Huron Statement," for "participatory democracy," a more organic call for remaking political and economic democracy.[8] In February 1964, Lyndon Johnson named the late President Kennedy's brother-in-law Sargent Shriver "chief of staff of the War on Poverty." Shriver had been the crusading director of Kennedy's Peace Corps, and he brought the same intensity to shaping domestic poverty programs. Shriver tapped comrades of the PCJD's Hackett—"Hackett's guerrillas" they were called, a wink, perhaps, at insurgent tactics to come. Jack Conway, a former trade union organizer, directed the Community Action Program, and a number of former PCJD officials moved into planning positions. These activist planners argued the poor needed access to power, not simply better social services. Drawing upon international development practices that emphasized community self-help, Conway's planners, likely led by former PCJD staffer Richard Boone, inserted "maximum feasible participation" provisions into the legislation creating Community Action.[9] Local Community Action Agencies (CAAs) would become entirely new local administrative outposts within the Office of Economic Opportunity (OEO), the new executive branch agency headed by Shriver. Shriver soon set out on a campaign of "maximum feasible public relations" to raise awareness among the poor about federal funding opportunities. In October 1964, just six weeks after OEO launched, the agency announced its first grants.[10]

The federal government was funding an entirely new range of public-private partnerships with social welfare and service organizations, clergy, and civil rights groups, a highly visible effort, in effect, to expand liberals' midcentury commitment to democratic pluralism. Within fourteen months, some six hundred CAPs were in operation, less than 15 percent of which were run by local governments.[11] Shriver's and Hackett's "guerrillas" had explicitly designed this structure "to avoid having the program channeled through and taken over by the 'establishment'—the network of existing leadership" composed of "local government" and elite "private groups."[12] Frequently, CAAs established storefront service centers to expand access to public services including welfare entitlements, urban renewal relocation assistance, legal aid, and public health clinics. A Chicago CAA worker described helping citizens for whom "bureaucratic procedures . . . are forever breaking down," people "who have become . . . habituated to injustice" and are "kept in ignorance of their rights." These neighborhood centers also hired and trained local residents. By 1968, some 870 communities had CAP-sponsored, independently administered neighborhood service centers, which, according to one estimate, employed more than 100,000 residents and professionals.[13]

CAAs were, by their very nature, confronting existing administrative power structures, leaders of which were loath to concede authority to neighborhood people. Cleveland's CAPs were stymied by Mayor Ralph Locher's meddling in the application process, and his Economic Opportunities Council was dominated by business elites. Faced with anger at the lack of community representatives, Locher appointed a black former insurance company director as chair—"a willing tool of interests other than those of the poorer neighborhoods," as one critic complained. While members of the NAACP and Urban League eventually joined the council, a subsequent report found that "community leaders, residents and poor involved . . . regarded this as a 'sell out' by the middle-class Negro leaders." This was the sort of leadership that led CORE's Ruth Turner to call Cleveland "a citadel of tokenism."[14] Where black residents were consulted, property owners, not the poorest, dominated.[15] These controversies spurred a report coauthored by Kenneth Clark, which described Cleveland's "program" as marked by "bitterness . . . and a sense of alienation among the Negro poor."[16]

In many other cities, however, CAPs were "organizing the poor politically," as a Johnson administration official noted with trepidation in the fall of 1965. Simply accessing public resources in many places necessitated challenging the myriad ways the political and economic structures marginalized and preyed upon poor people. In Syracuse, a Community Action Training Center organized protests, rent strikes, and sit-ins. In New York City, residents mobilized with OEO funding to confront public school administrators, the city welfare department, and slumlords. The welfare rights organizer Beulah Sanders advocated using CAP funding to build networks of welfare rights activists who could challenge racist and intransigent local welfare administrators.[17]

CAPs also targeted local businesses and elite civic associations. As the March 1966 cover of *Nation's Business*, the publication of the U.S. Chamber of Commerce worried, "Is [the] War on Poverty Becoming [a] War on Business?" Businesspeople, the magazine noted, "admit to a feeling of 'sheer fright' over the influences which people lacking a business grounding can bring to these" taxpayer-supported programs. The article highlighted a litany of complaints about CAP activists, including those pursuing "consumer education" programs and boycotts in Washington, D.C., and "consumer advisers" in San Francisco who steered shoppers away from businesses that refused to stock certain goods and fresh produce.[18] Particularly worrisome was the specter of civil rights organizations using federal funds to challenge "local and regional balances of power," in the words of Boston CORE leader Alan Gartner.[19] As Gartner argued, "we must be the unreasonable ones, who can

Figure 4. The March 1966 edition of *Nation's Business*, the magazine of the U.S. Chamber of Commerce. Courtesy of Hagley Museum and Library.

spot an inequity wherever it may exist and demand that it cease—and now."[20] Cleveland CORE, too, worked "to 'watch dog' this federal program . . . so the money . . . is controlled in the right ways."[21]

To many local elites, then, Johnson's program appeared to be funding a direct assault on the existing power structure—as, indeed, it was. In 1965, the U.S. Conference of Mayors nearly passed a resolution charging OEO with "fostering class struggle" and pressed Chicago mayor Richard Daley to lobby administration officials to rein in the programs. The Conference of Mayors and National League of Cities endorsed resolutions urging OEO to recognize only city-hall-sponsored CAPs.[22] As Daley fumed to LBJ, activists were "trying to snatch . . . control of this country, control of everything, just under this program." The idea that "only the poor can control these programs," Daley protested, "doesn't bear the right of logic."[23]

Johnson had hardly had a revolutionary vision of democratic structural reform in mind with CAPs. In selling the program, he often described a paternalistic project of disciplining young, disproportionately African American men to the norms of breadwinning and the fiscal savings reaped as a result. In April 1964, Johnson pitched the War on Poverty to the U.S. Chamber of Commerce as a way to avoid violence, impose discipline, and produce taxpayers. "Unless you attack the causes of poverty itself," he advised, "you are going to be shoveling it out to the taxeaters instead of producing and training taxpayers."[24] As he put it on another occasion, he would "clear up these damn [welfare] rolls," by "teach[ing] them some discipline and when to get up, and how to work all day, and in two years, I'll have them trained where they can at least drive a truck instead of sit around a pool room." This was LBJ's sense of how New Deal works and youth projects, which he administered as a young man, had worked. As he explained to poverty aide Bill Moyers, "I thought we were going to have [Civilian Conservation Corps] camps.... I thought we were going to have community action [programs] where a city or county... could sponsor a project... and we'd pay the labor and a very limited amount of materials on it."[25]

Rather than bolster the supply-side state through elite-led developmental solutions for poverty that also yielded lighter welfare rolls, the War on Poverty instead shone a bright light on white elites' paternalistic racial assumptions, producerist privilege, and acceptance of and often investments in received inequities. Faced with a revolt among core constituencies of Democratic mayors, their private partners, and growing ranks of southern members of Congress, Johnson moved to resecure elite control over federal programs. He named Vice President Hubert Humphrey the administration's "special liaison" to local officials, a role Humphrey characterized as a "built-in Special Agent" for local executives.[26] Consulting with mayors, Humphrey worked with Congress to draft amendments to tighten local administrative controls over CAPs, including implementing "check point" procedures that empowered local officials to authorize proposals. Mere months following the Community Action Program's unveiling, local elites secured regulations to slow the dispersal of funds to community groups. By the spring of 1967, formal proposals to muzzle "maximum feasible participation" began emerging from the White House.

But the principle still had supporters within the administration. Testifying before Congress, Shriver offered a number of defenses, including the fiscal rationale: "Community action," he said, "is a democratic antidote to the dole." But he also warned about the explosive risks of dashing raised expectations through reforms that "leave the form but bleed the substance from these achievements."[27] Shriver's concerns flowed from his awareness of how stiffly the winds were blowing against his participatory principle. Johnson had just appointed a National Advisory Council on Economic Opportunity to assess the programs and to begin the administration's negotiations with Congress over their future.[28] In a message to the council, Johnson made clear that he expected members to recommend that "public officials and other interested groups in the community" should be given a "voice in forming policy for community action agencies."[29] Appearing before Congress ten days later, Johnson was more explicit. He sought not only local regulatory oversight over CAP hiring and salaries but also demanded that "community action agencies ... design and conduct programs with full participation by the private sector."[30] Johnson hoped that amplifying business involvement would salvage his relationship with local elites and, perhaps, his poverty agenda.

Confronted by militant poverty groups, businesspeople, meanwhile, began framing their guidance of federal programs as both more balanced and in the interest of the total community. This position was reinforced by representatives of the U.S. Chamber of Commerce in the same hearings at which Shriver defended the participation principle. By amplifying local businesspeople's involvement in poverty programs, chamber officials testified, the administration might address "the prostitution of community action for partisan purposes." They praised the Job Corps program—which largely operated through corporate contracts that offset the costs of hiring and training long-term unemployed citizens—as a promising model of public-private antipoverty partnership built through established channels within the supply-side state. Local chambers and city halls wrote scores of supportive letters for Job Corps. In an ironic twist, then, Job Corps, Shriver's chief manpower development program, was held up by supply-side state builders as evidence of their commitment to fighting poverty, evidence that they believed obviated the need to democratically empower the poor. As one businessman put it, "anyone who has been watching this is bound to be very conscious of almost a revolution in business thinking." In "city after city now we have many of our top business leaders, supported by people from the companies they are associated with, spending many hours and tackling problems of this kind."[31] To defend their access to and visions of federal subsidies, businesspeople were learning to frame themselves as poverty warriors.

While the administration maintained rhetorical support for "maximum feasible participation," to lead his reform council Johnson appointed Morris I. Leibman, an attorney at Chicago's corporate law firm Sidley and Austin and an outspoken critic of the civil rights movement's direct-action tactics.

Leibman gained notoriety for a speech to the American Bar Association subsequently published as, "Civil Disobedience: A Threat to Our Society Under Law," in which he argued, "Our imperfections do not justify tearing down the structures which have given us our progress." The concept of "righteous civil disobedience," he maintained, is "incompatible with the American legal system and society." Leibman's appeal to gradualism—clear rebukes of CAP activism—was widely reported.[32] As top Johnson aide Joseph Califano wrote in recommending Leibman, Mayor Daley considered the attorney "exactly the right guy for this job."[33] He is "all the way with us on our domestic program. . . . *He would be totally our man*" (emphasis in original).[34]

Leibman's council assessed CAPs and made recommendations for their reform. Its 1968 report *Focus on Community Action* found that "local struggles for control were generated" by "advocates of power for the poor . . . characterized by factionalism based on desire for personal power, special axes to grind, or promotion of different ideologies."[35] The report was designed to mollify southern Democrats, perhaps none more so than the War on Poverty's congressional sponsor, Georgia's Phil Landrum, and big city mayors such as Daley. The report detailed the administration's commitment to reforming OEO in ways that would save the programs by stifling "maximum feasible participation."[36] Doing the latter, they believed, would ensure the former. In the summer of 1967, which saw scores of cities explode in revolt, the White House and Congress made progress on the "city hall" amendments to CAP. As passed in December 1967, these amendments ultimately appropriated $1.773 billion for the poverty program but mandated that all CAPs either be public agencies or private agencies "designated" by state or local officials. The Johnson administration thus routed federal poverty funds through administrative structures most concerned with white elites' developmental preferences, a direct affront to the voluntary groups that had so enthusiastically and rapidly organized CAAs.[37] These were precisely the kind of reforms Shriver had warned about—stripping the program of its democratic substance while maintaining its ostensible social, participatory purposes.

In March 1968, Johnson called fifty businessmen to Washington to enlist them in his reformed War on Poverty. G. J. Tankersley, a Cleveland corporate executive, attended and reported to chamber members that the "President believes that if businessmen would go to work on this 'national crisis'" that "it can be solved." As another executive put it, "Most of us . . . haven't felt it the province of business to get into social problems." Yet "businessmen can put together more sheer power for good or evil than all the rest of the elements of the community combined." As Tankersley concluded, businessmen must "make a commitment to use our forces of free enterprise to help solve a very serious social problem."[38] Just as supply-side state builders had successively remade the Housing Act in their image, with Lyndon Johnson, they succeeded in remaking the War on Poverty. In reasserting control over federal subsidies, their defensive deployment of producerism was expanding to include not only taxes, jobs, and affordable housing, but also fighting poverty.

Cleveland: Now!

In the late 1960s, perhaps no city seemed better positioned to pursue the hopeful possibilities of interracial coalition building and the fusion of business and neighborhood concerns than Cleveland. Despite having run a candidate against him, in the spring of 1968, Mayor Carl Stokes won support from the city's business elite when he helped keep African American wards peaceful the night of Martin Luther King Jr.'s assassination. Stokes parlayed business leaders' confidence into a massive revitalization plan, Cleveland: Now!, designed to benefit business interests and black neighborhoods. Observers "marveled at how [Stokes] was able to speak the language of both the boardroom and the poolroom."[39] From leading business interests, galvanized by Johnson's call for elites' involvement in poverty, he secured commitments of jobs for thousands of chronically unemployed residents and $10 million in development seed funding.[40] On May 1, 1968, Stokes unveiled his ambitious public-private partnership, which envisioned building $1.5 billion in public and private contributions over ten years, with $177 million earmarked for the first two. The city would offer generous subsidies and tax abatements for downtown business development, restore urban renewal funding for the frozen Erieview project, and pursue funding for 4,600 new or rehabilitated affordable housing units, improved social services, and investments in education. Cleveland: Now! also aimed to create 16,000 new jobs in marginalized communities.[41] He secured $143 million in federal commitments, and voters, led by enthusiastic turnout in black neighborhoods, approved $100 million in bonds for chamber-backed infrastructure improvements and pollution abatement. Business leaders took out a full-page ad in the *Wall Street Journal* trumpeting a new day in the nation's eighth largest city.[42] "This time things are different," exclaimed the *Cleveland Press*.[43]

Stokes's partnerships extended beyond the chamber to include neighborhood and poverty groups, though funding here was considerably less than for urban renewal projects. Still, with OEO resources, Stokes subsidized a broad range of community groups, often primarily focused on economic development. In 1968, the Hough Area Development Corporation (HADC) received OEO's largest single award to a community development corporation, $1.5 million. The HADC incorporated a business, Community Products, Inc., that envisioned employing five hundred, primarily female, residents in manufacturing automobile components. In addition to delivering venture capital for fledgling businesses, the HADC offered small business consultation and job training.[44] Stokes seemed to be building his equitable development agenda, and in black neighborhoods, especially, spirits were high. "He's the best damn mayor Cleveland ever had," one resident affirmed. As summer approached, Stokes's youth initiatives were fully funded, offering employment for black teens. He was a darling of the national media.[45]

These grand expectations came to a violent end. Stokes had also deployed Cleveland: Now! funds with pragmatic politics in mind, institutionalizing a campaign strategy dubbed "Keep It Cool for Carl" in which black nationalist groups like Ahmed Evans's Black Nationalists of New Libya received grants for projects including cultural centers. Evans, however, used part of a $10,300 grant to rent a Glenville apartment where he stockpiled weapons. On July 23, 1968, Evans and comrades mistook two white truck drivers for undercover police officers and opened fire. As police arrived, a massive firefight erupted. Evans's nationalists killed three officers and, with their artillery, managed to explode a patrol car. In the Glenville shootout, seven Clevelanders—three police officers, three New Libyans, and one bystander—lost their lives. Responding to a harsh police crackdown, black youths looted white properties, moving east along Superior Avenue and west toward Rockefeller Park. Damage reached as far as a mile north of Superior, affecting some forty blocks east to west. To promote peace, Stokes forbade white officers from patrolling black neighborhoods, generating harsh, racist criticism from white officers. "Fuck that nigger mayor," said one. But Stokes's all-black officer corps restored calm.[46]

What did not hold together was Cleveland: Now!, as reports surfaced that Evans had used Stokes's grants to purchase weapons used to kill cops.[47] A Stokes ally later explained, "The funds allocated to Ahmed were a sincere effort . . . to work in a positive way in the community."[48] Sincerity, however, would not win back the support of Cleveland's white business community, convinced now that not even Stokes could keep black neighborhoods quiet. James Davis, a leading chamber member and president of the Cleveland Bar Association, defined the crisis in terms of a looming race war: "Today there are close to 30 million Negroes in the United States." Meanwhile, "the relatively small North Vietnamese population has tied down more than one million allied troops. . . . Should the majority of the Negro populations move from passive acquiescence in riots to active participation in rebellion, it is obvious what the result would be."[49] The mere fact of a large urban black population raised the specter of a race war. Davis argued that a war on crime, vigorous redevelopment efforts, and ousting Stokes were essential to restoring elite control of Cleveland.[50]

Stokes barely won reelection in 1969, but his relationship with the white-ethnic-dominated city council had fallen apart entirely. Stokes stopped attending council meetings. He would not run again. He had hit the limits of the white majority's narrow acceptance of an agenda that empowered African Americans but failed to discipline more militant proponents of black freedom. Each politically potent white constituency, ethnics and business, strategized paths to power.

The Battlegrounds of the Poverty War

The reality of black political power hardened rather than brokered racist antagonisms. Indeed, Davis's race war analogy and whites' broader rejection of black political leadership and empowerment was a direct rebuke to the notion, championed by the Ford Foundation and the Johnson administration, that urban pluralism could be made to work if black communities could organize effectively. As an older white ethnic complained, "If we'd have a Hungarian mayor, he'd take care of us. The black mayor takes care of them." The Buckeye Boys, a white ethnic gang in the once overwhelmingly Hungarian Buckeye neighborhood, terrorized black residents and businesses in the late 1960s. They repeatedly smashed the front window of Sir Rah's, a black realty company, and targeted African Americans' homes in the night with potshots, BB guns, and bricks. Nazi swastikas and spray paint scrawls of "White Power" appeared on street signs.[51] The neighborhood was sadly typical. A white advocate of racial reconciliation lamented that white residents refused interracial cooperation—Buckeye "was just impenetrable."[52]

This overtly racist politics fused with long-simmering and often legitimate anger at the growing costs and administrative inequities of liberals' supply-side state. Cleveland pursued its redevelopment agenda by taking on greater debt to fund infrastructure, capital investments, and urban renewal matching obligations. Thanks to deindustrialization and capital flight, homeowners' property taxes covered an ever-greater share of Cleveland's revenue needs.[53] Issues of fiscal equity and democratic accountability inspired Ralph Perk's entry into city politics. Born in 1914, Perk was raised in the Czech neighborhood on Cleveland's southeast side along Broadway Avenue and became a ubiquitous presence in practically every fraternal, ethnic, or Catholic organization. Perk, who dropped out of high school at fifteen, bucked ethnics' fealty to the Democrats and believed Republicans' emphasis on individual liberty, anticommunism, frugal governance, and moral traditionalism better reflected ethnic values. By 1949, Perk found his core political issue: limiting government spending in order to limit voters' property tax assessments. Perk managed Republican Franklin Polk's quixotic campaign for mayor, the central theme of which was opposing plans to borrow $22 million from the Reconstruction Finance Corporation for chamber-advocated infrastructure investments.[54] Perk was elected county auditor in 1962, a position from which he highlighted the costs to white property owners of liberal development programs. By the early 1970s, as his star rose, *Time* described Perk's "purposeful ethnic Bunkerism."[55] But if television's Archie Bunker won laughs for being comically behind the times, Perk's longstanding anti-tax politics had met its moment.

Even before Stokes's mayoralty, Perk sensed an opportunity to bring ethnics into Cleveland's largely dormant Republican Party. In March 1965, supported by ethnic leaders, Perk created the Nationalities Movement of Cuyahoga County. He inaugurated a "Nationality Unity Drive," sponsoring events including the 1967 "Captive Nations Week" rally in Public Square, where some 20,000 Clevelanders heard Perk celebrate their homelands locked behind the iron curtain.[56] Perk was invited to speak at Princeton University's Woodrow Wilson School, where, in 1968, he argued that white ethnics "have not been brain-washed by the Roosevelt era." Eliding ethnics' experiences of the Depression—when many stormed relief centers, protested evictions and foreclosures, and demanded public assistance—Perk argued that ethnics pulled themselves up by their bootstraps: "They stand for free enterprise and against federal controls."[57] Their thrifty virtues would save the country "from the tempest and chaos of America today."[58]

In his 1971 mayoral campaign, Perk linked these antigovernment, limited taxation values with thinly veiled racist invocations of crime and government waste. He pledged to take the "hand-cuffs off" the police department; his supporters wore star-shaped sheriff badges.[59] Perk painted Stokes's expansion of municipal employment as a threat to homeowners' tax rates, and he pledged to deliver the same level of services at lower cost. Stokes had added more than three thousand city workers, through which the municipal workforce began to reflect the diversity of its residents.[60] Perk would remove Stokes's "drones" from the city's payroll.[61] Perk's homeowner conservatism also contained a strong critique of Cleveland: Now!'s corporate tax breaks. Property taxes were high, Perk explained, because businesses got a break at the expense of small homeowners. Perk's small-propertied populism was echoed by Bishop William Cosgrove in the *Cleveland Catholic Universe Bulletin*. Cosgrove castigated suburban business elites for "parasitically" manipulating the city, gutting its tax base, and pitting whites and blacks "against each other."[62] As a structural diagnosis of the city's power imbalances, Cosgrove effectively echoed arguments that CORE's Ruth Turner was making. But these white men were not calling for interracial solidarity.

In 1971, despite no support from the national Republican Party, Perk won the mayoralty by dominating the city's once-Democratic white ethnic wards. His fusion of fiscal and racial grievances, which challenged the two halves of 1960s liberalism—its supply-side state and its efforts to empower poor and black Americans—won the day. Perk's inauguration brought into the open a range of erstwhile white Democratic supporters, including the United Auto Workers' Sherwood "Bob" Weissman who gave a fiery speech, blasting "corporate liberalism" and "downtown political power brokers."[63] Perk singled out a young Democratic councilman who had been instrumental in his election. Dennis Kucinich had organized "Democrats for Perk" and was often the opening act on the stump, vilifying Stokes Democrats' ties to business and racial preferences in hiring.[64] Kucinich underscored just how racially divided the city was: "There's only two parties in Cleveland," he said, "white and black."[65] As he put it, "The power is with the people."[66] He did not need to say which people.

Ralph Perk inherited a city nearing fiscal crisis—and so perhaps his fiscal conservatism had met its moment. Between 1960 and 1970, Cleveland's manufacturing employment declined by 34 percent.[67] Yet, over the same period, the suburban labor force had grown by 35 percent. Between 1960 and 1975, the city's population declined from nearly 900,000 to barely 600,000, yet suburban growth exceeded the city's population loss. Cleveland's property values plummeted as industry and residents decentralized, sending property tax receipts tumbling from $41.4 million in 1969 to $23.2 million in 1976.[68] By decade's end, only Newark, New Jersey, ranked higher than Cleveland in wealth disparity between city and suburb.[69] Despite such structural and spatial factors in driving the city's crisis, Perk was adamant: "To talk of increasing taxes now" would "take the pressure off this administration to modernize and streamline city government."[70] Cuts alone would not close the growing budget shortfall, and Perk also sold city assets, including land on which Stokes had planned 8,000 desperately needed units of public housing.[71] Selling assets, however, was not a long-term strategy and ultimately threatened future revenues.[72]

Mainly, Perk turned to Washington. Indeed, without some sort of regional tax sharing agreement with the suburbs, the entire viability of his low-tax high-service conservatism depended upon securing greater federal assistance—much of which would come through supply-side subsidies or by redirecting antipoverty funding. Roughly 40 percent of the city's budget was already subsidized by federal or state resources, and Perk sought to expand that figure.[73] Visiting Vice President Spiro Agnew, Perk reminded him that Cleveland was the nation's largest city with a Republican mayor. He presented a $200 million shopping list of funding requests and received assurances the White House would expedite aid to the city.[74] His timing was fortuitous. Nixon was developing a white ethnic political outreach strategy for his 1972 reelection.[75] As Nixon's staffers understood, "there is a changing of attitudes on the part of the ethnic population, prompted by the pressure from the Blacks."[76] Perk was soon consulting for the National Republican Party Heritage Groups Council, the organization driving Nixon's "white ethnic strategy." As a Nixon staffer wrote, we have been able to assist [Mayor Perk] in arranging considerable Federal assistance."[77] Nixon's staffers would also guide Perk in redirecting antipoverty funds.

As the Johnson administration defanged maximum feasible participation, it had also debuted the Model Cities program, superficially aimed to "coordinate" various War on Poverty programs and to fund a broad range of improvements to narrowly demarcated, predominantly minority neighborhoods. But it also reflected the Johnson administration's efforts to return to city officials control over federal subsidies.[78] A local Model Cities board, appointed and overseen by the mayor and city council, oversaw funding with the stipulation that "citizens have clear and direct access to the decision-making process." Yet, as Johnson put it in a private phone call, his goal was for officials to "take charge of the goddamn thing ... let's just sidestep [CAPs], let's start some new projects, and let their old ones kind of wither a little, transfer them, and let's get completely in charge."[79] Poverty groups would not give up without a fight, and in many cities, Model Cities became the final battlegrounds of the War on Poverty.

Model Cities Cleveland's area, which residents called the "model neighborhood," covered twenty-five square blocks, primarily in Hough. As conceived under the Stokes administration, the program would invest resources in jobs and jobs training, health services, improved education, housing, business stimulus, and infrastructure.[80] Stokes established a Citizens Participation Association (CPA), which, along with a neighborhood-elected Resident Board of Trustees, amplified residents' voices in consultations with the Model Cities administrator, the city's economic development office, and the city council, which had the final say. But rancor between Stokes and the city council, dominated by white Democrats, meant Cleveland struggled, as a postmortem explained, "to agree upon a single program."[81]

Ralph Perk inherited a fraught situation and, with the Nixon administration's assistance, made it much more so. HUD's regional director assured Perk that he could determine the structure, type, and procedures for citizen participation.[82] Perk allowed the Resident Board of Trustees' mandate to expire and populated his own board. Wilbur Warren, a Hough resident and member of the dissolved board, excoriated Perk in terms echoing the participatory principle Perk had trampled: this was an "act of maximum feasible manipulation to disenfranchise and shortchange widespread citizen participation."[83] Though their patrons had for a moment been federal agencies, residents understood they were once again confronting a hostile local administration without federal support. Even Cuyahoga County Republican Party executive Saul Stillman urged Perk to be more sensitive to "what [model neighborhood residents] consider . . . the erosion of their responsibilities and duties."[84] Despite new obstacles, residents worked to get the program moving again—indeed they considered it their duty.[85] Perk's goal was to get federal money moving into the city's coffers.

Nixon's HUD staffers explained that Perk could develop and implement "locally established procedures" for Model Cities, while paying lip service to "continued involvement of . . . citizen participation organizations."[86] With HUD's blessing, Perk redesigned the program to provide budgetary relief by using the health and welfare departments to administer social service programs, rather than establishing separate Model Cities agencies.[87] The funds would offset the costs of existing services, freeing resources to be shifted elsewhere. Within Model Cities, Nixon's OEO further loosened regulations to emphasize "local discretion," "additional authority to local chief executives," and even recommended expanding "the program . . . to include entire cities" rather than distinct neighborhoods, which would further empower public officials. Housing secretary George Romney considered these experimental reforms to Model Cities, dubbed "planned variations," a way to test the viability of the block grant model at the heart of what would become Nixon's "New Federalism."[88]

With the new board in place, bickering only worsened. Perk lashed out, contending that he no longer needed their consultation.[89] Neighborhood people argued the mayor threatened the "moral and legal commitment between the City of Cleveland and the residents of . . . Model Cities Neighborhoods."[90] Perk hit back in baldly racialized terms: "I am going to present my program to this board in three weeks. . . . If you do not wish to accept it, I will cut the program off." Said Perk, "People on the [nearly all white] west side don't want Model Cities anyhow. I can always get some other program."[91]

Fannie Lewis became the model neighborhood's chief advocate. The resolve with which Lewis approached her role surely reflected her roots in the Jim Crow South. Lewis was born and initially raised in Arkansas. There, she was intimately exposed to the worst of Jim Crow violence. In the late 1920s and early 1930s, she worked summers picking cotton with her family, and one horrific day she watched as a plantation overseer on horseback shot and killed a young boy, a classmate of hers, simply because he was lagging behind. Soon after, one of her teachers was tied to a tree and burned to death for teaching Fannie's class to read—a note attached to his remains read, "Niggers, read and run!" By the 1960s, Lewis, a single mother of three, now faced the devastation urban renewal was unleashing in black neighborhoods. Indeed, her first entry into organizing was to oppose Cleveland's clearance programs.[92] During the first wave of War on Poverty programs she worked as an intake counselor with the Hough Neighborhood Youth Corps. Lewis went on to direct the Model Cities Citizens Participation Association outreach centers. Throughout this work Lewis, too, lived in poverty.[93]

Lewis felt deeply empowered by her administrative role, which, as for many other women, launched her nearly three-decade career in community organizing and, eventually, electoral politics. Describing these early experiences, Lewis wrote, "it has been a pleasure for me to serve these young persons amid all the heartaches and opposition that I have encountered. . . . I have been in touch with some one's life to the extent that, what I have said and done has made a change for the better in them. I have caused them (in my unskilled an [sic] untrained way in the area of professional counseling but richly and

Figure 5. Fannie Lewis, citizen director of the Model Cities program, 1971. Cleveland Press Collections, courtesy of the Michael Schwartz Library Special Collections, Cleveland State University.

fervently, an most decidingly) to make a start upward by believing in them an respecting them as the important person when and where ever we Meet."[94]

What she lacked in formal training, Lewis more than made up for with tenacity. She watchdogged Model Cities funds, which she understood were slipping away.[95] She wrote (to no avail) for support from regional HUD officials: "Cleveland's Model Cities program is again in jeopardy."[96] The city's black newspaper lamented the situation facing black Clevelanders just two years after Stokes's departure: "Isn't it strange indeed that Cleveland is the only city where Negroes are retreating politically rather than advancing?"[97]

By September 1973, as rumors of corruption and fiscal impropriety reached mainstream white news organizations, Perk agreed to an independent audit. "The dismal record of Model Cities programs across the nation has been one of failure to the point of disaster and disappointment beyond belief," investigators began. "Cleveland has been no exception." Yet, Cleveland was unique for the extent of its failures. Residents, "the almost forgotten people whom the program was intended to benefit," were ignored by city hall.[98] On the eve of New Federalism, expenditures across all Model Cities programs were only 54 percent of the total allocated in 1972.[99] Funding was not getting to people and neighborhoods in need. Yet, the publicity generated by Model Cities' failures generally centered on the $9.3 million that the government "wasted" on Cleveland's poor communities, entrenching racist perceptions that efforts to fight poverty were futile, wasteful uses of public resources.[100]

When Model Cities was closed out on June 30, 1974, Cleveland's funding was rolled into the city's first Community Development Block Grant (described below), funds dispersed largely at local leaders' discretion. Fannie Lewis understood the importance of staying organized in the face of Nixon's New Federalism. Because "Model Cities will . . . be moving into a City Wide Program under Community Development" Block Grants, Lewis would "form a Coalition to . . . immediately become organized, chartered, [and] start to provide workshops and orientation to the Community."[101] She understood that, beneath the language of "community development," barriers for poor people's access to federal antipoverty funds were being fortified.

New Federalism

To woo the primary beneficiaries of the New Deal, Richard Nixon would restore much of the New Deal's model of fiscal federalism. The slate of intergovernmental reforms that Nixon called "New Federalism" constituted a policy expression of his efforts to court local businesspeople and cement his "silent majority" of working-class and suburban white voters. New Federalism's central theme was empowering local elected officials—and thereby local electoral and white racial majorities—by stripping the Democratic Congress of regulatory authority over local uses of national resources. As one staffer explained, New Federalism would reestablish "political ideas of American federalism plowed under by the Great Society," which made it "extremely difficult for chief executives at the State and local levels to set and implement their own priorities."[102]

Beyond Nixon's partisan rationale for reforming federalism, however, by 1969, signs abounded that the federal system had entered a sustained period of fiscal and administrative crises: its nested layers of governance had become scrambled by crisscrossing mandates, financing, and competing authorities. The nonpartisan Advisory Commission on Intergovernmental Relations

(ACIR) found that local governments suffered operating deficits tied to growing commitments (often due to unfunded or underfunded federal mandates), and inflation was driving up municipal costs of services and contracts.[103] State and local governments also relied on the most visible and volatile tax receipts. Sales taxes were particularly fickle since inflation drove up receipts in some years but could crash when consumer spending contracted. And by 1972, Americans believed the property tax was "the least fair of the major tax sources."[104] Yet, with rising costs and obligations to service bonded debt, officials hiked taxes throughout the 1960s. In 1960, only nineteen states imposed general sales and personal income taxes; by 1970 thirty-three did so. In the 1960s, increased state and local tax collection actually outpaced economic growth, a remarkable fact given the decade's galloping economy.[105]

Nixon's silent majority perceived these crises in two primary ways. Though black homeowners often suffered disproportionately predatory property assessments and taxes, as municipal governments computerized notoriously corrupt property tax assessment practices, the average property tax bite increased, seeding anti-property-tax movements across the country.[106] Meanwhile, many white voters associated public spending with liberal policies that seemed relentlessly focused on business-backed redevelopment schemes or redressing black poverty. To sell New Federalism, then, Nixon fused these racial and fiscal discontents. New Federalism would bolster local majoritarianism and "stabilize" or even reduce local property taxes.[107] In a primetime speech in August 1969, Nixon detailed "general revenue sharing" (GRS), New Federalism's initial gambit, which would share string-free federal tax receipts with subnational governments. This was "a gesture of faith in America's State and local governments and in the principle of democratic self-government."[108] In his 1971 State of the Union address, Nixon explained that "the further away government is from the people, the stronger government becomes and the weaker people become." "Local government," he said, invoking the racially freighted, majoritarian notion of "the people," "is the government closest to the people, it is most responsive to the individual person."[109] Nixon used localist language and communitarian framings that echoed Johnson's arguments for the War on Poverty, but tied them instead to a different definition of local community. And while Johnson's fiscal argument was based on putting the unemployed to work, Nixon emphasized how New Federalism might limit the silent majority's property taxes. Less than two weeks ahead of his 1972 reelection, Nixon signed the GRS bill alongside Philadelphia's white ethnic mayor Frank Rizzo. "Revenue sharing," said Nixon, "can provide desperately needed tax relief for millions of Americans."[110]

Though GRS did, in fact, contain the potential to remake fiscal federalism, framing that potential in conservative terms of limiting the significance of the federal government obscured the enduring—and expanding—importance of federal resources in underwriting localism, however defined. New Federalism enabled politicians such as Ralph Perk to continue railing against and limiting *local* taxes while using *federal* funds to pad budgets. Though Nixon sold GRS as a sort of municipal analogue to critiques of welfare dependency, calling to dial back federal influence in each area, in the fiscal and economic crises of the 1970s, municipal governments would become more dependent on federal aid: GRS alone sent string-free checks to practically every government in the United States—some 37,000 units of government. By the end of 1976, more than $30 billion in GRS funds had flowed to state and local governments.[111]

The most significant of New Federalism's reforms were in the Housing and Community Development Act of 1974, Title I of which created Community Development Block Grants (CDBGs). CDBGs bundled together funding from a range of liberal urban programs, stripped them of most regulations, and sent most funds to local governments via formula rather than applications. If the steady expansion and reform of categorical programs within, for instance, the various amendments to the Housing Act, reflected liberals' ongoing prioritization of local elites' preferences, the move to block grants offered a way to deliver flexible funding without having to pass new legislation. Rather than view Nixon's reforms as a fundamental break from an era liberal governance, both supply side liberals and Nixon's staffers viewed the War on Poverty's more targeted partnerships with the poor as having been an essential rupture; Nixon was restoring a New Deal model of elite-centered federalism. Indeed, the liberal economist Walter Heller had developed the rationale for block grants and revenue sharing in the mid-1960s, revealing administrative and philosophical continuities between seemingly oppositional eras of government reform.[112]

But intentions and context matter. While Johnson had begun inviting private-sector leadership to steer poverty programs, his efforts to stifle dissent functioned within the context of the broader raft of Great Society poverty programs and entitlements—including Head Start, Medicaid, and education spending—which made genuine differences in the lives of impoverished Americans. Nixon viewed localism and public-private partnerships as tools for unwinding and devolving federal regulatory and social support favoring for poor Americans. Nixon's staffers described public-private partnerships as ways of ensuring "local autonomy" in determining "community" priorities. But in the context of strained local budgets, they recognized that "local autonomy without [federal] financial resources may be a meaningless concept."[113] Indeed, while his Republican successors would pair Nixonian regulatory devolution with an emphasis on *defunding* federal programs, Nixon used liberal means—direct federal spending—to support businesses as well as burgeoning Republican constituencies across the suburbs and the Sunbelt.[114]

Critics warned that sending loosely regulated antipoverty-oriented "community development" funds to state and local governments would inevitably yield fewer resources for marginalized Americans.[115] But Nixon's staffers believed the federal government had little role left to play in redressing racial inequalities. Top urban policy aide Daniel Patrick Moynihan was clear on the administration's position on race. "Mostly," he said, Nixon's policy team "doesn't think at all" about race or racial inequality.[116] While Moynihan's critique of the War on Poverty argued that the poor were not "ready" to administer federal funds, a Model Cities activist offered the opposite critique of New Federalism: "Local government is not ready for the burdens which Nixon wants to give it." As he explained, "the only real salvation for the disadvantaged, and for poor blacks in particular, is the direct intervention of the federal government."[117] Testifying before Congress, Georgia's governor Jimmy Carter essentially agreed, warning that when "funds are taken away from the poor and put into general revenue sharing or block grants, even the most enlightened legislature is not going to take these funds and put them back exclusively into programs that benefit the poor."[118] Reflecting his material interests as governor, however, Carter supported New Federalism's deregulatory thrust.

While Nixon's recourse to federalism was not new, his expansive emphasis on elite-led public-private partnerships as directly beneficial to poor people planted a key conceptual seed for neoliberal policy ideas and more muscular forms of business producerism to come. As the legislation gained momentum, Nixon and, later, Gerald Ford began selling public-private partnerships not only as Republican innovations but as ways to generate private-sector solutions for "community development" and poverty. In CDBGs, Nixon's team crafted vague language that could be understood either as a ratification of the War on Poverty's goals or as a loophole through which nearly any local development program could be pulled. CDBG funds were to be used in one of three areas: (1) to benefit low- and moderate-income persons; (2) to clear slums and blight; or (3) to "meet an urgent local need." Aping the War on Poverty's participation principle, the final bill also called for "maximum feasible priority" to ensuring community input. Just about anything, however, could fit into these categories.[119]

The administration worked especially closely with business associations to sell its solutions for urban poverty. Vice President Agnew participated in a U.S. Chamber sponsored closed-circuit telecast with 26 urban chamber leaders along with "thousands of business and community leaders" who beamed in to exchange "views on the vital role of voluntary action in attacking community problems."[120] At another gathering, Agnew ratified businesspeople's commitment to fighting poverty.[121] By 1973, Nixon's team explicitly urged business leaders to make plans to secure CDBGs, and HUD partnered with the U.S. Chamber of Commerce on a series of videos about the promise of block grants. The tapes, the chamber explained, were a "must for all community planners, chambers of commerce, city officials and local businessmen."[122]

The Housing and Community Development Act of 1974 sailed through the Democrat-controlled legislature, becoming law nearly ten years to the day after Johnson established his War on Poverty. LBJ, of course, had taken the first steps toward curtailing citizen participation in poverty programs. A Democratic Congress joined Nixon and Ford in finishing the job, re-empowering supply-side state builders by endowing them with broad discretion not only in development initiatives but also in fighting poverty. Though Nixon resigned a month before the legislation was signed, in a final victory, under Title I of the 1974 legislation, CDBGs' funding formula favored population growth, poverty rates, and levels of crowded housing, privileging Republicans' emerging base in suburbs and the fast-growing, low-wage Sunbelt. As one contemporary understood, far from fighting poverty, New Federalism's "real agenda was to get money to the suburban communities—to spread the money around" to the Silent Majority.[123]

Contesting Community Development

The deregulatory ethos of the 1970s, then, most often linked to sectoral deregulations during the Carter years, had philosophical roots in the Johnson and Nixon administrations. In New Federalism, the deregulatory thrust manifested a marked drop in paperwork required to win federal aid. No book of rules was sent to local administrators. The guidelines issued in the Federal

Register, too, went little beyond the vague language of the bill itself. Periodically, President Gerald Ford's HUD director David Meeker sent memos of clarification, but these missives—dubbed "Meeker Memos"—were regarded as rules of thumb. Rather than audit programs, HUD asked cities to sign "assurances" that their proposals met the spirit of the law. To one local official, a staffer stressed local autonomy: "This is your program. We are not going to second-guess you, nor look beyond your certifications and if we get citizen complaints about your performance, we will simply refer them to you."[124]

Cleveland's byzantine political system, however, was a direct rebuke to the notion that local government was intrinsically more effective at identifying and solving local problems. Each of the city's thirty-three wards elected its councilperson to two-year terms, yielding a constant state of campaigning punctuated by volatile factions, backroom deals, and petty scandals. The mayor, also elected to two-year terms, was supposed to herd the council. The corrosive politics only worsened with the arrival of millions in loosely regulated funding. One of the few federal mandates demanded that mayors and councils jointly approve spending priorities. Rather than agree to omnibus spending packages, Cleveland's council members demanded to vet each proposal. Annually, this could mean more than one hundred individual pieces of legislation bogged down in a quagmire of politicking and grandstanding.[125]

The arrival of CDBGs, Fannie Lewis wrote, inaugurated an "era of fast changing federal, state and local programs." Community groups must "provide the needed source for citizens to get instantaneous information, interpretation of policies, and Technical Assistance."[126] She established the Cleveland Citizens Participation Association (CCPA), which raised concerns with Mayor Perk that "the community will . . . be forced to accept or reject" rather than offer input on CDBG plans.[127] Lewis's group also contacted Meeker and planned a trip to Washington.[128] "New Federalism," CCPA members maintained, "means we as Citizens have to demand from City Hall what is rightfully ours."[129] As Lewis feared, Perk developed his own priorities for padding the budget. Activists clashed with Perk over plans to use CDBGs to pay nearly two hundred police officers' salaries. The administration held rushed community hearings, and, though HUD initially rejected the project, Perk won an exception from Meeker who ruled "Concentrated Crime Patrol" was a "supportive service" fundable with CDBGs.[130] Lewis excoriated Perk for "provid[ing for] citizen participation in its lowest form."[131] A Brookings study found that "protests were largely ignored by the city."[132]

The administration's actions, however, inspired intensified activism among groups formed over the previous decade. The Buckeye-Woodland Community Congress (BWCC) had roots in 1960s Ford Foundation programs to foster interracial dialogue.[133] By the 1970s, the BWCC focused on interracial, cross-class economic opportunity and, in particular, improving residents' homes, joining a national movement of neighborhood groups—some of which did secure modest CDBG funding and even fought successful battles against bank redlining.[134] And the BWCC was just that: more than seven hundred Buckeye-Woodland residents and representatives of 105 social, civic, and church groups attended its founding conference.[135] The fresh memory of the War on Poverty's participation mandate endowed BWCC members with high expectations for programs ostensibly meant to benefit their neighborhoods. Kenneth Kovach, a white sociology professor at Notre Dame College, served as inaugural president. Georgiana Watts, a black resident, was housing committee chair, and she, like others, worried New Federalism was enabling the city to direct community development funds to downtown business interests. As Thomas Gannon, Kovach's twenty-six-year-old deputy put it, politicians "respond, it seems, only to pressure . . . from well-organized groups like the downtown merchants and owners and managers of industry."[136] Cleveland, one commentor explained, "was undergoing a veritable revolt of the neighborhoods," and the new activism combined older direct-action tactics with rigorous studies on issues facing the neighborhoods. Similar groups emerged across the city, including one in Hough led by Fannie Lewis.[137]

Activists did score a victory over one of Perk's plans to direct CDBG funds to business elites. In 1976, Nick Mileti, owner of Cleveland's professional basketball and hockey franchises, moved the teams to a new arena in Richfield thirty miles south of the city in hopes of attracting suburban revenue. Mileti still owned an arena on the city's east side, and after failing to find a buyer, he turned to Perk.[138] News leaked that Perk planned to buy the arena using $1 million in CDBGs (along with $1 million in other federal grants). Perk argued the investment would generate a meager $15,000 to $25,000 a year in public revenue.[139] Though it had no connection to revitalizing struggling neighborhoods, HUD officials assisted Perk. The CDBG legislation did not allow for purchasing developed property. HUD helped Perk reconfigure the transaction: if Mileti donated the arena, Perk could purchase the land with CDBGs.[140] In the wake of urban renewal and decades of overcrowding, the BWCC's Margaret Foster was furious: "Our houses are falling down and Mayor Perk's city is deteriorating—this is where we need the money."[141]

Barbara Pertz, a Buckeye resident and homeowner, fumed about obstructive participation practices: "I don't want to read in the newspaper that the mayor is going to spend $1 million for the Arena. . . . I want him to come here and suggest it first."[142] Perk ultimately faced resistance from the city council, which saw little to gain from the plan. The combination of neighborhood protest and council indifference scuttled the purchase. It was a rare victory for citizen engagement in Cleveland's CDBG process.

More than any other aspect of the program, however, CDBGs inspired hope for working-class and poor residents that federal resources would support the revitalization of their homes and neighborhoods in the aftermath of urban renewal and predatory housing programs. Particularly promising were Titles II and III of the Housing and Community Development Act of 1974, which offered financing for home renovations. These titles were themselves a remedy for earlier housing programs that promoted poor citizens' access to homeownership without corresponding support for making the often run-down homes they purchased safe and viable. Following the discontents of FHA Section 220 financing for multifamily developments on urban renewal sites, the 1968 Housing and Urban Development Act extended the Johnson administration's efforts to bring the private sector to bear more centrally in affordable housing. Rather than build public or private affordable housing projects, the new programs would enable poor people to purchase existing houses—and thus also avoid racially contentious efforts to place public or affordable housing in white neighborhoods. The 1968 act created entirely new unregulated FHA-backed mortgage markets for poor people's homeownership through the Section 235 mortgage insurance program, which secured mortgages in formerly redlined, deeply segregated neighborhoods with old and deteriorating housing stock.[143] The renovation subsidies in the 1974 act were an acknowledgment that many homes purchased in blighted areas with FHA-backed mortgages were poorly inspected, if at all, and that the costs of maintaining substandard homes were breaking the nation's poorest homeowners.

The BWCC made the pernicious combination of redlining and the failures of Title III's 518b program, which they argued benefited better-off homeowners, their focus. The 518b program set aside funds to reimburse homeowners for the costs of repairs. The legislation also sought to encourage private lending for home improvements by relaxing regulations on the amount local savings and loans could offer. Local Community Development officers could make small, low-interest loans: $200 for a new furnace; $750 for roof work. But the program also offered direct loans at fixed 3 percent interest for twenty years with a maximum loan of $17,400. As BWCC's Margaret Foster testified before Congress, "many homes in our community would not even be appraised at $17,000 and it would be foolish to pour that much money into rehabilitation." HUD's "inept administration and 'hands-off' policy," she explained, "let city officials use the funds for political projects which bypass the people."[144] Much of Cleveland's home rehabilitation loans were directed to white ethnic or gentrifying neighborhoods, such as Ohio City on the west side. When neighborhood groups accused officials of ignoring their needs, administrators "asserted that 'priority areas for receiving low-interest loans for new construction or housing rehabilitation were those where it was deemed that the money would go the farthest'"—an early example of the fiscal "triage" argument that would soon become prevalent.[145] Cleveland was typical in this regard—the 3 percent loan program also subsidized gentrification in Atlanta, Boston, Dallas, and San Francisco.[146] Likewise, in Tampa and Jacksonville, the program underwrote "above-code rehabilitation" designed to promote "fluidity in the housing market." When a HUD official inquired about subsidies going to middle- rather than lower-income homeowners, a Jacksonville official was incredulous: "that bothers you?"[147] Subsidies designed not only to fight poverty, promote access to homeownership, and remedy earlier programmatic inequities were instead seeding gentrification.

Perhaps most insidious, this failure to deliver rehabilitation loans to struggling homeowners created publicly structured incentive systems that reinforced private banks' unwillingness to lend. Foster testified before the Senate Banking Committee on Neighborhood Preservation and described how the process worked. Once a neighborhood like Buckeye was redlined, the best options for potential home buyers were purchasing FHA or VA-backed mortgages. One neighborhood in Buckeye, for instance, once dominated by white ethnic Hungarians, saw 224 of its 281 residences change hands between 1965 and 1975, creating a majority African American community. Nearly three-quarters (73 percent) of the new mortgages were secured through the FHA or VA, "but in most cases no inspection [took] place."[148] As Foster continued, "The home buyer, thinking the house has met standards of the federal government, moves in. Then the first time he turns on the furnace he finds it out of order." Had city officials been more responsive with 3 percent loans, perhaps homeowners could have shouldered the burden of their collapsing homes. Instead, a "tight financial situation makes the homeowner face a decision to make a major repair or be late on his mortgage payment." A pernicious structure had ensnared them. Financially strained by the costs of misleading mortgages and unable to secure a loan from the city's development office, homeowners fell behind on mortgage payments. Banks invalidated late payments and demanded late fees. After just two or three late payments, mortgage companies foreclosed. Homeowners were trapped in what activists called "fast foreclosure." The process, Foster testified, was "systemic." By backing the mortgage and not the home buyer or the actual home, and by allowing local officials' discretion in lending, the FHA incentivized the process. Owners were evicted, houses were abandoned, and government delivered lenders the full value of the mortgages. Foster provided Congress with information on 300 such foreclosures in Buckeye alone.[149] East Cleveland saw 233 fast foreclosures between 1973 and 1975.[150] Funds that had originally been created to fight a War on Poverty were speeding the foreclosure and eviction of thousands of aspiring homeowners, speeding gentrification, and padding the pockets of private lenders.[151]

It was these circumstances that led Buckeye resident Sarah Turner to bring pieces of her home's broken banister to Washington in the summer of 1976 for demonstrations and public hearings organized by National People's Action (NPA), the Chicago-based neighborhood organization that fought mortgage redlining and fast foreclosure. As an activist from Providence, Rhode Island, put it, "We got community development money in our cities and all we really got was political patronage. . . . We know where the money is going . . . while our houses are going down the drain." As hundreds of protesters gathered outside HUD's headquarters in support of Turner and her allies, barricaded inside, HUD officials set up a public-address system from which they promised investigations. "We don't want any more big government programs," complained Gail Cincotta, NPA's leader. "It was big government programs that destroyed our cities."[152]

* * *

During the 1976 presidential campaign, Gerald Ford's surrogates traveled the country articulating their public-private, loosely regulated, elite-led vision of community development. A particularly fraught visit to Cleveland by Ford's HUD director, Carla A. Hills, offers a telling example of just how decisively the War on Poverty's emphasis on resident participation was defeated. After the NPA demonstrations in Washington, the BWCC invited Hills to meet, but activists were furious when they were granted just forty minutes and that twenty other people, including Perk staffers, were also invited. "For these reasons," Kovach wrote Hills, "this was a bogus meeting and phony attempt to discuss new ways to revitalize neighborhoods."[153] Meanwhile, Hills spent over an hour with business and civic elites, underscoring the importance of private-sector-led solutions for housing and poverty.[154] Hills flew back to Washington on the private jet of Eaton Corp., among the city's most powerful corporations.[155]

Building on Lyndon Johnson's initial retreat, Nixon and Ford laid down the nation's arms in the War on Poverty. But the massive federal subsidies set aside to fight that war lived on in New Federalism. So too did a rhetorical commitment to community participation and fighting poverty that increasingly centered businesspeople as the proper administrators not merely of growth but also of community uplift. The second half of the 1970s and 1980s would see Cleveland's business elites, led by the brash James Davis, pursue a much more vigorous campaign to recover control over development and antipoverty subsidies. That Cleveland's businesspeople had to wage a battle against highly mobilized community organizations would have been shocking to many rural or smaller-city southern elites. These supply-side state builders had never faced much of a challenge to their access to federal subsidies. When those challenges came, however, boosters incorporated ways of managing community participation that would soon offer a model for business's reconstruction of northern urban democracies, too. North or South, large city or small, local businesspeople were learning the value of framing their partnerships with government in terms of fighting poverty and finding proactive ways of managing and neutralizing community participation—key steps toward the neoliberalization of poverty policy and, perhaps, democracy itself.

CHAPTER 6

Making Poverty Pay

It took a last-minute telegram, but in January 1965, the Office of Economic Opportunity approved Jimmy Carter's application to develop his region's Community Action Program under the auspices of the West Central Georgia Area Planning and Development Commission (WCGAPDC). A precocious supply-side state builder freshly elected to a second two-year term as state senator, Carter, just forty years old, organized civic and business elites across southwest Georgia to secure federal support for regional economic development. But his APDC's initial application had not included requisite language about poor people's participation. Final approval required that Carter send an amendment stating: "Provisions for incorporating the poor in the actual planning of our program have been made. Poor have been in the actual power structure itself. We plan to use their talents and suggestions in all plans under the Economic Opportunity Act."[1] Carter's planning commission would be a "launching pad" for the region's war on poverty, which, beyond a Head Start program, primarily focused on workforce development.[2] The commission appointed program developers to set the agenda, oversee the work of the Community Action Council (CAC), and "explain the program[s] to top officials and . . . communicate and work with the poverty stricken."[3] Though the council did include minority members, their selection reflected white elites' labor- and development-oriented vision of Community Action rather than any bottom-up plans coming from poor communities: black CAC members included Napoleon Williams, principal of the segregated Vienna High and Industrial School, and H. J. Ladd, vocational agriculture teacher at the segregated Douglass High School. Carter's commission's model of Community Action thus reflected the adaptability of decentralized, supply-side administrative structures. They could at once

Figure 6. Jimmy Carter (standing, second from left) and the West Central Georgia Area Planning and Development Commission, ca. 1965. Courtesy of Georgia Archives, Vanishing Georgia Collection, sum084.

incorporate vestiges of Jim Crow, approximate the participatory spirit of a more modern liberalism, and still underwrite elite development priorities.

As the War on Poverty's "maximum feasible participation" mandate ignited clashes in larger cities, in many smaller rural or developing communities with less highly concentrated minority populations, white elites had freer rein to develop novel ways of managing citizen participation. Moreover, in the context of national repudiation of Jim Crow, supply-side liberalism's emphasis on localism, economic growth, and fiscal moderation offered these elites an ostensibly moderate vernacular that could be understood as tempering Johnson-era liberalism's seeming overreach even as elites continued to pursue federal subsidies. In a harbinger of highly brokered, neoliberal forms of democracy to come, in Georgia's smaller communities, the War on Poverty provided an impetus and institutional proving ground for tightly managing poor citizens' participation in local administration. Supply-side state builders' position at the nexus of public and private, local and national power well situated them to manage the transition from Jim Crow to a "post-racial"

South whose more subtle forms of market and civic exclusions and hierarchies of power were converging with those of the rest of the country.

The reasons for these regional convergences had less to do with any stated racial or political ideologies than with the evolving structures and priorities of the liberal state and its continued articulation through the interests of local public and private sector elites. In the wake of urban uprisings of the late 1960s, some liberals even viewed small-scale urban development of rural areas as a solution for the broader urban crisis. And, as federal urban planning grants, urban renewal, and the War on Poverty arrived in smaller and rural communities, these programs required elites to develop indexes of local privation, encouraging them to frame their developmental agendas in terms of ameliorating poverty. Urban renewal especially encouraged rural and small-city officials to highlight "blight" and "slums" within their communities, dynamics more often associated with larger cities. Indeed, by the time the federal urban renewal program came to an end in 1974, the majority of renewal-funded municipalities had populations, like Rome, of fifty thousand or fewer. And at the peak of the civil rights movement, smaller cities often displaced considerably higher proportions of minority residents than did larger cities. Even as the formal Jim Crow order fell across the South, then, liberal development initiatives empowered seemingly "moderate" elites to simply wipe out black communities in the name of progress.[4]

As Jimmy Carter's political ambitions grew, his network of supply-side state builders became an essential springboard to the governor's mansion and key policy development allies once there. Between a first failed campaign in 1966 and his successful effort in 1970, Carter used the state's APDC network to build his reputation and hone his politics. Against an earlier persona built around progressive inclusion of women, young people, and minority Georgians, by the late 1960s Carter positioned public-private regional institutions such as APDCs as defensive bulwarks against federal incursions—expressions of elite-led localism that incorporated aspects of Franklin Roosevelt's New Deal and Richard Nixon's New Federalism. By 1970, Carter sold himself to Georgia's white voters as a conservative champion of local majoritarianism, a protector of his own silent majority. Though national news outlets heralded Carter's gubernatorial election as the dawning of a new "New South," his calls to transcend racism had more in common with Roosevelt's and Nixon's willful neglect of discrimination than with the sort of racial progressivism and calls for structural reform associated with the civil rights movement.

As civil rights activists pressed for equal rights and as liberal programs ostensibly intended to empower poor or marginalized citizens continued to benefit elites, these structures of incremental, elite-brokered progress would be strained to the breaking point. By the early 1970s, when Carter declared a "post-racial" politics, black frustration and anger would erupt in Rome, just as it did in hundreds of other American municipalities between 1965 and 1972.[5] That these tensions exploded years after the passage of the Civil Rights and Voting Rights Acts reflected the fact that formal disfranchisement and segregation constituted the more visible surface of much deeper forms of inequality that were national rather than regional, structural rather than exceptional, embedded in and reproduced by the evolving liberal state.

Brokering Progress, Managing Participation

When school let out on a Thursday in March 1963, some one hundred students from Rome, Georgia's segregated high school joined the sit-in movement sweeping the South. At least sixty-two were arrested for refusing "to obey store owners," the *Atlanta Daily World* reported. The students' actions had been closely monitored by black ministers and the city's chapter of the Human Relations Council of Georgia, an interracial organization affiliated with the liberal Southern Regional Council.[6] Despite the role played by interracial progressives—who alerted the chamber of commerce of the students' plans—when NAACP field secretary Vernon Jordan Jr. took up the teenagers' case, a judge denied his motion for dismissal. Students would have to pay a $50 fine (over $400 in 2020) or spend five days in jail.[7] Nevertheless, black and white leaders soon negotiated the integration of the city's public library.[8] This highly brokered, limited, and tightly managed integration—in which black teenagers still earned heavy fines, jail time, and criminal records—defined the outer limits of racial progress under late Jim Crow across much of the South: violence was avoided, a modicum of integration was achieved, and Rome's white business and civic leadership maintained control—some even touted their progressivity.[9]

Meanwhile, though the U.S. Chamber of Commerce decried the War on Poverty as "a billion-dollar boondoggle," many southern elites were firmly and enthusiastically in control of the initiative from the start, particularly in smaller, developing communities.[10] Like many of their northern brethren, southern supply-side state builders' sense of social progressivity was also informed by the shifting programmatic language and goals within the federal programs they pursued. Initially, however, elites primarily viewed the War on Poverty as "manpower development" initiatives that might boost their development agendas. Indeed, in its annual report, Rome's Coosa Valley APDC (CVAPDC) included updates on OEO programs between discussions of a minerals development study and industrial and building codes.[11] These infrastructural and developmental conceptions of antipoverty programs were largely in line with President Johnson's vision of the poverty war.[12] Local elites were happy to develop cheap, government-subsidized labor.

Like Carter's commission, Rome's Coosa commissioners appointed the region's initial Community Action Committee until plans for ensuring "maximum feasible participation" of the poor could be established.[13] Richard McCullough, clerk of the Floyd County Board of Roads and Revenue, was named chairman. Mather Payne, Rome chamber president and owner-operator of the regional news radio station WRGA, chaired the Community Action nominating committee. Others included white school superintendents Harold Lindsey and Milton McDonald, Donald Jackson, a black businessman "representing the Negro community," and representatives from the Floyd Health Department and the Junior Chamber of Commerce (neither the Jaycees nor the chamber had black members). W. T. Levins of the CVAPDC was brought in as a "technical advisor." The commission quickly won $2.7 million in federal funding across a number of different poverty programs.[14]

As they pursued a multitude of federal spending programs, commissioners and chamber members shared expertise and counsel. The regular "Eggs and Issues" breakfast hosted by state legislators and the governor's office in Atlanta, for instance, provided "a wonderful opportunity for fellowship and political skullduggery," as Rome's chamber put it.[15] Jimmy Carter modeled his APDC on Romans' example, and his commission's executive director, Hugh Davis, traveled the state meeting other APDC officials to assess "whether or not our progress has been in line with theirs." Happily, he reported, given "the short time we have been operational, our progress has been very good."[16] The CVAPDC strengthened these networks by hosting a conference on the issue of "comprehensive planning" within Community Action Programs (CAPs) including best approaches "to train the unemployed and underemployed citizens to fill job needs and thus become useful, productive citizens," the *Rome News-Tribune* reported. Attendees included the Atlanta regional OEO director, as well as CAA officials from Knoxville, Tennessee, and Florence, Alabama. Organizers anticipated hosting between 250 and 350 "labor leaders, industrialists," and "CAP directors and staff."[17] These well-networked officials envisioned subsidized labor programs jump-starting New Deal–style developments. As Carter explained, his commission pursued Community Action to "work for [the] total economic development of the entire area."[18] Though Americus, a larger community within the jurisdiction of Carter's commission, saw robust civil rights organizing, black civil rights leaders were seemingly never consulted for its CAC, which instead appointed black vocational educators.[19]

While elites were most concerned with economic development, these new federal programs required them to develop indexes of poverty in their applications. Carter's commission partnered with a neighboring APDC on one grant application, which explained that the region's "economic torpor" derived from the "general lack of industrial skills, . . . isolation . . . and general impoverishment," which was "to a significant extent a matter of racial circumstance."[20] In tiny Alma, in southeastern Georgia, officials generated reports estimating that 1,038 out of a total 2,380 housing units were "substandard, i.e., dilapidated and deteriorating." The region's crisis of poverty manifested itself in other ways, with families "subjected . . . to considerable stress." In 1969, Alma's Bacon County had the third highest number of admissions to mental health hospitals of all Georgia counties, a remarkable fact given its population, which officials emphasized on behalf of winning development-oriented grants.[21] Liberals' emergent social priorities were expanding elites' sense of producerist justifications—not only would they deliver jobs and bustling communities, they were addressing a variety of social crises.

But the necessity of working with the poor injected new frustrations into officials' usual complaints about sluggish bureaucracy and inequitable funding decisions. Testifying before Congress, leaders of the Lower Chattahoochee Valley APDC explained that they struggled with impoverished residents' "apathy" when officials attempted to correct their habits. As commissioners explained, "For people who have for years conditioned themselves to living under adverse conditions," white or black, "it is very difficult to adjust to change." Yet, APDC "aids and staff [sic]" conducted "visits and followup visits" among rural families "in order to create motivation and self-confidence." Ultimately, "we have been fairly successful in breaking the communication barrier."[22] The lines of communication mainly flowed from elites to the poor, though, and some APDC leaders disparaged maximum feasible participation mandates. Oliver Terriberry, director of the Georgia Mountains APDC and formerly an engineer at Georgia Tech's Industrial Development Division, explained to the National Advisory Commission on Rural Poverty that his organization "concentrated on developing work discipline" among the poor in order to end "the need for welfare." But he bemoaned the "extreme emphasis" on "the involvement of minorities." Getting them to "participate in planning" was rendering "purely secondary" what he considered "the meaningfulness of the programs." A commission member pressed him on the point, however, noting that "the coming together of the races in these communities . . . may leave a far more valuable aftereffect" than simply generating economic growth. Terriberry did concede that "this is the first time we are having some interplay between two races."[23]

While Terriberry's conception of the War on Poverty was clearly at odds with those of certain liberals, he was wholly in line with Georgia's network of supply-side state builders. In 1962, leaders in Alma formed the Bacon County Development Corporation devoted to "the economic welfare of the community." Their primary activity was applying for federal aid, and among their earliest prospects was Community Action. In a letter to OEO director Sargent Shriver, one local businessman practically screamed the entitlement elites felt toward federal aid: "WE DESIRE IMMEDIATE CONSIDERATION TOWARDS OUR REQUEST FOR A GRANT [caps in original]."[24] After being twice denied, in 1968 their third application was accepted. Alma became the smallest municipality in the country to receive a federal Model Cities grant. "A great event has taken place," Wm. W. Lee, the co-owner of Lee Feston Chevrolet-Olds of Alma, Georgia, wrote to his congressman William S. Stuckey. The grant, he predicted, "will probably push Alma further into the present than any other event in its history. . . . We now have a future."[25]

To white elites in larger cities, the enthusiasm for Model Cities among their cousins in smaller, rural, developing communities might have been astonishing. But the relative disempowerment of less densely populated African American communities, their regional networking, and their embrace of liberal planning techniques enabled small-city and rural elites to establish strategies for minimizing poor and minority residents' involvement. In Alma, officials structured Model Cities in ways that respected the letter but not the spirit of the participatory mandate. Rather than designate specific areas the Model Cities neighborhood, officials designated the entire region. They created an administrative structure and community "task force" model that included minority and poor participants but that isolated them as individual representatives across twelve different task forces, each of which was "chaired by a respected and informed lay citizen"—an elite, white male. These twelve units were, in turn, embedded within a broader structure beneath the mayor, city council, and county commissioners. This organization diffused the potential influence of African Americans and poor or working-class whites whose interests might have otherwise disrupted what civic leaders had begun calling their "new politics of development."²⁶

Georgia's network of regional elites helped Alma's leadership devise their system for managing community participation, which emerged from communication with the Slash Pine APDC, based in Waycross. For federal officials, the administrative structure ticked the box of "citizen participation," ensuring funds flowed to the community. But, as L. W. Taylor Jr., Bacon County manager, explained, their program for brokering poor and minority participation would help "lay a solid foundation for a true community improvement and development program." It would be spearheaded by "the community establishment, the people with the wallets and the power to permit and to bring about change." "Soon," he reported, "we had the complete involvement by the community power structure."²⁷ Having established a way to manage the poor's participation, elites plunged into their development initiatives.

For liberal politicians and policymakers, meanwhile, there were at least three reasons for sending antipoverty funds to the rural South. First, and most obviously, local elites were hungry for development subsidies, and given Democrats' precarious electoral position in the region by the late 1960s, these programs, like the Appalachian Regional Commission (ARC), might bind fraying alliances. Second, many of these communities did, in fact, possess rural versions of "blight" or impoverishment including tar-paper shacks and homes lacking plumbing. And, while deindustrialization was a slow-moving crisis in larger cities, when a rural carpet factory closed, a small community could be devastated literally overnight. Indeed, following the consolidation and mechanization of Alma's small-scale agriculture, the town relied on tourism fed by surface routes to Florida. The completion of the interstate highway system shattered the tiny community's already fragile economic base. Third, during the 1960s and into the 1970s, larger cities' crises encouraged members of Congress and policymakers to think of rural development as a potential pressure valve. This rationale updated New Deal–era rural conservation and development efforts that had targeted many of the same areas. As a 1972 congressional report explained, "78 percent of all Americans" had "crowded together on less than 2 percent of the land." Pilot programs, such as Model Cities in Alma-Bacon County, "show[ed] clearly" to advocates of rural urbanization "that a level of bountiful living can be established in the countryside."²⁸

As in many of liberals' other supply-side initiatives, officials assessed the success of rural antipoverty or development programs in terms of jobs or businesses created and tax yields boosted. Alma's elites credited its Model Cities programs with more than 425 new private-sector jobs and a tax yield increase "of 25 percent between 1967 and 1970, from $16,401,000 to $20,048,000."[29] Despite the initiatives' ostensible antipoverty thrust, most new jobs were not available to African Americans. Black community leader Bennie Moore hoped the program might help "keep our young people from leaving town." "We need Negro councilmen, firemen, police clerks, cashiers and sales people," he said. But white officials "say that they're not qualified for these jobs." Moore planned to run for the Model Cities council, but he was circumspect: "I don't think I'm going to win . . . but I'm going to try. It's the principle of the thing."[30] Moore's aspirations for state support of local, rural black economic development quietly echoed decades of African American critiques of liberalism's inordinate support for "lily-white" economic progress.[31]

Alma ultimately received nearly $5 million in Model Cities funds, which elites invested in improvements to the county airport and a 200-acre industrial park.[32] Alma's Model Cities Commission chairwoman Omi Walden credited the program with "returning decision making to the local level by making block grants to accomplish objectives we couldn't do otherwise." The program was "an experiment to prove that if people and industry had a hospitable model community—from the political, social, and economic standpoint—they would remain in small towns."[33] The OEO shared these goals. By 1972, the agency funded 125 Model Cities programs, nearly half of which were in cities of 100,000 residents or fewer: four were in cities with populations between 5,000 and 10,000; sixteen between 10,000 and 25,000; and fifteen between 25,000 and 50,000.[34] In many communities, however, those resources all but bypassed residents in crisis. While that reality was nothing new, something subtle had shifted in the rhetorical self-presentation of rural southern supply-side state builders: they were learning to articulate their agendas not only on behalf of economic growth but also in terms of ameliorating poverty. Whether in the urban North or rural South, the administrative structure of liberals' social-qua-development programs increasingly invited businesspeople to view themselves and their interests as operating on behalf of and even in dialogue with marginalized citizens.

Making Poverty Disappear

Another liberal program that invited local elites to take account of poverty was urban renewal. Of course, sparsely developed, small southern cities in rural areas with underdeveloped land were not the communities Alvin Hansen and the designers of urban redevelopment had in mind. As Coosa commissioners noted after having secured urban renewal subsidies for Rome, the city had "a substantial amount of vacant land . . . suitable for development."[35] While cities like Cleveland faced fiscal strictures structured by the legacies of industrial development and hard spatial boundaries, elites in small cities such as Rome adopted urban renewal for a different set of reasons. Indeed, liberal officials encouraged local leaders to think of impoverished slums as a national rather than big city or even regional phenomenon. In the contentious 1960s, this could be an especially appealing framing of racial poverty for southern elites, many of whom fumed at northern charges of southern racial exceptionalism. As the Jim Crow order fell and the civil rights movement gained momentum, urban renewal offered southern leaders both an exculpatory explanation for pockets of entrenched racial poverty—they were nationally endemic—as well as capacities to simply remove black neighborhoods.

According to federal officials, urban blight and slums were a form of urban "pathology" that might soon infect all American cities and towns. Like the medical term upon which it was based, the pathology rationale for urban renewal framed "blight" as a communicable "disease of urban life." In 1955, James W. Follin, commissioner of the federal Urban Renewal Administration, detailed this framework before an audience at the University of Michigan's School of Public Health. Blight was an "insidious disease which advances steadily once it gains a foothold." Follin's was a sweeping diagnosis, at once capacious in terms of identifying symptoms while remaining utterly silent about causes. Blight could be "residential structures in need of major repairs"; "dwellings" with "incompatible types of living accommodations or . . . excessive occupancy"; "inadequate public utilities or recreational or community facilities"; or simply "changes in the pattern of urban living" or parcels of land associated with "increased local governmental costs." Blight's essential quality, he explained, was that it was "an ailment that is indigenous to almost all our cities" no matter their size or location. "It is the same in Washington, New Orleans, New York, and Louisville," he said." It was "not so different either in Miami, Austin, San Antonio, and Durham." He offered metrics to identify blight—rates of juvenile delinquency, incidences of tuberculosis, population density—all of which, once established, could authorize federal support for clearance. In a sense, of course, Follin was absolutely right—slum conditions *were* a national phenomenon created by racially discriminatory practices of government and markets. Yet, the pathology rationale demanded no assessment or reform of existing political or economic institutions. Rather than view racialized poverty as structured by racially discriminatory practices, pathology instead rendered racial poverty a blandly natural and exogenous threat, a disease corrupting otherwise healthy cities, which, like a cancer, would overtake them unless they were excised. Follin's presentation was turned into a cartoon-illustrated brochure distributed to cities and towns across the country.[36]

Rome's urban renewal authority, composed of the usual white elites, firmly embraced the pathology rationale for clearance. During the New Deal, Millard I. "Jack" Frost had overseen the Civilian Conservation Corps in six southeastern states.[37] A quarter century later, Frost led Rome's renewal efforts.[38] Along with Frost, the five-member Urban Renewal Board was populated by white elites: W. T. Maddox, president of National City Bank; A. L. Barron, secretary of the Rome Coca-Cola Bottling Company (and former president of the Rome chamber, head of the Rotary Club, and chair of the Georgia Bottlers Association); Charles Hight Sr., owner of Hight Insurance Co.; John Jervis, president of Citizens Federal Savings and Loan Association (an active chamber and Kiwanis member); and J. Dan Hanks, director of development for the exclusive Darlington Schools.

In 1962, upon securing a $15,000 planning grant, Rome's planners targeted for clearance the bustling Five Points black community along East First Street (see Map 1). Planners envisioned improving "traffic flows, parking, shopping facilities and [the] appearance" of downtown Rome to entice suburban and county shoppers.[39] While the neighborhood had its share of dilapidated homes, it was also the primary black business district—cafés, drugstores, barbershops, a pool hall, and churches dotted Cothran, East and West Ross, East First, and North Broad Streets. Some of the businesses were regional institutions—Webb's Café was famous for its cabbage and cornbread, and Hubert Holland's barbershop was known for its lively political discussions and, for black long-haul truckers crisscrossing the Jim Crow South, its comfortable and safe shower facilities.[40]

Drawing upon Follin's pathology rationale, one renewal advocate explicitly equated Five Points with the northern urban crisis: "Although 'Urban problems' are normally associated with larger urban centers . . . several of the same problems exist in Rome."[41] The primary reasons Coosa commissioners advocated for clearance were largely social and prophylactic. They argued for razing Five Points because "persons living in blighted areas tend to develop a feeling of alienation from the society of which they are a part." Clearance was in order since "the legal and moral codes of society are less effective in regulating the conduct of these persons."[42] They targeted all 285 homes in the neighborhood, and, when demolition was complete, all but one building had been destroyed.[43] White elites would break an alleged chain of alienation, pathology, and dependence in Rome's historic African American center by simply destroying it.

In adapting urban renewal for their small city, Rome's elites joined a national movement that made renewal a disproportionately small-city program. This process reflected converging interests between local officials and Democratic party builders and policymakers in the Kennedy and Johnson administrations. Supply-side liberals hoped expanded access to renewal would bolster the reindustrialization efforts of the Area Redevelopment Administration and its successors, the Economic Development Administration and ARC, each of which lacked robust capacities for clearing and preparing land.[44] To maximize smaller cities' access to federal aid, liberals also established subnational "economic development districts," regional commissions that effectively disseminated the Coosa commission and ARC models nationally—by 1967 at least seventy-five regional councils operated across the country.[45] Beyond amplifying local and regional planning capacities, in June 1963, Congress also responded to pressure from local officials by liberalizing small communities' matching requirements. For all communities of fifty thousand or fewer residents or those that met the ARA's designation of a redevelopment area (formerly a "depressed area"), Congress raised the federal share from two-thirds to three-fourths of project costs.[46]

The carrot of renewal funding was another way liberals sought to incentivize the modernization of small-city and rural-community governing capacities—and to hone those capacities by scrutinizing and redeveloping blighted, impoverished, and disproportionately black communities. Securing renewal funds required applicants to complete a "workable program" report. Often subsidized by 701 planning grant funds, creating these reports generated data and assessments of slums and blight. They also included proposals for new codes, zoning, and ordinances to be "vigorously enforced"; a general plan of the city including traffic and land use plans; proposed administrative structures for renewal; and, in a limp gesture at urban renewal's origins as a housing program, some "consideration" as "to the problem of rehousing displaced minority group families." Follin extended the pathology metaphor: any project could emphasize different "treatments for the blight disease—conservation, rehabilitation, and redevelopment, or in public health terms, prophylaxis, medical treatment and surgery."[47] Developing "workable programs" thus encouraged elites to read race and poverty in their communities in new ways: as problems, certainly, but also funding and modernization opportunities for government and business.

Clearance and redevelopment in small communities took on an especially intimate cast—those administering displacement and those displaced were often familiar. Indeed, Donald Jackson, who represented African Americans on Rome's Community Action Council, lost his business to urban renewal. He despaired of ever reopening and aired his grievances in a letter to the *News-Tribune*. "About dislocated business . . . the Rome Housing Authority said 'We would love for 'em (this 'em is [their] way of saying black businessmen) to come back in there." But this "is an inside joke for it has been known . . . that once blacks were out of the Five Points and East First area that there would be no way for them to get back." As he concluded, "Between the money lenders, developers, and the power of the Housing Authority . . . we can forget Five Points."[48] Echoing national patterns, some of Rome's black community leaders had been initially optimistic about using relocation funds to purchase new homes on the outskirts of town or to make new homes in their old neighborhood. Rather than relocate his barbershop, Hubert Holland planned to reopen in the redeveloped area. But, like Jackson, he found it impossible to submit a winning bid for property that had once been his—officials created shifting requirements for securing land, including rules stipulating the purchase of multiple lots, an impossibility for many black Romans. Businesspeople who relocated suffered, too, as did their employees. Callie Martin worried that her business, Let's Eat Café, would not recover. In the old neighborhood, she said, "I was able to give work to two people. But now I'm just working by myself and not really making ends meet." Renewal "really caused me to lose a decent living." Hers was one of sixteen black-owned businesses that were displaced by Rome's East First Street Urban Renewal Project. By 1971, only four businesses had reopened. Said Holland, "The way I see it, they destroyed the Negro businesses, what little they had. . . . They just destroyed it."[49]

Between 1962 and 1974 almost three hundred Southern municipalities undertook their first federally funded urban renewal projects, a number that rose alongside the intensity of the civil rights movement. By the time urban renewal concluded in 1974, small cities like Rome, rather than large cities like Cleveland, were the preponderant sites of urban renewal projects. Between 1950 and 1974, 75 percent of the municipalities receiving urban renewal funds had populations of 50,000 residents or fewer; a plurality of those communities had populations of 25,000 or fewer. While the War on Poverty was meant to empower or at least employ the poor, urban renewal offered elites the power to simply wipe out poverty by razing poor neighborhoods and neighborhoods of color. And, while big cities displaced considerably larger numbers of residents, smaller cities often displaced much higher percentages of their families of color. In Rome, 96 percent of the families displaced were African American, a slightly higher rate than the state as a whole. Beyond Atlanta (which displaced more than 4,000 black families and just 449 white), 33 municipalities in Georgia carried out urban renewal programs, displacing a minimum of 7,223 families of color and only 1,509 white families. While African Americans comprised just 14.5 percent of Georgia's population in 1960, they counted for more than 80 percent of those displaced.[50]

One white Roman urged black residents to look on the bright side. "Urban-Renewal is the best thing that ever happened to North Rome! Sure," Mrs. W. T. Skelton wrote the *News-Tribune*, "it's been long going," and there have been "hardships of re-locating families and disturbing businesses." Of destroyed churches, she reminded readers that many "of the best churches were started with a bush Arbor or tent." She accentuated the positive: "We are getting a new drive-in bank, larger and more convenient North Rome Fire Department, New North Rome School . . . [and] the Atlanta expressway will be closer to Rome." "So," she concluded, "let's exercise our faith in the future and our government . . . and brighten the corner where we are and I am sure this time next year if God lets us live, things will look much better."[51] For many black residents and business owners, however, the damage was done.

By 1971, Rome's black residents were mobilizing for a meaningful share of administrative power over the local use of national resources. The Housing Authority and Urban Renewal Board, they argued, "ought to have at least one member who knows and understands the problems of poor blacks." When pressed on adding a black representative to the board, a white official equivocated, saying it was "a reasonable area in which we would benefit from another point of view." But, "I wouldn't say that a man who might be eligible for reappointment would be automatically removed to be replaced by a black person simply for the sake of putting a black name on the roll."[52] Despite securing the ballot and formally desegregated public space, the enduring domination of "moderate" white power meant African Americans faced persistent and, in some ways, far worse forms of disfranchisement well into the "post"–civil rights era.[53] Under supply-side liberalism's mantra of fighting poverty and blight with development, hundreds of black Romans lost their homes, communities, businesses, and jobs. In the aftermath of Jim Crow, they now faced the more subtle forms of civic and market barriers to full enfranchisement that had become entrenched nationally through liberal's supply-side state.

And so a rising generation of black Romans demanded meaningful political empowerment rather than the kind of token representation in city government that, as Donald Jackson's destroyed business suggested, rendered fundamentally contingent even the "best" black citizens' opportunities. Jimmy Hardy, organizer of Rome's Black Coordinating Committee, spoke for this younger generation, saying, "It's to the point now, especially with the young blacks . . . that we don't care, really, how you feel about us. But we want to see some effective action taken on what we want." White residents did not understand, he said, "what happens in the black community." "They leave their jobs, and get in their cars, and roll up their windows and turn on their air conditioners and they go back home" to "their side of town." Another black activist warned the *News-Tribune*, "You haven't had a demonstration yet . . . you haven't had any real serious vandalism or rioting . . . but you see it's something that can happen."[54]

It remains unclear who perpetrated the violence or what sparked it—some said police aggression following allegations of black on white crime—but, within forty-three minutes on the night of August 30, 1971, five downtown white-owned businesses were hit with Molotov cocktails.[55] Three days later, a small bomb exploded near the main entrance to a bowling alley. The city commission and chamber hosted a series of meetings with black leaders, after which commission chairman Ben Lucas conceded that "qualified blacks" should be given positions on the Urban Renewal and Housing Authorities. Like other white leaders before him, he rejected calls to replace white members with black representatives, insisting that commissioners serve out their terms.[56] Two weeks later, three hundred African American students walked out of Rome's East High School to demand equal representation in student affairs and equal access to extracurricular activities. Sixteen students were arrested, and the Georgia National Guard was put on alert.[57]

Rome's white leadership responded with another round of interracial meetings led, once again, by the city commission and chamber. Once again, black residents demanded meaningful positions in the police and fire departments, representation on the city's various commissions and boards, and equal employment and educational opportunities. Jeffrey Jackson charged that members of "the white business and industrial world" were guilty of perpetuating the "stereotype . . . that blacks, regardless of their education [were] simply not capable of performing well in anything but menial jobs."

Meanwhile, white business owners were "getting rich off the black community. They're taking the money out of the black community and into [white subdivisions of] . . . Horseleg Estates or wherever they live."[58] Self-described white moderates struggled to understand black residents' anger. One white resident believed they had been "coming around" in recent years to correcting their "misconception of our black fellow man." And yet, "some small minority" was committing violence. "How," they asked, in an ironically telling expression of white racial innocence, "can anyone hate something or someone so much that they know so little about?" That they "burned what honest people worked for" indicated "evidently they must have a great hatred."[59] It was in this moment—when rebellions continued to ripple across black communities and white Americans stirred a roiling brew of racial innocence and racial grievances—that Jimmy Carter celebrated the South's rendezvous with its "post-racial" future.

Jimmy Carter's Silent Majority

Governor Jimmy Carter gained national acclaim in the early 1970s when *Time* magazine made him the focus of a cover story on a new generation of racially moderate southern Democrats. Along with Governors Reubin Askew of Florida, Dale Bumpers of Arkansas, and Linwood Holton of Virginia, Carter's election in Georgia signaled, as *Time* put it, "that the region is abandoning the fateful uniqueness that has retarded its development and estranged its people."[60] Carter's initial political persona had little to do with the politics of race. In the early 1960s, he branded himself a New South "business progressive" in the mode of Governor Carl Sanders. In 1966, Carter entered the Democratic primary for governor on a platform blending aspects of liberalism's progressive and supply-side sensibilities, focusing on education reform, expanded mental health services, and the fiscal gains to be won from boosting growth and employment. His platform, "Forward Georgia," urged "greater interest and participation in matters of government on the part of young people, women and responsible business leaders."[61] By uniting a constituency of Sanders's moderate businesspeople with younger, progressive voters, Carter mounted a surprisingly strong campaign. But in the midst of rising white anger over the pace of federally directed racial change, and thanks to residue of the state's undemocratic political structure, Carter lost the primary to the reactionary segregationist Lester Maddox. Maddox owned Atlanta's Pickrick, a fried chicken restaurant near Georgia Tech's thriving campus, and made a name for himself when, in 1964, he brandished a pistol at three black activists attempting to integrate his restaurant. Between 1966 and 1970, when Maddox would be term-limited out of office, Carter worked to redefine his politics in ways that belied *Time*'s admiring coverage of his ostensibly post-racial politics.

Carter spent these years absorbing white grievances about the pace of racial change, a dynamic whose hyperbole only added to the force with which it defined the contours of state and national politics. Despite the disparate effects of urban renewal and white control over the War on Poverty, many white Georgians inflated African Americans' seeming gains, charging that federal desegregation mandates, the Civil Rights and Voting Rights Acts, and antipoverty programs signified the elevation of minority and poor citizens at the expense of traditional white power and authority. In Rome, Johnson's support for the Civil Rights and Voting Rights Acts began a sustained period of racist fearmongering on the *News-Tribune*'s usually boosterish editorial pages—editors warned readers about the arrival of "all-powerful, centralized government." In a letter to the editor, the Reverend Thomas Wheelis of the First Methodist Church of Rome argued the Civil Rights Act meant "every person in America has less freedom."[62] Other white Romans complained about the seemingly peaceful and tolerant ways local officials and police had treated black activists: "you have allowed countless thousands of Negroes to demonstrate without so much as touching them. Is this 'Civil Right'?"[63]

Though some white southerners continued to defiantly support Jim Crow–style segregation, many others understood that the Civil Rights and Voting Rights Acts signified a decisive shift in the boundaries of acceptable political expression. Rather than fulminate against the acts themselves, many whites pivoted to raging against adjacent policies, claiming that they augured federal domination. Particularly useful in this regard were caricaturized versions of the Great Society and the War on Poverty. As the *New York Times*' Tom Wicker reported, in a matter of months, a cross-section of white voters quickly decided the War on Poverty meant "aid to Negroes."[64] Though Lyndon Johnson had anticipated this move, which represented not so much a racial backlash as a venue shift for racial reactionaries, he was alarmed by its ferocity. Mississippi's governor Paul Johnson Jr., a moderate Democrat aligned with LBJ, warned him that he was receiving seventy letters of protest each day, some with death threats. On a phone call with labor secretary Willard Wirtz, LBJ worried that liberals failed to grasp the threat to traditional bases of support in the South and big cities.[65]

The *News-Tribune*'s editors, meanwhile, signaled the rising salience of another racist venue shift, this one focusing on the wastefulness of new federal expenditures, particularly in the context of having to service the interest on the federal debt, the "most disturbing built-in [spending] increase."[66] When the *News-Tribune* endorsed Barry Goldwater for president, the editors charged Johnson with a "program of taxing and spending in the guise of 'serving' the people." They married their call for fiscal responsibility to a more sweeping warning about a "philosophy of government which cannot operate successfully unless it is total and that can only be arrived at by the gradual erosion of every individual liberty and privilege."[67] Even Rome's leading union, Local 689 of the Textile Workers Union of America, endorsed Goldwater, underlining his "strong stand for states' rights, for integrity, morality, and fiscal sanity in government."[68] Gardner Wright Jr. was thrilled after a local rally demonstrated growing support for Republicans: "we have a larger crowd for our meeting than the Democrats had for theirs," a sign "of the [growth of the] Republican party in Floyd County in the last three years."[69]

Despite having signed the Southern Manifesto in 1956, north Georgia congressman Phil Landrum's sponsorship of the Economic Opportunity Act provoked a flood of racist demagoguery sometimes disguised as calls for fiscal restraint from a set of Democrats, too. Georgia's Zell Miller is a case in point. Miller hailed from the northeastern Georgia mountain town of Young Harris and initially focused on improved education and development in his largely white, rural, and poor district. After serving two terms in the state house, however, in 1966, Miller embraced the politics of racial resentment and fiscal restraint in a campaign to unseat Landrum. The War on Poverty, he charged, had been "laid by Lyndon Johnson and hatched by Phil Landrum" and contained "some of the most wasteful uses of the taxpayers' money ever conceived by man."[70] His themes were localism, waste, and Lyndon Johnson: "I shall work for federal cooperation, rather than federal domination," he promised.[71] Though Landrum defeated Miller in the primary and held his seat in Congress, in the 1966 midterms, Democrats lost forty-seven seats in the House, largely in southern and suburban districts.

This was the year Jimmy Carter lost the Democratic gubernatorial primary to Lester Maddox. While Carter avoided the metastasizing politics of racial resentment in 1966, the lesson he took was the necessity of accommodating them. As he traveled the state and region, Carter learned to finesse the racially inflected politics of localism and moderation, drafting on more overtly racist politics that associated federal spending with racial unrest. In one case, a U.S. senator called for investigating an OEO-funded summer school in Nashville, which, he charged, was "subsidizing riots" by "teaching Negro children to hate white people." The *News-Tribune* reported these allegations on its front page.[72] North Carolina's Republican congressman James Gardner charged that poverty-funded groups were spending "taxpayers' dollars to create and organize a political machine."[73] Jesse Helms, then a newsman in Raleigh, went even further, arguing that the War on Poverty could not fix problems "for people . . . who [choose] to live like pigs." The initiative was "a literal manifestation of pouring money down rat holes."[74]

It was in this political environment, then, that Carter began arguing that "the major goals of the next administration in Georgia" must "be to return control of government to the people of our state."[75] As his Washington, D.C.–based pollster found, 81 percent of the Georgia electorate reported feeling alienated from government, and 54 percent felt integration was moving too fast.[76] Georgians, Carter explained, "feel threatened" and "often distrust the rich, the poor, students, politicians." Describing this average, normatively white voter to an Atlanta Kiwanis club, Carter noted they "sometimes forget that their taxes go for education, highways and national defense"—areas of seeming consensus for the booster types in his audience. Many white voters instead focused on "the welfare programs and the pockets of dishonest public officials. Their government seems to have most concern for the 'loafing' class . . . and for the poor who seem to get along pretty well without working."[77] Carter was learning to craft his own silent majority appeal, blending the technocratic aspects of his background in economic planning with claims rooted in localism and barely veiled appeals to racial majoritarianism.

He also discovered that his regional planning and development efforts could be reframed to fit the moment. Carter redoubled his APDC work, secured a seat on the State Advisory Committee, and became its vice-chairman, serving alongside Chairman Fred Starr, Rome's commission director.[78] Carter later estimated that he gave some 1,800 speeches during these years, traversing Georgia on a perpetual campaign. In these speeches, he reframed his planning partnerships as both bulwarks against federal overreach and conduits for decentralizing federal largess, symbols of his commitment to localism and majoritarianism. He sharpened this message in the pages of *The Activator*, his commission's newsletter. In one piece, Carter stoked concerns about federal meddling with local prerogatives, arguing that the "most important factor in the maintenance of constitutional government in our nation is to nourish strong local governments." Only if "we fail to meet the needs of our people . . . will [we] be faced with the specter of interference by our state and national governments."[79] Elite-led planning, supported by decentralized federal funds, could ensure the local majority's autonomy.

Rather than craft a message about the collective value of government and the need to expand participation, as he had in 1966, Carter opted to politicize white anger. Once the 1970 Democratic gubernatorial primary was underway, in which he faced his former ally Carl Sanders, he had so honed his talking points that he rarely wrote out his speeches, instead jotting key words on three-by-five-inch cards. The most frequent included "Control government—individual," "Failures—dissatisfaction," "individual freedom = freedom of the nation," "heritage," and "conservatism."[80] Carter blasted Sanders for trying "to please a group of ultra-liberals . . . in Washington."[81] A television ad tied Sanders to national liberals, featuring a Sanders campaign button that, when rubbed with a rag, transformed Sanders's face into Hubert Humphrey's.[82] Carter explicitly distanced himself from his 1966 campaign, proclaiming, "I was never a liberal; I am and have always been a conservative."[83] A campaign pamphlet titled "Jimmy Carter's Philosophy of Government" laid out his blend of majoritarian politics, rhetorical commitment to equality, and his emphasis on localism and economic growth. "Georgia is a conservative state," Carter wrote, and the best guarantee of freedom was the federal system itself: "We believe in the principle of federalism with a fair distribution of power and responsibility between the local, state and federal governments." Conservatism meant local, majoritarian control backed, perhaps, by loosely regulated federal resources.[84] The southeastern *Laurens County News* endorsed Carter in the primary because "[we] are convinced that he is a man susceptible to the will of the majority of the people." Carter "is a conservative . . . [and he] speaks the language of the people of Georgia."[85]

As election day approached, beyond making "law and order" and "system of justice" the first two planks in his platform, Carter had not crafted a policy-oriented appeal to the cross-section of white constituencies opposed to desegregation mandates, the voters Carter felt were decisive in 1966 and would be again in 1970.[86] When President Nixon's Internal Revenue Service called into question the tax-exempt status of "segregation academies"—private or religious schools established in the wake of the *Brown* decision to take advantage of federal tax exemptions for donations to educational institutions—Carter seized on the issue. Tax exemption enabled churches to bundle resources, sometimes reaching into the millions of dollars, to build new schools and offer poor, rural, and working-class white families reduced tuitions.[87]

Campaigning on behalf of protecting private schools' tax exemption, then, offered a way not only to signal his sympathy for white voters' outrage at government overreach but, more subtly, to indicate support for their sense of entitlement to its protections.[88] Carter visited a number of segregation academies, including a new private school in Swainsboro. Speaking in its all-white sixth-grade classroom, Carter drew an applause when he praised Lester Maddox as a potential partner in government.[89] Near his hometown of Plains, Carter appeared at Americus's Southland Academy, where, for a time, his brother Billy sent his children. Southland's officials had reportedly burned books with images of African Americans in them and had also purchased texts from the American Opinion Company, an offshoot of the John Birch Society.[90] Carter praised Southland as "an excellent example of what interested parents can do in establishing an educational institution of superior quality and with educational opportunities for children of widely varying economic resources." Under his administration, he pledged, and "in spite of court rulings, school integration, or any other obstacle, the quality of education in our state will not suffer."[91] Georgia's most prominent segregationists, including former governor Marvin Griffin, celebrated Carter's victory. Not everyone was impressed with the candidate's tactics. The *Macon News* decried his "bitter campaign," calling Carter "a classic example of a good man whose high standards have been undermined by political ambition."[92] Carter's courting of reactionary white voters revealed not only how ideologically malleable supply-side politics could be, but also the thin and liminal space between the very live politics of an older South and those of new, "New South" Democrats. The "post-racial" politics of a rising generation of Democrats would transcend the politics of race not only by accommodating racial resentments but also by emphasizing the limits of liberal governance.

"Post-Racial" Politics

While *Time*'s cover feature on Carter and New South Democrats made a passing reference to the racial opportunism of his 1970 campaign, it led with the line that made Carter's inaugural address so famous: "I say to you quite frankly that the time for racial discrimination is over." Yet the national media overlooked much of the rest of his inaugural address. "Our people," Carter's next, more defensive and qualified line began, "have already made this major and difficult decision." "We Georgians are fully capable of making our judgments and managing our own affairs."⁹³ While the national media may not have been sensitive to Carter's subtleties, his invocations of localism and majoritarianism were clear to supporters. Carter would put civil rights questions in the past by simply declaring a post-racial Georgia where local decisions could be made without the interference or regulation of the federal government. "We've been able to overcome the handicap of being preoccupied in every decision we made with the race issue," Carter later said, downplaying the ongoing reality of significant forms of racial inequality and obscuring the ways in which his own policy agenda would soon exacerbate them.⁹⁴

Like Nixon's New Federalism, Carter's post-racial politics and policies reframed New Deal–style, elite-led cooperative federalism for an age of white anger at government. Rather than focus explicitly on racial grievances, both men spoke in broad terms about how out of touch the federal government had grown from average—that is, white—Americans. Each politician cultivated what might be described as "antigovernment governance"—they worked to keep voters focused on government's inefficiencies, overreach, and limits and framed their policy goals less in terms of using government to solve social problems but rather as solving problems caused by government. Like New Federalism, Carter's major initiative would be reorganizing and rationalizing government bureaucracy on behalf of enhancing his silent majority's access to efficient and effective services. For minority or poor Georgians who were at last securing some benefits of War on Poverty programs, the twin impacts of Carter's reorganization and Nixon's New Federalism would be to undermine access to public services. Despite his blandly populist ways of talking about technocratic government reforms, the racialized sense of federal overreach was never far from the surface of Carter's proposals. His initiatives, he explained, would produce a "simple government which our people can understand and control," characterized by more robust "local and state control over the management of federally financed programs in Georgia." After singling out the "more vocal" residents of "urban or industrial" areas, Carter did not need to define who constituted "our people."⁹⁵

Carter launched a public outreach campaign titled "Goals for Georgia," which solicited input and complaints from Georgians through a series of regional meetings. He tapped Sam Nunn, a thirty-two-year-old rising star in Georgia's Democratic Party, to run the initiative.⁹⁶ Nunn had succeeded Carter as president of the APDC oversight board, and he chaired Carter's campaign in Houston County. Under Nunn, "Goals" created the Citizens Committee for Reorganization, which posted fifty thousand handbills throughout the

Figure 7. Jimmy Carter campaign material, ca. 1970–71.

state on which Governor Carter was depicted as a sword-wielding St. George, slashing a hydra-headed dragon with heads named "Waste," "Inefficiency," "Special Interests," and "Petty Politicians."[97] In his second State of the State address, Carter struck a more aggressive and aggrieved chord. "How much have you read about the thousands of Georgians who are not organized to represent a particular interest, but who are merely confused, frustrated, and even alienated from our government because of its complexity, inefficiency, and inability to meet their legitimate demands?"[98] It was on their behalf, Carter's silent majority, that he sought reform.

While Carter framed his antigovernment governance in populist terms, in actually developing his program he worked most closely with business elites. If, in the receding era of county courthouse politics racial resentments limited business' ability to promote developmental governance, New South Democrats such as Carter borrowed some of the old racial resentments on behalf of championing business-like, ostensibly limited but quite active government shaped in close partnership with businesspeople. His public awareness task force solicited feedback from local business leaders through thousands of mailers dispersed through the APDCs. With their support and that of the State Chamber of Commerce, Carter's plan received a full hearing from local business leaders, Jaycees, Lions, Kiwanians, and chambers. Their endorsements rolled in.[99] But Carter also empowered businesspeople to design and implement the reorganization of state government. The head of the influential Georgia Poultry Federation, Tom Linder Jr., led Carter's policy planning team. Linder had previously run an APDC, and he was a vigorous advocate of reorganization.[100] The poultry king gathered an informal committee of management consultants, corporate executives, and several public officials.[101] Leaders of major Georgia companies including Delta Air Lines, Coca-Cola, Lockheed, Southern Railway, and Georgia Power shaped the reorganization plans.[102] They also loaned corporate executives to the state to begin implementing reforms: 48 businesses ultimately loaned the administration 65 employees, meaning privately salaried government volunteers composed a majority of the 117 reorganization staffers.[103] Over the spring and summer of 1971, Carter's business consultants conducted a thorough assessment of the institutional layout, function, and accounting of every unit of government.[104] In February 1972, the reorganization package passed the state legislature: 198 of his consultants' 243 proposals for streamlining government were approved.

At least three significant developments resulted from Carter's business-led government reorganization. First, in institutionalizing his campaign against government, Carter made a name for himself as a businessman-turned-politician who would tame public institutions. But the reality was far different, and Carter's career delineates an increasingly common genus of politician in the final quarter of the twentieth century: the outsider candidate whose more modest reform agenda once in office only frustrated and entrenched the antigovernment expectations they stoked. Indeed, Carter's reorganization did little to tame the size or scope of government. Though he dissolved a number of agencies and departments, none of the state's fifty thousand employees were laid off. Carter planned to cut the workforce through attrition.[105] Later, top aide Jody Powell admitted the administration had no idea how much or whether the reorganization had even saved taxpayer dollars: "We [said] $50 million, but no one really knows how much it saved or cost."[106]

Second, and more materially, following Nixon's assault on the War on Poverty and by bolstering supply-side state builders' control over federal subsidies, Carter's reorganization created new obstacles for marginalized

Georgians' access to already attenuated antipoverty programs. The administration's goals for the various poverty programs, Linder explained, was establishing "coordination ... between these agencies."[107] Linder implemented this tighter administrative control by requiring the state's Economic Opportunity Authorities (EOAs) to match their territories to the state's APDCs to enable their oversight of poverty programming. In north Georgia, this led to a year of delayed payments for Head Start and other programs when the North Georgia EOA protested losing not only administrative autonomy but also two counties (and funding) to a neighboring APDC.[108] As Community Development Block Grants (CDBGs) came online, the reorganization also made the APDCs regional CDBG administrators. While CDBGs were ostensibly required to maintain "citizen participation," a subsequent report on CDBGs in twenty-six southern cities found that "citizen participation was low and the application and administration of grants was dominated by local political leaders." As in the North, the "projects were not serving the needs of the poor, but actually benefitted middle- and upper-income areas."[109] In Georgia, the Black Leadership Coalition, a political action group, charged Linder's reorganization team with having a "lily-white staff," and the *Baltimore Afro-American* paraphrased their most trenchant critique: "Gov. Carter's non-discriminatory policies are limited to public relations, [while] his political actions are concentrated with overt racism."[110]

In practice, then, Nixon's New Federalism and Carter's reorganization converged at the very moment when many impoverished citizens were finally securing new benefits and a range of black activists in the rural South were pursuing alternative developmentalist, black capitalist, and sometimes nationalist visions.[111] As reports circulated that Nixon planned to shutter the OEO entirely or at least end its categorical poverty programs, Georgians appealed to their representatives. A car accident had left Pamela Vaughn a paraplegic, and she described how, for three years after high school, she struggled to find steady employment. Through the OEO's Operation Mainstream she got "a job doing clerical work for the Franklin County Neighborhood Service Center." "Now that I have this job," Vaughn wrote, "I'm off welfare and out of the house, but more important I now can do my part to contribute to society. . . . If OEO is cut out I will have to go back home and back on welfare as will others."[112] Juanita Johnson of Augusta described how federally funded job opportunities had empowered her community: "they have instilled within the individuals a feeling of self-pride and a sense of belonging." The programs were also breaking down "the barrier that existed between the 'haves' and the 'have nots'" because "each group now has a better understanding of the other."[113] Like Cleveland's model neighborhood residents, many African Americans in Georgia viewed access to federal programs not simply in terms of rights but also in terms of securing more robust responsibilities for and opportunities in their communities.

Even some skeptical white Georgians recognized that far from creating dependency many programs fostered self-reliance. The principal of Franklin County Junior High School allowed that he "would be the first Georgian to support cutting funds for giveaway programs of the 'Great Society.'" Yet, "I do feel that some programs need not be cut simply because it was an outgrowth of President Johnson's Administration." He supported Neighborhood Youth Corps and Operation Mainstream because "the people involved . . . earn their way. For me, they have been given a dollars work for a dollars pay [sic] . . . I came up hard and I appreciate people who will work."[114] The realities of newly empowered citizens doing valuable work in their communities, however, were no match for the racialized myths about the War on Poverty and, increasingly, liberal government itself.

If Carter's reorganization made it more difficult for the intended beneficiaries of poverty programs to secure their rights, its third major effect was to further entrench the power and authority of business elites and supply-side practices. By the early 1970s, many were looking to develop international business opportunities, export markets, and new sources of cheap finance as inflation exerted upward pressure on domestic interest rates. Despite a growing budget crunch and a worsening recession, Carter expanded funding for Industry and Trade (I&T), the state's main industrial recruitment and business promotion agency. I&T had offices in Brussels and Tokyo, and Carter opened new outposts in Europe, Asia, and South America.[115] In the process, I&T's international recruitment bureaus became more closely tied to the APDCs.[116] At the end of 1972, foreign firms had invested some $5 billion in the South, and by the end of 1974, that figure had grown to nearly $8 billion. Georgia paced the region in foreign business and capital recruitment.[117] Most of the state's exports went to Western Europe and Canada, though the Middle East and South America were growing partners, too. By the mid-1970s, then, Georgia's public and private leadership had secured tighter control over poverty spending and redoubled the state's increasingly globalized commitment to economic development.

* * *

By the end of his term as governor, Carter was receiving national acclaim for his role in leading the South, as the *Christian Science Monitor* described it, to a "new-found" period of "racial and political quiet."[118] Yet that quiet was largely the result of ignoring or silencing the voices of poor and marginalized residents. "The South made some very difficult decisions on race over the last few years," Carter said in 1972, "and doesn't want to go through them again."[119] Despite such defensive constructions of a post-racial politics, Carter was surely aware of the fictions he was spinning. The years 1968 to 1971 saw violent insurgencies by rebelling African Americans in at least twenty-six Georgia municipalities with some, like Rome, seeing multiple incidents.[120]

Carter's home county, Sumter, was riven by confrontations over white racism. In 1971, hundreds of black students undertook a three-day boycott of the public schools. The school board was dominated by outspoken supporters of private academies who orchestrated the sale of a shuttered public school to a segregation academy for $1,001.50 (a contemporary estimate suggested that a similar facility would cost $100,000). Southland Academy, where Carter campaigned in 1970, had also been parasitically launched in a shuttered public school. The board slashed taxes that funded public schools and delivered public-school resources and equipment to private academies. As one black parent made clear, "We're concerned the county school system might be wrecked financially" as the all-white board made new cuts to a school system that was underfunded, overcrowded (thanks to closures), and which, in a majority white county, had become 74 percent black.[121] Under scrutiny, the governor's brother Billy eventually pulled his children out of Southland. In 1972, limited to one gubernatorial term and already eyeing national office, Carter walked back his support of segregation academies. But the sustained protest in Sumter County gave the lie to Carter's "racial" pivot. The all-white board continued its assault on the public schools, firing not just white officials sympathetic to integration but ousting black officials, too. One Mrs. Fuchs, a black counselor at Plains High School, was fired, a board member reported, because "no nigger woman should make $12,000 a year."[122]

Carter's post-racial pivot, of course, had nothing really to do with ameliorating racial inequality. Rather, it reflected the sense among many white citizens who, in more or less accepting the civil rights gains of the 1960s, felt they had no further obligations to African Americans. Carter's language was about absolving those citizens of past complicity in systems of political and economic disfranchisement and turning the page on debates about racial inequality, a source of exhaustion and anger for white Georgians. As Carter's career in Georgia suggests, conservatives held no monopoly on the post-racial politics of white racial innocence and its aggrieved analogue, white victimhood. Nor did Richard Nixon have a monopoly on localist and majoritarian politics and the politics of antigovernment governance, each of which offered ways of reorganizing and remobilizing the energies of old racial grievances.

As white liberals and conservatives together brought what remained of the War on Poverty to heel, Rome's chamber began to more forcefully articulate their producerist self-conceptions. Supply-side state builders' encounter with liberal poverty and development programs in the 1960s shaped what would become one of the War on Poverty's most durable and unexpected developments: businesspeople's newly expansive claims that their growth agenda, their businesses, and their partnerships with government would not only deliver economic progress but also ameliorate poverty. Faced with the violence and protests of 1971, Rome's leaders developed a more sharply delineated sense of the community's racial and political boundaries. As the chamber's newsletter explained, "There are three classes of residents in any community: (1) Those who live off it; (2) Those who live in it; and (3) Those who live for it."[123] Chamber types across the rural South had always viewed themselves as their community's essential providers: "Those who live for it." Carter and Nixon's silent majority comprised the racially bounded sense of "those who live in it." But when pushed by mobilized minority groups or other activists—"those who live off it"—Rome's once mild-mannered business elites joined businesspeople across the nation in embracing a much harder-edged version of business producerism.

The business producerism that would take off in the 1970s undercut the claims of labor, the working class, or the poor to government support on behalf of businesspeople's heightened sense of entitlement to public authority and control over public funds. In the economic and fiscal crises of the 1970s, the plausible claim that business growth might also ameliorate poverty became another way businesspeople, liberals, and conservatives alike sought to newly legitimize public support for the types of development programs and public-private governance that had always composed liberalism's supply side. The harder-edged producerism that crept into northwest Georgia's business politics was not unique to the region. Few supply-side state builders mobilized more aggressively than those in Cleveland, Ohio.

PART III

Reinventing Government

CHAPTER 7

Settling Liberalism's Debts

In the 1970s, American businesspeople believed they were under siege. Consumer advocates and "public interest" campaigners such as Ralph Nader joined environmentalists in pushing for new national regulations, while local poverty organizers, activist attorneys, and civil rights groups pressed to democratize the administration of development, poverty, and welfare programs.[1] Many activist groups had been emboldened by the prospect of the War on Poverty or welfare programs and were doubly motivated by their obstruction or withdrawal. They sought greater community-level empowerment across a broad range of public or partisan institutions: community control over schools in Harlem; leadership positions within the Democratic Party in Philadelphia; citizen oversight of police in Chicago.[2] In Cleveland, activists including Fannie Lewis and Sarah Turner organized for economic justice and fundamental political reforms. Whether or not these initiatives actually threatened businesses' bottom lines, for local white elites, at stake was both a legacy and a principle of elite supremacy.

Cleveland's businesspeople faced a triple threat: their heretofore natural position administering federal programs was in question; alternative, neighborhood-based definitions of development were gaining popularity; and a white ethnic, small-propertied populism was cohering as a political force, calling into question costly business-backed developments and tax abatements. Add to those fears the specter of black citizens achieving formal political power in Carl Stokes's mayoralty, and the entire power structure and subsidies that defined an era of supply-side liberalism were suddenly in question. Their fears came to a head when, in 1977, a broad coalition of neighborhood activists secured the mayoralty for Dennis Kucinich, a brash young populist who set aside an earlier, cynical racial populism to mount a direct assault on the city's business leadership, which he called a "shadow government." Kucinich's election signaled broad-based rejection of key assumptions of supply-side liberalism and none more so than the privileged place of private-sector elites in liberals' visions of progress. Business interests must serve the public interest, Kucinich argued, not vice versa.

But Kucinich took office at a singularly inauspicious moment for progressive urban reform movements. As the Watergate crisis reached its culmination in the summer of 1974 and as the nation slunk away from Vietnam, a less sensational but no less momentous set of public-sector crises threatened to undercut the relative capacities and autonomy of city governments. Squeezed by inflation, pressures to increase municipal workers' wages, suburban outmigration, and plummeting property values and tax yields, many cities faced intractable budget crises. Cleveland's business community monitored the city's finances and repeatedly warned Kucinich and his predecessor of mounting debt burdens the chamber had so enthusiastically helped create. Meanwhile, the cost to borrow on municipal bond markets—cities' traditional fiscal pressure valves and New Dealers' preferred means of structuring local fiscal-political autonomy—skyrocketed as inflation and shifting investment practices pushed interest rates higher. In one of his first acts as president, Gerald Ford convened the State and Local Governments Conference on Inflation, at which New York City's mayor Abraham Beame spoke for many local officials who "plead for Federal cooperation."[3] Over the summer of 1974, cities' cost to borrow rose some 30 percent, and yet many had no choice but to ramp up their borrowing. With New York City's 1975 fiscal crisis following quickly on the heels of Nixon's resignation, for many voters, governments across the federal system seemed not only incapable of meeting the decade's challenges: they seemed somehow to be at the root of the problems.[4]

"How," asked *Nation's Business*, the flagship publication of the U.S. Chamber of Commerce, "did these cities and states get themselves into this predicament?" Writing in October 1975, the author had an answer: "Obviously, many committed themselves to spending more than was coming in."[5] The moral of the crisis was that governments that "lived beyond their means"—that is, governments that responded too generously to the demands of insurgent poor, working-class, and neighborhood groups—were learning the "lessons of New York City."[6] That same month, the *Wall Street Journal* editorial board warned local officials that "the most important lessons to be learned from New York City's financial crisis is that government had better start keeping their books" like a "good housewife" or a corporation.[7] On the liberal end of the spectrum, the *Christian Science Monitor* editors agreed: New York "is in effect dramatizing a condition which needs correction in the whole body politic." "No longer can municipal, state, and federal bureaucracies go on spending beyond their capacity to pay . . . they must learn to be better managers of the public wealth."[8] In many cities, fiscal "correction" seemed in order.

But if the lesson so many took from New York City was of the overgenerosity of its local social welfare state, a questionable proposition in any event, it was a lesson grossly misapplied to virtually any other city. To be sure, New York's high debt load was, in part, the result of its inability to secure revenues to support its better developed, sovereign social welfare systems, which included community health centers and free tuition at the city's public colleges and universities.[9] But New York City's ability and willingness to finance those social goods at all lays bare just how exceptional were its midcentury fiscal capacities and social democratic aspirations. Much more common was Cleveland's type of budget crunch, which was punctuated not by debates about the city's profligate generosity but by its inability to cover basic operations. In the face of declining property tax yields and population decline, its debts covered expenses associated with municipal utilities, construction or maintenance of new capital facilities like sewage treatment plants, or improvements to meet new federal pollution control standards; debts that covered routine operating and administrative expenditures such as police and fire protection or to contribute to public employees' pension funds (whether legally or, in Cleveland's case, extralegally); or debts floated to subsidize urban renewal and redevelopment agendas pressed by the organized business community and which local administrations hoped would stimulate the tax revenues essential to transcending fiscal instability.[10] These were debts, in other words, associated with maintaining cities at the height of midcentury liberalism and in partnership with local business elites—not debts associated with extravagant local social welfare states.

Rather than receive their rightful portion of the blame for cities' outsized debts, businesspeople went on the offensive, using the crises to reconstruct their authority over local democracies. These producerist campaigns sought not simply to roll back hated regulations or wasteful programs but to fundamentally reconstitute businesses' privileged relationship with government—what attorney and future Supreme Court justice Lewis Powell called the "American system of business and government" in his famous, but, as this chapter maintains, only partially understood memo to the U.S. Chamber of Commerce. The success of that campaign rested not only on the crisis of legitimacy facing public institutions but also on the political logics reinforced by four decades of liberal policies that framed businesspeople and market mechanisms as efficient and effective deliverers of social goods. Liberal policies had taught businesspeople to think of themselves in these terms, and the seeming fiscal efficiency and social efficacy of business became both a model for government reform and an object and means of public policy, defining political-cultural assumptions in the emergence of a neoliberal age. And, by the mid-1970s, businesspeople's efforts to reestablish their advantaged relationship with government was underwritten not only by the weight of this history but also by a newly assertive and quintessential institution of that neoliberal age, credit rating agencies, whose rising influence created new types of leverage for businesspeople intent on reorganizing and reclaiming political authority. Few did so more aggressively than Cleveland's, where, faced with the Kucinich insurgency, the business community took the extreme measure of calling the city to repay several short-term loans held by local banks. Cleveland's elites moved literally to discredit Kucinich and, in so doing, engineer the city's default and their own redemption.

To view Cleveland's 1978 default as an exceptional event triggered by backlash to the Kucinich insurgency is to miss the ways in which Cleveland's businesspeople were participants in a national movement of local businesspeople to reclaim their authority in local affairs. This movement was animated by a harder-edged version of business producerism, situating businesspeople's economic and administrative expertise, discipline, and vision as the essential ingredients in urban and ultimately national revitalization. Leveraging decades' worth of municipal debt associated with running cities at the high tide of liberalism—debts from which the business community continued to profit in numerous ways—was certainly an important step on the road to the neoliberal city. But it was also a culmination of liberal forms of midcentury city building.

Liberalism's Debts

Municipal borrowing had been a steadily growing reality, prerequisite even, of midcentury city and market making, incentivized by federal programs, championed by supply-side liberals such as Alvin Hansen, and bolstered by contingent structural dynamics. Urban renewal, suburban school construction, infrastructure investments, and more were all underwritten or augmented by borrowing, which, as Hansen argued into the 1960s, helped direct private capital toward stimulative and publicly useful projects, smoothing speculative cycles of booms and busts, and boosting employment and purchasing power. As one contemporary expert put it, the 1950s had been the "best of all possible worlds" for sellers on the tax-exempt municipal bond market when fixed interest payments averaged 3.5 percent.[11] In an era when individual taxable income was subject to federal rates as high as 91 percent, the relatively lower yields on federally tax-exempt municipal debt offered high-earning individuals an attractive place to shield and steadily grow their wealth.[12] These dynamics created an inadvertently virtuous circle between national tax policy and municipal fiscal requirements and help explain why the growth of state and local debt outpaced federal aid during decades when the federal government seemed most generous to its subnational siblings.[13] Bonded debt, which accounted for just 7.3 percent of state and local capital in 1960, rose to 22.4 percent by 1973, even as federal aid grew significantly.[14] Federal programs, many of which required matching contributions, and fiscal policy habituated municipalities, no matter their size, to the increasingly humdrum but essential necessity of borrowing private capital to deliver public services.

For city officials confronting decades of deindustrialization and white flight, the interest rate hikes and inflation of the late 1960s and 1970s must have seemed like a cruel change of the rules, midgame. Beginning in 1966, as interest rates on U.S. Treasury bills rose, investors sought higher-yield instruments, which in turn, pushed up municipal interest payments on long-term bonds—that year's 3.92 percent average rate was the highest since 1934, and it would continue to rise.[15] Low interest rates and federal tax exemption made the local debt regime work, but these structural factors were totally beyond city officials' control and both shifted decisively against them in the late 1960s and 1970s. They not only faced soaring interest rates, but with inflation ticking upward in the late 1960s, the Federal Reserve tightened the money supply, producing a constricted market for municipal securities in 1969–70 as investors sought higher returns at shorter intervals. Meanwhile, Congress faced its own budget problems and drafted legislation proposing an end to tax exemption for municipal securities. Though the plan was tabled, its mere consideration, along with the Fed's tight money policy, pushed interest rates still higher.[16]

Meanwhile, the simultaneous upward pressure inflation exerted on public sector wages and contracts drove up the costs of municipal services at a moment when, as one mayor testified before Congress, the "overburdened property tax," which accounted for three quarters of municipal revenue,

Table 1. City of Cleveland tax revenue (in millions of dollars)

	1970	1971	1972	1973	1974	1975	1976	1977	1978
Actual	91.9	68.4	85.9	78.7	85.8	92.2	95.9	104.0	115.6
Inflation adjusted	91.9	65.2	81.8	70.0	69.2	68.4	67.7	68.7	70.8

Source: Richard F. Tompkins, *"All the Necessary Service the People Need and Deserve: Federal Grants in Cleveland During 1978": A Case Study for the Brookings Institution* (Cleveland: Cleveland Foundation, 1979), 6.

was "effectively exhausted" and, unlike income or sales tax revenue, barely tracked inflation.[17] Public-sector employees struck frequently in the 1970s, demanding their wages keep pace with inflation.[18] Cities implemented austerity budgets, ensuring longer waits for services for frustrated residents, even as greater shares of funds went to servicing debt.[19] A midwestern mayor testified before Congress in 1974, demanding that representatives "think of where the cuts or the revenue are going to come from."[20] Even Richard Nixon, no real friend to cities, argued that his revenue sharing bill was essential to preventing "states, cities, and counties [from] going bankrupt."[21] As cities leaned heavily on federal aid, most were forced to find alternative sources of capital as inflation weakened the real value of their tax receipts (Table 1).[22]

Many did so by borrowing even more and at shorter intervals. For decades, commercial banks had offered cities short-term loans on the order of months, sometimes termed "bond anticipation notes" or "tax anticipation notes," to be converted into general obligation bonds or retired with general funds. By the 1970s, the annual volume of short-term borrowing actually surpassed traditional bond issuances.[23] These short-term loans, often offered by local banks, created the potential for recurrent choke points between municipal solvency and lenders. That is, if bankers lacked faith in a city's ability to retire or convert these loans, they could recall them, raising the specter of default. In addition to the emergence of national credit-rating agencies, which began charging cities to rate their creditworthiness in 1968, short-term borrowing bound cities' fiscal well-being much more closely to the interests and oversight of local commercial banks.[24]

The two forms of fiscal surveillance, one national, the other local, could be mutually reinforcing. That is, as rating agencies such as Moody's and Standard and Poor's (S&P) expanded their scrutiny, many municipal ratings were downgraded, and cities increasingly turned to short-term borrowing.[25] Fernand St. Germain, representative from Rhode Island, remarked that local commercial banks' "credit powers, alone, can be literally life or death for . . . municipalities." He also speculated about the implications of business elites' frequent interlocking financial and political interests: "When these credit functions are enhanced by trust investments, linked directorships and other ties" among business elites, "the potential for control and power is awesome." A subsequent House report described how, in this emerging political-fiscal environment, "the decisions of loan officers and the board of directors of financial institutions are critical; at times carrying far more impact than the decisions of thousands of citizens of a municipality."[26] Far from a dramatic break with earlier eras of municipal finance and business elites' oversight of municipal affairs, the 1970s witnessed an acceleration into an era of higher costs and greater surveillance. By 1980, fully one-third of local governments' capital requirements were met by borrowing. That year, on the precipice of an age of federal austerity, municipalities had accumulated some $365 billion in debt; by 1994 the figure soared to $1.2 trillion.[27]

The situation reached its inflection point in the mid-1970s, as inflation and rising interest rates encouraged investors to exit municipal bond markets in search of higher-yield instruments. In July 1974, New York City declined an unprecedentedly high bid of 7.923 percent on $438 million in bonds; the following day, Chicago rejected a bid of 6.96 percent for $40 million in general obligation bonds. San Antonio, Texas, and Santa Clara, California, offered millions in routine bonds but received no bids.[28] Such dry figures fail to capture the full significance of the merest uptick in interest rates on municipal securities. In New York City in the 1960s, a 1 percent increase amounted to $30 million per year in additional interest payments—revenue that might have hired thousands of teachers.[29] In Cleveland, debts associated with the unfinished Erieview urban renewal project alone cost the city $50,000 in monthly interest payments.[30] Cleveland was not alone in having to service debts related to renewal: as of February 1981, local public agencies still held nearly $400 million in outstanding notes related to urban renewal, a program whose federal contributions ended in 1974.[31] By 1975, local governments accounted for more than two-thirds of the roughly eight thousand offerings of state and local debt.[32] While the *uses* of municipal debt had often underwritten the reproduction of gross racial inequalities and violence—witness urban renewal—the shifting fiscal-financial landscape of the 1970s meant that greater shares of scant municipal revenues went to creditors, who enjoyed legal priority for repayment prior to funding for essential services like schools, parks, housing, and community health facilities.

The municipal debt load would have been higher still had voters not begun rejecting bond referenda with greater frequency, a leading indicator of looming tax revolts. In 1968, voters rejected nearly half of municipal bond proposals; by election day in 1975, 93 percent of nearly $6 billion worth of bond referenda were rejected.[33] San Francisco's mayor Joseph Alioto called the situation "a story of horror."[34] As the National League of Cities and U.S. Conference of Mayors put it, despite the reality that demands for social services continued to rise, large cities, especially, had simply "reached their taxing limit," and, in many communities rocked by deindustrialization and suburbanization, the absolute value of property was declining in any event.[35] Though the media explained the 1970s' urban fiscal crisis in terms of "the lessons" of New York City's seemingly profligate welfare state, the fiscal foundations of midcentury urban liberalism were crumbling for much deeper structural reasons.

Reinventing Business Producerism in the 1970s

Some of the strongest supporters of the midcentury municipal debt regime had always been local business elites—and not simply because that borrowing often underwrote their development agendas. Individual and institutional purchasers of that debt profited from the federal tax exemptions on the interest cities paid; banks that marketed and purchased debt enjoyed commissions on nearly every transaction associated with municipal borrowing; and law firms offered profitable bond counseling services for issuers and purchasers. Even as voters began rejecting bonds with greater frequency, Cleveland's business leaders pressed forward with an ambitious debt-based development agenda. In late 1967, the chamber of commerce and industry associations created the Greater Cleveland Growth Association, the *Plain Dealer* reported, so the "city's future business growth can be planned, programmed, and pinpointed from one dynamic headquarters."[36] The association poached William Adams II, the executive vice president of Seattle's chamber, to serve as director, thanks in part to his sterling record of passing bond referenda. Adams, a Texas native, had also worked for chambers in San Antonio, Pasadena, and Los Angeles, and his arrival in Cleveland was delayed while he orchestrated thirteen Seattle debt issuances totaling $820 million. As Adams told the *Plain Dealer*, "My research on Cleveland shows there are exciting things to be done" there, too.[37] Growth Association members were thrilled when Seattle voters bucked national trends and passed the bulk of his measures, which included financing to build a domed stadium.[38] The Growth Association predicted a future of "rosy" progress.[39]

Such was not to be the case. By 1971, the association was "in a leadership crisis." Adams had seemingly spent more time boasting about past successes before other chambers than in developing new projects. This was especially galling because he enjoyed a staff of seventy-two and an annual budget of $1.3 million, far exceeding that of most urban chambers or development organizations. Dues-paying members threatened to quit if the leadership issues were not addressed. One board member drew the bottom line: "This organization is supposed to keep companies from moving away and entice new ones here. It has done too little in either direction."[40]

As voters turned against bonded debt, business associations continued to look to the federal government for subsidies. By the early 1970s, however, many had begun to recognize that their national lobbying associations, particularly the National Association of Manufacturers (NAM), were fighting to kill many of the federal programs they most valued. As a result, a growing number of firms and business associations began quitting the NAM, which hired consultants to assess its "serious membership erosion." The desire of Cleveland's businesspeople for closer relationships with government at all levels, NAM discovered, defined the kind of "political action group" local affiliates sought. The firms polled, all of which were still members, felt the NAM was wasting resources on programs such as "Promoting Concepts of Free Enterprise" and should instead focus on "the health of the national and local economies." At a moment when "4 out of 5 members hoped to see NAM get more involved in local politics and in forging local congressional contacts," members called for "aids and courses on practical politics." Though NAM opposed Nixon's revenue-sharing program, supply-side state builders strongly supported his New Federalism agenda.[41] Frustrated by the ideological edge of groups like NAM, squeezed by inflation, boxed in by voter-imposed municipal austerity, and facing insurgent civil rights, neighborhood, and poverty groups, local business elites felt their once unquestioned political authority under siege. To restore their influence over public resources, many chambers applied the lessons they had learned in skirmishes over the War on Poverty: their growth agendas might be profitably reframed in terms of solving poverty and municipal fiscal crises.

A decade earlier, business leaders primarily viewed poor neighborhoods as ripe for removal. But, as the Johnson administration rolled out its War on Poverty, designed to balance historical and racial deficits of economic and democratic opportunity, the U.S. Chamber of Commerce undertook a series of studies recommending that local "businessmen in every community . . . involve themselves" in federal programs targeting "the problems of low-income people."[42] Writing for the U.S. *Chamber of Commerce Newsletter*, Fred Burtner, of the Greater San Antonio chamber, warned that poor and minority groups were forming their own organizations to win federal aid. "Recently," he wrote, "I discovered a private organization in San Antonio duplicating many of the programs of our Chamber. I was shocked to learn it has nearly twice as many employees and a larger budget than our Chamber—80% of which is federal money." While both organizations claimed to have the best intentions of San Antonio at heart, "the Chamber speaks and acts for the business community in behalf of the total community while the other organization is minority oriented, seeking jobs only for ethnic group citizens." Burtner put part of the blame for the proliferation of "minority"-dominated organizations on chambers themselves, conceding that "too often we have not done our job well, leaving a vacuum which has been filled by some other organization." He titled his piece "A Matter of Survival."[43]

Along with emphasizing social investments, chambers developed initiatives highlighting racial inclusion. These often transparently tokenized gestures dovetailed with an emerging set of white-collar, professional, and suburban liberals' embrace of individualist solutions for poverty or integration.[44] They encouraged local elites to think of themselves, their businesses, and their associations as contributing to social progress and inclusion even as they more aggressively policed the boundaries of public resources. They also subjected minority community members to what must have been excruciating scrutiny—and then, given the power dynamics at play, made them feel compelled to offer thanks for the privilege. Orlando's chamber began a program for "community communications and understandings" in which a "white member of the [chamber] would introduce a black member who told of some personal examples of discrimination. . . . In most cases, this was the first time any of our white civic clubs had ever heard the problem from a black man."[45] In a particularly stark example, the U.S. Chamber highlighted the "colorful success story" of Elias "Chino" Valdes, who rose from an "agricultural worker picking fruits and vegetables" to owning a small business. When he was elected president of the chamber of commerce of Santa Paula, California, businesspeople celebrated his "rise from 'wetback' to his present civic and business stature in the community."[46]

While national business associations like the NAM or ideologues such as Milton Friedman scoffed at the idea of business's "social responsibility"—in 1970 Friedman plausibly derided it in the pages of the *New York Times* as "hypocritical window-dressing" that "cloak[ed]" "their self-interest"—supply-side state builders argued their businesses and associations could benefit a broader range of constituencies than ever before.[47] Creating minority business development initiatives or supporting schools, many chambers recognized, could bolster their civic standing while possibly enabling them to redirect more aggressive constituencies or programs. By the early 1970s, the U.S. Chamber's *Newsletter* noted that nearly three hundred chambers reported some kind of "socio-economic program expenditures" totaling $13.5 million, almost a quarter of the $55 million in total programming. Unsurprisingly, vocational education represented the largest investment. Farther down the list were youth activities (seventh), while support for minority enterprise development ranked last, though, they noted, "this type of activity was virtually non-existent even three years ago." From internal polling, the U.S. Chamber concluded, "Business people are willing to pay their local chambers to take the lead in organizing effective community improvement programs."[48] So much the better if it meant chambers captured federal resources in the process.

Indeed, the U.S. Chamber identified ways its affiliates could claim their "vital stake" in the Model Cities program, explaining that an "*important feature of the supplemental funds is that they can be used in any way a city chooses so long as the city gives emphasis to high-priority actions in the model neighborhood area*" (emphasis in original). Model Cities offered "flexibility," and federal spending could hit "$1.5 billion!" Seattle's chamber, Boeing, the American Medical Association, and the Weyerhaeuser Company created a $30 million economic development corporation and a $6 million housing corporation, each run by "stockholders from industry, government, and the neighborhood." In Houston, a "prominent" chamber leader led the Model Cities citizen participation and oversight board. The U.S. Chamber also urged business leaders to overcome their discomfort speaking "before vocal minority groups." Too often, "one unpleasant confrontation" led elites to "lose enthusiasm." But affiliates must press on: Model Cities "offers a means for decentralizing Federal aid and for sharing Federal revenues."[49] Commandeering antipoverty programs offered businesspeople affirmation of their producerism, even as they steered federal subsidies away from the poor.

If supply-side state builders' aggressive mobilization on behalf of renewed partnerships with government seems to cut against the grain of business's antigovernment politics in the 1970s and after, much of that dissonance might derive from prevailing interpretations of corporate attorney Lewis F. Powell's famous memorandum to the U.S. Chamber of Commerce, "Attack on American Free Enterprise System." At a time when business faced new and costly regulations as well as criticism "from the college campus, the pulpit, the media, the intellectual and literary journals," Powell called on business elites to overcome their historical "reluctance" to "aggressively" pursue political power. "Business," Powell wrote, "must learn the lesson, long ago learned by labor and other self-interest groups." In contrast to the "quite new" crisis of business's legitimacy, Powell conjured the middle decades of the twentieth century as a golden age of public and private partnership. Alternating between what he called the "American free enterprise system," "the system," and "the American system of government and business," Powell described a time when businesspeople were respected leaders in all facets of American life—as job creators, drivers of "the standard of living," "community leaders," and partners to government. But because businesspeople had taken for granted these self-evident roles, "few elements of society today have as little influence in government as the American businessman." In contrast to decades past, "one does not exaggerate to say," Powell wrote, that "the American business executive is truly the 'forgotten man.'"[50]

Widely read since its public disclosure as a call for big business to mobilize against government intrusion in the market, Powell's memo is better understood as a call for reinvigorating and insulating the close ties between business and government that flourished since Franklin Roosevelt first invoked "the forgotten man."[51] Powell crafted his manifesto at the behest of his friend and longtime neighbor Eugene B. Sydnor Jr. Sydnor owned a regional chain of department stores in and around Richmond, Virginia, and his career was a direct rebuke to the notion that businesspeople preferred government's powers to be strictly limited. In the 1950s, Sydnor served in Virginia's House and Senate where he advocated technical- and higher-education-based economic development. He also served as the first chairman of the State Technical Education Board and directed the Virginia Division of Industrial Development and Planning, its version of Georgia's Area Planning and Development Commissions. Sydnor was a leader of Richmond's chamber of commerce, the Virginia Retail Merchants Association, and, in the early 1970s, was appointed chairman of the U.S. Chamber of Commerce's Education Committee. It was in this last role that Eugene asked his friend and neighbor Lewis to write a memo outlining the forgotten importance of business in American politics.⁵² Sydnor had a clear sense of how the "American system of business and government" should work: each had much to gain from the other and in no domain so much as the pursuit of economic growth. By the 1970s, insurgent groups and costly new regulations wrought by a "new class" of activist lawyers and bureaucrats were displacing heretofore-unchallenged public-private partnerships, which businesspeople had never before had to expend much energy justifying. Sydnor asked his friend to give businesspeople a more aggressive language of business producerism that would inspire a campaign for restoring the kinds of public-private partnerships that had flourished since the 1930s.

During the 1970s, then, the U.S. Chamber nurtured a campaign to help affiliates reframe business as the forgotten and abused but still-beating hearts of their communities—and to exercise their leverage over local governments. The *Chamber of Commerce Newsletter* wrote that local businesspeople held an "unparalleled opportunity": the decade's fiscal and political crises "have forced political leaders . . . to search for better ways to perform their respective jobs."⁵³ With rising interest rates, inflation, and resistance to taxation, mayors recognized the need to streamline service delivery. Businesspeople could offer guidance, burnish their legitimacy as community leaders, and reclaim their commanding positions. As one chamber writer argued, Americans must understand that "business creates the economy upon which a community is built." A "prosperous economic climate" ensures "that our job level and tax base meet our needs."⁵⁴ The U.S. Chamber urged affiliates to tout business's role as the nation's producers—of jobs, of opportunity, of tax revenues, and even, perhaps, as local fiscal crises rippled across the county, of cost-efficient governance and services.

A sharp edge could creep into these priorities, especially in the face of new claimants to government largesse and rights. An Atlanta banker put a fine point on business's sense of privilege. Speaking to the chamber in Rome, Georgia, he explained that private enterprise, is "the keystone to all we have." It is "the country's provider." "It's no longer a democracy when we are governed by minority interests," he said. "When those who pay no tax use their vote to dictate how the taxes are spent . . . we're in trouble."⁵⁵ Businesspeople—job and tax producers—deserved once again to both steer and benefit from those public-spending decisions. In Rome, business's authority had yet to be seriously challenged. But in Cleveland, neighborhood activists and a range of populists, conservative and progressive, threatened to sunder the supply-side partnerships business elites had too long taken for granted.

Stacking the Deck

As Cleveland's business leaders nurtured their more muscular producerism, they grew quickly frustrated that the city's Republican mayor was a less than willing or even competent partner in securing federal subsidies. Thanks in large part to his resistance to new spending or debt, Growth Association members complained that Ralph Perk "is in a box of [white] ethnic support."[56] Ever concerned with Cleveland's reputation, elites must have cringed at national news coverage of Perk's folksy gestures, such as declaring August 16, 1972, "Bowlers' Day" in Cleveland. These efforts could get the better of him, as when Perk reached for a blow torch rather than oversized scissors to cut the ribbon at a steelworkers' convention. When he brought the torch too close, his Vitalis-oiled shock of hair went up in flames as photographers snapped away.

Most significant, however, was the Perk administration's sheer incompetence when it came to securing and dispersing federal aid at a moment when Cleveland's share of the national pie was shrinking. As midcentury categorical grants were folded into Community Development Block Grants (CDBGs), cities like Cleveland lost funding in absolute terms (though, given its Republican mayor, Cleveland fared somewhat better than other northern cities). Cleveland's total aid slipped by about 10 percent, while rural, suburban, and southern municipalities gained considerably. While 71 percent of Great Society–era categorical grants were disbursed to central cities, in CDBGs, only 42 percent was.[57] Perhaps recognizing that his administration was not up to the task of securing and administering federal aid, Perk asked the Nixon administration to "lend-lease a bright young man from Washington" to teach his aides how to secure "federal grants as expeditiously as possible."[58] By 1975, however, *Cleveland Magazine* reported that Perk had "no long-range planning for the use of federal subsidies." Between 1974 and 1977, the city was awarded nearly $50 million in CDBGs but failed to disperse or contract more than $22 million in grants. Of the $26 million that was deployed, some $5 million was absorbed into the budget for "administrative" purposes.[59] Despite the fact that every interest group in the city sought greater public spending, Perk could not get the money out the door. Under an aggressive new chairman, the Growth Association mounted an offensive.

James C. Davis was an attorney and partner at Squire, Sanders & Dempsey, Ohio's top bond firm, and he had garnered much attention in the late 1960s when he not only blamed white ethnics for the city's decline, but took to the stage to debate Martin Luther King Jr. on the merits of civil disobedience.[60] He quickly undertook a pressure campaign, peppering Perk with offers of assistance and words of unsubtle intimidation. The Growth Association's Governmental Affairs Division lobbied in Washington to expand federal aid.[61] But, as the older chamber had always done, it also studied the intergovernmental transfer of funds, generating its own snapshot of the city's finances.[62] Armed with this data, Davis barraged the mayor with correspondence, sometimes with praise, sometimes with threats, but always with clear articulations of the association's agenda.[63] When it leaked, for instance, that Perk's planning commission was contemplating expanding the city's publicly owned electric utility, Cleveland Municipal Light (often called Muny Light), to the competitive detriment of its privately held rival, Cleveland Electric Illuminating, Davis admonished Perk: it would be "destructive of general business confidence in the administration." Davis was confident that Perk would "make it clear that this was simply a planning exercise by the Commission and does not reflect the official views of the administration." He hoped not to have to take the issue public.[64] Perk disavowed the plan.

Davis also "shocked and challenged the business community," seeking a colossal $6 million operating budget to implement what he called Greater Cleveland Forward, explicitly based on Forward Atlanta, Mayor Ivan Allen's public-private partnership; Davis also consulted with Houston's chamber.[65] Association members soon raised $4.8 million in private contributions with which they would leverage public investments.[66] But if the Growth Association sought to learn the secrets of the Sunbelt's boom, they grasped only partial lessons. Rather than use public investments to make structural interventions that might remake or diversify Cleveland's economic base, elites remained bound to flashy, large scale physical redevelopment projects to entice suburbanites into the city—essentially replicating the rationale for the stalled Erieview project. Nearly half of the funds, for instance, were devoted to planning a fantastical "jetport," an airport floated five miles into Lake Erie.[67] Meanwhile, in 1972 real estate mogul Sheldon Guren sought $25 million in revenue bonds to develop a new stadium, hotel, and office complex, dubbed "Gateway," along the Cuyahoga River—that project would remain a priority until it was at last completed in the mid-1990s.[68] The Growth Association also funded plans by the San Francisco architect Lawrence Halprin, a guru of planning's "new urbanism." Rather than a new pedestrian mall, however, with industry closing down, suburbanizing, or heading to the south and global south, what Cleveland really needed was balanced and robust solutions for rising poverty rates and remaking its economic base. At the vanguard of using recreation and mixed-use public space to lure suburban retail and tax dollars, Halprin was optimistic. "What I'm really good at," he said in Cleveland, "is getting things built."[69]

The Growth Association worked with consultants to cohere a rationale for directing greater levels of community development and antipoverty funds toward their physical redevelopment plans favoring suburban commuters and retail. They were assisted by former Ford administration HUD official David Meeker who had taken an urban planning position at Cleveland State University. Meeker continued to bluntly articulate his outlook: established neighborhoods and business districts should be "enhanced so that Cleveland will not become a Black ghetto of lower income classes," he wrote. Investing in poor neighborhoods simply threw good money after bad.[70] As one Growth Association member explained, white suburbanites "think of downtown as a black area and [they] fear blacks."[71] Investing CDBGs in Halprin's redevelopment plan could reverse that perception and thus reverse the outflow of retail and tax dollars. Here was the wisest use of antipoverty-oriented "community" development funds. Perk acquiesced. The city soon invested several hundred thousand dollars of CDBGs to pursue Halprin's plan.[72] Business elites formed the Downtown Cleveland Corporation to steer these efforts. Overseeing its work was James Davis. *Plain Dealer* editor Thomas Vail called to invest millions more to help "bury our 'Rubesville' image."[73]

Reflecting the sustained political salience of the 1960s' participatory ethos, the Growth Association funded a two-and-a-half day "Take Part Workshop," a signature of Halprin's design process. Thirty-six Clevelanders participated, including the usual public and private elites but also some regular people—a student, a public housing resident, homemakers, blue-collar workers. While Halprin championed the exercise as part of his "ethic of inclusion," the city's business leadership recognized its utility for engineering consent and fulfilling the new necessity of community participation. Roldo Bartimole, a muckraking chronicler of Cleveland politics, described the workshop as "pure, unadulterated bull." It was a "stacked deck" intended to "create the façade . . . behind which the profit-makers" pressed their interests.[74]

More than flashy new urbanist plans, feints toward democratic participation, or quasi-intellectual justifications for defunding poor neighborhoods, however, the city's mounting fiscal crisis afforded the association its greatest leverage. In the summer of 1974, when costs to borrow were soaring, the association produced a report that found the city would be $18 million in the red in 1975. Perk's gimmicks and short-term measures—privatizing the sewer system and repurposing federal grants to cover operating expenses—papered over an intractable crisis. That year, too, voters defeated a Growth Association–backed income tax hike while the depreciation of Cleveland's property values was sending tax receipts tumbling. Cleveland was not alone—in Chicago in 1971, Mayor Daley hiked city property tax rates by 18 percent, but depreciation meant yields plummeted.[75] Congress, meanwhile, sat on revenue sharing's reauthorization throughout 1975, contemplating solving its own fiscal crunch by ending the formula-based program that offered few obvious rewards for members. Cleveland's fiscal year (FY) 1975 budget was set at $126 million, which included $76.4 million for the fire and police departments alone; city tax receipts would only bring in $74.1 million, a growing portion of which was devoted to debt service. As Perk put it, without federal funds, "this would be a one-department town."[76]

Faced with the desperate need to generate revenue, in 1976, Perk fully acceded to the Growth Association's plan for downtown redevelopment, which went further than the direct subsidies of liberalism's supply side to include massive tax abatements. That officials turned to tax abatements as a primary means of delivering growth and tax resources suggests business' rising clout in the context of local governments' diminishing capacities—it was no accident, perhaps, that the practice was popularized by Southern states during the capital-scarce opening decades of the twentieth century.[77] Though he had never believed it himself, Perk tried to persuade his ethnic base that their fate as well as that of their city was inextricably linked to that of the city's businesses. Perk announced the plans without a shred of optimism: "Cleveland has a disease. It is mentally crippling, it is spiritually crippling, and it is psychologically crippling." He described "this urban masochism" that had seized the city.[78] His "Twenty Point Action Program" had all the hallmarks of Jim Davis's plan. It included a land bank (the legislation for which was written by Davis's firm); "an equitable tax-abatement formula" (also written by Davis's firm); a "Businessman's Advisory Council" (to be chaired by the CEO of National City Bank, which would receive one of the first abatements); and an Economic Growth Commission "to pull all these points together, and to serve as the central force to develop a series of long-range economic growth plans." When the Growth Commission debuted, redubbed the Mayor's Economic Coordinating Commission, Davis became head.[79] Sohio (now British Petroleum) secured land on Public Square to build a new corporate headquarters. In the negotiations,

Davis's firm represented Sohio, and Davis represented the city. Sohio soon won a $21 million abatement paired with millions in CDBG-funded site improvements.[80]

Perk's political legitimacy had totally collapsed. His economic planning department was in shambles, and the city's budget was declared unauditable in 1977 by Price Waterhouse and again in 1978 by Ernst and Ernst. A Brookings study found the city's published data for CDBG expenditures "was greatly at variance with financial reports filed with the federal government," indicating fraud, incompetence, or both. The city's fiscal crisis meant that "each department is truly a creature of the federal government."[81] A subsequent audit found that Perk had even misappropriated $52 million in revenue bonds, routing them into the general budget.[82] Because the bonds failed to support revenue-generating operations, they would have to be repaid from general funds.

A range of left-progressives in Ohio, many associated with the Ohio Public Interest Campaign (OPIC), began organizing in Cleveland to roll back Perk's handouts and sought explicitly to work across lines of race and space. Made up of labor organizations, particularly statewide UAW chapters threatened by plant closures, senior citizens groups, and neighborhood associations, OPIC made corporate civic responsibility and tax fairness its central issues.[83] They sought to close corporate tax loopholes and abatements, and one of their chief pieces of proposed (but never passed) legislation, the Community Readjustment Act, would have required corporations planning to close plants to give two years' notice and severance pay to workers and municipalities.[84] OPIC's first major campaign in Cleveland took on Mayor Perk and council president George Forbes's corporate tax breaks, which they estimated would cost some $35 million in foregone revenue.[85] On August 1, 1977, OPIC flooded the city with fifty thousand leaflets targeting the city's business leadership: "You can't run Cleveland if you sell it out," it read. "We need revenues to run our city and schools," but Perk was "giving away taxes to downtown businesses."[86] Who, they asked, was city government for?

The 1977 mayoral election was a referendum on this question. Councilman Dennis Kucinich—always opportunistic, sometimes racially cynical, but reliably anti-corporate—made opposition to the privatization of the city's public electric utility, Muny Light, the centerpiece of his campaign. Business interests were behind the proposed sale to its private rival, Cleveland Electric Illuminating (CEI), and Kucinich claimed a "shadow government" led Cleveland, headed by the Growth Association, CEI, its bank Cleveland Trust, and the city's major law firms Jones Day and Jim Davis's Squire Sanders. In one of the campaign's signature moments, Kucinich supporters coordinated a Saul Alinsky–inspired demonstration at National City Bank, a recipient of one of Perk's abatements. Nearly 22 percent of National City's deposits came from within the city, but the bank only lent 5 percent of its mortgages there.[87] Echoing the 1976 National People's Platform action in Washington, D.C., the neighborhood groups piled debris on the sidewalk in front of the bank's headquarters, dramatizing National City's unwillingness to lend locally.

The governing logic of four decades of supply-side liberalism was under sustained political scrutiny and fiscal strain. The failure of liberalism's social promises was particularly glaring compared to its continued empowerment—and enrichment—of business interests. As one OPIC leader put it, "Liberals will either have to give up on the social spending commitments that have made them liberals, or they'll have to become whatever we are—progressives, populists, whatever." This tradeoff, he said, will put "them right up against the corporations, and that threatens their political careers. What we have to demonstrate is that people like us—who are an increasing majority and who can deliver on referenda and initiatives—threaten their careers even more."[88] As a diagnosis of the contradictions and tensions at the heart of liberalism's supply side—its soaring commitments to social and racial empowerment advanced through economic means and public-private partnerships—OPIC was spot on. But whether they spoke for a majority of Americans was less clear. Indeed, liberalism's supply side had also created forms of soft power, new types of political-cultural common senses, that lent legitimacy to business's claims as social and political actors. In the clash with Dennis Kucinich, businessmen would cash in not only decades of structural equity. They would also tout their producerist bona fides, positioning the sober leadership of businesspeople and the apolitical rationality of market logics as the solution for the city's—and nation's—fiscal and political volatility.

Progressive Populism Versus Business Producerism

Dennis Kucinich was heralded by the nation's left as a sign of hope, an electoral breakthrough for a coalition of neighborhood groups and activists desperate for a victory. Just thirty-one when he took office, Kucinich, *The Nation* reported, "may well signal a new era in American politics" driven by young people calling for "a program of economic justice and economic democracy."[89] If the 1970s was the "decade of the neighborhood," a period when working-class white and black homeowners and the poor mounted sustained insurgencies against unresponsive public officials and private practices of redlining and disinvestment, Cleveland was among the few cities to elect a populist mayor.[90] Advised by the progressive urban planner Norman Krumholz, who came to Cleveland to work for Mayor Stokes, Kucinich argued that tax abatements were primarily political rather than economic tools. They robbed the city's neighborhoods of valuable capital in order to signal to businesses an administration's pliability. Kucinich quashed Perk's abatements for Sohio and National City Bank. Though the city council overturned his veto, Kucinich froze federal funds and halted infrastructure improvements for such corporate projects, terminating—for the moment—the Sohio and National City developments. In planning circles, Krumholz was a leading advocate of what he later termed "equity planning," a strategy for the long-term development of declining cities that focused on shoring up services for lower- and middle-class residents without unduly pandering to business and suburbanites.[91] Equity planning was about maximizing resident choice and opportunity, which could also lead Krumholz to support the quasi-privatization of certain public goods, such as Perk's sale of the city transit system to a regional authority, which Krumholz saw as a way to provide Clevelanders access to suburban work.[92] This emphasis on choice also led Kucinich and Krumholz to fight to keep Muny Light public.

But Kucinich's political style quickly threatened to swamp his substance. Kucinich's politics were anti-corporate, redistributionary, and, thanks to his intemperate, impetuous, and often incoherent style, ultimately unsustainable. Though Kucinich touted Krumholz's ideas in the campaign, his increasingly entrenched battle with the city's business elites led him to abandon judicious planning. He and Krumholz rarely met.[93] Beyond attacking corporations, Kucinich lacked a governing agenda akin to Carl Stokes's Cleveland: Now!, which conditioned support for business development on their support for affordable housing and jobs initiatives. While Krumholz's planning ideas gained sway in other cities, Cleveland continued to lurch from crisis to crisis.[94]

Kucinich also needlessly alienated neighborhood groups, his core constituency. One typical confrontation pitted Kucinich and Citizens to Bring Broadway Back (CBBB). CBBB had petitioned Perk to demolish an abandoned home that was a danger to the neighborhood. When Kucinich ignored the same requests, CBBBers demolished the structure and hauled scraps into the Community Development Department. "We went into the building carrying all this charred wood," a member remembered, "dropping ashes and junk everywhere, and [Community Development director Betty Grdina] started screaming, 'Call the police.' . . . She was literally shoving people out of the office."[95] They called confrontational actions like these "hits," a tactic that neighborhood groups would turn to in the fractious and desperate years to come.

As frustration with Kucinich mounted, a decade of uphill organizing, constrained budgets, and debates about priorities made neighborhood organizations' unity a fragile thing. Exhaustion and intramural resentments exploded at a 1978 Neighborhoods Conference. Ten groups—more than seven hundred Clevelanders—and Kucinich staffers had hoped to reboot their relationships. It was a disaster. Grdina refused to answer questions until several unannounced city officials were permitted to speak. Kucinich's chief of staff explained to the activists "how you're going to have to behave if you want to come down to city hall and see us." Residents chanted over him, "You work for us!" Diane Yambor of the Buckeye Woodland Community Congress (BWCC) seized the microphone. A struggle erupted. Fannie Lewis, the Model Cities veteran, Hough resident, and Kucinich supporter (he delivered her a patronage post), mounted the stage. An attendee recalled, "Lewis walked up and hit Agnes Jackson [of the BWCC] over the head with the microphone . . . Sarah Turner [also of BWCC] picked up a chair and was going to hit Fanny [sic] over the head . . . at which point one of the organizers took the chair away, and Sarah grabbed another one, and that's when all hell broke loose." Administration officials fled. They soon severed ties with the neighborhood coalitions. By the following year, the BWCC petitioned HUD to issue CDBG funds directly to neighborhood groups, bypassing city hall entirely. Responding to the activists' complaints, Kucinich made matters worse: "Activist community groups are unnecessary with a mayor who understands their needs."[96] Despite having employed Saul Alinsky's confrontational tactics to get elected, as Kucinich put it, "Alinsky was never on the inside."[97] As the austerity of the 1980s arrived, many neighborhood groups would abandon the quest for political reform amid an increasingly desperate search for economic sufficiency.

The main front in Kucinich's wars, however, was with the city's business leadership. Incensed by the conflict over tax abatements and frustrated by Kucinich's plans to use CDBGs for fundamental needs such as sewer improvements, the Growth Association pursued a multifront assault. It did so in dialogue with national business associations. In April 1978, more than three hundred association members hosted a day of workshops jointly sponsored by the U.S. Chamber of Commerce, NAM, and the National Federation of Independent Business. The Sunbelt was prominently represented. Speakers detailed "programs by which businessmen could influence the political process and encourage their employees and shareholders to do the same." In his keynote, Senator Harry Byrd (D-Va.) urged Cleveland's power elite to make their voices heard. Inefficiency, waste, and mismanagement were rampant in government, he said, because "the commodity in shortest supply" was businesslike "common sense."[98]

Just five months into his term, Cleveland's business community mounted a campaign to recall Kucinich. He survived the August recall by a mere 236 votes out of 120,300 cast. Neighborhood groups refused to support him, and turnout in key wards sagged.[99] Kucinich surmised that business leaders had organized and funded the effort. Brock Weir, the chairman of Cleveland Trust bank and a Growth Association leader, had become an increasingly vocal opponent, and a subsequent investigation confirmed that much of the campaign's funding had come from the suburbs.[100] Blocked at the polls, Weir and the largely suburb-residing organized business community reached for more subtle points of leverage over the city.

Kucinich had inherited a precarious budget and an external audit underscored the city's dependence on debt in general and accelerating dependence on short-term borrowing in particular: the city's current long-term debt included $231,976,000 in general obligation bonds and $182,780,000 in revenue bonds. But it also held $41,115,000 in short term loans, bringing the total load to nearly $500 million. When that audit become public in 1978, Moody's downgraded the city's debt rating, pushing up future borrowing costs. The city was forced to double down on short-term loans from commercial banks.[101]

As Brock Weir later conceded, the banks used the city's short-term debt as leverage. New York City's crisis, he said, "taught us a lesson about asking questions" about Cleveland's fiscal situation. But the crisis that mainly concerned Weir was political. It was about "the present administration. The Perk administration was not as antagonistic toward the business community and the banking community as to precipitate a showdown," he said.[102] While credit rating is ever and always an inherently subjective political project, it was rare to have a bank official come right out and say so. On June 5, 1978, amid the recall effort, an analyst at Cleveland's Society National Bank produced a report that the city's credit rating "should be" lowered to the equivalent "of a low 'Baa' with a declining trend to 'Ba.'" On June 22, barely two weeks after the report's completion, Moody's downgraded Cleveland's credit rating to "Baa," with disastrous implications for the city's interest rates on future debt. On June 29, Weir's Cleveland Trust informed the city that it would not refinance its short-term notes. Kucinich called a meeting with Weir, who told the mayor, as the city's finance officer recalled, "that 'default might not be bad for the City' because it would, he felt, force the City to address its long term financial problems."[103] Standard and Poor's soon suspended its ratings for the city, and Moody's again downgraded its rating.

Kucinich turned to the national media, calling attention to the banks' political exploitation of their economic leverage. Left-progressive activists descended on Cleveland, attracted by the chance to study and protest the power of finance capital in action. In "Cleveland: An Autopsy," Barbara and John Ehrenreich highlighted how corporate elites strategically aggregated individual power; indeed, "simply adding up" the corporations would not produce "a true measure of . . . business leaders' collective economic power." Cleveland Trust, for instance, had a controlling interest in thirty companies, while its board members had "direct interlocks" with nineteen other corporations. A similar set of interlocking directorates, board positions, and stock holdings characterized other banks, too.[104] Cleveland's business leaders had even deployed their unity to resist external capital during the 1960s' conglomerate boom. Like a threatened lizard that puffs up to exaggerate its size, "when one Cleveland company was threatened, other Cleveland companies would . . . announce . . . plans to merge with it, thus creating the possibility of a new company too large for the outsider to swallow." They also intuited the affective and deeply local basis of business's producerism, which animated elites' sense of producerist entitlement and the intensity of their mobilization. The difficulty in confronting Cleveland's business community, the Ehrenreichs argued, was that "they *do* care about Cleveland. Their company headquarters are downtown, their plants are in the Flats, and to the extent that neither can be moved or replaced, their corporate futures are bound up with the fate of the city."[105]

Kucinich grasped the stakes of this fiscal and political war, and he sought to make its subtle terms as visible as possible. In an incendiary press release, he proclaimed, "The banks . . . represent raw economic power. . . . They won't buy Cleveland's bond offerings and they continue their systematic looting of Cleveland's financial resources in the pursuit of maximum profits." They "say that the public must pay the price for economic development . . . [and] to insure the profit margins of the banks and corporations won't be disturbed. It's time to turn the tables on this sort of self-serving logic. Those who are in a position to gain the most, the banks and corporations, should be required to take the risks."[106] Kucinich took dead aim at the fiscal foundations and political assumptions undergirding decades of supply-side state building—and none more so than the notion that the public sector's fiscal well-being and progressive possibilities necessarily rested on private profits and the taxes they might produce.

As December 15, 1978 loomed, the deadline for the city to refinance or pay back its short-term notes, Cleveland Trust executives and Loan Review Committee members, which included figures such as Jones Day attorney Richard Pogue, moved decisions about municipal borrowing from technical staff within the commercial banking division to executives at the holding company level. Bank executives and trustees, not loan officers, would determine the city's financing.[107] Kucinich prepared an omnibus package of bonds that, in the past, would have guaranteed the banks' willingness to work with the city, but executives would not budge. The banks' political power was clear. And, in stark contrast to New York City's crisis, in which its debt was in the billions and its month-to-month borrowing in the hundreds of millions, Cleveland's banks took their stand over a mere $15.5 million.

The engineered crisis entered its end stage at a December 15 meeting at which Maurice Saltzman, owner of Bobbie Brooks women's wear, and Brock Weir presented Kucinich and council president Forbes with an ultimatum. To secure the bank's willingness to refinance the debt, the city would have to sell Muny Light to Cleveland Electric Illuminating, which had long coveted its public rival's market share. As Saltzman recalled, "I told the mayor to sell MUNY," and Weir confirmed that "he would then consider providing assistance to the city in selling its bonds." Kucinich remembered the exchange differently, claiming Weir proffered the demand himself.[108] That same afternoon, Moody's again lowered Cleveland's bond rating to the level New York City reached in the depths of its 1975 crisis, and on a live edition of the six o'clock news, Kucinich rejected both a compromise measure and the sale of Muny, calling the proposals "Baloney!" While the other banks ultimately agreed to refinance their holdings, Weir's Cleveland Trust would not budge on a mere $5 million. As midnight approached, Kucinich led an emergency city council meeting and refused the council members' entreaties to sell Muny. When council president George Forbes, a chief advocate of compromise and the sale of Muny, rapped his gavel at 12:06 a.m., the city entered default.[109] Cleveland was the first major city to default on debt obligations since the Great Depression. "We had been kicked in the teeth for six months," Weir later said; "On December 15 we decided to kick back."[110]

While activists such as Ralph Nader tried to rally support for Kucinich, business leaders crafted a narrative in which Kucinich was to blame. As the *Washington Post* reported, Cleveland still "boasts 33 national corporate headquarters and, after New York and Chicago, is home to more of the nation's top 1,000 corporations than any other metropolitan area."[111] In May 1979, business leaders crafted an object lesson about Kucinich's threat to the city's business climate when Diamond Shamrock, one of Cleveland's venerable firms, announced that it was moving its headquarters to Dallas. Despite later analysis suggesting the move was mainly about new opportunities in the Southwest, the company's president and CEO gave city business leaders a boost by saying "the anti-business attitude on the part of the city administration" had contributed to their decision, laying the loss of two thousand jobs at Kucinich's feet.[112] Rumors circulated that the managing partner of Jones Day, Allen C. Holmes, had requested the statement.[113] Kucinich thanked them for "the gratuitous kick in the teeth."[114]

If the city's fiscal precarity had given business elites certain structural advantages, it was the producerist gloss on their position that translated into an emerging and increasingly durable form of politics resonant with voters. Despite Weir's spasms of intemperate rhetoric, he dressed his bank's decision in producerist garb, emphasizing corporate responsibility for the city's welfare.[115] He called the debt, he said, because of "how we view our responsibility to the city and the people of Cleveland." "Your bank has a commitment to Cleveland that stretches back 85 years." It was a "very difficult decision, made in the hope that it would help mobilize the city's government to begin to deal realistically with Cleveland's financial problems." Public-sector officials, he charged, "don't have the standards of accountability of the private sector." He unleashed his producerist ire at Kucinich in testimony before Congress: "It seems a topsy-turvy world of values indeed when by reckless and unsubstantiated charges, a delinquent, deceitful and defiant debtor can call his all-too-patient creditors to account." In the wake of the crisis, polls found that Weir enjoyed a higher favorability rating in Cleveland than did Kucinich.[116]

If the Perk and Kucinich years taught Cleveland's business leadership anything, it was the importance of having pliant officials in city hall. With the city barred from credit markets, power brokers wooed Ohio's Republican lieutenant governor George Voinovich to come home to run for mayor. Beyond campaign contributions, business leaders offered to lend his administration hundreds of hours of their time as well as hundreds of private employees, overhauling city administrative processes and planning. Most of these loaned executives' salaries would be paid by their private employers. Just as Jimmy Carter's private business consultants had done in Georgia, businesspeople would move into Voinovich's government to modernize, streamline, and reform public institutions.

In the 1979 mayoral campaign, Kucinich tried to revive his populism. He explored creating a city-owned bank and putting workers' pension funds to use as part of a new investment-oriented development strategy. His administration applied for federal funds to study the bank proposition. He also backed an OPIC corporate tax reform proposal to "get corporate America out of the business of government."[117] Voinovich, meanwhile, pledged moderation and "a very businesslike atmosphere at City Hall," joining an emerging set of politicians of both parties who promised stability through businesslike budgetary discipline and market-like efficiency in public administration. Voinovich promised to "run the city like the president of a corporation would run a corporation. I look at the taxpayers as shareholders and they have a right to get a return on their tax dollar."[118] While Kucinich framed voters as literal stockholders in an expansive social enterprise, Voinovich's market-oriented language implied efficiency and limited government.

Voinovich's emphasis on businesslike discipline and market-inspired governance were newly resonant with Cleveland's white voters, especially. He won a commanding 13 percentage point victory. While Kucinich's support in lower-income and black wards remained steady, his support among white voters declined precipitously.[119] Kucinich, many voters believed, rode his antibusiness rhetoric to default and, in so doing, in the wake of Watergate, Vietnam, and the widespread fiscal crises of the 1970s, provided further local impetus for white voters' declining faith in public institutions. Business producerism thus provided a political-cultural logic that facilitated key aspects of the neoliberal world emerging—business and markets, rather than government, might be more effective and efficient provisioners of social goods. They could perhaps even offer models for reforming government itself.

* * *

Cleveland's debt crisis certainly played out in extremis. But the fiscal pressures the city faced were increasingly common, and, in the absence of federal assistance, the necessity and costs of municipal borrowing soon became unsustainable even for seemingly booming Sunbelt cities.[120] An interregional convergence of sorts was increasingly apparent among big cities with vastly different histories and political economies. By the late 1970s, commercial banks held nearly half the municipal debt in the United States, much of it the sort of short-term loans on which Cleveland defaulted.[121] The historical legacies of liberalism's supply-side partnerships, the midcentury prerogative to borrow, and the ascending power of credit-rating agencies and finance capitalism strengthened profound structural advantages for local business elites that cut across regional distinctions of politics or culture—the relative success or failure navigating fiscal policy and development remained contingent, but, to politicians and even voters, the range of political options seemed only to narrow.

With producerist rhetoric soberly emphasizing fiscal realities, bankers, businesspeople, and credit-rating officials promoted the notion that growing constraints on cities were hardly political at all—they were the natural order, the rules of the game. As Hyman Grossman, an S&P official, put it, cities that failed to "budget realistically" and instead chose to "'do what the heck we feel like'" would see their ratings downgraded.[122] The priorities of figures such as Dennis Kucinich were thus irresponsible political flights of fancy; bankers and ratings officials simply defined the terms of reality. Increased borrowing and credit surveillance and the austerity of the Reagan years would only lend further legitimacy to business's development agendas.

But in the fiscal and governing crises of the 1970s and 1980s, the political-cultural common senses attached to business producerism and the seeming rationality of markets also lent credence to using businesslike and market methods—and businesspeople themselves—to remake government. Far from simply a local phenomenon, by the late 1970s the entire structure of fiscal federalism seemed to be in crisis as more and more interest groups—poor and working-class Americans, women and minorities, as well as businesspeople—pressed their demands for empowerment and subsidies up the federal ladder. In search of efficiency, savings, and restored order, politicians across the partisan spectrum sought to borrow the growing cachet of the market and private sector partners—less as vehicles of auxiliary or enhanced state capacity, as New Deal liberals had, but as models for remaking the state itself, perhaps even insulating it from the democratic claims of mobilized publics.

CHAPTER 8

Federalism in Crisis

By the late 1970s, democracy itself, a set of political scientists and economists argued, had become "overloaded" by "interest groups" who demanded increasingly unsustainable levels of public spending. The era's prevailing claims that cities brought their debt crises on themselves thus prefigured broader assertions about the relationship between inflation, federal spending, and the limits of democracy— citizens were fattened by entitlements and disinclined to pay up or accept less. Each of these claims also abetted elite efforts to bring progressive insurgents to heel. In 1980, the economist Lester Thurow described the United States as "the zero-sum society," fractured by distributional battles that broke along lines of race, class, identity, region, and neighborhood. For many scholars and commentators alike, fiscal crises, tax revolts, and inflation were at bottom crises of democracy.[1] The *Atlanta Constitution*'s editors published an especially bleak assessment. "Inflation," they wrote, "is messing us up." Many would have to make "severe sacrifices," but "Americans may no longer be capable" of sacrificing for the greater good.[2] As in the case of municipal debt crises, however, popular and often deeply racialized grievances about America's seemingly out-of-control welfare state obscured the realities of who mainly benefitted from public subsidies.

These crises were articulated through less familiar but no less significant clashes within the system of fiscal federalism and the increasingly strained Democratic coalition. Jimmy Carter's political career illuminates how the legacies of liberalism's supply side shaped both the battle lines as well as available forms of political power. In the 1960s, his Area Planning and Development Commission commandeered regional war on poverty programming. By 1971, elite-led regional development-qua-social policy animated the creation of the Southern Growth Policies Board (SGPB), an interstate compact of governors and regional planners underwritten by corporate and philanthropic sponsors. The board would create a "postindustrial" and "post-racial" South, deploying many of the same public resources for which mobilized marginalized groups contested. Explicitly pursuing white-collar, well-educated, high-tech, and white-dominated forms of work, the SGPB also rejected older development agendas oriented around low-wage "smokestack chasing," championing instead a suburban, environmentally friendly quality of life politics. Governor Carter served an influential early chairmanship, and the SGPB soon became an institutional, political, and intergenerational bridge between older, southern supply-side commitments and an emerging generation of "New Democrats."

As historically marginalized citizens won provisional forms of enfranchisement and learned to play the federal funding game, they joined supply-side state builders in pressing demands for greater political and economic empowerment up the federal system. Elites' concerns that democracy was being overloaded by selfish interest groups, were thus animated by battles between progressive advocates of increasingly targeted spending that might favor historically marginalized groups—African Americans seeking federal job guarantees, unions pushing for full employment legislation, activists' seeking to stabilize or expand welfare entitlements—and those, like the SGPB, who sought loosely regulated aid over which they enjoyed disproportionate control. Globalization, deindustrialization, and inflation all brought these distributional battles to an inflection point. And these pressures were intensified by an increasingly professionalized set of lobbyists, associations, and activists. While they reflected vast asymmetries of power, as political scientist Samuel Beer noted in 1977, these groups "march[ed] hand in hand" for "steady expansion" of federal spending.[3] Lobbyists' hands were more often at each other's throats, however, given the vast and asymmetrical array of interests they represented.[4]

The terms of engagement and the stakes of the battles—which saw elite groups such as the SGPB legitimize their claims to federal aid in terms of fighting poverty—were defined by the historical inequalities and assumptions built into the New Deal's decentralized supply-side state. Those inequalities were effectively reproduced by elites' claims that democracy was being overloaded, a seemingly descriptive term that instead mobilized negative political attention on the latest claimants to public resources: the so-called "special interests."

As he rose from supply-side state builder to the presidency, Jimmy Carter's political career offers a distinctive and distinctly ironic vantage point from which to view the crises of fiscal federalism in the 1970s. Carter arrived in the White House determined to rationalize the intergovernmental system and to prove to Americans that government could work. In the wake of the 1973–75 recession, however, a broad antipoverty coalition regrouped around demands for a full employment agenda.[5] In combination with mounting calls for regional equity in federal grants, which pitted the regional bases of the historical New Deal coalition, the urban North and developing South, Carter faced mounting pressure to add new policies and spending to an intergovernmental system he and his aides believed was inefficient, overstretched, and overheating, particularly as inflation surged in 1978.[6] Carter's failure to balance so many competing demands, which effectively meant balancing the demands of a fracturing Democratic coalition, would consume his presidency.

Zero-Sum Politics and the Problem of Public Authority

If inflation presented one constraint on federal spending, mounting taxpayer discontent with tax rates and public accountability provided another. While voters in Cleveland were furious about tax rates tied to municipal debt burdens and corporate tax abatements, other voters, often white citizens in lower-tax states such as Georgia, focused on the seemingly undemocratic, anti-majoritarian means by which elites imposed their development agendas. The rights-based and majoritarian grievances of taxpayer authority, which suffused tax revolts in high-tax and suburbanized states such as California and Massachusetts, also animated an adjacent but sometimes overlooked strain of white anger in low-tax states and rural communities. In such largely white communities, this majoritarian politics took hold as resentful voters increasingly believed that public resources flowed out of their communities and into cities. By the early 1970s, Nixon's majoritarian rhetoric—the effort to define and derive legitimacy from a racially bounded and mythically consensual majority—reflected a growing trend in which a number of white majorities were named and claimed by conservative activists: these included "the silent majority," "the new majority," "the real majority," "the emerging Republican majority," and, eventually, the Moral Majority.[7] Like Ralph Perk's and Dennis Kucinich's critique of developmental and abatement politics in Cleveland, however, the democratic compromises encouraged by liberal's supply-side state lent urgency, staying power, and at least a veneer of legitimacy to critiques of taxes and spending, which were often as much about racial majoritarianism as they were about democratic accountability over governing institutions that had the authority to spend public resources in ways that circumvented popular control.

In Georgia, rural taxpayers' anger was a growing concern for the Coosa Valley Area Planning and Development Commission (CVAPDC). The APDCs were akin to a type of a proliferating form of post–New Deal administrative governance, the "public authority," which enhanced government's abilities to plan and carry out programs and projects but often did so without a direct referendum on new revenue-raising or spending capacities. In fact, New Dealers encouraged the creation of public authorities specifically to avoid having to go to voters to raise revenues. Many were endowed with the authority to float their own bond instruments, which nevertheless required taxpayer revenue to secure and retire the debts. As a scholar of the public authority has put it, "the choice to build government capacity using what is essentially a strategy of circumvention comes with real costs," particularly given that "the possibility of open, democratic decision making about how to allocate available resources becomes elusive."[8] In times of growth and relative abundance, the stakes of such public and quasi-public systems of governance and administration are relatively low. But in periods of economic instability, austerity, and inflation—all of which converged in the 1970s—the costs and accountability of government become more hotly contested. While Georgia's APDCs rarely if ever created such debt financing themselves, they propagated their use by municipalities and other public authorities across the state, and, in any event, the commissioners often held multiple positions: serving on, for instance, an urban renewal authority that floated debt; an unelected APDC board; and an elected county commission. In Rome and Floyd County, small taxpayers' frustrations landed on all three types of governmental or quasi-governmental bodies, especially as the economic downturn began to cast shadows over these striving Sunbelt counties.[9]

Small-business owner Roy Knowles led the charge in northwest Georgia. Knowles owned and operated Roy's Little Garden, a variety store on the Floyd County side of the line with Rome. An outspoken supporter of Lester Maddox and George Wallace, Knowles made his first entry into electoral politics in 1967 when he challenged the incumbent county sheriff of nearly two decades. Anticipating the emergence of "law and order" politics in the post–civil rights years, Knowles's campaign was based on his conviction that there was "a dire need for honest government." The sheriff's office was as good a place to start as any.[10] Though Knowles lost, he became a key organizer of

George Wallace's 1968 presidential campaign. Liberal threats to segregation had launched Wallace's campaign, but they proved less essential to sustaining his career. Once he began looking for examples of "undemocratic" governance, white majoritarian discontent, and outrage over wasteful spending, Wallace easily broadened his base beyond self-identifying segregationists. Knowles tapped into these same discontents and, in 1970, he founded Concerned Citizens for a Better Government and directed its wrath upon city and county government and the Coosa commission.

Through Concerned Citizens, Knowles convened "town hall meetings" at which rural and working-class white residents complained about everything from "race mixing" to water rates and officials' unwillingness "to 'listen' to the complaints of the taxpayers." At a December 1970 meeting, a "fired-up, standing room only crowd," the *News-Tribune* reported, demanded the resignation of the county administrator and members of the board of commissioners. Rather "than tightening their belts a little bit," Knowles charged, the board continued its "foolish spending," drawing "the noose of higher taxes around our necks until we just about can't breathe anymore."[11] Calling out the CVAPDC, one woman described herself as "personally overwhelmed by the control these men already have over us." A Rome realtor rose to defend the besieged commissioners, urging attendees to develop solutions, rather than just "cussin'" and "tearing . . . everybody to pieces." He received a chorus of boos. Knowles summed up the situation: "we've had a Boston Tea Party going on in Floyd County long enough, and it's time to stop this taxation without representation."[12] The sense that out-of-touch elites perverted majoritarian institutions and wasted taxpayers' hard-earned money was metastasizing in rural and suburban communities alike.[13]

The perception that federal spending was disproportionately lavished on urban America also stoked resentments among residents of nonmetropolitan communities who felt they were being left behind. Georgia's Senator Herman Talmadge—an archetypal segregationist southern Democrat—sought one last time to use a New Deal-style spending program to renew white, rural voters' support for the party. By the late 1960s, many rural regions were reaching the end of a period of profound and protracted structural readjustment, one accelerated by U.S. farm policies and which yielded low employment, low wages, and population flight.[14] Talmadge used his position as chairman of the Senate Agricultural Committee to spearhead the legislation that became Richard Nixon's Rural Development Act of 1972, an effort to bring industrial employment to rural areas. As in the proposals for Community Development Block Grants (CDBG), Talmadge's legislation defined and legitimized "development" through its ability to solve poverty, as the Senate version detailed, "rais[ing] per capita income" or "directly inreas[ing] the employment or income or otherwise benefit[ing] the residents of a rural area."[15] Upon signing the final bill, Nixon emphasized "marshal[ing] . . . the energies of the private sector and of government at all levels." But, rather than offering direct grants, as in CDBGs and Revenue Sharing, most of this rural aid would come in the form of "commercial, industrial, and community development" loan programs in which subnational governments awarded recipients low-cost federal financing.[16] The federal government would act as a "catalyst, a coordinator, a stimulator, but," in classic supply side fashion, would work primarily through "local agencies and governments, local lending institutions, and local business enterprise."[17] The bill held special promise for rural Georgia, the *Atlanta Constitution* reported, because it would "quickly" "channel money to" the APDCs.[18] If, however, Talmadge imagined the program would win over angry rural voters like Roy Knowles, such reliance on well-established decentralized, public-private administrative channels risked cutting in the opposite direction.

The program ran into a number of other difficulties. Its passage coincided with Nixon's efforts to battle inflation by limiting federal spending in discretionary programs, which slowed the pace of awards.[19] While Georgia did receive the program's first loan—a Calhoun firm planned to hire 100 new employees with the financing—it took nearly a year for the subsidies to arrive. More fundamentally, however, many rural communities lacked the infrastructure necessary for supporting the resource heavy industry the bill hoped to cultivate. To simply begin the industrial recruitment process, a Georgia official estimated, would require $500 million of investments in rural sewage improvements.[20] Public water systems, workforce training, and improvements to rural housing all presented other costs associated with industrialization, or "smokestack chasing" as it would soon be derided. In the 1970s, those costs amounted to unfunded prerequisites for federal aid, costs far beyond the means of many strained state and local governments.

And in any event, rural residents' sense that federal funding often ended up in cities, large or small, was mainly correct. This was because the APDCs, most of which were based in Georgia's cities, followed Great Society–era program mandates that focused development initiatives on "growth centers"—small to larger cities within rural development districts. In this regard,

Governor Carter's state reorganization had significant if unintended consequences for Georgians' perceptions of the APDCs. In 1971, Carter moved the commission system into the governor's budget department in hopes that placing a broader range of social service programs in the hands of APDCs might endow social services with greater legitimacy. The inverse occurred. White, rural voters' anger at social spending and welfare programs rubbed off on the APDCs, slanting perceptions toward the public side of privately led partnerships.[21] By 1974, the CVAPDC managed regional child development programs, and the following year its funding in that area grew to $687,590 in state and federal aid, its largest budget line item. The APDC system's future had never been more secure, but its once-laserlike focus on economic development had become one among a growing number of priorities undertaken with state and federal funding.[22]

By 1974, Lester Maddox, Carter's lieutenant governor, had begun to hear from allies like Knowles that the APDCs operated above electoral control but with a hand in rural taxpayers' pockets. Allies in Georgia's Senate introduced legislation to require all APDCs to prepare comprehensive annual budgets for circulation among local governments for some form of approval. Carter was furious, complaining that commissions support "as many as 60 separate governmental units." "Sending a budget to all of them" for comment "would be a waste of time, money, and paper."[23] Though Maddox's allies fell three votes short, an older form of white-dominated, elite-directed localism was crashing up against another form of white-dominated, small-taxpayer majoritarianism.

Though the commission system survived, the flow of public administrative authority to a public-private commission posed important questions of accountability and legitimacy. The Georgia State House debated whether state law even authorized APDCs, with appointed rather than elected commissioners, to administer so many public programs. In 1978, Georgia's legislature created a five-year window during which commissions would be permitted to administer social programs after which they would have to subcontract with public agencies—a circuitous solution to the problem of democratic accountability. Parallel legislation also mandated that APDCs increase the number of publicly elected officials on their boards to two-thirds of total membership.[24] By the early 1980s, the majority of Coosa commission members were mayors or county commissioners.[25] That year, the CVAPDC moved into new headquarters, leaving the space it had shared for two decades with Rome's chamber of commerce.

Post-Racial, Postindustrial Policy

In the early 1970s, a group of on-the-rise New South politicians, largely Democrats, sought to adapt Roy Knowles' hated regional planning model into a postindustrial growth paradigm. Beyond Georgia's APDCs and their partnerships with Georgia Tech, these politicians were inspired by North Carolina governor Luther Hodges's pioneering Research Triangle Institute. If Hodges's economic vision, which took root in the 1950s, suggested a more modern outlook (R&D, he said, could pack "tremendous economic wallop"), he was also firmly planted in the Jim Crow South.[26] Hodges was a textile magnate long before he was an advocate of a postindustrial future, and he had also been an outspoken opponent of *Brown v. Board*. Hodges's career, which included a stint as John F. Kennedy's commerce secretary, suggests how futuristic economic outlooks and seemingly antiquated racist views could prove easily assimilable and mutually reinforcing. Indeed, elites' emergent postindustrial vision became increasingly tied to a vision of a "post-racial" South—one in which questions of racial equality were simply set aside.

Recognizing that the high infrastructural and other costs of "smokestack chasing" and environmental pollution went hand in hand, Jimmy Carter joined a group of "progressive" southern governors who aimed to change the kinds of business and industry southern states recruited. They did so with the northern urban crisis squarely in view. As northern cities struggled with deindustrialization, pollution, and escalating racial violence, in 1971, Duke University's president and former North Carolina governor Terry Sanford organized a conference in Atlanta, titled, "The Urban South: Northern Mistakes in a Southern Setting?" Sanford hoped to create an interstate board of governors and southern businesspeople who would explicitly plan southern growth, as one of his associates recalled, to avoid "turning our landscapes into industrial wastelands."[27] Virginia's governor Linwood Holton described the region's "planning" as "too little and too late," rendering leaders "oblivious to one of the greatest migrations in our history—the migration from countryside to cityside." The result was distinct but related rural and urban crises. Rural areas were either abandoned or transformed into "wasteland[s] of urban sprawl," while cities became "ghettos of rot and riot."[28] Following Sanford's 1971 conference, thirteen governors established the Southern Growth Policies Board (SGPB), a partnership between dues-paying states and southern business leaders with a mission to deploy Research Triangle assets to "manage" the transition from "smokestack chasing" to postindustrial economies.

In changing the structure of the southern economy and by courting higher-educated, higher-wage, disproportionately white workers, officials also imagined pivoting to a "post-racial" South, transcending—or, rather, sidelining—the racial struggles of the 1960s. West Virginia governor Arch Moore hoped the board would help "save us from the fate of all of the New Yorks and the Newarks and the Philadelphias and the Detroits in this country"—cities where oppressed African Americans had undertaken major revolts. Such "post-racial" politics operated as thinly disguised branding exercises rather than credible desires for racial reconciliation. Covering the board's early days, the *Washington Post* reported that southern leaders had, "by simple fiat, declared an end to racism." Displaying a shameless disregard for the South's history of racial violence, Sanford gushed that after "a century of being the whipping boy and backward child . . . the South can lead the nation, must lead the nation." South Carolina's governor John West envisioned "a truly post-racial society." An attendee of the initial meeting in Atlanta recalled the mood: "For most of us in that ballroom, it was a Southern Epiphany."[29] If any southerners felt truly liberated in the early 1970s, then, it was this set of "moderate" white political and business leaders who extolled economic growth as a path between economic and racial justice activism to their left and Wallace and Maddox coalitions to their right. These white politicos simply plucked the nagging thorn of racism and disfranchisement from their sides and heralded the South's "post-racial" future, one to be anchored by a postindustrial economy.

As they set aside live questions of equality and enfranchisement, southern Democrats also embraced aspects of the quality-of-life politics taking root in predominantly white suburbs. While the Northeast and West Coast have been most closely associated with this version of "New Democrat" politics, a sturdy southern variant was taking hold. This emerging synthesis fused attention to environmental quality, higher education, and seemingly meritocratic white-collar careers in high tech or well-paying service sectors. At one SGPB meeting, Linwood Holton underscored the urgency of environmentalism with an ominous anecdote. The "other day as we were taking off," he said, "the Eastern [Airlines] pilot said . . . look at the haze over Chicago. And he said you think that is clouds. That is pollution. As we approached Richmond he said you see that haze down there. That is the same thing as it was over Chicago."[30] In 1973, Holton chaired the SGPB and made clear that it was not another "'Industrial Development Board.'" It was a "planning and research agency that will help us study and develop and recommend policies . . . to keep a quality of life that we value, while at the same time" ensuring "the benefits of . . . desirable economic developments."[31] A younger generation of Democrats just taking political office embraced this outlook, including future Democratic Leadership Council members Lawton Chiles, elected to the U.S. Senate from Florida in 1971; Georgia's Sam Nunn, elected to the U.S. Senate in 1972; Arkansas's Bill Clinton, elected state attorney general in 1976 and governor in 1978; and Tennessee's Al Gore, elected to the U.S. House in 1976. The SGPB, then, became an institutional nexus for younger Democrats to exchange policy ideas and strategies and build networks and influence, nurturing the political economy of "post-racial" and "class-blind" politics usually associated with middle-class, white, and white-collar suburbanization.[32]

As they began mapping out this post-industrial policy, the board drew from an array of Cold War–era institutions and development experts.[33] Georgia Tech's Dr. Ross Hammond, who began his career at Rome's Industrial Development Branch, was a frequent consultant. Speaking at a 1973 meeting in Montgomery, Hammond urged "a conscious and coordinated effort to attract highly sophisticated, and hence, higher wage, economic activities to the area" by pouring resources into high-tech industries, job training, and scientific education for young people.[34] Another consultant emphasized the importance of high-tech R&D as a way to survive looming shifts in the international political economy. Walt Whitman Rostow, an influential international development and security adviser to Presidents Kennedy and Johnson and archetypal Cold War liberal, called for heavy public subsidization of research and development. In "our time," he explained, echoing Alvin Hansen's concern for investments and innovation, "the equivalent of open frontiers is going to be research and development; that is, the creation and application of new technologies" and "energy-related investment" as global oil shocks rocked domestic markets.[35] In seeking to "manage growth," Southern leaders plotted an entirely new economy.[36]

Governor Jimmy Carter served as SGPB director in 1973–74, the first year its professional research staff was fully operational (thanks, in part, to a $225,000 grant from the Ford Foundation). To cohere a balanced R&D agenda that might address urban and rural poverty even as officials championed postindustrial sectors, Carter appointed a twenty-member Commission on the Future of the South to establish a statement of objectives. Carter was careful to include two African American representatives: James Huger, business manager of Bethune-Cookman College in Daytona, Florida, and Athalie Range, Miami civil rights leader, city commissioner, and the owner of substandard rental properties in Miami.[37] To lead the commission, composed of academics, businesspeople, and public officials, Carter appointed Jim Cushman, a developer known for revitalizing Atlanta's tony Midtown. Cushman acknowledged southern sentimentality for the "good small town" life, but he believed it was "unrealistic to think we can ever go back to that." His goal was to make some "small towns more viable" but also to think carefully about the structure and location of economic developments. "We may [argue]," he said, "that growth shouldn't go . . . in this direction, but should be more in that direction."[38] Working with Cushman's commission, SGPB staffers produced a report sketching development goals for the region and states. Carter unveiled this report, "The Future of the South: A Statement of Regional Objectives for the Southern States," at the annual meeting in Atlanta in November 1974.[39]

Presenting the report, Carter rehashed his experience with the West Central Georgia APDC, which had taught him the importance of countering the "direct adverse impact of unplanned societal development" and of cultivating the federal government as a partner. We "cannot separate ourselves from government entities in the federal system," he said, "mainly because of finance, among other things."[40] In gently signaling the importance of federal aid, Carter underscored the imbalance in revenue capacities across the federal system, a fact that as Georgia's governor amidst rising inflation was becoming clear. SGPB staffers developed reports detailing the importance of federal funds for regional development, crediting CDBGs for its "reluctance to prescribe federal solutions" while also underwriting "capital requirements for financing the South's economic expansion." Generating new sources of capital by mastering federal programs would be increasingly important as credit markets strained under high interest and inflation rates.[41]

Though "The Future of the South" laid bare the uneven nature of southern development, including ongoing racial disparities and the emerging rural-metropolitan divide, Carter and his allies remained just as buoyant about the South's "post-racial" future in the mid-1970s as they had upon the board's conception a few years earlier. The *Atlanta Daily World*, a leading black newspaper, covered the November 1974 meeting at which Carter released their first major report. In a front-page article beneath a skeptical headline—"South Has 'Outgrown' Segregation"—editors allowed white liberals' racial obliviousness to speak for itself. Florida's governor Reubin Askew, the board's incoming director, explained that the region had "outgrown" racism thanks to rapid economic progress and generational change.[42] The *Norfolk*

Journal and Guide, another leading black paper, quoted Carter at length: "We are free for the first time to look to the future without preoccupation with . . . the color of our skins."⁴³ Carter reiterated his belief, as the *Daily World* reported, "that the civil rights movement of the 1960s 'liberated' southern whites from past prejudices and prepared the South for national leadership." Perhaps the *Daily World* was winking at Carter's well-known presidential aspirations. As Carter sought that higher office, however, the crosscutting demands on the federal system, the economy, and the liberal coalition itself were under unprecedented strain.

Humphrey-Hawkins and the Crisis of Federalism

Jimmy Carter began seriously exploring a run for the White House in 1972. That year, he became chairman of the Democratic Governors Campaign Committee, his first position in the national party. Carter did not shrink from controversy or confrontation and, ahead of the 1972 Democratic Convention, joined a bloc of southern and Border South governors at West Virginia's Greenbrier Hotel to discuss derailing George McGovern's candidacy. Carter was especially outspoken, warning that nominating McGovern would risk "decimating our ranks in the national congress and in state houses." McGovern's liberalism was "completely unacceptable to the majority of voters in many of our states." Carter even drew the ire of Georgia state house representative and civil rights icon Julian Bond, who charged Carter with perpetuating Jim Crow politics. Carter accused Bond of making a "racist statement," noting that Democrats had lost Georgia in 1964 and 1968 because they failed to seek Georgians' support.⁴⁴ He did not specify which Georgians he meant.

At the 1972 Democratic Convention in Miami Beach, Carter claimed the party's right flank, continuing to undermine McGovern while simultaneously lobbying to be McGovern's vice presidential nominee. Speaking before the delegates, Carter argued for the role of the states, rather than the national government, in innovating policy within the federal system. He cited the Appalachian Regional Commission as a signal example of states taking their own initiative—albeit with "substantial" "federal investments." He also touted Georgia's APDCs, in which "the Federal government played a supporting role, not the primary role."⁴⁵ Even as Carter championed those aspects of liberalism's supply side that could be read as conservative—the same aspects Barry Goldwater saluted in Rome in 1961—he took his place in the long history of southern politicians who did so on behalf of states' rights to greater federal assistance. As president, however, Carter would view the federal government's "supporting role" in far narrower terms.

On the campaign trail, Carter's efforts to bind a fraying Democratic coalition suggested just how untenable a proposition that was becoming. Elites, public officials, and growing ranks of white voters were deeply suspicious of minority administration and quota-based regulations while mobilized minority groups called for targeted, compensatory spending after decades of neglect and violence. To straddle the issue, Carter blended his personal conservatism—his born-again Christianity and his roots as a small-town businessman turned outsider politician—with a technocratic SGPB-style approach to policymaking. Carter emphasized an awkward blend of traditional liberal commitments to boosting employment, the era's customary calls to tame inflation, and a pledge to support struggling state and local governments by restoring "a true system of federalism."[46] His personal career with federal aid, marked in equal parts by criticism and dependence, suggested how thorny these dynamics could be. Moreover, Carter struggled to differentiate his vision of intergovernmental reform from Nixon and Ford's New Federalism precisely because they largely agreed on maintaining local elites' administrative authority within decentralized federal programs.

But Carter's election fundamentally depended upon his ability to court minority voters at a moment of profound and progressive change in the party's electorate. Newly mobilized constituencies within the party's growing base—welfare rights activists and advocates of full employment and authentic community development—hoped for more tightly targeted and regulated federal spending, since, as Carter himself acknowledged, "funds have been channeled, through administrative negligence or because of political pressures, into providing services for those who don't need them nearly so much." Block grants, he conceded, "designed for the ghetto families have too often been shifted to further benefit affluent families whose political influence . . . prevail[s]." He sought a "balanced national partnership" that would "grant to the local governments the administrative freedom needed for innovative, creative programming" while somehow ensuring that minority or poor residents received their share."[47] With this precarious balancing act, Carter hoped to hold together the traditional Democratic coalition.

Meanwhile, the liberal antipoverty coalition, which had recently splintered over debates about a guaranteed income, was organizing a full-employment campaign with the goal of establishing a right to a job. Such a program struck many as more pragmatic, even if it "helped to narrow the liberal economic justice agenda" by "eliminat[ing] broader claims for a 'right to live' irrespective of labor market participation."[48] Black activists particularly emphasized the disproportionate costs of the 1973–75 recession, in which the black unemployment rate was often double that of whites; in some places, the rate among young black men reached nearly 50 percent. As the Urban League's Vernon Jordan put it, what was merely a recession for most Americans amounted to "a major depression for black workers."[49]

Pushed by these groups along with organized labor, liberal legislators Augustus Hawkins, Hubert Humphrey, and Jacob Javits worked on a range of proposals to stimulate "full employment," by which they meant an overall unemployment rate of 3 percent or less. The first iteration, the proposed Balanced Growth and Economic Planning Act, dubbed "Humphrey-Javits," called for a new executive branch Economic Planning Board to formulate two-year growth plans. These plans would determine federal stimulus allocations to create maximum employment and productivity, blending macro-style Keynesian spending, micro-style sectoral planning and industrial policy, and public works spending in communities with chronic unemployment.[50] Hawkins, who represented the Watts district of Los Angeles, would solve African American unemployment with programs that offered "targeting through universalism," as one scholar described it.[51] President Ford would surely veto the bill, however, and so Humphrey-Javits was intended to build momentum.

In 1976, with unemployment still high, Humphrey partnered with Hawkins on another bill. Humphrey-Hawkins would rely upon traditional Keynesian stimulus and public works employment and direct the Federal Reserve to work with Congress and the president to seek full employment. Rather than create a new, centralized executive branch planning body, the bill called for creating local planning councils to initiate public and private works and development projects to be funded with countercyclical stimulus. A leading historian of Humphrey-Hawkins described the initiative as "a bold, even grandiose plan for a social democratic America."[52]

Perhaps nothing better illustrates the ways in which Humphrey-Hawkins aimed to update New Deal–style planning, spending, and revenue creation schemes than did the vision of Leon Keyserling, who ghostwrote many of its amendments to the Full Employment Act.[53] By the 1970s, Keyserling was one of twentieth-century liberalism's most venerable demand- and supply-side fusionists. In addition to playing a pivotal role in drafting the National Labor Relations Act in 1935, he wrote the legislation that created the slum clearance provisions of the U.S. Housing Act of 1937 and drafted the executive order creating the National Planning Agency (which later became HUD). Under President Kennedy, Keyserling was a chief advocate of the regional economic planning that had breathed brief life into the Area Redevelopment Administration. For Keyserling, the 1970s' crises flowed from decades of misplaced and paltry spending priorities and a lack of comprehensive regional economic planning. Inflation and fiscal crises, in other words, were supply-side planning issues.

In January 1976, Keyserling published a white paper titled *Toward Full Employment in Three Years*. As he described it, the problems of public revenue, employment, wages, and overall economic performance in the 1970s were both interwoven and historical. First, "high unemployment and deficient production cut grievously into public revenues at all levels of government." This explained "why public outlays for the great domestic priorities ... have fallen so lamentably short to date." The deficiency in public spending was both "the result" and an "important cause ... of the poor economic performance." He projected that public spending between 1976 and 1980 would fall some $425 billion short "without sweeping economic priorities to activate the economy fully."[54] Keyserling's depiction of a virtuous circle of social and economic priorities and of demand- and supply-side stimulus and public revenue generation went further still. The president's economic advisers must "abandon the artificial dichotomy between economic and social purposes, and stop pretending that we can 'efficiently' pursue the former by neglecting the latter."[55] He was emphasizing the economic value of social spending, but he argued the inverse just as powerfully. In the case of environmental conservation and cleanup, for instance, he warned that "'no growth' or slow growth" positions would only "frustrat[e]" environmentalism since the best way "to support the cleansing of our air and waters" was "with the dividends of more jobs, investment, and output."[56] Keyserling was reasserting the supply-side basis of social and even environmental progress.

To blend the growing commitments of modern liberalism, which was expanding to include not just environmental concerns but also quality of life issues related to workplace safety and satisfaction, Keyserling called for local and regional planners to shift the structure of the economy. Like the SGPB and NRPB before it, he urged planners to think carefully about the nature of the employment they sought. No longer should polluting manufacturing sectors with their workplace drudgery receive most-favored status from planners and politicians. As liberals pivoted toward a full-employment agenda, Keyserling called for stimulating "slower growth in factories producing gadgets, relative to growth in human services."⁵⁷ He envisioned Humphrey-Hawkins's federal spending, managed through local and regional planning councils, as a step toward cleaner economic sectors while also generating full employment and producing public revenues. Keyserling even emphasized deeply rooted ideals about employment and family formation: the bill "would . . . reduce the conditions which force so many mothers to work instead of staying home," a reality of the 1970s that "has grave social consequences."⁵⁸ This New Dealer was envisioning a blend of supply- and demand-side liberalism that would fight poverty and restore male breadwinning in a postindustrial age. But the plan would have to contend with more than the austerity politics of inflation.

Jimmy Carter owed much of his political career to the institutional legacies of New Deal planning, which had inspired the commissions that nurtured Carter's ideal vision of government. For Carter, steeped in nearly two decades of regional planning and its bureaucratic and intergovernmental battles, the call to create *new* local or regional economic planning bodies appeared at best redundant and at worst to add further complexity to the already muddled intergovernmental system. Carter thus gave Humphrey-Hawkins a tepid endorsement, which he couched in terms of his "commitment to the free enterprise system. I'm a businessman," he said, and "I would opt for equality of the state and local government [with the federal government]." A chief economic aide explained that Carter "believes in long-range planning," but he "has reservations about the specific economic planning requirements" of the proposed legislation, "fearing the creation of yet another bureaucracy."⁵⁹ In this sense, Carter had the support of the U.S. Chamber of Commerce. In assessing Humphrey-Hawkins, a U.S. Chamber report reflected the quiet reality of regional economic planning that had emerged across the country by the 1960s: "nationwide, decentralized, planning already exists and is not at issue." The Chamber opposed "national economic planning—centralized planning."⁶⁰ Carter viewed new intergovernmental programs and bureaucratic oversight with wariness—not because he did not believe in the model, but rather because he believed the structures already existed. They simply needed to be clarified and reformed.

The toothless and underfunded version of Humphrey-Hawkins that Carter ultimately signed was not simply a victim of his resistance to new bureaucracies or his fiscal conservatism.⁶¹ By 1978, many dyed-in-the-wool congressional liberals shared Carter's instincts for limiting public spending which many perceived as contributing to increased prices. As inflation surpassed 8 percent, the liberal watchdog organization Americans for Democratic Action (ADA) tracked declining fealty to liberal causes among congressional Democrats. House Democrats slid from an average ADA score of 62 percent in 1975 (100 percent was perfectly liberal) to 48 percent in 1978. Northern representatives earned the most rapid decline in ratings, a twenty-one-point drop. In 1979, Chicago's liberal representative Abner Mikva predicted "the most conservative Congress since Harry Truman's time" and warned that even Carter might be "unpleasantly surprised" by liberals' budget-cutting mood.[62] Senator Edmund Muskie, a dependable liberal, related allies' fears of being called "budget busters," lending credence to ADA's explanation that liberals' rightward turn had more to do with "cowardice" than any decisive ideological shift.[63] As the socialist Michael Harrington noted, "the conventional wisdom" was changing. "This is like 1931. Just as the conventional wisdom of the 1920s was shattered by the depression, the conventional wisdom of the 1960s has been shattered by inflation."[64] Vice President Mondale, the administration's resident New Dealer, underscored the mortal threat inflation posed for traditional liberal approaches to party building, public finance, and the economy: "If we don't solve inflation ... everything we stand for will be eroded ... when we press for real income improvement, inflation burns up the increase; when we push for growth, our standard of living deteriorates."[65] Republicans were thrilled. Representative Barber Conable gleefully cheered the "Republican Congress, full of Democrats."[66]

If inflation had effectively tabled the issue of generous new federal jobs and development spending, the questions of federalism, intergovernmental reform, and what to do about existing spending programs were as urgent as ever. If anything, inflation and rising interest rates increased pressure on Carter to come up with a workable solution for federalism, since so many constituencies expected support in hard times. But Carter's own instincts for fiscal moderation meant that as he contemplated winners and losers of various reform schemes, he resisted the traditional carrot of new funding—the lubricant that had kept the party machine running since the New Deal and had also ensured the passage of Nixon's New Federalism. Nixon, however, did not seek to appeal to nearly so diverse a roster of mutually quarrelsome constituencies as Carter. Rather than reform the system, however, Carter would mainly bring the crisis of federalism into the open.

"I Owe the Special Interests Nothing"

The personnel Carter cultivated in Georgia shaped his approach to federalism. For his chief congressional liaison, Carter tapped Frank Moore.[67] A management specialist by training, Moore worked for two different APDCs in Georgia before becoming special assistant for Carter's state reorganization plan and later a top legislative liaison. To oversee the administration's approach to federalism, Carter appointed James McIntyre who had served as the administrative head of Georgia's APDC system. Jack Watson served Carter as chairman of the Georgia Human Resources Board, which, in 1972, oversaw the reorganization of state poverty programs. As Watson put it, those reforms were "the most controversial aspect of [Carter's] entire state reorganization plan," and he had been tasked with "helping to sell the concept."[68] Watson would eventually become President Carter's chief of staff, and his experiences in Georgia handling the contentious issues of participation and administrative empowerment loomed large. The major question, Watson wrote in the summer of 1977, was "whether we are philosophically in favor of more grant consolidation and fewer program requirements, or whether we favor greater targeting and more prescriptive requirements." In short, "questions of categorical versus block grants and targeting versus revenue sharing raise fundamental philosophical questions on which we need to develop consistent policy soon."[69]

Carter's inclination was to maximize the authority and administrative flexibility of state and local executives, regional planners, and private-sector elites. Despite business's central role in Georgia's reorganization, Carter never thought of business as the kind of "special interest" he believed was creating pressure on the federal system. In his presidential campaign, he repeatedly called out other "special interests"—African Americans, the poor, organized labor—who had in fact delivered his thin margin of victory. But, as he liked to say, "I owe the special interests nothing."[70]

Within his first six months in office, Carter tasked the Advisory Commission on Intergovernmental Relations (ACIR) with reviewing all federal categorical grants to state and local governments, requesting proposals for consolidations and reform. Chaired by Robert E. Merriam, the son of the New Dealer Charles Merriam, the ACIR found some 442 categorical grants in operation at an annual cost of $74 billion. Merriam, like his father, had been active in Chicago politics, and he made a series of recommendations for sorting out the intergovernmental aid system. Merriam's ACIR report was little concerned with local battles or questions of equity. His commission recommended consolidating hundreds of grants into twenty to thirty categories of programs and to standardize application and reporting requirements across all programs. With the majority of the electorate in a cost-cutting mood but unwilling to see cuts to programs they valued, Merriam's approach harmonized with Carter's technocratic instincts: savings might be found in bureaucratic efficiencies and Carter's "zero-base" budgeting, not by cutting programs.[71]

The politics of such a slate of reforms, however, would prove more difficult. Carter had signaled support to the many groups now pressuring his administration: the pro-spending but anti-regulation planners and state executives; the mayors who eyed their governors with jealousy; and the community activists and advocates of minority or poor citizens who called for federal guarantees for local control and minority or community participation. In 1977, he called to reduce "the number and complexity of planning requirements," many of which, of course, were established to increase minority citizens' access to federal programs.[72]

Letters and telegrams poured into the White House from officials complaining about intergovernmental regulations. As one New York official put it, he experienced repeated "mixups, delays, and 'try again next time.'" "It's tough for a Democrat to criticize Washington," he wrote, but he had not received "a straight answer on our project."[73] Municipal officials, meanwhile, called for a greater share of spending to bypass governors.[74] Decatur, Georgia's mayor called for maximizing "the options of local governments," since mandates to target federal aid "often wasted money on areas which could not be rehabilitated." She sought a program that allowed local officials to start in better-off neighborhoods. In asking to be allowed to write off poor neighborhoods, the mayor closed with a plaintive appeal: "Please trust us to care about our communities."[75]

Still others, however, warned against trusting mayors to care for minority or impoverished communities. The Legal Services Community Development Task Force, a self-described "nationwide group of legal services attorneys and their low-income clients," urged the administration to push Congress to require "75% of CDBG funds to be spent for the benefit of low and moderate income persons and to specify that low income people must receive a portion of those funds in accord with the relative severity of their needs." Even the best estimates of the program's use for lower- and moderate-income Americans suggested funds were shunted away from these citizens. As they put it, "HUD guidelines must be precise ... since the qualitative guidelines

... allowed flagrant diversion of funds away from low and moderate income people."[76] Other community advocates echoed these arguments, engaging in professionally coordinated campaigns of telegrams, letter writing, op-eds, and media appearances. In one telegram to the White House, Gary, Indiana's mayor Richard Hatcher and Vernon Jordan charged that "for more than eight years ... we have seen the communities we represent ignored ... by the ... programs and policies supposedly being designed to benefit them." Carter had to ensure "structured citizen participation" and the "active involvement of non-governmental organizations with established records of working effectively with low-income and minority communities."[77] They sought guarantees of administrative enfranchisement.

Yet, the administration's progress on answering the philosophical questions of federalism, which was as much about Democratic Party maintenance as it was intergovernmental reform, remained halting and ambivalent.[78] Carter's task forces generated many memos and reports, but they yielded weak executive orders that simply drew further attention to problems of "administrative inefficiencies" without offering solutions. Carter regularly called for agencies "identify redundancy and gaps in coverage so that we can develop simpler, uniform requirements."[79] And he often passed the buck to executive agencies, urging them to eliminate, correct, or rewrite regulations. Eighteen months into his term, Carter's goal, he explained, was simply making the federal system as understandable and equitable "as human beings can make" it—as if it had been called to life on its own.[80] This was neither inspiring rhetoric nor a clear mandate.

Growing Apart

The White House's Conference on Balanced National Growth and Economic Development, a "national town meeting" held January 29 to February 2, 1978, was intended to spur new policy approaches to energy crises, stagnant wages, inflation, and global competition.[81] Two years of planning went into the conference, which included five hundred representatives of state and local government, business, academia, and citizens' groups. Conference director Michael Koleda had absorbed the nearly universal frustration with the confused and competitive state of intergovernmental relations, and he hoped the conference would generate a "breakthrough idea," something, *National Journal* reported, "as dramatic as the New Deal in the 1930s ... to make the federal system more responsive to real problems." Many businesspeople were among the delegates. As the president of a steel company from Jamestown, New York, put it, "I'm obviously no economic liberal," but he hoped the conference would galvanize new development policies. As the conference approached, the White House's goal was becoming simpler: to take weight off the president's shoulders. As Jack Watson put it, the administration hoped to convince state and local officials to "pull away from this notion that everything has to fall squarely on the lap of the federal government." There are "not enough dollars in the federal budget," said Watson, and "we must start acclimating people's thinking along those lines."[82] Instead, the conference became a venue for airing grievances about federal programs and interregional jealousies, and dreaming up spending programs better suited to alternative political realities and leaders.

The conference was dominated by the historical rivalry between northern and southern boosters and their political representatives, made fresh by the economic transformations of the 1970s. In the bicentennial year of 1976, two widely observed articles stirred the American bugbear of sectionalism. In May, *Business Week* published "The Second War Between the States," which highlighted the battle for industry the South appeared decisively to be winning. In June, *National Journal* published "Federal Spending: The North's Loss Is the Sunbelt's Gain," which poured salt into northern economic wounds by documenting how the region's taxes were redistributed to southern states.[83] The northern reaction was swift and drew upon long-standing southern approaches to organizing through federalism. Massachusetts congressman Michael J. Harrington organized the Northeast-Midwest Congressional Coalition to revise federal funding formulas.[84] "Regionalism, which everyone [in the North] decries," Harrington said, "has been a Southern specialty for the better part of the post-Civil War period."[85] The North, said the coalition's executive director, would emulate the SGPB's model of regional cooperation and federal lobbying: "We're trying to learn . . . how to make the federal government responsive." Said Harrington, the SGPB "taught us some valuable lessons . . . about long-range planning and what a region needs to do."[86] Since the New Deal, the South had enjoyed favorable federal funding status. "Now it's our turn," said Harrington.[87] More than two hundred northern and midwestern members of Congress joined Harrington's coalition. As cities such as Cleveland teetered on the brink of fiscal ruin, federal funds could quite literally be the difference between bankruptcy and solvency, between hiking property taxes and voters' rage and reelection. Cleveland's congressman Louis Stokes, Carl Stokes's brother, commissioned a Congressional Budget Office study arguing for routing federal spending to northern cities.[88] Northerners must "demand equity," an ally contended. New England newspaper editors complained that states paid $30 billion more in federal taxes than was returned in federal aid, services, or contracts.[89] Cleveland's *Plain Dealer* reported that Ohio paid "Uncle Sam $4.6 billion more in taxes than the state gets in return."[90] Cleveland's Growth Association denounced the disparities.[91]

Northern action paid quick dividends. In early 1977, when Carter and Congress expanded the $2 billion anti-recessionary local public works program, a vestige of Carter's campaign commitment to boosting employment, Northeast-Midwest Congressional Coalition members wrote allocation formulas favoring their states. New York's share soared from $232.9 million to $488.1 million, and Pennsylvania's rose from $83.3 million to $182 million. North Carolina's allotment, meanwhile, increased more modestly, from $28 to $43.8 million.[92] As northerners pressed their advantages, Harrington wrote a *New York Times* op-ed calling for a TVA-style energy and economic development program for the region.[93] In a political setting in which a national economic plan like Humphrey-Hawkins struggled to gain traction, however, a new TVA was hardly in the offing. For members of Congress, then, the most realistic goal was reorienting allocation formulas and tweaking the regulatory thrust of CDBGs, which was up for reauthorization in 1977.

The northern offensive and the prospect of rejiggered allocation formulas triggered a rapid redeployment of SGPB resources. Though its founders had conceived of the board as a postindustrial planning organization and not a lobbying outfit, in 1976–77 it quickly plunged into the battle over federal funding formulas.[94] Carter's successor as Georgia's governor, George Busbee, was SGPB chairman, and, in his keynote before the 1977 Southern Governors Association meeting, he joined the fight over federal funding. "Since the *National Journal* printed its now famous 'Sunbelt versus Snowbelt' article," he fumed, "it seems that everyone has been hellbent on creating another sectional war between the states." Busbee pressed his audience to action.[95] Southern papers duly printed his charges, portraying the region as an underdog in the fight for federal aid.[96] Busbee exhorted the governors, "you can pay Southern Growth Policies Board now, or pay the North later."[97]

Countermobilization by southern and western members of Congress forced a compromise, which only entrenched regional jealousies despite the fact that all regions received more funding. Brookings scholar and New

Federalism architect Richard Nathan brokered the solution. Nathan's "dual formula" created two tracks. The original formula emphasizing population growth and poverty remained, favoring the South and growing suburbs. But a second formula emphasizing pre-1939 housing stock and "growth lag" was added, which would expand CDBG spending overall and send more funds northward.[98] As *National Journal* put it, "Nobody loses absolutely under either proposal, but the degree of winning varies considerably."[99] The dual-track formula offered $2.24 billion in grants in FY1980 alone, with $1.18 billion set aside for cities with populations below fifty thousand.[100] The North, SGPB analysts reported, would see a bump of 40 percent in 1978 and 71 percent in 1980. Southern states enjoyed increases of just 7 percent and 12 percent, respectively. Under the dual formula, the board warned, "a great many Southern cities will lose in relative terms."[101] The normally mild-mannered Busbee proposed an alternative formula: "Let's go back to 1864 and count the number of burned homes we had in the state after Sherman went through Georgia."[102]

Elites' squabbles over relative losers and winners elided the reality that the poor were losing in much more material terms. Carter's HUD secretary Patricia Harris had proposed a "social-targeting" regulation in CDBG—had it passed, 75 percent of CDBG spending would have been directed to low- and moderate-income residents. But she faced a brick wall of opposition from local officials and members of Congress who believed that targeting undermined block grants' intrinsic flexibility.[103] The opposition also underscored the reality that poverty, like New Deal employment programs or Cold War defense spending before, served as a useful fig leaf for supply side state builders' publicly-underwritten growth agendas. Indeed, the ongoing reality of southern poverty became elites' fallback position for legitimizing federal favoritism. The rhetorical contrast with the board's optimism just a few years earlier was striking. "As long as the South has more people in poverty than any other part of the nation," said Busbee, and "as long as our family income is less than any other part of the nation, then we will work against all forms of domestic colonialism."[104] As an SGPB draft statement put it, "any notion that we in the South have arrived, that there are no more serious problems to be dealt with, that we can turn the keys to the federal treasury over to the other regions because we have no more need of outside help, is nonsense."[105] A 1978 SGPB report underscored the poverty rationale for boosters' designs: contrary "to rather widely held beliefs, the problem of poverty is more pervasive in the South than in the North," where one in five residents lived in poverty as opposed to one in ten in the North.¹⁰⁶ To maintain federal spending they would direct toward a high-tech, high-skill economy, the SGPB forcefully highlighted regional poverty.¹⁰⁷

Regional jealousies and demands on the federal government practically defined the Conference on Balanced National Growth and Economic Development, where debates centered on how to support differing regional approaches to development and local budget crunches; how to address the federal aid question; how to strike the proper balance between macroeconomic stimulus and micro-level, targeted structural policies; and how to design and implement proper federal regulations to ensure minority constituencies' access, empowerment, and support.¹⁰⁸ As the sessions unfolded, the Conference Advisory Committee's leaders lowered their expectations from forging a new national development agenda to simply getting the various groups to embrace a spirit of interdependence.¹⁰⁹ But without Carter's or Congress's support, the federal funds that might buy such comity were not forthcoming.

These dynamics were on display at the Conference's most anticipated panel, which featured George Busbee and New York senator Daniel Patrick Moynihan, each of whom had deep commitments to regionally inflected and historically informed visions of liberalism's supply side. Despite each region's abiding interest in federal aid, and despite the fact that both were Democrats, the fear and loathing generated by austerity, rivalry, and decades of competitive federalism had foreclosed a chance at constructive mutuality. Moynihan's remarks were notable for their sensitivity to the New Deal's commitment to federalism and economic development. "What will become of this tradition of national liberalism," he wondered, "if it turns out that the New Deal was a one-way street, that the policies of the New Deal brought about the downfall of the region which nurtured them and gave them to the nation? I will tell you what will happen. There will be a response of bitterness and reaction which will approach in duration if not in intensity the response of the South to defeat in what we now call the War Between the States."¹¹⁰ Moynihan understood that New Deal federalism and partnerships had offered a political and economic basis for interregional peace if not unity. Its withdrawal would produce gridlocked political institutions, interregional bickering, and economic volatility. Appearing with Busbee and Moynihan, Walt Rostow tried to offer a Cold War–style synthesis, urging officials to think of "the energy problem" as the opportunity "to make investments which would, in themselves," bring about "full employment." Rather than frame various forms of stimulus in terms of employment or industrial policies, he urged attendees to use some of that Cold War Keynesian alchemy: identify a pressing national need—new sources of energy—and quietly develop economic plans and investments under that guise.[111] In the crossfire between Busbee and Moynihan, Rostow's suggestions received little coverage. Instead, news outlets covered Busbee's overheated attacks on Moynihan's "fire and brimstone regionalism" as "bunk, pure bunk."[112]

On the eve of Reagan's election, northern and southern officials and their private-sector allies were organizing in lockstep to maintain the federal aid they felt they deserved. Americans of all stripes demanded this support beneath rhetoric that emphasized wasted spending on other regions, trumpeted racist or majoritarian grievances about welfare or unworthy recipients, shouted loudly about out-of-control property tax rates that funded programs and public authorities that seemed beyond taxpayers' control—all of which fed a sense that government was beholden to every special interest except one's own.

* * *

By January 1979 Carter and his advisers were in bunker mode. Their refusal to countenance greater spending meant they were under siege from essentially every group, class, and constituency whose expectations for government support the New Deal, New Frontier, Great Society, and New Federalism had raised. The administration, top aides wrote, struggled with how to manage "the intensity of interest" in the "various development assistance proposals by Congress, State and local officials and interest groups." They essentially shut down. Carter's advisers "agreed that there should *not* be consultations or discussions with Congress, the interest groups or the press on these matters, other than those scheduled" in a manner tightly controlled by the White House.[113] As the administration closed ranks and Carter contemplated a course-altering speech, aides reached out to allies for ideas. Among those who came to Washington was George Busbee. Carter's aides were so impressed with his proposals that they asked him to draft a memo for Carter, which he delivered in January 1979.

Busbee began by offering his political impressions, fresh on the heels of Michael Dukakis's surprising defeat by a radical anti-taxer in the Massachusetts Democratic primary elections. "While I am not panicking over [California's] Proposition 13" and the tax revolt in Massachusetts, "there is a . . .

growing concern on the part of the American people . . . that we curb both [government] growth and spending." "President Carter," Busbee predicted, "has approximately twelve months to produce sufficient results in slowing down government spending, in balancing the budget, and in constraining government growth . . . to run successfully for reelection."[114] Busbee saw firsthand in Georgia, too, the changing political mood.[115] In 1976, as frustration with government at all levels was hardening, Floyd County voters rejected a number of growth-oriented bond issues and ousted a number of incumbents. A long-standing Floyd County commissioner called it "the worst year in history for incumbents."[116] That year, too, Roy Knowles scored his first political victory, a seat on the Floyd County Commission.

Busbee's recommendations were clear: maximize cuts to "non-essential" federal spending to rein in inflation and develop a comprehensive sorting-out program for federal versus state versus local responsibilities. "What I am suggesting," he wrote, is "for the Federal government to either fully get in or get out of many of the existing national programs." New block grants could replace the bevy of federal categorical grants in education, social services, vocational training, and nutrition assistance; development programs offered "the most impressive area of consolidation." To implement these reforms, Carter would have to confront what Busbee called the "Federal Powers," a "triangle composed of the committee staffs in Congress, mid-level bureaucrats in the Federal government, and public interest groups" representing minorities and poor citizens, especially. Ultimately, "the candidate, republican or democrat, who captures these themes in his or her campaign will be the victor whether the race is a primary or a general election." On his copy of the memo, Carter scrawled a note to aides Jim McIntyre and Stu Eizenstat: "This is one of the best memoranda I've ever seen. . . . Assess for me how we can proceed."[117]

They urged caution. Busbee's suggestions contained "highly controversial" questions. Local officials "would strongly resist any" initiative that "was perceived to increase State control over Federal grants-in-aid that currently go directly to local government." Moreover, "minorities and the disadvantaged are even more skeptical about the responsiveness of State governments to their concerns" and would view shifting power to states "as a retreat from our commitment to the poor, the minorities and the disadvantaged." With more white voters supporting insurgent candidates like Roy Knowles, the president's support depended on turning out minority voters. In short, even pursuing "a study could be very damaging."[118] Carter yielded. But by failing to tackle these issues head on, either through boosted spending or with a more clearly conservative line, the administration lacked any political stance, especially in the face of challenger who offered a striking alternative to Carter's muddling-along federalism and mismanagement of the decade's distributional clashes.

Ronald Reagan's inauguration, noted incoming Coosa commission director C. D. Rampley, meant "we are apparently entering an era in which" the growth of government "will be curtailed, with the emphasis on planning and development shifted to state and local governments." He predicted the commission would "narrow its focus, operate in fewer and more defined areas of community and economic development."[119] As boosters across the country would discover, however, for Reagan, cutting "into the waste," "the needless federal programs," most often meant slashing antipoverty programs, threatening the very funding upon which boosters relied for so many development plans.[120] As the Reagan administration undermined federal aid, boosters would turn to state governments, where a new generation of Democrats was reinventing supply-side liberalism, the Democratic Party, and perhaps even government itself.

CHAPTER 9

Reinventing Democrats

Two years into his first term in the U.S. Senate, Colorado's Gary Hart described the dilemma facing a new generation of Democrats: by the second half of the 1970s, Americans had "healthy skepticism about Government's ability to solve every problem." Yet they also expect "Government to solve the problem[s]" but "not . . . administer" the solutions; "I don't know what you can do about that."[1] By then, Democrats, the party of good government, wrestled with the fact that the state itself was more hotly politicized and discredited than even during the 1950s' red scare when three-quarters of Americans still trusted government to do what is right "just about always" or "most of the time." By 1978, that figure had plunged below 30 percent.[2]

As liberal governance strained beneath the weight of its legitimacy crisis, New Democrats also developed a certain skepticism for programs and policies as usual, thanks, in part, to their wariness about certain interest groups—"special interests"—who competed for them.[3] Indeed, Republicans were not alone in highlighting waste and inefficiency in government, and, in the 1970s, some Democrats joined in racializing and discrediting social welfare programs, particularly Aid to Families with Dependent Children (AFDC). But those politics were also often at the cynical end of a wide, bipartisan, and frequently earnest spectrum of frustration with government's costs and ineffectiveness. A generational suspicion about traditional public programs hardened as younger liberals reckoned with the reality that even initiatives they supported were often underfunded, disjointed, and difficult to reform thanks to crosscutting intergovernmental administration and funding.[4] But rather than confront constitutional, fiscal, or capitalist root causes, New Democrats, rather like New Dealers, sought creative ways to work through and around the institutional and political status quo.

To restore Americans' faith in government, New Democrats would seek to reorient the means and ends of governance itself. They increasingly emphasized growth—technical, apolitical, efficient. Growth would be a solvent within which interest group clashes over political power and public programs might be diluted, delayed, or obviated entirely. They would even come to imagine their growth agenda, which in fact depended upon significant redistribution of public resources, as apolitical, indeed even *anti*-political. Soon, their frustration with government was matched by a newfound enthusiasm for entrepreneurial and increasingly postindustrial supply-side development policies.

In certain ways, these growth and investment-oriented initiatives echoed New Dealers' emphases on shaping private investment patterns, relying on decentralism, and working through private intermediaries. But, their new partners in high tech and financial sectors were considerably less labor intensive or locally rooted than were liberals' partners in earlier supply side initiatives. As New Democrats championed innovation and investment and developed publicly subsidized venture capital pools and entrepreneur incubator programs, they also raised funds from and rubbed shoulders with Wall Street financiers—perhaps even coming to identify with them. Indeed, their success in stimulating high-tech sectors introduced them to a world of entrepreneurs and an emerging "investment" mentality at a moment when inflation and high interest rates constricted private investment markets and public capacities. If midcentury liberals relied upon private actors to enhance and carry out the public good, New Democrats increasingly viewed private sector growth and entrepreneurialism as proxies for the public good.

Spurred along by the belief that proliferating state and local high-tech investment initiatives were working, New Democrats also began framing the updated tools of liberalism's supply side as "entrepreneurial" alternatives to discredited public "programs." As two leading liberal consultants argued, in contrast to rigid "programs," markets might be "self-correcting" since market "demand creates its own supply." If, as they explained, public programs "rarely die" even as they often "fail to meet the real needs of those they are intended to help"—they highlighted Head Start's failure to reach two-thirds of eligible families—market-based solutions, structured by government, might ebb and flow along with demand.[5] Liberal policy ideas became flecked with buzzy tropes like "entrepreneurialism," "competition," "innovation," "human capital," and "investment."

In a limited sense, such "marketized" discourse reflected its origins in postindustrial public-private partnerships meant to put a zippy gloss on public policies. But it also augured a significantly narrowed political imagination for the practice and purpose of government, mass democracy, and democratic accountability.[6] New Democrats possessed earlier generations' instinctual faith in capitalism, but they lacked a willingness to develop "programs" to protect citizens from its excesses. Along with public-private partnerships, New Dealers had also emphasized "cooperation" and pluralism—inherent was a sense of collective effort and jockeying toward consensus in which public resources played a boundary-setting role in securing the economic and social opportunities that might make democratic citizenship meaningful. New Democrats remained ostensibly committed to such social goods, but they increasingly believed that their delivery through public programs or entitlements was inevitably inefficient; pluralism had metastasized into special interest-group battles, driving the party's declining fortunes.

As they sought a way out of the interest-group politics of programs, New Democrats began to conceive of enfranchisement, especially for the poor, as primarily an economic rather than democratic condition. Rather than secure rights and social outcomes through the pluralistic interplay of democratic publics or expand opportunities for citizens' administrative enfranchisement, many New Democrats came to view market-based policies as ways to depoliticize the delivery of positive individual economic and social outcomes, limiting the democratic excesses they believed defined the post–civil rights era. The consultant David Osborne, a chief ally of the centrist Democratic Leadership Council, explained that, "unlike the 1960s, when the primary focus was on bringing the poor into the *political* process—through civil rights legislation and community organizing, and federal efforts like the Community Action Program—today's efforts focus primarily on bringing them into the *economic* process."[7] New Democrats were recognizing in market-based solutions a means of diluting and deflecting the confrontational, fiscally fraught politics of contested social policies. They were reconceptualizing citizens as entrepreneurs; taxpayers deserved returns on their investments; and market mechanisms and incentives or fees for services might even replace certain programs and regulations. Significantly, too, against President Reagan's efforts to outright destroy the social safety net and the welfare provisions in AFDC, they touted the relative progressivity and entrepreneurial ways in which they would reform and save liberal social commitments. In an age of widespread mistrust of government, the market became the solution to Hart's dilemma.

New Democrats' path to embracing a neoliberal, market-based social contract was paved by ostensibly good intentions winnowed down and transformed by both perceived and real limitations of government, Reagan's austerity, and a generational encounter with ascendant forms of financial capitalism and skepticism for certain interest group politics. Marketized growth politics described not only a set of policy tools but also an emerging ethos about democracy, governance, and rights, a fundamentally depoliticized vision of democratic participation that obscured just how hungrily in-groups—business constituencies chief among them—continued to consume public resources. In the allegedly "free market" 1980s, hundreds of millions of taxpayer dollars supported high-tech incubators, public venture capital funds, and more, all to perfect the "climate . . . for the entrepreneur."[8] In their emerging framework of "entrepreneurial governance," seemingly short-term tradeoffs in terms of social welfare entitlements or democratic accountability became increasingly acceptable compromises for liberals such as Bill Clinton, who foretold fantastic economic futures for all, just around the corner.

Tough Choices for Special Interests

Sometimes dubbed the "Watergate babies," the overwhelmingly white, male New Democrats who came to office in the mid-1970s confronted party "leadership badly out of touch, and a system of failing institutions," as Gary Hart complained in 1973 after managing George McGovern's failed bid for the presidency in 1972. This rising generation of liberals included Joseph Biden (b. 1942), Christopher Dodd (b. 1944), Charles Schumer (b. 1950), Paul Tsongas (b. 1941), and Timothy Wirth (b. 1939). Bill Clinton (b. 1946) narrowly lost a bid for Congress in 1974 before pursuing state office. Jerry Brown (b. 1938), Michael Dukakis (b. 1933), Hart (b. 1936), and Georgia senator Sam Nunn (b. 1938) also took office in the early and mid-1970s. As Hart argued, many believed that voters' affective concerns about government itself and the era's distributional battles more than any longstanding ideological or partisan commitments defined the emerging contours of American politics.[9]

It was in this context, and at a moment when government seemed fiscally incapacitated, that AFDC, popularly called "welfare," became an outsized lightning rod (compared to its slice of the federal budget), offering politicians an opportunity to focus a majority of voters' frustration on the costs of a program that benefited a narrow, racialized, and recently mobilized set of interests. Indeed, as activists sought to connect citizens to programmatic entitlements, between 1965 and 1970 alone, AFDC grew from 3.3 million to 7 million recipients. The costs associated with these entitlements were unevenly distributed across the country—California and New York accounted for 40 percent of the total increase in caseloads in the 1960s, and rising costs in those major media centers helped define the terms of national debate.[10]

Yet the discontents with AFDC cut across the ideological spectrum and had roots in the program's stingy provisions and intergovernmental administrative structures. Begun in the New Deal, liberals had never sufficiently funded or mobilized AFDC to support the number of citizens whose poverty entitled them to assistance.[11] In the 1960s, a potent left-leaning critique held that AFDC was a "miserly, ill-conceived destroyer of families" that encouraged men's abandonment because male-headed families were denied assistance. An emergent "antipoverty coalition" composed of welfare rights activists sought "fundamental income redistribution" that would underwrite a guaranteed income, regardless of marital status, in part to overcome local administrative impediments to aid.[12] Indeed, local officials from New York to Las Vegas threw up considerable administrative impediments to poor people's access to welfare.[13] Meanwhile, as poverty activists and feminists called attention to the growing necessity and, for some, desirability of women's wage work, an emerging cadre of feminist critics situated gainful employment, perhaps augmented by AFDC benefits, as the best guarantee for women's independence.[14] Among liberal and left activists of the late 1960s and early 1970s, then, welfare was viewed as insufficient, a disincentive for work and family formation, and too often undermined by local administrative intransigence.

Feminists and poverty activists were drowned out, however, by a bipartisan group of largely white men who defined the nation's welfare predicament in terms of different sorts of fiscal and moral crises. As welfare rights activists mounted successful grassroots legal strategies to overcome local barriers to deserving citizens' access to the program, growing numbers of welfare recipients meant state governments faced significant new costs in an era of already strained budgets. While New York's Republican governor Nelson Rockefeller instituted an 8 percent reduction of the welfare budget, California's governor Ronald Reagan pursued a different tactic. He would "purify" the system of those who "didn't belong." Because AFDC payments were generally well below subsistence levels, recipients often blended wage work and welfare, making fraud a "predictable, if not inevitable" fact of life on welfare.[15] As Reagan's administration rooted out fraud, he popularized a racialized association of welfare with criminal raids on the public treasury—here was his "welfare queen." By then, the welfare rights movement had gained footholds in the

Deep South, too. In Georgia, AFDC enrollees soared from just 74,757 in 1965 to 359,510 by spring 1975.[16] By 1976, and as a number of states with large urban populations pursued increasingly aggressive tactics to expose fraud, one poll found that 85 percent of respondents agreed that "too many people on welfare cheat by getting money they are not entitled to."[17]

Rather than focus on fundamental causes of poverty or the structural deficiencies of AFDC, politicians instead highlighted visible, proximate battles over budgets, bureaucracy, and special interests' access to programs. While Reagan and Republicans drummed up scandals and associated them with liberalism, liberals, too, signaled their commitments to rooting out public corruption and waste. Many Democrats joined conservatives in entrenching suspicions that public institutions were increasingly inefficient and captured by special interests. They emphasized the "tough choices" they would have to make, as Massachusetts governor Michael Dukakis explained in an interview with *Nation's Business*. Dukakis evinced a steely realism in frankly acknowledging government's limitations and citizens' responsibilities. Massachusetts was "paying dearly for our past spending habits, and no one is very happy about it." "If people on welfare have the capacity to work, then we ought to expect them to work." "The bottom line," he explained to a business readership, is "that hard budget choices have to be made"—for some.[18]

Senator Sam Nunn of Georgia, who would become an influential founding member of the Democratic Leadership Council (DLC), sharpened his political themes in the 1970s, focusing on government waste and special interests. His career illuminates a bridge between "New South" Democrats like Jimmy Carter and the incremental evolution of southern Democrats—their rejection of overt racism—but also the ways in which they continued to use antigovernment rhetoric that spoke volumes to racial conservatives. By 1965, Nunn, twenty-seven years old, was the president of Perry, Georgia's chamber of commerce, led the Middle Georgia Area Planning and Development Commission, and would soon win a seat in the state House. Like Carter, an early ally, Nunn was captivated by economic planning and the pursuit of federal development dollars. He became a lieutenant in Carter's state reorganization plan and spent the summer of 1971 visiting local elites frustrated by regulations and intergovernmental relations.[19] Like Carter, as Nunn sought higher office, he campaigned on his "conservative" bona fides. Nunn tied rising consumer prices and taxes to federal spending: "Cutting the budget and giving taxpayers a break," he said, "will give the Washington bureaucrats something useful to do for a change."[20] His campaign slogan was "Get Tough in Washington." Nunn secured endorsements from segregationists including George Wallace and unreconstructed racists Marvin Griffin and Herman Talmadge.[21] His politics resonated with New South Democrats and Jim Crow Democrats alike.

Nunn was part of a rising generation of Democrats who did not need Reagan's presidential election to recognize that attacking bureaucracy, welfare, and taxes was gaining political salience. By 1975, reforming welfare and saving revenues by securing paternal child payments had become hot button issues. Nunn worked closely with Senator Russell Long of Louisiana on a bill to authorize the IRS to support surveillance of parents who failed to provide for their children. Under the bill, states that failed to enforce child support obligations would lose federal AFDC funds.[22] The proposal was a political show of fiscal discipline in the form of class and race discipline. More broadly, Nunn illuminated government's cost and inefficiency. An early cosponsored bill would have required representatives supportive of new programs to "explain to their constituents that the effect of their vote requires the imposition of additional taxes."[23] Nunn partnered with Wisconsin senator William Proxmire to call attention to the high costs of big government, claiming that maintaining the bureaucracy "exceeds $8 billion a year." Proxmire demanded all federal agencies send him a copy of every form they used. When stacked up, he claimed, the Census Bureau's forms measured six feet.[24] By 1978, Senators Hart, Nunn, and Proxmire considered joining Republicans in seeking constitutional spending limits.[25] If these Democrats struggled to articulate an affirmative role for government, however, long-standing liberal commitments to economic growth and boosting fiscal capacities would provide a way forward. The Reagan administration's assaults on the welfare state would also bolster their sense of progressivity.

Reagan's *New* New Federalism

Ronald Reagan's attacks on welfare entitlements were part of a broader effort to overturn the New Deal by undoing its model of fiscal federalism. This was a far more revolutionary vision than most initially understood. Perhaps because he redeployed Nixon's "New Federalism" moniker, through which his predecessor had restored aspects of New Deal federalism, or perhaps because Americans tend not to think much about federalism at all, Reagan's initial calls for federalism reforms were viewed as less momentous than his tax cutting agenda.[26] As Reagan's staffers developed their federalism proposals, they delegated tax policy negotiations to Congress, where there was bipartisan enthusiasm for the project. Rather than check Reagan's fiscal program, congressional Democrats joined a bidding war over tax cuts.[27] The Economic Recovery Tax Act of 1981 (ERTA) moved swiftly through Congress, and its three-year, 23 percent reduction in federal income tax rates was the single largest tax cut in U.S. history. The administration also cut $35.2 billion from the federal budget, ending 400,000 Americans' AFDC benefits and slashing payments for another 279,000. One million Americans lost access to food stamps. Though some Democrats chafed at targeting programs for the poor, most agreed on the importance of reducing federal spending. Some 60 percent of the cuts came from antipoverty programs that only amounted to 18 percent of "universal" federal income maintenance entitlement programs such as Social Security, which went unscathed.[28] With the economy in recession, slashed budgets and taxes generated even greater subnational fiscal pressures and poverty. It seemed the dawning of a new political age: as *Newsweek* put it, "Rest in Peace, New Deal."[29]

Though Reagan had scored a major blow, it was not decisive. To truly unravel the New Deal, he would have to do more than starve the state; he would have to quash its fiscal federal structures—the ways national resource sharing supported state and locally administered programs. Reagan understood this. On February 18, 1981, he laid out his New Federalism agenda before a joint session of Congress, calling to "convert a number of categorical grant programs into block grants to reduce wasteful administrative overhead and to give local governments and States more flexibility and control." He engaged, too, in some critiques of bureaucracy in the style of Nunn and Proxmire, decrying the "7 million man and woman hours of work by State and local officials . . . required to fill out government forms."[30] Beneath these critiques of inefficient governance, staffers' guiding principle was restoring "power and authority and revenue sources back to state and local governments."[31]

Returning power, authority, and revenue to state and local governments sounded good to many veterans of the 1970s Sunbelt-Frostbelt wars. Indeed, Reagan's rhetoric recalled Nixon's New Federalism, which yielded general revenue sharing (GRS) and CDBGs, mother's milk for local governments and business associations.[32] GRS supplied an average of 8.5 percent of Georgia's local government revenue, and even Republican congressman Newt Gingrich believed "revenue sharing should be the last program we cut."[33] Gingrich's position was echoed in a U.S. Chamber of Commerce–conducted survey, which found "overwhelming support for the program" among local affiliates: 73 percent of local chambers supported its reauthorization.[34]

Reagan had no plans for the kind of cooperative federalism that had underwritten New Deal and Nixonian federalism. His "dream," as he put it, was "that the block grants are only a means to an end. And the end is that the [national] government, which has preempted over the years so much of the tax revenue potential in this country" would devolve as much fiscal and programmatic authority as possible back to the states and localities.[35] Block grants were simply a step toward complete devolution and destruction of federal programs, which state and local governments could choose to reestablish and fund on their own.[36] After Reagan called a group of governors to the White House to enlist their support, the *Atlanta Constitution* reported that his plans "wiped the smiles right off their faces." Reagan proposed ending all federal support for transportation, development, AFDC, and food stamps, among other programs.[37] As widespread anti-tax sentiment continued to simmer across the country, particularly anti-property-tax sentiment, the governors understood that Reagan's New Federalism would ruin them, fiscally and politically. Georgia's Democratic governor George Busbee, a keen supporter of a federal "sorting out" initiative, complained that Reagan blithely ignored the fiscal disparities between levels of government: "Does federalism just mean that states and localities should absorb all excess federal costs that stand in the way of balancing the federal budget?"[38]

Instead of moderating his position, Reagan ramped up calls for what he and his aides had begun calling a "swap": the federal government would take over the administration and funding of Medicaid in an effort to cut costs (and subsequently devolve the program back to states); and the states would administer and fund AFDC and other social welfare programs including food stamps.[39] This swap would encourage efficiency and accountability, said Reagan, because Americans were essentially rational, like businesses: "we've seen industries driven out of some States by adverse tax policies." "The built-in guarantee of freedom is our federalism . . . the right of a citizen to vote with his feet. If a State is badly managed, the people will . . . either use their power at the polls," Reagan said, "or they'll go somewhere else."[40] With such austere views of federalism, however, Reagan lost the governors' support as well as that of a majority in Congress.[41]

Having failed to overhaul federalism and, in 1983, forced to accept tax hikes, Reagan instead pursued haphazard spending cuts, injecting greater uncertainty into the intergovernmental system. While nearly all programs sustained cuts, with the exception of GRS, which expired in 1986, most survived thanks to bipartisan support for federal aid to localities; put another way, national politics was still shaped by local interests. Though wounded, New Deal federalism persisted.

Reinventing Supply-Side Liberalism

Ronald Reagan's assaults on the social welfare state and cooperative federalism are essential for understanding New Democrats' evolution toward embracing a more neoliberal social contract. Which is not the same thing as saying New Democrats borrowed their ideas from Republicans. They did not. Rather, their defense of the welfare principle and the importance of helping the poor informed both their ongoing sense of progressivity while their perceptions of fiscal limitations and wariness about special interests authorized experiments with reforms. Though AFDC survived the Reagan years, its future was far from certain. When its demise came at the hand of a Democratic president the following decade, however, it would not be because conservative ideas about welfare had won a decisive victory among liberals. Rather, it would be because, in the face of conservative critiques of welfare and efforts to limit taxation, New Democrats believed they had discovered winning approaches to reinventing government and reimagining the social contract. Many of those ideas emerged from liberalism's supply side.

In 1982, a number of self-consciously centrist Democrats sought to rebrand the party around a slate of new priorities. The first product of these efforts was a series of reports, *Rebuilding the Road to Opportunity*, prepared by members of the Democratic Caucus Committee on Party Effectiveness. It was an attempt to take a long, deep look at "the changing nature of the economy," its regional variations, and it culminated with calls for new "investments" and "partnership[s] among all sectors of the economy."[42] These Democrats framed long-standing social commitments to housing, the environment, crime, or national security in economic terms. Particularly influential in shaping the document were Representatives Richard Gephardt of Missouri, Gillis Long of Louisiana, and Tim Wirth of Colorado, who authored the volume's cornerstone report on long-term economic policy. Authors and staff members, many of whom would soon help create the Democratic Leadership Council (DLC), consulted with economists and economic thinkers, including Lester Thurow and Robert Reich, as well as "leaders of business, industry, and labor" and "governors ... and mayors."⁴³ Republicans' "trickle down" approach, they argued, was already discredited. It fell to Democrats to "rekindle the entrepreneurial spirit in America, to encourage the investment and the risk taking—in private industry and in the public sector—that is essential if we are to maintain leadership in the world economy."⁴⁴ While the document had little immediate impact, its significance lay in Democrats' thematic discovery of entrepreneurialism and their policy emphasis on boosting investments. They were discovering liberalism's supply side all over again.

Many political-economic analysts were coming to see the era's fiscal crises and unfinished economic transitions as symptoms of underlying crises of entrepreneurialism and innovation. The 1970s had been a decade of consultant-led disaggregation and reorganization as corporate conglomerates built in the 1960s spun off or closed down less profitable divisions. Meanwhile, finance for entrepreneurial businesses, whether early or late stage, ran up against constricted capital markets, soaring interest rates, and conservative investors. Some $170 million was invested in the fledgling venture capital market in 1969; by 1975, the figure was just $10 million. Simultaneously, the emerging shareholder value movement prioritized short-term profits rather than riskier, long-term investments in R&D. The result was a decline in private-sector innovation. New patents issued between 1971 and 1984 dropped 31 percent. Initial public offerings plunged as well: one thousand companies went public in 1969; just one hundred did so between 1973 and 1977. "No subject is more central to our hopes for the future," said William Simon, President Ford's treasury secretary, than the question of capital formation for innovation.⁴⁵ The so-called "Volcker Shock" of 1980 made the investment climate even worse. Appointed Federal Reserve chair by Jimmy Carter and retained by Reagan, Paul Volcker moved aggressively to curb inflation by raising interest rates. By the summer of 1981, the federal funds rate surpassed 19 percent. Inflation did fall, but soaring interest rates meant that capital for entrepreneurs and small businesses was expensive and scarce. Sam Nunn even tied his support for Reagan's tax cut to freeing capital for early-stage entrepreneurs, a logic that effectively echoed Walter Heller and John F. Kennedy's supply-side rationale for tax cuts twenty years earlier.⁴⁶ But tax cuts offered an imprecise approach to structuring supply-side investments. Active government might be necessary to steer capital toward innovative sectors and entrepreneurs.

Liberals also embraced entrepreneurial innovation because it promised to solve a nagging problem of the twentieth-century political economy. Southern governors had created the Southern Growth Policies Board (SGPB) to transition away from "smokestack chasing," a zero-sum race to the bottom in terms of wages and pollution. By the late 1970s, the SGPB called for a new "generation of... economic policies" in which the goal was supporting "local entrepreneurs" and diversifying local economic bases. "The 'grow your own' approach," had "the advantage of being other than a zero-sum game."[47] Interregional competition over public subsidies and escalating state and local tax incentives had defined regional battles throughout the twentieth century but had also bypassed many small, innovative businesses that might have taken off with a little financing or technical assistance. By the mid-1980s, SGPB executive director Stuart Rosenfeld underscored the need for governments to broker technology transfer and deliver patient capital—that is, to socialize the risks of innovation and commercialization. He offered the example of Japanese domination of the LCD television market, a technology developed in the United States that was lost because public officials lacked entrepreneurial vision.[48] While the entrepreneur has a long history of veneration in American life, *entrepreneurialism* as a social and political mindset and orientation toward public policy took off in the 1970s and 1980s.

Entrepreneurialism also harmonized with emerging social and cultural ideas about the relationship between state and market: calls for decentralism, and small-scale, "authentic" forms of commerce and politics flourished in the 1970s. If Sam Nunn reflected the southern branch of New Democrats, Robert Reich was characteristic of a strand emerging from elite institutions of higher education where young leftists and liberals critiqued the Vietnam War and the machinelike bureaucratic state. Interviewed for a *Time* feature on the "cynical idealists" of the graduating class of 1968, Reich, a Dartmouth graduate, imagined "putting the political decisions back down where the people are—making more room for self-initiative and creativity." Reich described himself as against "status quo-ism" and was skeptical of those who were blindly "loyal to an abstract group."[49] This outlook reflected a generational mood that also suffused movements for community development, black capitalism, and "moral capitalism," which critiqued prevailing institutions and imagined new political formations grounded in human-scale economies.

Reich would become a leading member of a group of economic thinkers who rediscovered and reinvented supply-side liberalism. He joined Harvard's Kennedy School of Government after studying antitrust at Yale Law School and a stint in Carter's Federal Trade Commission. As he became a public intellectual, Reich argued that the major institutions of the American economy—government, corporations, and labor—had become too large, rigid, and beholden to entrenched interests to foster entrepreneurial innovation. Corporate executives were "paper entrepreneurs," pioneering innovative legal strategies to avoid taxes and regulations, externalize costs, and horde profits.[50] With Ira Magaziner, a business consultant with experience in state-level postindustrial policies, Reich published *Minding America's Business: The Decline and Rise of the American Economy* (1982). They called for a forceful new national industrial policy, one that might update and rationalize the existing decentralized and defense-oriented systems, which they derided as "industrial policy by default." Not since Alvin Hansen's heyday had such influential economic thinkers advocated aggressive government economic planning and restructuring of private investments. Reich also drew sharp contrasts with Reagan's tax-cutting approach to the supply side, envisioning instead a "truly 'supply side' series of policies" that systematically "address[ed] the pattern of investment, the mechanisms for industrial transitions, and the development of human resources."[51] In his book heralding the New Democrats, *The Neoliberals*, Randall Rothenberg described "supply-side liberalism" as "policy that promotes investment, cooperation, and the use of market forces" to boost national competitiveness.[52] The economist Lawrence Klein published "The Supply Side" in the *American Economic Review*, warning that traditional macroeconomic "demand oriented model[s]," including tax cuts, were ill-suited to stimulating new sources of energy and innovation.[53]

With *Rebuilding the Road to Opportunity*, then, New Democrats hoped to take command of supply-side policies at a moment when an industrial policy debate captured national attention thanks to Senator Edward Kennedy's presidential primary challenge of Jimmy Carter. Kennedy's plan for a $1 billion American Reindustrialization Corporation made industrial policy the "year's hot economic topic," the *New York Times* reported.[54] Kennedy's emphasis on traditional industries was backed by leading labor organizations. But a range of other interests also urged government to take a more assertive role in shaping sectoral economic developments, especially as global competition surged from Germany and Japan, both of which operated robust industrial policies. A broad range of corporate executives and business association leaders, including even the vice president of the archconservative National Association of Manufacturers, weighed in affirmatively.[55] *Rebuilding*'s authors called for "strategic" investments in emerging "service and information" sectors led by a congressional "commission on capital formation" and an economic cooperation council, made up of leaders of business, labor, and academia, to work with federal officials to oversee some $20–30 billion in targeted investments in new sectors and worker retraining.[56]

Private-sector support for public investments and planning also reflected the fact that capital itself was now the inducement business sought from government—in addition, of course, to R&D and technology transfers, land preparation, infrastructure subsidies, contracts, and public insurance of private investments. Writing in the *New York Times*, Lehman Brothers officials called for government to provide "patient capital" for innovative firms. As they wrote, "venture capitalists are not very venturesome" and "rarely back companies that cannot go public within two or three years." They envisioned "a national development bank ... accelerat[ing] the transition from invention to commercial application," which had been so hampered by tight venture capital and other investment markets in the 1970s.[57] Even tiny Rome, Georgia's chamber of commerce argued that government must "make sure that venture capital is available" since "small business and rural entrepreneurs often have trouble securing loans" in the high interest rate environment of the early 1980s.[58]

Advocating a national postindustrial policy, however, created some cognitive dissonance for Democrats, many of whom spent the previous decade describing government's inefficiencies and ineffectiveness. They tried to finesse distinctions between supporting high technology but not "technocracy"; they asserted the "national interest" but rejected definitions of the nation grounded in "the sum of special interests"; they championed industrial policy while evincing skepticism about government's efficacy.[59] Perhaps not surprisingly, postindustrial policy's momentum stalled in Washington.

Meanwhile, state and local officials were seizing the initiative. Belden Hull Daniels, founder of Boston's Economic Innovation International, was an early champion of socially responsible investing, or, as he later defined it, "building ... privately capitalized innovative institutions to accomplish public purposes."[60] In the mid-1970s, Governor Michael Dukakis tapped Daniels to serve on Massachusetts's Capital Formation Task Force, which recommended creating the Massachusetts Technology Development Corporation (MTDC), a *public* venture capital fund. Capitalized with federal and state resources, the MTDC took equity stakes in high technology and computing startups with the goal of generating jobs and tax revenues in struggling communities. By the mid-1980s, the MTDC was widely heralded and self-sustaining: the state no longer needed to deliver subsidies. By then, too, the MTDC debuted a new partnership with the Pension Reserves Investment Board, in which the MTDC invested $2 million of state employees' pension reserves in early-stage technology companies. The Massachusetts AFL-CIO even grew interested in the venture capital game, contemplating "privatizing" and managing its own pension-reserve-backed product development fund in which labor and the state could invest. As a consultant put it, "if we are successful, we shall have created a permanent financial institution to channel capital to traditional manufacturing," which means "supporting the jobs they provide, as well as generating revenues to the state"—in other words, workers would own the means of production.[61] Nationally, meanwhile, Daniels helped establish twenty-six public venture capital funds that delivered some $3.2 billion in public and private capital to entrepreneurs.[62]

As officials pursued innovative new entrepreneurial investment policies, they often relied upon the expertise and personnel of an earlier era. Georgia Tech's Advanced Technology Development Center captures this phenomenon. In 1979, Governor Busbee instructed Georgia Tech's Engineering Experiment Station to study the state's scientific and technological assets and their potential for growth in new, entrepreneurial sectors. After visiting Silicon Valley and North Carolina's Research Triangle, Georgia Tech experts recommended creating an "incubator" for "a community of advanced technology companies in Georgia." The center's founders understood their project as a high-tech update of the older APDC–Georgia Tech partnerships.[63] Wayne Hodges, the center's founding director, even began his career at an APDC. As he recalled, Rome's APDC was the "genesis of everything." Despite whatever paradigm-shifting gloss politicians sought to attach to the efforts, many of the people doing the work understood their efforts as extending initiatives with roots in midcentury economic planning.[64] By the spring of 1984, Georgia Tech's incubator had "graduated" six companies, and thirty more were in residence.[65] Among the most successful graduates was Digital Transmission Systems whose high-speed modems led to a multimillion-dollar contract with telecommunications giant MCI. Spurred by local officials and business, the Advanced Technology Development Center established branches across the state.[66] One rural chamber called a prospective office "a tremendous asset" for meeting the "unique needs and concerns" of community entrepreneurs.[67] A 1985 McKinsey report celebrated Georgia Tech as "a national model for technology transfer."[68] In 1988, a businesswoman in Rome cheered Georgia Tech's assistance in terms that suggested that she, like earlier generations of businesspeople, had naturalized the public's role in private development—"The great American free enterprise system continues to tell us: 'only in America, and better still . . . IN GEORGIA,' are these ventures not only possible, but ultimately successful!"⁶⁹

As the Reagan administration destabilized intergovernmental aid, Georgia also created capital formation programs, since smaller, particularly rural firms, struggled to secure private credit or investment capital.⁷⁰ Working with Belden Hull Daniels, Georgia created a publicly subsidized fund to support entrepreneurs unlikely to receive "private financing."⁷¹ A chief advocate used a New Deal analogy to sell the program: the state would pair direct subsidies with "long-term [seven- to twenty-year] loans by local banks and offer them at sub-market rates." He called it a "sort of Fannie Mae for [development] finance." Firms in rural areas would especially benefit as Georgia's VC-like fund made the state akin to "a private investor in a seed capital fund . . . designed to make a market rate of return on investment, not to make grants."⁷² In a poll of businesspeople, the Business Council of Georgia found overwhelming support: 96 percent "agree[d] that 'managing growth through coordinated planning at the local, regional, and state level is important to Georgia's future.'"⁷³ By the mid-1980s, many states had begun blending New Deal–style risk abatement measures with more aggressive entrepreneurial investments to create new businesses and markets.⁷⁴ In the ostensibly "free market" eighties, governments, most often led by Democrats, took a more interventionist stance in the workings of the market than New Deal or Cold War liberals ever had. Many New Democrats soon viewed entrepreneurial investment initiatives as more than just a way to create jobs or restore government solvency—the entrepreneurial, investment-oriented mindset might provide a model for remaking the party and reinventing government.

Reinventing Government

In 1985, a cohort of New Democrats created the Democratic Leadership Council to raise their status within the national party and rebrand the party with entrepreneurial growth at its center. While Ronald Reagan's landslide 1984 reelection was the catalyst, the outlooks and instincts, interests and agendas the DLC represented reflected deeper roots in the party, particularly in its southern, white, growth-oriented branch. Despite losing national influence since the 1950s, southern Democrats, especially governors, continued to thrive at the state level where they were captivated by the possibilities of post-industrial development policies. DLC member and Arkansas governor Bill Clinton was among the many politicians who hired Belden Hull Daniels, and Clinton created the full range of entrepreneurial development initiatives. The Arkansas Industrial Development Corporation used $5 million in annual CDBGs to deliver loans to small and medium-sized businesses; the Arkansas Development Finance Authority floated development bonds and made loans to entrepreneurs; the Arkansas Science and Technology Authority delivered millions in annual state grants to development-related research at universities and colleges, and, by 1988, was operating four "rural, community-based incubators" to support homegrown entrepreneurs.[75] As Clinton put it in 1985, "The process of . . . restructuring our economic base cannot occur overnight," but he had made a start.[76]

Governor Charles Robb, who led Virginia's postindustrial policy, announced plans for the DLC at the National Governor's Association meeting in February 1985, a sign that Robb, along with Governors Bruce Babbitt of Arizona and Robert Graham of Florida sought to boost the voices of state executives in the party. Ten governors were founding members, as were Senator Sam Nunn (Georgia) and Representative Richard Gephardt (Missouri), its first chairman.[77] Throughout 1985, DLC members, including Clinton, conducted a "political road show—a touring company of like-minded" politicians who appeared at "lunches or dinners with business leaders and party activists, meetings with editorial boards, press conferences and fundraisers."[78] Their primary concern, said Nunn, was that the party had "moved away from mainstream America in the 1970s." They would "move it back."[79]

If DLCers emphasized "mainstream" values, their accent on investments—in both entrepreneurial sectors and in the DLC itself—led them to spend a lot of time hobnobbing with Wall Street financiers. They formed an outreach organization, NETWORK, to cultivate private-sector partners and raise funds, particularly from this economically and culturally ascendant set. At one New York City NETWORK event, Nunn discussed American foreign policy as well the DLC's broader growth agenda. The event was hosted by Goldman Sachs partner Barrie Wigmore and was attended by more than forty New York–area NETWORK members. Wigmore and a Goldman Sachs colleague would become board members of the DLC's Progressive Policy Institute (PPI), its in-house think tank. Other New York events were hosted by Robert M. Brown III, managing partner of Shearson Lehman Hutton and a charter member of NETWORK.[80] While it is tempting to presume that financiers and their donations—which were becoming significant—were driving the DLC's policy positions, the opposite was also the case: as New Democrats emphasized investments and entrepreneurialism that might boost the real economy, they attracted the attention and resources of Wall Street.[81] After having developed venture capital funds, politicians such as Clinton may have even seen something of themselves in Wall Streeters, a very different class and scale of businessperson as compared to supply side liberalism's historical partners. There were other material reasons for their growing partnerships: business and political action committee fundraising, which, historically, had been rather evenly distributed between the parties, began skewing heavily toward Republicans in the late 1970s. As organized labor's power waned, Democrats sought any fundraising advantages they could find. These relationships would only deepen over time as New Democrats also recruited former Wall Streeters to serve in administration positions in hopes of boosting not only the high tech but also financial sectors.[82]

Despite the long history of liberalism's supply side, the extent to which new generations of business elites and liberals alike naturalized and submerged those commitments abetted the sense that New Democrats' emphasis on the supply side was novel—instead, it was their increasing emphasis on particular sectors and their suspicion of special interests that was distinctive. New Democrats sought to distance themselves from midcentury liberalism's association with bureaucracy and the interplay of interest groups, which earlier liberals venerated as pluralism. In this sense, Randall Rothenberg's *The Neoliberals* was not simply an account of the new generation; it also reflected and curated their collective, partial memory of New Deal and midcentury liberalism. "Loss of faith in the private sector," he explained, "allowed the New Dealers freedom to indulge in solutions requiring absolute federal authority." As he put it, "centralization, macroeconomics, interest-group politics—these were and are the chief elements of modern liberal ideology." By the 1970s, the "forty-year-old group imperative still existed—something *had* to be done about the blacks, something *had* to be done about the elderly.... But as more slices were cut from the economic pie, few noticed that the pie itself was shrinking."[83] All that was left, Rothenberg lamented, were greedy groups picking at the bones of a sclerotic state.

Anxiety about "special interests" thus became the mean underbelly of and politically safe proving ground for New Democrats' optimism about entrepreneurial growth. Indeed, PPI consultant Will Marshall called for disassociating the party from special interests. New Democrats must become champions of fiscal discipline and address the fact that an "explosion of new rights and entitlements"—including rights to "remedial and college education, to abortion, to equal pay for women, to child and health care, to free legal counsel, to public facilities for the disabled, and many, many more"—meant "higher taxes to pay for public transfers to 'special interests.'"[84] Lester Thurow urged Democrats to reject, as Rothenberg put it, the "appeasement of group interests ... via transfer payments."[85] As Charles Robb lamented, the party was "preoccupied with wealth redistribution." All of this, of course, obscured the fact that these positions *did* reflect a clear stance on distributing resources and power, which reinforced and entrenched existing inequalities by framing public support for private-sector growth as somehow fundamental or even apolitical.

Their focus on economic growth and denigration of special interests led critics within the broader party to charge DLCers with purposeful neglect of poverty, labor, and civil rights. Some mocked them as the "white male caucus." As Jesse Jackson quipped, the DLC rather stood for "Democrats for the Leisure Class." DLCers shot back that their approach was about returning to foundational growth policies. New Jersey Democrat Bill Bradley was explicit: "social issues *are* secondary ... to the health of the economy."[86] As Clinton put it, for too long the "party has been too concerned with dividing the fruits of our labors when the real need is to increase them."[87]

In intramural battles over liberalism's social commitments, entrepreneurialism moved easily from describing policies' outcomes to describing an approach to reforming government. A report of the Council of State Planning Agencies (CSPA), a research and lobbying organization of state planners, argued that reforming government to support new sectors might inspire voters' faith in government not only by yielding public wealth but also generating models of efficient, entrepreneurial governance.[88] Clinton worked so closely with the CSPA that one commentator described Arkansas as "something of a laboratory" for economic planners and government reformers.[89] Inspired by the work of economists like David Birch and Lester Thurow, the CSPA published a series of policy briefs that urged governments to use entrepreneurialism and markets as a model for reforming or retiring traditional "programs" on behalf of a broader project of reinventing government.[90]

In the 1980s, the writers and consultants David Osborne and Ted Gaebler researched a book with precisely that title. *Reinventing Government: How the Entrepreneurial Spirit Is Transforming the Public Sector* chronicled the widespread but largely ad hoc adoption of the entrepreneurial mentality among public officials in the 1980s (Clinton provided the forward to Osborne's 1988 book *Laboratories of Democracy: A New Breed of Governor Creates Models for National Growth*). Osborne and Gaebler championed what they called the "investment mentality"—a new way of thinking for public servants that "maximize[s]" the "long-term return" on government spending. They opened a chapter titled "Enterprising Government: Earning Rather Than Spending" with an epigraph from a former California city manager: "The tax revolt . . . is here to stay. We have to guarantee future revenues by creating new revenue sources." The chapter detailed examples of how public employees began to "think about revenues" and profits. Beyond high-profile examples like Los Angeles' $225 million windfall from the 1984 Olympics, they cataloged case studies of subcontracting, private-sector sponsorships, creative land acquisitions and leasing, profit-sharing arrangements through private contracts and partnerships, public and private joint financed businesses (like hotels, a favorite use of Urban Development Action Grants, described in Chapter 10), and revenue bond sales. The new paradigm was rooted in a vision of active if frugal government that developed the "habit of gauging the return on their spending as if it were an investment."[91]

Reinventing Government culminated with Osborne and Gaebler's call for "market-oriented government," which they contrasted with "programs"—"administrative mechanisms" run by "public employees, that spend appropriated money to deliver a service." The problems with "programs," they argued, were many: they were designed for constituencies who may not need them rather than "customers" who might opt into the service. They fostered bureaucratic "turf" and clientelism, which generated fragmentation, interest groups, and rigidity. They rarely "measure[d] results," self-corrected, or "die[d]." And they were often underfunded and failed to achieve economies of scale necessary to meet their goals. Entrepreneurial, market-based policies, however, might yield a state whose initiatives waxed and waned along with need, perhaps shedding divisive democratic battles over regulatory targeting and funding. They held up the FHA's creation of thirty-year fixed-rate mortgages as an example of solving "a problem generated by the market" by "*restructur*[ing] that market."[92] By restructuring the mortgage market with insurance rather than direct subsidies, the FHA created a scalable social and economic good that tracked demand. User fees for services could replace taxes across a wide range of domains. Marketized governance, they proclaimed, was prone neither to stagnation nor bloat, might evolve alongside needs, and offered greater efficiency and return on investments for taxpayer-shareholders.

Reimagining Poverty

Despite the proliferation of entrepreneurial policies, Democrats were at least nominally committed to using government to raise up the poor and marginalized. And many places and people were being left behind in the 1980s. Critiquing welfare and other programs could only get them so far—as the DLC's Al From explained, they had to find "new ways to further" the party's "first principles."[93] Indeed, following the Volcker Shock, construction starts and car sales nose-dived, pushing unemployment past 10.8 percent in December 1981. While Volcker allowed interests rates to fall alongside inflation, the employment recovery was uneven—the unemployment rate for African Americans did not peak until 1983, when it hit 21 percent. The Fed's high interest rates also invited foreign investments in U.S. bonds, which strengthened the dollar, making foreign goods cheaper for American consumers, putting domestic manufacturers at a disadvantage. Americans still employed in manufacturing faced pressure to accept lower or stagnant wages, a fate preferable to the many thousands laid off as firms closed down or moved overseas.[94]

In glittering capitals such as Atlanta, deep racial poverty and underemployment meant thousands of citizens lived in the Sunbelt's shadows, unable to find work in emerging, higher-paying tech or service economies. These shadows were cast across rural communities, too. In Georgia, where the unemployment rate peaked at 8.6 percent in January 1983, academics and journalists warned that "two Georgias" were rapidly diverging, cleaving the Atlanta boom region from the rest of the state.[95] The Atlanta area enjoyed wage levels above the national average, the only counties in the state that did so.[96] By the middle of the 1980s, only fourteen of 159 counties in the state had a per capita income above the state average, suggesting just how much of an outlier was the Atlanta region. The divergence would become more extreme: between 1985 and 1992, nearly three hundred manufacturing plants, predominantly in smaller cities and rural communities, closed down, wiping out some 38,000 jobs.[97] These dynamics had stark racial dimensions, reflecting regional trends. In 1980, 34.1 percent of southern African Americans lived below the poverty line, compared with just 10.2 percent of white families.[98] For much of the 1980s, in Atlanta, the black unemployment rate was double that of whites.[99] As the "new" economy took off, the poor constituted a particularly "significant underutilized human resource," as the SGPB put it in marketized terms. The "hope for the large adult population living in the South," was new investments in "training work forces for the increasingly sophisticated . . . jobs . . . in services and manufacturing." "Most importantly," they argued, fusing the economic and social, these investments would be "the gift of the future for Southern children."[100]

Perhaps no politician more thoroughly merged the themes of poverty, education, and entrepreneurialism than Bill Clinton. Governor Clinton positioned public school reform as a foundational piece of the broader development agenda that he hoped would rapidly modernize Arkansas's economic base. But, in his first term, allies lamented, Clinton took on too many powerful interests.[101] He lost his reelection bid to a Republican who pilloried his spending amid a recession.[102] In 1982, though, voters returned Clinton to office, and he focused on education reform. In a state with adult functional illiteracy rates reaching 25 percent, Clinton emphasized adult education since, as one staffer explained, any high-tech job training programs would fail to reach "a whole base of people out there" who struggled to read. By 1986, adults composed nearly 15 percent of high school degrees awarded in Arkansas.[103]

As his star rose, Clinton secured leadership positions in regional and national organizations, helming the SGPB in 1985–86. If southern underdevelopment had been the nation's No. 1 economic problem in Franklin Roosevelt's day, for Clinton, the problem was pockets of poverty amid abundance. Clinton appointed the SGPB's Commission on the Future of the South led by former Mississippi governor William Winter. As Winter put it, "there remains that other South, largely rural, underedeucated, underproductive, and underpaid that threatens to become a permanent shadow of distress." Their mission, Clinton wrote, was "to mobilize support for those public policies and public-private partnerships which will increase the per capita income, reduce poverty, and reduce unemployment for Southerners by 1992."[104]

Like many southern Democrats before him, Clinton was learning to frame poverty as an economic opportunity. Clinton and Winter's commission report, titled *Halfway Home and a Long Way to Go*, was the product of working groups focused on human resource development, technology and innovation, and government structure and fiscal capacity. The report began by lamenting that too many southerners "can read the ripeness of a tomato or the sky's forecast of rain, but not the directions for installing new machinery." The South "must decide how to rescue those Southerners left behind" by plugging them into innovative sectors. The commission featured varieties of supply-side stimulus, including "the economic development role of higher education"; enhancing "the South's capacity to generate and use technology";

fostering "new economic development strategies aimed at home-grown business and industry"; and improving "the structure and performance of state and local governments." Clinton established the board's Southern Technology Council (STC) to unite the "technological and scientific resources of business, government, labor, and educational institutions" in order to "contribute to technology based development."[105] The STC established a regional consortium to "expand" the abilities of "technical and community colleges" to support entrepreneurs' and workers' ability to adopt "new process technologies and innovations."[106] Funded largely by such venerable supply-side liberal institutions as the Tennessee Valley Authority and the Appalachian Regional Commission, the STC would help rural regions pursue the high-tech economy and, to a lesser extent, help workers adapt to the innovative new environment.[107] In terms of structuring private investments and innovation, Clinton's supply-side liberalism stood on the shoulders of earlier liberal institutions and ideas.

But Clinton's approach to poverty marked a significant conceptual break with New Deal and midcentury liberalism. Rather than guarantee public employment or envision growth as sustaining forms of security that might shield Americans from the ravages of poverty and markets, Clinton framed the individual entrepreneurial capacities of poor people themselves as the ultimate solution for poverty. Clinton understood that education and new high-tech, service, or financial sectors would never deliver sufficient employment for the many adults in rural communities where those sectors were unlikely to settle. An experiment in entrepreneurialism in Chicago's South Shore neighborhood offered a possible solution. In the 1970s, community development advocates sought to overcome the limitations of private lending and public programs that failed to deliver affordable capital for small businesses or home rehabilitation. ShoreBank, as they called their "microlending" initiative, won support from the Ford Foundation, which arranged for Shore-Bank's founders to serve as consultants to a similar endeavor in Bangladesh. Muhammad Yunus established the Grameen Bank in 1983, and within a couple of years, his program, which emphasized lending to women, operated 226 branches serving 3,600 villages. Invited by ShoreBank's founders, Bill and Hillary Clinton met Yunus in Washington, D.C., in 1986. As Bill Clinton later put it, "the parallels" between Yunus's efforts in Bangladesh and rural poverty in Arkansas were "obvious."[108]

The very next week, Yunus flew to Arkansas where he and the Clintons toured Pine Bluff, a city suffering high unemployment and capital flight.

They remarked at the similarities between Bangladeshis and Arkansans, particularly their can-do spirit. But they also elided essential differences, especially the fact that Arkansas's population density—an entrepreneur's customer base—was about 1 percent of Bangladesh's.[109] Nevertheless, in 1988 Governor Clinton established the Good Faith Fund with $500,000 in seed capital from the Ford and Levi Strauss Foundations. The fund opened in Pine Bluff, whose surrounding counties were among the nation's poorest. Like Grameen, the fund offered small loans with exceedingly high interest rates. Yet, in its opening years, when it financed "snack wagons and catering firms," car washes and silk-screen printing shops, the fund saw high rates of defaults. The Clintons accentuated the positive. Hillary Clinton, who served on the fund's board, described the initiative as "the best method we found after looking around the world for a solution accessible to the people who need help the most." The program's twenty-eight-year-old director Julia Vindasius, whom the Clintons recruited from ShoreBank, was more circumspect: "I don't imagine the bulk of our borrowers will be able to support themselves full time with these businesses right away."[110]

Yet, it would be imprecise to view these developments in purely cynical terms. Microlending programs enabled the Clintons to tout their support for single minority mothers in ways they believed transcended questions about black family formation, pathology, and female wage-earning that had fueled criticism of welfare and the War on Poverty. Entrepreneurship highlighted poor women's economic agency rather than dependency.[111] They might even become engines of community development. This entrepreneurial reframing of the poor was amplified by influential economists and scholars, such as Harvard Business School's Michael E. Porter, who later published "The Competitive Advantage of the Inner City." Far from pathologically dependent, the poor were "industrious and eager to work," Porter argued. "In fact, there is a real capacity for legitimate entrepreneurship among inner city residents." But much of that energy had been "channeled into the provision of social services" by "social, fraternal, and religious organizations"—put another way, poverty was the cost of misspent energies by the so-called "special interests." The key would be "redirect[ing] some of that talent and energy" away from interest-group squabbles and "toward building for-profit businesses and creating wealth."[112] The Clintons joined middle-class feminists in arguing that welfare disempowered women, while "self-employment, especially home-based businesses" offered "women a way to balance the demands of work and family."[113] Whether single mothers could find the time and energy to nurture children and businesses while servicing high interest loans ultimately redounded to the scope of their entrepreneurial spirit.

New Democrats were also increasingly confident that using government to structure varieties of entrepreneurial economic activity—whether personal or business—*did* offer a sharp contrast with Reagan's assaults on the social safety net. Yet if Reagan's vision of the market was a space freed from public responsibilities or social obligations, a different dynamic defined the ideological drift of New Democrats, in which the language of social progress, of democracy itself, was often collapsed into and used to legitimize their emerging economic agenda. Entrepreneurial rationale and market metaphors suffused their entire social vision. SGPB staffers championed "development investing" or "social investing," frames meant to encourage officials to sell "social objectives" in terms of their market-making possibilities and vice versa—in one case highlighting the developmental potential of making riskier investments with state pension funds.[114] Stuart Rosenfeld urged officials to frame primary and secondary schools as growth engines, marketizing the value of schools. "Once schools are perceived as a way to create and hold jobs and as contributing to local development," Rosenfeld wrote, "cities and towns may think differently about bond issues and school taxes."[115]

The neoliberal political rhetoric of "human capital" also exemplified the entrepreneurial "marketization" of economic security—that is, explaining the political or social value of work in terms of carefully cultivated personal characteristics or individual assets that also stimulated market expansion. In 1988, while advocating greater spending on education, Clinton waved an edition of *Business Week*, its cover story titled "Human Capital."[116] Robert Reich argued that "human capital"—"people, their skills and education"—was the "centerpiece" of Clinton's entrepreneurial "philosophy" of politics.[117] While New Democrats may have understood these marketized frames as essential for legitimizing social spending, this rhetoric also revealed the narrowing of the liberal social and moral imagination—individuals would raise themselves up by fitting themselves in to entrepreneurial initiatives, and social programs were legitimate primarily in service of this economic vision.

In contrast to the mythologized "bleeding heart" redistribution of earlier liberal social initiatives, New Democrats were coming to believe that economic and fiscal realism—Dukakis's "hard choices" and Nunn's "get tough" provisos—provided sturdier justifications for liberalism's social commitments than did redistribution or direct social welfare spending. As Reich argued in his 1983 book *The Next American Frontier*, rather than prioritize social justice to achieve a more equal or expansive economy, social justice must flow from growth. "Social concerns," Reich argued, "are the ends that economics seek to serve. It is perverse to relegate them even implicitly to a separate and subordinate status."[118] Yet, New Democrats were doing just that by conflating economic and social ends while privileging entrepreneurial policies. In his 1988 book *Laboratories of Democracy*, David Osborne included an entire section devoted to "The Lessons" of state-level economic innovation in the 1980s: "The First Agenda" was creating economic growth; "The Second Agenda" was "bringing the poor into the growth process."[119] Government's role no longer necessarily included providing a baseline of protection or support from the market's excesses. The state must prepare the poor to meet the market.

Unlike social spending on education or job training, then, AFDC appeared less and less compatible with entrepreneurialism. In the new world of markets and entrepreneurial poor people, welfare was not simply a drain on public resources, a disincentive to work, or an impediment to family formation. It threatened to sap impoverished people's entrepreneurialism, encouraging them to form interest groups to pressure the state rather than direct that energy toward individual economic improvement. Though Clinton's SGPB report recommended entrepreneurial investments in education, welfare and even Medicaid deserved more careful scrutiny. As staffers wrote in marketized terms, "the lower productivity of so many families guarantees [not only] that the future South will have higher rates of poverty, infant deaths, and teen pregnancy" but also that "we will be able to collect fewer taxes to pay for bandaging these running sores." Welfare ought to be conditioned upon attendance at "programs in remedial education, parenting, or job training aimed at employment available in the area." As staffers maintained, reflecting the era's mentality of fiscal triage, "with too much need and too little money, the South must spend local, state, and federal money where return will be highest."[120]

If earlier liberals viewed AFDC as a necessary if regrettable bulwark against abject poverty, New Democrats were coming to see welfare as a poor investment of scarce resources, perhaps even an impediment to economic expansion. As the PPI, the DLC's policy shop, worked on welfare reform proposals, staffers also emphasized initiatives that might "make work pay." The growing ranks of the working poor—full- or near-full-time workers whose earnings were below the poverty line—became their focus. Rather than make work pay by legislating a higher minimum wage (which was not raised in the 1980s when its real value fell by 25.2 percent), the PPI proposed expanding the Earned Income Tax Credit (EITC), a highly technocratic, depoliticized social benefit that would operate through the tax code, by formula, rather than through more visible, democratically contestable "programs."[121] By delivering income through tax credits rather than wages, PPI's "American Working Wage" also constituted a massive stimulus to businesses, which could continue to pay exploitative wages.[122] And even then, the program was designed simply to bring working people up to the poverty line—not to transcend poverty. As long as labor markets remained favorable, businesses would have few incentives to raise wages.

New Democrats' confidence in their entrepreneurial policies and simultaneous denigration of special interests and the politics of redistribution led some DLC consultants to dismiss even soliciting poor and minority citizens' votes. As William Galston and Elaine Kamarck explained in their forceful 1989 memo "The Politics of Evasion," for two decades Democrats were mired in "myths" about voter mobilization and redistribution. Jesse Jackson's 1984 and 1988 presidential campaigns were premised on the "myth of mobilization"—of turning out voters of color. Appealing to minority Americans with traditional commitments to redistribution—what they called the myth of "liberal fundamentalism"—might drive turnout. But the trouble "with selective mobilization is that in politics, as in business, it's not the gross that counts, it's the net." Republicans' countermobilization of the white majority would swamp these efforts. The solution was confronting "an inhospitable ideological climate" with "consistent use of middle-class values—individual responsibility, hard work, equal opportunity—rather than the language of compensation."[123] The survival of the party depended upon flattering the biases and self-conceptions of white, suburban, professional voters who, like many New Democrats, misremembered or simply denied the state's role in their own economic security. As one of Michael Dukakis's chief political strategists put it, growth offered "an approach" to politics that "everybody can rally behind." New Democrats' programs, he said, were "not driven by constituency politics."[124] New Democrats thus advanced their own politics of evasion—evasion of the realities of who continued to benefit from state power and redistribution.

With supply side tools in hand, DLCers soon became enthusiastic proponents of reforming welfare, and the entrepreneurial investment ethos suffused their alternatives. Proposed investment instruments, "individual development accounts," would help low-income families "build financial assets," which could be used for higher education, home ownership, self-employment, or retirement. As the DLC's 1990 "New Orleans Declaration" put it, "all claims on government are not equal." This "means taking a hard look at federal entitlements and subsidies; cutting spending for low priorities and eliminating outmoded programs." "In the long run," DLC operative Bruce Reed summarized, "the way to overcome Republican deficits is to do what the Republicans haven't done: neither tax and spend nor borrow and spend, but invest, save, and grow."[125] Though DLC members liked to say they believed in "growth with equity," their order of operations was clear: "Mainstream Democrats believe in putting economic growth before redistribution; we are unabashedly for democratic capitalism."[126] Yet even an enthusiastic supporter such as Randall Rothenberg recognized the dangers of such a constricted view of democracy and social citizenship. As he mused, did New Democrats' outlook simply mean "that the 'national interest'"—as contrasted with special interests—was "nothing more than the special interests of the liberal upper middle class"?[127] The answer, increasingly, was yes.

* * *

To demonstrate that their message resonated with a broad and diverse set of Americans, in the spring of 1991, the DLC held its annual convention in Cleveland, Ohio. By then, DLC members cultivated an image as iconoclastic policy entrepreneurs, with the PPI pumping out white papers and proposals. DLC leaders Sam Nunn, Al From, and Bill Clinton aimed for the Cleveland event to look as much as possible like a presidential nominating convention.[128] As if confirming a platform, they voted to ratify their "New American Choice Resolution," a document that reflected the process of ideological transformation DLCers had undertaken since 1982, when *Rebuilding the Road to Opportunity* was released. DLCers would pursue "a set of common beliefs and broad national purposes" rather than a "set of programs" promised "to disparate interest groups." States and local governments had been "laboratories of innovation" in the 1980s, offering lessons in fiscal responsibility, industrial policy, and entrepreneurial solutions for poverty and welfare reform. The Cleveland convention would bring those commitments to the center of the party's governing vision and launch one of their own to the presidency.

Bill Clinton delivered the keynote address. Against a critique of Republican "denial, evasion, and neglect," he championed opportunity, responsibility, and community. He called for giving "people a new choice, rooted in old values, a new choice that is simple, that offers opportunity, demands responsibility, gives citizens more say, provides them responsive government." The language of community, however, was designed to soften a clear hierarchy of priorities. "Opportunity for all means first and foremost a commitment to economic growth," he said, pivoting to his by-then-stock commitments to "emerging technologies," "incentives to invest," and developing "world-class skills, for people who live here while money and management may fly away." For the poor, Clinton drew upon the PPI's plan to expand the EITC and create work training programs and demanded "that everybody who can go to work do it, for work is the best social program this country has ever devised." For all his optimism, Clinton could not resist casting fiscal aspersions on welfare: "Forty percent, forty percent," he repeated himself, "of our welfare dollars would not have to come out of the taxpayers' hides," he said, "if the men who owe child support and can pay it, did it."[129] Clinton's vision for the state's obligation to the poor thus remixed older, Johnson-era ideas—that welfare should be short term, that the burden to taxpayers should be minimized, and that economic growth was the basis of self-sustaining families. But Johnson never denied the importance of having subsistence-level income maintenance entitlements in place.

Instead, Clinton and New Democrats envisioned their growth and antipoverty policies—"making work pay" through the EITC and emphasizing work obligations—ultimately obviating the need for a welfare entitlement at all (see epilogue). The following summer, when he accepted the Democratic Party's nomination for the presidency, Clinton depicted an "America that says to entrepreneurs and businesspeople: We will give you more incentives and more opportunity than ever before to . . . create . . . American wealth in the new global economy." For the poor, Clinton offered "an America where we end welfare as we know it."[130] By the early 1990s, Clinton would frame these transformations in characteristically optimistic, marketized terms: "We need to create a small business entrepreneurial economy in every underclass urban area and rural area in the country." He continued, railing against traditional programs or entitlements, "whenever the power of the government can be used to create market forces that work, it's so much better than creating a bureaucracy to hire a bunch of full-time people to give somebody a check."[131]

Clinton and the New Democrats succeeded in remaking the Democratic Party. But the lopsided economic developments and entrenched poverty of the 1980s and 1990s belied their faith in entrepreneurialism and markets as solutions for poverty. Nowhere, perhaps, were the contradictions more glaring than in Cleveland, where by the time of the DLC convention in 1991 the city was heralded as a shining success—a beacon of the promise of entrepreneurial public-private partnerships—even as the city became one of the nation's poorest.

CHAPTER 10

Leveraging Poverty

"One lesson Americans learned in the Eighties was that they had to take responsibility for their own fates." So began Myron Magnet's article, "How Business Bosses Saved a Sick City," published in the March 27, 1989 edition of *Fortune* magazine. Magnet, a neoconservative urban policy analyst, described how in the 1980s, "no city has battled more cannily than Cleveland. A microcosm—almost a caricature—of all the recent ills of urban industrial America," Cleveland "achieved a unity almost startling in this every-man-for-himself epoch." Magnet's "unity" comprised the city's business leadership, which, facing economic and population decline, formed an "executive cabal," "a *formal* conspiracy of CEOs to provide leadership." The fruits of Cleveland's public-private partnerships were apparent to anyone visiting the newly sparkling downtown. Plans were moving forward for new stadiums and arenas for the city's beloved sports franchises. Downtown, Magnet proclaimed, "is springing up as rapidly, extensively, and glitteringly as if by Prospero's magical conjuration." The conjurers were the city's major law firms, banks, and real estate developers: Forest City Enterprises (real estate), Society (now Key) Bank, the Jacobs brothers (real estate), and the Cleveland Clinic. The "cabal" had even pooled resources to create a venture capital fund to support a biomedical postindustrial policy. With a supportive relationship with Mayor George Voinovich, the economy seemed to be taking off. As Magnet concluded, "you can't help thinking that *this* is what community is all about."[1]

Beneath such bluster, the transformations of urban governance in the 1980s were rather like the Progressive Era in reverse. Then, officials employed businesslike methods to establish "good government," stifle corruption, and underwrite the progressive expansion of city services if not democracies—albeit often with capital and labor recruitment as underlying goals. In the postwar decades, however, public debt and fiscal precarity empowered the growing sectors of financial, real estate, and legal services. By the 1980s, rather than businesspeople serving as external partners in social, economic, or political reforms, private-sector elites moved aggressively to penetrate, capture, and redirect local governance. "Businesslike" reforms still emphasized capital recruitment, but local elites sought to shear off the costs of social services in order to capture an ever-greater share of public resources, including through tax abatements, an inversion of supply-side liberalism's commitment to boosting public wealth. The results were often spectacular and spectacularly inequitable.

Magnet's celebration of Cleveland's renaissance was a particularly frothy example of the Reagan era's veneration of "free markets" and business leadership. But Cleveland's "comeback" did not reflect Reagan's vision of governance. Reagan's notion that markets alone could produce more equitable outcomes than government was the rhetorical gloss on an effort to destroy the New Deal state by undoing its social entitlements and systems of cooperative federalism. As businesspeople tried to explain to his administration, however, Reagan's austerity, devolution, and free market shibboleths, operationalized in his enterprise zone urban development proposals, actually threatened to stymie supply-side state builders' development agendas. Their vision of governance was more aligned with New Democrats' entrepreneurial version of liberalism's supply side. Cleveland's business elites' redevelopment agenda and biomedical postindustrial policies were underwritten with hundreds of millions of dollars in public subsidies, suggesting just how central public resources continued to be in "market-based solutions."

Reagan's austerity, however, did contribute in an oblique way to businesspeople's enhanced leverage over what public spending remained. The concept of "urban triage" captures the rationale for the systematic public disinvestment of poor neighborhoods that underwrote Cleveland's "comeback" and formed an urban corollary to the New Democrats' more austere vision of supply-side liberalism. As articulated by Anthony Downs, a Brookings Institution fellow and Carter administration consultant, urban triage held that rather than invest increasingly scarce resources in declining neighborhoods, "the worst-first strategy," Downs called it, cities should invest in areas of "existing strengths"—sturdy neighborhoods and businesses likely to attract greater private investment. Such "leveraging" of antipoverty and development dollars, which defined Carter's Urban Development Action Grant (UDAG) program, might reverse processes of private disinvestment. Fundamentally, however, it also authorized public disinvestment from impoverished neighborhoods as policy: "a logical implication of this principle," Downs explained, was that many officials, though they would not "admit it publicly," had "decided to 'write off' such neighborhoods." To save cities, then, Downs and others advocated urban triage as a way to maximize scarce resources. Echoing New Democrats' critiques of welfare and their turn toward an investment mentality, Downs urged officials to make "tough choices" on behalf of leveraging private investments with resources redirected or extracted from poor and working class communities.[2]

Structuring this disinvestment and redistribution in a city almost evenly divided between working-class and poor white and black residents also required remaking local democracies in ways that socialized residents to those tough choices. In partnership with politicians and from seats of authority within government, supply-side state builders adapted the sorts of tokenized, individualist, and highly managed participation that Jim Crow states had constructed in the 1950s and 1960s. This interregional convergence on attenuated, tightly managed, and neoliberalized forms of democratic "participation" was also the result of businesspeople and white liberals alike having learned the lessons of the participatory battles of the 1960s and 1970s: better to organize citizen participation on elites' terms than risk more fundamental structural democratic and economic reforms.[3]

As the participatory ethos of the 1960s was hollowed out and redeployed on behalf of elites' development priorities, in Cleveland, as in other many other cities of the post–civil rights era, a new generation of black political leaders proved, over time, quite amenable to elites' developmental priorities and managed democratic participation. Indeed, Cleveland's chief black power broker, city council president George L. Forbes, became a signal example of what historian Keeanga-Yamahtta Taylor calls an "indispensable" partner to white elites at a moment when many cities became majority minority.[4] Forbes became a chief advocate of the era's more muscular and extractive forms of business producerism. As he put it, "government does not create jobs," but rather creates the "political climate . . . incentives and tax relief" through which jobs would materialize.[5] That Forbes profited handsomely from his place atop the city's Democratic machine also reflected the hybridized form urban democracies assumed by the 1980s, blending aspects of Jim Crow, machine politics, and the casual and profitable conflicts of interest that had often been a part of liberalism's supply side.[6]

By the early 1990s, when Bill Clinton delivered the keynote address at the Democratic Leadership Council conference in the "comeback city,"

Cleveland had the second highest percentage of economically dependent residents among twenty-three of the nation's largest cities.[7] In the 1980s, the percentage of Cleveland's residents living below the poverty line soared from 28 to 43 percent.[8] As New Democrats and Republicans championed different versions of market-based solutions for poverty, the former centered on state action and resources and the latter on state withdrawal, together they sped the arrival of a newly austere social contract, in which austerity, economic development, and entrepreneurialism authorized the withdrawal of even the most meager income maintenance programs, abetted by the hollowing out and co-optation of the 1960s' participatory principle. Effectively abandoned by public institutions, many marginalized citizens stopped voting. Neoliberal democracy, then, emerged through the engineered withdrawal of hope and opportunities, in which managed democratic participation and disempowerment faded into sustained democratic disengagement.

The Big Business of Urban Bondage

As cities were remade in the 1980s—physically, politically, economically—the interests of external actors came to matter more than even before. Certainly, suburb-residing businessmen maintained their power in city government. But in their efforts to remake the city as a destination for white-collar work and suburban recreation, they were aided by the seeming actuarial rationalities of national credit rating agencies. Rating the worthiness of municipal debt is always a subjective and political process, one in which cities with large minority populations have often been deemed riskier bets and so paid higher interest rates to borrow.[9] Those higher interest rates, in turn, accelerated recourse to short-term borrowing in Cleveland, which had amplified the power of local banks, enabling them to profoundly undercut Mayor Dennis Kucinich and neighborhood interests. Cleveland was hardly alone in this respect: in the 1980s, the quest to get back into the good graces of credit rating agencies constrained Mayor Harold Washington in Chicago; it determined draconian budget cuts in Philadelphia; and it led public authorities and special districts everywhere to hike fees and fares.[10]

Following Cleveland's 1978 default, Mayor Voinovich made significant reforms simply to reenter bond markets. Taking office in the winter of 1979–80, Voinovich drafted a legion of private-sector conscripts to tackle the city's fiscal crisis and modernize city governance. Like Governor Jimmy

Carter in Georgia, who conscripted business executives to reorganize the state government, Voinovich's Operations Improvement Task Force invited scores of private-sector executives and their associates into city hall to reform city operations. At least eighty-nine executives, on loan from sixty-two businesses, composed a "brigade of missionary businessmen," as the *Plain Dealer* put it, and, as in Georgia, their purview encompassed questions of form and priorities. The *Plain Dealer* reported that "the several hundred businessmen" brought in to "form his government . . . are largely males and part of the city's white power structure . . . [who] live in the suburbs." The city's law director, Thomas Wagner, Voinovich's second in command, was loaned by Voinovich's old law firm, Calfee Halter & Griswold. Wagner's assistants came from Calfee, Jones Day Reavis & Pogue, and Baker Hostetler & Patterson. As the *Plain Dealer* noted, Voinovich "did not invite any of the grass-roots neighborhood people to participate."[11] Instead, over its first two years and with some 37,000 hours of private-sector labor, Voinovich built an entirely new city government in the image of white, suburban business executives.[12]

The most significant factor in stabilizing Cleveland's fiscal crisis and ensuring reentry into debt markets, however, was voters' passage of an increased city wage tax, which advocates, including business elites, strategically branded a "commuter tax." The tax increase was essential to restoring positive bond ratings, and finance director William Reidy (on loan from Pricewaterhouse-Coopers) pressed it at the behest of New York's Lazard Freres & Co. In the 1970s, Lazard had become the go-to consultant for governments in fiscal crisis after Felix Rohaytn, a lead council at Lazard, chaired New York City's Municipal Assistance Corporation (MAC), the state body charged with restructuring the city's finances after its debt crisis.[13] Rohaytn also advised officials in Illinois, Detroit, and Washington, D.C.[14] With Lazard's counsel, Voinovich orchestrated a deal with Cleveland's financiers: the city would supplement its declining property tax revenues with the wage tax increase, and the banks would refinance the city's short-term notes. Initial estimates forecast a $35 million windfall largely funded by suburban commuters thanks to the 0.5 percent tax increase (bringing the city levy to 2 percent). New revenue would go primarily to retiring old debts, which, Voinovich's aides suggested, would save the city some $21 million in interest payments.[15] Twenty months after default, Voinovich forged an agreement with the city's banks to refinance older notes—those on which the city had defaulted—and also to sell $36.2 million in new bonds, officially exiting default.[16] Voinovich was effusive in his gratitude to the banks, but they were not acting altruistically. Offering the city financing at 9 percent interest meant that, over their fourteen-year life, the *new* bonds could yield some $26.7 million in transfers of tax dollars to purchasers of federally tax-exempt debt.[17] Voinovich wasn't merely good politics for the city's business community; the return to debt markets meant real profits for purchasers of municipal securities.[18] The city continued to engage Lazard to manage debt, maximize credit scores, and minimize interest payments.[19]

While the income tax hike was a more progressive source of revenue, external capital demanded other more regressive reforms. One investment firm applauded Voinovich's willingness to make "expenditure cuts" to ensure a balanced budget and his "strong management actions, including sizable city employee lay-offs."[20] Voinovich, however, worried about overly aggressive cuts: "if you cut the city's level of services any more than they are now being delivered, we won't have a city." But even as he argued for preserving services, he conceded the value of regressive new forms of municipal finance: boosting "Court fees, fines, and costs would," he said, "be very good."[21] As in many other cities, officials turned to fees for services in order to resist new tax levies, which credit ratings officials worried were inherently unstable thanks to voters' shifting moods. Indeed, ratings officials were coming to believe that democracy itself was not such a good bet.[22]

Credit rating agencies' sustained surveillance of urban finances went beyond periodic reports sent via FedEx or fax. Voinovich, his aides, and business allies made regular trips to New York to present Cleveland's financial standing. Agents also regularly visited to assess progress on, as Voinovich explained to them, "the promises Cleveland has made to you [regarding] our financial plan."[23] In 1986, beyond such accounting reports, audits, budget forecasts, and wish lists for new debt instruments, Moody's and S&P officials climbed onto buses to view major development projects forecast to attract suburban workers and retail dollars: the new Sohio building, Tower City, the Galleria, the Halle Building, and Playhouse Square.[24] Wrapping up a visit with a "ratings increase pitch," city financial officers reassured ratings agents: it is "no longer an issue if [the] city can manage—we have proven we *can*" through "reduced city services in response to tax base decline, yet not so much as to be a deterent [sic] to development."[25] Local business elites, who had always policed the boundaries of municipal government, were now backed—and supervised—by powerful credit rating agencies.

Firms such as Lazard and credit raters like Moody's and S&P were not alone in profiting from urban fiscal distress. McKinsey & Co. and Booz-Allen developed considerable public-sector consulting practices in the 1960s. In 1969 alone, New York City paid a reported $75 million in fees to external consultants, and, by the 1980s, they expanded their municipal consultancies to capitalize on fiscal crises.[26] Voinovich hired a McKinsey team to develop an economic redevelopment plan, and those consultants, in concert with local business leaders Stanley Pace, of TRW, and Richard Pogue, managing partner of Jones, Day, Reavis & Pogue, urged Voinovich to back the creation of what they called the Cleveland Roundtable. Publicly, the Roundtable was portrayed as a bridge organization between corporate leaders, labor, elected officials, and the various ethnic and racial groups in the city. Privately, however, its purview was wider and its impact greater than that of a discussion group. Consultants argued that the Growth Association's mandate and membership had become too broad, its effectiveness blunted. A smaller organization, with membership limited to the CEOs of major corporations, could focus primarily on "long-range strategies and programs for economic development" and, given the corporations' importance to the city, would possess natural leverage to implement the programs.[27]

Cleveland's business elites, like those in the South, were also learning the lessons of War on Poverty–era battles with community groups: preemptive inclusion structured by elites was far preferable to confronting organized activists with more robust demands for empowerment. Funded by private contributions and the Cleveland Foundation, upon whose board sat a number of Roundtable members, the business executives hired a staff to support committees focused on economic development, housing and neighborhood development (this committee was later dropped), education, and "race relations," upon which minority community and religious leaders were invited to sit.[28] Rather than blanket rejection of minority involvement, as had been James Davis's preference in the wake of urban rebellions and the collapse of the Stokes mayoralty, business elites would cultivate their own structures for "community" participation.

McKinsey's consultants also recommended the Roundtable create another organization, Cleveland Tomorrow, established in 1982, which would begin to focus on the nitty-gritty of the city's postindustrial economic planning by creating a venture capital fund and a "center for small business development."[29] To direct Cleveland Tomorrow, business leaders poached Richard Shatten from McKinsey. The Roundtable and Cleveland Tomorrow would soon become a hybrid planning commission, upon which government and business relied, serving as a steering committee for nearly every major public or private undertaking.[30] For the first time, Cleveland's business leaders were creating what many Sunbelt businesspeople had forged decades earlier: durable public-private planning institutions capable of shaping policy, lobbying Washington, managing interest group participation, and, soon, developing postindustrial policy and development plans geared toward white suburbanites.

Managing Urban Democracy

While the interests and perspectives of external capital were coming to matter more than ever before, the city, along with leading philanthropies, could not simply withdraw funding from neighborhood groups—the explosive violence of the late 1960s powerfully highlighted the folly of neglect. Instead, officials developed strategies for managing various neighborhood, development, and activist groups. First would be elevating the prestige of key groups whose agendas dovetailed with or did not directly challenge elites' emerging development agenda, often by making strategic grants.[31] The second was creating a durable structure for managing demands from neighborhoods and their council members, which both released political pressure and, ideally, induced residents' compliance with austerity.

The need to manage community participation was underscored by a 1982 "hit" orchestrated by affiliates of National People's Action (NPA), the group behind Sarah Turner's 1976 trip to Washington, D.C. Voinovich had reactivated the tax abatement for the downtown headquarters of Standard Oil of Ohio (Sohio), which his predecessor Dennis Kucinich had vetoed. Activists had spent the previous winter and spring agitating against Sohio's excessive prices for home heating fuel. In September, when Gail Cincotta brought an NPA caravan to Cleveland, locals invited organizers to join them as they "hit" Sohio's CEO Alton Whitehouse on his home turf. They bused out to the exclusive Gates Mills Hunt Club, where hundreds of neighborhood activists confronted a veranda of lunching club members. One activist recalled that the "Hunt Club had never before seen so many African-Americans." Gates Mills' tiny police force was called, but it was overwhelmed by the crowd. While leaders demanded to see Whitehouse (he was not there), others drank from members' wine glasses. It was "the pinnacle for Cleveland groups," one activist gleefully recalled. Others, however, agreed with a woman who worried that it "was an embarrassing thing, very embarrassing." When the foundations that supported many of the groups simply ended or slashed their funding, it was more than just embarrassing—it was crippling. The group that led the hit soon collapsed.[32]

With the violence of the late 1960s a live memory, business elites also understood that cultivating neighborhood associations would offer the legitimizing veneer of community participation. Community development corporations (CDCs), growth-oriented associations formed through the War on Poverty, became elites' favored neighborhood associations.[33] The Hough Area Development Corporation (HADC), established in the late 1960s, initially reflected a push for "community capitalism," emphasizing not simply job creation but, for a time, community ownership of businesses.[34] It was also committed to the era's community uplift agenda—one program, "Project Afro," would develop "self-identity, self-pride, self-respect and positive ambitions among youth in Negro poverty stricken areas."[35] By the 1980s, these CDCs had a Washington lobbying group, the Campaign for Community-Based Economic Development.[36] Often, however, CDCs depended upon local philanthropies and government, and during the 1970s and into the 1980s, officials invested token sums in groups like the HADC, incentivizing the transition away from politicized definitions of "community development" to less confrontational forms of "business development."[37] Spurred by modest Community Development Block Grant (CDBG) funds— a 1983 grant of $53,697 went to revitalize a commercial strip on Hough Avenue—as well as other, smaller grants from the Cleveland Foundation, and a $90,000 line of credit from a local bank, by the early 1980s the HADC's activities focused solely on "venture investments." The Roundtable even invited an HADC leader to join its board meetings—a meaningful gesture for the HADC, albeit one that cost elites nothing. Despite city, philanthropic, and business support, however, given Hough's staggering poverty, one leader worried in late 1982 that their investments faced a "bleack [sic] future."[38] With federal aid destabilized by the Reagan administration, HADC, like other CDCs, saw few public alternatives to private and voluntary funding.

Voinovich understood the difficulties and opportunities of Reagan's austerity and drafted a memo explaining the complex relationship between citizens' expectations for local government and the dynamics of federal funding. The relative invisibility of federal aid was especially significant. Since residents often missed the federal role in local services, Voinovich cautioned municipal officials against assuming federal "grants will continue; therefore, any use of grants must be made with future commitments of local funds held to a minimum." The city "must be on guard that it does not assume the position of trying to cover the costs of programs which have been deleted by a higher level of government."[39] In such uncertain times, spending on physical infrastructure or, better yet, using federal aid to stimulate private-sector development or voluntary actions would be a wiser use of subsidies.

The trick would be getting the neighborhoods and city council members to sign off on disinvestment. During the summer of 1980, the administration organized a series of neighborhood "Block Grant Workshops." A sequence of three meetings—on "needs," "priorities," and "the plan"—was designed to build resident and councilmanic consensus around the diminished use of block grants in neighborhoods. Some frustrated citizens complained that the meetings, which were frequently held on weekday mornings, "skirted around neighborhood people."[40] But offering neighborhoods a real chance to direct city priorities was never the goal. Rather, they were meant to offer lessons in budgetary discipline and to invite citizens to sign off on austerity. As officials explained, while the city would "rate highly those activities which everyone can agree upon," the limited "dollar figures should encourage the people involved to realize the hard decisions that prioritization brings."[41] In 1981, the city distributed seventeen one-time grants, ranging from $45,000 for rehabilitating a playground in Hough to $300,000 for improvements to a park in Glenville.[42] Each council member was also given a small annual allotment of discretionary block grant funds of around $75,000. Roughly half of the funds underwrote new sidewalks for which the city had previously charged property owners; other funds supported nascent housing rehabilitation efforts.[43] While the improvements were undoubtedly valued, the overall lesson for residents, council members, and neighborhood groups was to expect diminishing support.

This sort of closely managed administrative participation had become a hallmark of Sunbelt growth strategies, and Voinovich would employ a hybridized, machinelike version throughout the 1980s. In addition to the Block Grant Workshops, the mayor formed a "commission on neighborhoods" to build consensus and to perhaps co-opt neighborhood groups. Its structure, which included but also effectively isolated poor or minority representatives, echoed those established by Georgia's Area Planning and Development Commissions. Cleveland's commission comprised some thirty member-organizations, each of which sent a representative. While each neighborhood group, including the HADC and Citizens to Bring Broadway Back, sent one member, representatives of the Roundtable, Growth Association, and banks spoke in more unified terms.⁴⁴ Even the Roundtable's dedicated "race relations" committee was more of a PR and management exercise (by 1986, Voinovich charged that the group failed to develop "a positive agenda").⁴⁵ But for Roundtable leaders, the desired result was to create a pressure valve for neighborhood or racial frustration with the city's business-directed development priorities in order to smooth a path toward those very plans. To get there, however, elites also had to navigate a very different set of challenges: the Reagan administration's austerity.

Supply-Side Fiscalism and Reagan's Austerity

The greatest obstacle to the Roundtable's economic vision was the Reagan administration. To "pay" for his initial round of tax cuts, Reagan abolished the Comprehensive Employment and Training Act (Nixon's jobs-training block grant) and slashed poverty programs such as AFDC, food stamps, Medicaid, and HUD's housing and Section 8 vouchers. Given their ostensible association with ameliorating poverty, rumors swirled that the administration was also considering killing or slashing CDBGs, revenue sharing, the Appalachian Regional Commission, and Jimmy Carter's Urban Development Action Grants (UDAGs). One Georgia official was outraged by indiscriminate cuts to CDBGs. Despite talk of local empowerment, he fumed, "All we received are the cuts."⁴⁶ Two years later, when the administration and its few congressional allies again sought to cut or defer $500 million in FY1986 CDBG commitments, Georgia's Republican senator Mack Mattingly joined fourteen colleagues in protest: "many local communities across this nation took the 'word' of the federal government and believed that if an appropriations bill was passed by congress and signed by the President, then the money could be counted on"—"let's be fair!"⁴⁷ The result was an urban policy that was ideologically charged but often incoherent and which proceeded through three discernable phases: an early period of slashing spending and regulations associated with antipoverty programs; a second phase that trumpeted "free market" solutions for urban poverty; and a third phase of indiscriminate cuts and urban abandonment, in which the administration gestured at balanced budgets on the backs of poor people and cities.⁴⁸

Despite their pleas for administrative autonomy, Reagan's dismantling of key regulations in CDBGs turned out to be a mixed blessing for local officials. In May 1981, HUD eliminated reviews of CDBGs benefits for low- and moderate-income people, and, in its reauthorization removed "front-end review" of local programs, freeing up communities to move more quickly and with less oversight. Poverty groups cried foul, and a group of mayors conceded "a certain ambivalence" about deregulation. As a representative of the U.S. Conference of Mayors put it, "What we are looking for, I think, is procedural deregulation, and not philosophical deregulation." Federal regulations, he recognized, provided political cover for local officials to invest in needed social programs in the face of intense pressure from elites. In 1983, Congress responded to these concerns by issuing new regulations mandating that 51 percent of CDBG spending target low- and moderate-income beneficiaries, a decision it had resisted in 1977. In 1987, it upped the threshold to 60 percent.[49] Nevertheless, given the lack of expanded appropriations, when accounting for inflation, from 1980 to 1990 CDBGs' effective value declined by 49.6 percent.[50] Social targeting may have taken a growing share of funds, but the pool was drying up.

In addition to fighting to preserve CDBGs, Tom Duffy, Cleveland's first full-time Washington lobbyist, worked to secure Urban Development Action Grants, a program with ostensible antipoverty goals and which was invaluable for private development interests.[51] The Carter administration created UDAGs to forge yet another "new partnership" between government and business, emphasizing neither the large-scale "superblock" developments of urban renewal, nor a primary focus on impoverished communities as in the War on Poverty. Instead, the program was more akin to urban triage, which, like the battlefield usage from which it was drawn, meant focusing dwindling resources in areas likely to generate the most positive fiscal and developmental impacts. In 1975, the economist and HUD consultant Anthony Downs, later one of President Carter's policy advisers, explained this outlook in Cleveland. Downs argued that investing in solid neighborhoods rather than those in the early stages of decline was "a far more effective use of resources than the worst-first strategy in terms of attracting private dollars into further investment." Such "leveraging" of private investment was "crucial . . . to really improve conditions in the city." Residents "of the worst-condition area will oppose [such an approach]—naturally," Downs conceded. "But you must face up to it if you want funds spent on neighborhoods to have any positive long-run impacts." By "leveraging" private "investments," public inputs would produce private growth and boost tax yields down the road.[52]

The supply-side liberalism that suffused UDAGs anticipated and dovetailed with New Democrats' veneration of entrepreneurial investments. UDAGs required local officials to use federal funds to "leverage" private investment. Certainly, urban renewal had a similar logic: local administrators helped acquire, clear, and prepare land for private developments. But UDAGs contained far broader possibilities for public sculpting of markets. The program could be applied to just about any public-private partnership for industry, commerce, retail, or housing. Cities often set up economic development corporations (Cleveland's was the Citywide Development Corporation) that offered publicly subsidized, sub-market-rate, low-interest loans to developers, which, given inflation and skyrocketing interest rates, was valuable. As loans were repaid, cities often used the capital to establish new revolving loan or venture capital pools. Officials could also stipulate that, as a condition of a loan, a portion of the subsequent profits would accrue to the municipality: 50 percent of the profit in one development in Newark, New Jersey, went to the city.[53] To qualify for a federal UDAG, cities and business had to demonstrate projected employment benefits, a high ratio of prospective private to public investment, and, most important, sign a statement affirming that, "but for" the UDAG subsidy, the private entity would not pursue the project. In identifying new market possibilities, teaming with business, and literally investing federal dollars, governments were taking on not just an interventionist role in markets: local government was becoming an investment bank, choosing private partners and creating markets where, "but for" the public subsidy, there had plausibly been none.[54]

As they assessed existing urban policies, one Reagan administration official described UDAG as "pure Reaganism."[55] Though the program's emphasis on markets appeared to dovetail with Reagan's rhetoric, the government's aggressive shaping of markets through blended public-private capacities was much more a creature of liberalism's supply side than conservative's tax-and-regulation-slashing version. Reagan's urban policy was primarily concerned with devolution and laissez-faire, hacking back government to free private markets and capital from public preferences. Even UDAG was perennially on the chopping block until it was finally defunded in 1988. Indeed, Reagan formed a task force on private-sector initiatives to explore areas where markets might fully replace government taxing and programmatic authority. Even a sympathetic American Enterprise Institute analyst recognized, however, that the "the private sector" would never "compensate for the slowdown in the growth of federal social spending on a 'dollar-for-dollar' basis." That researcher understood that Reagan instead used the prospect of private-sector action as cover for slashing federal aid.[56]

Reagan's ill-fated "enterprise zones" legislation characterized the second phase of his urban policy. A municipal microcosm of his administration's "supply-side fiscalism"—the notion that tax cuts rather than direct stimulus or publicly structured private investments might produce economic productivity, employment, and growing tax revenues—"enterprise zones" fused Reagan's critique of government and his veneration of markets into a simple formulation.[57] These "zones," he argued, will "demonstrate that freedom of enterprise can succeed where government has failed—if given the chance."[58] Reagan offered caricaturized contrasts with the War on Poverty, describing its "heavy government subsidies and central planning." Evincing little awareness of how often business interests had enthusiastically captured poverty subsidies, "Enterprise Zones," he said, were "the direct opposite of the Model Cities Program of the 1960's."[59] Nudged along by figures such as Milton Friedman, by the late 1970s and early 1980s, Reagan began to argue that simply removing government programs would uncover latent market forces that would, in themselves, produce positive social outcomes for the neediest Americans.

Reagan was popularizing a truly revolutionary shift in thinking about the relationship between government, the market, and social provision. Some five decades of liberal economic and social programs had rested on the state nudging along social progress; that is, however, thin their ultimate commitment was to fighting poverty, liberal initiatives or officials were ultimately accountable for setting goals and policy, structuring investments, and partnering with a variety of actors. Reagan offered the *disembodied* market as a way to provision social goods, an utterly unfalsifiable political claim so long as government existed.[60] As if there had never been poverty or unemployment before liberal efforts to solve those problems, Reagan told a gathering of black Republicans in 1982 that the "binge" of social spending of the Great Society produced a "tragic halt" to the economic advancement of poor and black citizens.[61] The best way to expand economic progress for all Americans, Reagan told a group of minority businesspeople, was to roll back government programs and "mobilize the power of private enterprise" to "work your magic."[62] The siren song of free markets offered politicians nearly limitless opportunities to avoid taking political responsibility for social and economic outcomes.

Enterprise zones became the way in which the administration sold the "magic" of the market as solutions for poverty and urban problems. Though his first attempt to get the legislation through Congress stalled in 1981, when he mainly emphasized its growth potential, Reagan resubmitted the package in 1983.[63] A 1982 memo signaled the shifting emphasis from growth to uplifting poor people: the "natural market forces . . . unleashed in central cities would . . . lead to the economic redevelopment of these areas and to real, private sector jobs for . . . disadvantaged individuals."[64] By 1983, Reagan argued the legislation "will be of primary benefit to America's disadvantaged citizens in our most depressed areas"—he used the phrase "depressed areas" six times.[65] At the moment New Democrats were reimagining public policies and poverty assistance in entrepreneurial terms, the Reagan administration went considerably further. The market itself, Reagan said in his 1984 State of the Union, would "break the bondage of dependency" in the nation's poorest communities. If governance is defined as state action—independent or through civil or private intermediaries—New Democrats' entrepreneurial governance was still that; Reagan's was state withdrawal as policy.

Sharp criticism of the enterprise zones program came from within the administration as well as from the very businesspeople meant to be the primary beneficiaries. Dan J. Smith, a top adviser in the Office of Policy Development and one of the legislation's architects, warned that Reagan was generating misconceptions about the program's potential. Smith cautioned that enterprise zones are "unlikely to affect in any significant way areas containing chronic unemployment and major infrastructure deficiencies."[66] The most incisive criticism, however, came from members of the private sector, scores of whom the administration invited to workshops to solicit their support. Instead, business leaders picked apart the proposals, particularly Reagan's claims that the zones would stimulate small, labor-intensive businesses. His emphasis on tax incentives, they noted, was largely redundant since the 1981 tax cuts had already lowered businesses' liabilities. They also estimated that any new "business activity will come from businesses outside the zone who were deciding to expand into a zone." But even this outcome was unlikely. Most significantly, because the proposals were overwhelmingly geared toward tax relief, the zones would be "most attractive to capital-intensive firms and those having significant tax liabilities"—meaning big, existing businesses. They were simply "not likely to attract small, labor-intensive businesses who create the bulk of new jobs in America."[67]

In contrast to marginal tax or regulatory relief, businesspeople called for the full suite of liberal supply-side policies: "access to capital"; "availability of training for unskilled labor"; infrastructure, transportation, and "proximity to markets"; "local government commitment"; quality services (including transit, fire, and police); and "strong, resourceful business and community leadership dedicated to revitalization." Beyond their usual call for lower "wage rates," growing businesses sought the types of robust subsidies that characterized supply-side liberalism.[68] With support for the program flagging, the administration let the proposal fade away, suggesting, perhaps, what most urban advocates had long suspected—the administration didn't much care about cities or poverty.

The third phase of Reagan's urban policy began in 1985 as the administration contemplated new cuts to federal spending to reduce soaring deficits. Cleveland's Republican mayor George Voinovich was the president of the National League of Cities, and he was forced to bring his critiques of the administration—which had been strategically muted—into the open. While his critiques were pointed, he directed much of his ire at the Democratic Congress rather than his party's leader. As plans circulated in Washington for some $5 billion in cuts to urban programs, Voinovich charged Congress with "cowardice." They lacked "guts" and threatened cities with "irreparable damage."[69]

Much worse, however, was the "bombshell" news that the administration was contemplating closing all federal tax exemptions for municipal borrowing. Since the landmark Revenue Act of 1913, interest paid to purchasers of municipal securities had been exempted from federal taxation, an essential indirect subsidy for municipal governments, which could never afford to compete with higher yield corporate bonds or securities. Federal tax exemption quite literally made the market for the debt that made modern American cities possible. In March 1986, however, when the "mind-boggling" news leaked, as one Chicago official characterized it, the municipal bond market slammed to a halt.[70] Voinovich had just appeared before Congress pleading for greater flexibility in raising local revenue, and now the administration seemed poised to move decisively in the opposite direction.[71] Voinovich traveled to New York to rally officials at Bear Stearns and other investment banks, urging them to use their clout to protect cities' ability to borrow. Writing to one banker, Voinovich conceded that he was not toeing the Republican Party line, though "with the problems I have ... as a result of what is happening in Washington, it is a wonder I am not a flaming liberal."[72] The mayor of the largest city to default on its bonds since the 1930s had become "the most dedicated champion" of cities' right to take on tax-advantaged debt.[73]

While Voinovich and his allies succeeded in preserving tax exemption for general obligation bonds, the Tax Reform Act of 1986 ended the subsidy for industrial development bonds (IDBs), a loosely regulated form of development financing. Since the 1930s, IDBs and other forms of tax-exempt bond financing enabled local governments to deliver low-interest, long-term financing for new or expanding businesses. Congress had never mandated comprehensive reporting of their use and so had only a vague sense of their cost to the treasury. This was largely because their usage was historically limited to smokestack chasing in Deep South states including Arkansas, Mississippi, and Alabama, which, along with Kentucky, accounted for around 80 percent of the total IDB market by the early 1960s—an estimated $80 million in annual financing. As deindustrialization accelerated, however, by 1968, forty states authorized the instruments when, that year, an estimated $1.8 billion in federal tax-exempt IDBs were issued by state and local governments.[74] But the total value of IDBs and their cost to the treasury remained opaque. As Congress mulled various deficit reduction measures, members urged the Treasury Department to mandate IDB reporting. When the figures came in, the cost to the treasury obliterated expectations. Federally tax exempt development bond financing issuances in just FY1984 totaled $17.4 billion, and that year's bonds alone carried a cumulative tax loss over time of $7.9 billion.[75] That year, Cleveland issued $179 million in new IDBs, delivering sub-market-rate financing to 108 businesses.[76]

The sheer scale of the little-understood program yielded a bipartisan consensus. Democrat Dan Rostenkowski, chair of the House Ways and Means Committee, worried "that bonds are being issued without any sense of public priorities," highlighting subsidies "for a liquor store and luxury boxes for a sports stadium." Kmart received $220.5 million in federally tax-exempt financing with which it opened ninety-six stores in nineteen states.[77] While critics charged that many of these projects would have been built regardless of financing, others, including the director of Ohio's Development Financing Commission, claimed that in the context of high interest rates, tax-free bonds were "the only game in town" for communities desperate to create jobs and tax revenues.[78] Like tax abatements, in the context of federal austerity and economic challenges, a developmental initiative pioneered in the capital-starved, early twentieth-century South had gone national. When Congress ended IDBs' exemption, issuances plummeted. In 1985, governments in Georgia issued $859 million in IDBs. The next year, the market was $25 million.[79] While Voinovich and his allies saved the market for general municipal securities, between the end of IDBs' tax exemption and the Reagan administration's austerity, local governments and businesses faced a harsh new world when it came to funding economic development.

The New Politics of Race, Patronage, and Poverty

As Reagan's austerity lashed the poor and struggling cities, minority coalitions seized a greater share of political power—a "hollow prize" as scholars have described cities in the wake of deindustrialization and as the tide of generous liberal spending rolled out.[80] In Cleveland, as in many other majority or near-majority minority cities, the consolidation of black political power also reflected a post–civil rights era unity born of pragmatic alliances. This unity was fragile, cloaking personal tensions and rival ideas about empowerment and community development. The city's political fragmentation—symbolized by its thirty-three-member city council—also meant the battle lines were relatively stable. Since each member represented a small, fixed ward, council members often spread spending across councilmanic districts, purchasing a degree of support for downtown development by enabling members to modestly serve constituencies.[81]

In Cleveland, councilwoman Fannie Lewis and council president George Forbes occupied two ends of the delicate but durable black political coalition. In 1979, Lewis, the veteran of battles over War on Poverty spending, was elected councilwoman for Ward 7, which included Hough. Lewis served until her death in 2008, becoming the longest serving councilperson in Cleveland's history. Like Lewis, Forbes was the child of sharecroppers, born in Tennessee in 1931. Forbes served in the U.S. Marines before settling in Cleveland, where he worked his way through college and law school. He won his first council seat in 1963, representing Glenville, and by the end of the decade was a top lieutenant in Carl and Louis Stokes's potent Twenty-First Congressional District Caucus.

Unifying the black vote to secure Carl Stokes's mayoralty, however, did not mean the city's black political leadership was internally unified—slights, rivalries, and deals with other interests hampered the coalition. Feeling overlooked by the Stokes brothers, Forbes built his career by advancing charges that black political elites too often ignored poor residents, and he worked to ingratiate himself with the county Democratic Party, Carl Stokes's foe. This maneuvering served Forbes well in the 1970s when he won two significant positions—county Democratic Party cochair and city council president—and maintained his profile in his shrinking district (in 1979, a mere 1,800 voters reelected Forbes).[82] Forbes fought for black municipal employment and demanded minority hiring quotas in city contracts and construction projects—no small commitments to black economic advancement. And he routinely called out racially biased policing and shoddy public housing and ensured that black-owned firms won city contracts. But by controlling city council committee assignments, budget debates, and party patronage, Forbes amassed a greater degree of personal loyalty and political debts than appeals to racial unity might have generated.

Among Forbes's greatest political assets was the uncertainty surrounding federal aid and his tight rein on city council, its commissions and board seats, which yielded control over nearly 10 percent of the city's block grant funds—some $33 million in grants between 1974 and 1983. Forbes distributed these funds to favored churches, projects, neighborhood organizations, and council members, ensuring loyalty, but often of a grudging sort. The *Call and Post*, a Forbes supporter, conceded that his main "failure . . . has been his inability" to convince black Clevelanders that he was committed "to the advancement of the entire community, instead of just chosen allies and friends."[83] The muckraker Roldo Bartimole leveled a more biting critique, charging that Forbes "operates on fear and intimidation" and by "rigidly controlling and keeping silent . . . black members of council on issues and votes of importance to him."[84] One black councilman described how Forbes "punish[ed]" him for his independence by withholding several hundred thousand dollars in federal aid.[85]

Forbes was also a businessman, and his law firm Rogers, Horton & Forbes, established in 1971, would become the largest minority-owned firm in Ohio. Like many white liberals and businesspeople before him, Forbes engineered ways to profit through casual conflicts of interest, particularly through his firm's work for businesses seeking government contracts or favors such as zoning changes. In 1984, the firm secured a $60,000 fee from the Ozanne Construction Company for serving as general counsel in negotiations with the city over a housing development contract. The firm also represented interests seeking work on the city's convention center, the transit system, and the North Shore office project, which the law firm Jones Day would make the headquarters of its growing international practice. By the mid-1980s, however, according to available records, the firm's most significant revenue was generated through bond counseling—legal work essential for the underwriting, issuance, and purchase of government debt.[86] In one case, the firm served

Figure 8. Cleveland City Council president George Forbes's calculated distribution of increasingly precious federal funds was well known. Ray Osrin, editorial cartoon, *Cleveland Plain Dealer*, April 17, 1985. Ray Osrin Editorial Cartoons Collection, courtesy of the Michael Schwartz Library Special Collections, Cleveland State University.

as underwriting counsel for the State of Ohio on a prison bond, earning a $45,000 fee. By the middle of the 1980s, Forbes was almost certainly a multimillionaire, profiting handsomely from the ancillary wages of his council presidency.[87]

Cleveland's business elites recognized in Forbes a man with whom they could deal, and by the late 1970s he had cultivated close ties with James Davis and the Growth Association. At the nadir of the Kucinich years, Forbes announced his support for plans to shrink the city council from thirty-three to twenty-one wards, charging that the outsized body neither produced rational development planning nor effectively represented the city, whose population was rapidly shrinking. The Growth Association backed Forbes, and, after a campaign in which twenty council members supported the proposal, Cleveland's council was reduced to twenty-one wards, and council members' terms (and the mayor's) were increased to four years. To protect his seat and amplify his control, Forbes's district was redrawn to include not only his old ward in

Glenville, but also much of University Circle, the tree-lined campus featuring the city's art museum, Case Western Reserve University, and Severance Hall, home to the renowned Cleveland Orchestra. Forbes purchased a $13,500 lot at the corner of 115th Street and Bellflower, amid the city's "cultural citadel," and hired an in-demand architect to design a four-thousand-square-foot home.[88] By 1989, the *Plain Dealer* described Forbes as the "darling of much of corporate Cleveland," an indispensable power broker in the postindustrial, post–civil rights city.[89]

Fannie Lewis, meanwhile, used her council seat to fight for the decade's only new affordable housing project, Lexington Village. As she had in the Model Cities wars and in the early days of CDBGs in the 1970s, she continued to fight "to keep the federal dollars for the Black people it was intended for."[90] Most significantly, she spearheaded a low-density, affordable housing project, the first phase of which opened on October 1, 1985. Lexington Village included a pool, playground, tennis and basketball courts, and one- and two-bedroom apartments and larger townhouse-style homes. Diminished federal aid and ambivalent support from Voinovich and Forbes forced Lewis to turn

Figure 9. Cleveland city councilwoman Fannie Lewis at the Lexington Village affordable housing development, February 10, 1989. David I. Andersen/ *The Plain Dealer* © 1989. All rights reserved. Reprinted/used with permission.

to nonprofits and the private sector to finance the project. She partnered with the Famicos Foundation, a nonprofit formed in 1970 to rehab houses and apartments, which, by 1985, despite little public support, had rehabilitated over 350 homes and six apartment buildings.[91] Lexington Village soon housed two thousand Clevelanders in Hough, still one of the city's poorest neighborhoods. While Voinovich helped link private funds to the project and delivered modest CDBG funding, Lewis was the prime mover.[92] "Lexington Village," she declared, "proves that the city bureaucracy can function. A lot of people doubted whether the city could work with the developers and the bank" to create homes for poor and working people, "but the city proved it could deliver."[93] Lewis's point was clear: elites' abandonment of poor and working people and their neighborhoods was a choice repeatedly made.

Development and Democracy in the Dual City

With the city's financial situation stabilized and Forbes commanding the city council, Voinovich and the Roundtable planned the city's economic future with suburban residents' work and recreational opportunities squarely in view. Voinovich consulted closely with Mandell "Del" de Windt, initially the Roundtable's most influential member, on the "Dual Hub Corridor" plan.[94] The city's downtown, resting on the southern shore of Lake Erie, was one of two "hubs" designated for subsidies for office, recreation, and retail development. The second was University Circle, five miles east of downtown, occupying much of Forbes's council district. Linking the two hubs were the east-west arteries of Euclid and Chester Avenues, along which the Cleveland Clinic's expanding campus occupied more than twenty blocks. "Obviously," Voinovich wrote to his private-sector allies, "the agreed corridor from downtown to University Circle seems ... to be the City's best opportunity for future development." "If you concur," we should "develop an overall plan and strategy for the area" that "would represent our civic vision ... and would ultimately be adopted by our City Planning Commission."[95]

Rather than simply use businesspeople as advisers or consultants, Voinovich formalized their role in policymaking and execution. Cleveland Tomorrow designed a postindustrial policy, while the Roundtable became Voinovich's planning and development committee.[96] The organizations produced "Civic Vision," a "general plan" for redevelopment. Unveiled November 8, 1984, in a special section of the *Plain Dealer*, Civic Vision championed downtown redevelopment led by "business and civic leaders." As in the managed participation of the Block Grant Workshops, Civic Vision invited citizens to participate in listening sessions detailing the reasons why the vast majority of subsidies would support the dual hubs.[97]

Alongside the physical redevelopment of the hubs, the Roundtable heeded McKinsey consultants' counsel that Cleveland needed a postindustrial development policy. In 1980, planners recognized the potential of targeting "advanced technology related to Cleveland's medical services," especially in partnership with the Cleveland Clinic.[98] The Clinic, as Clevelanders call it, had an international reputation for its pioneering work in heart surgery, and it had also navigated unrest thanks to its central role in some of the most egregious displacements of the urban renewal era, learning, as many businesses had, the value of token community outreach measures in the process.[99]

In 1982, Voinovich aimed for the private hospital to be the first beneficiary of a state-originated enterprise zone–type tax rebate program.[100] The Clinic's leadership, though, remained concerned about the "character" of the neighborhood surrounding the Chester Avenue site where it planned to expand its campus. Like the business consultants who warned Reagan that tax and regulatory breaks were thin stimulus, the hospital's leaders sought broader "incentives": "Financial assistance to the adjacent local development corporations"; "the establishment of a non-profit or a for-profit corporation to provide security services in the area" (the clinic had once contemplated a private "guard force" composed of "men with previous military service, especially combat experience"); and they asked that publicly underwritten "consultants . . . develop a physical redevelopment" and an "investment strategy for the larger area focusing on medically related industries."[101] The Clinic sought an entirely new market and redeveloped environment geared toward the medical industry.

While the private hospital had historically relied on federal contracts to drive its research-oriented expansion, Cleveland Tomorrow created the Primus Venture Fund, a $25–30 million venture capital fund design to support early-stage startups. They imagined raising much more, and hoped for public support, too: Cleveland banker Brock Weir, writing in *Industry Week*, urged the Reagan administration to create "a National Industrial Policy Board . . . with quasi-independent status like the Federal Reserve Board." Weir imagined representatives of business, academia, and labor serving ten-year terms during which they would "analyze and deliberate on the long-range industrial needs and opportunities . . . and [have] limited powers to influence the flow of capital."[102] Though these ideas were lost on Reagan, subnational governments took the initiative.

Ohio created the $80 million Thomas Edison program in 1983, as the *Wall Street Journal* put it, to "provide seed capital, establish incubators and fund technology centers."[103] The *Journal* held up Ohio's Edison program, which invested more than $250 million by 1988, as an exemplar of entrepreneurial postindustrial policy.[104] By the summer of 1986, former McKinsey consultant and Cleveland Tomorrow director Richard Shatten lauded two new publicly subsidized research centers that matched public or private venture capital to commercializable R&D. With initial investments of $3.5 million from Ohio's Edison program, the centers would build "a base of new medical technology businesses." As Shatten exclaimed, Cleveland would "make love to our entrepreneurs."[105] The Cleveland Clinic's Foundation Research Institute tapped these funds and recruited more subsidies from the National Institutes of Health. As Dr. Bernadine Healy, the foundation's chairwoman put it, Cleveland would become "one of the major centers in the country for biomedical research and biomedical technology." Between 1985 and 1989 the institute's budget grew from $5 million to $36 million, employing some 160 scientists and an overall staff of 355. The growing enterprise would soon have a new home, the Clinic's Health Sciences Center, a thirty-thousand-square-foot building between Cedar and Carnegie Avenues. Soon, a second ninety-thousand-square-foot facility was on the drawing board.[106] Bill Sanford, whose medical technology and sterilization start-up Steris benefited from early-stage Edison VC investments, was grateful for the public assistance: "People in start-up businesses tend to underestimate the amount of time and money involved in starting a business." Cleveland's incubators, venture funding, and public-to-private technology transfers could help generate faster, more cost-effective start-ups. In 1988 Steris hired its thirty-eighth employee.[107] By 2014, Steris was a publicly traded company with $2.6 billion in annual revenues.[108]

George Forbes was instrumental in shepherding many of these developments through the council and often in ways that symbolically if not substantively signaled he had black residents' interests at heart. When Voinovich proposed financing a loan program for *middle*-income homebuyers near the Clinic development—sandwiched between deeply impoverished black neighborhoods of Hough and Fairfax—Forbes repudiated the plan. The corridor, he charged, would act as precisely the kind of gentrified "buffer zones between the Clinic and the residents of Fairfax" that the Clinic had asked the city to create. He blasted the proposal at a council meeting: "if you think you are going to start building rose bushes and trees on Cedar [Road] to buffer white folks from black folks you are out of your damn mind.... It's just plain, down-South segregation." In what was becoming classic Forbes fashion, however, his bluster provided cover—at the same meeting he and a majority of the council voted for the loan subsidies.[109]

Most important, Forbes used the sustained crises of declining population, federal austerity, deindustrialization, and fiscal instability to argue on behalf of business's most aggressive demands: tax abatements. Here the historical arguments for liberalism's supply side were turned inside out. Rather than use federal spending to boost local developments and tax yields to shore up municipal fiscal autonomy, the city justified tax abatements as the last, best way to boost development and produce a modicum of employment—in search of mystical future tax yields.

Yet, at a time of federal austerity, abatements also offered fiscally straitjacketed municipal officials a means of action in step with the era's antigovernment sentiment and veneration of risk-taking entrepreneurs. Indeed, Mayor Voinovich often submerged government's role in structuring the city's major developments. At a ribbon cutting for a development along the dual hub corridor, he celebrated private developers as "the new urban pioneers, rebuilding an old city with vision, courage and commitment."[110] This was a vision he sold as president of the National League of Cities. In Baton Rouge, Voinovich explained how, in Cleveland, "44 corporate leaders" rebuilt city government and created the Roundtable "to take the economic destiny of the city into their hands."[111] Abatements then, signified politicians' willingness to create space for and get out of the way of heroic entrepreneurs and risk-taking investors.

At a moment when city schools were deteriorating and black neighborhoods, including Forbes's district, were sliding into catastrophic poverty, however, Forbes's defense of abatements was also politically indispensable for businesspeople. Blocking tax abatements, Forbes argued, only "consigns" Clevelanders "to a future without hope for... job[s] or any reasonable opportunity for escape from poverty."[112] "Long term [fiscal] stability," he argued, depends on making "Cleveland attractive to new economic development."[113] By 1988, Forbes engineered a political solution to defuse anger over the fact that abatements robbed schools of funds. To ensure support for the Tower City and Ameritrust abatements, for which the city would forgo some $128 million in revenues, Forbes pledged to "share [with the schools] on a 50/50 basis, all increased tax revenue generated by development of these new projects"—though those proceeds, were they to materialize, could be shared in cash or "in-kind services such as waste collection."[114] Regardless, the schools would have to wait years for the abatements to end. With abatements ensuring the further withdrawal or destabilization of municipal resources, "popular marketization"—the turn by regular people to markets and other nongovernmental organizations for support—became entrenched. Community activists, parents, and residents turned to market alternatives or nonprofits not by preference but in desperate efforts to maintain essential goods and services.[115]

Yet the city did have resources. Indeed, Civic Vision's downtown hub depended upon considerable sums of federal community development and antipoverty funds.[116] The Roundtable, armed with its own lobbyists and consultants in Washington, kept the pressure on city officials: "Al Ratner and Shellie Guren," Voinovich wrote to his development director, "are interested in getting one half million to one million dollars' worth of money for their Tower City project." The mayor delivered far more for this high-end retail and hotel project in the Van Sweringens' Terminal Tower. Tower City ultimately received five UDAGs totaling $31.5 million. And, as the Roundtable noted with relief, Congress's protection of CDBGs "paved the way for ... Tower City ... by furnishing $12.5 million" for crucial infrastructure improvements.[117] Ultimately, it took $54 million in state and federal resources to ensure the project's completion in 1988, nearly fifteen years after it had been conceived. Rather than inject federal and state funding into neighborhoods where it was desperately needed, Cleveland pumped millions of dollars into ensuring Tower City's developers would take UDAG financing. Private developers had not been waiting all those years for a freer market to break ground.

The community development subsidies lavished on Tower City only scratched the surface of the vast public underwriting of private profit that transformed the city into a retail and recreational destination for suburbanites. On Ninth Street, officials devoted another $3.5 million UDAG to finance the Galleria, a glass atrium, high-end shopping center that finally completed the Erieview urban renewal site. The Galleria's boosters made cheerful comparisons to other developments courting white suburbanites in cities including Baltimore (Harborplace), Boston (Faneuil Hall), Chicago (Water Tower Place), Denver (Tabor Center), and Minneapolis (City Center).[118] On Public Square, across from Tower City, the Jacobses received another $10 million in UDAGs to begin redeveloping land on which they would raise the city's tallest building, the Society (now Key) Bank tower. Meanwhile, the city directed millions of UDAGs to a housing scheme for the Flats and Warehouse entertainment districts along the river in hopes of attracting young professionals. Over seven years, the city directed $80.5 million of UDAGs to the dual hub project and a major renovation of the moribund theater district. Together, they represented 80 percent of the city's total UDAG spending.

Though Voinovich's use of CDBGs was initially more in line with actual neighborhood development than was the Perk administration's (in part because of tightened regulations), when Reagan's cuts came, neighborhoods suffered the bulk of the reductions. From 1985 to 1986, when Reagan slashed CDBGs, Cleveland's share shrank from nearly $29 million to $19 million. Voinovich faced hard choices, certainly, but housing received the most drastic cuts. Formerly, the city set aside $3.3 million for housing and rehab programs. The bulk of those funds went to a program for weatherizing homes, but that total was cut from $2.8 to $1.2 million. The greatest housing department expenditure became code enforcement ($2.2 million), which enhanced the city's capacity to force residents to use their own capital to make renovations—or face fines and eviction.[119] The city did, however, offer a $500,000 program to community development corporations to stimulate private investment in market-rate housing for new middle-class residents, which, officials claimed, would yield eight hundred new housing units. This funding was often geared toward gentrification rather than existing residents. Easily the city's largest CDBG expenditure was the $3.567 million it set aside for "administration" purposes, funds that could be moved through various departments to support whichever programs it saw fit.

Throughout, the city's impoverished neighborhoods continually faced the intentional public disinvestment that flowed from urban triage. In one policy memo, an official urged colleagues to recognize "the seriousness of demographic changes." The city should deny subsidies even to groups like the Hough Area Development Corporation operating in neighborhoods deemed beyond repair. "It is difficult," she noted, to "threaten the existence of certain organizations. Nevertheless, we find it unconscionable to continue throwing good money after bad." The city must "redirect critical assets to help good organizations and make wise investments."[120] The mayor's business allies were even clearer about redirecting community development funds away from poor, minority neighborhoods. Prior to coming to Cleveland to take up the presidency of Tower City, Inc., Richard Green was community development director in Columbus, where he oversaw neighborhood redevelopment around the Battelle Institute, a science and technology development center. As he explained in one memo, "*Under no circumstances should family low income housing be allowed* as it will defeat market upgrading and the program of 'renaissance.'" Housing for the elderly and "for handicapped persons," however, could be included, since they provide a "buffer zone (protecting against the poor)," as well as "good PR." All of this would "demonstrate concern and creativity while further segmenting the lower income, radical population."[121] In Cleveland, George Forbes was even rumored to have told developers that "there's no advantage to being around poor people."[122] Redirection, segmentation, and active public disinvestment and segregation of impoverished citizens constituted urban policy in the 1980s.

Forbes's primary base of political support shifted during the decade, and so would his tactics for maintaining power. In 1981, when white west-side council members attempted to recruit disgruntled east-side black representatives to oust him, Forbes raised the specter of white dominance of city council. Councilwoman Fannie Lewis, whom the *Call and Post* dubbed "the conscience of City Council," joined with a young black councilman, Michael R. White, to begrudgingly rally behind Forbes.[123] As White put it, despite his own considerable critiques of Forbes, "What we did was no different from what the Irish or Italians would have did [*sic*]."[124] By the end of the 1980s, however, when Forbes faced another west-side mutiny, he drew upon a deep well of business support. The Growth Association organized a "Good Government Committee," composed of a who's who of financial and legal services elites.[125] They filled a war chest for Forbes to distribute campaign funds to council members, buying their support. Top donors included scores of attorneys at Squire, Sanders, and Dempsey, principals at Forest City Ratner, contractors, and many suburb-residing businesspeople.[126] Forbes showered black neighborhoods with leaflets urging voters to support the city's chief "black leader," "champion," and the "*President . . . we* could *trust.*" "Don't let them do it," a flyer warned. "Black leadership is hard to get, but it's harder to keep."[127] Often skeptical of others' calls for black unity, Forbes was not above invoking it when his seat was on the line.

Yet, residents of African American neighborhoods understood that they were being slowly, progressively, intentionally abandoned. Armstrong Grace, a Glenville resident, described the situation: "I am writing this to inform the City of Cleveland, that there are people living in the Glenville area, specifically the area southeast of Superior. I say this because, at this time, I am at the end of my patience with this city. The area I'm referring to is part of our most well-known Council President's district. No one, however, in this entire city, including George Forbes, seems to acknowledge our existence."[128] For African Americans in Cleveland, the increasing hollowness of Forbes's advocacy and their literal abandonment contributed to the collapsing legitimacy of local institutions. In his plaintive letter to the *Call and Post*, Grace noted that the city's paper of record, the *Plain Dealer*, would not even deliver to his house. Community activist Don Freeman, a longtime Hough resident, explained that "Twenty-five years ago," on the eve of the 1966 Hough riots, "people were not abandoned." By 1989, Cleveland may have been the national media's comeback city, but thousands of residents were "abandoned and relegated to permanent poverty by this society and its institutions."[129]

* * *

Sitting just behind Bill Clinton when he delivered the keynote address at the 1991 Democratic Leadership Council convention in Cleveland was the city's new mayor, Michael White. In 1989, when George Voinovich won the governor's office, White, then a thirty-eight-year-old state senator and former city councilman, defeated the fifty-nine-year-old George Forbes in a mayoral contest pitting different generations of black power brokers. By then, Forbes's legitimacy had collapsed in black neighborhoods, and he hoped a few black stalwarts, white voters, and businesspeople would secure his victory. Campaigning in black wards, Forbes took credit for Fannie Lewis's Lexington Village and charged White with being "a slum landlord" thanks to some two hundred code violations in rental properties White owned.

White and Forbes, however, split the black vote, and the support White earned from white voters ensured his victory. White pledged a city "free of division and hatred," and he accused Forbes of abusing his power to gin up the code violations and cynically stir racial animosities.[130] Perhaps most important, White emphasized individual responsibility and a tough-on-crime agenda. The centerpiece of his campaign was his call for individuals in black neighborhoods to take responsibility for themselves and their communities while he worked on the city's ongoing economic revitalization.

These themes resonated with the central thrust of Clinton's address, in which he called for balancing government's role in promoting economic opportunity with the personal obligation of individual responsibility. The New Democrat leaned heavily on images of urban pathologies—drug abuse, broken families, and crime. Such social crises, Clinton argued, ultimately depended upon individual solutions. As he put it, "governments do not raise children, people do, and it is time they were asked to assume their responsibilities and forced to do it if they refuse." As he explained "if you give opportunity without insisting on responsibility, much of the money can be wasted, and the country's strength can still be sapped." By delivering these words in a city nearly evenly split between white and black working-class and poor voters, Clinton hoped to establish himself as a white liberal who was, as he put it, "not afraid to tell the people the truth." Clinton's target audience, then, was clearly not most poor people. Rather, he hoped to convince "the very burdened middle class" that Democrats would "take their tax money and spend it with discipline."[131]

For his support of such "centrist" values, Michael White received a glowing profile in the DLC's publication, the *Mainstream Democrat*, which called him "Cleveland's new mainstream Democratic mayor."[132] "Cleveland has become known as the Comeback City," said White upon learning that Cleveland would host the DLC convention. "By coming here in 1991, the DLC will give Democrats a great chance to become the Comeback Party."[133] In highlighting the support of a moderate, black rising star, DLCers hoped to deflect criticism that their agenda lacked racial inclusivity. But it was inclusivity of a particular sort. Northeastern Ohio was home to working-class white "Reagan Democrats," whom the DLC aimed to bring back to their fathers' party. A conservative Democratic city councilman who had voted for Reagan and Bush supported White because his "message . . . in the black community is that you can't go blaming people anymore. . . . There comes a point where people have got to take control of their own destiny." That conservative Democratic councilman was convinced—he would vote for Clinton.[134]

White's and Clinton's emphasis on growth, individual responsibility, and a hard line on crime also played well with Cleveland's business leadership. White enthusiastically extended his predecessor's suburban-oriented development plans. New bond issues and state and federal funding were crucial for the redevelopment of the inner harbor and other projects, including the Rock and Roll Hall of Fame. But White's biggest undertaking—a massive new sports complex to house the professional baseball and basketball franchises, "Gateway," conceived by supply-side state builders in the mid-1970s—was funded by a highly regressive countywide tax on alcohol and cigarettes, which, like abatements, redistributed resources from regular residents to business elites. Though government continued to be blamed for neighborhoods in crisis, its foundational, stimulative role was all but ignored in the national

Figure 10. Mayor Michael White at the lakefront site of the future Rock and Roll Hall of Fame, January 4, 1991. Behind him, from left, the striped North Point building, home to the law firm Jones, Day, Reavis & Pogue (now Jones Day); behind it, the Erieview Tower and Erieview urban renewal site; and, at right, the pyramidal Sohio Tower, the Key Bank Tower under construction, and the Van Sweringens' Terminal Tower, site of the Ratner's Tower City luxury retail and hotel development. Steve Kagan/ The Chronicle Collection/ Getty Images.

media's fawning coverage of Cleveland's bifurcated comeback. Instead, that comeback fundamentally rested on the diversion of community development funds and, through abatements and sin taxes, direct, upward redistribution of resources out of poor neighborhoods.

Between 1980 and 1988, Cleveland's poverty rate increased by more than a third, and over 65 percent of the population in three predominantly black neighborhoods on the east side—including Hough and Glenville—lived below the poverty line. By 1988, over half the residents of 40 percent of the city's census tracts lived in poverty; in 1970 the figure had been just 3.5 percent.[135] Without meaningful representation, with activist groups fractured and drained, hope dashed, and with residents increasingly ground down by and accustomed to the new style of hollowed out participation, many African Americans understood turning out to the polls to be an empty exercise. Many simply stopped voting. In 1967, when Carl Stokes won the mayoralty, voter turnout in black wards reached 80.4 percent. In the mayoral election of 1985, the figure was just 36.77 percent.[136] "Black voters won a resounding victory in the primary election" of 1985, one frustrated citizen wrote. "Their candidate, *Black apathy*, defeated every other runner-up by a wide margin."[137]

Though black citizens had for decades demanded administrative empowerment within the decentralized administrative state, the neoliberalized and tightly managed forms of participation realized by the 1980s more often excused and enabled entrenched inequalities rather than challenged them. The public private policy tools, political-cultural veneration of business producerism, imbalanced fiscal federal structures, and the racial exclusion built into liberalism's supply side state, then, helped produce the entrenched, racialized poverty, diminished democracy, and public disinvestment and electoral demobilization characteristic of neoliberal cities. Indeed, real estate, banking, and financial and legal services firms—the businesses most associated with the neoliberal turn—had always been among the most ubiquitous supply-side state builders. Rather than offer sustained and frank appraisals of the ongoing significance of public resources, of the ongoing realities of political power in shaping markets and social opportunity, in the 1990s, New Democrats would increasingly apply supply side tools and market-based solutions across a widening array of social policies—from welfare to health care—and in so doing further drain democratic contestation from the workings of the state itself.

Epilogue:
The New Democrats and the Idea of the State

"It was an orgy of austerity," recalled Robert Reich of President Bill Clinton's first cabinet meeting.[1] Reich had played a leading role in Clinton's campaign, and his ideas suffused its bible, *Putting People First*. For Reich, the spiritual foundations of their agenda were expansive new "investments" in high-tech sectors of the economy as well as in "human capital"—education and worker retraining. While he imagined restoring faith in active if lean and entrepreneurial government, Reich's marketized ideas dovetailed with more overtly antigovernment aspects of Clinton's campaign. Featured prominently in *Putting People First* were pledges to slash the deficit, cut "100,000 unnecessary positions in the bureaucracy," and, most famously, "end welfare as we know it."[2] Still, as he arrived in Washington to lead Clinton's Labor Department, Reich was optimistic.

Yet from the start Reich's vision of supply-side investments to remake the "real economy" crashed up against a very different set of ideas about government's role emanating from financial markets. Wall Street, particularly the bond traders and financiers New Democrats courted in the 1980s, warned that the growing deficit would produce higher interest rates, diminished investments, and perhaps even inflation, finance capitalists' greatest fear. A newly assertive financial sector had strong advocates in Treasury Secretary Lloyd Bentsen, National Economic Council Director Robert Rubin, and Federal Reserve Chair Alan Greenspan. These advisers reminded Clinton that they best understood the economy—or at least, Wall Street's version of it. To protect Wall Street's margins, which they framed in terms of producing jobs, they ordered similar fiscal fetters on national budgets that credit rating agencies and lenders pressed on debt-saddled municipal governments. Wall Street was flexing its own producerist muscles.

After a decade during which New Democrats argued for making hard choices on social spending, Clinton's Wall Street whisperers tasked him with making some of his own. Reich was incredulous "that *the deficit* [was] . . . framing our discussions about what we want to accomplish." They spent that first cabinet meeting, and much of the first term, coming "up with symbolic ways to show taxpayers we intend to do government on the cheap." The administration, wrote Reich, was "building [its] own conceptual prison."[3]

But New Democrats' increasingly asymmetrical partnership with Wall Street was not primarily to blame. Nor was their conceptual prison particularly new. Instead, New Democrats' desiccated imagination for public endeavor and the habit of doing "government on the cheap" had roots in New Deal and Cold War liberals' own ideas about the relationship between the state and markets as well as their wariness about the state they built.

A State of Denial

In the shadow of global fascism and communism, New Deal and midcentury liberals were anxious about the clear aggrandizement and exercise of state power. As they constructed their hesitant leviathan—discursively and in actual fact—political struggle and public authority took receding roles in narratives about the organization of political power, citizenship, and the state. By midcentury and as Cold War anticommunism suffused American politics, denial became built into the very bones of the liberal state—they delegated authority, lionized the local, and constructed public-private partnerships. Their stars were the genius of market capitalism and the "American way"—scrappy individuals and businesspeople, intrepid inventors and entrepreneurs, the nuclear families whose consumption made it all go. The transformational technological advancements of the Cold War and supply-side states, the creation of a vast white middle class through restructured housing markets and higher education, and public investments that drove the explosive economic expansion of the Sunbelt were markers of modern democratic capitalism, not the engineered products of the distribution and redistribution of political power and resources.[4]

Here was the midcentury liberal consensus: the overt exercise of the state's developmental or regulatory power was rarely an end in itself; rather, they were deployed to meet temporary expediencies, ensure earned forms of social security, and execute momentary course corrections to more securely and broadly diffuse market opportunities and capitalist development. For liberals during Cold War decades characterized by relative bipartisan political acceptance if not full consensus about the state's positive but restrained domestic role, spinning such mythologies came with few obvious political costs. Moreover, they maintained, the state owed its very existence, its fiscal lifeblood, to markets. And, in initiatives where the state's power was undeniable, as in urban renewal, liberals excused its often brutal costs as temporary exceptions to their broader consensus, costs more easily accepted, of course, because of the racially disparate ways they were borne. And in any event, markets for housing and much else were being reformed and restarted and cities were being returned to fiscal autonomy, which might preclude the need for government to take such action in the future.

But, as liberals constructed what one scholar has called a "Rube Goldberg state," submerging and naturalizing its advantages for white citizens and business, they handed up to future generations impaired and partial memories of its benefits, of just how far reaching and enduring its programs and policies had become, and of just how tenaciously—if behind the scenes rather than in the streets—elite interests fought to maintain structural advantages.[5] Even as liberals committed themselves to formal racial enfranchisement and civil rights, then, structural inequalities compounded for poor, minority, and even rural citizens. Midcentury liberals at once pushed considerable fiscal, social, spatial, racial, and political inequalities onto future generations while entrenching political structures and common senses that emphasized market outcomes over frank appraisals of state power, of economic growth over redistribution. The greatest proponents of a mythically weak American state, then, were often midcentury liberals themselves.[6] New Democrats' "conceptual prison" was built from their conceptual inheritances.

As marginalized citizens sought the kinds of state support that had ensured the explosive growth of the white middle class, many white liberals and New Democrats, already primed to mistrust public institutions in the age of Vietnam and Watergate, viewed those claims with a suspicion also born of racial privilege and the historical amnesia that abetted it. In fashioning their own illusions of progress, New Democrats reinvented many of the orientations of liberalism's supply side, which, they perhaps intuited, tended to insulate administration from broader publics. Reframed in marketized terms, the tools of liberalism's supply side—decentralism, public-private partnerships, fiscal realism—might even enable liberals to shear off the most obviously contested public policies, draining politics from controversial social questions while ostensibly maintaining them as secondary priorities within a broader growth agenda. As PPI fellow and Clinton adviser David Osborne explained, the primary issues "are those of adjustment" to new economic realities: "battles over distribution and power will await a more stable time."[7]

As if politics was not ever and always a battle over distribution and power. In historical fact, of course, the inverse logic had more often been the case—public power and political choices had driven both the affluence and the compounding disparities that shaped the political contestations New Democrats now hoped to sidestep or forestall by recentering growth. By imagining the pursuit of economic growth and fiscal solvency as somehow outside of or before politics, New Democrats effectively dealt themselves out of momentous contests over political and economic power. At best, they became unwitting handmaidens to neoliberal processes unfolding. Often, however, as in their destruction of welfare entitlements dating to the New Deal, New Democrats' anti-politics made them active agents in these transformations.

Indeed, if progressives and social democrats had imagined *decommodifying* social goods like housing by taking them out of the market, by the 1990s New Democrats imagined *depoliticizing* social policies like welfare by injecting supply-side logics into them. When Bill Clinton signed the Personal Responsibility and Work Opportunity Reconciliation Act of 1996, the developmental and governing priorities of liberalism's supply side helped eclipse a long-standing social entitlement for Americans in economic crises. In place of the modest income support of Aid to Families with Dependent Children, Temporary Assistance to Needy Families (TANF) offered block grants to states, instituted stringent work requirements, set strict lifetime limits, and built a thicket of bureaucratic rules and surveillance that disincentivized citizens from seeking public assistance.

While this was a far harsher bill than Clinton envisioned—his signing statement was notably defensive—he quickly moved to accentuate the positives, highlighting how supply-side sensibilities had moved from the politics of development to shaping the anti-politics of ending redistribution for the poor. Speaking in Nashville, Clinton explicitly highlighted the depoliticization of welfare, celebrating how the bill "could take poverty out of politics." "Now," he said, "everybody who has ever said a bad word about the welfare system has nothing left to cuss; there is nothing there anymore. [*Laughter*] And now, there is no politics in poverty any more." Clinton's anti-politics echoed Wall Street's producerism and evinced New Democrats' characteristic skepticism for "programs": "The government has to balance the budget to keep interest rates down, to keep the economy strong, so we can keep creating jobs for everybody. We cannot have a government-created program that hires all these folks."[8]

In its place, he offered public-private partnerships. Businesses and nonprofits would now receive subsidies that had once gone directly to the poor: "just think what would happen if every business, every nonprofit . . . in this country took what used to go to the welfare recipient in the welfare check as a supplement and hired just one person—just one person—and took responsibility for training that person."[9] Clinton urged states "to take advantage of [the] new flexibility to use money formerly available for welfare checks to encourage the private sector to provide jobs."[10] He created the "Welfare to Work Partnership," a public-private partnership aimed at moving one million Americans from welfare to work by 2000. Hardly just jawboning, the partnership was backed with $3 billion in federal subsidies. The funds would "help cities and States to create jobs and subsidize jobs," said Clinton, "either community service jobs or subsidized private sector jobs." It also offered tax credits to companies that hired former welfare recipients.[11] In signing away welfare, Clinton simultaneously created entirely new subsidies for businesses, further ratifying their role in solving poverty. Like so many liberals before him, Clinton invested significant energy, resources, and political capital in trying to incentivize, structure, or cajole businesses and businesspeople to deliver social goods that might have been more efficiently and democratically delivered by the state.

By block granting the program's federal contributions and failing to index the subsidies to inflation, TANF declined in value over time. Though supporters highlighted how many Americans moved off of welfare rolls, those figures also included impoverished Americans no longer entitled to cash assistance. Moreover, by denying millions of Americans support, TANF also created slack in labor markets, exerting downward pressure on wages. By 2020, only twenty-one out of every one hundred families in poverty received cash assistance, down from sixty-eight in 1996. If TANF had supported the same number of families in poverty as AFDC, 3.44 million families would have received support in 2020; but only 1.06 million families received aid, and, thanks to meager benefit levels, TANF lifted many fewer families out of deep poverty than AFDC, putting families and children at greater risk.[12] While poor and marginalized Americans like Sarah Turner had always had to fight for state support, the wider safety net was there if you knew how to access it. By the 1990s, New Democrats employed the tools and instincts of supply-side liberalism on behalf of a much more austere vision of sufficiency and a fundamentally antipolitical view of democracy and governance.

Development, Democracy, and Discontents

If midcentury liberalism's electoral dominance and Cold War era concerns about totalitarian communism together abetted a certain ideological and political ambivalence about the liberal state, its antipolitical legacy among New Democrats would prove crippling in the face of a resurgent and power-hungry conservatism catalyzed by Newt Gingrich's 1994 Contract with America. Republicans were learning to marshal their own version of class warfare, pitting a class of "worthy" taxpayers against a highly racialized bogeyman of Democrat-favored tax-eaters. To liberals, Gingrich's New Majority advanced patently abstract, even absurd grievances about government overreach, liberal threats to democracy, and confiscatory taxation. But much of the effectiveness of his appeal—particularly its emphasis on fiscal ceilings, democratic transparency, and term limits—tapped into and harnessed white suburban and rural voters' anger at the supply-side shape of decades of liberal governance. One way to read Gingrich's success in 1994 was as a culmination, a national gathering in of long simmering local discontent with the fiscal and administrative practices of decades of local-national, public-private development politics. Those discontents would also kill Clinton's attempt to create a *national* postindustrial development policy.[13]

Long before 1994, anger with the supply-side state had shredded the peppy growth politics that narrowly but confidently defined civic life in Rome and much of Georgia since the Second World War. In 1983, when the Floyd County Commission sought approval for a $3.4 million bond issue for a new county library to anchor Rome's downtown revitalization, voters' response illustrated just how discredited that civic vision had become. The plan's champion was Anne Rigas who, that year, had become the Coosa Valley Area Planning and Development Commission's first chairwoman. Rigas had gotten a taste of city-county acrimony in the 1970s—she endured Roy Knowles's Wallace-ite campaigns against the Coosa and county commissions and had even faced him in earlier campaigns.[14] Knowles's antiestablishment politics had become popular, and voters increasingly rejected bonds for new civic and developmental assets. In 1983, Floyd County residents defeated Rigas's library bond, which nevertheless won a majority of Romans' votes.

After so many defeats it might have seemed silly for commissioners to solicit a new bond. But they saw it as the first step in a dance that officials had learned over years of voters' mounting resistance. They would work behind the scenes to secure public subsidies. In 1979, after voters three times declined a sales tax increase, commissioners engineered one themselves.[15] They also secured a federal judicial order that the jail be renovated or rebuilt; ensuring that the county ultimately footed the bill. For a new courthouse, commissioners secured more than $2 million in federal grants. For the library, they won $3 million in state funds and unilaterally floated $3 million in revenue bonds. By the time the library was completed three years later, all of its advocates on the commission had been voted out of office.[16] They had gotten their improvements, but they had also undermined democratic transparency, the will of the majority, and, ultimately, trust in democracy itself.

The seemingly disproportionate anger over the construction of a library, then, is incomprehensible absent the longer context of the sorts of insular commissions, boards, and elite- and expert-led governance incentivized by decades of liberalism's supply side and its reliance on bond markets. "The Day Democracy Died in Floyd County" boomed one political ad. "*Tomorrow* will be your last opportunity for 4 years," one candidate exhorted voters, "to return the government of Floyd County back to the people and stop this runaway spending that can only lead to higher property taxes, deficits and less jobs."[17] "What happened to DEMOCRACY in Floyd County?" asked another ad: "What we have now is an unelected dictatorship!"[18]

Still, Rigas persisted. In 1990, she pursued an open seat on the county commission. Her opponent that year was Roy Knowles. Knowles was seventy-five years old and suffering from emphysema and, soon, lung cancer. His campaign slogan was familiar: "Your tax dollars vs. the special interests," by which he meant not only a racialized version of special interests, but also officials like Rigas.[19] Despite his age and infirmity, Knowles defeated Rigas's developmentalism.[20] Midway through his term, however, Knowles succumbed to his illnesses. Among those who called his widow with condolences was Lester Maddox.[21] Knowles may have been dead, but his fiery low-tax, racial-majoritarian, antiestablishment politics soon went national when Gingrich's Contract with America swept Republicans to the House majority in 1994.

This was also the moment when the Clinton administration unveiled its national postindustrial policy. In his campaign, Clinton proposed creating

170 locally administered, federally funded technology and manufacturing "extension centers" that could do for the economy "what the interstate highway of the 1950s did for the productivity of the nation's travel and distribution system."[22] While administration deficit hawks and a Republican filibuster stymied these initiatives, in 1994, Clinton announced more measured plans to expand three existing federally subsidized commercial technology development centers, including one in Cleveland, into one hundred Manufacturing Technology Centers (MTCs) across the country. Clinton raised the funding for the MTCs' parent agency, the Advanced Technology Program, from $68 million to $441 million.[23] The initiative looked like nothing so much as Georgia Tech's regional R&D centers, the first of which was located in Rome, thanks to the work of the CVAPDC, itself a legacy of the New Deal's National Resources Planning Board and Works Progress Administration.

The kind of elite- and expert-led pragmatism that undergirded those initiatives was on its heels in Washington and locally. Gingrich's confederates targeted the programs "as particularly worthy of extinction." The new generation, reported the *Washington Post*, "reserve[s] a special circle in their political hell for anything that remotely smacks of 'industrial policy.'"[24] Killing the Commerce Department, under which the MTC operated, became Republicans' top target in the symbolic quest to slay a branch of the administrative state. As a Gingrich ally put it, "We're trying to . . . [prevent] a Federal command-and-control system."[25]

Clinton struggled to mount a compelling defense. Without a robust collective memory of liberalism's supply side, indeed, without much of a language to defend state action at all, the best precedent Clinton could offer was the interstate highway system—hardly a compelling analogy. His attempt at speaking explicitly was similarly doomed by collective amnesia about just how far-reaching publicly underwritten development investments continued to be. As he put it, "the Federal Government will directly support commercial technology through industry consortia [and] regional technology alliances."[26] The *Economist* offered a quizzical critique of the proposal, suggesting just how naturalized and submerged liberalism's supply side had become: "Mr. Clinton is embarking on an overt industrial policy just as America looks poised to win a great technology race precisely because it eschewed such direct government meddling."[27]

Clinton moved some funding into commercial research and development, but the figures paled compared to his earlier aspirations. By the end of his term, if Clinton had a coherent economic strategy, it was unleashing the very financial sectors whose warnings about the deficit helped cement the administration's conceptual prison and social austerity. Meanwhile, the rise of a less-regulated, finance-driven, globalizing economy exerted other significant but less evident changes that threatened not only greater inequality but also the local foundations of liberals' supply-side state.

The Splintering of the Local Power Elite

By the 1990s, the foundations of liberalism's supply side, its elite-led public-private partnerships, were crumbling. Some causes, like the Knowles and Gingrich movements, were clear enough, even if their connections to liberalism's local face was less apparent. Others, however, particularly the bipartisan choice to embrace finance capitalism and globalization, and with them the mergers and acquisitions frenzies of the 1980s, sped the local power elite's fragmentation in ways more fundamental.[28]

In the 1980s and 1990s, Cleveland's Roundtable and Cleveland Tomorrow underwent significant shifts in leadership. Retirements, mergers, and company takeovers, the *Plain Dealer* reported, "led to an unusually high turnover in the membership." In just four years, 50 percent of the CEOs who composed Cleveland Tomorrow's leadership changed. New members were younger and non-native: in 1986, just two of twenty-two new members of Cleveland Tomorrow were native northeastern Ohioans.[29] By 2001, when the CEOs of Eaton Corporation, TRW, Sherwin-Williams, KeyCorp, and Steris announced their retirements, a business journal explained that "the moves sweep away some of the primary civic architects of the city's comeback," leaders possessed of "nearly a century of combined" service to their firms and community.[30]

Beyond replacing natives with non-Clevelanders, significant structural changes within corporate capitalism also meant "the intensity level" of executive involvement in civic affairs had "weakened." By the 1990s, "companies suddenly were no longer local institutions," but were "fragmented and disconnected in the global marketplace," reported *Inside Business*. One official emphasized how the ascension of shareholder value had increased "focus on CEO performance," which meant unprecedented shareholder demand on executives' time and energies. As a CEO and member of Cleveland Tomorrow put it, attendance at board meetings was flagging, and coordinating meetings with other CEOs was "almost impossible." Meanwhile, shareholder prerogatives exerted downward pressure on corporate civic donations and spending since, as one CEO lamented, "Shareholders ... question it much more than they would" have in the past. A nonprofit advocate lamented that CEOs had only recently served on multiple philanthropic boards but "that leadership" had become "more spread out."[31]

Cleveland Tomorrow, which had so captivated Cleveland's CEOs, was dissolved in 2004. The rapidity of the transformation was striking: just six years earlier, it had been the subject of a glowing Harvard Business School case study. By 2018, civic-minded businesspeople seemed unable even to imagine mastering the local political economy. As one respondent in an article on Cleveland's "leadership vacuum" lamented, things had become so fragmented that, "even if you had a superior being at the top (guiding the region's economic development), would things be different? I don't know."[32] Shareholder value, the rise of finance, and the mergers and acquisitions movements of the 1980s and 1990s had siphoned off and fractured the old power elites' leadership, attention, autonomy, and philanthropy. Like credit rating agencies' power over municipal budgets, external financial interests were coming to matter as much or more in shaping local business and civic dynamics, and the federal government was no longer the reliable financial and organizing partner it had once been.

Similar developments emerged in Georgia where an elegiac 1987 article in *Georgia Trend* described how, "in the past 20 years, power has splintered." But in this former Jim Crow state, these processes also reflected an expansion of democracy, which editors viewed with ambivalence. "So many more people have a say that no public project can be accomplished without the painstaking building of coalitions." Civic leaders "have to fret about satisfying outsiders, ranging from housing-project residents ... to middle-class whites protesting highways that slice through their neighborhoods." As the CEO of SunTrust Bank put it, "The days when a few guys could decide what went on are over."[33]

Meanwhile, outside investors often took the lead in local developments. "Canadians and Texans often count for more than Georgians in ... area real estate" where they financed new malls, housing developments, and towers. The banking sector, too, as reliable a producer of supply-side state builders as law firms, "succumbed to outside investment." North Carolina's First Wachovia Corp. gobbled up First Atlanta. In Rome, Georgia State Bank was sold to AmSouth; National City Bank of Rome and Home Federal were acquired by First Union; First Rome Bank by Regions Bank.[34] Nationally, between 1984 and 2011, total federally insured banks and thrifts fell by 59 percent, from 17,901 to 7,357.³⁵ The new, larger institutions often imported managers who hoped to move up the corporate ladder and out of communities like Rome or Cleveland.

In manufacturing and retail, too, outside conglomerates or larger corporations took ownership positions in Georgia companies. At midcentury, department store magnate Richard Rich was one of Atlanta's most influential businesspeople. But in 1976 a Cincinnati conglomerate acquired Rich's empire.³⁶ As a leading businessman put it, Rich's successor has "to check in with Cincinnati before he can do anything . . . Dick Rich didn't have to call anyone." Lawrence Gellerstedt, a construction firm president, longed for "the old Camelot" days under "our benevolent dictatorship" of business leaders.³⁷

The result of the "benevolent dictatorship," once it was established in Cleveland, and for decades in Georgia, had been relatively smooth implementation of publicly sponsored development projects and a dynamic, expansive, and publicly secured economy for businesspeople and many, disproportionately white middle- and upper-class Americans. All of this was threatened, *Georgia Trend* implied, by greater democratic accountability and mounting antigovernment sentiment. Editors, liberals, and supply-side state builders, however, all failed to see that businesses' dominance of community and economic development had also engendered much of the anger and inequality that threatened their existence.³⁸

Even Georgia's vaunted postindustrial policy was under assault. In 2011, Republican governor Nathan Deal, riding the Tea Party wave, cut funding for Georgia Tech's Research Alliance by nearly 75 percent. As a businessman and supporter of Georgia Tech's incubator put it, "the money that the state puts into GRA is multiplied by federal grants and private dollars, historically at a factor of 5 to 1. . . . We have a lot at stake."³⁹ Rather than make a clear call for public investment in private-sector innovation, business interests worked behind the scenes to successfully fight the cuts. As its director explained in 2019, the initiative still funded "great opportunities to improve the human condition." He detailed the fund's public purpose in classic supply-side liberal terms: "Having a diverse, technology-driven economy benefits everyone. The state benefits from payroll taxes and high-quality jobs. . . . It's a virtual cycle. . . . [We] look at these young companies and help them . . . recognize that in any company's lifetime, moments of success aren't going to last forever."⁴⁰ The state stood ready with more investments and expertise to nurture entrepreneurs, to help them overcome adversity.

The public energy, resources, and imagination that offered such patient, generous, and nurturing finance and political capital to businesspeople, however, was never offered to the poor. Nor did the initiatives necessarily produce grateful, civic-spirited businesses. While an incalculable number of American companies have benefited from a fantastic array of public resources, their muscular producerism authorized ever more audacious extractions from the public trust. In 2014, Steris, which received important early seed capital from Ohio taxpayers in the 1980s, joined the "tax inversion" trend, moving its headquarters to Ireland to limit domestic tax liabilities.[41] Publicly supported corporations drained public resources in other, less obviously direct ways. The Cleveland Clinic, like many universities, used its leverage to expand its campus with public subsidies but pays no property taxes. The billion-dollar not-for-profit instead touts its impact on the local economy as well as the income taxes its employees pay, much of which, however, ends up in federal rather than local coffers.[42] The city of Cleveland cannot afford to lose the Clinic. But thanks to tax abatements, write-offs, and direct subsidies, it also cannot afford investments in basic goods and services for its residents. Such are the everyday trade-offs and devil's bargains of a governing structure that has bound itself to private profit. Except for a matter of months during the War on Poverty, when impoverished Americans had momentary access to federal community development funds—a use of resources most municipalities have never felt fiscally secure enough to imagine allocating—the United States has never trusted poor people to administer resources that might enable them to determine their own fates.

Yet even that vanishingly short window of support empowered many, and many women especially, launching careers in community organizing, community development, and formal politics, as in the case of Cleveland's longest-serving councilwoman, Fannie Lewis.[43] Long after her battles over Model Cities, Lewis championed poor and marginalized Clevelanders, fighting for every scrap of public, private, and nonprofit subsidy to make her district a better place to live. The "Fannie Lewis Law" is still on the books, mandating that city residents compose at least 20 percent of the workforce on any city construction project with public investments of more than $100,000. She also devoted herself to voter organizing and, in the face of cutbacks, succeeded in expanding access to ballot boxes. Some of the most lasting public goods she delivered were the Lexington Village and Crawford Estates public and affordable housing developments, which continue to serve her community.

In Rome and Floyd County, Georgia, too, pressure from African American residents finally broke the grip of white administrative supremacy when Samuel Burrell Sr. won an open seat on the county commission in 1992. Burrell had been principal of the segregated Main High School, but despite his qualifications, his victory was far from assured.[44] Over the course of twenty-six secret ballots, the commission deadlocked between Burrell and Lucian Oldham, a retired, white business owner. After a frustrated commissioner forced the votes into the open, Burrell won in two rounds.[45] As Alvin Jackson, vice president of Rome's NAACP put it, with an African American at last granted a degree of administrative enfranchisement, "we can begin to see equal treatment in government." Perhaps more meaningfully, the seat Burrell would occupy was that of the late Roy Knowles. Not all progress, then, was illusory. But much of the expansion of democratic representation or economic opportunity in the twentieth century was driven not by any inherent commitment or allyship of American liberalism but often despite it—and thanks to the hard work and tenacity of individuals like Fannie Lewis in concert with their communities.

Pressed on the question of the United States' deeply entrenched poverty, rather than advocate for directly empowering the poor and marginalized, business leaders and politicians more often advocate bootstraps initiative. "The opportunity we have is to give them the opportunity to help themselves," Albert Ratner told *Newsweek*. The CEO of Forest City, a founding member of Cleveland's Roundtable, and the developer of Terminal Tower's Tower City and its publicly subsidized Ritz-Carlton Hotel, Ratner was unabashed about directing free market shibboleths at the poor, while his company helped itself to public subsidies. "Individuals," he said, "have to save themselves."[46] As of 2023, however, thanks to regional competition and suburban alternatives, Ratner's Tower City struggles with low occupancy and is now home to a massive, extractive casino. The city, desperate as always for capital thanks in part to a budget pockmarked with tax abatements, struck a buyout agreement on the remainder of Forest City's public debt. Rather than receive payment for the total value of UDAG loans, Cleveland cut a third of its publicly owed debt to secure a one-time payment—another subsidy for a dying development.[47] A similar fate befell the Jacobs brothers' Galleria on the Erieview urban renewal site, which is nearly empty and at one point was converted into a giant urban greenhouse for organic produce. As one farmer put it, "It's not really a shopping mall anymore."[48] Thirty years later, however, Fannie Lewis's Lexington Village is still a viable, at-capacity community in the heart of Hough, one of the poorest neighborhoods in one of the nation's poorest cities.

Essential to modern liberals' self-conception has always been a progressive vision of uplifting the poorest, of pursuing equality of opportunity. Yet, reconciled to the constitutional structure of American fiscal federalism and market capitalism, liberals chose to work through elite, private intermediaries and state and local governments, honoring, they believed, Americans' preference for civil society, for localism. In these cyclical returns to public-private partnerships, however, liberals invented ever more circuitous and improbable ways of delivering social and economic opportunity, empowering conservative white business elites, bond holders and credit raters, and tax-hungry subnational governments. Rather than merely work around Americans' presumed anti-statism, liberals' supply-side state ultimately entrenched and provoked it—inviting deserving skepticism at the unequally distributed costs, unfulfilled promises, and undemocratic practices enabled by government through delegation and debt. Imagining alternatives to the United States' stark racial and class inequalities, then, whether rural or urban, big city or small, will mean undoing the democratic disfranchisement and demobilization wrought by the American public-private state, which, as Philip Selznick warned in 1949, risked turning "democracy" into little "more than honorific symbols" that obscured the actual working out of power.[49] Making American democracy meaningful, then, demands decoupling the interests of capital from our visions of progress. It means making peace with democratic contestation, empowering marginalized citizens, and, above all, trusting and joining with them in confronting the root causes of our inequalities.

ABBREVIATIONS

AC	*Atlanta Constitution*
ACIR	Advisory Commission on Intergovernmental Relations
ADW	*Atlanta Daily World*
APP	American Presidency Project, John Woolley and Gerhard Peters, University of California, Santa Barbara
Brown	Walter J. Brown Media Archives & Peabody Awards Collection, University of Georgia Library, Athens
Burton	Harold Hitz Burton Papers, Western Reserve Historical Society, Cleveland, Ohio
Carter	Jimmy Carter Pre-Presidential Papers, Jimmy Carter Presidential Library, Atlanta, Georgia
CCB	*Crain's Cleveland Business*
CCUS	Papers of the Chamber of Commerce of the United States, Hagley Museum and Library, Wilmington, Delaware
CDF	Cleveland Development Foundation Records, Western Reserve Historical Society, Cleveland, Ohio
CM	*Cleveland Magazine*
CP	*Cleveland Call and Post*
CSM	*Christian Science Monitor*
CT	*Chicago Tribune*
Davis	James W. Davis Papers, Richard B. Russell Library for Political Research and Studies, University of Georgia, Athens
Forbes	George L. Forbes Papers, Series II, Western Reserve Historical Society, Cleveland, Ohio
Ford	Gerald R. Ford Presidential Library, Ann Arbor, Michigan
Gaither	James C. Gaither Files, War on Poverty, 1964–1968, Part 3: White House Aides Files, LBJ Library, Austin, Texas, ProQuest History Vault, American Politics and Society from Kennedy to Watergate

GCGA	Greater Cleveland Growth Association Papers, Western Reserve Historical Society, Cleveland, Ohio
Gingrich	Newt Gingrich Papers, University of West Georgia Special Collections, Carrollton
GPCA	Georgia Power Corporate Archives, Atlanta
GT	*Georgia Trend*
Hargrett	Hargrett Rare Book and Manuscript Library, University of Georgia, Athens
Hills	Carla Anderson Hills Papers, Hoover Institution Library, Stanford, California
Hough	Hough Area Development Corporation Records, Western Reserve Historical Society, Cleveland, Ohio
JFKOH	President John F. Kennedy Oral History Collection, John F. Kennedy Presidential Library, https://www.jfklibrary.org/asset-viewer/archives/JFKOH
LAT	*Los Angeles Times*
Lewis	Fannie M. Lewis Papers, Western Reserve Historical Society, Cleveland, Ohio
Mattingly	Mack F. Mattingly Papers, Richard B. Russell Library for Political Research and Studies, University of Georgia, Athens
Mayor	Records of the Mayor of the City of Cleveland, George V. Voinovich, Western Reserve Historical Society, Cleveland, Ohio
Miller	Zell Miller Papers, Richard B. Russell Library for Political Research and Studies, University of Georgia, Athens
NAACP	Papers of the NAACP, ProQuest History Vault
NB	*Nation's Business*, Hagley Museum and Library, Wilmington, Delaware, https://digital.hagley.org/nationsbusiness
Nixon	Richard M. Nixon Presidential Library, Yorba Linda, California
NJ	*National Journal*
NYAN	*New York Amsterdam News*
NYT	*New York Times*
PAL	Public Administration Library, City Hall, Cleveland, Ohio
PD	*Cleveland Plain Dealer*
Perk	Ralph J. Perk Papers, Western Reserve Historical Society, Cleveland, Ohio

RCCP	Rome Chamber of Commerce Papers, Special Collections, Sara Hightower Regional Library System, Rome, Georgia
Reagan	Ronald Reagan Presidential Library, Simi Valley, California
RFCL	Rome-Floyd County Library, Sara Hightower Regional Library System
RNT	*Rome News-Tribune*
SGPB	Southern Growth Policies Board Papers, Southern Historical Collection, Wilson Library, University of North Carolina, Chapel Hill
Stuckey	William S. Stuckey Papers, Richard B. Russell Library for Political Research and Science, University of Georgia, Athens
Talmadge	Herman E. Talmadge Papers, Richard B. Russell Library for Political Research and Studies, University of Georgia, Athens
Voinovich	George V. Voinovich Papers, Western Reserve Historical Society, Cleveland, Ohio
WHCF	White House Central Files, Jimmy Carter Presidential Library, Atlanta, Georgia
White	White House Staff Files of Lee C. White, John F. Kennedy Presidential Library, Boston
WP	*Washington Post*
WSJ	*Wall Street Journal*

NOTES

Introduction

1. Thomas S. Andrzejewski, "Neighborhood Chiefs Force HUD to Action," *PD*, June 15, 1976, 1; Randy Cunningham, *Democratizing Cleveland: The Rise and Fall of Community Organizing in Cleveland, Ohio, 1975–1985* (Cleveland: Belt Publishing, 2018), 116–17; on these programs, see Keeanga-Yamahtta Taylor, *Race for Profit: How Banks and the Real Estate Industry Undermined Black Homeownership* (Chapel Hill: University of North Carolina Press, 2019).

2. See especially Greta Krippner, *Capitalizing on Crisis: The Political Origins of the Rise of Finance* (Cambridge: Harvard University Press, 2011); Judith Stein, *Pivotal Decade: How the United States Traded Factories for Finance in the Seventies* (New Haven: Yale University Press, 2011); and Daniel Rodgers, *Age of Fracture* (Cambridge: Belknap Press of Harvard University Press, 2012).

3. See, for instance, Nancy MacLean, *Democracy in Chains: The Deep History of the Radical Right's Stealth Plan for America* (New York: Penguin, 2017).

4. "Agnew Stresses Role of Private Sector in Meeting Urban Crisis," *Association Letter*, February 1969, box 5, series II, CCUS.

5. Carla A. Hills, speech, City Club of Cleveland, October 8, 1976, folder City Club of Cleveland, 10/8/76, box 40, Hills; President Ford's Neighborhood Policy Address, Draft 1, October 19, 1976, folder Urban Development and Neighborhood Revitalization Committee, 6, box 11, Myron B. Kuropas Papers, Ford.

6. On the New Deal order, see especially Steve Fraser and Gary Gerstle, eds., *The Rise and Fall of the New Deal Order* (Princeton: Princeton University Press, 1989). On the neoliberal order, see Gary Gerstle, "The Rise and Fall (?) of America's Neoliberal Order," *Transactions of the Royal Historical Society* 28 (2018): 241–64.

7. Midcentury anticommunism and McCarthyism did significant violence to the left-liberal coalition, purged untold numbers of leftists from the administrative state, and considerably narrowed social-democratic opportunities for state building. But, as this book argues, midcentury liberals' attachment of social aspirations to markets, public-private partnerships, and decentralism reflected a continuity with and expansion of certain aspects of New Deal governance. On the McCarthy era and the evisceration of the American left, see especially Ellen Schrecker, *Many Are the Crimes: McCarthyism in America* (Boston: Little, Brown, 1998); and Landon Y. R. Storrs, *The Second Red Scare and the Unmaking of the New Deal Left* (Princeton: Princeton University Press, 2013). John F. Kennedy, Remarks in Heber Springs, Arkansas, at the Dedication of Greers Ferry Dam, APP, https://www.presidency.ucsb.edu/node/236260.

8. Ted Sorensen, *Counselor: A Life at the Edge of History* (New York: HarperCollins, 2008), 140.

9. On growth liberalism, see Robert M. Collins, *More: The Politics of Economic Growth in Postwar America* (New York: Oxford University Press, 2002).

10. Marisa Chappell, *The War on Welfare: Family, Poverty, and Politics in Modern America* (Philadelphia: University of Pennsylvania Press, 2010), 21–35; and Annelise Orleck and Lisa Gayle Hazirjian, eds., *The War on Poverty: A New Grassroots History, 1964–1980* (Athens: University of Georgia Press 2011).

11. On historical blind spots associated with organizing political history around ideological orders or partisan divisions, see Brent Cebul, Lily Geismer, and Mason B. Williams, "Beyond Red and Blue," in Cebul, Geismer, and Williams, eds., *Shaped by the State: Toward a New Political History of the Twentieth Century* (Chicago: University of Chicago Press, 2019).

12. On the American fiscal state, see W. Elliot Brownlee, ed., *Funding the Modern American State, 1941–1995: The Rise and Fall of the Era of Easy Finance* (New York: Cambridge University Press, 1996); Ajay K. Mehrotra, *Making the Modern American Fiscal State: Law, Politics, and the Rise of Progressive Taxation, 1877–1929* (New York: Cambridge University Press, 2013); and Daniel Wortel-London, "The Tax Trap," *Dissent*, Winter 2021.

13. Scholars have illuminated how works programs revolutionized working-class politics, the nation's infrastructural assets, and forged a more inclusive public sphere. See Lizabeth Cohen, *Making a New Deal: Industrial Workers in Chicago, 1919–1939* (New York: Cambridge University Press, 1990); Jason Scott Smith, *Building New Deal Liberalism: The Political Economy of Public Works* (New York: Cambridge University Press, 2009); and Mason B. Williams, *City of Ambition: FDR, LaGuardia, and the Making of Modern New York* (New York: W. W. Norton, 2014).

14. "Foresight in Traffic," *PD*, May 18, 1936, 6.

15. "A New Meaning for WPA," *Augusta Chronicle*, April 9, 1936; and "How Augusta and Richmond County Will Share in WPA Funds," *Augusta Chronicle*, September 8, 1935.

16. "Program Launched to Expand Work of Experiment Station," *Brownsville Herald*, March 22, 1936.

17. Joe W. Fleming II, interview by Stephen Goodell, February 19, 1969, interview 1, transcript, p. 13, Lyndon Johnson Oral History Project, Miller Center, University of Virginia, http://web2.millercenter.org/lbj/oralhistory/fleming_joe_1969_0219.pdf. On decentralized, public-private development as a "discourse of progress," see Nathan D. B. Connolly, *A World More Concrete: Real Estate and the Remaking of Jim Crow South Florida* (Chicago: University of Chicago Press, 2014), 211.

18. On modernization theory and development programs abroad, see Michael E. Latham, *Modernization as Ideology: American Social Science and "Nation Building" in the Kennedy Era* (Chapel Hill: University of North Carolina Press, 2000); Nils Gilman, *Mandarins of the Future: Modernization Theory in Cold War America* (Baltimore: Johns Hopkins University Press, 2004); David Ekbladh, *The Great American Mission: Modernization and the Construction of an American World Order* (Princeton: Princeton University Press, 2009); Daniel Immerwahr, *Thinking Small: The United States and the Lure of Community Development* (Cambridge: Harvard University Press, 2015); Stephen J. Macekura and Erez Manela, eds., *The Development Century: A Global History* (New York: Cambridge University Press, 2018); and Amy C. Offner, *Sorting Out the Mixed Economy: The Rise and Fall of Welfare and Developmental States in the Americas* (Princeton: Princeton University Press, 2019).

19. On recourse to public and private credit as alternatives to direct public expenditure, see, Sarah L. Quinn, *American Bonds: How Credit Markets Shaped a Nation* (Princeton: Princeton

University Press, 2019). On municipal borrowing, see Destin Jenkins, *The Bonds of Inequality: Debt and the Making of the American City* (Chicago: University of Chicago Press, 2021).

20. On breadwinner liberalism, see Robert Self, *All in the Family: The Realignment of American Democracy Since the 1960s* (New York: Hill and Wang, 2013).

21. On the submerged system of social and economic, largely white, middle-class entitlements born in the New Deal, see, Jennifer Klein, *For All These Rights: Business, Labor, and the Shaping of America's Public-Private Welfare State* (Princeton: Princeton University Press, 2003); Ira Katznelson, *When Affirmative Action Was White: An Untold History of Racial Inequality in Twentieth-Century America* (New York: W. W. Norton, 2005); and Suzanne Mettler, *The Submerged State: How Invisible Government Policies Undermine American Democracy* (Chicago: University of Chicago Press, 2011).

22. On the growing disconnect between liberals' discourse of rights and the policy apparatus constructed to deliver them, see Karen Orren and Stephen Skowronek, *The Policy State: An American Predicament* (Cambridge: Harvard University Press, 2017); see also Samuel Moyn, "The Second Bill of Rights: A Reconsideration," in Silja Voeneky and Gerald L. Neuman, *Human Rights, Democracy, and Legitimacy in a World of Disorder* (New York: Cambridge University Press, 2018), 111–35.

23. I do not mean for the decentralized administrative state and liberals' supply-side state to be synonymous. Rather, the latter, through which public-private partnerships were often forged, emerged through the former. And, while they are conceptually and institutionally distinct entities, they did often overlap. Over time, supply-side sensibilities captured other domains, as in the rise of for-profit prison contracting. On federalism and the emergence of legal protections and procedures within the administrative state, see Daniel Ernst, *Tocqueville's Nightmare: The Administrative State Emerges in America, 1900–1940* (New York: Oxford University Press, 2016); Jessica Bulman-Pozen, "Administrative States: Beyond Presidential Administration," *Texas Law Review* 98, no. 2 (2019): 267–325; Sara Mayeux and Karen Tani, "Federalism Anew," *American Journal of Legal History* 56, no. 1 (2016): 128–38; and Karen Tani, *States of Dependency: Welfare, Rights, and American Governance, 1935–1972* (New York: Cambridge University Press, 2016). On the administrative state more broadly, see especially Joanna Grisinger, *The Unwieldy American State: Administrative Politics Since the New Deal* (New York: Cambridge University Press, 2012); and Anne Kornhauser, *Debating the American State: Liberal Anxieties and the New Leviathan, 1930–1970* (Philadelphia: University of Pennsylvania Press, 2015).

24. See, for example, Kenneth L. Kusmer, *A Ghetto Takes Shape: Black Cleveland, 1870–1930* (Urbana: University of Illinois Press, 1976); Karen Ferguson, *Black Politics in New Deal Atlanta* (Chapel Hill: University of North Carolina Press, 2002); Khalil Gibran Muhammad, *The Condemnation of Blackness: Race, Crime, and the Making of Modern Urban America* (Cambridge: Harvard University Press, 2010); Nayan Shah, *Contagious Divides: Epidemics and Race in San Francisco's Chinatown* (Berkeley: University of California Press, 2001); Julie Weise, *Corazon de Dixie: Mexicanos in the U.S. South Since 1910* (Chapel Hill: University of North Carolina Press, 2014); and Brian Purnell and Jeanne Theoharis, eds., *The Strange Careers of the Jim Crow North: Segregation and Struggle Outside of the South*, with Komozi Woodard (New York: New York University Press, 2019).

25. Ira Katznelson, *Fear Itself: The New Deal and the Origins of Our Time* (New York: Liveright, 2013), 7 and 22.

26. See, for instance, Matt Garcia, *A World of Its Own: Race, Labor, and Citrus in the Making of Greater Los Angeles* (Chapel Hill: University of North Carolina Press, 2002); Nayan Shah,

Stranger Intimacy: Contesting Race, Sexuality, and the Law in the North American West (Berkeley: University of California Press, 2012); and Kelly Lytle Hernandez, *City of Inmates: Conquest, Rebellion, and the Rise of Human Caging in Los Angeles* (Chapel Hill: University of North Carolina Press, 2017).

27. See, especially, Cohen, *Making a New Deal*; Robert Zieger, *The CIO, 1935–1955* (Chapel Hill: University of North Carolina Press, 1997); Gail Radford, *Modern Housing for America: Policy Struggles in the New Deal Era* (Chicago: University of Chicago Press, 1996); Howard Brick, *Transcending Capitalism: Visions of a New Society in Modern American Thought* (Ithaca: Cornell University Press, 2006); Doug Rossinow, *Visions of Progress: The Left-Liberal Tradition in America* (Philadelphia: University of Pennsylvania Press, 2007); and Meg Jacobs, *Pocketbook Politics: Economic Citizenship in Twentieth-Century America* (Princeton: Princeton University Press, 2007).

28. "Report of Committee on Increased Opportunity for Employment and Economic Security," 10, folder National Conference on Problems of Negro Youth, 1937, Administrative File: Group 1, Subject File—American Fund for Public Service, Part 03: The Campaign for Educational Equality, Series A: Legal Department and Central Office Records, 1913–1940, NAACP.

29. W. O. Walker to Walter F. White, October 10, 1941, folder 001521-006-0351, NAACP.

30. See Paige Glotzer, *How the Suburbs Were Segregated: Developers and the Business of Exclusionary Housing, 1890–1960* (New York: Columbia University Press, 2020), chaps. 5 and 6.

31. Jacquelyn Dowd Hall, "The Long Civil Rights Movement and the Political Uses of the Past," *Journal of American History* 91 (March 2005): 1233–63.

32. See Fraser and Gerstle, *The Rise and Fall of the New Deal Order*; Lizabeth Cohen, *A Consumer's Republic: The Politics of Mass Consumption in Postwar America* (New York: Vintage, 2003); and Cohen, *Making a New Deal*.

33. On the construction of white homeowner politics and the splintering of the New Deal coalition, see Thomas Sugrue, *The Origins of the Urban Crisis: Race and Inequality in Postwar Detroit* (Princeton: Princeton University Press, 1996); Kevin Kruse, *White Flight: Atlanta and the Making of Modern Conservatism* (Princeton: Princeton University Press, 2005); Robert Self, *American Babylon: Race and the Struggle for Postwar Oakland* (Princeton: Princeton University Press, 2005); David M. P. Freund, *Colored Property: State Policy and White Racial Politics in Suburban America* (Chicago: University of Chicago Press, 2007); Matthew Lassiter, *The Silent Majority: Suburban Politics in the Sunbelt South* (Princeton: Princeton University Press, 2007); and Lily Geismer, *Don't Blame Us: Suburban Liberals and the Transformation of the Democratic Party* (Princeton: Princeton University Press, 2017). On deindustrialization, see especially Jefferson Cowie, *Capital Moves: RCA's Seventy-Year Quest for Cheap Labor* (Ithaca: Cornell University Press, 1999). On deindustrialization and the unraveling of the public-private union and employment-based system of social security, see Gabriel Winant, *The Next Shift: The Fall of Industry and the Rise of Health Care in Rust Belt America* (Cambridge: Harvard University Press, 2021).

34. Gary Gerstle, "The Protean Character of American Liberalism," *American Historical Review* 99, no. 4 (October 1994): 1043–73. Robert Self describes liberalism's "plastic" qualities in Self, *American Babylon*, 13.

35. This book defines "governance" and identifies "the state" not only in terms of what government and state actors *did* but in the broad exercise of public authority by state and non-state actors alike. In this sense, state power and public authority operate not only in the formal realms of state apparatus, power, and coercion, but through a spectrum of creative relationships

and tensions across civil society and markets. I borrow the "multiplication" of state authority from James Sparrow, William Novak, and Stephen Sawyer, "Introduction," in Sparrow, Novak, and Sawyer, eds., *The Boundaries of the State in U.S. History* (Chicago: University of Chicago Press, 2015), 1. On models of statebuilding through civil society, the voluntary sector, and private interests, see Brian Balogh, *The Associational State: American Governance in the Twentieth Century* (Philadelphia: University of Pennsylvania Press, 2015); Margot Canaday, Nancy F. Cott, and Robert O. Self, *Intimate States: Gender, Sexuality, and Governance in Modern U.S. History* (Chicago: University of Chicago Press, 2021); and William J. Novak, "The Myth of the 'Weak' American State," *American Historical Review* 113, no. 3 (June 2008). My conceptions of state power have also been shaped by Michael Mann's notion of "infrastructural power" and Beatrice Hibou's conception of the state's tendency to "discharge" authority to nonstate actors. See Michael Mann, "The Autonomous Power of the State: Its Origins, Mechanisms, and Results," *European Journal of Sociology* 25, no. 2 (1984): 185–213; and Beatrice Hibou, ed., *Privatizing the State* (New York: Columbia University Press, 2004), 18–28. On conservative campaigns against left-liberalism, see especially Kim Phillips-Fein, *Invisible Hands: The Making of the Conservative Movement from the New Deal to Reagan* (New York: W. W. Norton, 2009); and Storrs, *The Second Red Scare*.

36. On midcentury liberals' wariness about centralized authority, see Ira Katznelson, *Desolation and Enlightenment: Political Knowledge After Total War, Totalitarianism, and the Holocaust* (New York: Columbia University Press, 2003); Wendy Wall, *Inventing the "American Way": The Politics of Consensus from the New Deal to the Civil Rights Movement* (New York: Oxford University Press, 2008); Reuel Schiller, *Forging Rivals: Race, Class, Law, and the Collapse of Postwar Liberalism* (New York: Cambridge University Press, 2015); and Katrina Forrester, *In the Shadow of Justice: Postwar Liberalism and the Remaking of Political Philosophy* (Princeton: Princeton University Press, 2019).

37. David Kennedy, *Freedom from Fear: The American People in Depression and War, 1929–1945* (New York: Oxford University Press, 1999), 210.

38. Nancy Weiss, *Farewell to the Party of Lincoln: Black Politics in the Age of FDR* (Princeton: Princeton University Press, 1983); Cheryl Greenberg, *"Or Does It Explode?": Black Harlem in the Great Depression* (New York: Oxford University Press, 1991); and Eric Schickler, *Racial Realignment: The Transformation of American Liberalism, 1932–1965* (Princeton: Princeton University Press, 2016).

39. This book follows federal resources as they intersected with and were in turn reshaped by actors and interests across multiple political scales and structures. On the concept of "multiple political orders," see Margaret Weir, "States, Race, and the Decline of New Deal Liberalism," *Studies in American Political Development* 19 (Fall 2005): 157–72. On creative federalism, see Martha Derthick, *Keeping the Compound Republic: Essays on American Federalism* (Washington, D.C.: Brookings Institution Press, 2001), 122–25.

40. In his pathbreaking study of federal investments in Sunbelt development, Bruce Schulman called them "neo-Whigs." Schulman, *From Cotton Belt to Sunbelt: Federal Policy, Economic Development, and the Transformation of the South, 1938–1980* (New York: Oxford University Press, 1991).

41. See especially C. Wright Mills, *The Power Elite* (New York: Oxford University Press, 1956); Robert H. Wiebe, *The Search for Order, 1877–1920* (New York, 1967); and Alfred Chandler, *The Visible Hand: The Managerial Revolution in American Business* (Cambridge: Belknap Press of Harvard University Press, 1977). Much work remains to be done to add greater specificity to local capital's varied political scales, cultures, and classes. For differing approaches, see

Sven Beckert, *The Monied Metropolis: New York City and the Consolidation of the American Bourgeoisie, 1850–1896* (New York: Cambridge University Press, 2001); Victoria de Grazia, *Irresistible Empire: America's Advance Through Twentieth-Century Europe* (Cambridge: Harvard University Press, 2006), chap. 1; Bethany Moreton, *To Serve God and Wal-Mart: The Making of Christian Free Enterprise* (Cambridge: Harvard University Press, 2009); Patrick Wyman, "Trump and the American Gentry," *Atlantic*, September 23, 2021; and Melinda Cooper, "Family Capitalism and the Small Business Insurrection," *Dissent*, Winter 2022.

42. Victor R. Fuchs, "The Growing Importance of the Service Industries," *Journal of Business* 38, no. 4 (October 1965): 344; "The 'Commercializing' of Civic Movements," *American City*, April 1914, 321, cited in Alison Isenberg, *Downtown America: A History of the Place and the People Who Made It* (Chicago: University of Chicago Press, 2005), 36; Robert Putnam, *Bowling Alone: The Collapse and Revival of American Community* (New York: Simon and Schuster, 2000), 48–64; Suzanne Mettler, *Soldiers to Citizens: The GI Bill and the Making of the Greatest Generation* (Oxford: Oxford University Press, 2005), 123–35. On the reciprocal growth of voluntary associations and government, see Theda Skocpol, Marshall Ganz, and Ziad Munson, "A Nation of Organizers: The Institutional Origins of Civic Voluntarism in the United States," *American Political Science Review* 94, no. 3 (September 2000).

43. On producerism, see, Michael Kazin, *The Populist Persuasion: An American History* (Ithaca: Cornell University Press, 1995). On producerism and labor's consumerist turn, see Lawrence Glickman, *A Living Wage: American Workers and the Making of Consumer Society* (Ithaca: Cornell University Press, 1997).

44. Clarence N. Stone, *Regime Politics: Governing Atlanta, 1946–1988* (Lawrence: University Press of Kansas, 1989), 56.

45. Phillips-Fein, *Invisible Hands*; Angus Burgin, *The Great Persuasion: Reinventing Free Markets Since the Depression* (Cambridge: Harvard University Press, 2012); Benjamin Waterhouse, *Lobbying America: The Politics of Business from Nixon to NAFTA* (Princeton: Princeton University Press, 2013); and Lawrence Glickman, *Free Enterprise: An American History* (New Haven: Yale University Press, 2019).

46. On cultures of state building, see James Sparrow, *Warfare State: World War II Americans and the Age of Big Government* (New York: Oxford University Press, 2011). More broadly, the public-private war mobilization and the myth of the private sector's primacy capture these dynamics. See Mark Wilson, *Destructive Creation: American Business and the Winning of World War II* (Philadelphia: University of Pennsylvania Press, 2016).

47. See Daniel Stedman Jones, *Masters of the Universe: Hayek, Friedman, and the Birth of Neoliberal Politics* (Princeton: Princeton University Press, 2012); and Gerstle, "The Rise and Fall (?) of America's Neoliberal Order." On historians' ambivalence about the concept of neoliberalism, see Kim Phillips-Fein, "The History of Neoliberalism," in Cebul, Geismer, and Williams, *Shaped by the State*.

48. See especially Brian Goldstein, *The Roots of Urban Renaissance: Gentrification and the Struggle over Harlem* (Cambridge: Harvard University Press, 2017); Lily Geismer, "Agents of Change: Microenterprise, Welfare Reform, the Clintons, and Liberal Forms of Neoliberalism," *Journal of American History* 107, no. 1 (June 2020): 107–31; and Benjamin Holtzman, *The Long Crisis: New York City and the Path to Neoliberalism* (New York: Oxford University Press, 2021).

49. Important exceptions include Shane Hamilton, *Trucking Country: The Road to America's Wal-Mart Economy* (Princeton: Princeton University Press, 2008); and Moreton, *To Serve God and Wal-Mart*.

50. On New Dealers' decentralism and cooperation with local governments, see Daniel Rodgers, *Atlantic Crossings: Social Politics in a Progressive Age* (Cambridge: Belknap Press of Harvard University Press, 1998), 448–61; and Alan Brinkley, *Voices of Protest: Huey Long, Father Coughlin, and the Great Depression* (New York: Vintage, 1982), 247–48.

51. Fiscal federalism, the New Deal, and the role of federal policies in incentivizing these ways of organizing "growth coalitions" remain underexplored. For powerful exceptions, see John Mollenkopf, *The Contested City* (Princeton: Princeton University Press, 1983); and Eric H. Monkkonen, *The Local State: Public Money and American Cities* (Stanford: Stanford University Press, 1995). Relatively few histories of the New Deal center the perspectives of municipal officials or local businesspeople. Key exceptions include Williams, *City of Ambition*; and Mark Gelfand, *A Nation of Cities: The Federal Government and Urban America* (New York: Oxford University Press, 1975). An older literature explored the New Deal's impact on voting patterns and party coalitions. See Bruce M. Stave, *The New Deal and the Last Hurrah: Pittsburgh Machine Politics* (Pittsburgh: University of Pittsburgh Press, 1970); and Cohen, *Making a New Deal*.

52. Scholars have illuminated the dynamics of urban-suburban and metropolitan fiscal fragmentation and competition. See especially Self, *American Babylon*; and Colin Gordon, *Citizen Brown: Race, Democracy, and Inequality in the St. Louis Suburbs* (Chicago: University of Chicago Press, 2019).

53. On nineteenth-century developmentalism, see Brian Balogh, *A Government Out of Sight: The Mystery of National Authority in Nineteenth-Century America* (Cambridge: Cambridge University Press, 2009); John Lauritz Larson, *Internal Improvement: National Public Works and the Promise of Popular Government in the Early United States* (Chapel Hill: University of North Carolina Press, 2001). On decentralized economic planning and industrial policy, see Peter K. Eisinger, *The Rise of the Entrepreneurial State: State and Local Economic Development Policy in the United States* (Madison: University of Wisconsin Press, 1989); Guian McKee, *The Problem of Jobs: Liberalism, Race, and Deindustrialization in Philadelphia* (Chicago: University of Chicago Press, 2008); and Fred Block, "Swimming Against the Current: The Rise of a Hidden Developmental State in the United States," *Politics & Society* 35, no. 2 (2008): 169–206. On historical debates about industrial policy, see Otis Graham, *Losing Time: The Industrial Policy Debate* (Cambridge: Harvard University Press, 1992).

54. Alan Brinkley, *The End of Reform: New Deal Liberalism in Recession and War* (New York: Vintage, 1995), 3–4; on Keynesianism, see also Collins, *More*; Jacobs, *Pocketbook Politics*; Cohen, *A Consumer's Republic*; and Zachary D. Carter, *The Price of Peace: Money, Democracy, and the Life of John Maynard Keynes* (New York: Random House, 2020).

55. U.S. National Resources Committee (NRC), *Our Cities: Their Role in the National Economy* (Washington, D.C.: U.S. Government Printing Office, 1937), 51.

56. Charles E. Merriam, "The Federal Government Recognizes the Cities," *National Municipal Review* 23, no. 2 (February 1934): 107–10.

57. NRC, *Our Cities*, 51.

58. Franklin D. Roosevelt, "Message to Congress Recommending Legislation," November 5, 1937, APP, https://www.presidency.ucsb.edu/documents/message-congress-recommending-legislation.

59. On localism, see Thomas J. Sugrue, "All Politics Is Local: The Persistence of Localism in Twentieth-Century America," in Meg Jacobs, William Novak, and Julian Zelizer, eds., *The Democratic Experiment: New Directions in American Political History* (Princeton: Princeton University Press, 2003). On military Keynesianism as regional development policy, see Kari Frederickson,

Cold War Dixie: Militarization and Modernization in the American South (Athens: University of Georgia Press, 2013); and Michael Brenes, *For Might and Right: Cold War Defense Spending and the Remaking of American Democracy* (Amherst: University of Massachusetts Press, 2020). On universities as brokers of federal developmentalism, see Margaret Pugh O'Mara, *Cities of Knowledge: Cold War Science and the Search for the Next Silicon Valley* (Princeton: Princeton University Press, 2004); and Christopher Loss, *Between Citizens and the State: The Politics of American Higher Education in the 20th Century* (Princeton: Princeton University Press, 2011). On the Cold War construction of the "American Way," see Wall, *Inventing the "American Way."*

60. My approach to urban development and federalism is indebted to Arnold Hirsch, *Making the Second Ghetto: Race and Housing in Chicago, 1940–1960* (Chicago: University of Chicago Press, 1983); on urban historians' blind spots for smaller or rural cities, see Richard Harris, "A Portrait of North American Urban Historians," *Journal of Urban History* 45, no. 6 (2019): 1237–45.

61. On growth coalitions, see especially Stone, *Regime Politics*; for an incisive update that incorporates neoliberalism, see Tracy Neumann, *Remaking the Rust Belt: The Postindustrial Transformation of North America* (Philadelphia: University of Pennsylvania Press, 2016).

62. Brent Cebul and Robert Nelson, "Toward a More Complete Reckoning: Renewing Inequality and New Histories of Urban Renewal," in Douglas Appler, ed., *The Forgotten Geographies of Urban Renewal: How Title I of the Housing Act of 1949 Shaped Small Cities, Suburbs, Territories, and Other American Communities* (Philadelphia: Temple University Press, forthcoming).

63. On twentieth-century economic planning, see Otis L. Graham, *Toward a Planned Society: From Roosevelt to Nixon* (New York: Oxford University Press, 1976); Michael Reagan, *Designing a New America: The Origins of New Deal Planning, 1890–1943* (Amherst: University of Massachusetts Press, 1999); and Robert Fishman, ed., *The American Planning Tradition: Culture and Policy* (Washington, D.C.: Woodrow Wilson Center Press, 2000). On the growth of regional planning councils inspired by the NRPB, see Gregory S. Wilson, *Communities Left Behind: The Area Redevelopment Administration, 1945–1965* (Knoxville: University of Tennessee Press, 2009), 34–47.

64. On local political and business elites' relative moderation, see Kruse, *White Flight*; and Lassiter, *The Silent Majority*; on infrastructural violence, see Jenkins, *The Bonds of Inequality*.

65. Interregional convergences, political learning, and continuities constitute an underappreciated aspect of twentieth-century politics and urban development. For exceptions, see Lassiter, *The Silent Majority*; and Matthew Lassiter and Joseph Crespino, eds., *The Myth of Southern Exceptionalism* (New York: Oxford University Press, 2009).

66. Theodore Rosenof, *Economics in the Long Run: New Deal Theorists and Their Legacies, 1933–1993* (Chapel Hill: University of North Carolina Press, 1997), 44–86.

67. For a sociological account of elite agency and economic decline, see Sean Safford, *Why the Garden Club Couldn't Save Youngstown: The Transformation of the Rust Belt* (Cambridge: Harvard University Press, 2009).

68. My use of the terms "Sunbelt" and "Rustbelt" and the historical contingencies involved in their social and political production have been informed by Andrew Needham, *Power Lines: Phoenix and the Making of the Modern Southwest* (Princeton: Princeton University Press, 2014), esp. 14–16. On development and the low-wage Sunbelt, see Elizabeth Tandy Shermer, *Sunbelt Capitalism: Phoenix and the Transformation of American Politics* (Philadelphia: University of Pennsylvania Press, 2013). James Cobb emphasizes a range of inducements for capital mobility.

See Cobb, *The Selling of the South: The Southern Crusade for Industrial Development, 1936–1990* (Urbana: University of Illinois Press, 1993).

69. On community control movements, see Matthew Countryman, *Up South: Civil Rights and Black Power in Philadelphia* (Philadelphia: University of Pennsylvania Press, 2006); and Donna Murch, *Living for the City: Migration, Education, and the Rise of the Black Panther Party in Oakland California* (Chapel Hill: University of North Carolina Press, 2010).

70. On the "structuralist critique," see Alice O'Connor, *Poverty Knowledge: Social Science, Social Policy, and the Poor in Twentieth-Century U.S. History* (Princeton: Princeton University Press, 2001), 146–51.

71. Ronald P. Formisano, *Boston Against Busing: Race, Class, and Ethnicity in the 1960s and 1970s* (Chapel Hill: University of North Carolina Press, 2004); Sugrue, *Origins of the Urban Crisis*; Lassiter, *The Silent Majority*.

72. On the state's legitimation crisis, see Krippner, *Capitalizing on Crisis*.

73. See especially Thomas Edsall, *The New Politics of Inequality* (New York: Penguin, 1984); Lily Geismer, *Left Behind: The Democrats' Failed Attempt to Solve Inequality* (New York: Public Affairs, 2022); and Geismer, *Don't Blame Us*.

74. David Osborne and Ted Gaebler, *Reinventing Government: How the Entrepreneurial Spirit Is Transforming the Public Sector* (Reading, Mass.: Addison-Wesley, 1992), 25.

75. On the "new participation," see Caroline W. Lee, Michael McQuarrie, and Edward T. Walker, eds., *Democratizing Inequalities: Dilemmas of the New Public Participation* (New York: New York University Press, 2015).

76. Barry Karl, *Charles E. Merriam and the Study of Politics* (Chicago: University of Chicago Press, 1974), 50–53; Reagan, *Designing a New America*, 60–61.

77. Charles E. Merriam, *Public and Private Government* (New Haven: Yale University Press, 1945), 16, 8, and 57; Merriam, *Prologue to Politics* (Chicago: University of Chicago Press, 1939), 7.

78. On debates about "representative bureaucracy," see Kornhauser, *Debating the American State*, chap. 2, Lewis quotation at 62; Philip Selznick, *TVA and the Grass Roots: A Study of Politics and Organization* (Berkeley: University of California Press, 1949), 264.

Chapter 1

1. Franklin D. Roosevelt, radio address from Albany, New York, April 7, 1932: "The 'Forgotten Man' Speech," APP, https://www.presidency.ucsb.edu/node/288092.

2. On business and Progressive Era urban reforms, see especially Kenneth Feingold, *Experts and Politicians: Reform Challenges to Machine Politics in New York, Cleveland, and Chicago* (Princeton: Princeton University Press, 1995); Rodgers, *Atlantic Crossings*; and Daniel Amsterdam, *Roaring Metropolis: Businessmen's Campaign for a Civic Welfare State* (Philadelphia: University of Pennsylvania Press, 2016).

3. Joanna Grisinger, "The (Long) Administrative Century," in Stephen Skowronek, ed., *The Progressives' Century: Political Reform, Constitutional Government, and the Modern American State* (New Haven: Yale University Press, 2016), 363.

4. W. H. Foster to Lincoln McConnell, December 13, 1933, box 2, RCCP.

5. *Final Report on the WPA Program, 1935–43* (Washington, D.C.: U.S. Government Printing Office, 1946), 9 and 48.

6. Harry L. Hopkins, *Spending to Save: The Complete Story of Relief* (New York: W. W. Norton, 1936), 169.

7. On the WPA, see generally, Smith, *Building New Deal Liberalism*.

8. On opposition to the New Deal among elite national business conservatives, see Phillips-Fein, *Invisible Hands*, chap. 1.

9. Numan V. Bartley, *The Creation of Modern Georgia*, 2nd ed. (Athens: University of Georgia Press, 1990), 147–208.

10. Franklin D. Roosevelt, "Message to the Conference on Economic Conditions of the South," July [4], 1938, APP, https://www.presidency.ucsb.edu/node/209037.

11. Michelle Brattain, *The Politics of Whiteness: Race, Workers, and Culture in the Modern South* (Athens: University of Georgia Press, 2004), 18–44; and Douglas Flamming, *Creating the Modern South: Millhands and Managers in Dalton, Georgia, 1884–1984* (Chapel Hill: University of North Carolina Press, 1992), 9–55.

12. Kenneth Sturges, *American Chambers of Commerce* (New York: Moffat, Park and Co., 1915), quotation at 231; three thousand figure at 45; and on local chamber of commerce development overall, see 11–54.

13. "Birth of the SCSA," *Southern Secretary*, August 1937, box 1, RCCP.

14. Foster's household information is from U.S. Department of Commerce, Bureau of the Census, *Sixteenth Census of the United States: 1940*, enumeration district 57-8 [Rome, Floyd County, Georgia].

15. Wilton E. Cobb to W. H. Foster, March 12, 1929, box 2, RCCP.

16. W. H. Foster to D. Hodson Lewis, March 3, 1931, box 2, RCCP.

17. W. H. Foster to Commercial Secretaries of Georgia, March 24, 1930, box 2, RCCP.

18. George Magruder Battey, *A History of Rome and Floyd County* (Atlanta: Webb and Vary, 1922), 325; and Roger Aycock, *All Roads to Rome* (Roswell, Ga.: W. H. Wolfe Associates; sponsored by Rome Area Heritage Foundation, 1981), 164–65.

19. J. M. Ashley to W. H. Foster, March 14, 1929, box 2, RCCP.

20. Robert McMath, "Infrastructure for the New South: Dalton Utilities and the Development of an Industrial City," unpublished paper in author's possession.

21. Rome to Chattanooga, undated, box 2, RCCP.

22. "Number Miles of Road Paved in Past Five Years in Floyd County," undated, box 2, RCCP; Roads Group, Meeting Minutes, February 15, 1929 box 2, RCCP.

23. W. H. Foster to O. N. Richardson, February 26, 1929, box 2, RCCP.

24. President, Bainbridge Chamber, to W. H. Foster, March 30, 1931, box 2, RCCP.

25. W. H. Foster to Wesley Shropshire, January 12, 1931, box 2, RCCP.

26. Columbus Roberts to W. H. Foster, May 6, 1930, box 2, RCCP.

27. Aycock, *All Roads to Rome*, 423–24.

28. 1940 U.S. Census, Floyd County, Georgia.

29. Morrell Johnson Darko, *The Rivers Meet: A History of African-Americans in Rome, Georgia* (Kearney, Neb.: Morris Publishing, 2003), 16–19.

30. August Meier and Elliott Rudwick, "The Boycott Movement Against Jim Crow Streetcars in the South, 1900–1906," *Journal of American History* 55, no. 4 (1969): 756–75.

31. John Dittmer, *Black Georgia in the Progressive Era, 1900–1920* (Urbana: University of Illinois Press, 1977), 114–15.

32. Darko, *The Rivers Meet*, 42.

33. Crystal Nicole Feimster, *Southern Horrors: Women and the Politics of Rape and Lynching* (Cambridge: Harvard University Press, 2009), 189; "Negro Lynched in Georgia," *Los Angeles Herald*, April 2, 1902.

34. Emory University, Georgia Lynching Project Circa 1875–1930, https://scholarblogs.emory.edu/galynchings/lynchings/.

35. Isabel Wilkerson, *The Warmth of Other Suns: The Epic Story of America's Great Migration* (New York: Knopf, 2010), 104.

36. R. W. Bullock, "A Brief Statement Concerning Conditions Among Negroes in Georgia and the Program of the National Youth Administration in the State," prepared for the Conference on the Future of America's Negro and Negro Youths under the auspices of the National Youth Administration, Washington, D.C., January 6–8, 1937, pp. 1–2, folder 001509-005-0220, NAACP.

37. "Terrapin Race Feature of Labor Day Program," September 7, 1931, box 1, RCCP; and Battey, *A History of Rome and Floyd County*, 484.

38. J. L. Storey to General Committee, Labor Day Program, August 6, 1931, box 1, RCCP.

39. John W. Bale to J. L. Storey, August 5, 1931, box 1, RCCP.

40. Elna C. Green, ed., *The New Deal and Beyond: Social Welfare in the South Since 1930* (Athens: University of Georgia Press, 2003), ix.

41. Flamming, *Creating the Modern South*, chaps. 6–9. On southern paternalism more broadly, see Jacqueline Dowd Hall, *Like a Family: The Making of a Southern Cotton Mill World* (Chapel Hill: University of North Carolina Press, 1987).

42. Brattain, *Politics of Whiteness*, 49–63 and 75–77; and Flamming, *Creating the Modern South*, 195–97.

43. William H. Courtney to W. H. Foster, September 21, 1932, box 2, RCCP; Andrew J. Calhoun to A. M. Bergstrom, November 28, 1933; and A. B. Gelt to W. H. Foster, December 12, 1933, box 2, RCCP.

44. W. H. Foster to Richard B. Russell, October 19, 1932, box 2, RCCP.

45. "Rome Backs Roosevelt on Recovery Program," *Chattanooga Daily Times*, July 25, 1933, 2.

46. W. H. Foster to D. B. Lasseter, March 20, 1934, box 1, RCCP.

47. David Lilienthal to W. H. Foster, November 2, 1936, box 1, RCCP.

48. Patrick Maney, *The Roosevelt Presence: The Life and Legacy of FDR* (Berkeley: University of California Press, 1992), 42.

49. Franklin D. Roosevelt, "Remarks to Directors of the National Emergency Council," February 2, 1934, APP, https://www.presidency.ucsb.edu/documents/remarks-directors-the-national-emergency-council.

50. Franklin D. Roosevelt: "Second Fireside Chat," May 7, 1933, APP, https://www.presidency.ucsb.edu/documents/second-fireside-chat.

51. Franklin D. Roosevelt: "Message to Congress Recommending Legislation," November 5, 1937, APP, https://www.presidency.ucsb.edu/documents/message-congress-recommending-legislation.

52. "Road Report" attached to Lincoln McConnell Jr. to W. H. Foster, December 10, 1930, August 20, 1928, box 2, RCCP.

53. David E. Lilienthal, "Address Before the Tennessee Valley Institute," April 21, 1934, box 2, RCCP.

54. J. G. Bent Jr. to W. H. Foster, September 19, 1933, box 2, RCCP.

55. W. H. Foster to J. G. Bent Jr., September 21, 1933, box 2, RCCP. Material in this paragraph was previously published in Brent Cebul, "Creative Competition: Georgia Power, the Tennessee Valley Authority, and the Creation of a Rural Consumer Economy, 1934–1955," *Journal of American History* 105, no. 1 (2018): 45–70.

56. W. H. Foster to Lincoln McConnell, December 14, 1933, box 2, RCCP; "Elbert P. McGhee," *AC*, July 16, 1970, 3C. On businessmen in the CWA, see Bonnie Fox Schwartz, *The Civil Works Administration, 1933–1934: The Business of Emergency Employment in the New Deal* (Princeton: Princeton University Press, 1984).

57. Michael Stephan Holmes, "The New Deal in Georgia: An Administrative History" (Ph.D. diss., University of Wisconsin, 1969), 137–40.

58. "To Speed Public Works," in Summary of the Proceedings of the Southeastern Divisional Meeting of the Chamber of Commerce of the United States, November 20 and 21, 1933, box 1, RCCP.

59. "Loaned to CWA," *Snap Shots*, January 1934, box 477, GPCA.

60. Michael S. Holmes, *The New Deal in Georgia: An Administrative History* (Westport: Greenwood Press, 1975), 169–75.

61. Franklin D. Roosevelt, Executive Order 7034—Creating Machinery for the Works Progress Administration Online by Gerhard Peters and John T. Woolley, APP, https://www.presidency.ucsb.edu/node/208644

62. Jason Scott Smith, *A Concise History of the New Deal* (New York: Cambridge University Press, 2014), 84–88.

63. Bartley, *Creation of Modern Georgia*, 173–74.

64. Brattain, *Politics of Whiteness*, 13.

65. Holmes, *New Deal in Georgia*, 168–69.

66. James T. Patterson, *The New Deal and the States: Federalism in Transition* (Princeton: Princeton University Press, 1969), 28; Gavin Wright, "The New Deal and the Modernization of the South," *Federal History* 2 (2010): 59.

67. Gavin Wright, *Old South, New South: Revolutions in the Southern Economy Since the Civil War* (Baton Rouge: LSU Press, 1996), 260.

68. Aycock, *All Roads to Rome*, 420–24.

69. *RNT*, July 3, 1942; Aycock, *All Roads to Rome*, 487–88.

70. Henry Curran Wilbur to R. A. Palmer, July 15, 1929, box 2, RCCP. On Southern boosters' fights against New Deal labor laws, see Katherine Rye Jewell, *Dollars for Dixie: Business and the Transformation of Conservatism in the Twentieth Century* (New York: Cambridge University Press, 2017), chap. 3.

71. W. J. Cash, *The Mind of the South* (New York: Knopf, 1941), 398.

72. Paul E. Mertz, *New Deal Policy and Southern Rural Poverty* (Baton Rouge: LSU, 1978), 229.

73. Franklin D. Roosevelt, "Address at Gainesville, Georgia," March 23, 1938, APP, https://www.presidency.ucsb.edu/documents/address-gainesville-georgia.

74. Franklin D. Roosevelt, "Address at University of Georgia, Athens, Georgia," August 11, 1938, APP, https://www.presidency.ucsb.edu/documents/address-university-georgia-athens-georgia.

75. William E. Leuchtenburg, "Franklin D. Roosevelt: Domestic Affairs," Miller Center, University of Virginia, https://millercenter.org/president/fdroosevelt/domestic-affairs.

76. Rosenof, *Economics in the Long Run*, 44–45; and Paul A. Samuelson, "Alvin H. Hansen, 1887–1975," *Newsweek*, June 16, 1975, 72.

77. John Kenneth Galbraith, *A Contemporary Guide to Economics, Peace, and Laughter* (New York: Signet, 1971), 49–50.

78. Quoted in Rosenof, *Economics in the Long Run*, 54.

79. Ibid., 56.

80. J. K. Galbraith, *The Economic Effects of the Federal Public Works Expenditures, 1933–1938*, prepared with the assistance of G. G. Johnson Jr., for the Public Works Committee, National Resources Planning Board (Washington, D.C.: U.S. Government Printing Office, 1940), quotation at 12; for "off-site" data, 38–56.

81. Alvin Hansen, *Full Recovery or Stagnation?* (New York: W. W. Norton, 1938), 318 and 326–27.

82. Schulman, *From Cotton Belt to Sunbelt*, 42.

83. David L. Carlton and Peter A. Coclanis, eds., *Confronting Southern Poverty in the Great Depression* (Boston: Bedford Books of St. Martin's Press, 1996), 13.

84. Ibid., 14.

85. Ibid., 21–25; and Katznelson, *Fear Itself*, 168–72.

86. Quoted in William Leuchtenburg, *The White House Looks South: Franklin D. Roosevelt, Harry S. Truman, Lyndon B. Johnson* (Baton Rouge: LSU Press, 2005), 48.

87. Roosevelt, "Message to the Conference on Economic Conditions of the South."

88. Franklin D. Roosevelt, "Fireside Chat," April 14, 1938, APP, https://www.presidency.ucsb.edu/node/209619.

89. Franklin D. Roosevelt, "Address at University of Georgia, Athens, Georgia," August 11, 1938.

90. Ferguson, *Black Politics in New Deal Atlanta*, 166–85.

91. Robert D. Leighninger Jr., *Long-Range Public Investment: The Forgotten Legacy of the New Deal* (Columbia: University of South Carolina Press, 2007), 121–27.

92. "DeSoto Homes," Historic American Buildings Survey, No. GA-2403, National Parks Service, undated, http://lcweb2.loc.gov/master/pnp/habshaer/ga/ga1000/ga1020/data/ga1020data.pdf.

93. Bullock, "A Brief Statement Concerning Conditions Among Negroes in Georgia," 7–8, and 9–21.

94. Schulman, *From Cotton Belt to Sunbelt*, 118.

95. Mertz, *New Deal Policy and Southern Rural Poverty*, 238.

96. Hansen quoted in Rosenof, *Economics in the Long Run*, 63.

97. *Southern Secretary*, December 1937, box 2, RCCP.

98. Holmes, *New Deal in Georgia*, 333.

99. "An Overview of Rome in the Twentieth Century," January 10, 1989, National Register of Historic Places Continuation Sheet, U.S. Department of the Interior, National Park Service.

100. Mississippi Valley Association, "The Alabama-Coosa River Project," undated pamphlet, box 2, RCCP; Battey, *A History of Rome and Floyd County*, 315–32.

101. W. H. Foster to W. H. Butler, June 26, 1929, box 2, RCCP.

102. E. L. May to W. H. Foster, June 13, 1929, box 2, RCCP.

103. M. C. Tarver to J. J. McDonough, April 19, 1941, box 1, RCCP.

104. Franklin D. Roosevelt to M. C. Tarver, December 26, 1940, box 1, RCCP.

105. Thomas M. Robbins to M. C. Tarver, January 6, 1941, box 1, RCCP.

106. "Coosa Meeting Called April 16," *RNT*, April 3, 1941, box 2, RCCP; and "Coosa Waterway Action Gladdens Local Citizens," *Gadsden Times*, November 9, 1941, box 1, RCCP.

107. J. R. Hornady to J. J. McDonough, April 21, 1941, box 1, RCCP.

108. J. R. Hornady to Henry W. Pyne, May 8, 1941, box 1, RCCP.

109. "Crucial Event April 28," *RNT*, April 22, 1941, box 2, RCCP.

110. "Coosa Waterway Action Gladdens Local Citizens," *Gadsden Times*, November 9, 1941, box 1, RCCP.

111. I. M. Levinson to Sen. Walter F. George and Sen. Richard Russell, undated (December 1941), box 1, RCCP.

112. Ed L. Cantrell to Walter F. George and Richard B. Russell, December 6, 1941, box 1, RCCP.

113. M. C. Tarver to C. A. Milhollin, December 4, 1941, box 1, RCCP.

114. Franklin D. Roosevelt, "Address at Gainesville, Georgia."

115. Sparrow, *Warfare State*, 167–69.

116. "Crucial Event April 28," *RNT*, April 22, 1941.

117. Phillips-Fein, *Invisible Hands*, 3–33.

118. *Southern Secretary*, December 1937, box 2, RCCP.

119. Radio Script No. 1-A, "Taxes—and the Stockholder," U.S. Chamber of Commerce, January 1939, box 2, RCCP.

120. Smith, *Building New Deal Liberalism*, 64–65.

121. Franklin D. Roosevelt, "Address Before the American Retail Federation, Washington, D.C.," May 22, 1939, APP, https://www.presidency.ucsb.edu/node/209670.

122. *Southern Secretary*, August 1937, box 2, RCCP.

123. Schulman, *From Cotton Belt to Sunbelt*, 129.

124. "Governor Arnall Points the Way to Greater Progress in Georgia," *Georgia Progress*, September 15, 1944, binder 1, Economic Development, GPCA.

125. Rosenof, *Economics in the Long Run*, 49; Alvin Hansen, "Mr. Keynes on Underemployment Equilibrium," *Journal of Political Economy* 44, no. 5 (1936): 667–86, quotations at 680, 681, 683.

126. Hansen, "Mr. Keynes on Underemployment Equilibrium," 683.

127. "Governor Arnall Points the Way to Greater Progress in Georgia"; and Bartley, *Creation of Modern Georgia*, 196–97.

128. Franklin D. Roosevelt: "Transmittal to Congress of the Progress Report of the National Resources Committee," January 11, 1940, APP, https://www.presidency.ucsb.edu/node/209648.

129. "Industry Panel Program Goes Forward at Meetings in 200 Georgia Towns," *Georgia Progress*, January 1, 1945, binder 1, Economic Development, GPCA.

130. "What Others Say About Georgia," *Georgia Progress*, December 1, 1945, binder 1, Economic Development, GPCA.

131. Schulman, *From Cotton Belt to Sunbelt*, 129.

132. John Chamberlain, "Arnall of Georgia," *Life*, August 6, 1945, quoted in Stephen G. N. Tuck, *Beyond Atlanta: The Struggle for Racial Equality in Georgia, 1940–1980* (Athens: University of Georgia Press, 2001), 42–43.

133. "Good Government Is Good Business in Georgia," ca. 1944, binder 1, Economic Development, GPCA.

134. Holmes, *New Deal in Georgia*, 83; Bartley, *Creation of Modern Georgia*, 196.

135. "A Talk by Ernest L. Wright, Kiwanis Club of Rome, May 30, 1949," quotations at 3, 8, 6, and 10, States' Rights Council of Georgia, Inc., May 30, 1949–February 8, 1960, MS.76.5 / Hall Hoag 683, Reel 5, Filmed from the holdings of The Hall-Hoag Collection of Dissenting and Extremist Printed Propaganda, John Hay Library, Brown University, Gale Primary Sources, Document Number DSECMS238442550.

136. "Roland Hayes Returns to Native Georgia and Is Beaten by Whites," *Chicago Defender*, July 25, 1942, 1; "Beaten in Georgia, Says Roland Hayes," *NYT*, July 17, 1942, 9.

137. Ed Bridges, "Roland Hayes Claims He Was Beaten in Rome," *AC*, July 17, 1942, 16.
138. Roy Wilkins, "The Watchtower," *NYAN*, August 1, 1942, 7.
139. W. E. B. Du Bois, "As the Crow Flies," *NYAN*, August 15, 1942, 6.

Chapter 2

1. John T. Flynn, "The Betrayal of Cleveland," *Harper's Magazine*, January 1934, 142-150.
2. Barney Warf and Brian Holly, "The Rise and Fall and Rise of Cleveland," *Annals of the American Academy of Political and Social Science* 552 (May 1997): 210.
3. Louis B. Seltzer, *The Years Were Good* (1956), 150, accessed online at http://www.clevelandmemory.org/ebooks/tywg; Herbert H. Harwood Jr., *Invisible Giants: The Empires of Cleveland's Van Sweringen Brothers* (Bloomington: Indiana University Press, 2003), 211 and 253-54; Albert Miller Hillhouse, *Municipal Bonds: A Century of Experience* (New York: Prentice-Hall, 1936), 22 n. 82.
4. While the rate of borrowing varied greatly across municipalities (often because of state restrictions instituted after fiscal crises of the 1870s), the most dramatic growth of bonded indebtedness in the 1920s was concentrated in northern industrial cities undergoing suburbanization, including smaller cities like Jersey City, New Jersey, or Utica, New York. Relatively fewer southern municipalities borrowed at similar per capita rates, though raw municipal default numbers in several southern states, particularly Florida and North Carolina, were higher than in many northern or western states. See Samara Gunter and James Siodla, "Local Origins and Implications of the 1930s Urban Debt Crisis," paper presented at the 111th Annual Conference of the National Tax Association, 2018, available online, https://ntanet.org/wp-content/uploads/2019/03/Session1202_Paper1566_FullPaper_1.pdf; and Hillhouse, *Municipal Bonds*, 24-30.
5. Harwood, *Invisible Giants*, 253-54 and 261.
6. Ibid., 253.
7. Clevelander Richard F. Grant of the M. A. Hanna mining company served as U.S. Chamber president. Frederick C. Crawford, head of the Cleveland manufacturing firm Thompson Products, served on the National Association of Manufacturers' finance committee and chaired its executive board. "U.S. Chamber of Commerce Parley to Open Tuesday," *WP*, May 17, 1925; "NAM Asked Balanced U.S. Budget," *WSJ*, December 8, 1945; "Crawford Urges Lifting of Curbs on Business," *WSJ*, July 21, 1945.
8. Families, friends, and professional contacts also played an important role in subsidizing business growth. Naomi Lamoreaux, Margaret Levenstein, and Kenneth Sokoloff, "Mobilizing Venture Capital During the Second Industrial Revolution: Cleveland, Ohio, 1870-1920," *Capitalism and Society* 1, no. 3 (2006): 26 and 38-39. Georgia banking statistics in Board of Governors of the Federal Reserve System, *Banking and Monetary Statistics, 1914-1941* (Washington, DC: Board of Governors of the Federal Reserve System, 1943), 26; on interest rates by region, see ibid., 463-64.
9. Monkkonen, *The Local State*, 20 and 19.
10. Hillhouse, *Municipal Bonds*, 238-39. On these dynamics in Detroit, see Amsterdam, *Roaring Metropolis*, 64-65.
11. Amsterdam, *Roaring Metropolis*, 9-10, 43-47, 54-56, 114-20.
12. Hillhouse, *Municipal Bonds*, 4-5.
13. Ibid., 3.
14. "New Bond Issues to Be Offered to Investment Bankers and the Public," *NYT*, September 3, 1930, 46; *Financial Statistics of Cities Having a Population of over 100,000* (Washington, D.C.: U.S. Department of Commerce, 1934), 172.

15. Flynn, "The Betrayal of Cleveland," 150.
16. Monkkonen, *The Local State*, 25.
17. Hillhouse, *Municipal Bonds*, 240–41.
18. Monkkonen, *The Local State*, 26.
19. Warren Roberts, "Behind the Cleveland Relief Problem," *Bulletin of the National Tax Association* 25, no. 6 (March 1940), folder 5, container 2, Burton. On Georgia, see Hillhouse, *Municipal Bonds*, 42.
20. Michael Katz, *In the Shadow of the Poorhouse: A Social History of Welfare in America* (New York: Basic Books, 1986), 155–63.
21. Kenneth Feingold, *Experts and Politicians: Reform Challenges to Machine Politics in New York, Cleveland, and Chicago* (Princeton: Princeton University Press, 1995), 84 and 105–6.
22. Cleveland Chamber of Commerce Executive Committee Minutes, December 11, 1931, vol. 2, container 44, GCGA.
23. Daniel Kerr, *Derelict Paradise: Homelessness and Urban Development in Cleveland, Ohio* (Amherst: University of Massachusetts Press, 2011), 80.
24. Katz, *In the Shadow of the Poorhouse*, 214; "Money Mobilization," Annual Report, 1931–32, container 75, GCGA.
25. Kerr, *Derelict Paradise*, 80.
26. "Cities Prefer Own to Federal Relief," *NYT*, September 6, 1931, 23; Amsterdam, *Roaring Metropolis*, 1–14.
27. Meeting of the Executive Committee of the Cleveland Chamber of Commerce, December 11, 1931, p. 7, vol. 2, container 44, GCGA.
28. City Plan Committee, Housing Meeting Minutes, April 7, 1933, vol. 2, container 47, GCGA.
29. Committee on Public Finance and Taxation to the Board of Directors, Cleveland Chamber of Commerce, May 17, 1932, attached to Board of Directors Meeting, May 25, 1932, vol. 1, container 45, GCGA.
30. Committee on Public Finance and Taxation to Board of Directors of the Cleveland Chamber of Commerce, February 20, 1933, vol. 1, container 45, GCGA.
31. Executive Committee Meeting Minutes, December 11, 1931, container 44, GCGA.
32. Committee on Public Finance and Taxation to Board of Directors of the Cleveland Chamber of Commerce, February 20, 1933, vol. 1, container 45, GCGA.
33. Committee on Public Finance and Taxation to Board of Directors of the Cleveland Chamber of Commerce, October 27, 1932, vol. 1, container 45, GCGA. The levy passed, and the city planned to apply to the RFC for additional relief funding. "City Still Faces Financial Crisis," *PD*, November 10, 1932, 5.
34. Sparenga paid $8,800 for the house in 1928. In the 2008–9 mortgage crisis, the home sold for $5,000. See Brian Albrecht, "Cleveland Eviction Riot of 1933 Bears Similarities to Current Woes," *PD*, March 8, 2009.
35. Kerr, *Derelict Paradise*, 89.
36. "14 Hurt as Crowd Fights 160 Police," *PD*, July 19, 1933, 1; Albrecht, "Cleveland Eviction Riot"; James Steele, "Home-Owners in Revolt," *The Nation*, September 6, 1933, 266.
37. See, e.g., "Repulse Cleveland Mob," *NYT*, September 9, 1932, 42; "50 Seized in Cleveland Relief Riot," *NYT*, January 31, 1933, 11; "Cleveland Raises Relief Standard," *NYT*, June 18, 1933, E6; see also "Troubles Beset Ohio Relief After Long Political Fight," *CT*, March 19, 1935, 2.

38. Edward M. Miggins, "Between Spires and Stacks: The People and Neighborhoods of Cleveland," in W. Dennis Keating, Norman Krumholz, and David C. Perry, eds., *Cleveland: A Metropolitan Reader* (Kent, Ohio: Kent State University Press, 1995), 186–89.

39. "Asks Principals to Seek Hungry," *PD*, September 29, 1931, 3.

40. Kerr, *Derelict Paradise*, 75–78.

41. Kusmer, *A Ghetto Takes Shape*, 101, 140–43, 42–46, 97–99.

42. Ibid., 40–43, 56, 10, 161–67, Hughes quotation at 167.

43. Ibid., 178–79, 187.

44. See Kimberley L. Phillips, *AlabamaNorth: African-American Migrants, Community, and Working-Class Activism in Cleveland, 1915–45* (Urbana: University of Illinois Press, 1999).

45. "Mayor Linked with Rioting in Cleveland," *Chicago Daily Tribune*, undated, folder 14, container 23, Burton.

46. Zieger, *The CIO*, 42–55; Heidi Fearing, "Fisher Body Strike," *Cleveland Historical*, accessed May 9, 2022, http://clevelandhistorical.org/items/show/393; Len De Caux quoted in Frances Fox Piven and Richard A. Cloward, *Poor People's Movements: Why They Succeed, How They Fail* (New York: Vintage Books, 1979), 50.

47. Kevin Boyle, "'There Are No Union Sorrows the Union Can't Heal': The Struggle for Racial Equality in the United Automobile Workers, 1940–1960," *Labor History* 36, no. 1 (1995): 5–32; and Bruce Nelson, *Divided We Stand: American Workers and the Struggle for Black Equality* (Princeton: Princeton University Press, 2001).

48. City Plan Commission Report, Board of Directors Minutes, July 20, 1932, vol. 1, container 45, GCGA.

49. National Planning Board, *Final Report—1933–34* (Washington, D.C.: U.S. Government Printing Office, 1934), 22; quoted in Reagan, *Designing a New America*, 188.

50. City Plan Commission Report, Board of Directors Minutes, July 20, 1932, vol. 1, container 45, GCGA.

51. Radford, *Modern Housing for America*, chaps. 1 and 2.

52. *Public Works Engineers' Yearbook, 1944, Including the Proceedings of the 1943 Public Works Congress, Held at Chicago, Illinois, October 24–27, 1943* (Chicago: American Public Works Association, 1944), 21.

53. Mabel Walker, *Urban Blight and Slums* (Cambridge: Harvard University Press, 1938), 112–14, 40, 48, 117, 122–23.

54. Committee on City Plan to Board of Directors, Cleveland Chamber of Commerce, July 5, 1932, vol. 1, container 45, GCGA.

55. City Plan Commission Report, July 8, 1932, quotations at 7, 2, 4, and 5, attached to Board of Directors Minutes, July 20, 1932, p. 7, vol. 1, container 45, GCGA.

56. City Plan Commission Report, Board of Directors Minutes, December 7, 1932, quotations at 2 and 9, vol. 1, container 45, GCGA.

57. James Monnett Jr., "U.S. Offers 12 Million on Housing Here," *PD*, September 7, 1933, 1; Kerr, *Derelict Paradise*, 93–104; Manufacturers' Committee, Subcommittee on Industrial Mortgage Loan Company Minutes, October 25, 1933 and November 6, 1933, vol. 2, container 46, GCGA.

58. Office of the Secretary of the Treasury, *Final Report on the Reconstruction Finance Corporation* (Washington, D.C.: U.S. Government Printing Office, 1959), 29, https://fraser.stlouisfed.org/files/docs/publications/rcf/rfc_19590506_finalreport.pdf.

59. Federal Reserve Bank of Cleveland, "Matthew J. Fleming," accessed May 9, 2022, https://www.federalreservehistory.org/people/matthew_j_fleming; "Loan Heads Appointed," *LAT*, February 8, 1932, 1.

60. Iver C. Olsen, *Revenue Bond Financing by Political Subdivisions: Its Origin, Scope, and Growth in the United States* (Washington, D.C.: U.S. Government Printing Office, 1936), 4.

61. Ibid., 7.

62. David Schleicher, "Hands On! Part 2: The Trilemma Facing the Federal Government During State and Local Budget Crises," working paper, Wharton Legal Studies and Business Ethics Workshop, October 22, 2020, 41–45.

63. Olsen, *Revenue Bond Financing*, 11, 4.

64. Monkkonen, *The Local State*, 31–33.

65. *First Deficiency Appropriation Bill for 1936: Hearings Before the Subcommittee of the Committee on Appropriations, U.S. Senate, on H.R. 12624*, 74th Cong. (Washington, D.C.: U.S. Government Printing Office, 1936), 323.

66. "Slum Clearance Nears," *CP*, September 8, 1934, 4.

67. On processes described in this and the preceding paragraph, see Kerr, *Derelict Paradise*, 93–104.

68. Olsen, *Revenue Bond Financing*, 22–23.

69. Smith, *Building New Deal Liberalism*, 97–98.

70. Smith, *A Concise History of the New Deal*, 52.

71. Report from the Committee on Public Finance and Taxation, Board of Directors Meeting Minutes, June 20, 1933, vol. 1, container 46, GCGA.

72. Industrial Development Committee Meeting Minutes, December 26, 1933, vol. 2, container 47, GCGA.

73. J. C. Argetsinger to A. Z. Baker, October 14, 1935, vol. 1, container 49, GCGA.

74. Smith, *Building New Deal Liberalism*, 85–86.

75. "Politics Wins," *PD*, March 31, 1936, 8; "Slate Alexander for Railway Head," *PD*, October 15, 1926, 8; John P. Leacacos, "Alexander Out as County WPA Chief," *PD*, July 23, 1938, 1.

76. "Backs Plan to Put Lawyers on WPA," *PD*, December 1, 1936, 4.

77. "Asks Jobs for 500 in Traffic Survey," *PD*, May 17, 1936, 4.

78. "Foresight in Traffic," *PD*, May 18, 1936, 6.

79. William Ganson Rose, *Cleveland: The Making of a City* (1950; repr., Kent: Kent State University Press, 1990), 877.

80. "WPA Workers to Be Expo Guests," *PD*, September 16, 1936, 1.

81. "WPA Begins Work on Lake Drive Bridges," *PD*, April 6, 1937, 19; Policy Committee, Construction Industries Meeting Minutes, May 19, 1938, Chamber of Commerce Meeting Minutes, vol. 2, container 52, GCGA; and "Start Next Week on Two WPA Jobs," *PD*, December 19, 1936, 1.

82. Executive Board of the Manufacturers' Committee Minutes, September 27, 1934, vol. 2, container 48, GCGA.

83. "Leaders Meet to Map Road to Recovery," *WP*, December 10, 1934, 1.

84. Executive Board of the Manufacturers' Committee Minutes, December 10, 1934, vol. 2, container 48, GCGA.

85. Charles W. Lawrence, "WPA Chief Spurs Work with Humor," *PD*, January 24, 1937, 7.

86. Argetsinger to Baker, October 14, 1935, vol. 1, container 49, GCGA.

87. Lawrence, "WPA Chief Spurs Work with Humor."

88. Howard Whipple Green, *Nine Years of Relief in Cleveland, 1928–1937* (Cleveland: Cleveland Health Council, 1937), 2.

89. Rose, *Cleveland*, 986.

90. Slovenian Cultural Garden, *Cleveland Historical*, accessed May 9, 2022, http://clevelandhistorical.org/items/show/138#.UrIyW2RKl0I.

91. "Turnstiles Tick 154,407 for Sunday," *PD*, June 29, 1936, 1.

92. Chads O. Skinner, "Find City's 'Big Shot' Is Uncle Sam," *PD*, May 21, 1938, 1.

93. Policy Committee, Construction Industries Meeting Minutes, May 19, 1938, Chamber of Commerce Meeting Minutes, vol. 2, container 52, GCGA.

94. "Huge WPA Street Grant Approved," *PD*, September 16, 1938, 9.

95. Policy Committee, Construction Industries Meeting Minutes, May 19, 1938, Chamber of Commerce Meeting Minutes, vol. 2, container 52, GCGA.

96. National Resources Planning Board, *National Resources Development: Report for 1942* (Washington, D.C.: U.S. Government Printing Office, 1942), 58.

97. National Resources Planning Board, *Security, Work, and Relief Policies, 1942* (Washington, D.C.: U.S. Government Printing Office, 1942), 295.

98. Karl, *Charles E. Merriam*, 50–53.

99. Michael Willrich, *City of Courts: Socializing Justice in Progressive Era Chicago* (New York: Cambridge University Press, 2003), 32–34.

100. Esther Fuchs, *Mayors and Money: Fiscal Policy in New York and Chicago* (Chicago: University of Chicago Press, 1992), 54–55; Reagan, *Designing a New America*, 61–67.

101. Charles Merriam, *American Political Ideas: Studies in the Development of American Political Thought, 1865–1917* (New York: Macmillan, 1920), 308–9.

102. Quoted in Reagan, *Designing a New America*, 67.

103. Merriam, "The Federal Government Recognizes the Cities," 107–10.

104. Merriam quoted in James Sparrow, "Charles Merriam and the Search for Democratic Power After Sovereignty," in Gary Gerstle and Joel Isaac, eds., *States of Exception in American History* (Chicago: University of Chicago Press, 2020), 211–12.

105. Quoted in Rosenof, *Economics in the Long Run*, 54 and 56.

106. Alvin H. Hansen, *The American Economy* (Westport: Greenwood Press, 1977), 32–33.

107. Hansen, *Full Recovery or Stagnation?*, 318 and 326–27.

108. David Ciepley, *Liberalism in the Shadow of Totalitarianism* (Cambridge: Harvard University Press, 2006), 127.

109. Merriam, "On Planning," in Seymour Harris, ed., *Saving American Capitalism* (Cambridge: Harvard University Press, 1948), 160–61.

110. Ibid., 163; Philip Funigiello, *The Challenge to Urban Liberalism: Federal-City Relations During World War II* (Knoxville: University of Tennessee Press, 1978), 166.

111. National Planning Board, *Final Report—1933-34*, 15–16.

112. Merriam, "On Planning," 161.

113. Hansen, *Full Recovery or Stagnation?*, 327 and 329.

114. Charles Lawrence, "County Mappers to Work to Inch," *PD*, June 30, 1937, 7.

115. John T. Howard, "City Planning in Cleveland," 2, PAL; Director's Progress Report, April 1, 1940 to April 1, 1941, folder Regional Association of Cleveland, PAL.

116. "Mall Will Get Housing Center," *PD*, August 2, 1938, 13.

117. Howard, "City Planning in Cleveland."

118. "Lausche Pleads for City Planning," *PD*, August 22, 1942, 10.

119. Report of the Mayor's Advisory Committee on Planning Organization, July 10, 1942, PAL.

120. Alvin Hansen and Guy Greer, "The Federal Debt and the Future," *Harper's*, March 31, 1942, 489–500.

121. Kerr, *Derelict Paradise*, 101–2.

122. Joel Schwartz, *The New York Approach: Robert Moses, Urban Liberals, and Redevelopment of the Inner City* (Columbus: Ohio State University Press, 1993), 25–26.

123. Samuel Zipp, "The Roots and Routes of Urban Renewal," *Journal of Urban History* 39, no. 3 (2013): 371.

124. Walker, *Urban Blight and Slums*, 137.

125. Ibid., 17–72, quote on 68.

126. Kerr, *Derelict Paradise*, 95–96.

127. "Building with Vision," *PD*, February 3, 1937, 6.

128. Walker, *Urban Blight and Slums*, 69.

129. James R. Barrett and David R. Roediger, "The Irish and the 'Americanization' of the 'New Immigrants' in the Streets and in the Churches of the Urban United States, 1900–1930," *Journal of American Ethnic History* 24, no. 4 (2005): 3–33.

130. Anna M. Spodnik, interview by Jeanette E. Tuve, September 24, 1986, Ethnic Women of Cleveland Oral History Project, Cleveland State University.

131. "Ohio: The Lonely One," *Time*, February 20, 1956; "Ohio: Pursuing the Artful Dodger," *Time*, October 8, 1956.

132. "Ness, Eliot," *Encyclopedia of Cleveland History*, accessed May 9, 2022, https://case.edu/ech/articles/n/ness-eliot.

133. Seltzer, *The Years Were Good*, 230–31.

134. Author interviews with Andrew Hudak, December 22, 2010, and Taras Szmagala, January 4, 2011, Cleveland, Ohio.

135. Department of Finance, City of Cleveland, Ohio, *Financial Report*, year ending December 31, 1943, Mayor's Budget Estimates, PAL.

136. Alvin Silverman, "Offers Plan Jobs to Bohn, Howard," *PD*, July 21, 1942, 1.

137. Todd M. Michney, "Constrained Communities: Black Cleveland's Experience with World War II Public Housing," *Journal of Social History* 40, no. 4 (Summer 2007): 936 and 938.

138. Clayborne George to Walter F. White, October 8, 1941, folder 001521-006-0351, NAACP.

139. Nathan Straus to Mark J. Grossman, October 28, 1941, folder 001521-006-0351, NAACP.

140. W. O. Walker to Walter F. White, October 10, 1941, folder 001521-006-0351, NAACP; "Brief Report by Special Committee of the Cleveland Branch NAACP Investigating Alleged Discriminatory Practices of the Cleveland Metropolitan Housing Authority," attached to Willard White to Thurgood Marshall, October 16, 1941, folder 001521-006-0351, NAACP.

141. W. O. Walker to Walter F. White, October 10, 1941, folder 001521-006-0351, NAACP.

142. "Report of Committee on Increased Opportunity for Employment and Economic Security," 10, folder 001509-005-0220, NAACP.

143. Michney, "Constrained Communities," 933.

144. Parker James, "This Is Cleveland," in "This Is Cleveland as Others See Us," September 1943, folder Cleveland 1940–1949, PAL.

145. "Impact of the War on the Cleveland, Ohio Area," U.S. Department of Labor, Bureau of Labor Statistics, July 1944, PAL.

146. Walter Beam to Members of the Cleveland Chamber of Commerce, in *This is Cleveland as Others See Us*, September 1, 1943, 1, folder Cleveland 1940–1949, PAL.

147. "The Best Location in the Nation," folder Cleveland 1940–1949, PAL.

148. "Cleveland: All Geared Up to Serve Industry," Chamber of Commerce, April 1945, folder Cleveland 1940–1949, PAL.

149. Jewell R. Dean, "Postwar Days to See River Improvement Work Pushed," *PD*, September 24, 1944, 9A.

150. Alvin Silverman, "Council Ready to Listen on Main Ave. Bridge Removal," *PD*, June 12, 1945, 1.

151. Alvin Silverman, "'Treat All Alike' Marks Pay Veto," *PD*, June 29, 1944, 1.

152. Department of Finance, City of Cleveland, Ohio, *Financial Report*, year ending December 31, 1943, Mayor's Budget Estimates, PAL.

153. Alvin Silverman, "15 Millions in Postwar City's Bag," *PD*, July 23, 1944, 1.

154. Board of Directors Meeting Minutes, December 18, 1945, GCGA Meeting Minutes, vol. 1, 1945–46, container 59, GCGA.

155. Alvin Silverman, "Council Ready to Listen on Main Ave. Bridge Removal," *PD*, June 12, 1945, 1.

156. "Impact of the War on the Cleveland, Ohio Area," U.S. Department of Labor, Bureau of Labor Statistics, July 1944, PAL; Report of the Committee on Taxation, April 12, 1944, GCGA Meeting Minutes, vol. 1, 1944–45, container 58, GCGA.

157. "Report to Mayor Frank Lausche on the Status of Plan Preparation for the 1944–1949 Capital Improvement Budget & Program," 2, April 1, 1944, PAL.

158. "Cleveland's Planners," *Time*, July 22, 1946, folder Cleveland 1940–1949, PAL.

159. "Greater Cleveland," September 27, 1945, 69, folder Finance 1940–1949, PAL; and John O'Donnell, "Public Finance in a Growing Economy: Some Postwar Trends in Municipal Bond Financing," *Journal of Finance* 17, no. 2 (May 1962).

160. *Fifth Annual Six-Year Capital Improvement Program, 1948–1953*, June 1947, City Planning Commission, PAL.

161. *Sixth Annual Capital Improvement Program, 1949–1954*, June 1948, City Planning Commission, PAL.

162. Jacobs, *Pocketbook Politics*, 230–31; *Sixth Annual Capital Improvement Program, 1949–1954*, June 1948, City Planning Commission, PAL.

163. Department of Finance, City of Cleveland, Ohio, *Financial Report*, year ending December 31, 1946," Mayor's Budget Estimates, PAL; and Ray Dorsey, "O Debt, Where Is Sting, Asks City," *PD*, July 22, 1949, 4; Jon Teaford, *Rough Road to Renaissance: Urban Revitalization in America, 1940–1985* (Baltimore: Johns Hopkins University Press, 1990), 68.

164. "Purse Strings Pulled Tighter," *PD*, December 21, 1948, 14.

165. "Roosevelt Lists Post-War Rights," *PD*, January 15, 1942, 2.

166. Brinkley, *End of Reform*, 250–53.

167. Phillips-Fein, *Invisible Hands*, 31–34.

168. William McDermott, "McDermott on the Future," *PD*, January 29, 1942, 7.

169. Brinkley, *End of Reform*, 254–55.

170. Russell Weisman, "An Economist's Point of View," *PD*, August 18, 1942, 8.

171. Brinkley, *End of Reform*, 255–57; George Griswold, "Pennywise, Says FDR of Critics," *PD*, February 17, 1943, 1; "Half Slave, Half Free," *PD*, March 20, 1943, 8.

172. John Grabowski, introduction to Rose, *Cleveland*, xiii.

173. Rose, *Cleveland*, 876.

174. Ibid., xiv.

175. Karl, *Charles E. Merriam*, 279–80.

176. Moyn, "Second Bill of Rights: A Reassessment."

Chapter 3

1. John F. Kennedy, "Remarks at Muscle Shoals, Alabama, at the 30th Anniversary Celebration of TVA," May 18, 1963, APP, http://www.presidency.ucsb.edu/node/236379.

2. Council of Economic Advisers (Walter Heller et al.), interview by Joseph Pechman, August 1, 1964, transcript, p. 37, JFKOH.

3. Collins, *More*, 40–68.

4. Kennedy, "Remarks at Muscle Shoals, Alabama."

5. Advertisement, "Goal for 1952—1000 Members," *RNT*, February 24, 1952.

6. "Rome Is Growing," *RNT*, February 24, 1952, 4.

7. Sparrow, *Warfare State*, 243–47; and Mettler, *Soldiers to Citizens*.

8. Wilson, *Communities Left Behind*, 34–47; and Cobb, *The Selling of the South*, 35–95.

9. Handwritten notes, January 19, 1945, box 2, RCCP.

10. Minutes of Meeting with Representatives from Rome, Dalton, and Cartersville, January 19, 1945, box 2, RCCP; Minutes of Meeting of Representatives of Northwest Georgia Counties, February 16, 1945, box 2, RCCP.

11. Robert Nelson, "Report Dealing with the Potentialities of Northwest Georgia from the Standpoint of the Tourist Trade," undated, box 2, RCCP.

12. Richard Snyder Combes, "Origins of Industrial Extension: A Historical Case Study in Georgia" (master's thesis, Georgia Institute of Technology, 1992), 42, folder EES-Industrial Extension Division, GTA Subject File, Georgia Institute of Technology Archives, Atlanta, Georgia.

13. "Economic-Industrial Research at Tech," *Georgia Progress*, January 1, 1945, binder 1, Economic Development, GPCA.

14. Thomas A. Scott, "Winning World War II in an Atlanta Suburb: Local Boosters and the Recruitment of Bell Bomber," in Philip Scranton, ed., *The Second Wave: Southern Industrialization from the 1940s to the 1970s* (Athens: University of Georgia Press, 2001), 1–23; and Richard S. Combes, "Aircraft Manufacturing in Georgia: A Case Study of Federal Industrial Investment," in Scranton, *Second Wave*, 24–42.

15. Charles S. Bullock III and Mark J. Rozell, *The New Politics of the Old South: An Introduction to Southern Politics* (New York: Rowman and Littlefield, 2009), 50.

16. Bartley, *Creation of Modern Georgia*, 204.

17. Calvin Kytle, "A Long Dark Night for Georgia?" *Harper's*, September 1948, 55–64.

18. Calvin Kytle and James A. Mackay, *Who Runs Georgia?* (Athens: University of Georgia Press, 1948), 256.

19. Robert L. Scoggin to Herman Talmadge, September 12, 1971, folder 20, box 211, series II, Talmadge.

20. Winston A. Bowman, "Gray v. Sanders, 372 U.S. 368 (1963)." *Encyclopedia of the Supreme Court of the United States*, edited by David S. Tanenhaus, vol. 2, Macmillan Reference USA, 2008, pp. 358–359.

21. Minutes of Meeting of Representatives of Northwest Georgia Counties, February 16, 1945, box 2, RCCP.

22. "Rome Leaders Await Area Tourist Meet," *RNT*, August 24, 1955, 1.

23. O'Mara, *Cities of Knowledge*, 202.

24. Margaret O'Mara notes that Georgia Tech lagged behind the example of Stanford University in terms of transforming Atlanta's urban political economy. But Georgia Tech's obligation to the entire state was unique. Ibid., 221–22.

25. Combes, "Origins of Industrial Extension," 46.

26. "25 Years of Progress: Coosa Valley Area Planning and Development Commission, 1958–1983," July 21, 1983, 2; in author's possession.

27. Author interview with W. Gardner Wright, June 27, 2013, Rome, Georgia.

28. "New Harper-Nichols Furniture Store Graces Rome Cotton Block," *RNT*, April 27, 1954.

29. "25 Years of Progress."

30. Author interview with W. Gardner Wright. On the emergence of southern Republicans and "the myth of moderation," see Joseph Crespino, *In Search of Another Country: Mississippi and the Conservative Counterrevolution* (Princeton: Princeton University Press, 2007), 136–40.

31. "Area Planning Group Maps Broad Program," *RNT*, June 24, 1959, 2.

32. "25 Years of Progress," 2.

33. James T. Sparrow, "A Nation in Motion," in Lassiter and Crespino, *The Myth of Southern Exceptionalism*, 169.

34. Carl Feiss, "The Foundations of Federal Planning Assistance: A Personal Account of the 701 Program," *Journal of the American Planning Association* 51, no. 12 (1985); Peter Dreier, John Mollenkopf, and Todd Swanstrom, *Place Matters: Metropolitics for the Twenty-First Century*, 2nd ed., rev. (Lawrence: University Press of Kansas, 2004), 113.

35. Alan J. Howard, "Home Rule in Georgia: An Analysis of State and Local Power," *Georgia Law Review* 9 (1974–75): 757.

36. "25 Years of Progress," 3.

37. "Area Planners Set Budget, Sign New Tech Contract," *RNT*, July 19, 1963, 3.

38. Michael Bradshaw, *The Appalachian Regional Commission: Twenty-Five Years of Government Policy* (Lexington: University Press of Kentucky, 1992), 27.

39. "Coosa Planners to Hold Annual Session Thursday," *RNT*, July 17, 1960, 1.

40. Bartley, *Creation of Modern Georgia*, 181.

41. CVAPDC Newsletter, May 1969, RFCL.

42. CVAPDC Newsletter, February 1969, RFCL.

43. Ibid.

44. "Coosa Valley Program Speeded in 11 Counties," *RNT*, September 21, 1961, 20.

45. Bernard Street, "Coosa Valley Planning Program Taking Shape," *RNT*, September 19, 1961, 8.

46. "25 Years of Progress," 4.

47. "Rome Chosen as Site for Area Engineering Branch," *RNT*, July 21, 1960, 1.

48. "A Time for Moderation," *RNT*, January 24, 1957, 4.

49. "President Shows Irresponsibility," *RNT*, July 19, 1963, 4.

50. Rome-Floyd County Chamber of Commerce News-Letter, September 1963, Hargrett.

51. Combes, "Origins of Industrial Extension," 47.

52. Northwest Georgia Branch to CVAPDC, January 14, 1963, RFCL.

53. *IDeas*, vol. 5, no. 2, April 1965, folder Industrial, Engineering Experiment Station, Georgia Tech Archives, Atlanta, Georgia.

54. Rome-Floyd County Chamber of Commerce News-Letter, July 1962, Hargrett.

55. Howard A. Schretter, "The Area Planning and Development Commission: Its Relationship with Local Planning Programs," Institute of Community and Area Development, University of Georgia, Athens, Georgia, October 18, 1963, folder Speeches, Draft of Speeches, Notes [2], box 5, Carter.

56. "West Central Georgia Area Planning and Development Commission: Area Planning and Development Commissions in Georgia," undated, folder Speeches, Draft of Speeches, Notes [2], box 5, Carter.

57. Burton Sparer, "Area Planning and Development Commissions in Georgia Today," prepared by the Legislative Research Division of the Institute of Government, University of Georgia, February 1975, 7, in author's possession.

58. "25 Years of Progress," 3.

59. Seymour E. Harris, interview by Arthur M. Schlesinger Jr., June 16–17, 1964, transcript, pp. 9–11, 24–27, JFKOH.

60. Julian Zelizer, *Taxing America: Wilbur D. Mills, Congress, and the State* (New York: Cambridge University Press, 1998), 170–71.

61. Kenneth Casebeer, "Drafting Wagner's Act: Leon Keyserling and the Precommittee Drafts of the Labor Disputes Act and the National Labor Relations Act," *Berkeley Journal of Employment and Labor Law* 11, no. 1 (March 1989): 73–131.

62. Collins, *More*, 43.

63. Storrs, *The Second Red Scare and the Unmaking of the New Deal Left*, chap. 4.

64. Collins, *More*, 44–45.

65. Wilson, *Communities Left Behind*, 34–53.

66. Joseph A. Pechman, "Walter W. Heller, 1915–1987," *Brookings Papers on Economic Activity* 1987, no. 2 (1987): viii–xi, https://www.brookings.edu/wp-content/uploads/1987/06/1987b_bpea_pechman.pdf.

67. Walter W. Heller, "The Role of Fiscal-Monetary Policy in German Economic Recovery," *American Economic Review* 40, no. 2 (May 1950): 532.

68. Ibid., 546.

69. Walt W. Rostow, *Stages of Economic Growth: A Non-Communist Manifesto* (Cambridge: Cambridge University Press, 1960), 13 and 15.

70. Zelizer, *Taxing America*, 179–81.

71. John F. Kennedy, "Address and Question and Answer Period at the Economic Club of New York," December 14, 1962, APP, https://www.presidency.ucsb.edu/node/236775.

72. Council of State Chambers of Commerce, "Federal Tax Facts," bulletin no. 22, June 4, 1958, attached to Walter W. Heller, Memorandum for the president, April 5, 1963, folder Council of Economic Advisors, April 1963: 1–7, collection Papers of John F. Kennedy, Presidential Papers, President's Office Files, John F. Kennedy Presidential Library, Boston, MA, Digital Identifier: JFKPOF-075a-007-p0005.

73. Collins, *More*, 53.

74. Kyle Crichton, "Walter Heller: Presidential Persuader," *New York Times*, June 21, 1987, 1, 13.

75. Zelizer, *Taxing America*, 204–7.

76. Harris interview, 63, JFKOH.

77. John F. Kennedy to Seymour E. Harris, April 8, 1957, attached to Harris interview, 15, JFKOH.

78. O'Connor, *Poverty Knowledge*, 147.

79. On Harrington's book and its impact, see Maurice Isserman, *The Other American: The Life of Michael Harrington* (New York: Public Affairs, 2000), 175–220.

80. On Appalachian stereotypes including "state of nature" metaphors, see Dwight B. Billings, introduction, in Billings, Gurney Norman, and Katherine Ledford, eds., *Back Talk from Appalachia: Confronting Stereotypes* (Lexington: University Press of Kentucky, 1999).

81. Heller, "The Role of Fiscal-Monetary Policy in German Economic Recovery," 532 and 546.

82. Stefan Grüner, "Ensuring Economic Growth and Socioeconomic Stabilization: Industrial Policy in West Germany, 1950–1975," in Christian Grabas and Alexander Nützenadel, eds., *Industrial Policy in Europe After 1945: Wealth, Power, and Economic Development in the Cold War* (London: Palgrave Macmillan, 2014), 86–112.

83. Glen Edward Taul, "Poverty, Development, and Government in Appalachia: Origins of the Appalachian Regional Commission" (Ph.D. diss., University of Kentucky, 2001).

84. Rome-Floyd County Chamber of Commerce News-Letter, February 1963 and April 1963, Hargrett.

85. Appalachian Regional Commission, *The Appalachian Experiment, 1965–1970* (Washington, D.C.: Appalachian Regional Commission, 1972), 90; Bradshaw, *The Appalachian Regional Commission*, 26–28.

86. Eisinger, *Rise of the Entrepreneurial State*, 9.

87. Wilson, *Communities Left Behind*, 88–89.

88. Well-mobilized counties won the lion's share of support. Bradshaw, *The Appalachian Regional Commission*, 29.

89. "Texans Resent U.S. Listing as Depressed Area," August 1, 1961, news clipping, Area Redevelopment Administration, July 31, 1961–October 2, 1962, General File, 1954–1964, series 1, White; Wilson, *Communities Left Behind*, 52.

90. John F. Kennedy to John Horne, February 27, 1962, Area Redevelopment Administration, July 31, 1961–October 2, 1962, White.

91. James Miller et al. to William Batt, September 3, 1965, folder VI B, ARA General 1961–1965, box 69, series VI, Davis.

92. James Davis to Gray Burch, September 2, 1965, folder VI B, ARA General 1961–1965, box 69, series VI, Davis; and CE 7 008, 8/31/1965, attached to Davis to Burch, September 2, 1965.

93. G. G. Burch to James Davis, August 27, 1965, folder VI B, ARA General 1961–1965, box 69, series VI, Davis.

94. Sar Levitan and Harold Sheppard, "Impact of Technological Change upon Communities and Public Policy," undated, 15, Area Redevelopment Administration, July 31, 1961–October 2, 1962, General File, 1954–1964, series 1, White.

95. Nicholas deB. Katzenbach to Lee C. White, Civil Rights Problems in Programs of the Area Redevelopment Administration, November 9, 1961, Area Redevelopment Administration, July 31, 1961–October 2, 1962, General File, 1954–1964, series 1, White.

96. William L. Batt, interview by Larry J. Hackman, May 10, 1967, transcript, p. 165, JFKOH.

97. Daniel J. Galvin, *Presidential Party Building: Dwight D. Eisenhower to George W. Bush* (Princeton: Princeton University Press, 2010), 174–75.

98. Batt interview, 180–81, JFKOH.

99. "Coosa Area Planners Praised by Roosevelt," *RNT*, October 4, 1964.

100. Bradshaw, *The Appalachian Regional Commission*, 43.

101. Appalachian Regional Commission, *The Appalachian Experiment, 1965–1970*, 90; Bradshaw, *The Appalachian Regional Commission*, 26–28.

102. "The Valley of Poverty," *Life*, January 31, 1964.

103. *Annual Report of the Appalachian Regional Commission* (Washington, D.C.: Appalachian Regional Commission, 1965), 4.

104. Joe W. Fleming II, interview by Stephen Goodell, February 19, 1969, interview 1, transcript, p. 13, Lyndon Johnson Oral History Project, Miller Center, http://web2.millercenter.org/lbj/oralhistory/fleming_joe_1969_0219.pdf.

105. Batt interview, 194, JFKOH.

106. Ibid., 199.

107. Ibid., 179.

108. CVAPDC Annual Report, June 30, 1966, 15–16.

109. CVAPDC Annual Report, 1971.

110. CVAPDC Newsletter, August 1970, RFCL.

111. CVAPDC Newsletter, November 1969; and CVAPDC Newsletter, August 1969, RFCL.

112. CVAPDC Newsletter, June 1969, RFCL.

113. Charles Prejean, "Georgia and Local Government Modernization: Area Planning and Development Commissions," report, 1973, 31, in author's possession. I am grateful to Alec Fazackerly Hickmott for sharing this resource.

114. "Coosa Valley Planners Win Worldwide Fame," *RNT*, July 15, 1966, 3.

115. *Atlanta Constitution*, undated clipping, Planning Commission, RFCL.

116. Sparer, "Area Planning," 11–12.

117. "Goldwater Attacks 'Indecision' of JFK," *RNT*, November 19, 1961, 1.

118. "Sen. Goldwater Lauds Coosa Valley Planning," *RNT*, November 20, 1961.

119. "Landrum Linked to LBJ," *People's Choice*, News of the 9th District, September 1966, folder 15, box 1, series II, Miller.

120. Press release, July 15, 1966, folder 7, box 276, series II, Talmadge.

Chapter 4

1. *Investigation of Housing, 1955–56: Hearing Before the Subcommittee on Housing of the Committee on Banking and Currency, House of Representatives*, 84th Cong., on H. Res. 203, February 13, 1956, part 4, Cleveland, Ohio (Washington, D.C.: U.S. Government Printing Office, 1956), 118.

2. See especially Nathan Connolly, *A World More Concrete: Real Estate and the Remaking of Jim Crow South Florida* (Chicago: University of Chicago Press, 2014); Hirsch, *Making the Second Ghetto*; Samuel Zipp, *Manhattan Projects: The Rise and Fall of Urban Renewal in Cold War New York* (New York: Oxford University Press, 2010); and Elihu Rubin, *Insuring the City: The Prudential Center and the Postwar Urban Landscape* (New Haven: Yale University Press, 2012).

3. Kerr, *Derelict Paradise*, 131.

4. LaDale C. Winling and Todd M. Michney, "The Roots of Redlining: Academic, Governmental, and Professional Networks in the Making of the New Deal Lending Regime," *Journal of American History* 108, no. 1 (June 2021): 42–69.

5. Leo Grebler, *The Role of Federal Credit Aids in Residential Construction* (New York: National Bureau of Economic Research, 1953), 27.

6. Miles L. Colean, "FHA and the Welfare State," *House & Home*, January 1953, 180–81.

7. "Apartment Boom: FHA's Impact on the Financing and Design of Apartments," *Architectural Forum*, January 1950, 98.

8. On the conservative turn framework, see Marc A. Weiss, "The Origins and Legacy of Urban Renewal," in J. Paul Mitchell, ed., *Federal Housing Policy and Programs, Past and Present* (New Brunswick, N.J.: Center for Urban Policy Research, Rutgers University, 1985), 253–74. On left-progressive movements for public housing, see Radford, *Modern Housing for America*; Rhonda Williams, *The Politics of Public Housing: Black Women's Struggles Against Urban Inequality* (New York: Oxford University Press, 2004); and Joshua B. Freeman, *Working-Class New York: Life and Labor Since World War II* (New York: New Press, 2001), 105–24.

9. Nikhil Pal Singh, *Black Is a Country: Race and the Unfinished Struggle for Democracy* (Cambridge: Harvard University Press, 2004), 142.

10. Grebler, *Role of Federal Credit*, 63; Comptroller General of the United States, *Summary Report to the Subcommittee on Housing Committee on Banking and Currency, United States Senate: Information Relating to Certain Aspects of Multifamily Housing Programs* (Washington, D.C.: U.S. Government Printing Office, 1963), 487.

11. Eugene Segal, "Upshur Evans: Key Man on City's Looks," *PD*, November 17, 1963, 13; Minutes of the Meeting of the Committee on Urban Redevelopment, May 19, 1953, p. 2, vol. 2, container 65, GCGA; James Yeilding to Urban Redevelopment Citizens Committee, January 29, 1954, vol. 2, container 65, GCGA; "The Future Is Worth $500—Plus," *PD*, June 8, 1954.

12. Kerr, *Derelict Paradise*, 131.

13. Segal, "Upshur Evans."

14. Cleveland Chamber of Commerce Annual Report for 1955–56, folder Annual Reports–Industrial Development Committee, container 153, GCGA.

15. Director's Progress Report, April 1, 1940–April 1, 1941, folder Regional Association of Cleveland, PAL.

16. "Annexations in Houston," City of Houston Planning and Development Department, accessed May 10, 2022, https://www.houstontx.gov/planning/Annexation/docs_pdfs/HoustonAnnexationHistory.pdf. See also Lassiter, *The Silent Majority*, 52–53, 180–84, and 280–85.

17. These included WWII FHA housing programs for veterans and war workers, including FHA Section 608–backed Cleveland Parkway Gardens (449 units) and Knollwood Apartments (329 units). U.S. Department of Housing and Urban Development, Terminated Multifamily Mortgages Database, accessed May 10, 2022, https://www.hud.gov/program_offices/housing/comp/rpts/mfh/mf_f47t.

18. 1960 U.S. Census, Parma, Ohio.

19. David Stradling and Richard Stradling, "Perceptions of the Burning River: Deindustrialization and Cleveland's Cuyahoga River," *Environmental History* 13, no. 3 (2008): 515–35, figures at 528; "Cleveland Hard Hit by Factory Closings Since 1960," *Toledo Blade*, July 3, 2016, http://www.toledoblade.com/business/2016/07/03/Cleveland-hard-hit-by-factory-closings-since-1960.html.

20. Nishani Frazier, *Harambee City: The Congress of Racial Equality in Cleveland and the Rise of Black Power Populism* (Fayetteville: University of Arkansas Press, 2017), 35–42.

21. "Pastor Hits Bias as Main Cause of Slums," *CP*, March 5, 1955, 4A.

22. Nate Silverman, "Plant Tax Cut Raises City's Fear," *PD*, October 14, 1955, 1.

23. On northern cities and discriminatory policing, see Muhammad, *Condemnation of Blackness*.

24. Neal R. Peirce, "Fiscal Federalism: Revenue Sharing Is Not Enough," *Publius* 6, no. 4 (Autumn 1976): 177–84; and Alvin D. Sokolow, "The Changing Property Tax and State-Local Relations," *Publius* 28, no. 1 (Winter 1998): 168.

25. Guy Greer and Alvin H. Hansen, *Urban Redevelopment and Housing* (Washington, D.C.: National Planning Association, 1941), 4.

26. Alvin Hansen, "The City of the Future," *National Municipal Review* 32 (1943): 70.

27. Guy Greer, "Urban Redevelopment," in Harris, *Saving American Capitalism*, quotations at 196 and 199–200; Greer and Hansen, *Urban Redevelopment and Housing*.

28. Weiss, "Origins and Legacy of Urban Renewal," 253–74; and Gelfand, *A Nation of Cities*, 136–56.

29. Walker, *Urban Blight and Slums*, 129–30, 68.

30. Hansen and Greer, "The Federal Debt and the Future," 500.

31. On the Cold War and liberal developmentalism abroad, see Gilman, *Mandarins of the Future*; Immerwahr, *Thinking Small*; and Offner, *Sorting out the Mixed Economy*.

32. Harry Truman, "Annual Message to the Congress on the State of the Union," January 5, 1949, APP, https://www.presidency.ucsb.edu/node/230007.

33. Gunnar Myrdal quoted in Alec Fazackerly Hickmott, "Living in the Country: Imagining Development and Remaking the Black Rural South, 1933–1986" (Ph.D. diss., University of Virginia, 2016), 39.

34. Truman, "Annual Message to the Congress on the State of the Union," January 5, 1949.

35. I borrow "discourse of progress" from Connolly, *A World More Concrete*, 211.

36. Alexander von Hoffman, "A Study in Contradictions: The Origins and Legacy of the Housing Act of 1949," *Housing Policy Debate* 11, no. 2 (2000): 299.

37. Urban Redevelopment Conference Minutes, May 7, 1952, vol. 2, 1952–53, container 64, GCGA.

38. "Cleveland Housing Head Speaks Feb. 7," *Pittsburgh Courier*, February 8, 1958, 4.

39. Urban Redevelopment Conference Minutes, May 7, 1952, vol. 2, 1952–53, container 64, GCGA.

40. Minutes of the Meeting of the Committee on Urban Redevelopment, March 24, 1954, vol. 2, container 65, GCGA.

41. *Urban Renewal Project Characteristics* (Washington, D.C.: Housing and Home Finance Agency, Urban Renewal Administration, June 30, 1961), 33; Kerr, *Derelict Paradise*, 130–35.

42. James T. Patterson, *Grand Expectations: The United States, 1945–1974* (New York: Oxford University Press, 1996), 336.

43. Gelfand, *A Nation of Cities*, 168.

44. "Inflation Spills Red on City Budgets," *Business Week*, January 5, 1952, 80–81; International City/County Management Association, *The Municipal Year Book* (Chicago: International City Manager's Association, 1952), 4.

45. *Housing in America: Its Present Status and Future Implications; A Factual Analysis of Testimony and Studies* (Washington, D.C.: U.S. Government Printing Office, 1948), 155–56.

46. President's Advisory Committee on Government Housing Policies and Programs, *Recommendations on Government Housing Policies and Programs* (Washington, D.C.: U.S. Government Printing Office, 1953), 218–19.

47. Ibid., 151–54.

48. On debates about public housing, see D. Bradford Hunt, "How Did Public Housing Survive the 1950s?," *Journal of Policy History* 17, no. 2 (2005): 203–4.

49. *Housing in America*, 64.

50. Ibid., 6.

51. *FHA Investigation: Report of the Senate Committee on Banking and Currency*, 84th Cong., January 6, 1955 (Washington, D.C.: U.S. Government Printing Office, 1955), 2; Leo Grebler, David M. Plank, and Louis Winnick, *Capital Formation in Residential Real Estate: Trends and Prospects* (Princeton: Princeton University Press, 1956), 147.

52. House Committee on Banking and Currency, Subcommittee on Housing, *Slum Clearance and Urban Renewal* (Washington, D.C.: U.S. Government Printing Office, 1956), 12–13; Housing and Home Finance Agency, *Tenth Annual Report* (Washington, D.C.: U.S. Government Printing Office, 1957), 52.

53. "FHA's Five-Year-Old Scandal," *House & Home*, May 1954, I-H.

54. Hunt, "How Did Public Housing Survive," 203–4.

55. On Brooklyn and Queens, see Nicholas Shatan and Kathe Newman, "The State Market Relationship as a Real Estate Technology: FHA Multifamily Development and Preservation, 1934–Present," *Urban Geography* 41, no. 8 (2020): 1076–77.

56. Housing Act of 1954, Public Law 83-560, approved August 2, 1954, 68 Stat. 590, at 607–8.

57. Ibid., 623.

58. *Replacing Blight with Good Homes: FHA's Section 220 Mortgage Insurance for Urban Renewal*, issued jointly by Federal Housing Administration and Urban Renewal Agency, Housing and Home Finance Agency (Washington, D.C.: U.S. Government Printing Office, October 1955), 10, 3, 2 (last two ellipses in original); *Investigation into FHA Multiple Dwelling Projects: Report of the Committee on Government Operations, United States Senate* (Washington, D.C.: U.S. Government Printing Office, 1967), 9–10; *FHA Mortgage Foreclosures: Hearings Before a Subcommittee of the Committee on Banking and Currency, U.S. Senate*, 88th Cong., January 27–28, 1964 (Washington, D.C.: U.S. Government Printing Office, 1964), 55–65.

59. Minutes of the Meeting of the Committee on Urban Redevelopment, March 24, 1954, p. 2, vol. 2, container 65, GCGA; Eugene Segal, "Five Top Banks Here Plan $185,000,000 Slum Housing Pool," *PD*, April 1, 1955, 1.

60. Todd Michney, "White Civic Visions Versus Black Suburban Aspirations: Cleveland's Garden Valley Urban Renewal Project," *Journal of Planning History* 10, no. 4 (2011): 292.

61. "Seek Capital Funds Today for Garden Valley Housing," *PD*, December 7, 1954, 4; Eugene Segal, "Garden Valley Parley Called," *PD*, December 12, 1954, 10B.

62. Kerr, *Derelict Paradise*, 131.

63. "Virden Outlines Kingsbury Plan," *PD*, May 28, 1954, 25.

64. "The Future Is Worth $500—Plus," *PD*, June 8, 1954, 14.

65. Board of Directors Meeting, October 2, 1952, Chamber of Commerce Minutes, 1952–53, vol. 1, container 64, GCGA.

66. "Push Kingsbury Housing Project," *PD*, February 8, 1955, 5.

67. Eugene Segal, "FHA Hesitation Sets Back Start of Garden Valley," *PD*, May 12, 1955, 13.

68. Todd Simon, "City Aims to Force Owners to Fix Houses Near Project," *PD*, September 1, 1955, 45.

69. "Garden Valley Pledged $2,090,700 by FHA," *PD*, March 22, 1956, 6.

70. "FHA Shifts Stand, to Back Garden Valley Home Plan," *PD*, September 8, 1955, 4.

71. House Committee on Banking and Currency, Subcommittee on Housing, *Slum Clearance and Urban Renewal*, 9, 11 n. 1.

72. *Investigation of Housing, 1955–56*, 7.

73. Ibid., 118 and 123 (testimony of Upshur Evans); Eugene Segal, "Lawmakers Get Earful on FHA," *PD*, February 14, 1956, 1.

74. *Investigation of Housing, 1955–56*, 123 (Evans testimony).

75. Miles Colean, "Impotency of FHA Policies," *Architectural Forum*, June 1955, 162.

76. *Investigation of Housing, 1955–56*, 123 (Evans testimony).

77. Oscar Steiner, *Our Housing Jungle—and Your Pocketbook: How to Turn Our Growing Slums into Assets* (New York: University Publishers, 1960), 83 and 85.

78. "FHA Should Trust Local Agencies," *PD*, February 15, 1956, 16.

79. Housing Act of 1956, Public Law 84-1020, approved August 7, 1956, 70 Stat. 1091, at 1096–98.

80. "New Profits in the New Housing Bill," *House and Home*, March 1959, 47; "1956 Housing Bill Highlights," *American Builder*, September 1, 1956, 26.

81. *FHA Mortgage Foreclosures*, 78. Some builders urged Congress to implement a "high-cost area amendment" to the Housing Act. See *Investigation of Housing, 1955–56*, 91.

82. *FHA Mortgage Foreclosures*, 484–85 and 31; and *Investigation into FHA Multiple Dwelling Projects*.

83. Eugene Segal, "Urban Program Showing Defects," *PD*, January 1, 1959, 1; Michney, "White Civic Visions," 296.

84. "Ask Mayor to Form Citizens Group for Urban Redevelopment," *CP*, April 30, 1955.

85. "Let the Community in on Redevelopment Plans," *CP*, April 30, 1955.

86. Rey Gillespie, "Community Relations," *PD*, May 12, 1957, 36.

87. Kerr, *Derelict Paradise*, 132.

88. "A View of the Garden Valley Urban Renewal Project as Seen by Staff of Garden Valley Neighborhood House," February 16, 1961, 6, folder Garden Valley Neighborhood House, box 30, CDF.

89. "Garden Valley Protests Today," *PD*, December 2, 1964, 32; William Nelson Jr. and Philip Meranto, *Electing Black Mayors: Political Action in the Black Community* (Columbus: Ohio State University Press, 1977), 78–79.

90. Eugene Segal, "Huge Sums Are Lost on Longwood," *PD*, April 18, 1963, 13.

91. "FHA May Foreclose Mortgage of Garden Valley Development," *PD*, December 27, 1963, 5.

92. *Investigation into FHA Multiple Dwelling Projects*, 10 and 6.

93. Vivian Aplin, "Garden Valley Project Is Hit by Foreclosure," *PD*, May 26, 1973, 1.

94. Kerr, *Derelict Paradise*, 132; Carol Poh Miller and Robert Wheeler, *Cleveland: A Concise History*, 2nd ed. (Bloomington: Indiana University Press, 1997), 161–62.

95. Michney, "White Civic Visions," 296.

96. *Urban Renewal: Hearings Before the Subcommittee on Housing of the Committee on Banking and Currency, House of Representatives*, 88th Cong., part 1, October 22–24, 1963, part 2, November 19–21, 1963 (Washington, D.C.: U.S. Government Printing Office, 1963), 393 (statement of William L. Slayton).

97. Guian A. McKee, "The Hospital City in an Ethnic Enclave: Tufts–New England Medical Center, Boston's Chinatown, and the Urban Political Economy of Health Care," *Journal of Urban History* 42, no. 2 (2016): 259–83.

98. On white gentrification, see Suleiman Osman, *The Invention of Brownstone Brooklyn: Gentrification and the Search for Authenticity in Postwar New York* (New York: Oxford University Press, 2011); and Judah Gribetz and Frank P. Grad, "Housing Code Enforcement: Sanctions and Remedies," *Columbia Law Review* 66, no. 7 (1966): 1254–90.

99. *Urban Renewal: Hearings*, 469, 408, 426–27 (Slayton testimony and appendixes).

100. Ibid., 175 (testimony of Cleveland mayor Ralph Locher).

101. Minutes, Joint Meeting of the Executive Committee of the Greater Cleveland Growth Board, Board of Directors of the Cleveland Chamber of Commerce, and Executive Committee of the Cleveland Development Foundation, November 24, 1964, container 163, GCGA.

102. Theodore Hall, "Planning in Cleveland, 1903–1968," in *A History of Planning in Cleveland, 1903–2000*, 27, PAL.

103. "Mayor and Council Team Up on Bonds," *PD*, October 8, 1960.

104. *Urban Renewal: Hearings*, 181 (statement of Edward W. Sloan Jr.).

105. "Garden Valley Protests Today," *PD*, December 2, 1964.

106. Nelson and Meranto, *Electing Black Mayors*, 81.

107. Frazier, *Harambee City*, 78–105, Turner quote at 105.

108. David Cohen, in Ruth Turner interview with Robert Penn Warren, May 7, 1964, *Robert Penn Warren's Who Speaks for the Negro? An Archival Collection*, Robert Penn Warren Center for the Humanities, Vanderbilt University, http://whospeaks.library.vanderbilt.edu/interview/ruth-turner.

109. Ruth M. Turner, "Black Power: A Voice Within," *Oberlin Alumni Magazine*, May 1967, 17–19; reprinted in John H. Bracey Jr., August Meier, and Elliott Rudwick, eds., *Black Nationalism in America* (Indianapolis: Bobbs-Merrill, 1970), 465–70.

110. Turner interview with Warren, May 7, 1964.

111. "Mayor and Council Team Up on Bonds," *PD*, October 8, 1960.

112. "3 City Issues Are Headed for Approval," *PD*, November 9, 1960.

113. Comparative figures available at D.3 Credit Market Debt Outstanding by Sector, Federal Reserve Economic Data, https://fred.stlouisfed.org/categories/32256.

114. *Cleveland Press*, April 6, 1971, in folder 88, container 6, Perk.

115. *Moody's Municipal and Government Manual* (New York: Moody's Investor's Service, 1963), 1642; Ray Dorsey, "Levy Defeat Hurls Issue into Politics," *PD*, August 15, 1962, 1.

116. Eugene Segal, "Urban Bond Issue 1st Opposed Here," *PD*, November 2, 1963, 7; Eugene Segal, "Urban Renewal Issue to Be Put to Voters Again, Locher Says," *PD*, November 7, 1963, 2.

117. John T. McGreevy, *Parish Boundaries: The Catholic Encounter with Race in the Twentieth-Century Urban North* (Chicago: University of Chicago Press, 1996), 228.

118. "West Side Solons Debate Free Drives for Poor," *CP*, April 2, 1966.

119. Eugene Segal, "City Renewal 'Ball' Tossed to Council," *PD*, January 15, 1960, 5.

120. *Urban Renewal: Hearings*, 226 (testimony of James Lister).

121. "Celebrezze Steps Up Pace on Downtown Renewal Work," *PD*, June 1, 1960, 54.

122. *Urban Renewal*, 505–6 (Slayton testimony).

123. I. M. Pei and Associates, *Erieview, Cleveland, Ohio: An Urban Renewal Plan for Downtown Cleveland* (New York: I. M. Pei, 1961), https://dome.mit.edu/handle/1721.3/175665.

124. Kerr, *Derelict Paradise*, 138.

125. "Levin's Plan for Building Gets City OK," *PD*, March 25, 1962, 6.

126. Theodore Hall, "Planning in Cleveland, 1903–1963," 27.

127. *Federal Urban Renewal Program: Special Report*, undated, 22, folder Publications—not contained in the bound volumes for Chamber Publications, box 5, series III, CCUS.

128. David Stradling and Richard Stradling, *Where the River Burned: Carl Stokes and the Struggle to Save Cleveland* (Ithaca: Cornell University Press, 2015), 105–6; The Journal of the Supreme Court of the United States, 1962, Case No. 353, Monday November 5, 1962, 74, https://www.supremecourt.gov/pdfs/journals/scannedjournals/1962_journal.pdf.

129. Judge John V. Corrigan, opinion, July 16, 1963, cited in *Urban Renewal*, 522.

130. Norman Krumholz, "Cleveland: The Hough and Central Neighborhoods—Empowerment Zones and Other Urban Policies," in W. Dennis Keating and Norman Krumholz, eds., *Rebuilding Urban Neighborhoods: Achievements, Opportunities, and Limits* (Thousand Oaks: SAGE, 1999), 88.

131. W. O. Walker, "Downtown Cleveland, a Victim of Prejudice and Selfishness," *CP*, February 24, 1962, 10.

132. Mark Souther, *Believing in Cleveland: Managing Decline in the Best Location in the Nation* (Philadelphia: Temple University Press, 2017), 87–88.

133. Krumholz, "Cleveland," 90–91.

134. "Hough Citizens Continue on Bad Housing Assault," *CP*, December 12, 1964.

135. "'Ghost Town' Residents Want City Action Now," *CP*, March 16, 1963; "Congressman Rips Hough Enforcement," *CP*, January 4, 1964, 1A.

136. "Urban Renewal Plans Scored as Cause of Decay," *NYT*, April 5, 1966.

137. Annual Report, Greater Cleveland Growth Board, February 11, 1963, 18, container 132, GCGA.

138. "NAACP Branch Says City Fiddles with Urban Renewal as Town Decays," *CP*, October 31, 1964.

139. Charles Loeb, "Cleveland's Urban Renewal—A Fiasco," *CP*, November 26, 1966, 8B.

140. *Hearing Before the United States Commission on Civil Rights: Hearing Held in Cleveland, Ohio, April 1–7, 1966* (Washington, D.C.: U.S. Government Printing Office, 1966) (hereafter *CCR*), 37 (testimony of Morris Thorington Jr.).

141. U.S. Advisory Commission on Intergovernmental Relations (ACIR), *Relocation: Unequal Treatment of People and Businesses Displaced by Governments* (Washington, D.C., January 1965), 25.

142. "Did We Vote for Poverty or Progress?" *CP*, February 6, 1965.

143. Robert E. Baker, "U.S. Rights Unit Opens Hearings in Cleveland," *WP*, April 3, 1966.

144. *CCR*, 37–38 and 42 (Thorington testimony).

145. Baker, "U.S. Rights Unit Opens Hearings in Cleveland."

146. *CCR*, 609, 613, and 615–16 (Jack Reavis testimony).

147. *CCR*, 619 (Carl Stokes testimony).

148. On the Hough uprisings, see "The Hough Uprisings of 1966," *Cleveland Historical*, accessed August 4, 2022, https://clevelandhistorical.org/items/show/7; Joseph Crespino, *Strom Thurmond's America* (New York: Hill and Wang, 2012), 104–5.

149. J. Edgar Hoover, Report, U.S. Department of Justice, FBI, attached to John J. Gunther, Executive Director of the U.S. Conference of Mayors, "Federal-City Reporter," memorandum, September 30, 1964, folder Negro–Miscellaneous Info., container 102, GCGA.

150. Recommendations for Greater Cleveland Growthland 1964 Advertising, vol. GCGB Special Meeting of Executive Committee, January 15, 1964; and 1962 Annual Report, First Year Activities and Progress, Greater Cleveland Growth Board, February 11, 1963, 1, vol. GCGB

Executive Committee Meeting Minutes February 23, 1963, container 132, GCGA; Greater Cleveland Growth Board advertisement, October 23, 1962, *WSJ*, vol. January 10, 1963, GCGB Executive Committee Meeting Minutes, January 10, 1963, container 132, GCGA; and "Racial Powder Keg," *WSJ*, March 14, 1967.

151. Roldo Bartimole, "Who Governs: The Corporate Hand," in Keating, Krumholz, and Perry, *Cleveland*, 165.

152. "CORE Leader Sparks New Civil Rights Coalition," *CP*, April 23, 1966; and "CORE Leader McKissick Takes Leave of Absence," *CP*, October 14, 1967.

153. Turner interview with Warren, May 7, 1964.

154. Target City Assessment, August 1969, 6, Target City Reel, Ford Foundation Archives, New York; Karen Ferguson, "Organizing the Ghetto," *Journal of Urban History* 34, no. 1 (2007): 78.

155. "Civil Rights Drive Planned in Cleveland," *CT*, June 15, 1967.

156. "Rights Leaders Hold Unity Talks; Map Effort to Ease Tension in Cleveland," *NYT*, June 15, 1967.

157. "Every City Is a Summer 'Test Case,'" *LAT*, June 16, 1967.

158. "Bought and Paid For or Just Plain Stupid?," *CP*, July 8, 1967; "Dems Courage Falters, in Denying Stokes OK," *CP*, August 12, 1967.

159. "Leo Jackson to Ride the Fence Again," *CP*, July 22, 1967.

160. Nelson and Meranto, *Electing Black Mayors*, 125 and 127; Laurette White, "Dents for Stokes Is Elegant Fare," *CP*, September 16, 1967; "'The Feminine Touch' in Dollars for Stokes Drive," *CP*, September 16, 1967.

161. Nelson and Meranto, *Electing Black Mayors*, 114–15.

162. Carl B. Stokes, *Promises of Power: A Political Autobiography* (New York: Simon and Schuster, 1973), 100–102.

163. Quoted in Estelle Zannes, *Checkmate in Cleveland: The Rhetoric of Confrontation During the Stokes Years* (Cleveland: Press of Case Western Reserve University, 1972), 57.

164. "The Making of a Mayor," *PD*, December 10, 1967.

165. Nelson and Meranto, *Electing Black Mayors*, 158.

166. Ferguson, "Organizing the Ghetto," 92–93.

167. Donald Sabath, "Urban Renewal Attacked Again," *PD*, November 16, 1966, 8.

Chapter 5

1. *CCR* (Paul Younger and Ruth Turner testimony); "Rep. Powell Snubs Petitioners Here," *PD*, October 31, 1964, 14; "Proceed with Caution," *CP*, October 10, 1964, 8B.

2. On the War on Poverty's domestic and international origins, see, O'Connor, *Poverty Knowledge*; Immerwahr, *Thinking Small*; and Offner, *Sorting Out the Mixed Economy*.

3. Daniel P. Moynihan, *Maximum Feasible Misunderstanding: Community Action in the War on Poverty* (New York: Free Press, 1969), 132 and 136–37.

4. Lyndon B. Johnson, "Commencement Address at Howard University: 'To Fulfill These Rights,'" June 4, 1965, APP, https://www.presidency.ucsb.edu/documents/commencement-address-howard-university-fulfill-these-rights; and Lyndon B. Johnson, "Special Message to the Congress Proposing a Nationwide War on the Sources of Poverty," March 16, 1964, APP, https://www.presidency.ucsb.edu/node/239636; Gareth Davies, *From Opportunity to Entitlement: The Transformation and Decline of Great Society Liberalism* (Lawrence: University Press of Kansas, 1996), 89.

5. Immerwahr, *Thinking Small*, 134; O'Connor, *Poverty Knowledge*, 113–29, quotations at 128 and 129.

6. Richard M. Flanagan, "Lyndon Johnson, Community Action, and Management of the Administrative State," *Presidential Studies Quarterly* 31, no. 4 (December 2001): 589–91.

7. O'Connor, *Poverty Knowledge*, 133.

8. Students for a Democratic Society, *The Port Huron Statement* (New York: Students for a Democratic Society, 1962). Available online via Wikisource (https://en.wikisource.org/wiki/Port_Huron_Statement), accessed May 20, 2022.

9. Lillian B. Rubin, "Maximum Feasible Participation: The Origins, Implications, and Present Status," *Annals of the American Academy of Political and Social Science* 385, no. 1 (September 1969): 14–29.

10. O'Connor, *Poverty Knowledge*, 167–69.

11. Donald Haider, "Governors and Mayors View the Poverty Program," *Current History*, November 1971, 276; Joseph Loftus, "How Poverty Bill Was Saved," *NYT*, December 25, 1967, 1.

12. ACIR, *Intergovernmental Relations in the Poverty Program* (Washington, D.C., April 1966), 25.

13. Frances Fox Piven and Richard Cloward, *Regulating the Poor: The Functions of Public Welfare*, updated ed. (New York: Vintage Books, 1993), 297, 288–89, and 303.

14. Turner interview with Warren, May 7, 1964.

15. Kenneth Clark and Jeannette Hopkins, *A Relevant War Against Poverty: A Study of Community Action Programs and Observable Social Change* (New York: Harper and Row, 1969), 164–65.

16. Al Sweeny, "Mayor Would Rather Starve Cleveland of Poverty Funds Than Enlarge Board," *CP*, January 30, 1965, 1A; "Powell Clarifies Poverty Agencies," *CP*, May 12, 1965, 1C; Clark and Hopkins, *A Relevant War Against Poverty*, 166.

17. O'Connor, *Poverty Knowledge*, 171–72; Elizabeth Hinton, *From the War on Poverty to the War on Crime: The Making of Mass Incarceration in America* (Cambridge: Harvard University Press, 2017), 53; Davies, *From Opportunity to Entitlement*, 90–91; and Rhonda Y. Williams, "'To Challenge the Status Quo by Any Means': Community Action and Representational Politics in 1960s Baltimore," in Orleck and Hazirjian, *The War on Poverty*, 83; Annelise Orleck, *Storming Caesar's Palace: How Black Mothers Fought Their Own War on Poverty* (Boston: Beacon Press, 2005), 110–15.

18. "Is War on Poverty Becoming War on Business?," *Nation's Business*, March 1966, 40–41, 58–61, quotations at 61.

19. August Meier, *CORE: A Study in the Civil Rights Movement* (New York: Oxford University Press, 1973), 336.

20. Hamilton Bims, "CORE: Wild Child of Civil Rights," *Ebony*, October 1965, 35–42.

21. Meier, *CORE*, 364.

22. Haider, "Governors and Mayors View the Poverty Program," 275–76.

23. Guian A. McKee, "'This Government Is with Us': Lyndon Johnson and the Grassroots War on Poverty," in Orleck and Hazirjian, *The War on Poverty*, 52–53.

24. Lyndon B. Johnson, "Remarks to the Members of the U.S. Chamber of Commerce," April 27, 1964, APP, https://www.presidency.ucsb.edu/node/239087.

25. McKee, "'This Government Is with Us,'" 38–39, 44–45.

26. Haider, "Governors and Mayors View the Poverty Program," 277.

27. *Economic Opportunity Act Amendments of 1967: Hearings Before the Committee on Education and Labor, House of Representatives*, 90th Cong. (Washington, D.C.: U.S. Government Printing Office, 1967), 887.

28. White House Daily Diary, March 16, 1967, pp. 8-9, LBJ Presidential Library, www.lbjlibrary.net/collections/daily-diary.html; and Joseph Loftus, "Council to Guide Poverty Agency," *NYT*, March 23, 1967, 23.

29. Bradley Patterson Jr., National Advisory Council on Economic Opportunity, Outline of Questions and Issues, May 17, 1967, folder 016516-010-0260, Gaither.

30. Lyndon B. Johnson, "Special Message to the Congress: America's Unfinished Business, Urban and Rural Poverty," March 14, 1967, APP, https://www.presidency.ucsb.edu/node/237975.

31. *Economic Opportunity Act Amendments of 1967: Hearings*, 3171, 515–627, 3174; on Job Corps, see Offner, *Sorting Out the Mixed Economy*, chap. 6.

32. Morris Leibman, "Civil Disobedience: A Threat to Our Society Under Law," *The Freeman*, December 1964, 262–65; see also "Bar Official Decries Civil Rights Tactics," *NYT*, July 9, 1965, 13.

33. Joe Califano to Lyndon Johnson, February 28, 1967, folder 016516-010-0260, Gaither.

34. Ibid., February 13, 1967, folder 016516-010-0260, Gaither.

35. *Focus on Community Action: Report of the National Advisory Council on Economic Opportunity* (Washington, D.C.: U.S. Government Printing Office, 1968), 29.

36. On Landrum's dismay over CAPs, see Davies, *From Opportunity to Entitlement*, 195. See also Joe Califano to Lyndon Johnson, October 16, 1967, folder 016516-010-0260, Gaither.

37. ACIR, *Intergovernmental Relations in the Poverty Program*, 30.

38. G. J. Tankersley Presentation on National Alliance of Businessmen to Greater Cleveland Growth Association Board of Directors, March 6, 1968, folder Board of Directors, March 6, 1968, container 146, GCGA.

39. Leonard N. Moore, *Carl B. Stokes and the Rise of Black Political Power* (Urbana: University of Illinois Press, 2002), 72.

40. Meeting Minutes, Greater Cleveland Growth Association Board of Directors, March 6, 1968, 3, folder Board of Directors, March 6, 1968, container 146, GCGA.

41. Board of Directors Meeting Minutes, November 29, 1967, vol. 1967–1968, container 165, GCGA; Moore, *Carl B. Stokes*, 72–74.

42. Bartimole, "Who Governs."

43. Moore, *Carl B. Stokes*, 74; "Carl Stokes' First Year as Mayor," *PD*, November 17, 1968, 1-AA.

44. Nishani Frazier, "A McDonald's That Reflects the Soul of a People: Hough Area Development Corporation and Community Development in Cleveland," in Laura Warren Hill and Julia Rabig, eds., *The Business of Black Power: Community Development, Capitalism, and Corporate Responsibility in Postwar America* (Rochester: University of Rochester Press, 2012), 68–92.

45. Moore, *Carl B. Stokes*, 76–77.

46. Ibid., 88.

47. Ibid., 80–85.

48. Kerr, *Derelict Paradise*, 174.

49. Davis quoted in Hinton, *From the War on Poverty to the War on Crime*, 132.

50. John E. Bryan, "City Awaiting Leadership Renaissance," *PD*, August 20, 1972, 1A.

51. Joe Eszterhas, "Buckeye Road: Neighborhood of Fear," *PD*, January 18, 1971, 10A.

52. McGreevy, *Parish Boundaries*, 228.

53. Seymour Sacks and William F. Hellmuth Jr., *Financing Government in a Metropolitan Area: The Cleveland Experience* (New York: Free Press of Glencoe, 1961); on postwar tax rates, 247; on debt, 297–300.

54. These revolts were echoed elsewhere. See Becky Nicolaides, *My Blue Heaven: Life and Politics in the Working-Class Suburbs of Los Angeles, 1920–1965* (Chicago: University of Chicago Press, 2002), 140–56; and, Lassiter, *The Silent Majority*, 175–84.

55. "Perk Out in Front," *Time*, October 15, 1973.

56. "Rally Set on Square for Captive Nations," *PD*, July 13, 1967, 61.

57. "Speech Delivered by Ralph J. Perk at Woodrow Wilson School—Princeton University," May 3, 1968, folder 2, Container 1, Perk.

58. Perk speech notes for the Italian Sons and Daughters of America Convention in Miami Beach, Florida, August 15–22, 1970, folder 18, container 2, Perk.

59. George Lardner, Jr., "More Slogans Than Issues," *WP*, October 31, 1971, A1; "Perk's Campaign Has Sharp Edges," *CP*, October 30, 1971, 8A.

60. Deborah Atwater Hunter, "The Aftermath of Carl Stokes: An Analysis of Political Drama in the 1971 Cleveland Mayoral Campaign," *Journal of Black Studies* 8, no. 3 (1978): 337–54.

61. Edward P. Whelan, "Perk Men Quietly Studying Ways to Cut City Workers," *PD*, November 5, 1971, 1.

62. *Cleveland Catholic Universe Bulletin*, May 29, 1970.

63. Bob Weissman [name misspelled as Wiesman in article] quoted in Mark Blacher, "Perk Inaugurated—Pledges Cooperation, *CP*, November 13, 1971, 1A.

64. Kucinich drafted Perk's speech for the important City Club debate. Todd Swanstrom, *The Crisis of Growth Politics: Cleveland, Kucinich, and the Challenge of Urban Populism* (Philadelphia: Temple University Press, 1985), 108.

65. Lardner Jr., "More Slogans Than Issues."

66. Kucinich quoted in Swanstrom, *Crisis of Growth Politics*, 108.

67. Richard Tompkins, *"All the Necessary Service the People Need and Deserve: Federal Grants in Cleveland During 1978"; A Case Study for the Brookings Institution* (Cleveland: Cleveland Foundation, 1979), 1.

68. Joseph L. Wagner, "U.S. Funds: Catch-22 for City Budgets," *PD*, April 18, 1976, 21.

69. Tompkins, *"All the Necessary Service,"* 13.

70. Press release, folder 831, container 54, Perk.

71. Dorothy Fuldheim, memo from Television Station WEWS, November 17, 1971, folder 831 container 54, Perk.

72. Edward P. Whelan, "Mayor Ralph J. Perk and the Politics of Decay," *CM*, September 1975.

73. Summary of Federal Grants Awarded Since November 1971, folder 996, container 65, Perk.

74. Edward Whelan, "Perk Is Hopeful of Major U.S. Funds for City," *PD*, November 22, 1971, 1.

75. See Thomas J. Sugrue and John D. Skrentny, "The White Ethnic Strategy," in Bruce J. Schulman and Julian E. Zelizer, eds., *Rightward Bound: Making America Conservative in the 1970s* (Cambridge: Harvard University Press, 2008), 171–92.

76. Bob Marik and Jeb Magruder to Ken Cole and Ed Harper, Confidential Memorandum re: Strategic Considerations for the 1972 Campaign, October 21, 1971, folder Campaign Administrative Files, box 9, Frederick Malek Papers, Nixon.

77. J. Marsh Thompson to Ken Cole, re Lunch Today with Mayor Ralph Perk, January 5, 1973, box 10, Local Governments, White House Central Files (WHCF), Nixon.

78. Alice O'Connor, "Swimming Against the Tide: A Brief History of Federal Policy in Poor Communities," in Ronald Ferguson and William Dickens, eds., *Urban Problems and Community Development* (Washington, D.C.: Brookings Institution Press, 1999), 104.

79. McKee, "'This Government Is with Us,'" 56.

80. Fact Sheet, Cleveland Model Cities, First Year Program, folder 793, container 53, Perk.

81. Report of the Model Cities Investigating Committee, Peat, Marwick, Mitchell and Company, September 25, 1973, folder 793, container 53, Perk.

82. Ibid.

83. Wilbur C. Warren to Ralph Perk, December 7, 1971, folder 789, container 52, Perk.

84. Saul G. Stillman to Ralph Perk, February 24, 1972, folder 715, container 48, Perk.

85. Model Cities election, folder 799, container 53, Perk.

86. Elmer C. Binford to Ralph J. Perk, March 5, 1973, folder 793, container 53, Perk.

87. George P. Rasanen, "U.S. Officials Skeptical of Model Cities' Impact," *PD*, April 13, 1973, 1A; George P. Rasanen, "Plan Offered to Break Model Cities Logjam," *PD*, March 28, 1972, 11-A.

88. Timothy Conlan, *From New Federalism to Devolution: Twenty-Five Years of Intergovernmental Reform* (Washington, D.C.: Brookings Institution Press, 1998), 48.

89. Alice Ashford to Robert Doggett, April 12, 1973, folder 793, container 53, Perk.

90. Statement of Fannie Lewis and Willie Tufts, August 1, 1971, folder 1, container 1, Lewis.

91. John Lenear, "Model Cities CPO Dir. Says City Is Stalling," *CP*, April 14, 1973, 16A.

92. Ted Schwarz, "I'll Get My Rest When the Lord Is Done with Me Here," *Cleveland Scene*, August 13, 2008, https://www.clevescene.com/cleveland/ill-get-my-rest-when-the-lord-is-done-with-me-here/Content?oid=1520629.

93. Troy Lee James to Ohio Bureau of Unemployment, October 4, 1971, folder 1, container 1, Lewis.

94. Fannie Lewis, "What My Job Means to Me," April 11, 1968, folder 283, container 13, Lewis.

95. Fannie Lewis to Tom Brown, August 9, 1973; Fannie Lewis to George Forbes, August 14, 1973; and Tom Brown to George Forbes, August 14, 1973, folder 792, container 53, Perk.

96. Fannie Lewis to Susan Schick, April 6, 1973, folder 793, container 53, Perk; Fannie M. Lewis to Ralph Perk, April 26, 1973, folder 792, container 53, Perk.

97. "Arnold Pinkney Follows The Script," *CP*, June 30, 1973, 1A.

98. Donald Jacobs and Herbert Whiting, Report of the Model Cities Investigative Committee, September 25, 1973, folder 747, container 50, Perk.

99. Bernard J. Frieden and Marshall Kaplan, *The Politics of Neglect: Urban Aid from Model Cities to Revenue Sharing* (Cambridge: MIT Press, 1975), 229.

100. Robert Holden, "Cleveland's Model Cities Program," *PD*, January 13, 1974, 28.

101. Fannie Lewis to community organizations, August 16, 1974, folder 35, container 2, Lewis.

102. Althusius, "Federalist No. 3," June 29, 1970, folder New Federalism, 1969–72, box 1, Richard P. Nathan Papers, Hoover Institution, Stanford University, Palo Alto, California.

103. ACIR, *Federalism in 1973: The System Under Stress* (Washington, D.C., January 1974).

104. ACIR, *Public Opinion and Taxes* (Washington, D.C., May 1972), 1–4.

105. ACIR, *Revenue Sharing—An Idea Whose Time Has Come* (Washington, D.C., December 1970).

106. Isaac Martin, *The Permanent Tax Revolt* (Stanford: Stanford University Press, 2008); and Bruce Schulman, *The Seventies: The Great Shift in American Culture, Society, and Politics* (New York: Free Press, 2001), 205–7. On racially discriminatory local tax assessment and collection practices, see Andrew W. Kahrl, "The Short End of Both Sticks: Property Assessments and Black Taxpayer Disadvantage in Urban America," in Cebul, Geismer, and Williams, eds., *Shaped by the State*, 189–217.

107. Raymond Waldmann to Ed Harper, February 23, 1971, folder Revenue Sharing, box 32, WHCF: Federal Aid, Nixon; John Murphy, "General Revenue Sharing's Impact on County Government," *Public Administration Review* 35, no. 2 (March–April 1975): 134; and Richard Nixon, "Statement About the General Revenue Sharing Bill," October 20, 1972, APP, http://www.presidency.ucsb.edu/node/255247.

108. Richard Nixon, "Address to the Nation on Domestic Programs," August 8, 1969, APP, http://www.presidency.ucsb.edu/node/239998.

109. Richard Nixon, "Annual Message to the Congress on the State of the Union," January 22, 1971, APP, https://www.presidency.uscb.edu/node/240562.

110. Nixon, "Statement About the General Revenue Sharing Bill."

111. David Caputo, "Richard M. Nixon, Revenue Sharing, and Federalism," in Leon Friedman and William Levantrosser, eds., *Richard M. Nixon: Politician, President, Administrator* (New York: Greenwood Press, 1991), 59–76; Conlan, *From New Federalism to Devolution*, 65–76; Amitai Etzioni, "Revenue Sharing Five Years Later," *WP*, April 4, 1976, C1.

112. Walter Heller, *New Dimensions of Political Economy* (Cambridge: Harvard University Press, 1966), chap. 3.

113. "Financing New Communities: Government and Private Experience in Europe and the United States," U.S. Department of Housing and Urban Development, Office of International Affairs, May 1973, 8–9.

114. Richard Nathan et al., *Block Grants for Community Development* (Washington, D.C.: Brookings Institution, 1977), 363.

115. Tom Johnson, "Hatcher Sees Revenue Sharing as a Threat to Blacks in Cities," *NYT*, February 23, 1971, 41.

116. William Safire, *Before the Fall: An Inside View of the Pre-Watergate White House* (New Brunswick, N.J.: Transaction Publishers, 2005), 224.

117. Taylor, *Race for Profit*, 242.

118. ACIR, *General Revenue Sharing: An ACIR Re-Evaluation* (Washington, D.C., October 1974), 48.

119. Internal Memo re: Community Development Legislation: Major Differences Between Administration's Urban Community Development Special Revenue Sharing Proposal and Community Development Grant Program Proposed by Housing Subcommittee's Study Panel III, June 25, 1971, folder Revenue Sharing, July 1–31, 19–71, box 34, FA7, Nixon.

120. "March 26th Telecast—Participating Cities," *Association Letter*, February 1969, box 5, series II, CCUS.

121. "Agnew Stresses Role of Private Sector in Meeting Urban Crisis," *Association Letter*, February 1969, box 5, series II, CCUS.

122. "The Better Communities Act," *U.S. Chamber of Commerce Newsletter*, August 1973, box 5, series II, CCUS.

123. "Government Seeks the Right Formula for Community Development Funds," *NJ*, February 12, 1977.

124. Donald Kettl, *Managing Community Development in the New Federalism* (New York: Praeger, 1980), 22.

125. CDBG Overview, folder 50, container 3, Buckeye-Woodland Community Congress Papers, Western Reserve Historical Society, Cleveland, Ohio.

126. Fannie Lewis to Community Agencies, Groups and Organizations, October 8, 1974, folder 36, container 2, Lewis.

127. Fannie Lewis and Joseph Hagerty to Ralph Perk, November 15, 1974, folder 36, container 2, Lewis.

128. CCPA Meeting Minutes, March 26, 1975, folder 36, container 2, Lewis.

129. CCPA Statement Prepared for the Community Development Block Grant Hearing, April 26, 1975, folder 52, container 3, Lewis.

130. Nathan et al., *Block Grants for Community Development*, 441.

131. Fannie Lewis to Ralph Perk, April 28, 1975, folder 200, container 9, Lewis.

132. Nathan et al., *Block Grants for Community Development*, 442.

133. McGreevy, *Parish Boundaries*, 227–28.

134. Suleiman Osman, "The Decade of the Neighborhood," in Schulman and Zelizer, *Rightward Bound*; on community movements against redlining, see Rebecca Marchiel, *After Redlining: The Urban Reinvestment Movement in the Era of Financial Deregulation* (Chicago: University of Chicago Press, 2020).

135. "Buckeye-Woodland Group to Fight Blight," *PD*, February 16, 1975, 35A.

136. William Miller, "Black and White Join to Fight City Hall," *PD*, April 27, 1975, 1.

137. "Buckeye-Woodland Group to Fight Blight."

138. Thomas Andrzejewski, "Buckeye-Woodland Residents Meet to Rap City Plan to Buy Arena," *PD*, July 14, 1976, 8E.

139. Thomas Andrzejewski, "200 Protest Perk's Plans to Buy Arena for Investors," *PD*, July 16, 1976, 7A.

140. Dean Clark to Paul Lydens, September 3, 1976; and Paul Lydens to William Slider re: Secretary's Briefing Paper—Cleveland, Ohio, September 21, 1976, folder City Club of Cleveland, 10/8/76, box 40, Hills.

141. "Neighborhoods First, City Told," *PD*, July 17, 1976, 6A.

142. Andrzejewski, "200 Protest Perk's Plans."

143. Taylor, *Race for Profit*, 55–56, 88–92.

144. *The Rebirth of the American City: Hearings Before the Committee on Banking, Currency, and Housing, House of Representatives*, 94th Cong., part 2, September 27–30 and October 1, 1976 (Washington, D.C.: U.S. Government Printing Office, 1976), 854 (statement of Margaret Foster, recording secretary, BWCC).

145. Nathan et al., *Block Grants for Community Development*, 475.

146. J. Thomas Black, Allan Borut, and Robert Dubinsky, *Private-Market Housing Renovation in Older Urban Areas* (Washington, D.C.: Urban Land Institute, 1977).

147. William Hamm to Paul O'Neill, Field Trip Report, August 16, 1972, box 3, WHCF, FG-24, HUD, Nixon.

148. Thomas Andrzejewski, "Fast Foreclosure: Neighborhood, Lenders at Odds on Extent of Risk," *PD*, October 19, 1975, A1.

149. *Neighborhood Preservation: Hearings Before the Committee on Banking, Housing, and Urban Affairs, United States Senate*, 94th Cong. (Washington, D.C.: U.S. Government Printing Office, 1976), 109–11 (statement of Margaret Foster, BWCC).

150. Andrzejewski, "Fast Foreclosure," A4.

151. Taylor, *Race for Profit*, 207–8 and 225–26.

152. Andrzejewski, "Neighborhood Chiefs Force HUD to Action"; Osman, "Decade of the Neighborhood," 119.

153. Secretary Carla A. Hills, Itinerary, City Club of Cleveland, October 8, 1976; and Kenneth J. Kovach et al., to Carla Hills, October 22, 1976; both in folder City Club of Cleveland, 10/8/76, box 40, Hills.

154. Carla A. Hills Speech, City Club of Cleveland, October 8, 1976, folder City Club of Cleveland, 10/8/76, box 40, Hills.

155. Asst. Sec. for Legislative Affairs re: Secretary's Trip to Cleveland—October 8, 1976, box 40, Hills.

Chapter 6

1. Jimmy Carter to Richard Housler, January 11, 1965, folder 1/65–3/65, box 20, Carter.

2. "WGCAC Approves Charter, Elects Officers At Meet," *Americus Times*, undated clipping, box 20, Carter.

3. West Central Georgia Area Planning and Development Commission, Meeting Minutes, January 27, 1965, 3, folder 1/65–3/65, box 20, Carter.

4. Cebul and Nelson, "Toward a More Complete Reckoning"; and Digital Scholarship Lab, "Renewing Inequality," *American Panorama*, ed. Robert K. Nelson and Edward L. Ayers, https://dsl.richmond.edu/panorama/renewal/#view=0/0/1&viz=map.

5. Elizabeth Hinton, *America on Fire: The Untold History of Police Violence and Black Rebellion Since the 1960s* (New York: Liveright, 2021).

6. "15 Sit In at Rome Counters," *AC*, February 15, 1963, 12; "62 Fined In Rome, Georgia Demonstrations," *ADW*, April 2, 1963, 1; Tuck, *Beyond Atlanta*, 139.

7. "Teenagers Stage Sit-Ins at Rome Drug Counters," *ADW*, March 29, 1963, 1; "62 Fined in Rome, Georgia Demonstrations," *ADW*, April 2, 1963, 1.

8. WSB-TV News film clip of police chief Nelson Camp and downtown Rome, Georgia, March 28, 1963, Brown.

9. On racial liberalism, integration, and elite brokers' self-conceptions as "progressive," see William H. Chafe, *Civilities and Civil Rights: Greensboro, North Carolina, and the Black Struggle for Freedom* (New York: Oxford University Press, 1981), 287–300.

10. "Poverty War Assailed as a Plan to Get Votes," *NYT*, February 6, 1964, 26. In other areas of the South, elites got involved retroactively to blunt minority empowerment. See, for example, Crespino, *In Search of Another Country*, 135–36.

11. CVAPDC Annual Report, June 30, 1966.

12. McKee, "This Government Is with Us," 39.

13. *Examination of the War on Poverty: Staff and Consultants Reports; Prepared for the Subcommittee on Employment, Manpower, and Poverty of the Committee on Labor and Public Welfare, United States Senate*, vol. 8, *Community Action Program: State Technical Assistance Agencies* (Washington, D.C.: U.S. Government Printing Office, 1967), 2335–50.

14. "Floyd Action Unite to Name Officers in 'Poverty' War," *RNT*, October 24, 1965, 3; CVAPDC Newsletter, January 1969, RFCL.

15. Rome-Floyd County Chamber of Commerce News-Letter, April 1963, Hargrett.

16. West Central Georgia Area Planning and Development Commission, Meeting Minutes, January 27, 1965, 4, folder 1/65–3/65, box 20, Carter.

17. "Community Planning Parley Set Saturday," *RNT*, May 5, 1967, 3.
18. "Sen. Carter Addresses W. Georgia Planners," *AC*, January 21, 1964, 14.
19. Tuck, *Beyond Atlanta*, 173–86.
20. "A Grants-in-Aid Proposal: An Identification of Economic Development Potentials of a Fourteen-County Area in Southwest Georgia," 6, folder 4/65, box 20, Carter.
21. Ibid., 25–26.
22. *Rural Poverty: Hearings Before the National Advisory Committee on Rural Poverty, Memphis, Tennessee, February 2 and 3, 1967* (Washington, D.C.: U.S. Government Printing Office, 1967), 268.
23. Ibid., 97–99, and 102; Charlie Black, "Columbine the Hungry Buffalo," *Georgia Tech Alumnus* 41, no. 8 (1963): 18, https://issuu.com/gtalumni/docs/1963_41_8.
24. Braswell Deen Jr. to Sargent Shriver, August 19, 1964, folder 101106-007-0278, War on Poverty, 1964–1968, Part 5: White House Central Files, Welfare and the Poverty Program Subject Files, Lyndon Johnson Presidential Library, ProQuest History Vault.
25. Wm. W. Lee to William S. Stuckey, November 23, 1968, folder 22, box 21, subseries B, series IV, Stuckey.
26. Robert E. Nipp, *The Alma-Bacon County Story: A Model for Rural America*, Farmers Home Administration, U.S. Department of Agriculture, July 24, 1972 (Washington, D.C.: U.S. Government Printing Office, 1972), 15–16.
27. Ibid., 9–10.
28. Ibid., 1–2. On the New Deal and rural conservation, see Sarah Phillips, *This Land, This Nation: Conservation, Rural America, and the New Deal* (New York: Cambridge University Press, 2007).
29. Nipp, *The Alma-Bacon County Story*, 5.
30. Sam Hopkins, "Town Getting Smaller—But Better," *AC*, November 15, 1970, 1C; Alex Coffin, "Alma-Bacon Pushing Model Cities Effort," *AC*, May 11, 1970, 1A.
31. John P. Davis and Charles Hamilton Houston, "TVA: Lily-White Reconstruction," *The Crisis*, October 1934, 290–291; and Alec Fazackerly Hickmott, "Black Land, Black Capital: Rural Development in the Shadows of the Sunbelt South, 1969–1976," *Journal of African American History* 101, no. 4 (Fall 2016): 504–34.
32. Department of Housing and Urban Development, Model Cities Grants, 8th Congressional District, undated, and "HUD Notification," Project Number ME-10-005, undated, folder 14, box 92, series IV, Stuckey.
33. Omi Walden to W. S. Stuckey Jr., November 19, 1970, folder 1, box 39, subseries B, series IV, Stuckey.
34. Nipp, *Alma-Bacon County Story*, 4.
35. CVAPDC, "Rome Urban Area Comprehensive Development Plan" (1968), 55, box 680, A1 145, Final Grant Reports, RG 207, Records of the Department of Housing and Urban Development, National Archives II, College Park, Md.
36. James W. Follin, *Slums and Blight . . . a Disease of Urban Life*, Urban Renewal Bulletin, no. 2 (Washington, D.C.: Urban Renewal Administration, Housing and Home Finance Agency, 1956), 2. For a broader discussion of "blight," see Wendell E. Pritchett, "The 'Public Menace' of Blight: Urban Renewal and the Private Uses of Eminent Domain," *Yale Law & Policy Review*, 21, no. 1 (Winter 2003), 1–52.
37. U.S. Department of Agriculture, *Directory of Field Activities of the Bureau of Biological Survey, 1939* (Washington, D.C.: U.S. Government Printing Office, 1939), 36.

38. "Plans Group to Move on Preliminary Study," *RNT*, June 10, 1959, 1.

39. CVAPDC, "Rome Urban Area Comprehensive Development Plan," 33.

40. Erin Demesquita, "Ghosts of Five Points," February 2018, https://readv3.com/2018/02/ghosts-of-five-points/.

41. "Area Engineers Join in Week's Observance," *RNT*, February 13, 1969, 5.

42. CVAPDC, "Rome Urban Area Comprehensive Development Plan," 29.

43. Housing and Home Finance Agency, Urban Renewal Administration News Release, November 22, 1963, folder VI C Floyd Co. 1960–1965, box 74, series VI, Davis; and CVAPDC, "Rome Urban Area Comprehensive Development Plan," 33.

44. Senate Committee on Banking and Currency, Executive Session on Housing Act of 1965, June 22, 1965, 44.

45. Eric Wentworth, "Planners Within Planners Festoon the Old Pork Barrel," *WP*, May 14, 1967, C3.

46. *Area Redevelopment Act Amendments: Hearings Before the Committee on Banking and Currency, House of Representatives*, 88th Cong., July 29–30, 1963 (Washington, D.C.: U.S. Government Printing Office, 1963).

47. Follin, *Slums and Blight*, 11–13.

48. Donald Jackson, letter to the editor, *RNT*, August 8, 1971.

49. Chris Frazier, "Urban Renewal: Promises or Progress? Four of 16 Firms Reopen After Property Is Taken," *RNT*, August 4, 1971, 3A.

50. Data compiled from Digital Scholarship Lab, "Renewing Inequality."

51. Mrs. W. T. Skelton, letter to the editor, *RNT*, August 8, 1971.

52. WSB-TV News film clip of a civil rights demonstration as well as a press conference with Ben Lucas, chair of the Board of Commissioners, in Rome, Georgia, September 15, 1971, Brown; and Chris Frazier, "Urban Renewal: Promises or Progress?: Many Descriptions Fit Much-Changed Program," *RNT*, August 6, 1971, 3A.

53. On moderate white elites' efforts to broker desegregation, see Lassiter, *The Silent Majority*.

54. Brattain, *Politics of Whiteness*, 273–74.

55. "Fire Bombs Hit Five Rome Firms," *RNT*, August 31, 1971, 3.

56. "Bomb Attempt Follows Race Relations Meeting," *RNT*, September 2, 1971, 3.

57. WSB-TV News, September 15, 1971, Brown.

58. Brattain, *Politics of Whiteness*, 275–76.

59. "Roman Forum," *RNT*, September 5, 1971, 5A.

60. "New Day A'Coming in the South," *Time*, May 31, 1971, 14–20.

61. Jimmy Carter remarks to Atlanta Press Club, June 30, 1966, folder Speeches, Draft of Speeches, Notes [1], box 5, Carter; "Blueprint for a Greater Georgia," Platform of Jimmy Carter, folder Speeches, Draft of Speeches, Notes [2], box 5, Carter.

62. Brattain, *Politics of Whiteness*, 247 and 231.

63. "Two Say Rights Bill Personal Infringement," *RNT*, June 24, 1964, 4.

64. Robert Korstad and James Leloudis, *To Right These Wrongs: The North Carolina Fund and the Battle to End Poverty and Inequality in 1960s America* (Chapel Hill: University of North Carolina Press, 2010), 306.

65. Telephone conversation no. 10904, sound recording, LBJ and Willard Wirtz, October 1, 1966, 10:03 a.m., Recordings and Transcripts of Telephone Conversations and Meetings, LBJ Presidential Library, accessed May 19, 2022, https://www.discoverlbj.org/item/tel-10904.

66. "Beaten Path," *RNT*, June 22, 1964, 4.

67. "Goldwater Charts Better Course," *RNT*, November 1, 1964, 4.

68. The labor vote was not, however, unanimously behind its local leadership's support of Goldwater, and several dissenters made their opposition to Goldwater—and their leadership—public in a letter. Brattain, *Politics of Whiteness*, 247–49.

69. "It's Our Choice," *RNT*, July 14, 1964, 4.

70. "Landrum Linked to LBJ," *People's Choice*, News of the 9th District, September 1966, folder 15, box 1, series II, Miller.

71. "Zell Miller Speaks on Issues," *People's Choice*, News of the 9th District, September 1966, folder 15, box 1, series II, Miller.

72. "Congress Investigates OEO Funds for 'Hate' School," *RNT*, August 4, 1967, 1.

73. Korstad and Leloudis, *To Right These Wrongs*, 291.

74. Ibid., 301.

75. Jimmy Carter, speech to Association of County Commissioners of Georgia, April 13, 1970, folder Speech Material [1], box 39, Carter.

76. Peter Bourne, *Jimmy Carter: A Comprehensive Biography from Plains to Post-Presidency* (New York: Scribner, 1997), 188–89.

77. Jimmy Carter, speech notes before the Atlanta Kiwanis, August 5, 1969, folder Speech Material [1], box 39, Carter.

78. Meeting Minutes, State Advisory Committee on Planning and Development, January 12, 1968, folder Area Planning and Development Advisory Committee, box 23, Carter.

79. Jimmy Carter, "Commission Growing in Usefulness as Channel to State Resources," *The Activator*, May 1966, box 5, Carter.

80. See, generally, folders Speech Notes by Community, box 40, Carter.

81. Betty Glad, *Jimmy Carter: In Search of the Great White House* (New York: W. W. Norton, 1980), 130.

82. Steven Brill, "Jimmy Carter's Pathetic Lies," *Harper's*, March 1976, 79.

83. Ibid., 84.

84. "Jimmy Carter Will Be Great for Georgia's Cities," undated, Campaign Platform for Cities, 1970, 19, folder Campaign Platform, 1970, box 23, Carter.

85. "Primary 1970: The Pick of the Press," *AC*, September 5, 1970, 4A.

86. Platform, Jimmy Carter for Governor, 1970, folder Campaign Platform, 1970, box 23, Carter.

87. Evan Jenkins, "School Conflict in the South Is Intensifying," *NYT*, August 19, 1973, 48.

88. On segregation academies, see Joseph Crespino, "Civil Rights and the Religious Right," in Schulman and Zelizer, *Rightward Bound*.

89. *Laurens County News*, September 5, 1970; *Decatur-Dekalb News*, September 16, 1970.

90. Cynthia Brown and Marlene Provizer, "The South's New Dual School System: A Case Study," *New South*, January 1972, 61.

91. *Americus Times-Recorder*, July 30, 1970.

92. *Macon News* reprinted as "Carter's Bitter Campaign," *AC*, September 3, 1970, 5A.

93. "Governor Jimmy Carter's Inaugural Address," January 12, 1971, https://www.jimmycarterlibrary.gov/assets/documents/inaugural_address_gov.pdf.

94. Jimmy Carter, speech to Coastal Area Community Action, July 11, 1974, transcript, RCB-9288, Governor, Executive Dept., Gov.'s Speech Transcripts, Gov. Jimmy Carter, Speeches, 1971–75, Georgia Archives, Morrow, Ga.

95. Jimmy Carter, budget address to Joint Session of the General Assembly, January 13, 1972, DOC-6982, Georgia Archives.

96. On "Goals for Georgia," see Mattie Sayrs Anderson, "Governor Jimmy Carter, Idealist or Realist: A Study of Carter's Commitment to Citizen Participation and Planning the Goals for Georgia Program" (master's thesis, Georgia State University, 1979).

97. Bill Shipp, "Campaign Team Helps Carter," *AC*, December 28, 1971, 15A.

98. Leslie Wheeler, *Jimmy Who?* (Woodbury: Barron's Educational Series, 1976), 72.

99. Weekly Progress Report—Public Awareness, July 5, 1971, DOC-2227, Governor, 1971–1972, Georgia Archives; and Public Awareness—Status Summary, September, 1971, DOC-2227, Governor, 1971–1972, Georgia Archives.

100. Tom Linder Jr., article for Georgia Poultry Federation, DOC-2227, Governor, 1971–1972, Georgia Archives.

101. Meeting Minutes, Reorganization and Management Improvement Study, July 28, 1971, DOC-2225, Georgia Archives.

102. Undated planning committee roster, DOC-2225, Georgia Archives.

103. Bourne, *Jimmy Carter*, 207.

104. "Reorganization and Management Improvement Study: Preliminary Review Summary," undated [April and May 1971], RCB-9313, Georgia Archives.

105. "Carter: No Power Play," *AC*, November 17, 1971; Reorganization and Improvement Study, November 24, 1971, DOC-2225, Georgia Archives.

106. John Dillin, "Carter: What Others Say About Him," *CSM*, July 21, 1976, 14.

107. *National Economic Development Program, Part 1: Hearings Before the Subcommittee on Economic Development of the Committee on Public Works, United States Senate*, 92nd Cong. (Washington, D.C.: U.S. Government Printing Office, 1971), 51 (statement of Tom Linder, Georgia planning and community affairs officer).

108. See generally, LC Adams to William "Sonny" Walker, February 4, 1974 and attached report, folder 8: OEO 1974, box 12, subseries B, series VI, Davis.

109. Legislative Issues Briefing Book, House Republican Conference, August 1976, 16–17, folder Decentralization 2, box 5, Gingrich.

110. "Coalition Charges Carter with Governmental Racism," *Baltimore Afro-American*, June 19, 1971, 9.

111. See Hickmott, "Black Land, Black Capital"; and Devin Fergus, *Liberalism, Black Power, and the Making of American Politics* (Athens: University of Georgia Press, 2009).

112. Pamela Vaughn to Herman Talmadge, received February 26, 1973, folder 24, box 148, series XI, Talmadge.

113. Juanita Johnson to Herman Talmadge, received March 13, 1973, folder 24, box 147, series XI, Talmadge.

114. Jim Gurley to Herman Talmadge, February 15, 1973, folder 24, box 148, series XI, Talmadge.

115. Jimmy Carter, Budget Message, November 17, 1974, DOC-6950, Governors' Messages to General Assembly, 1908–1974, Georgia Archives.

116. DOC-6823: Governor '71–'72 Reorganization Study, Advisory Commission Correspondence, 1971–1972, Georgia Archives.

117. Cobb, *Selling of the South*, 88–89.

118. John Dillin, "Southerners Lauded for Leading Change," *CSM*, October 1, 1973, 2.

119. Allen L. Otten, "The New South Still Conservative," *WSJ*, November 2, 1972, 20.

120. "Timeline of Black Rebellions," in Hinton, *America on Fire*, 313–38.
121. Charles Wheeler, "Sales of School Stirs Hassle," *AC*, May 23, 1971, 8.
122. Brown and Provizer, "The South's New Dual School System," 59–72.
123. W. G. McWilliams Jr., "President's Pen," *Forum*, October 1974, Hargrett.

Chapter 7

1. Waterhouse, *Lobbying America*, chap. 1.
2. See, for instance, Ansley T. Erickson and Ernest Morrell, eds., *Educating Harlem: A Century of Schooling and Resistance in a Black Community* (New York: Columbia University Press, 2019); Countryman, *Up South*; and Toussaint Losier, "'The Public Does Not Believe the Police Can Police Themselves': The Mayoral Administration of Harold Washington and the Problem of Police Impunity," *Journal of Urban History* 46, no. 5 (2020): 1050–65.
3. *The State and Local Governments Conference on Inflation*, September 23, 1974 [Report], (Washington, D.C., 1974), 376.
4. See especially Krippner, *Capitalizing on Crisis*, introd. and chap. 3; and Kim Phillips-Fein, *Fear City: New York's Fiscal Crisis and the Rise of Austerity Politics* (New York: Metropolitan Books, 2017).
5. "The Money Crunch for States and Cities," *NB*, October 1975, 23–28.
6. Ibid., 28; Kim Phillips-Fein, "The New York City Fiscal Crisis and the Idea of the State," in Sven Beckert and Christine Desan, eds., *American Capitalism: New Histories* (New York: Columbia University Press, 2018), 107.
7. "Learning from New York City," *WSJ*, October 15, 1975, 24.
8. "New York: A National Lesson," *CSM*, October 20, 1975, 21.
9. See generally Freeman, *Working-Class New York*.
10. ACIR, *City Financial Emergencies: The Intergovernmental Dimension* (Washington, D.C., July 1973), 31–48.
11. Sidney Homer, *The Great American Bond Market: Selected Speeches of Sidney Homer* (Homewood, Ill.: Dow Jones-Irvin, 1978), 15; Roland Robinson, *The Postwar Market for State and Local Securities* (Princeton: Princeton University Press, 1960), 1–18.
12. *Fundamentals of Municipal Bonds* (Washington, D.C.: Investment Bankers Association of America, 1959), 1–2.
13. On state-level indebtedness, see Michael R. Glass and Sean H. Vanatta, "The Frail Bonds of Liberalism: Pensions, Schools, and the Unraveling of Fiscal Mutualism in Postwar New York," *Capitalism* 2, no. 2 (Summer 2021): 427–72; and Nicholas Dagen Bloom, *How States Shaped Postwar America: State Government and Urban Power* (Chicago: University of Chicago Press, 2019), 27–31. For aggregate totals, see Board of Governors of the Federal Reserve System (U.S.), "State and Local Governments; Debt Securities and Loans; Liability, Level," retrieved from FRED, Federal Reserve Bank of St. Louis, https://fred.stlouisfed.org/series/SLGSDODNS.
14. Barry Bosworth, James S. Duesenberry, and Andrew S. Carron, *Capital Needs in the Seventies* (Washington, D.C.: Brookings Institution, 1975), 57.
15. Jenkins, *The Bonds of Inequality*, 119.
16. James Warren Beebe, "Retroactive Increases in Municipal Bond Interest: Revisiting Two Basic Municipal Financing Limitations," *Urban Lawyer* 3, no. 3 (Summer 1971): 311–12.
17. *State and Local Governments Conference on Inflation*, 12–13 and 204. See also ACIR, *Federalism in 1973*, 12.

18. Lane Windham, *Knocking on Labor's Door: Union Organizing in the 1970s and the Roots of a New Economic Decline* (Chapel Hill: University of North Carolina Press, 2017), 24–25 and 31.

19. "States, Localities Hard Hit by Recession," *Facts on File World News Digest*, May 3, 1975; "Taxpayers' Lament: 'Give Us Better Services,'" *U.S. News and World Report*, November 17, 1975, folder Decentralization, box 5, Gingrich.

20. *State and Local Governments Conference on Inflation*, 7. See also *The Growing Threat of a Domestic Financial Crisis: Hearings Before the Subcommittee on Financial Markets of the Committee on Finance, United States Senate*, 93rd Cong. (Washington, D.C.: U.S. Government Printing Office, 1974).

21. ACIR, *Understanding the Market for State and Local Debt* (Washington, D.C., May 1976), 3.

22. Bosworth, Duesenberry, and Carron, *Capital Needs in the Seventies*, 34–35.

23. ACIR, *Understanding the Market for State and Local Debt*, 12.

24. S&P began charging local governments for bond rating in 1968; Moody's and Fitch followed soon after. Roger Biles, "Public Policy Made by Private Enterprise: Bond Rating Agencies and Urban America," *Journal of Urban History* 44, no. 6 (2018): 1100.

25. Donald Halder, "The Financial Impact on Local Governments of Intergovernmental Aid Programs," in Sylvan Feldstein, Frank Fabozzi, and Irving Pollack, eds., *The Municipal Bond Handbook* (Homewood, Ill.: Dow Jones-Irwin, 1983), 47–53.

26. *The Role of Commercial Banks in the Finances of the City of Cleveland: Staff Study by the Subcommittee on Financial Institutions Supervision, Regulation, and Insurance of the Committee on Banking, Finance and Urban Affairs of the U.S. House of Representatives, June 1979* (Washington, D.C.: U.S. Government Printing Office, 1979), 1, PAL; Davita Silfen Glasberg, *The Power of Collective Purse Strings: The Effects of Bank Hegemony on Corporations and the State* (Berkeley: University of California Press, 1989), 2.

27. Timothy Sinclair, *The New Masters of Capital: American Bond Rating Agencies and the Politics of Creditworthiness* (Ithaca: Cornell University Press, 2014), 95.

28. *The Growing Threat of a Domestic Financial Crisis*, 3,

29. Alberta M. Sbragia, ed., *The Municipal Money Chase: The Politics of Local Government Finance* (Boulder, CO: Westview Press,1983), 70.

30. D. R. Bruckner, "Cleveland Urban Renewal Dream Turns into Financial Nightmare," *LAT*, March 5, 1967, J1.

31. "$50 Bil. in Urban Renewal Notes in 1954–1979," *Bond Buyer*, February 9, 1981, 14.

32. Sbragia, *The Municipal Money Chase*, 69.

33. Terry Robards, "Most Bond Plans Rejected by U.S. Voters," *NYT*, November 6, 1975, 1.

34. *The Growing Threat of a Domestic Financial Crisis*, 4.

35. *State and Local Governments Conference on Inflation*, 210.

36. "A New Force for City's Growth," *PD*, December 6, 1967, 22.

37. Michael Kelly, "Growth Group Chief to Look and Listen," *PD*, December 16, 1967, 10.

38. "Seattle's Thrust and Cleveland's," *PD*, February 15, 1968, 18.

39. "City's Economic Prospects Rosy," *PD*, January 4, 1968, 47.

40. "Growth Association in Leadership Crisis," *PD*, September 25, 1971, 1.

41. Guidelines for Action, NAM Government Finances Department, June 16, 1972, folder Field Division Bulletin (1972), box 3, series IV, National Association of Manufacturers Papers, Hagley Museum and Library, Wilmington, Del.

42. *Economic Opportunity Act Amendments of 1967: Hearings Before the Committee on Education and Labor*, part 3, July 1967, 3167–68 (statement of John Burkhart).

43. Fred Burtner, "A Matter of Survival," *Chamber of Commerce Newsletter* (hereafter *CCN*), December 1972, box 5, series II, CCUS.

44. See, generally, Geismer, *Don't Blame Us*.

45. "'Understanding' . . . A Big Step in Improving Racial Relations," *CCN*, October 1973, box 5, series II, CCUS.

46. "From 'Wetback' to Chamber President," *CCN*, September 1973, box 5, series II, CCUS.

47. Milton Friedman, "The Social Responsibility of Business Is to Increase Its Profits," *NYT*, September 13, 1970, SM17.

48. *CCN*, July 1971, box 5, series II, CCUS.

49. "Model Cities—Outlook for 70s," *CCN*, January 1970, box 5, series II, CCUS.

50. Lewis F. Powell Jr. to Eugene B. Sydnor Jr., "Attack on American Free Enterprise System," August 23, 1971, http://law.wlu.edu/deptimages/Powell%20Archives/PowellMemorandum Typescript.pdf.

51. Jacob S. Hacker and Paul Pierson, *Winner-Take-All Politics: How Washington Made the Rich Richer—and Turned Its Back on the Middle Class* (New York: Simon and Schuster, 2010), 117–19.

52. House Joint Resolution No. 208 (on the death of Eugene B. Sydnor Jr.), January 14, 2004, Virginia House of Delegates, https://lis.virginia.gov/cgi-bin/legp604.exe?041+ful+HJ208+pdf.

53. *CCN*, February 1975, box 5, series II, CCUS.

54. "A Need to Explain Business," *CCN*, August 1973, box 5, series II, CCUS.

55. Chris Drummond, "'It's Time to Keep the Faith': Statesman Challenges Rome Area Business Leaders," *RNT*, January 18, 1980.

56. John E. Bryan, "City Awaiting Leadership Renaissance," *PD*, August 20, 1972, 1.

57. ACIR, *Community Development: The Workings of a Federal-Local Block Grant* (Washington, D.C., March 1977), 64 and 73.

58. Ralph J. Perk to Harry Dent, December 9, 1971, folder 745, container 50, Perk.

59. Edward P. Whelan, "Mayor Ralph J. Perk and the Politics of Decay," *CM*, September 1975, in Dan Marschall, ed., *The Battle of Cleveland: Public Interest Challenges Corporate Power* (Washington, D.C.: Conference of Alternative State and Local Policies, 1979), 70–74, quotation at 72; "Mayor's Economic Coordinating Commission: Agenda for Initial Meeting," undated 1977, folder 995, container 65, Perk; Carla A. Hills, "Federal Fair Housing Policy and Our Ethnic Heritage," folder Community Development, April 27, 1976–May 10, 1976, box 8, James Cannon Files, Ford.

60. "Dr. King Organized E. Side for Vote, Jobs, Rent Unions," *PD*, April 5, 1967; Terence Sheridan, "Jetport!," *CM*, November 1, 1972.

61. Bryan, "City Awaiting Leadership Renaissance"; Greater Cleveland Growth Association Governmental Affairs Division Taxation Department Policy Statement, February, 1973, folder 752, container 50, Perk.

62. Greater Cleveland Forward Status Report, January 31, 1973, folder 997, container 66, Perk.

63. James Davis to Ralph Perk, August 30, 1972; James Davis to Jackie Presser, cc to Ralph Perk, October 23, 1972; James Davis to Ralph Perk, November 1, 1972; James Davis to Ralph Perk, February 7, 1973; all in folder 745, container 50, Perk.

64. James Davis to Ralph Perk, May 1, 1972, folder 753, container 50, Perk.

65. On Forward Atlanta, see Bartley, *Creation of Modern Georgia*, 225–26. See also "Council on the Future Is Organized in Cleveland," *CCN*, April 1971, box 5, series II, CCUS.

66. "To Those Interested in the Future of Greater Cleveland," Greater Cleveland Forward Status Report, January 31, 1973, folder 997, container 65, Perk; Bryan, "City Awaiting Leadership for Renaissance."

67. Greater Cleveland Forward Status Report; James Davis to John A. Volpe, Secretary of Transportation, Department of Transportation, December 2, 1971, folder 745, container 50, Perk.

68. "Colossal Project Unveiled," *PD*, June 15, 1972, 2A; Allen Wiggins and Harry Stainer, "The Hotel Squeeze," *PD*, June 18, 1972, 1.

69. "Halprin Begins Two-Day Study," *PD*, February 13, 1973, 10A.

70. Proposed Plan for Neighborhood Revitalization, Recommendations from Workshops on Cleveland Neighborhoods and Housing, Cleveland State University, 1976–77, folder Cleveland State University–Institute of Urban Studies, 1977–78 (2), box 5, David O. Meeker Papers, Ford.

71. Souther, *Believing in Cleveland*, 144.

72. Halprin Plan, folder 795, container 52, Perk.

73. "Downtown Revitalization Priorities Are Established," *PD*, December 11, 1975, 1A; Thomas Vail, "Cleveland Is on the Move," *PD*, February 3, 1974, 2AA.

74. Souther, *Believing in Cleveland*, 131–32.

75. Joseph Wagner, "U.S. Funds: Catch-22 for City Budgets," *PD*, April 18, 1976, 21; Andrew Diamond, *Chicago on the Make: Power and Inequality in a Modern City* (Berkeley: University of California Press, 2017), 233.

76. Joseph Wagner, "City Taxes Couldn't Support Safety Forces; Aid Pays Bills," *PD*, January 17, 1975, 2.

77. On Southern states and the proliferation of industrial tax exemptions, see Cobb, *The Selling of the South*, 46–50.

78. Mayor's Remarks, Land Use Conference, December 4, 1976, folder 997, container 65, Perk.

79. News release announcing formation of Mayor's Economic Coordination Commission, July 4, 1977, and Cleveland's Economic Development Commission, September 16, 1977, folder 995, container 65, Perk.

80. "Tax Reduction New Here, Works OK in St. Louis," *PD*, July 1, 1977, 3B.

81. Tompkins, *"All the Necessary Service,"* 25 and 27.

82. Todd Swanstrom, "Urban Populism, Fiscal Crisis, and the New Political Economy" in Keating, Krumholz, and Perry, *Cleveland*, 101.

83. On OPIC and the tax revolt, see David Osborne, "Renegade Tax Reform: Turning Prop 13 on Its Head," *Saturday Review*, May 12, 1979, in Marschall, *Battle of Cleveland*, 153–56.

84. On OPIC generally, see Austin McCoy, "No Radical Hangover: Black Power, New Left, and Progressive Politics in the Midwest, 1967–1989" (Ph.D. diss., University of Michigan, 2016).

85. "Rise of Public Interest Politics," in Marschall, *Battle of Cleveland*, 26.

86. "You Can't Run Cleveland If You Sell It Out," in Marschall, *Battle of Cleveland*, 34.

87. "2 of City's Top Banks Lowest in Home Loans," *PD*, June 25, 1977, 6B.

88. Osborne, "Renegade Tax Reform," quote at 154.

89. Fred Branfman, "The Cleveland Story: How the Banks Foreclosed Dennis Kucinich," *The Nation*, January 20, 1979, 43–46.

90. Osman, "The Decade of the Neighborhood," in Schulman and Zelizer, *Rightward Bound*.

91. The foundational document for "equity planning" was Krumholz's paper for the 54th Annual Conference of the American Institute of Planners. Norman Krumholz and Ernest R. Bonner, "Toward a Work Program for an Advocate Planning Agency," October 25, 1971, City Planning Commission, PAL.

92. Norman Krumholz, "Government, Equity, Redistribution, and the Practice of Urban Planning," in Keating, Krumholz, and Perry, *Cleveland*.

93. Author interview with Norman Krumholz, January 4, 2011, Cleveland, Ohio.

94. On Krumholz's legacy, see Pierre Clavel, *The Progressive City: Planning and Participation, 1969–1984* (New Brunswick, N.J.: Rutgers University Press, 1986), 94–95.

95. Cunningham, *Democratizing Cleveland*, 59.

96. Ibid., 61–68.

97. Swanstrom, *Crisis of Growth Politics*, 194–95, 122.

98. "Make Views Heard Sen. Byrd Advises Businessmen Here," *PD*, April 15, 1978, 7B.

99. Swanstrom, *Crisis of Growth Politics*, 195.

100. Joseph Rice, "Suburbanites Top List of Donors Backing Kucinich Recall," *PD*, September 28, 1978, 14A.

101. *Role of Commercial Banks*, 229, 16.

102. Ibid., 567.

103. Ibid., 27.

104. Barbara Ehrenreich and John Ehrenreich, "Cleveland: An Autopsy," in Marschall, *Battle of Cleveland*, 16–18; "Cleveland's Power Structure," in Marschall, *Battle of Cleveland*, 10.

105. Ehrenreich and Ehrenreich, "Cleveland: An Autopsy," 17–18 (emphasis in original).

106. *Role of Commercial Banks*, 31–32.

107. Ibid., 32–33.

108. Ibid., 819.

109. Ibid., 42.

110. Alexander Cockburn and James Ridgway, "The Mayor Who Said No: Is Dennis Kucinich as Mad as They Say?," *Village Voice*, January 22, 1979, in Marschall, *Battle of Cleveland*, 88.

111. "Nader Cheers Kucinich War," *PD*, January 19, 1979, 7A; Rudy Maxa, "Dennis Kucinich Is No Joking Matter," *WP*, February 25, 1979; quoted in *Role of Commercial Banks*, 4.

112. Todd Swanstrom, "Urban Populism, Uneven Development, and the Space for Reform," in Scott Cummings, ed., *Business Elites and Urban Development: Case Studies and Critical Perspectives* (Albany: SUNY Press, 1988), 134.

113. Mary Strassmeyer, "Principal Guest Conductor," *PD*, June 18, 1979, 4A.

114. "Diamond Shamrock Leaving Cleveland for the Southwest," *WSJ*, May 30, 1979, 22.

115. Davita Silfen Glasberg, "The Political Economic Power of Finance Capital and Urban Fiscal Crisis: Cleveland's Default, 1978," *Journal of Urban Affairs* 10, no. 3 (1988): 224.

116. James Ring Adams, "Drawing the Line in Cleveland," *WSJ*, August 17, 1979, 6.

117. Amos Kermisch, "Kucinich Comes Out Full Force for Tax Initiative," *PD*, April 29, 1979, 23.

118. Joseph Wagner, "Voinovich: Viewing the Front 4," *PD*, September 30, 1979, 4A; Joseph Wagner, "City Weighs Establishing Own Bank," *PD*, September 27, 1978, 1A, 10A, in Marschall, *Battle of Cleveland*, 137; and Dennis J. Kucinich, "How Kucinich Views Corporate Power," *CP*, May 9, 1979, in Marschall, *Battle of Cleveland*, 139–40.

119. Swanstrom, *Crisis of Growth Politics*, 223.

120. Jason Hackworth, "Local Autonomy, Bond-Rating Agencies and Neoliberal Urbanism in the United States," *International Journal of Urban and Regional Research* 26, no. 4 (December 2002): 707–25; and Jamie Peck, "Austerity Urbanism: American Cities Under Extreme Economy," *City* 16, no. 6 (2012): 626–55.

121. *Role of Commercial Banks*, 1.

122. "Moody's Downgrades Ratings for Boston and for Philadelphia," *WSJ*, January 28, 1976, 25.

Chapter 8

1. See Claus Offe, *Contradictions of the Welfare State* (Cambridge, MA: MIT Press, 1984); Lester Thurow, *The Zero-Sum Society: Distribution and the Possibilities for Change* (New York: Basic Books, 1980).

2. "Spoiler of the Dream," *AC*, August 24, 1978, 4A.

3. Beer quoted in ACIR, *The Federal Role in the Federal System: The Dynamics of Growth* (Washington, D.C., August 1981), 128.

4. Martha Derthick, *Between State and Nation: Regional Organizations of the United States* (Washington, D.C.: Brookings Institution, 1974).

5. Nancy MacLean, *Freedom Is Not Enough: The Opening of the American Workplace* (Cambridge: Russell Sage Foundation Books at Harvard University Press, 2008); Chappell, *The War on Welfare*.

6. W. Carl Biven, *Jimmy Carter's Economy: Policy in an Age of Limits* (Chapel Hill: University of North Carolina Press, 2022), 185–207.

7. William Rusher, *The Making of the New Majority Party* (New York: Sheed and Ward, 1975); Richard M. Scammon and Ben J. Wattenberg, *The Real Majority: An Extraordinary Examination of the American Electorate* (New York: Coward-McCann, 1970); Kevin Phillips, *The Emerging Republican Majority* (New Rochelle: Arlington House, 1969); and Daniel K. Williams, "Jerry Falwell's Sunbelt Politics: The Regional Origins of the Moral Majority," *Journal of Policy History* 22, no. 2 (2010): 125–47.

8. Gail Radford, *The Rise of the Public Authority: Statebuilding and Economic Development in Twentieth-Century America* (Chicago: University of Chicago Press, 2013), 155–56.

9. CVAPDC Annual Report, 1975.

10. "Adams, Knowles Will Seek Sheriff's Office," *RNT*, March 11, 1968, 3.

11. Chris Frazier, "'Town Meeting' Group Calls for Ouster of Commissioners," *RNT*, December 9, 1970, 3.

12. "'Town Hall' Meet Lacks Solutions," *RNT*, December 9, 1970, 4.

13. "Market Improvement Slows; Placement Ratio Declines," *Weekly Bond Buyer*, January 22, 1968, 49.

14. See especially, *Persistent Poverty in Rural America*, Rural Sociological Society Task Force on Persistent Rural Poverty (Boulder, CO: Routledge, 1993), 1–38 and 292–301.

15. *Rural Development Financial Resources Act of 1972*, Public Law 92-419, S. 3462, April 7, 1972, 110.

16. Richard M. Nixon, "Statement on Signing the Rural Development Act of 1972," August 30, 1972, APP, https://www.presidency.ucsb.edu/documents/statement-signing-the-rural-development-act-1972.

17. "U.S. Acts to Save Vanishing Farmer," *CT*, November 22, 1972, 12.

18. Reg Murphy, "The Need to Get It Altogether," *AC*, April 20, 1972, 4A; "U.S. Acts to Save Vanishing Farmer."
19. "Slashes in Farm Subsidies Planned; 1972 Income Cited," *LAT*, January 30, 1973, 14.
20. Cliff Green, "Rural Development Plan Stymied From Start," *AJC*, January 13, 1974, 12B.
21. CVAPDC Annual Report, 1971.
22. CVAPDC Annual Report, 1974.
23. "APDC Bill Being Reintroduced," *AC*, February 1, 1974, 7.
24. "'78 Big Year for Coosa Valley Planners," *RNT*, clipping, n.d., 1979, RFCL.
25. CVAPDC Annual Report, 1980–81.
26. Schulman, *From Cotton Belt to Sunbelt*, 169.
27. "An Exciting Beginning," *Anniston Star*, May 13, 2012.
28. "For the Record . . . the Regional Approach to Growth Problems," *WP*, October 18, 1972, A16.
29. "Compact Set Up for 'Post-Racial' South," *NYT*, October 5, 1971, 26; "SGPB: An Exciting Beginning," Southern Growth Policies Board 40th Anniversary Commentaries, 7–8, in author's possession; "Another of the 'New Souths,'" *WP*, October 10, 1971, F1.
30. Minutes, March 29, 1972, 50, folder Executive Committee Meeting, 3/29/72, box 22, subseries 1.3, SGPB.
31. Linwood Holton, "This Is the Southern Growth Policies Board," folder Annual Meeting, 3/15–3/17, 1973, subseries 1.3, box 22, SGPB.
32. Samuel Hays, *Beauty, Health, and Permanence: Environmental Politics in the United States, 1955–1985* (Cambridge: Cambridge University Press, 1989). On white, suburban class-blindness, see Geismer, *Don't Blame Us*.
33. Minutes, Executive Committee Meeting, October 17, 1975, folder Executive Committee Meeting, 10/16–10/17, 1975, Atlanta, subseries 1.3, box 22, SGPB.
34. Ross Hammond, "Southern Economic Development Trends and Some Policy Implications," folder Annual Meeting 3/15–3/17, 1973, Montgomery, box 22, subseries 1.3, SGPB.
35. W. W. Rostow, "The South and the Future of the American Economy," February 24, 1978, folder Southern Growth Policies Board, RCB-16535, Georgia Archives.
36. *Growth Management Policies for the South: The Report of the Growth Management Policies Committee of the Southern Growth Policies Board* (Research Triangle Park, N.C.: Southern Growth Policies Board, December 1974).
37. Connolly, *A World More Concrete*, 233–40.
38. Colleen Teasley, "Onward! Commission's Aim Is South's Gain," *AC*, May 6, 1974, 7D.
39. William L. Bowden to Governors of the Southern States, July 8, 1974, folder Executive Committee May 17, 1974, box 22, subseries 1.3, SGPB; Jimmy Carter, "The Future of the Southern States," Proceedings of the Annual Meeting of the Southern Growth Policies Board, November 12–14, 1974, folder 1974, box 22, subseries 1.3, SGPB.
40. Carter, "Future of the Southern States."
41. "National Growth Policy Research on the South," attached to Minutes, Executive Committee Meeting, September 24, 1976, folder Executive Committee, September 23–24, 1976, box 23, subseries 1.3, SGPB.
42. "South Has 'Outgrown' Segregation," *ADW*, November 19, 1974, 1.
43. William Cotterrell, "How the Rights Movement 'Liberated' Dixie Whites," *Norfolk New Journal and Guide*, November 23, 1974, 1.

44. R. W. Apple, "Governors Group Charts Anti-McGovern Strategy," *NYT,* June 4, 1972, 60; Warren Weaver Jr., "Drive to Stop McGovern Fails to Start," *NYT,* June 5, 1972, 26; "Bond's Remark on Democrats Was 'Racist,' Says Gov. Carter," *AC,* June 1, 1972.

45. Jimmy Carter, "State Concerns in the Seventies" (Suggestions for Miami), undated, 1972, RCB-9288, Governor, Executive Dept., Gov.'s Speech Transcripts, 1970, November—Gov. Lester Maddox: Speech Working Files thru 1970, December—Gov. Jimmy Carter/Speeches, 1971–75, Georgia Archives.

46. "Is the Man from Georgia Ready to Help the States and Cities?," *NJ,* January 22, 1977.

47. Carter quoted in Patricia Roberts Harris to Jimmy Carter, June 12, 1978, folder FA 6/1/78–6/15/78, box FA-3, WHCF.

48. Chappell, *The War on Welfare,* 126.

49. Jack Houston, "Jobless Rate Highest Among Blacks," *CT,* December 9, 1975, C9.

50. Hobart Rowan, "Humphrey-Javits Bill Urges Long-Term Economic Planning," *WP,* May 13, 1975, D8.

51. Theda Skocpol, "Targeting Within Universalism: Politically Viable Policies to Combat Poverty in the United States," in Christopher Jencks and Paul E. Peterson, eds., *The Urban Underclass* (Washington, D.C.: Brookings Institution, 1991), 411–36; Harvey L. Schantz and Richard H. Schmidt, "The Evolution of Humphrey-Hawkins," *Policy Studies Journal* 8, no. 3 (Winter 1979).

52. Stein, *Pivotal Decade,* 190; Jefferson Cowie, *Stayin' Alive: The 1970s and the Last Days of the Working Class* (New York: New Press, 2010), 269–70.

53. On Keyserling's role, see Kenneth M. Casebeer, "Holder of the Pen: An Interview with Leon Keyserling on Drafting the Wagner Act," *University of Miami Law Review* 42 (1987): 296.

54. Leon H. Keyserling, *Toward Full Employment in Three Years* (Washington, D.C.: Conference on Economic Progress, 1976), 10–11.

55. Ibid., 3.

56. Ibid., 14.

57. Ibid.

58. Chappell, *The War on Welfare,* 133.

59. Hobart Rowan, "Carving an Economic Platform," *WP,* April 12, 1976, A1.

60. Report of the Task Force on National Economic Planning, January 14, 1977, folder Board Reports, 1977, box 6, series I, CCUS.

61. Iwan Morgan, "Jimmy Carter, Bill Clinton, and the New Democratic Economics," *Historical Journal* 47, no. 4 (2004): 1023. Keyserling was furious that Humphrey-Hawkins was "ignored flagrantly and almost in its entirety," calling Carter's economics "conservative." Leon H. Keyserling, *"Liberal" and "Conservative" National Economic Policies and Their Consequences, 1919–1979: A Study to Help Implement Promptly the Humphrey-Hawkins Full Employment and Balanced Growth Act of 1978* (Washington, D.C.: Conference on Economic Progress, 1979), 2.

62. Dennis Farney, "The Dwindling Band of Liberals," *WSJ,* January 15, 1979, 20.

63. Jack Germond, "Congress and Carter: Who's in Charge?," *NYT,* January 30, 1977, SM11.

64. David Broder, "Children of the '60s Grow Up on Proposition 13," *WP,* July 17, 1978, A4.

65. William Leuchtenberg, "Jimmy Carter and the Post-New Deal Presidency," in Gary M. Fink and Hugh Davis Graham, eds., *The Carter Presidency: Policy Choices in the Post-New Deal Era* (Lawrence: University Press of Kansas, 1998), 20–21; Austin Scott, "Carter Signs $20.1 Billion Jobs, Stimulus Measure," *WP,* May 14, 1977, A2; Morgan, "Jimmy Carter, Bill Clinton, and the New Democratic Economics," 1021.

66. Farney, "The Dwindling Band of Liberals."

67. Jimmy Carter, *Keeping Faith: Memoirs of a President* (Fayetteville: University of Arkansas Press, 1995), 46–47.

68. Jack Watson, interview, December 13, 1980, transcript, p. 3, JCPL, https://www.jimmycarterlibrary.gov/assets/documents/oral_histories/exit_interviews/Watson.pdf.

69. Jack Watson and Larry Gilson to Jimmy Carter, July 18, 1977, folder FA 7/16/77–7/20/77, box FA-1, WHCF.

70. Leuchtenberg, "Jimmy Carter and the Post-New Deal Presidency," 11.

71. Robert E. Merriam to Jimmy Carter, June 28, 1977, folder FA 7/16/77–7/20/77, box FA-1, WHCF.

72. White House press release, July 19, 1977, folder, FA 7/16/77–7/20/77, box FA-1, WHCF.

73. James J. Coyne to Jack Watson, October 13, 1978, folder FA 11/20/78–12/31/78, box FA-3, WHCF.

74. Henry W. Maier to Jimmy Carter, December 22, 1977, folder FA 1/1/78–1/31/78, box FA-2, WHCF.

75. Ann Crichton to Bruce Kirschenbaum, September 26, 1977, folder FA 9/10/77–9/30-77, box FA-2, WHCF.

76. Comments of the Legal Services Community Development Task Force on the Proposed Amendments to 24 CFR Part 270, Subparts C, D, & G, undated [likely 1977 or 1978], Secretary of State Front Office, Sec. of State Subject Files, 1946–79, Ben W. Fortson Jr., RCB-1615, Georgia Archives.

77. Richard Hatcher et al. to Frank B. Moore, September 25, 1977, folder FA 9/10/77–9/30/77, box FA-2, WHCF.

78. Elmer B. Staats to Jack H. Watson, February 14, 1978, and attached report, folder FA 2/1/78–2/28/78, box FA-3, WHCF.

79. Statement by the President, September 9, 1977, folder FA 9/1/77–9/9/77, box FA-2, WHCF.

80. Jimmy Carter, Memorandum for the Heads of Executive Departments and Agencies, June 21, 1978, folder FA 6/1/78–6/15/78, FA-3, WHCF.

81. B. Drummond Ayres, "An Elusive Economic Goal," *NYT*, February 3, 1978, A11.

82. David S. Broder, "White House Balanced Growth Forum Promises Controversy," *WP*, January 1, 1978, A2; Neal Pierce, "Federalism—A 'Hell of an Experiment' in Resolving Economic Growth Dilemmas," *NJ*, January 21, 1978.

83. "The Second War Between the States," *Business Week*, May 17, 1976; "Federal Spending: The North's Loss Is the Sunbelt's Gain," *NJ*, June 26, 1976.

84. "Mr. Harrington Responds," *WSJ*, February 11, 1977, 8.

85. Ellen Hume, "'Frostbelt' Gains in Fight for U.S.," *LAT*, November 13, 1977, A1.

86. George P. Rasanen, "It's Frostbelt vs. Sunbelt for U.S. funds," *PD*, October 23, 1977, B8.

87. "North-Midwest Coalition Imitates South," *Raleigh News and Observer*, May 22, 1977, folder Southern Growth Policies Board, RCB-16535, Georgia Archives.

88. *Troubled Local Economies and the Distribution of Federal Dollars*, August 1977, Congressional Budget Office, Washington, D.C., http://www.cbo.gov/sites/default/files/cbofiles/ftpdocs/113xx/doc11362/1977_08_troubled.pdf.

89. Richard Lyons, "House Group Wants to Stem Sunbelt Flow," *WP*, September 2, 1976, B1.

90. Rasanen, "It's Frostbelt vs. Sunbelt for U.S. Funds."

91. William Miller, "Efforts to Save Jobs Must Await Decision of Defense Department," *PD*, May 27, 1977, 14A; George Rasanen, "House Coalition to Appeal Pentagon Cuts to Carter," *PD*, September 22, 1977, 9B.

92. "North-Midwest Coalition Imitates South."

93. Michael J. Harrington, "Rescuing the Region," *NYT*, July 1, 1977, 17.

94. Federal Policy Impacts on Southern Growth, October 19, 1977, attached to Minutes, Executive Committee Meeting, July 29, 1977, folder Executive Committee, July 29, 1977, Atlanta, box 23, subseries 1.3, SGPB.

95. George Busbee, "Remarks on Southern Growth Policies Board," August 30, 1977, folder Southern Growth Policies Board, RCB-16535, Georgia Archives; "South Said 'Asleep' on Programs, Losing Millions," *Huntsville Times*, August 31, 1977, folder Southern Growth Policies Board, RCB-16535, Georgia Archives.

96. "South Said 'Asleep' on Programs, Losing Millions."

97. Busbee, "Remarks on Southern Growth Policies Board."

98. Richard P. Nathan et al., "Monitoring the Block Grant Program for Community Development," *Political Science Quarterly* 92, no. 2 (Summer 1977): 240.

99. "Government Seeks the Right Formula for Community Development Funds," *NJ*, February 12, 1977.

100. Nathan et al., "Monitoring the Block Grant Program," 237–38.

101. SGPB, "Federal Allocation Formula Changes and Their Implications," September 8, 1977, folder Southern Growth Policies Board, RCB-16535, Georgia Archives.

102. Jim Merriner, "North's Grants Formula Rapes Dixie, Busbee Says," *AC*, August 31, 1977, 1A.

103. Nathan et al, "Monitoring the Block Grant Program"; and Michael J. Rich, "Community Development Block Grants at 40: Time for a Makeover," *Housing Policy Debate* 24, no. 1 (2014): 46–90.

104. B. Drummond Ayres Jr., "Parley on U.S. Policy Toward South Asked," *NYT*, October 20, 1977, 21.

105. B. Drummond Ayres Jr., "Sunbelt Organizing Washington Lobby in Hunt for Funds," *NYT*, December 18, 1977, 29.

106. Jim Montgomery, "Out of the Money: Deep Poverty Persists in the South Despite New Wealth of Area," *WSJ*, December 29, 1978, 1.

107. Statement by Incoming Chairman Governor George D. Busbee, attached to Summary of Minutes, Executive Committee Meeting, July 29, 1977, folder Executive Committee, July 29, 1977, Atlanta, box 23, subseries 1.3, SGPB.

108. *White House Conference on Balanced National Growth and Economic Development: Final Report*, vol. 1, *Summary of Conference Proceedings* (Washington, D.C., July 1978), 21.

109. Ibid., 4–5.

110. B. Drummond Ayres Jr., "Moynihan Warns on Aid for New York City," *NYT*, February 1, 1978, A18.

111. *White House Conference on Balanced National Growth*, 35.

112. "Yankee, Southerner Try to Mend Fences," *Boston Globe*, February 1, 1978; David S. Broder, "Moynihan vs. Busbee: Hoped-for Excitement at Meetings on Growth," *WP*, February 1, 1978, A7.

113. Jim McIntyre to Stu Eizenstat et al., January 22, 1979, folder FA 1/1/79–1/31/79, box FA-5, WHCF.

114. George Busbee to Charles Kirbo and Griffin Bell, January 5, 1978, folder FA 2/1/79–2/15/79, box FA-5, WHCF.

115. Charles N. Bailey to George Busbee, July 7, 1978, RCB-21816, Georgia Archives.

116. "Three Incumbent Commissioners Defeated, Two Face Runoff," *RNT*, August 11, 1976, 3.

117. Jimmy Carter handwritten note on memorandum to Jimmy Carter, January 9, 1979, folder FA 2/1/79–2/15/79, box FA-5, WHCF.

118. Stu Eizenstat and Ralph Schlosstein to Jimmy Carter, February 7, 1979, folder FA 2/1/79–2/15/79, box FA-5, WHCF.

119. CVAPDC Annual Report, 1980–81, Hargrett.

120. "Busbee Makes a Point," *RNT*, January 14, 1981, 4.

Chapter 9

1. Jack Germond, "Congress and Carter: Who's in Charge?," *NYT*, January 30, 1977, SM11.

2. Pew Research Center, "Public Trust in Government: 1958–2021," May 17, 2021, https://www.pewresearch.org/politics/2021/05/17/public-trust-in-government-1958-2021/.

3. On efforts to categorize and name the "New Democrats," see Charles Peters, "A Neo-Liberal's Manifesto," *WP*, September 5, 1982, C1; Kenneth S. Baer, *Reinventing Democrats: The Politics of Liberalism from Reagan to Clinton* (Lawrence: University Press of Kansas, 2000), 32-35; and Geismer, *Left Behind*, ch. 1.

4. On the crisis of public policy, see Orren and Skowronek, *The Policy State*.

5. Osborne and Gaebler, *Reinventing Government*, 284–88.

6. On marketization, see especially Holtzman, *The Long Crisis*, 3–5; and Suleiman Osman, "'We're Doing It Ourselves': The Unexpected Origins of New York City's Public-Private Parks During the 1970s Fiscal Crisis," *Journal of Planning History* 16, no. 2 (2017): 162–74. On market metaphors and the narrowing of the political imagination, see Rodgers, *Age of Fracture*, chaps. 1–2.

7. David Osborne, *Laboratories of Democracy: A New Breed of Governors Creates Models for National Growth* (Boston: Harvard Business School Press, 1988), 12 (emphasis in original).

8. David M. Erdman, "Politicians Picture High Tech as Elixir for Economic Ills," *Allentown Morning Call*, February 22, 1987, D6.

9. Gary Hart, *Right from the Start: A Chronicle of the McGovern Campaign* (New York: Quadrangle, 1973), 325.

10. Julilly Kohler Hausmann, *Getting Tough: Welfare and Imprisonment in 1970s America* (Princeton: Princeton University Press, 2017), 142.

11. Michael Katz, *The Undeserving Poor: America's Enduring Confrontation with Poverty* (New York: Oxford University Press, 2013), 68.

12. Chappell, *The War on Welfare*, 222.

13. Orleck, *Storming Caesar's Palace*; and Tani, *States of Dependency*.

14. Chappell, *The War on Welfare*, 226.

15. Ibid., 165.

16. LeeAnn B. Lands, "Lobbying for Welfare in a Deep South State Legislature in the 1970s," *Journal of Southern History* 84, no. 3 (August 2018): 653–96.

17. Julilly Kohler-Hausmann, "Welfare Crises, Penal Solutions, and the Origins of the 'Welfare Queen,'" *Journal of Urban History* 41, no. 5 (2015): 759 and 766.

18. "The Money Crunch for States and Cities," *NB*, October 1975, 24–25.

19. Roland McElroy, *The Best President the Nation Never Had: A Memoir of Working with Sam Nunn* (Macon, Ga.: Mercer University Press, 2017), 24–26, 29.

20. "Sam Nunn Campaigns on the Issues, Pledges to Get Tough in Washington," 1972, box 3, RCB-255, Legislature, State Programs Study Commission, Administrative Records, Georgia Archives.

21. McElroy, *The Best President the Nation Never Had*, 50–51.

22. Beau Cutts, "Congress Clears Nunn Support Bill," *AC*, December 21, 1974, 2B.

23. Bob Fort, "Nunn Wants Spending Explanations," *AC*, April 14, 1973, 5A.

24. "Like Counting Confetti: Forms Bog Down," *CT*, October 26, 1975, 4.

25. Andrew Mollison, "Proposed Amendment's Limit on Federal Spending Unveiled," *AC*, November 19, 1978, 16A.

26. The administration's attention to federalism has been largely overlooked by historians. In one excellent edited volume, for instance, Reagan's "New Federalism" received just four passing mentions. W. Elliot Brownlee and Hugh Davis Graham, eds., *The Reagan Presidency: Pragmatic Conservatism and Its Legacies* (Lawrence: University of Kansas Press, 2003). On optimism for intergovernmental reform, see, for instance, John Herbers, "Governors Ask Realignment of State and Federal Powers," *NYT*, August 6, 1980, A16.

27. Monica Prasad, "The Popular Origins of Neoliberalism in the Reagan Tax Cut of 1981," *Journal of Policy History* 24, no. 3 (2012) 351–83.

28. Gareth Davies, "The Welfare State," in Brownlee and Graham, *The Reagan Presidency*, 211–12. On Reagan's tax policy, see Molly Michelmore, *Tax and Spend: The Welfare State, Tax Politics, and the Limits of American Liberalism* (Philadelphia: University of Pennsylvania Press, 2012), 137–44. On Democrats' "bidding war" with Republicans over the tax cut package, see Prasad, "Popular Origins," 371–72.

29. Peter Goldman, "Rest in Peace, New Deal," *Newsweek*, August 10, 1981.

30. Ronald Reagan, "Address Before a Joint Session of the Congress on the Program for Economic Recovery—February 1981," February 18, 1981, https://www.reaganlibrary.gov/research/speeches/21881a.

31. Ronald Reagan, "Memorandum for Members of the Cabinet and Agency Heads," March 20, 1981, folder M, RCB-19481, Georgia Archives; "Reagan Federalism: Restoring the Balance," folder Federalism Initiative (1), box 13, series II: Subject File I, 1981–1984, White House Staff Member and Office Files, Media Relations, Reagan.

32. Henry Eason, "Governors, Reagan Don't See Eye to Eye on 'New Federalism,'" *AC*, March 1, 1981, 4D.

33. Article for Urban Georgia, Newt Gingrich, October 31, 1979, folder Revenue Sharing Article, box 147, Gingrich.

34. Report to the Board of Directors on General Revenue Sharing, February 6, 1980, folder Board Reports 409th Meeting, February 21, 1980, box 6, series I, CCUS.

35. Ronald Reagan, "Interview with Reporters on Federalism," November 19, 1981, APP, https://www.presidency.ucsb.edu/documents/interview-with-reporters-federalism.

36. "Reagan Federalism: Restoring the Balance."

37. Eason, "Governors, Reagan Don't See Eye to Eye ."

38. Charles Royer, "One Mayor on 'Fiscal Death Row,'" *LAT*, November 22, 1981, G5; Steven R. Weisman, "Reagan Will Seek Governors' Views on Transfer Plan," *NYT*, February 2, 1982, A1.

39. "Background and Status Report on Federalism Initiative" fact sheet, July 13, 1982, folder FG (Federal Government Organizations) 091600-091699, box 6, WHORM: FG, Reagan; Davies, "The Welfare State," 218.

40. Reagan, "Interview with Reporters on Federalism," November 19, 1981.

41. Bill Boyarsky, "Some States Are Likely to Sink in Ronald Reagan's New Federalist Sea," *LAT*, February 7, 1982, D1.

42. Gillis W. Long and Timothy W. Wirth, letter of transmission, in *Rebuilding the Road to Opportunity: Turning Point for America's Economy* (Washington, D.C.: House Democratic Caucus, September 1982), iii–iv, House Democratic Caucus Records, box 63, folder 2, Library of Congress.

43. Sidney Blumenthal, "Drafting a Democratic Industrial Plan," *NYT*, August 28, 1983, SM31.

44. *Rebuilding the Road to Opportunity*, 2.

45. Louis Hyman, *Temp: How American Work, American Business, and the American Dream Became Temporary* (New York: Viking, 2018), 170–86; Margaret O'Mara, "Startup Cowboys and High-Tech Pioneers," conference paper, Organization of American Historians Annual Meeting, April 2016, Providence, R.I., in author's possession.

46. Craig R. Hume, "Nunn Backs GOP Tax Cut," *AC*, June 15, 1978, 1A.

47. *Final Report of the Southern Growth Policies Board Task Force on Southern Cities* (Research Triangle Park: SGPB, 1981), 47.

48. Stuart Rosenfeld, "Technology Transfer: From Invention to Innovation to Industry," *SGPB Alert*, November 1984, 1–2, subseries 4.4, box 95, SGPB.

49. "The Cynical Idealists of '68," *Time*, June 7, 1968.

50. Graham, *Losing Time*, 60–70.

51. Ira C. Magaziner and Robert B. Reich, *Minding America's Business: The Decline and Rise of the American Economy* (New York: Harcourt Brace Jovanovich, 1982), 330.

52. Randall Rothenberg, *The Neoliberals: Creating the New American Politics* (New York: Simon and Schuster, 1984), 221–22.

53. Lawrence Klein, "The Supply Side," *American Economic Review* 68, no. 1 (March 1978): 6.

54. Edward Cowan, "Carter Economic Renewal Plan," *NYT*, August 22, 1980, D1.

55. T. R. Reid, "Kennedy: 'Reindustrialize' the U.S.," *WP*, May 21, 1980, A4; John Herbers, "Nationwide Renewal of Public Works Urged," *NYT*, April 5, 1981, 26; Graham, *Losing Time*, 53–55; Clyde H. Farnsworth, "U.S. Industry Seeking to Restore Competitive Vitality to Products," *NYT*, August 18, 1980, A1; and Stein, *Pivotal Decade*, 248–49, NAM quote on 245.

56. Margot Hornblower, "House Democrats Issue Ambitious Alternative to Reaganomics," *WP*, September 19, 1982, A11.

57. Roger C. Altman and Jeffrey E. Garten, "Business Forum: Why the U.S. Needs a Development Bank; The Only Source of 'Patient Capital,'" *NYT*, October 16, 1983, A3.

58. *Forum*, April 1983, Hargrett.

59. Dennis Wrong, "The Joy of Sects," *New Republic* 191, no. 7 (1984): 34; and Harvard Sitkoff, review of *The Neoliberals: Creating the New American Politics*, by Randall Rothenberg, *Political Science Quarterly* 100, no. 3 (Fall 1985): 532–33.

60. Economic Innovation International, Inc., http://www.economic-innovation.com/about_us.htm.

61. MTDC Annual Report, 1986, 2, and MTDC Annual Report, 1989, 7, MIT Library, Cambridge, Mass.; Samuel Leiken to Arthur R. Osborn, January 26, 1990, Massachusetts/AFL-CIO Executive Council Meetings, https://archive.org/stream/executivecouncil90215afl2/executivecouncil90215afl2_djvu.txt. One of the first companies in which Massachusetts pension funds were invested was Kronos, the workforce and labor management technology firm

whose software enabled businesses to closely monitor workers' hours—later leading to charges of wage theft. See Nate Anderson, "More 'Dell Hell': Employees File Class-Action Lawsuit," February 14, 2007, *Ars Technica*, http://arstechnica.com/uncategorized/2007/02/8847/.

62. Brent Cebul, "Supply-Side Liberalism: Fiscal Crisis, Post-Industrial Policy, and the Rise of the New Democrats," *Modern American History* 2, no. 2 (2019): 152–54.

63. Robert C. McMath Jr. et al., *Engineering the New South: Georgia Tech, 1885–1985* (Athens: University of Georgia Press, 1985), 446.

64. Author interview with Wayne Hodges, August 14, 2012, Atlanta, Georgia.

65. "From Missiles to Pole Beans," *Georgia Trend*, May 1986.

66. Kenneth Darnell to Joe Frank Harris, November 7, 1988, folder GA Tech Reg. Office, box RCB-1506, Georgia Archives.

67. Lindy Rodgers to Joe Frank Harris, November 29, 1988, folder GA Tech Reg. Office, box RCB-1506, Georgia Archives.

68. McKinsey findings summarized in "Beginning Thoughts on Georgia's Economy and Capital Markets," June 14, 1989, 10, folder Growth Strategies Commission, Capital Markets—June 1989, RCB-14937, Georgia Archives.

69. Julie V. Ouseley to Joe Frank Harris, November 7, 1988, folder GA Tech Reg. Office, RCB-1506, Georgia Archives.

70. "Finance for the Future: Capital Markets Analysis and Action to Enhance Georgia's Economic Development," November 30, 1989, 20–21 and 5, folder Growth Strategies Commission, Capital Markets—November 1989, RCB-14937, Georgia Archives.

71. James S. Balloun to Belden Hull Daniels, June 22, 1989, folder Growth Strategies Commission, Capital Markets—June 1989, RCB-14937, Georgia Archives.

72. John Sibley to Joe Frank Harris, December 7, 1989, folder Growth Strategies Commission, Capital Markets—December 1989, RCB-14937, Georgia Archives.

73. Sibley to Joe Frank Harris, December 2, 1988, folder Growth Strategies Commission: Correspondence—December 1988, RCB-14935, Georgia Archives.

74. Stuart Rosenfeld, "Sowing the Seeds for Growth: State Support for R&D," *SGPB Alert*, December 1985, subseries 4.4, box 95, SGPB.

75. Osborne, *Laboratories of Democracy*, 104.

76. "Clinton Running for Presidency," *Baxter Bulletin*, January 18, 1985, 4.

77. Tom Sherwood and James Dickinson, "Robb Trying to Form New Party Policy Group," *WP*, February 16, 1985, A9; Dan Balz and David Broder, "Rival Democratic Councils Forming," *WP*, February 27, 1985, A7.

78. Paul Taylor, "Democrats' New Centrists Preen for '88," *WP*, November 10, 1985, A1.

79. Phil Gailey, "Dissidents Defy Top Democrats; Council Formed," *NYT*, March 1, 1985, A1; Dan Balz, "Southern and Western Democrats Launch New Leadership Council," *WP*, March 1, 1985, A2.

80. "DLC Plans Busy Fall: Special Conference Is Highlight," *DLC Newsgram*, September 1989, 2, folder Democratic Leadership Council, box RCB-20213, Georgia Archives.

81. Timothy P. R. Weaver, *Blazing the Neoliberal Trail: Urban Political Development in the United States and the United Kingdom* (Philadelphia: University of Pennsylvania Press, 2016), 116.

82. On these dynamics, see Edsall, *The New Politics of Inequality*, chaps. 1, 4, 6, and pp. 78–89. See also, Lily Geismer, *Left Behind: The Democrats' Failed Attempt to Solve Inequality* (New York: Public Affairs, 2022), 147-49.

83. Rothenberg, *The Neoliberals*, quotations at 30 and 63.
84. Joan Didion, *Political Fictions* (New York: Vintage, 2001), 162.
85. Rothenberg, *The Neoliberals*, 63.
86. Ibid., 68, 17–20.
87. Clinton quoted in Osborne, *Laboratories of Democracy*, 109.
88. Neal R. Peirce, Jerry Hagstrom, and Carol Steinbach, *Economic Development: The Challenge of the 1980s* (Washington, D.C.: Council of State Planning Agencies, 1979), 7.
89. Osborne, *Laboratories of Democracy*, 89.
90. Leonard U. Wilson and L. V. Watkins, "How the States Plan," *Challenge* 18, no. 6 (January/February 1976): 43–51. On Birch and the CSPA, see Osborne, *Laboratories of Democracy*, 33–35.
91. Osborne and Gaebler, *Reinventing Government*, quotes on 208 and 206, 195, 196, 205.
92. Ibid., 285–86, 284.
93. Al From, interview by Russell L. Riley and Darby Morrisroe, April 27, 2006, Washington, D.C., transcript, 5, William J. Clinton Presidential History Project, Miller Center, University of Virginia.
94. Dean Baker, *The United States Since 1980* (New York: Cambridge University Press, 2007), 71–74.
95. U.S. Bureau of Labor Statistics, "Unemployment Rate in Georgia (GAUR)," retrieved from FRED, Federal Reserve Bank of St. Louis, https://fred.stlouisfed.org/series/GAUR, September 16, 2019.
96. "The Issue All the Politicians Love to Tout," *GT*, October 1985.
97. Carrie Teegardin, "Inside the Other Georgia," *AC*, June 28, 1992, C1.
98. *1980 Commission on the Future of the South: Final Report* (Research Triangle Park: SGPB, 1980), 29.
99. U.S. Bureau of Labor Statistics, "Unemployment Rate—Black or African American," retrieved from FRED, Federal Reserve Bank of St. Louis, https://fred.stlouisfed.org/series/LNS14000006, September 16, 2019; Morris Thompson, "Atlanta's Unequal Prosperity: Races' Fortunes Show Big Gaps," *WP*, July 18, 1988, A17.
100. *1980 Commission on the Future of the South: Final Report*, 12
101. Osborne, *Laboratories of Democracy*, 89–90.
102. Thomas Garrett, "White Says State Should Cut Back Spending and Prepare for Rough Economic Times Ahead," *Baxter Bulletin*, May 8, 1980, 3.
103. Osborne, *Laboratories of Democracy*, 92–93, 10–11.
104. Doris Betts, *Halfway Home and a Long Way to Go: The Report of the 1986 Commission on the Future of the South* (Research Triangle Park: SGPB, 1986), 4.
105. Stuart Rosenfeld to STC, May 16, 1986, folder STC Minutes, box 92, subseries 3.3, SGPB; "Regional Science and Technology Centers of Excellence: A Report from the Southern Technology Council of the Southern Growth Policies Board," September 1987, box 92, subseries 3.3, SGPB.
106. "A Project of the Southern Technology Council of the Southern Growth Policies Board, Regional Consortium of Advanced Manufacturing Technology, Training, Development, and Demonstration Centers," folder SGPB CMC Minutes/Process Reports, box 92, subseries 3.3, SGPB.
107. Southern Technology Council Newsletter, May 1988, folder SGPB, box 92, subseries 3.3, SGPB.

108. Geismer, "Agents of Change," 117.

109. Ibid.

110. "Good Faith Fund Aids Unlikely Borrowers," *Miami Herald*, May 3, 1990, 7B.

111. Geismer, "Agents of Change," 120–21.

112. Michael Porter, "The Competitive Advantage of the Inner City," *Harvard Business Review*, May–June 1995, https://hbr.org/1995/05/the-competitive-advantage-of-the-inner-city.

113. Geismer, "Agents of Change," 113.

114. Alton Skinner, "The Use of State Pension Funds for Venture Capital," *SGPB Alert*, January 1984, 1.

115. Stuart Rosenfeld, "Looking Back to the Future: Economic Roles for Public Schools," September 1982, 10–11, folder Staff Memos from Jesse (1985 back), box 20, subseries 1.2.3, SGPB.

116. Dennis Byrd, "Governor Unveils Legislative Package," *Baxter Bulletin*, October 3, 1988, 1.

117. David Wessel, "Tsongas, Clinton Differ on Strategies for Spurring U.S. Economic Growth," *WSJ*, March 2, 1992, A14.

118. Robert B. Reich, *The Next American Frontier* (New York: Times Books, 1983), 21.

119. Osborne, *Laboratories of Democracy*, 249–318.

120. Betts, *Halfway Home*, 17 and 9.

121. Baker, *The United States Since 1980*, 71–74.

122. Robert Shapiro, "An American Working Wage: Ending Poverty in Working Families," *PPI Policy Report*, February 1990.

123. William Galston and Elaine Kamarck, "The Politics of Evasion: Democrats and the Presidency," *PPI Policy Report*, September 1989, 3–4, 18.

124. David Broder, "'New Deal-Making' Politics: Massachusetts Governor Develops a Machine," *WP*, February 10, 1986.

125. Bruce Reed, "The New Orleans Declaration: A Reader's Guide," *Mainstream Democrat*, May 1990, 15.

126. "DLC Plans Busy Fall: Special Conference Is Highlight," *DLC Newsgram*, September 1989, 1, folder Democratic Leadership Council, box RCB-20213, Georgia.

127. Rothenberg, *The Neoliberals*, 247.

128. Al From interview, April 27, 2006, 39–40.

129. Bill Clinton, Democratic Leadership Council Keynote Address, May 6, 1991, https://www.c-span.org/video/?17869-1/democratic-leadership-council-keynote-address, accessed May 31, 2022.

130. William J. Clinton, "Address Accepting the Presidential Nomination at the Democratic National Convention in New York," July 16, 1992, APP, https://www.presidency.ucsb.edu/documents/address-accepting-the-presidential-nomination-the-democratic-national-convention-new-york.

131. Clinton quoted in Geismer, "Agents of Change," 123.

Chapter 10

1. Myron Magnet, "How Business Bosses Saved a Sick City," *Fortune*, March 27, 1989, 106.

2. Anthony Downs, "Using the Lessons of Experience to Allocated Resources in the Community Development Program," in Downs, ed., *Recommendations for Community Development Planning* (Chicago: Real Estate Research Corporation, 1976), 1–28, quotation at 13.

3. On the "new inclusion" see Lee, McQuarrie, and Walker, *Democratizing Inequalities*.

4. Keeanga-Yamahtta Taylor, *From #BlackLivesMatter to Black Liberation* (Chicago: Haymarket Books, 2016), 79.

5. George L. Forbes, Growth Association, *Questions for Candidates*, attached to William H. Bryant to George L. Forbes, August 8, 1989, folder 5, container 3, Forbes.

6. On black power brokers and the maintenance of the political-institutional status quo, see Adolph Reed, *Stirrings in the Jug: Black Politics in the Post–Civil Rights Era* (Minneapolis: University of Minnesota Press, 1999); Taylor, *From #BlackLivesMatter to Black Liberation*, 89–99; and, generally, Connolly, *A World More Concrete*.

7. Cleveland City Planning Commission, "Population: Trends," http://planning.city.cleveland.oh.us/cwp/pop_trend.php#11.

8. G. Thomas Kingsley and Kathryn L. S. Pettit, *Concentrated Poverty: A Change in Course*, Neighborhood Change in Urban America, no. 2 (Washington, D.C.: Urban Institute, 2003), https://www.urban.org/sites/default/files/publication/58946/310790-Concentrated-Poverty-A-Change-in-Course.pdf.

9. Jenkins, *The Bonds of Inequality*.

10. Biles, "Public Policy Made by Private Enterprise," 1103–9; Jason Hackworth, *The Neoliberal City: Governance, Ideology, and Development in American Urbanism* (Ithaca: Cornell University Press, 2007), 29–39.

11. Phillip Allen to George Voinovich, January 23, 1981, folder 53, container 2, Mayor; Gary Clark, "Voinovich Wants City to Help Businesses Grow," *PD*, January 18, 1982, 3C.

12. "Cleveland's Response to the New Federalism: The Private-Public Partnership," folder FG 006-07 096880 (2 of 9), box 14, FG 006-OPD, Reagan.

13. "Federal Spending Cuts Could Worsen Older Cities' Ability to Borrow Money," *NJ*, February 7, 1981.

14. Iver Peterson, "Cleveland Testing Advice of Rohaytn," *NYT*, February 15, 1981, 39.

15. Thomas W. Lippmann, "Cleveland's New Commuter Tax," *WP*, March 1981, A1. Council president George Forbes and black community leaders supported the tax. See "The Tax Levy Must Pass," *CP*, February 7, 1981, 1A.

16. Juan Williams, "Cleveland: The Politics of Default," *WP*, February 6, 1981, A15

17. Figure calculated by author.

18. Iver Peterson, "Cleveland's Council Clears Pact Ending City's Default," *NYT*, October 9, 1980, A22.

19. Joel W. Motley to George Voinovich, May 23, 1989, folder Bond Presentation, container 29, Mayor.

20. Amy Doppelt, Cleveland, Ohio, Various Purpose General Obligation Bonds Series 1986A, L. F. Rothschild, Unterberg, Towbin, July 17, 1986, 1–2, folder Bond Issue, container 33, Mayor.

21. George V. Voinovich to Bill Reidy, Finance Director, Financial Recovery Plan, April 7, 1980, folder 7, container 5, Mayor.

22. Paul J. Wiener to George V. Voinovich, December 13, 1985, folder 12, container 12, Mayor; and Jenkins, *Bonds of Inequality*, 201–2.

23. Preliminary Outline, Rating Agency Presentation, February 8, 1985, quotation on 2, folder Bond Presentation, container 29, Mayor.

24. Charles Brown to George Voinovich, April 25, 1986, folder 28, container 40, Mayor.

25. Preliminary Outlines, Rating Agency Visit, Standard & Poor's, June 23, 1986, Moody's, June 24, 1986, folder Bond Presentation, container 29, Mayor.

26. Martin Tolchin, "City Paid $75 Million in 1969 in Fees to Private Consultants," *NYT*, July 1, 1970, 1.

27. George Voinovich to Gary Conley et al., May 19, 1983, and Development Priority Memo, February 23, 1983, folder 1, box 13, Mayor.

28. Greater Cleveland Roundtable, Board of Trustees Meeting Minutes, January 19, 1983, folder 17, box 13, Mayor.

29. Greater Cleveland Roundtable, Board of Trustees Meeting, October 25, 1982, pp. 5–6, folder 17, container 13, Mayor.

30. Author interview with Richard Pogue, December 29, 2010, Cleveland.

31. Roldo Bartimole, "Neighborhoods Beware of Foundation Role," *Point of View* 11, no. 24 (1979): 1.

32. Cunningham, *Democratizing Cleveland*, 136–37.

33. On CDCs, see Julia Rabig, *The Fixers: Devolution, Development, and Civil Society in Newark, 1960–1990* (Chicago: University of Chicago Press, 2016).

34. Frazier, "A McDonald's That Reflects the Soul of a People."

35. Diana Tittle, *Rebuilding Cleveland: The Cleveland Foundation and Its Evolving Urban Strategy* (Columbus: Ohio State University Press, 1992), 171–72.

36. On their lobbying efforts, see folder 117, container 6, Hough.

37. William Myricks to Michael Benz, November 30, 1977, folder 43, container 3, Hough; and Rabig, *The Fixers*, chap. 8.

38. H. C. Mushangazhiki to Claude, November 24, 1982, folder 198, container 10, Hough.

39. George Voinovich, "Mayor's Statement of Fiscal Policy," undated, folder 53, container 2, Voinovich.

40. Phillip C. Allen to George Voinovich, June 20, 1980, folder 53, container 2, Voinovich; and Ellen Abraham to Diane Downing, April 8, 1982, folder 24, container 10, Voinovich.

41. Jack Krumhansl and John Wilbur to Citizen Participation Teams, Briefings for the Process, June 17, 1980, June 23, 1980, folder 11, container 6, Voinovich.

42. Vincent J. Lombardi to Phillip Allen, Block Grant Reimbursements, November 24, 1980, p. 3, folder 1, container 7, Mayor.

43. Vincent J. Lombardi to George V. Voinovich, November 28, 1988, folder CDBG, container 29, Mayor; and Cunningham, *Democratizing Cleveland*, 142–44.

44. "A Mayor's Commission on Neighborhoods," attached to Karl Bonutti to George V. Voinovich, February 6, 1980, folder 8, container 7, Mayor.

45. Roundtable, April 4, 1986, p. 12, folder 3, container 2, Mayor.

46. Linda Parham, "State Officials Decry Block Grant Inflexibility," *AC*, undated, folder 9, box 12, subseries C, series I, Mattingly.

47. Statement of Senator Mack Mattingly, February 19, 1986, folder 8, box 31, subseries C, series III, Mattingly.

48. Crime policy was also essential to Reagan's urban policy. See Hinton, *From the War on Poverty to the War on Crime*, 308–38.

49. Michael Rich, "Community Development Block Grants at 40: Time for a Makeover," *Housing Policy Debate* 24, no. 1 (2014): 58.

50. Eugene Boyd, *Community Development Block Grants: Summary of the Law and Its Implementation* (Washington, D.C.: Congressional Research Service, 1990), 6.

51. Tom Duffy coordinated his lobbying with the city's biggest firms. Thomas Duffy to George Voinovich, April 18, 1980, folder 1, container 6, Mayor.

52. *Cleveland Press*, January 9, 1976, folder 974, container 64, Perk.

53. Richard P. Nathan and Jerry A. Webman, eds., *The Urban Development Action Grant Program: Papers and Conference Proceedings on Its First Two Years of Operation* (Princeton: Princeton Urban and Regional Research Center, 1980), 28.

54. Eisinger, *Rise of the Entrepreneurial State*, 11–22; and Ingrid Reed, "The Life and Death of UDAG: An Assessment Based on Eight Projects in Five New Jersey Cities," *Publius* 19, no. 3 (1989): 93–109.

55. The Urban Development Action Grant, undated memo, folder Urban Development Assistance Program (2), OA 9460, box 36, Edwin Meese Files, Reagan.

56. Renée A. Berger, "Private-Sector Initiatives in the Reagan Era: New Actors Rework an Old Theme," in Lester M. Salamon and Michael S. Lund, eds., *The Reagan Presidency and the Governing of America* (Washington, D.C.: Urban Institute Press, 1985), 192 and 194.

57. Conservative economist Herbert Stein coined the term "supply-side fiscalist" to deride supply-side tax cuts. See Karen W. Arenson, "The New Economics View: From the Supply Side," *NYT*, March 5, 1981, A1.

58. Ronald Reagan, "Talking Points for State and Local Officials Briefing on Enterprise Zone Proposals," March 24, 1982, White House Subject Files, BE (Business—Economics), box 91, Reagan; Jones, *Masters of the Universe*, 317–18.

59. Ronald Reagan, "Message to the Congress Transmitting Proposed Enterprise Zone Legislation," March 23, 1982, APP, https://www.presidency.ucsb.edu/node/245885.

60. Brent Cebul, "The Antigovernment Impulse: The Presidency, the 'Market,' and the Splintering Common Good," in Roger Biles and Mark Rose, eds., *The President and American Capitalism Since 1945* (Gainesville: University Press of Florida, 2017), 99–122.

61. Herbert Denton, "Reagan's Reproach of the Great Society Overlooks a Few Facts," *WP*, September 27, 1982, A5.

62. Ronald Reagan, "Remarks at a White House Ceremony Honoring the Minority Small Business Persons of the Year," October 11, 1984, APP, https://www.presidency.ucsb.edu/node/260697.

63. Ronald Reagan, "The President's News Conference," November 10, 1981, APP, https://www.presidency.ucsb.edu/node/246952.

64. "The Administration Plan for Enterprise Zones," January 6, 1982, folder 24, container 10, Voinovich.

65. Statement by the President, March 7, 1983, folder Enterprise Zones (1), OA 12999, box 3, MB Oglesby Files, Reagan.

66. Dan J. Smith to Bob Carleson, November 5, 1981, folder HUD Enterprise Zone Panels, 05711, box 2, Dan Smith Files, Reagan.

67. On these meetings, see folder HUD Enterprise Zone Panels, 05711, box 2, Dan Smith Files, Reagan.

68. Dan J. Smith to Dennis Kass and Bob Carleson, re: Enterprise Zone Panel Responses, October 28, 1981, folder HUD Enterprise Zone Panels, 05711, box 2, Dan Smith Files, Reagan.

69. Victor Merina, "Head of Cities League Assails Budget Bill," *LAT*, December 9, 1985, A4.

70. Bill Barnhart and Herb Greenberg, "Muni Bond Bombshell: Senator Urges Income Be Taxed by U.S.," *CT*, March 20, 1986, B1.

71. Testimony of George V. Voinovich, House Budget Committee, Task Force on Community and Natural Resources, January 22, 1986, folder 4, container 8, Voinovich.

72. George V. Voinovich to Phil Cohen, December 31, 1985, folder Bond Issue, container 33, Mayor.

73. Frank Shafroth, "George Voinovich Remembered: A 21st Century Don Quixote," *Bond Buyer*, June 21, 2016.

74. L. A. Dinneen, "Alaskan View of Industrial Revenue Bonds," *Bond Buyer*, January 2, 1968, 17.

75. Eisinger, *Rise of the Entrepreneurial State*, 157 and 162.

76. Elroy M. Leach, "An Economic Analysis of Industrial Revenue Bonds and the Demand for Inputs" (Ph.D. diss., University of Illinois, Chicago, 1984), iv.

77. Alberta M. Sbragia, *Debt Wish: Entrepreneurial Cities, U.S. Federalism, and Economic Development* (Pittsburgh: University of Pittsburgh Press, 1996), 178.

78. Daniel Hertzeberg, "On the Bandwagon: Use of Tax-Exempt Financing for Stores and Other Business Soars, Stirring Critics," *WSJ*, October 8, 1980, 56; James O'Shea, "Development Bond Use Is Expanding, So Is Controversy," *CT*, November 2, 1980, N1; Matthew Purdy, "How Financier Raised Millions for Track," October 5, 1983, *Philadelphia Inquirer*, 1; Ward Sinclair, "Aid for Irish Dairy Operation in Georgia Stirs Bitter Protest," *WSJ*, April 12, 1986, A1.

79. "No More Small Development Bonds," *GT*, January 1988.

80. Neil Kraus and Todd Swanstrom, "Minority Mayors and the Hollow-Prize Problem," *PS: Political Science & Politics* 34, no. 1 (2001): 99–105.

81. Swanstrom, *Crisis of Growth Politics*, 147–48.

82. William Nelson Jr., "Cleveland: The Evolution of Black Political Power," in Keating, Krumholz, and Perry, *Cleveland*, 287–89.

83. Raymond Smith, "Forbes Viewed as City Council Architect/Leader," *CP*, February 18, 1988, 1A.

84. Roldo Bartimole, "Forbes Tightens Screws," *Point of View* 13, no. 16 (1981): 2–3.

85. Raymond Smith, "Oust Forbes Movement Quelled," *CP*, December 24, 1987, 4A.

86. Handwritten notes, RBJ, GLF, 1984 Major Projects, folder 14, container 13, Forbes.

87. Edward P. Whelan, "George Forbes: An Obsession with Power," *CM*, November 1986.

88. Ibid.

89. Steve Luttner, "Shoo-in Status Is Shattered," *PD*, January 1, 1989, 33.

90. Shelley M. Shockley, "Councilman Lewis Asks Where's the Money?," *CP*, November 30, 1989, 1A.

91. "Minter Named Foundation Director," *CP*, December 15, 1983, 4A; Michael McQuarrie, "Nonprofits and the Reconstruction of Urban Governance: Housing Production and Community Development in Cleveland, 1975–2005," in Elisabeth S. Clemens and Doug Guthrie, eds., *Politics and Partnerships: The Role of Voluntary Associations in America's Political Past and Present* (Chicago: University of Chicago Press, 2011).

92. William Wood, "Hundreds Attend Lexington Village Ground Breaking," *CP*, December 6, 1984, 1A.

93. Margaret Williams, "Councilwoman Lewis' Dream Village a Reality," *CP*, October 24, 1985, 6B.

94. See correspondence between George Voinovich and Del de Windt in folder 29, container 13, Voinovich.

95. George Voinovich to Del de Windt et al., February 23, 1983, 3, folder 1, container 13, Voinovich.

96. Don Plaskett to George Voinovich, re: Greater Cleveland Roundtable Meeting Notes, February 27, 1986, folder 17, container 13, Voinovich

97. Keating, Krumholz, and Perry, *Cleveland*, 127.

98. "Designing an Economic Development Strategy for Greater Cleveland, Prepared for the Second Annual Fall Seminar of the College of Urban Affairs, CSU, Governing Greater Cleveland: Options for the Eighties," October 1980, 4, folder 29, container 1, Dan J. Marschall Papers, Western Reserve Historical Society, Cleveland.

99. Merlin Chowkwanyun, "Cleveland Versus the Clinic: The 1960s Riots and Community Health Reform," *American Journal of Public Health* 108, no. 11 (November 2018): 1495–96.

100. Thomas Brazaitis, "Enterprise Zone Test Seen Here," *PD*, March 25, 1982, 15; and George Voinovich to Brian Bowser and Russ Geuther, June 4, 1982, folder 24, container 10, Voinovich.

101. Brian Bowser to George Voinovich and Russ Geuther, May 25, 1982, folder 24, box 10, Mayor; Chowkwanyun, "Cleveland Versus the Clinic," 1497.

102. M. Brock Weir, "Executive Exchange: Needed: The Recapitalization of America," *Industry Week*, October 18, 1982; and Voinovich to Weir, October 28, 1982, folder 4, container 6, Mayor.

103. Udayan Gupta, "Venture Capitalists in Midwest Finding Opportunity at Home," *WSJ*, June 24, 1986, 37.

104. Cebul, "Supply-Side Liberalism," 156.

105. Roger Lowe, "Planned Research Centers Could Spawn Medical Technology Firms," *CCB*, August 4, 1986; and "Richard Shatten," *CCB*, May 24, 2010.

106. Della LaFuente, "Clinic's Research Arm Dives into Growth Plan," *CCB*, February 26, 1990.

107. Mark Russell, "Entrepreneurs Temper Thrill of Own Business with Reality," *PD*, October 4, 1988, 10C.

108. "Steris to Acquire Synergy Health for $1.9 Billion in Cash and Stock," news release, October 13, 2014, https://sterisplc.gcs-web.com/news-releases/news-release-details/steris-acquire-synergy-health-19-billion-cash-and-stock.

109. William Wood, "Forbes Speaks Out Against Gentrification of East Side," *CP*, June 9, 1983, 1A.

110. Thomas Andrzejewski, "Growth Association Chief, Mayor Laud Each Other," *PD*, January 18, 1984, 4D.

111. "Remarks by Cleveland Mayor George Voinovich, Thursday, August 15, 1985, Louisiana Municipal Association, Baton Rouge, Louisiana," 12, folder 21, container 1, Voinovich.

112. George Forbes, draft "Letter to the Editor," undated, folder 4, container 3, Forbes; Roldo Bartimole, "Cost to Schools Abatement," *Point of View* 21, no. 21 (1989): 4, folder 15, container 1, Forbes.

113. George L. Forbes, Growth Association, *Questions for Candidates*, attached to William H. Bryant to George L. Forbes, August 8, 1989, folder 5, container 3, Forbes.

114. Announcement of Agreement, May 9, 1988, folder 14, container 1, Forbes; Ron Rutti, "School Board Urges to Fight Tax Abatement," *PD*, June 22, 1989, folder 13, container 1, Forbes.

115. See, generally, Holtzman, *The Long Crisis*.

116. By 1985, Cleveland ranked fourth in UDAG funding, behind only New York, Detroit, and Baltimore. Between 1981 and 1988 the city received over $103 million in UDAGs. Keating, Krumholz, and Perry, *Cleveland*, 130.

117. Greater Cleveland Growth Association, "Block Grant Primer Update," October 1982, folder 173, container 9, Hough; George Voinovich to Vince Lombardi, January 18, 1980, folder 5, container 6, Voinovich.

118. "Galleria Rekindles Downtown Retailing in Thriving Cleveland," news release, undated, folder 4, container 125, Mayor.

119. Figures compiled from Community Development Block Grant, Year XI Projected Use of Funds and Community Development Block Grant, Year XII Projected Use of Funds, Project Summary, folder 12, container 12, Voinovich.

120. Judith Ayers and Randall Short to Vincent Lombardi and Hunter Morrison, re: Commercial Revitalization, October 28, 1982, pp. 1–2, folder LDCs, container 15, Mayor. On CDBGs and LDCs, see Mayor's Local Development Corporation Meeting, November 1, 1982, folder LDCs, container 15, Mayor.

121. Roldo Bartimole, "Green: Keep Poor Out," *Point of View* 13, no. 20 (1981): 2–3 (emphasis in original).

122. Isabel Wilkerson, "Cleveland Mayoral Race Marked by a Bitter Feud," *NYT*, October 23, 1989.

123. "City Council Won't Be the Same," *CP*, November 2, 1989, 4A.

124. Joe Gilyard, "White Led Resistance to Forbes Ouster," *CP*, November 21, 1981, 1A.

125. Statement of Contributors, Good Government Committee, attached to Carole Hoover to George Forbes, April 6, 1988, folder 1, container 2, Forbes.

126. Roldo Bartimole, "The Forbes Kitty," *Point of View* 18, no. 12 (1986), folder 16, container 2, Forbes.

127. Campaign flyer, "Tuesday, April 5, 1988, Vote No," folder 2, container 3, Forbes.

128. D. Armstrong Grace, "Resident Questions Cleveland's Worth," *CP*, March 19, 1987, 8A.

129. Susan Griffith, "Hough: 25 years after the riots," *CP*, July 4, 1991, 1A.

130. Wilkerson, "Cleveland Mayoral Race Marked by Bitter Feud"; John Funk, "Call Him Mayor White," *Akron Beacon-Journal*, November 8, 1989, A1; Roldo Bartimole, "White Hits Hard," *Point of View* 21, no. 2 (1989).

131. Bill Clinton, DLC Keynote Address, May 6, 1991, accessed May 24, 2022, https://www.c-span.org/video/?17869-1/democratic-leadership-council-keynote-address.

132. David Kurapka, "A New Mayor for the New Cleveland: Michael White," *Mainstream Democrat*, December 1990, 17–18.

133. "Cleveland to Host Democratic Leadership Council's 1991 Convention," *PR Newswire*, September 10, 1990.

134. Thomas Edsall, "Clinton Gains from Eased Race Tensions in Big Cities," *WP*, October 8, 1992, A1.

135. *Poverty Indicators*, vol. 6, 1988, Council for Economic Opportunities in Greater Cleveland, 15, PAL.

136. William Nelson, "Cleveland: The Evolution of Black Political Power," 291.

137. Governor Foust, "A Resounding Victory," letter to the editor, *CP*, October 31, 1985, 9A (emphasis in original).

Epilogue

1. Robert Reich, *Locked in the Cabinet* (New York: Vintage, 1998), 29.

2. Bill Clinton and Al Gore, *Putting People First: How We Can All Change America* (New York: Times Books, 1992).

3. Reich, *Locked in the Cabinet*, 29, 79.

4. See, especially, Mettler, *The Submerged State*; and David M.P. Freund, "Marketing the Free Market: State Intervention and the Politics of Prosperity in Metropolitan America," in Kevin M. Kruse and Thomas J. Sugrue, eds., *The New Suburban History* (Chicago: University of Chicago Press, 2006).

5. Elisabeth Clemens, "Lineages of the Rube Goldberg State: Building and Blurring Public Programs, 1900–1940," in Ian Shapiro, Stephen Skowronek, and Daniel Galvin, eds., *The Art of the State: Rethinking Political Institutions* (New York: NYU Press, 2006).

6. Novak, "The Myth of the Weak American State."

7. Osborne, *Laboratories of Democracy*, 332.

8. William J. Clinton, "Remarks at Vanderbilt University in Nashville, Tennessee," October 27, 1996, APP, https://www.presidency.ucsb.edu/documents/remarks-vanderbilt-university-nashville-tennessee.

9. Ibid.

10. William J. Clinton, "Statement on Signing the Personal Responsibility and Work Opportunity Reconciliation Act of 1996," August 22, 1966, APP, https://www.presidency.ucsb.edu/documents/statement-signing-the-personal-responsibility-and-work-opportunity-reconciliation-act-1996.

11. William J. Clinton, "Remarks Launching the Welfare to Work Partnership, May 20, 1997," *Weekly Compilation of Presidential Documents* 33, no. 21 (1997): 744–47, quote at 746.

12. Aditi Shrivastava and Gina Azito Thompson, "Policy Brief: Cash Assistance Should Reach Millions More Families to Lessen Hardship," Center on Budget and Policy Priorities, updated, February 18, 2022, https://www.cbpp.org/research/family-income-support/cash-assistance-should-reach-millions-more-families-to-lessen.

13. American politics became increasingly nationalized over the 1970s and 1980s, but Republicans' success in the 1994 midterm congressional elections was a watershed in these developments. See Daniel J. Hopkins, *The Increasingly United States: How and Why American Political Behavior Nationalized* (Chicago: University of Chicago Press, 2018), chap. 3, esp. 48–51.

14. "GOPs Win Forsyth and Floyd Posts," *AC*, November 6, 1980, C1.

15. "Recall Petitions Circulated in Floyd," *AC*, April 11, 1979, 24.

16. "Library: Community Pleased with Results," *RNT*, December 19, 1988, 1.

17. "The Day Democracy Died in Floyd County," *RNT*, August 8, 1988, 9.

18. "Remember the Library?," *RNT*, August 4, 1988, 10A.

19. Knowles advertisement, *RNT*, October 28, 1990, 6A.

20. Karin Ronnow, "Tumult, Controversy Enliven Election Year," *RNT*, December 30, 1990, 7A.

21. John M. Willis, "Knowles Known for Strong Stands," *RNT*, May 14, 1992, 1.

22. William Broad, "Clinton to Promote High Technology with Gore in Charge," *NYT*, November 10, 1992, C1.

23. Block, "Swimming Against the Current," 185.

24. Michael Schrage, "Look for the New Majority in Congress to Shake Up High-Tech Partnerships," *WP*, November 11, 1994, C3.

25. Edmund Andrews, "Outlook 1995," *NYT*, January 3, 1995, 19.

26. William J. Clinton, "Remarks at the Technology Reinvestment Project Conference," April 12, 1993, APP, https://presidency.ucsb.edu/node/219663.

27. "Do Not Adjust Your Set," *The Economist*, February 27, 1993, 65–66.

28. For a similar sociological argument, see Josh Pacewicz, *Partisans and Partners: The Politics of the Post-Keynesian Society* (Chicago: University of Chicago Press, 2016).

29. Thomas Gerdel, "New Faces in the Board Rooms," *PD*, July 8, 1986, 1E.

30. Michael Zawacki, "Who's In Charge Here?," *Inside Business*, April 2001.

31. Ibid.

32. Jay Miller, "Region Has Leadership 'Vacuum,'" *CCB*, June 3, 2018.

33. Allen Myerson, "The Currents of Power," *GT*, February 1987.

34. Chris Marr, "Bank Bids Farewell to Founder," *RNT*, January 26, 2007; "Prime Bank Officers Bring Wealth of Experience to Gwinnett County," *AJC*, January 27, 1991, P-5.

35. FDIC Community Banking Study, December 2012, chap. 2, https://www.fdic.gov/regulations/resources/cbi/report/cbsi-2.pdf.

36. John A. Bolt, "Rich's Chain Key Part of Federated's Operations," AP News, February 18, 1988, https://apnews.com/article/f1b98e3157eef3bc944fe21a19fda03b; and Kruse, *White Flight*, 185–92.

37. Myerson, "The Currents of Power," *GT*, February 1987.

38. "The End of an Era for Public Works," *GT*, August 1989.

39. Maria Saporta and Urvaksh Karkaria, "Georgia Research Alliance Facing Crippling Cuts," January 28, 2011, Saporta Report (February 1, 2011, blog), https://saportareport.com/georgia-research-alliance-facing-crippling-cuts/sections/abcarticles/maria_saporta/.

40. Kurt Jacobus, "10 Years Later: GRA Venture Fund," Georgia Research Alliance, https://gra.org/stories/1031/.

41. "Corporate Inverter Steris Blindsided by Brexit," Cantillon, *Irish Times*, November 13, 2018, https://www.irishtimes.com/business/health-pharma/corporate-inverter-steris-blindsided-by-brexit-1.3696692.

42. "Cleveland Clinic Injects $17.8 Billion into Ohio's Economy," September 18, 2018, https://newsroom.clevelandclinic.org/2018/09/18/cleveland-clinic-injects-17-8-billion-into-ohios-economy/#:~:text=While%20most%20Cleveland%20Clinic%20operations,income%2C%20property%20and%20business%20taxes.

43. On the empowerment of minority women in the War on Poverty, see Nancy A. Naples, *Grassroots Warriors: Activist Mothering, Community Work, and the War on Poverty* (New York: Routledge, 1998); and, generally, Orleck and Hazirjian, *The War on Poverty*.

44. Marla Edwards, "Blacks: Action a Turning Point," *RNT*, June 28, 1992, 1A.

45. "County Names Black Member," *RNT*, June 28, 1992, 1A, 2A.

46. "Reversal of Fortune," *Newsweek*, September 9, 1991.

47. "Forest City Paying $10.3 Million to Close Out $15 Million in City Loans," *PD*, May 25, 2011.

48. "Galleria Mall Is Giant Greenhouse," *PD*, February 27, 2010.

49. Selznick, *TVA and the Grass Roots*, 264.

INDEX

ACIR (Advisory Commission on Intergovernmental Relations), 171–72, 257–58
Activator, The (newsletter), 200
Adams, William, II, 220–21
administrative enfranchisement: administrative disfranchisement, 17; African Americans call for, 9, 22, 58, 119, 135, 145, 328; battles over meaning of, 151; Community Action Program in expansion of, 154; drive for minority, 83; in Floyd County, Georgia, 241; Hatcher and Jordan on, 259; marginalized communities' movements for, 19; New Democrats and, 269; racial boundaries to, 116; simulacra of, 21; Turner on, 139; War on Poverty and African American, 4–5
administrative state: decentralized, 8, 9, 26, 152, 328; McCarthyism purges leftists from, 347n7; Republican opposition to, 336; supply-side state and, 349n23
Advanced Technology Program, 336
Advisory Commission on Intergovernmental Relations (ACIR), 171–72, 257–58
AFDC (Aid to Families with Dependent Children): entrepreneurialism and, 292; growth in, 270–71; as lightning-rod issue, 270; New Democrats on, 267; Reagan and, 269, 271, 272, 274–76, 308; Temporary Assistance to Needy Families replaces, 332, 333
affordable housing: activists call for federal support for, 1; business elites see as their task, 148; in Cleveland, 82, 162, 232, *317*, 317–18, 325, 340; congressional hearings on, 117; economic and moral arguments for, 80; Evans on FHA backing for, 129; FHA mortgage insurance for incentivizing, 118; FHA procedures undermine, 131, 132, 133; Housing and Urban Development Act of 1968 on, 178; multiple actors in programs for, 15–16; private development of, 12, 66, 117, 136; property taxes redistributed for, 140; as public good, 136; rental projects on renewal sites abandoned, 134; slum clearance and market's failure to deliver, 124; supply-side sensibilities capture development of, 137; for war workers, 66; in white neighborhoods, 178
African American Clevelanders: anger of, 20, 145, 164, 185, 197; blamed for effects of urban renewal, 140, 144; Buckeye Boys terrorize, 164; Cleveland housing projects criticized by, 134–36; desegregation actions by, 121–22; disinvestment and, 299; downtown seen as black area, 228; in early twentieth century, 63–64; emigrate from the South, 58; employment opportunities for, 65; Erieview project and, 142, 143; Forbes and, 320–21, 324–25; at Garden Valley groundbreaking, 131; housing for, 63, 66; leaders amenable to elite development priories, 299; middle-class leaders of, 157; on New Deal works programs, 9; political power increasing among, 314–15; poverty among, 327; racial inequalities in urban renewal, 138–39, 142–44; racism faced by, 64–65; riots of 1966, 145, 325; segregation of, 18, 64, 70, 82, 121, 122, 138; slum clearance of neighborhoods of, 69–70, 88, 125, 142; Stokes and, 146–47, 162, 163, 327–28; "Target City Cleveland" program and, 146; unemployment among, 63; voting declines among, 327–28; wartime housing shortage for, 82. See also *Call and Post* (newspaper); *and black Clevelanders by name*

416   Index

African American Romans: administrative power sought by, 195–96; Black Coordinating Committee of, 196; Burrell elected to county commission, 340–41; on Community Action Committee, 186; displacement of, 195; Five Points neighborhood of, 32, 192–94; Jim Crow experienced by, 32–33; middle-class, 32; sit-in of March 1963, 185; slum clearance in neighborhoods of, 45, 192–94; protest by, 185, 196; whites on demonstrations by, 198; on white stereotyping of, 196–97

African Americans: administrative enfranchisement sought by, 9, 22, 58, 119, 135, 145, 328; alienation from liberal state, 139; in Alma, Georgia, Model Cities program, 188–89; ARA exclusion of, 109–10; blamed for effects of urban renewal, 140, 144; businesspersons claim to represent, 99; capitalism of, 206, 278; on Carter's Commission on the Future of the South, 249–50; in Carter's West Central Georgia APDC, 182; on democratizing American state, 116; disparities in school improvements for, 46; displacement of, 16, 45, 53, 55, 69, 82, 83, 119, 125, 129, 184, 191, 195; elites stifle democratic participation of, 19; family formation among, 290; FHA discrimination against, 18, 118; in Floyd County, Georgia, 29, 32; in Georgia, 28, 33, 195, 206–8; on Georgia APDC boards, 114; homeowners, 143, 172, 175, 232; housing conditions of, 66, 118, 122, 124; insurgencies of late 1960s, 208; jobs created by Model Cities not available to, 190; middle class, 32, 83, 157; migration to northern cities, 82, 121; minimum wage and, 40; Myrdal on, 124; National Negro Business League, 64; "the Negro problem," 124; New Deal as watershed moment for, 10–11; persistent disenfranchisement in "post"-civil rights era, 195; political power for, 152, 164, 213, 314–15; poverty among, 28, 108, 287; Reagan on enterprise zones and, 310; in Rome, Georgia, 32–33, 45, 185, 186, 192–97; seek federal job guarantees, 241; "something must be done about," 284; as special interest, 257; supply-side liberalism and, 8–9, 22, 119; supply-side state builders' relationships with, 129; unemployment among, 63, 253, 287; urban renewal's violence to, 117, 169; War on Poverty and, 4–5, 19; waxing and waning of enfranchisement of, 16–17. *See also* African American Clevelanders; African American Romans; civil rights movement; Jim Crow; segregation

Agnew, Spiro, 167

Agricultural and Industrial Development Board (AIDB), 52–53

Aid to Families with Dependent Children. *See* AFDC (Aid to Families with Dependent Children)

Alexander, Joseph H., 71–74

Alinsky, Saul, 231, 233

Alioto, Joseph, 220

Allegheny Conference, 120

Allen, Ivan, 12, 227

Allen, Walter, 32–33

Alma (Georgia), 187–90

American Enterprise Institute, 309

American Political Ideals (Merriam), 76

Americans for Democratic Action (ADA), 256

"American Working Wage," 293

Americus (Georgia), 187, 202

anticommunism, 4, 10, 15, 165, 330, 347n7

antipoverty programs: barriers to poor peoples' access to, 171; battles over control of, 151; business elites and, 181, 221; business involvement in, 160, 175; Carter's state government reorganization and, 206, 207; chambers of commerce commandeer, 223; citizen participation in subsidies for, 4; coalition for, 242, 252, 271; Coosa Valley Area Planning and Development Association and, 114; critics on loosely regulated funding of, 174; democratizing administration of, 213; Greater Cleveland Growth Association seeks to draw funds from, 228; infrastructural conceptions of, 186; Perk seeks to divert funding from, 167; in phases of urban policy, 307; Reagan policies and, 266, 274; in rural South, 189, 190; supply-side state building and, 18, 91; two approaches to, 155; Watson and Georgia's, 257; white Georgians on, 198. *See also* War on Poverty; *and programs by name*

APDC. *See* Area Planning and Development Commissions (APDC)

Appalachia: discourse of progress regarding, 124; poverty in, 91, 107, 111, 112; President's Appalachian Regional Commission, 110. *See also* Appalachian Regional Commission (ARC)

Appalachian Regional Commission (ARC): ARA contrasted with, 112; for binding fraying political alliances, 189; Carter on, 251; Coosa Valley APDC and, 111, *111*; disseminating model of, 193; Georgia projects of, 113; market-making potential of, 6; as prototype for Local Development Districts, 111–12; Reagan considers cutting, 307; reindustrialization efforts of, 193; Southern Technology Council funding by, 289; on transportation and poverty, 112

ARA. *See* Area Redevelopment Administration (ARA)

ARC. *See* Appalachian Regional Commission (ARC)

Area Planning and Development Commissions (APDC): African Americans on, 114; Carter and, 184, 205, 251; Cleveland's commission of neighborhoods compared with, 306; Economic Opportunity Authorities matched to, 206; every Georgia county in, 103; expanding priorities of, 246; expansion of model, 114; as Georgia Local Development Districts, 112; Georgia Mountains APDC, 187; Industry and Trade agency tied to, 207; Keyserling and, 254; Lower Chattahoochee Valley APDC, 187; "maximum feasible participation" and, 187–88; Middle Georgia APDC, 272; outsized portions of federal aid secured by, 113; partnerships with Georgia Tech, 247, 281; proliferation of, 243; revenue sharing and, 245; Rural Development Act of 1972 and, 245; rural voters' anger at, 246; Slash Pine APDC, 189; state government reorganization and, 246. *See also* Coosa Valley Area Planning and Development Commission (CVAPDC); West Central Georgia Area Planning and Development Commission (WCGAPDC)

Area Redevelopment Administration (ARA): African Americans excluded by, 109–10; community participation in, 109; difficulties of, 108–9; local elites administer programs of, 109; 110; localism of, 108; range of actors in, 15–16; reindustrialization efforts of, 193

Arkansas: illiteracy in, 288; industrial development bonds in, 313; Little Rock, 47; Pine Bluff, 289–90; poverty in, 289

Arkansas Development Finance Authority, 283

Arkansas Industrial Development Corporation, 283

Arkansas Science and Technology Authority, 283

Arnall, Ellis, 51–53, 93

Arnett, Joyce, 145

Askew, Reubin, 197, 251

Associated Charities, 61, 62, 63, 70

Atlanta: Bell bomber plant near, 93; black families displaced in, 195; business people of, 12; federal-local "growth coalition" in, 16; Forward Atlanta partnership, 227; gentrification in, 179; Georgia Power favors, 36; Georgia Tech's Engineering Experiment Station in, 95; Midtown revitalization, 250; poverty in, 287; Rich's empire in, 339; slum clearance and urban renewal project, 45

Atlanta Constitution (newspaper), 240, 245, 275

Atlanta Daily World (newspaper), 185, 250, 251

Atwater, W. T., 32

Augusta (Georgia), 6, 45, 92

austerity: administrative governance in times of, 243; Busbee and Moynihan on, 263; in city budgets of 1970s, 218; Humphrey-Hawkins bill and, 255; inducing residents' compliance with, 304, 306; neighborhood groups affected by, 233; under Reagan, 7, 13, 239, 270, 298, 305, 307, 313–14, 321; Reich on Clinton's, 329, 337; state withdrawal authorized by, 300

Babbitt, Bruce, 283
Bacon County (Georgia), 187, 189
Bacon County Development Corporation, 188
Baltimore Afro-American (newspaper), 206
banking, consolidation in, 338–39
Barron, Alfred Lee, 45, 192
Bartimole, Roldo, 228, 315
Barton, R. D., Jr., 100

Batt, William, 110, 113
Beam, Walter, 84
Beame, Abraham, 214
Beer, Samuel, 241
Bentsen, Lloyd, 329
Biden, Joseph, 270
Biggers, George C., 46
Birch, David, 285
black Americans. *See* African Americans
blighted areas: CDBGs for, 175; in Cleveland, 66, 67, 79–80, 141; Coosa Valley APDC in war on, 100; FHA mortgage insurance denied to, 129; framing development agendas in terms of, 184; homes in as poorly inspected, 178; Housing Act of 1949 on, 124; New Dealers on clearing, 80; as "pathology," 191–93; real estate taxation and redevelopment of, 123; redlining keeps capital out of, 128; in Rome, Georgia, 192, 195; rural, 189; urban renewal for redeveloping, 117; in "workable program" reports, 193
block grants: Carter on, 174, 252, 265; categorical grants versus, 257–58, 265, 274; Cleveland Block Grant Workshops, 306, 319; Clinton on, 333; Forbes and, 315; Heller on, 173; Housing and Community Development Act of 1974 on, 153; HUD-U.S. Chamber of Commerce videos on, 175; for Model Cities, 169, 190; Reagan on, 275; targeting of, 262; in Temporary Assistance to Needy Families, 332. *See also* Community Development Block Grants (CDBGs)
Bohn, Ernest: on Advisory Committee on Housing Policies and Programs, 126; African American leaders meet with, 83; as Cleveland Municipal Housing Authority director, 82, 125; on costs of slum property, 122, 126; public housing supported by, 79–81, 122; on Regional Association of Cleveland, 79; on regionalism, 80; on rehousing displaced residents, 125
Bond, Julian, 251
bonds, municipal. *See* municipal bonds
Boone, Richard, 156
bootstrap initiatives, 341
Boston, 80, 179, 322
Bradley, Bill, 285
Brinkley, Alan, 15

Brook Park (Ohio), 121, 128
Brooks, Robert, 32
Brown, H. Rap, 146
Brown, Jerry, 270
Brown, Robert M., III, 283
Brown v. Board of Education (1954), 99, 201, 247
Buckeye-Woodland Community Congress (BWCC), 177–80, 233
Bumpers, Dale, 197
Burke, Thomas, 86
Burrell, Samuel, Jr., 340–41
Burtner, Fred, 222
Busbee, George: on changes in New Federalism allocation formulas, 262; debate with Moynihan, 263, 264; Georgia Tech Advanced Technology Development Center and, 281–82; memo for Carter of January 1979, 264–66; on Reagan spending cuts, 275; on sectional competition over federal aid, 261
Bush, George H. W., 14, 326
business: alcohol and cigarette taxes redistribute resources to, 326; anger at domination of development by, 339; antigovernment politics of, 223–24; in antipoverty programs, 160, 175; business-oriented infrastructure, 91; capital as inducement sought from government by, 280; chambers of commerce create minority business development initiatives, 223; climate, 92, 113; Clinton redirects subsidies to, 333; Community Action Programs target, 157; conservatives, 12; crisis of legitimacy of, 224; emerging class of businessperson with political clout, 99; enterprise zones criticized by, 311; federal spending is big for, 75; "good government" politics and, 53, 93; Johnson consults businessmen, 161–62; local government influenced by, 225, 229, 298; as model for government reform, 216; moderates in the South, 97, 110, 248; at National Conference on Balanced Growth and Economic Development of 1978, 260; National Negro Business League, 64; New Deal works programs as good for, 25–55; as no longer local, 337; planning commissions encourage rational development of, 98; Powell on American system

of government and, 215, 224–25; pro-business politics in the South, 82; progressives, 197; shareholder value movement, 277, 337–38; as under siege in 1970s, 213; as special interest, 257; supply-side policies desired by, 311–12; "technical assistance" programs for, 102; UDAGs as partnerships between government and, 308; U.S. Chamber of Commerce on Roosevelt's attacks on big, 50; War on Poverty seen as war on, 157, *158*. *See also* business associations; business elites; business producerism; chambers of commerce; free enterprise; private investment; private sector

business associations: broader range of constituencies sought by, 223; on business's alleged social responsibility, 223; Cleveland elite in, 18, 58; on federal spending, 50; federal subsidies sought by, 221; on industrial policy, 279; national, 18, 50, 86, 113, 221, 233; New Deal programs benefit, 73; Nixon administration works with, 175; on postwar fiscal restraint, 86; in Rome, Georgia, 20; in Urban Land Institute, 123; in urban planning, 17; War on Poverty funds sought to disrupt suburban elite remote control of city politics, 19. *See also* chambers of commerce

Business Council of Georgia, 282

business cycle, 41, 89, 90

Businessmen's Interracial Committee on Community Affairs, 144

business producerism: of business elites, 49, 148; in Cleveland, 61, 85, 226, 231, 237; Clinton and, 21, 333; commandeering antipoverty programs and, 223; common sense associated with, 239; community uplift in rhetoric of, 154; defined, 30; federal investments ratify and reinforce, 88; on fiscal realities, 239; Forbes as advocate of, 299; harder-edged version of, 209, 216; local basis of, 235; national versus local versions of, 50; neoliberalism and, 238; Nixon and, 174; political-cultural veneration of, 328; Powell and language of, 225; public resource extraction authorized by, 340; of Reavis, 144; regional boosters in emergence of, 28; social responsibility claimed by, 14; takes off in 1970s, 209, 215–16, 220–25; of Wall Street, 330; war preparedness strengthens, 49

BWCC (Buckeye-Woodland Community Congress), 177–80, 233

Byrd, Harry, 234

CAAs (Community Action Agencies), 156–57, 161

CAC (Community Action Council), 182, 187, 194

Califano, Joseph, 161

California: AFDC growth in, 271; Los Angeles, 134, 286; San Francisco, 157, 179, 219, 220; Santa Clara, 219; Santa Paula, 222; tax revolts in, 242

Call and Post (newspaper): on black representation in urban renewal, 135; on Economic Opportunities Council, 151; on Erieview project, 143; on Forbes, 315; Grace's letter to, 325; on Lewis, 324; on race prejudice in Cleveland, 64; on slum clearance and black families, 69, 143, 144; Walker as editor of, 83, 143; White criticized by, 146

Campaign for Community-Based Economic Development, 305

CAP. *See* Community Action Program (CAP)

capital: abundance of, 56; big cities raise for innovative projects, 59; black, 46; bonded debt as, 217; cities seek alternative sources of, 218; Cleveland's demand for, 58–59; Community Development Block Grants for underwriting, 250; competition over, 30; decoupling from visions of progress, 342; external, 38, 39, 235, 302, 305; federal aid enhances white, 46; finance, 235, 239; flight, 122, 165, 289; formation, 44, 105, 277, 279, 280, 282; human, 291, 329; as inducement business seeks from government, 280; infrastructure spending seen as stimulating self-sustaining, 28; jump starting, 68, 81; liquidity, 68, 78; local, 98, 217; local government requirements met by borrowing, 219; markets, 56, 58, 277; matching, 37; New Deal programs benefit, 73; patient, 278, 280; private, 28, 31, 44, 57, 67, 77, 81, 123, 128, 217, 280–82; public, 13, 44, 268, 270, 280, 281; recruitment, 71,

capital (*continued*)
207, 297, 298; redlining keeps it out of blighted areas, 128; Roosevelt on agglomerations of, 25; scarcity of, 17, 19, 27, 31, 56, 58, 77, 229, 342; tax cuts for freeing, 105, 106; undercapitalization in African American economy, 33; venture, 13, 163, 268, 270, 277, 280–82, 284, 297, 303, 309, 319, 320

capitalism: black, 206, 278; community, 305; corporate, 337; democratic, 57, 108, 115, 294, 330; finance, 239, 270, 329, 337; Hansen on, 41, 42, 78; midcentury liberal consensus on, 330, 331, 342; "moral," 278; New Democrats' faith in, 269; poverty seen as fluke of managed, 90; Progressives on democracy and, 25; as root cause of social problems, 267

CARIA (Coosa-Alabama River Improvement Association), 47–50, 101

Carmichael, James V., 93–94, 97

Carter, Billy, 202, 208

Carter, Jimmy: antigovernment governance of, 203–5; APDCs and, 184, 205, 251; on block grants, 174, 252, 265; Busbee's memo of January 1979, 264–66; business elites and, 204–5, 207, 238; as businessman-turned-politician, 205, 252; Commission on the Future of the South of, 249–50; conservatism of, 201, 252; at Coosa Valley APDC meeting, 103; crisis of fiscal federalism and, 241–42; at Democratic Convention of 1972, 251; as Democratic Governors Campaign Committee chair, 251; on deregulation, 174, 175; on economic planning, 200, 255, 272; election as governor, 184, 197, 202; failure to balance competing demands, 242; on federalism, 201, 203, 252, 256–59, 266; on federal spending, 252, 264, 265; "Goals for Georgia" campaign of, 203–4; gubernatorial campaign of 1966, 184, 197–98, 200, 201; gubernatorial campaign of 1970, 201–2; on Humphrey-Hawkins bill, 255; inflation and, 207, 250, 252, 256, 264; interest groups and, 264, 265; Kennedy's primary challenge to, 279; localism of, 184, 200–201, 203, 252, 255; majoritarianism of, 172, 200, 201, 203; minorities and, 184, 252, 265; national acclaim for, 208; National Conference on Balanced Growth and Economic Development of 1978, 259; New Federalism compared with, 184, 203, 206, 252; Nunn compared with, 272; populism of, 200, 203, 204; on "post-racial" politics, 185, 197, 202, 208, 251; public-private partnerships and, 103, 184, 207; on racial discrimination, 202; racism attributed to, 206; recession under, 207, 242, 252; regional planning and, 200, 255, 257–58; on revenue sharing and block grants, 174; on segregation academies, 201–2, 208; on Southern Growth Policies Board, 241, 249, 252; special interests and, 204, *204,* 257; state government desegregated by, 114; state government reorganized by, 205–7, 246, 257, 272, 301; as supply-side state builder, 182; technocratic background of, 200, 258; UDAGs of, 6, 298, 307, 308; Volcker appointed by, 277; West Central Georgia APDC of, 103, 111, 182–83, *183,* 186, 187, 240, 250; white anger politicized by, 201

Cash, W. J., 39

CBBB (Citizens to Bring Broadway Back), 232–33, 306–7

CDBGs. *See* Community Development Block Grants (CDBGs)

CDF. *See* Cleveland Development Foundation (CDF)

Celebrezze, Anthony, 122, 131, 132, 134, 141, 155

Chamber of Commerce Newsletter, 222, 223, 225

chambers of commerce: Agnew partners with, 175; on ARA, 109; ARC works with local, 113; as capital-starved, 27; commercial versions of community development sought from, 2; as drivers of municipal debt, 59; at Georgia's Agricultural and Industrial Development Board meetings, 52; Georgia Tech and, 92, 95; infrastructure development supported by, 30; interregional networks of, 27; on Job Corps, 160; in Kentucky regional development commission, 108; local chamber types, 11–12; members on Coosa Valley APDC, 100; New Deal works programs administered by, 3; in Progressive Era reforms, 14; on revenue sharing, 274;

in Rome, Georgia, 26, 29, 32–34, 38, 48, 90, 96, 102, 185, 196; Roosevelt administration reaches out to, 35; Southern Commercial Secretaries Association, 29, 30; on speeding public works, 37; Starr partners with, 95. *See also* Cleveland Chamber of Commerce; U.S. Chamber of Commerce

Chicago: bond bid rejected in, 219; business elites of, 57; City Beautiful planning in, 79; Community Action Program in, 156; credit rating agencies and, 300; Daley, 158, 161, 229; entrepreneurialism in South Shore, 289; labor campaigns in, 65; Merriam and, 76, 78; pollution in, 248; property taxes in, 229; total assessed value decline in 1930s, 66; Water Tower Place, 322

Chicago Defender (newspaper), 55

Chiles, Lawton, 249

Cincotta, Gail, 180, 304

cities: dependence on federal aid, 122–23, 126, 173, 218; as destinations for white-collar work and suburban recreation, 300, 302, 322; federal spending seen as disproportionately going to, 244, 245; homogenization of urban environments, 16; inflation affects budgets of, 126, 172, 214; majority minority, 299, 314; managing urban democracy, 304–7; Merriam on next generation of, 77; migration to, 247; National League of Cities, 158, 220, 312, 321; political autonomy wanes, 123; postwar urbanization in the South, 97; poverty in, 175, 249, 307; property values in, 122; revolts of 1967, 161; urban reform, 80, 214. *See also* city (municipal) government; city planning; municipal debt; municipal bonds; urban development; urban policy; urban renewal; *and cities by name*

citizen participation. *See* community (citizen) participation

Citizens for Better Housing, 143

Citizens Participation Association (CPA), 164, 168

Citizens to Bring Broadway Back (CBBB), 232–33, 306–7

city (municipal) government: dispersion of administrative authority to, 8; federal aid directly to, 258; federal-municipal policy relationships, 15; fiscal problems of, 122–23, 240; Housing Act of 1954 and, 16; inflation and, 126, 172, 214, 217, 218, 225; in liberal market-shaping efforts, 15; in national balance of power, 14; need to streamline service delivery, 225; Progressive Era reforms in, 14; Section 701 planning grants to, 98; as site of decentralized state building, 17; tokenism in, 157, 196; transformation in 1980s, 297; urban triage ethos in, 21

city planning: Cleveland Chamber of Commerce committee on, 61; Cleveland City Planning Commission, 85, 138, 318; Merriam and, 76, 78; new urbanism, 227, 228; NRPB and, 88. *See also* urban planning

civic associations: Community Action Programs target elite, 157; Regional Association of Cleveland as, 79; Roosevelt administration reaches out to, 35; War on Poverty and, 4, 19

"Civic Vision" plan (Cleveland), 318–19, 322

"Civil Disobedience: A Threat to Our Society Under Law" (Leibman), 161

civil rights: bills of 1960s, 139; Businessmen's Interracial Committee on Community Affairs and, 144; Democratic Leadership Council accused of neglecting, 285; elections of 1964 and mobilization for, 110; versus further obligations to African Americans, 208; groups press for democratizing of administration, 213; liberals' formal commitment to, 331; persistent disenfranchisement of African Americans in "post"–civil rights era, 195; rhetoric about attached to public-private partnerships, 88; Rome, Georgia, business leaders' position on, 101; Franklin D. Roosevelt, Jr., on federal aid and, 110; Truman on, 54, 124; U.S. Commission on Civil Rights, 144–45, 151. *See also* civil rights movement

Civil Rights Act, 145, 185, 198

civil rights movement: Americus, Georgia, Community Action Council never consults leaders of, 187; Big Six leaders of, 146, 147; business elites face, 221; Carter on, 251; Cleveland's Economic Opportunities Council excludes leaders

civil rights movement (*continued*)
of, 151; Leibman on tactics of, 160–61; liberal policymakers on local elites and, 109; liberals' gradual acceptance of, 91; local and regional power challenged by, 157; War on Poverty and, 156; sit-in movement, 185; structural reform associated with, 184; urban renewal and increasing momentum of, 191, 194; white liberals influenced by, 124. *See also* CORE (Congress of Racial Equality); NAACP (National Association for the Advancement of Colored People); *and other organizations and leaders by name*

Civil Works Administration (CWA), 26, 36–37, 45

Clark, Kenneth, 157

class: in battles over distribution, 240; class-blind politics, 249; exclusions in liberal state, 11; federal financing for blunting class conflict, 70; fiscal disciple as class discipline, 273; imagining alternatives to inequalities of, 342; interracial, cross-class economic opportunity, 177; OEO seen as fostering class struggle, 158; Republican class warfare, 334; Roosevelt on, 25; whites embrace racial antagonism over loyalty to, 147; working-class militancy in Cleveland, 63. *See also* middle class; white-collar work; working-class whites

Cleveland
 area, 121
 city agencies and government: city council, 314, 316–17; City Planning Commission, 85, 138, 318; Citywide Development Corporation, 309; Economic Growth Commission, 229; Economic Opportunities Council, 151, 157; modernization of governance, 300–301; War Housing Service, 82; Washington lobbyist, 308
 demographics: demographic change, 121, 323; population, 58, 166; working-class whites, 20, 60, 88, 299. *See also* African American Clevelanders; white ethnic Clevelanders
 development and renewal: community development, 163, 175–80, 322–24; fails to pursue structurally interventionist strategies until 1980s, 19; Gladstone renewal site, 143; profits from developing in suburbs, 128; public-private partnerships, 19, 67, 131, 134, 162–64, 296, 297; road to urban renewal, 120–25; slum clearance, 58, 66, 67, 69, 75, 79, 80, 120, 169; urban redevelopment, 75, 165, 215, 227–29; urban renewal, 129, *130*, 132, 135–36, 140–45, 165, 169, 178, 215, 319
 economy: comeback, 297–98, 325–27; corporate headquarters, 237; deindustrialization, 88, 165, 321; manufacturing jobs lost, 121, 166; unemployment, 60, 61, 63, 65–67, 162, 163
 events: Democratic Leadership Council convention, 294–96, 299, 325, 326; eviction riots, 62–63; Glenville shootout of 1968, 163; Great Lakes Exposition of 1936–37, 72, 74, 87; HUD secretary visits, 2; National People's Action caravan, 304–5; riots of 1960s, 145, 304, 305, 325; U.S. Commission on Civil Rights hearings, 144–45; Van Sweringen brothers' insolvency, 56–57, 60
 "Fannie Lewis Law," 340
 federal programs: Block Grant Workshops, 306, 319; CDBGs for, 171, 176–80, 226, 228, 230, 233, 305, 318, 323; Community Action Program in, 157, 158; Model Cities, 168–71; UDAGs for, 308, 322–23, 342; War on Poverty, 19, 164–71; WPA hires white-collar unemployed, 6, 72; WPA projects, 72, 74–75, 79, 82, 87; Younger on, 151
 finance: budget shortfalls in 1950s, 122; commuter tax, 301, 302; credit rating lowered, 234–36; default of 1978, 216, 236, 239, 300, 312; financial crises, 61, 166–67, 215, 228–30, 234–36, 260, 300–302; industrial development bonds, 313; monthly interest payments, 219; municipal bonds, 59, 85, 86, 126, 139, 140, 162, 230, 235, 236, 301–2, 326; municipal debt, 20, 59–61, 82, 84–86, 140, 165, 215, 229, 234, 236, 294, 300, 341; property taxes, 82, 86, 140, 165, 215, 229, 301; property values, 143, 166, 229; share of federal aid declines, 226; tax abatements, 162, 229–32, 242, 298, 304, 319, 321–22, 327, 340, 341; tax-base decline, 302; tax revenues in 1970s, *218*
 housing: affordable, 82, 162, 232, *317*, 317–18, 325, 340; public, 67–70, 79, 80, 125, 132, 136, 167, 315

neighborhoods and districts: Buckeye, 1, 164, 177, 179, 180, 233; Cedar-Central, 82, 125, 143; Downtown, 138, *142,* 228, 297, 318, 319, 322; Fairfax, 320, 321; Flats and Warehouse districts, 323; Glenville, 306, 314, 317, 324–25, 327; Hough, 143, 144, 145, 151, 152, 163, 168, 169, 177, 305, 306, 318, 320, 323, 325, 327; Kingsbury Run, 129; Ohio City, 179; University Circle, 317, 318

planning: "Civic Vision" plan, 318–19, 322; "Dual Hub Corridor" plan, 318, 321, 323; regional planning, 55, 58, 79–80; Stokes's Cleveland: Now! program, 162–64, 166; urban planning, 16, 17, 81, 82, 85, 162, 228

politics and activism: activism of 1970s, 213; byzantine political system, 176; Democratic machine, 146, 299; labor movement, 65; neighborhood groups, 177, 179, 231, 233, 306, 316; political fragmentation, 314

postindustrial policy, 318–19

projects: Erieview, 136, 138, 140–43, *142,* 162, 219, 227, 322, *327*; Galleria, 302, 322, 342; Garden Valley, 129, 131–33, *132,* 135–36; Gateway, 227, 326; Lexington Village, *317,* 317–18, 325, 340, 342; Longwood, 129, 133–36; Outhwaite Homes, 82, 125; Rock and Roll Hall of Fame, 326, *327*; Terminal Tower, 56, 322, *327*; Tower City, 302, 321, 322, 342

social characteristics: blight, 66, 67, 79–80, 141; homogenization of urban environments, 16; poverty, 60, 300, 327; racial tolerance, 58, 63; racism, 64–65; wealth disparity between suburbs and, 167

suburbanization, 80, 88, 121, 122

supply-side state builders, 58, 85, 117, 209, 299, 326

war effort, 83–84

See also Cleveland Chamber of Commerce; Cleveland's business elites; Greater Cleveland Growth Association; *and organizations and individuals by name*

"Cleveland: An Autopsy" (Ehrenreich and Ehrenreich), 235

Cleveland: The Making of a City (Rose), 87

Cleveland Bar Association, 72, 145, 164

Cleveland Catholic Universe Bulletin, 166

Cleveland Chamber of Commerce: business elites in leadership of, 56–57, 121; committees on policy issues, 61; on deficit spending, 87; discriminatory rents investigated by, 64; on doing nothing as prohibitively expensive, 65; as driver of debt, 59, 214; economic development agenda of, 71; on Erieview project, 140; federal subsidies become habit forming for, 70; Greater Cleveland Growth Association and, 220; in Great Lakes Exposition of 1936–37, 72; grievance sessions about Roosevelt, 72–73; on housing and slum clearance, 66–69; Lausche opposes plans of, 84; members administer regional WPA projects, 71–72; members live in suburbs, 138, 140; more debt for renewal advocated by, 139; postwar projects proposed by, 84–85; projects preferred by, 75; remote control over city politics, 58; square pursuit of federal subsidies with commitment to limited government, 72, 130; on unemployment relief, 60–62; urban redevelopment conference of 1952, 125; on white ethnics and riots of 1966, 145; working-class militancy and, 63

Cleveland Citizens Participation Association (CCPA), 176

Cleveland Clinic, 297, 318–21, 340

Cleveland Development Foundation (CDF), 120; Downtown Plan of 1959, 138; in Erieview project, 136, 140, 142; Evans's role in, 117, 120; FHA financing brought to Cleveland by, 121; in Garden Valley project, 131, 132, *132,* 135; housing as focus of, 117; plan for displaced families of, 129; renewal agenda dominated by, 135; residents' perspectives neglected by, 135; seen as model of public-private cooperation, 134; Taft's role in, 147

Cleveland Electric Illuminating (CEI), 84, 227, 230, 236

Cleveland Foundation, 60, 62, 303, 305

Cleveland Homes, Inc., 67, 69

Cleveland Metropolitan Housing Authority (CMHA), 82, 83, 125, 138

Cleveland Municipal Light (Muny), 227, 230, 232, 236

Cleveland: Now! program, 162–64, 166, 232

Cleveland Press (newspaper), 82, 162

Cleveland Roundtable, 303; on "Civic Vision" plan, 318; Cleveland Tomorrow and, 303–4; in commission of neighborhoods, 306–7; downtown development advocated by, 322; on "Dual Hub Corridor" plan, 318; Hough Area Development Corporation leader at, 305; leadership changes in, 337; on postindustrial development plan, 319; race relations committee of, 307; Ratner and, 322; Voinovich on businesspeople and, 321

Cleveland's business elites: African American leaders amenable to development priorities of, 299; on Businessman's Advisory Council, 229; business producerism of, 61, 85, 226, 231, 237; on Chamber of Commerce committees, 61; city government reorganization in image of, 301; on city's precarious budget, 122; city wage tax increase advocated by, 301; civic associations dominated by, 121; in Cleveland Roundtable, 303; in Cleveland's comeback, 297–98; Downtown Cleveland Corporation of, 228; Economic Opportunities Council dominated by, 157; on eviction riots, 63; on Forbes, 316, 324; "free enterprise" commitments of, 73; influence in city politics, 58, 121; Kucinich and, 216, 232–37, 300; on Lausche, 81; as "money changers," 56–57; national scope of, 18, 62; Perk and, 177–78, 226; on riot of 1966, 145; Stokes and, 146, 162–64; as suburbanites, 58, 80, 121, 138, 140, 146, 166, 301; supply-side liberalism and, 4, 5, 284, 311–12, 342; Taft supported for mayor by, 147; Turner on forging new strategies for countering dominance of, 145–46; Voinovich supported by, 237–38; on White, 326. *See also* Cleveland's business elites

Cleveland Tomorrow, 303–4, 318, 319, 337, 338
Cleveland Trust Company, 60, 230, 234–36
Cleveland Urban Renewal Authority, 135
Clinton, Bill: austerity attributed to, 329, 337; at Cleveland Democratic Leadership Council convention, 294, 295, 299, 325; compromises of, 270; Council of State Planning Agencies and, 285; in Daniels' hiring, 283; defeat and then reelection of, 288; deficit cutting by, 329, 337; Democratic Party remade by, 295; on economic growth, 285, 295, 326; on education, 288, 289, 291; ends welfare as we know it, 21, 295, 329; on entrepreneurialism, 283, 288–90, 295, 296; Good Faith Fund of, 290; on individual responsibility, 325–26; National Partnership for Reinventing Government, 14; on national postindustrial development policy, 334–36; as New Democrat, 20, 270; in new generation of Democrats, 249; nomination for president, 295; Personal Responsibility and Work Opportunity Reconciliation Act of 1996 and, 332; on public-private partnerships, 21, 288, 333; *Putting People First,* 329; as Southern Growth Policies Board head, 288; as supply-side liberal, 6, 289; Wall Street financiers and, 284; on welfare as disempowering women, 290; welfare depoliticized by, 332–33; Yunus and, 289–90
Clinton, Hillary, 289–90
Cloward, Richard, 155
code enforcement, 137, 323
Cold War: anticommunism, 4, 10, 15, 330; ARA in context of, 108; Cold War liberals, 124, 249, 282, 330, 331; fighting poverty in context of, 154–55; Kennedy on TVA and, 89; modernization during, 7, 105, 113; publicly funded economic planning gains legitimacy during, 100; technological advances during, 330
Cole, Albert M., 126
Colean, Miles, 118, 133
Collier, Charles, 92
Combs, Bert, 108
Commission on the Future of the South, 249–50
Commons, John R., 41
Community Action Agencies (CAAs), 156–57, 161
Community Action Council (CAC), 182, 187, 194
Community Action Program (CAP): administrative enfranchisement and, 154; black activists' understanding of, 152; businesses and civic associations targeted by, 157; Carter's

West Central Georgia APDC and, 182; "city hall" amendments to, 161; city-hall-sponsored, 158; in Cleveland, 157; Coosa Valley APDC conference on comprehensive planning within, 186–87; Eastern Hough Organized for Action and, 151; Johnson and, 158–60, 167; Leibman and, 161; local administrative controls over, 159; "maximum feasible participation" principle in, 152, 153, 156; New Federalism brings to an end, 151; Osborne on, 269; the poor organized by, 157; as primary initiative of War on Poverty, 154; storefront service centers of, 156

community development: anger at business domination of, 339; ARA act on community participation in, 109; Carter and advocates of, 252; in Cleveland, 163, 180, 322–24; Coosa Valley APDC in, 100; critics on loosely regulated funding of, 174; Ford administration on, 2, 180; funding for business and gentrifying housing markets as, 154, 180; Greater Cleveland Growth Association seeks to draw funds from, 228; Hough Area Development Corporation in, 163; Legal Services Community Development Task Force in, 258–59; Lewis on language and reality of, 171; New Federalism and elite control of, 5; Nixon pays lip service to, 153; participatory, 147; poor women as engines of, 290; Reagan policies and, 266; Republicans on, 174; Rural Development Act of 1972 on, 245; self-help, 152; Starr in, 95; subsidies underwriting elite developments, 1; subsidies used to fund growth agenda, 20; Turner on democratizing, 22; War on Poverty and, 4, 116; women in, 340

Community Development Block Grants (CDBGs): in Arkansas, 283; to central cities, 226; changes in New Federalism allocation formulas and, 262; for Cleveland, 171, 176–80, 226, 228, 230, 233, 305, 318, 323; community participation in, 178, 206; in Georgia, 206; for Hough Area Development Corporation, 305; in Housing and Community Development Act of 1974, 173; Legal Services Community Development Task Force

on, 258; Lewis on, 176; local battles over use of, 20; Perk and, 176–78, 323; Reagan and, 274, 307–8, 323; reauthorization in 1977, 261; as reluctant to prescribe federal solutions, 250; Rural Development Act of 1972 compared with, 245; social-targeting regulation proposed for, 262; three areas for, 174–75; War on Poverty and urban renewal mandates rolled into, 19

community development corporations (CDCs), 305

community (citizen) participation: activists call for, 258; in ARA, 109; in Carter's West Central Georgia APDC, 182; in CDBG process, 178, 206; in Cleveland Roundtable, 303; Greater Cleveland Growth Association and, 228; Hatcher and Jordan on, 259; managed, 183, 299, 304–7, 319, 328; in Model Cities, 167; Perk on, 168, 169; preemptive inclusion by elites, 303; rhetorical commitment to, 181; small-city and rural elites seek strategies for minimizing, 188, 189; southern boosters' model of, 181. *See also* "maximum feasible participation" principle

"Comparative Advantage of the Inner City, The" (Porter), 290

Comprehensive Employment and Training Act, 308

Conable, Barber, 256

Congress of Racial Equality. *See* CORE (Congress of Racial Equality)

conservatism: backlash of, 140; business conservatives, 12; of Carter, 201, 252; of FHA, 18, 119, 131, 141; fiscal, 71, 166, 255; homeowner, 166; of Lausche, 81; liberal price protection opposed by, 85; liberals empower, 342; low-tax high-service, 167; Merriam rejects, 76; new federal rights initiatives opposed by, 83; Nixon's public-private partnerships and, 153; of Nunn, 272; "post-racial" politics in, 209; postwar consensus on cultural, 92; racial, 131, 272; resurgence of, 10, 15, 334; seen as anti-state, 13; "silent majority" claimed by, 242; southern super-, 110; on state intervention in housing, 118–19; Sunbelt, 91; on tax cuts, 106; UDAGs and, 309

consultants, 302–3
Contract with America, 334, 335
Conway, Jack, 156
Coosa-Alabama River Improvement Association (CARIA), 47–50, 101
Coosa Valley Area Planning and Development Commission (CVAPDC), 98–103; ARC and, 111, *111*; child development programs of, 246; conference on comprehensive planning, 186–87; disseminating model of, 193; establishment of, 96; as "genesis of everything," 281; Goldwater on, 115; as international showpiece, 114; Kennedy administration takes as model, 108; members as mayors or country commissioners, 246; National Resources Planning Board and, 97, 336; on OEO programs and development, 186; partnership with Georgia Tech, 113, 247, 336; poverty alleviation and enfranchising the marginalized not priorities of, 114; Rigas as chairwoman of, 334; rural taxpayer anger at, 243, 244; Section 701 grants for, 97–99, 109; Talmadge on, 116; urban renewal funds secured for Rome, Georgia, 191, 192
CORE (Congress of Racial Equality): Businessmen's Interracial Committee on Community Affairs and, 144; Community Action Programs monitored by, 158; Euclid Beach Park desegregation effort of, 121–22; Ford Foundation grant to, 146, 147, 152, 155; forges new strategies for developing political power, 145–46; Longwood ceremony picketed by, 134; protests at school construction sites, 138–39; rent strikes organized by, 143; structural critiques of liberalism and machine politics, 147; Turner on white activists in, 139; works with Garden Valley residents, 136
Cosgrove, William, 166
Council of State Planning Agencies (CSPA), 285
Cowan, Charles, 99
Cox, Archibald, 103
CPA (Citizens Participation Association), 164, 168
credit-rating agencies: Cleveland's rating downgraded, 234–35; fiscal fetters imposed by, 300, 329–30; liberals empower, 342; as new type of leverage for businesspeople, 216, 218, 239, 302

Cushman, Jim, 250
Cuyahoga County (Ohio): Nationalities Movement of Cuyahoga County, 165; new levy for welfare spending proposed, 62; Relief Administration, 63; Van Sweringen brothers owe back taxes to, 60; wartime production in, 84; WPA projects in, 74. *See also* Cleveland
CVAPDC. *See* Coosa Valley Area Planning and Development Commission (CVAPDC)
CWA (Civil Works Administration), 26, 36–37, 45

Daley, Richard J., 158, 161
Dallas, 179, 247
Daniels, Belden Hull, 280, 281, 283
Davis, Hugh, 186
Davis, James C., 226–27; campaign for business elite to recover control over development, 181; Downtown Cleveland Corporation and, 228; Forbes and, 316; Greater Cleveland Forward budget of, 227; law firm of, 226, 230, 231; as Mayor's Economic Coordinating Commission chair, 229; on minority participation, 303; Perk and, 227, 229; on race war, 164; on white ethnics, 145, 226
Deal, Nathan, 339
debt: Great Depression made worse by debt-fueled development of 1920s, 57; public, 77, 85; U.S. Chamber of Commerce on national, 50. *See also* municipal debt
decentralism: Carter on, 201, 252; in Carter's West Central Georgia APDC, 182; Clinton offers, 21; decentralized administrative state, 8, 9, 26, 152, 328; drive for minority administrative inclusion and, 83; entrepreneurialism and, 278; of Georgia Tech's Industrial Development Board, 102; Heller on German federalism and, 105; of industry and population, 166; Jim Crow associated with, 58, 182–83; liberals adopt, 15; local chamber types and, 11; local elites' decentralized administrative partnerships with Kennedy administration, 91; Magaziner and Reich on, 279; Merriam on, 57, 77, 78; Model Cities as means of, 223; New Deal and, 7, 26, 35, 43, 45, 241, 268; in public-private development commissions,

108; Franklin D. Roosevelt, Jr., on, 110; Rural Development Act of 1972 and, 245; Selznick on dilemma of, 22; in supply-side liberalism, 5, 8, 101, 139, 140, 331; urban governance as site of decentralized state building, 17; U.S. Chamber of Commerce on, 255

deficit spending: Clinton and, 329, 337; Hansen on, 77, 78; Kennedy and, 103, 106; Keynesianism on, 71, 78; New Deal, 86; U.S. Chamber of Commerce on, 50

deindustrialization: in Cleveland, 88, 165, 321; distributional battles affected by, 241; Douglas's depressed areas bill on, 104, 105; industrial development bonds and, 313; inflation of 1960s and 1970s and, 217; Kennedy on, 107; minorities' increasing political power in context of, 314; need for social services due to, 220; New Democrat initiatives in context of, 21; northern elites and, 55, 88; in rural South, 189; southern governors on, 247

Delano, Frederic, 50–51, 76

democracy: African Americans seek to democratize American state, 116; African Americans urged to work within hierarchies and systems of, 152; civil rights groups press for democratization, 213; Cleveland's Ukrainian Cultural Garden dedicated to, 74; democratic capitalism, 57, 108, 115, 294, 330; democratic participation, 17, 19, 228, 270, 299, 300; democratic pluralism, 152, 156; diminishing democratic contestation, 328; disengagement from, 300; economic, 155, 231–32; expands in Georgia, 338; Floyd County, Georgia, commissioners undermine, 335; Hansen on, 78; insulating the state from democratic claims, 239; liberal, 155; liberalism and government's undemocratic practices, 342; local, 25, 152, 215, 299; making it meaningful, 342; managing urban, 304–7; mass, 269; minority interests and, 225; neoliberal, 20, 183; New Dealers fail to address structure of, 44; New Democrats on, 270, 291, 294; Nixon on revenue sharing and, 172; participatory, 155; Progressive idealized image of local, 25–26; racially restricted, 101; Republicans on liberal threats to, 334; seen as overloaded by interest groups, 240, 241; strategy of circumvention and, 243; structural inequalities in, 155; supply-side New Dealers emphasize economic development over, 28; Wright on perfect, 54. *See also* democratic accountability

democratic accountability: of APDCs, 246; battles over, 17; in Cleveland, 141, 165; critiques of taxes and spending and, 243; marketized discourse narrows views of, 269; neoliberalism hollows out, 153; New Democrats and, 270; white working-class protest politics in Georgia and, 20

Democratic Advisory Council, 104

Democratic Caucus Committee on Party Effectiveness, 276

Democratic Leadership Council (DLC): Cleveland convention of, 294–96, 299, 325, 326; criticisms of, 285; on economic growth, 283, 294; on entrepreneurs, 283; establishment of, 282, 283; on growth with equity, 294; ideological transformation of, 294; mainstream values of, 283, 326; new generation of Democrats in, 249; "New Orleans Declaration," 294; Nunn in, 272; Osborne and, 269; Progressive Policy Institute of, 283, 292–95; *Rebuilding the Road to Opportunity* report and, 276; Wall Street financiers and, 283–84; on welfare reform, 293–94; on White, 326

Democratic Party: Cleveland machine, 146, 299; complacency in, 334; converging interests between local officials and, 193; "Democrats for Perk," 166; Keyserling as adviser to National Committee, 104; losses in midterms of 1966, 199; on national postindustrial policy, 280; New Deal Democrats, 140; in New South, 202, 204, 272, 273; as party of good government, 267; racism in Georgia, 27; Reagan Democrats, 326; reinventing, 267–96; southern, 8, 40, 43, 161, 189, 197–99, 244, 248, 272, 282–83; strains in coalition of, 240, 242, 252; white Democrats, 147, 168; white ethnics support, 81, 165, 166; "yellow dog" Democrats, 96. *See also* New Democrats

428　Index

depressed areas: ARC projects in, 113; Coosa-style commissions for, 108; Douglas's bill on, 104–5, 108; "economic development" replaces "depressed areas," 110; locals resent being characterized as, 109; in postwar Germany, 108; Reagan on, 311; as "redevelopment areas," 193
deregulation: ambivalence toward, 308; block grants as, 153; Carter on, 174, 175; Ford administration calls for, 2–3
desegregation: administrative enfranchisement contrasted with, 4–5; Batt on Appalachian governors and, 110; Carter and mandates for, 201; Carter desegregates Georgia state government, 114; CORE efforts in Cleveland, 121–22; defensive localism for opposing, 20; southern white resistance to, 198; as too narrow a goal for Turner, 139. *See also* integration
Detroit, 65, 80, 242, 301
developing nations, 105, 114, 124, 155
development: black alternatives for, 206; democratizing administration of, 213; developmental governance, 115, 204; international, 7, 124, 156, 249; investment, 28, 291, 336; neighborhood-based definitions of, 213; politics, 112, 189, 334; Rural Development Act of 1972 on, 245. *See also* community development; economic development; regional development; urban development
devolution: Ford administration calls for, 3; municipal governments strain under, 21; Nixonian regulatory, 173–74; of Reagan administration, 7, 13, 275, 298, 309
de Windt, Mandell, "Del," 318
disinvestment: community acquiescence sought for, 21, 306; in impoverished neighborhoods, 324; neighborhood insurgencies against, 232; in neoliberal cities, 328; UDAGs for reversing, 298–99; urban-triage abetted, 21, 298, 323; white racism countenances, 152
DLC. *See* Democratic Leadership Council (DLC)
Dodd, Christopher, 270
Douglas, Paul, 104–5, 108
Downs, Anthony, 298–99, 308
Drake, Robert, 64

Du Bois, W. E. B., 55
Duffy, Tom, 308
Dukakis, Michael, 264, 270, 272, 280, 291, 293

Earned Income Tax Credit (EITC), 293, 295
Eastern Hough Organized for Action, 151, 152
economic development: in amelioration of poverty, 7, 43, 44, 91, 209, 221; anger at business domination of, 339; ARA act on community participation in, 109; Arnall on racial progress and, 52; block grants for, 265; Campaign for Community-Based Economic Development, 305; Cleveland Roundtable on, 303; Cleveland's Economic Growth Commission on, 229; Coosa Valley APDC in, 98–101; "depressed areas" shifts to "economic development," 110; Georgia business elites use federal resources for, 88, 91, 92; Georgia Power's vested interest in, 37; Georgia's Agricultural and Industrial Development Board, 52–53; higher education in, 288–89; Lilienthal's letter regarding, 35; as "lily-white," 190; local businesspeople on expanded spending on, 36; market-making potential of programs for, 6–7; Merriam on, 77; National Conference on Balanced Growth and Economic Development of 1978, 259–60, 263–64; politics and, 30; President's Appalachian Regional Commission on, 110; Reagan policies and, 13, 266; regional planning for rationalizing, 75; rural, 19, 188, 189, 244; Stokes on, 163; subnational economic development districts, 193; supply-side New Dealers emphasize over democracy, 28; supply-side state builders in, 12; Sydnor on, 224; urban renewal pivots toward, 137; war preparedness and, 49
Economic Development Administration, 193
economic growth: in amelioration of poverty, 7, 43, 44, 91, 209, 221; ARC and private-sector, 112; "breadwinner" liberalism and, 7; business boosters on, 97; Clinton on, 285, 295, 326; Democratic Leadership Council on, 283, 294; Douglas's depressed areas bill on, 104; Eisenhower favors price

stability over, 104; emphasized over redistribution, 331; Kennedy on, 89, 103, 104; liberal economic policies for sustained, 90; managing, 249, 282; New Democrats emphasize, 268, 282, 285, 332; Osborne on, 292; planning commissions shepherd, 98; politics of, 270, 334; pro-growth regionalism, 95; public investment as means to, 92; in Roosevelt's vision of reform, 43–44, 46; social progress rooted in, 28, 44, 46, 53, 90, 103, 106, 107, 124, 154, 254; southern moderates on, 248; supply-side liberalism on, 4, 183
Economic Innovation International, 280
Economic Opportunities Council, 151, 157
economic opportunity: Arnall on, 52; attach rhetoric about to public-private partnerships, 88; in Cleveland, 65; interracial, cross-class, 177; liberals and expansion of, 341; supply-side liberals help entrench racial inequalities of, 4
Economic Opportunity Act, 199
Economic Opportunity Authorities (EOAs), 206
economic planning: Arkansas as laboratory for, 285; business elites use federal resources in Georgia, 88, 91, 92; Carter and, 200, 255, 272; Cleveland Tomorrow in, 303–4; Coosa Valley APDC in, 97, 98–101; democratic accountability lacking in public-private, 20; as feature of northwest Georgia boosterism, 100; federal investments become expectations, 88; Foster on new generation of businessperson and, 27; by Georgia's Agricultural and Industrial Development Board, 52; Humphrey-Javits bill on, 253; ideological hostility toward, 86; Keyserling on, 254, 255; liberals adopt decentralized rather than national, centralized approach to, 15; Magaziner and Reich on, 279; Merriam on, 57, 76–79; midcentury, 281; national, 57, 78, 79, 255; National Resources Planning Board on, 75–76, 79; New Deal encourages new capacities for, 15; NRPB as model for, 75–76, 79, 102; Nunn on, 272; Rome, Georgia, Chamber of Commerce on, 90; supply-side liberalism's contrasting modes of, 16; by WPA, 27. *See also* regional planning; urban planning

Economic Recovery Tax Act (ERTA) of 1981, 274
education: African American Romans on, 196; *Brown v. Board of Education,* 99, 201, 247; Busbee on block grants for, 265; Carter on, 197, 200, 202; Cleveland Roundtable on, 303; Clinton on, 288, 289, 291; Commission on the Future of the South on, 288–89; consumer, 157; Coosa Valley APDC on, 100; Great Society spending on, 173; individual investment accounts for, 294; integration of schools, 202, 208; Kennedy on, 106; Miller on, 199; New Deal and, 2, 45–46; New Democrats on, 248; Reich on, 329; on schools as growth engines, 291; segregation in Cleveland, 138; in the South, 39, 52; Southland Academy, Americus, Georgia, 202, 208; Stokes and, 162, 168; tax abatements versus funding for schools, 321–22; vocational, 223
Ehrenreich, Barbara and John, 235
Eisenhower, Dwight D., 104, 125–26
EITC (Earned Income Tax Credit), 293, 295
Eizenstat, Stu, 265
elites. *See* business elites; local elites; white elites
Ely, Richard T., 41
eminent domain, 67, 83, 125, 131
employment. *See* full employment; unemployment
enfranchisement: African American disenfranchisement, 195; Coosa Valley APDC and, 114; decentralized supply-side state seen as primary impediment to, 139; formal racial, 331; liberalism and democratic, 9; marginalized citizens win provisional forms of, 241; market barriers to, 196; southern Democrats and, 248; waxing and waning of African American, 16–17. *See also* administrative enfranchisement
enterprise zones, 298, 310–12, 319
entitlements: business elites oppose, 39; citizens fattened by, 240; Clinton on, 295; Community Action Programs expand access to, 156; Democratic Leadership Council on, 294; economic development seen as replacement for, 7; higher taxes to pay for, 285; New Democrats on, 21, 269, 270, 332; Reagan on, 298; supply-side tools seen as depoliticized versions of, 7

430 Index

entrepreneurs and entrepreneurialism, 270, 277–79, 281, 282, 285–86, 292–94, 309, 311, 329; African American, 64; Clinton and, 283, 288–90, 295, 296; community entrepreneurs, 281; in Coosa Valley, 90; Daniels' funds provide capital to, 281; entrepreneurial government, entrepreneurial postindustrial policy, 320; in Georgia, 282, 339; interest rates affect, 277, 280; midcentury liberals on, 330; New Democrats on, 268–70, 277, 282, 284, 291–93, 296, 298, 309, 311; policy, 152; politicians' willingness to create space for, 321; of poor women, 290, 291; Rostow on growth and development and, 105; as solution for poverty, 294; Southern Technology Council on, 289; state withdrawal authorized by, 300
environmentalism, 213, 241, 247, 248, 254, 276
equity planning, 232
Evans, Ahmed, 163
Evans, Upshur, 120; in Cleveland Development Foundation, 117, 120; on Cleveland of the future, 120; Garden Valley project and, 131, 136; on Housing Act of 1954, 120, 125; on Kingsbury Run project, 129; on Longwood project, 129; renewal agenda dominated by, 135; on urban renewal for revitalizing urban resources, 137
eviction riots, 62–63, 145, 165
executive branch: aggrandizement of, 15, 78; alternative vision of liberal democracy in, 155; Cleveland businesspeople on, 62; Humphrey-Javits bill on new agency for, 253. *See also presidents and other officials and agencies by name*

Fair Labor Standards Act (FLSA), 40
Famicos Foundation, 318
federal aid (subsidies): balance between macro-level stimulus and micro-level structural policies, 253, 263; boosters unite in order to win, 48–49; business associations and, 50, 221; businesspeople as recipients of, 12, 88, 91; for business poverty warriors, 160; Carter and, 252; chambers of commerce steer funds away from the poor, 223; cities' dependence on, 122–23, 126, 173, 218; Cleveland Chamber of Commerce seeks postwar, 84–85; Cleveland elites resist, 60, 85; for Cleveland housing redevelopment, 67–68; Cleveland's share declines, 226; Clinton redirects, 333; competition for, 51, 80; Democratic Leadership Council on, 294; deregulatory thrust and reduction of paperwork for, 175; elites' sense of entitlement to, 26, 49, 188, 235; Forbes and, 315, *316*; Greater Cleveland Growth Association lobbies for, 222; as habit forming, 70; Housing Act of 1949 on, 124; ideological instincts versus lure of, 73; imbalance in revenue capacity across federal system and, 250; indirect subsidies offered by New Deal works programs, 68; intergovernmental federal transfer system, 49; Jim Crow violence quelled by prospect of, 54; legitimized in terms of fighting poverty, 241; local elites' opportunistic use of, 75; local governments and, 37, 130, 258, 276; local matching grants for obtaining, 37, 67, 69–71, 84, 98, 122, 165, 217; markets remade by, 75; Model Cities as means of decentralizing, 223; naturalizing and regionalizing, 46–51; naturalizing New Deal subsidies, 70–75; in New Federalism, 181; Nixon's use of direct, 174; OEO publicity campaign about, 156; outsized portions for Georgia, 113, 114; Perk and, 167, 226; private investment and, 46, 306; Reagan undermines, 266, 305, 310; Reconstruction Finance Corporation delivers, 57; Franklin D. Roosevelt, Jr., on civil rights reform and, 110; rural Georgia's economy shaped by, 102; sectional competition over, 260–64, 278; seen as acceptable when controlled by local elites, 115; Southern Commercial Secretaries Association conference on winning, 51; square pursuit of with commitment to limited government, 130–31; state and local debt outpaces, 217; for subnational economic development districts, 193; supply-side state builders and, 13, 129, 205; unfunded prerequisites for, 245; U.S. Chamber of Commerce on minority groups receiving, 222; Voinovich on, 305–6; white capital enhanced by, 46. *See also federal grants*

Federal Emergency Relief Administration, 37, 46
federal government: Carter's antigovernment governance, 203–5; cities' dependence on, 122–23, 126, 173; complaints about regulatory and labor-related excesses of, 54; contested extensions of authority of, 101; debt, 199; federal-municipal policy relationships, 15; Foster's regionally based federal lobbying project, 27; infrastructural power of, 45; localism and self-help seen as antidotes to, 115; municipal borrowing incentivized by, 70, 216; national business associations oppose overreach by, 113; participatory community development sought from, 147; revenue sharing limits, 173; seeds administrative partners throughout the country, 98; Talmadge on centralizing power in, 38. *See also* executive branch; federal aid (subsidies); federal spending
Federal Housing Administration (FHA): conservatism of, 18, 119, 131, 141; discourages projects due to surrounding environment, 141; expanding mandate of, 118; fast foreclosure process incentivized by, 180; focus on white, suburban housing, 118, 127, 133; Hansen on, 78; Housing Act of 1954 on, 120; multiple actors in programs of, 15–16; protests of 1976, 1, 2, *2*, 20, 180; racism of, 18, 119, 131; redlining by, 118, 131; seen as expanding welfare state, 118; supply-side liberal commitments in, 4. *See also* Federal Housing Administration (FHA) mortgage insurance; Federal Housing Administration (FHA) mortgages
Federal Housing Administration (FHA) mortgage insurance: Cleveland's business elites on, 128–29; expansion of 1961, 137; Housing Act of 1954 on, 125, 128; multifamily programs, 18, 118; Osborne and Gaebler on, 286; Section 235 program, 178; suburbanization encouraged by, 121
Federal Housing Administration (FHA) mortgages: for Cleveland's Garden Valley project, 131; cost certification regulations, 127, 128, 133; Housing Act of 1949 on, 124; inflating land values for, 134; isolating from incompatible neighborhoods, 141; Lockwood on, 126; in Parma, Ohio, 121; for redlined neighborhoods, 179; Section 203 program, 127; Section 220 program, 118, 127–29, 131–34, 136, 178; Section 608 program, 127, 133; supply-side liberals' use of, 118
federalism: Carter and, 201, 203, 252, 256–59, 266; competitive, 73, 263; cooperative, 203, 275, 276, 298; crisis in, 171–72, 240–66; Great Society and, 171; Heller on German, 105, 108; of Kennedy, 108; liberalism on centralized authority and, 10; New Deal, 19, 51, 73, 153, 173, 263, 273, 276; Reagan on, 275; states' rights, 54, 110, 199, 252. *See also* fiscal federalism; New Federalism
Federal Reserve Bank, 68, 217
federal spending: business associations' complaints about, 50; Carter on, 252, 264, 265; constitutional limits called for, 273; in crisis in federalism, 240; Georgia shaped by, 102; interest groups seek steady expansion of, 241; is big for business, 75; Keyserling on, 255; liberal wariness of, 7; New Democrats on, 21; Nixon on limiting, 245; racial unrest associated with, 199–200; Reagan's cuts in, 274–76, 312, 323; on research and development, 95, 102; Roosevelt on unemployment and, 44; seen as disproportionately going to cities, 244, 245; southern social progress and, 46; in the South exceeds federal taxes from, 54; tax abatements contrasted with, 321; taxpayer discontent and, 242; U.S. Chamber of Commerce on, 50, 51, 61. *See also* deficit spending; federal aid (subsidies)
FHA. *See* Federal Housing Administration (FHA)
fiscal federalism: clashes within system of, 240; Cleveland's fiscal precarity due to, 122; in crisis by late 1970s, 239, 242; defined, 15; fluid politics of, 115; in legitimation crisis of 1970s, 20; liberalism as reconciled to, 341; New Federalism restores, 171, 173; Reagan and, 273, 274; in reorganization and structural convergence of local power dynamics, 16; unbalanced structures of, 328

fiscal policy: for analyzing modern liberalism, 9–10; crises of 1970s, 238; equity in, 165; fiscal conservatism, 71, 166, 255; fiscal discipline as class and race discipline, 273; fiscal realism, 239, 291, 332; Kennedy and, 103, 105; Keynesian, 4, 90, 107; New Deal's early fiscal conservatism, 71; New Democrats and, 284–85; postwar trend favoring restraint, 86; Revenue Act of 1964 and, 107; *Rome News-Tribune* on responsible, 199; supply-side fiscalism, 310; supply-side liberalism's moderate, 119, 183. *See also* deficit spending; fiscal federalism

Fisher Body Company strike (1936–37), 65

Fleming, Matthew J., 68

Flory, Walter, 79, 85

Floyd County (Georgia): African Americans in, 29, 32; bond issues rejected in, 265, 334–35; Burrell elected to county commission, 340–41; Civil Works Administration jobs in, 26; hospital for, 39; manufacturing increases in, 113; population of, 29; Republican Party in, 199; roads in, 30; small taxpayer frustration in, 243, 244. *See also* Rome (Georgia)

Follin, James W., 191–92

food stamps, 274, 275, 308

Forbes, George L., 314–15; African American constituents on, 324–25; city council district of, 316–17, 318; on city council reduction, 316–17; on Cleveland Municipal Light sale, 236; commitment to black interests of, 315, 320–21; corporate tax breaks of, 230; defeated for mayor, 325; law firm of, 315–16; Lexington Village project and, 317; on no advantage being around poor people, 324; as partner of white elites, 299, 316, 324; tax abatements defended by, 321–22

Ford, Gerald: Carter compared with, 252; on community development, 2, 180; Humphrey-Javits bill and, 253; more austere social contract of, 3; New Federalism of, 5; on public-private partnerships, 2–3, 174; State and Local Governments Conference on Inflation of, 214

Ford Foundation, 146, 147, 152, 155, 177, 249, 289, 290

foreclosure, fast, 180

Foreman, Clark, 43

Foster, Margaret, 177, 179–80

Foster, Wyatt, 29; on business complaints about infrastructure, 30; on Roosevelt administration's plans, 35–36; Coosa-Alabama River Improvement Association of, 47; Etowah River dam project and, 48; on levees for Rome, Georgia, 38–39; Lilienthal's letter to, 35; as local broker of public investment, 44; on New Deal discrimination against Rome, Georgia, 26, 36–37; on new generation of businessman, 27; regionally based federal lobbying project of, 27; RFC loan sought by, 34; in Southern Commercial Secretaries Association, 29, 51; on TVA versus Georgia Power, 36

free enterprise: Carter and, 255; Cleveland businesspeople's commitment to, 73; Coosa Valley APDC seen as example of, 115; federally funded cooperative regionalism as threat to, 99; governments' interventionist stance in markets in 1980s, 281; National Association of Manufacturers program on, 221; NRPB's rights initiatives and, 86; in phases of urban policy, 307; *Plain Dealer* editorial on public-private partnerships and, 87; Powell's defense of, 215, 224–25; for solving poverty, 162; supply-side state builders champion, 13; white ethnics support, 165. *See also* capitalism; markets

Freeman, Don, 325

Friedman, Milton, 14, 223, 310

From, Al, 287, 294

Frost, Millard I. "Jack," 192

full employment: antipoverty coalition regroups around, 242, 252; campaign for, 252–53; Humphrey-Hawkins bill on, 253; Kennedy on, 106; Keyserling's *Toward Full Employment in Three Years*, 254; Rostow on, 263; unions push for, 241

Full Employment Act of 1946, 104, 253

Full Recovery or Stagnation? (Hansen), 41

"Future of the South, The: A Statement of the Regional Objectives for the Southern States" (report), 250

Future Outlook League, 64–65

Index   433

Gaebler, Ted, 285–86
Galbraith, John Kenneth, 40–42, 103, 104, 107
Galston, William, 293
Gannon, Thomas, 177
Garden Valley Neighborhood House, 135
Gardner, James, 200
Gartner, Alan, 157–58
Gellerstedt, Lawrence, 339
gentrification: Cleveland private-investment program as geared toward, 323; community development funds speed, 180; federal subsidies for, 154; FHA mortgage insurance and, 137; Forbes on Cleveland Clinic proposal as, 321; rehabilitation loans for, 179
George, Walter F., 43
Georgia
  African Americans: access to federal programs desired by, 207; Black Leadership Coalition, 206; displacement of, 195; franchise denied to, 28, 33; poverty among, 28, 33; violent insurrections in in 1960s and 1970s, 208
  Chamber of Commerce, 95
  cities, towns, and counties: Alma, 187–90; Augusta, 6, 45, 92; Bacon County, 187–89; Gainesville, 49; Macon, 45, 92; Sumpter County, 208; Warm Springs, 39; Waycross, 92, 189. See also Atlanta; Floyd County (Georgia); Rome (Georgia)
  development: concern about means by which elites pursue their agendas, 242; development commissions, 18; industrial development bonds, 313; public investment sought by boosters, 27; regional development, 48, 52, 92, 96–98, 240; road construction, 37, 38
  economy: bank deposits, 59; entrepreneurialism, 282, 339; family income increases, 113–14; federal spending shapes, 102; industrial recruitment in, 95, 102, 207, 245; international trade relations, 207; manufacturing increases, 113; unemployment, 287; white-collar employment, 99
  federal programs: AFDC growth, 272; ARA programs, 109; ARC projects, 113; outsized portions of federal aid for, 113, 114; revenue sharing, 274; Rural Development Act of 1972, 245; work relief programs federalized, 38; WPA projects, 47
  planning: multicounty regional public-private planning and development organizations, 88, 91, 92; Planning Enabling Act of 1957, 98; regional planning, 16, 18, 52, 88, 91, 92, 98, 103, 110. See also Area Planning and Development Commissions (APDC)
  politics: alienation from government, 200; county courthouse politics, 18, 27; electoral system, 93–94, 197; growth politics, 334; hardening political mood in 1970s, 265; labor militancy, 34; rural taxpayer anger, 243; white working-class protest, 20; "wool hat" faction, 91, 112
  racial issues: Carter desegregates Georgia state government, 114; Jim Crow, 54–55; "post-racial" Georgia, 203; racial demagoguery, 37–38; racism, 27, 91, 208
  social characteristics: splintering of local elites, 338–39; two Georgias emerging, 287
  state agencies and government: Agricultural and Industrial Development Board, 52–53; Economic Opportunity Authorities, 206; "Eggs and Issues" breakfasts, 186; "Good Government is Good Business in Georgia," 51–55; home rule, 98; Human Resources Board, 257; Industry and Trade agency, 207; reorganization of state government, 205–7, 246, 257, 272, 301
  supply-side state builders, 188
  See also office-holders and other individuals by name
Georgia Institute of Technology. See Georgia Tech (Georgia Institute of Technology)
Georgia Mountains APDC, 187
Georgia Power Company: on Agricultural and Industrial Development Board, 52; in Carter's state government reorganization, 205; Collier's role in, 92; Georgia Progress publication, 93; "Good Government is Good Business in Georgia" ad, 53; Industrial Development Board and, 92; McDonough's role in, 48, 53, 101; in Planning Enabling Act of 1957, 98; "Planning for an Area Development Program" brochure, 102; Starr's role

Georgia Power Company (*continued*)
  in, 94, 95, 100; TVA rates compared with those of, 36; vested interest in economic development, 37, 48
Georgia Tech (Georgia Institute of Technology): Advanced Technology Development Center, 281–82; APDC partnerships of, 247, 281; city planning program, 92; Coosa Valley APDC studies with, 113, 247, 336; Engineering Experiment Station, 95–96, 281; Industrial Development Boards, 92–93, 249, 336; Industrial Development Division, 187; Maddox and, 198; Research Alliance, 339; Rome, Georgia, outpost of, 101–2, 249, 336
Gephardt, Richard, 276, 283
Gingrich, Newt, 20, 274, 334–37
globalization, 13, 21, 207, 241, 295, 337
Goldwater, Barry, 114–15, 199, 251
Good Faith Fund, 290
Gore, Al, 249
government: administrative governance, 243; antigovernment governance, 203–5; antigovernment sentiment, 54, 165, 205, 272, 321, 329, 339; big, 180, 273; business as model for reform of, 216; business's antigovernment politics, 223–24; capital as inducement business seeks from, 280; Carter reorganizes Georgia's state, 205–7; cost-efficient, 225; entrepreneurial, 270, 285–86, 311, 329; expert-led, 335; good, 25, 53, 54, 93, 94, 267, 297, 324; intergovernmental reform, 171, 252, 256, 259; liberal governance, 2, 153, 173, 202, 207, 267, 334; liberalism and undemocratic practices of, 342; marketized governance, 285–86; new ideas about state and markets, 278; Osborne on role of, 292; Powell on American system of business and, 215, 224–25; Reagan's shift in relationship between markets and, 310; reinventing, 211–342; rising expectations for, 264; seen as beholden to special interests, 264; skepticism and mistrust of, 267, 269, 270; strategy of circumvention in, 243; UDAGs as partnerships between business and, 308. *See also* city (municipal) government; federal government; limited government; local government; public sector; public spending; state, the

Grace, Armstrong, 324–25
Graham, Robert, 283
Grameen Bank, 289, 290
Graves, Bibb, 38
Gray Areas program, 152, 155
Grdina, Betty, 233
Great Depression: debt-fueled development of 1920s worsens, 57; property taxes and, 59–60, 66; Rose's history of Cleveland on, 87; stock market crash of 1929 leads to, 59; unionization and, 34; Van Sweringen collapse and, 56; white ethnics' experience of, 165. *See also* New Deal
Greater Cleveland Growth Association: Cleveland Roundtable and, 303; in commission on neighborhoods, 306; creation of, 220–21; Davis as chair of, 226–27; downtown redevelopment plan of, 227–29; Forbes and, 316; Good Government Committee of, 324; income-tax hike proposed by, 229; Kucinich and, 230, 233–34; lobbies for federal aid, 222; on regional disparities in federal spending, 261; renamed Mayor's Economic Coordinating Commission, 229; "Take Part" workshop, 228; workshops of April 1978, 233–34
Great Lakes Exposition (1936-37), 72, 74, 87
Great Society: aid to central cities during, 226; American federalism affected by, 171; expectations for government raised by, 264; growth centers emphasized in, 245; Johnson stifles dissent in context of, 173; Nixon's initiatives and, 153; Reagan on, 310; support for cutting programs of, 207; whites' caricatured versions of, 198. *See also* War on Poverty; *and programs by name*
Green, Richard, 323–24
Greenspan, Alan, 329
Greer, Guy, 80, 123
Griffin, Marvin, 202, 273
Grisanti, Teresa, 142
Grossman, Hyman, 239
growth, economic. *See* economic growth
growth centers, 245
growth coalitions, 16, 17
GRS. *See* revenue sharing
guaranteed income, 252, 271
Guren, Sheldon, 227, 322

Hackett, David, 155, 156
HADC (Hough Area Development Corporation), 163, 305, 306, 323
Halfway Home and a Long Way to Go (report), 288, 292
Halprin, Lawrence, 227–28
Hammond, Ross, 249
Hanks, J. Dan, 192
Hansen, Alvin: on cities' financial bind, 123; on deficit spending, 77, 78, 139; on economic planning, 78, 279; *Full Recovery or Stagnation?*, 41; Heller compared with, 105–6; on innovation, 17, 41–42, 52, 78, 105, 249; Keynesianism and, 17, 27, 40–42, 52, 78; Merriam and, 77, 78; on municipal borrowing, 216–17; on private investment, 17, 41, 42, 57, 77, 80, 105, 128; on public investment, 42, 44, 46, 47, 51, 57, 77–78, 80, 249; on public-private partnerships, 51, 77, 78; on stagnation, 17, 41, 42, 77; as supply-side liberal, 6, 216; on urban redevelopment, 80
Hardy, Wilson M., 45
Harper, T. Harley, 96–97, 110, 115
Harrington, Michael, 107, 152, 256
Harrington, Michael J., 260, 261
Harris, Patricia, 262
Harris, Seymour, 103, 107
Hart, Gary, 267, 269, 270, 273
Hatcher, Richard, 259
Hawkins, Augustus, 253
Haynes, Roland, 54–55
Head Start, 154, 173, 206, 268
Healy, Bernadine, 320
Heller, Walter, 105; on block grants and revenue sharing, 173; on federalism, 108; in German postwar reconstruction, 105, 108; Kennedy's economic-growth policy and, 103; on Revenue Act of 1964, 107; on tax cuts, 105, 106, 277
Helms, Jesse, 200
Hight, Charles, Sr., 192
high tech: Clinton and, 288, 289; Democrat support for, 280; Georgia Tech Advanced Technology Development Center, 281–82; Hammond on, 249; New Democrats on, 21, 248, 268, 284; Reich on, 329; Southern Growth Policies Board and, 241, 263; Southern Technology Council on, 289; taxpayer dollars support incubators for, 270
Hills, Carla A., 2, 180–81, 347n5

Hodges, Luther, 247
Hodges, Wayne, 281
Holland, Hubert, 32, 192, 194
Holliday, W. T., 120
Holmes, Allen C., 237
Holton, Linwood, 197, 247, 248
homeowners: associations oppose public housing, 125; black, 143, 172, 178, 232; conservatism of, 166; FHA-backed mortgages for poor peoples' homeownership, 178; growing alienation from liberal state, 139; Housing and Community Development Act of 1974 on, 178; individual investment accounts for, 294; 1970s as "decade of the neighborhood," 232; white homeowner politics, 9, 20. *See also* mortgages; property taxes; property values
home rule, 98
Hoover, Herbert, 25, 34, 57, 68
Hopkins, Harry, 26–27
Hornady, J. R., 48, 49
Hough Area Development Corporation (HADC), 163, 305, 306, 323
housing: Advisory Committee on Housing Policies and Programs, 126; CDBG cuts affect, 323; Cleveland Development Foundation's emphasis on, 117; Cleveland Roundtable on, 303; conditions of African American, 66, 118, 122, 124; Housing and Home Finance Agency, 126; market, 82, 122, 125, 135, 154, 179, 331; planning commissions encourage rational development of, 98; public-private system of, 118; rhetoric about attached to public-private partnerships, 88; supply-side liberal approach to, 118–19, 125–28; wartime crunch in, 82. *See also* affordable housing; Federal Housing Administration (FHA); public housing; rental housing
Housing Act of 1934, 118
Housing Act of 1937, 254
Housing Act of 1949, 118, 120, 123–26
Housing Act of 1954: commercial redevelopment emphasized in, 119, 125; cost certification requirement in, 128; on eminent domain, 125; evolution away from housing, 137; Hansen's influence on, 123; local officials empowered by, 120–21; public housing in, 118, 119, 127; remarries private profit with public endeavor, 127–28, 136; Section 701

Housing Act of 1954 (continued) planning grants, 16, 97–99, 103, 109, 193; "urban renewal" in, 120
Housing Act of 1956, 133
Housing and Community Development Act of 1974, 153, 173, 175, 178–79
Housing and Home Finance Agency, 126
Housing and Urban Development, Department of (HUD): on community development grants in Cleveland, 176, 177, 179; demonstrations of 1976 against, 1–2; Lewis writes to, 170; partners with U.S. Chamber of Commerce, 175; Perk and, 168
Housing and Urban Development Act of 1968, 178
Howard, John T., 79
Howell, Ulysses N., 45
HUD. See Housing and Urban Development, Department of (HUD)
Huger, James, 249
Hughes, Langston, 64
Human Relations Council of Georgia, 185
Humphrey, Hubert, 159, 201, 253
Humphrey-Hawkins bill, 253–56, 261

Ickes, Harold, 67, 71
Industrial Development Board, 92–93, 101–2
industrial development bonds (IDBs), 91, 313
industrial policy: Clinton and, 336; Democrat support for, 280; in Humphrey-Javits bill, 253; liberals adopt decentralized approach to, 15; liberals and supply-side state builders in local and regional, 15; Magaziner and Reich on, 279; national debate over, 279–80; NRPB on, 93; regionally targeted, 108; Rostow on, 264; state and local governments offer lessons on, 294; Weir on a National Industrial Policy Board, 319–20. See also postindustrial policy
industrial recruitment: in Cleveland, 84, 85; in Georgia, 95, 102, 207, 245; "smokestack chasing," 241, 245, 247, 278, 313
inequalities: businesslike reforms produce, 298; entrenched, 328; historical, 241; local elites exacerbate, 11; in local government, 10; in markets, 152, 155; New Democrats positions entrench existing, 285; public-private partnerships exacerbate, 5; in supply-side-liberal outcomes, 21–22, 119, 164; supply-side state builders and, 6. See also racial inequality
inflation: administrative governance in times of, 243; block grants fail to index for, 333; business elites squeezed by, 221; Carter and, 207, 250, 252, 256, 264; CDBGs affected by, 308; city budgets affected by, 126, 172, 214, 217, 218, 225; as constraint on federal spending, 242; as crisis of democracy, 240; economic development corporation loans and, 309; Eisenhower prefers recession to, 104; family income affected by, 114; Humphrey-Hawkins and, 255; investors exit municipal bond market due to, 219; Keyserling on, 254; liberals become concerned about, 255; National Conference on Balanced Growth and Economic Development of 1978 on, 259; Nixon and, 245; private investment restricted by, 268; surge in 1978, 242; tax-free bonds' importance due to, 313; Volcker fights, 277, 287; Wall Street on deficits and, 329; after wartime price controls were lifted, 85; white homeowner politics as response to, 20
infrastructure: antipoverty programs conceived in terms of, 186; ARC projects in Georgia, 113; borrowing for, 216; business-oriented, 91; businesspeople desire, 30, 75, 84–88, 97–98, 280, 311; Douglas's depressed areas bill on, 104; federal financing for strengthening local, 70; Hansen on public spending for, 42; Heller on public investment in, 105; infrastructural violence, 17; Kennedy on, 107; municipal bonds for, 139; municipal debt threatens projects, 59; private investment stimulated by, 28; RFC loans for, 34; Rome, Georgia's, improved, 90; Rural Development Act of 1972 requires, 245; self-liquidating projects, 34, 37, 68, 69; UDAGs for Cleveland, 322; WPA in development of, 37. See also New Deal works programs
innovation: big cities raise capital for, 59; Daniels on, 280; entrepreneurial, 105, 277, 279; *Halfway Home and a Long Way to Go* report on, 288; Hansen on,

Index 437

17, 41–42, 52, 78, 105, 249; Heller on, 105; Keynesianism seen as insufficient to create private-sector, 40; Klein on, 279; New Democrats on, 268; Osborne on state-level, 292; private-sector, 277, 339; Rostow on, 105; socializing risks of, 278; Southern Technology Council on, 289; state and local governments seen as laboratories for, 294; supply-side liberalism's emphasis on, 16, 106; venture capital for, 278, 280

Institute for Research in Social Science, 42–43

integration: attempt to integrate Maddox's restaurant, 198; Georgia voters on, 200; individualist solutions for, 222; Myrdal on, 124; in Rome, Georgia, 185; of schools, 202, 208; as too narrow a goal for Turner, 139. *See also* desegregation

interest groups: Carter and, 264, 265; in Cleveland, 226; demands for empowerment by, 239; democracy seen as overloaded by, 240, 241; Democratic Leadership Council on, 294; managing participation of, 304; multiracial, 5, 20; New Democrats on, 21, 267–70; politics of, 21, 269, 270, 284; Porter on, 290; Powell on, 224; programs generate, 286, 292; public spending demanded by, 240; supply-side state builders never cohere as national, 51. *See also* special interests

interest rates: Carter and, 256; for cities with minority populations, 300; Clinton on balanced budget and, 333; for economic development corporation loans, 309; entrepreneurs affected by, 277, 280; FHA and, 118; inflation pushes up, 207, 214; municipal governments affected by, 214, 217, 219, 225, 234; private investment and public capacities affected by, 268; Volcker's inflation fight and, 277, 287; Wall Street on deficits and, 329

interests, special. *See* special interests

investment: development, 28, 291, 336; individual investment accounts, 294; local government as investment bank, 309; outside investors, 338; socially responsible, 280; supply-side, 78, 277, 329. *See also* disinvestment; private investment; public investment

Jackson, Agnes, 233
Jackson, Alvin, 341
Jackson, Donald, 186, 194, 196
Jackson, Jeffrey, 196
Jackson, Jesse, 285, 293
Jackson, Leo, 146
Jacobs brothers, 322, 342
Javits, Jacob, 253
Jervis, John, 192
Jim Crow: Bond on Carter and, 251; built into New Deal developments, 45–46; decentralism associated with, 58, 182–83; declines in South, 191; futuristic economic outlooks and, 247; in Georgia, 54–55; Jim Crow-like policies, 8, 17, 18, 58; Lewis on violence of, 169; limits of racial progress under, 185; national repudiation of, 183; New Deal and preservation of, 35, 39; in New Deal works programs in Cleveland, 9; in New South, 91; poverty as consequence of, 28; in Rome, Georgia, 32–33, 54–55; Roosevelt on southern poverty and, 40; supply-side liberalism not concerned with, 55; supply-side state builders and, 28; in urban democracies of 1980s, 299; white southerners continue to support, 198. *See also* segregation

Job Corps, 154, 160
job training, 164, 168, 249, 288, 292, 295, 308
Johnson, Hugh, 35
Johnson, Juanita, 206–7
Johnson, Lyndon: ARC and, 110; businessmen consulted by, 161–62; Clinton compared with, 295; on Community Action Programs, 158–60, 167; deregulation's roots in administration of, 175; Howard University speech of 1965, 154; "maximum feasible participation" principle and, 152, 153, 160, 175; Zell Miller on, 199; National Advisory Council on Economic Opportunity, 160; on private-sector in poverty programs, 153, 173; Revenue Act of 1964 signed by, 107; *Rome News-Tribune* on, 199; supply-side state builders' authority reasserted by, 19; War on Poverty of, 4, 5, 19, 115, 147, 151, 154–56, 159, 172, 181, 186, 198, 221–22. *See also* Great Society

Johnson, Paul, Jr., 198
Jones Day (law firm), 231, 236, 237, 301, 303, 315
Jordan, Vernon, Jr., 185, 253, 259

Kamarck, Elaine, 293
Katzenbach, Nicholas, 109
Keel, H. H., 38, 39, 45, 47, 48
Kennedy, Edward, 279
Kennedy, John F.: accedes to march on Washington, 101; administration as maturation of supply-side liberalism, 91; ARA and, 108, 109; on Coosa-Alabama River project, 90; deficit spending by, 103, 106; on economic growth, 89, 103, 104, 106; economics education of, 103; election of, 139; federalism of, 108; fiscal policy of, 105; Goldwater criticizes, 114–15; on infrastructure, 107; Keyserling in administration of, 254; localism of, 90; planning and development organizations as model for, 91; on poverty, 89, 107–14, 155; President's Commission on Juvenile Delinquency, 155; on "rising tide that lifts all the boats," 4, 90; synthesis of demand- and supply-side policies of, 90; tax cut of, 91, 105–7, 277; on TVA, 89
Kentucky, 108, 110, 313
Keynesianism: on deficit spending, 71, 78; fiscal policy, 4, 90, 107; "growth liberalism," 4; Hansen and, 17, 27, 40–42, 52, 78; in Humphrey-Javits bill, 253; Kennedy and ascension of, 89; Keyserling and, 103–4; in New Deal and wartime state-building, 27; New Dealers adopt, 15, 71; in poverty's elimination, 90; Revenue Act of 1964 and, 107; Rostow on, 264; seen as insufficient to create private-sector investment, 40; social, 103–5; in Sunbelt-Rustbelt divergence, 18
Keyserling, Leon, 40, 43, 103–4, 253–55
Keyserling, Mary Dublin, 104
King, Martin Luther, Jr., 146, 147, 162, 227
Klein, Lawrence, 279
Klunder, Bruce, 139
Knowles, Roy, 243–44; backlash of, 337; Burrell occupies county commission seat of, 341; Floyd County Commission seat won by, 265; Maddox and, 243, 246, 335; on regional planning, 247; Rigas and, 334, 335; Talmadge attempts to win over, 245
Koleda, Michael, 259
Kovach, Kenneth, 177, 181
Krumholz, Norman, 232
Kucinich, Dennis: budget crisis of, 234; Cleveland's business elites and, 216, 232–37, 300; elected Cleveland mayor, 213–14, 231; mayoral campaign of 1977, 230–31; mayoral campaign of 1979, 238; neighborhood groups and, 231–34; in Perk campaign, 166; as populist, 213, 232, 238; priorities seen as irresponsible, 239; recall campaign, 234; on tax abatements, 232, 242
Ku Klux Klan, 33, 101

labor: business producerism undercuts claims of, 209; Democratic Leadership Council accused of neglecting, 285; Fair Labor Standards Act, 40; local elites employ cheap, government-subsidized, 186; market, 102, 253, 293, 333; National Labor Relations (Wagner) Act, 43, 104, 152, 253; right-to-work laws, 91, 109; as special interest, 257; traditional industries as concern of, 279. *See also* working-class whites; labor movement
Laboratories of Democracy (Osborne), 286, 292
labor movement: in Cleveland, 65; lacks clout in the South, 109; Lausche bucks, 81, 82; Massachusetts AFL-CIO, 281; in Ohio Public Interest Campaign, 230; waning power of, 284. *See also* unions
Ladd, H. J., 182
La Guardia, Fiorello, 80
Landrum, Phil, 161, 199
land-use planning, 93, 97, 193
Lausche, Frank, 79, 81–82, 84–86, 145
"law and order," 201, 243
Lazard Freres & Co., 301, 302
Lee, William W., 188
Lehman Brothers, 280
Leibman, Morris I., 160–61
Lester, Richard, 103
Levin, Albert, 141
Levins, W. T., 186
Levinson, I. M., 49
Levi Strauss Foundation, 290

Lewis, Fannie, 169, *170*; affordable housing fought for, *317,* 317–18, 325, 340; on CDBGs, 176; on city council, 314, 317, 324; Cleveland Citizens Participation Association of, 176; "Fannie Lewis Law," 340; Hough neighborhood group led by, 177; Lexington Village project of, *317,* 317–18, 325, 340, 342; as model neighborhood's chief advocate, 169; at Neighborhoods Conference of 1978, 233; organizes in face of New Federalism, 171; in political activism of 1970s, 213; tenacity of, 170, 341

Lewis, Hod, 47

Lewis, John D., 22

Lewis, Oscar, 155

liberalism: "breadwinner," 7; Cold War, 124, 249, 282, 330, 331; CORE's structural critique of, 147; corporate, 166; development alliance with local business boosters, 91; fiscal policy for analyzing modern, 9–10; gradual acceptance of civil rights movement by, 91; "growth," 4; liberal democracy, 155; liberal fundamentalism, 293; in local and regional industrial policy, 15; local elites engage with liberal policies, 10; local political and business elites empowered by, 3; market-oriented policies called for in place of programs of: 1-2; markets and, 3, 10, 15; midcentury, 12, 106, 215, 268, 284, 289, 330–31, 334, 347n7; as multiracial political coalition, 9; national, 201, 263; New Deal, 9, 106, 239, 330; participatory spirit of modern, 183; private sector in administration of initiatives of, 3, 11; progressive vision of, 8; public-private partnerships and, 3, 5, 330; public spending associated with policies of, 172; racial, 124; rightward turn in 1970s, 256; settling debts of, 213–39; Turner's criticism of, 139; vision versus reality of, 341–42; white liberals, 124, 209, 250, 299, 315, 326, 331. *See also* liberal state; neoliberalism; supply-side liberalism

liberal state: African American challenges to, 8, 119; barriers to enfranchisement entrenched through, 196; Cleveland elites and, 55; complaints about regulatory and labor-related excesses of, 54; democratic compromises of, 242; denial built into, 330; growing alienation from, 20, 139; liberal governance, 2, 153, 173, 202, 207, 267, 334; local business elites forge relationships with, 6; midcentury consensus regarding, 330–31; postwar businesspeople expand partnerships with, 88; public-private partnerships as check on, 3, 19, 153; racial, class, and ethnic exclusions in, 11; racial and gendered assumptions undergird, 116; regional convergences and evolving structures of, 184; structural inequalities in, 185

Liberty League, 12–13

Lilienthal, David, 35, 36

limited government: business elites square pursuit of federal subsidies with commitment to, 130–31; Carter and, 204; Cleveland Chamber of Commerce members' commitment to, 72, 130; efficiency attributed to, 238; Sydnor on, 224; U.S. Chamber of Commerce calls for, 50

Linder, Tom, Jr., 205, 206

Lindsey, Harold, 186

Lister, James, 129, 136, 141

local elites: ARA programs administered by, 109, 110; ARC and, 112; block grants controlled by, 153; in building new forms of sub-national supply-side capacity, 55; Carter and, 252; CDBGs and, 173; cheap, government-subsidized labor employed by, 186; in Cleveland, 55, 338; Community Action Programs and, 159; competition and jealousy between and among, 26, 51; decentralized administrative partnerships with Kennedy administration, 91; engage with liberal policies, 10; entitlement felt by, 26–27; federal aid seen as acceptable when controlled by, 115; federal capacities commandeered by, 22; FHA's expanding mandate and, 118; inequalities exacerbated by, 11; Jim Crow-like policies championed by, 17; Johnson and, 160; liberal state's articulation through, 184; on "maximum feasible participation" mandate, 5, 19; Merriam on participation of, 78; municipal crises of 1970s and, 215; New Deal programs empower, 3,

local elites (continued)
34–36, 45, 54, 58; opportunistic use of federal subsidies, 75; "participation" in management of marginalized communities, 20, 21; producerist ethos in, 49; public investment used for regional development by, 92; RFC and, 68–69; seen as leading in the public interest, 26; splintering of, 337–42; think of themselves as contributing to social progress, 222; in urban renewal, 144, 190, 191, 195; War on Poverty as seen by, 158. *See also* business elites

local government: Advisory Commission on Intergovernmental Relations on, 172, 257; ARA creates partnerships between federal agencies and, 108; blight and increased costs for, 191; block grants for, 153, 275; businesspeople desire commitment from, 312; business's leverage over, 225, 229, 298; capital requirements met by borrowing, 219; Carter on, 200–201, 203, 252, 255; CDBGs send funds by formula to, 173; civic associations work with, 20; Community Action Programs and, 156; converging interests between Democrats and, 193; in default in 1930s, 68; deficits due to federal mandates, 172; Democratic Leadership Council on, 294; federal aid and, 37, 130, 258, 276; fiscal crisis during Great Depression, 60; Greer on federal aid for, 123; *Halfway Home and a Long Way to Go* report on improving, 289; home rule for Georgia, 98; Humphrey as liaison with, 159; increasing state control over grants to, 265; inequalities in, 10; as investment bank, 309; liberals work through, 342; limitations on prolonged debt, 139; local chambers of commerce shape, 12; at National Conference on Balanced Growth and Economic Development of 1978, 259; National Resources Planning Board and, 75, 76; New Federalism and, 171; Nixon on, 172; Ohio restrictions on creating new forms of taxes by, 59; property values and revenues of, 81; racist and acquisitive structures of, 11; Reagan policies and, 266, 274; RFC and, 57, 68; Roosevelt administration reaches out to, 35; seen as not ready to administer federal funds, 174; social hierarchies in, 8; supply-side state builders turn to, 13–14; tax-exempt financing for, 313; for unemployment relief, 61; unfunded prerequisites for federal aid, 245. *See also* city (municipal) government

localism: of ARA, 108; of Carter, 184, 200–201, 203; Cleveland Chamber of Commerce turns from, 85; defensive, 20, 61; elite-led, 153, 184, 246; federal resources underwrite, 173; Goldwater on, 115; of Kennedy, 90; liberalism's deference to, 10, 15; local basis of business producerism, 235; local majoritarianism, 142, 184; marginalized communities challenge supply-side liberalism's versions of, 19; of Zell Miller, 199; New Deal and American democratic, 35; Nixon and, 153, 172–74, 209; Progressive Era's idealized image of local democracy, 25–26; in relief efforts, 61; of RFC, 68; seen as barrier to state building, 15; self-liquidation and matching requirements for promoting, 37; of supply-side liberalism, 19, 183, 342; of supply-side state builders, 15, 51; of white ethnic Clevelanders, 147. *See also* local elites; local government

Locher, Ralph, 144–47, 157
Lockwood, Rodney, 126–28
Long, Gillis, 276
Long, Russell, 273
Los Angeles, 134, 286
Loveman, Louis, 49
Lower Chattahoochee Valley APDC, 187
Lucas, Ben, 196
lynching, 10, 32–33

Macon (Georgia), 45, 92
Maddox, Lester: on APDCs, 246; Carter defeated by, 197–99; Carter praises, 202; Knowles and, 243, 246, 335; southern moderates versus, 248
Maddox, W. T., 192
Magaziner, Ira, 279
Magnet, Myron, 297
majoritarianism: of Carter, 184, 200, 201, 203; concern about anti-majoritarian means by which elites pursue their development agendas, 242; elites seen

as perverting, 244; Gingrich's New Majority, 334; in grievances over welfare, 264; New Federalism and, 172; of Nixon, 209, 242; politics of, 20, 201, 209, 242; racial, 200, 243; white, 20, 242, 244, 246. *See also* "silent majority"
managerial revolution, 76
marginalized communities: abandoned by public institutions, 300; accessing public resources, 157; businesspeople see themselves acting on behalf of, 190; Carter's state government reorganization and, 205–6; Cleveland: Now! on jobs for, 162; Coosa Valley APDC and enfranchising, 114; Democrats' commitment to raising up, 287; directly empowering, 341, 342; have to fight for state support, 333–34; Lewis champions, 340; multiplication of political authority and, 10; New Democrats on, 21, 331; New Federalism and resources for, 174; "participation" in elite management of, 20, 21; in participatory community development, 147; programs for benefit elites, 184–85; provisional forms of enfranchisement won by, 241; public-private partnerships exacerbate inequalities for, 5; silencing voices of, 208; Southern Growth Policies Board competes for resources with, 241; supply-side liberal policies and, 7, 8, 19; War on Poverty seeks to empower, 4. *See also* African Americans; minorities
market-oriented policies: of ARA, 108; congressional hearings on solutions for affordable housing from, 117; in economic crises of 1970s, 13; liberals employ, 5, 14; in New Deal, 3; New Democrats employ, 21, 269–70, 300, 328; public resources in, 298; for social progress, 112
markets: capital, 56, 58, 277; efficiency attributed to, 238; fails to provide affordable housing, 136; federal subsidies for remaking, 75; financial, 10, 77, 329; "free market" rhetoric, 13, 270, 298, 307, 310, 342; global, 337; housing, 82, 122, 125, 135, 154, 179, 331; idealization of, 13; inequities in, 152, 155; infrastructure spending for stimulating creation of, 28; labor, 102, 253, 293, 333; liberals and, 3, 10, 15; market barriers to enfranchisement in, 196; marketized governance, 285–86; market-making potential of liberal initiatives, 6–7; mortgage, 118; municipal bond, 17, 86, 214, 217, 219, 312, 335; New Deal in remaking of, 14–15; New Democrats on, 21, 291, 296; new ideas about state and, 278; Osborne on government and, 292; political power in shaping, 328; popular marketization, 322; Powell and government intrusion in, 224; racial discrimination in, 191; rationality attributed to, 239; Reagan on, 291, 298, 309–11; as self-correcting, 268; the state and, 282, 330, 331; stock market crash of 1929, 59; structural interventions in, 4; UDAGs for sculpting, 309. *See also* market-oriented policies
Marshall, Stewart A., 45
Marshall, Will, 284–85
Mason, Norman, 131
Massachusetts: Boston, 80, 179, 322; Capital Formation Task Force, 280; industrial decline of, 103, 107; as paying for their past spending habits, 272; tax revolts in, 242, 264
Massachusetts Technology Development Corporation (MTDC), 280–81
matching grants, local: borrowing for, 217; in Cleveland, 67, 69, 165; as difficult in states such as Georgia, 37; federal grants for obtaining, 70–71; liberalization of, 193
Mattingly, Mack, 307
"maximum feasible participation" principle: APDC leaders on, 187–88; in Community Action Program, 152, 153, 156; defeat of, 180; in Housing and Community Development Act of 1974, 175; Johnson and, 152, 160, 175; Moynihan on, 152–53; Rome's Community Action Committee and, 186; Shriver's defense of, 159–60; in smaller cities, 183; stifling of, 159, 161, 167; in War on Poverty, 4–5, 17, 115–16, 151–52, 154, 175, 177, 180, 183
Mayor's Economic Coordinating Commission, 229
McConnell, Eli, 32
McCormack, Walter, 67

McCullough, Richard, 186
McDermott, William, 86
McDonald, Milton, 186
McDonough, John J. "Jack," 48, 53, 101
McGhee, E. Pierce, 36–37
McGovern, George, 251, 270
McIntyre, James, 257, 265
McKinsey & Co., 302, 303, 319
McKissick, Floyd, 145–46
Medicaid, 154, 173, 275, 292, 308
Meeker, David, 176, 228
mergers and acquisitions, 337, 338
Merriam, Charles, 76–77; *American Political Ideals,* 76; decentralism of, 57, 77, 78; on economic planning, 57, 76–79; new personal rights proposed by, 86; NRPB and, 65, 76; "A Plan for Planning," 65–66; on policymakers discovering urban communities, 15; *Public and Private Government,* 21–22; on public-private cooperation, 21–22, 57, 66, 76, 77; on rational and evolutionary development, 65–66; on regional planning, 78
Merriam, Robert E., 257–58
microlending, 289–90
middle class: black, 32, 83, 157; in Cleveland, 140, 232, 323; Clinton on burdens of, 326; culturally conservative version of economic citizenship of, 92; feminists, 290; as special interest, 294; structural barriers to entering, 155; values, 293; white, 9, 19, 249, 330, 331, 338, 339
Middle Georgia APDC, 272
Mikva, Abner, 256
Mileti, Nick, 177–78
Miller, Zell, 115, 199
Mills, Wilbur, 107
minimum wage, 40, 293
Minneapolis, 322
minorities: in Busbee's Federal Powers triangle, 265; Carter and, 184, 252, 265; chambers of commerce create business development initiatives for, 223; on Cleveland Roundtable committees, 303; demands for empowerment by, 239; displacement of, 16, 195; FHA and, 118, 119; Jim Crow-like policies circumscribe citizenship for nonwhite, 8; locked into untenable mortgages, 1; majority minority cities, 299, 314; Model Cities for neighborhoods of, 167; political power increases for, 314; quotas for, 252, 315; rehousing after urban renewal, 193; scrutiny of, 222; in selective voter mobilization, 293; simulacra of administrative enfranchisement for, 21; single minority mothers, 290–91; U.S. Chamber of Commerce on federal aid for, 222; white Georgians on elevation of, 198. *See also* African Americans
Mitchell, George S., 43
Model Cities: in Alma, Georgia, 188–90; in Cleveland, 167–71; end of, 171; enterprise zones contrasted with, 310; U.S. Chamber of Commerce on, 223
modernization: during Cold War, 105, 113; Housing Act of 1954 and, 16; of infrastructure, 97; islands of poverty left behind, 107; Kennedy and modernization theory, 89; Myrdal on integration as problem of, 124; New Deal roots of, 7; race and poverty seen as opportunities for, 194; Rostow on, 105; urban renewal funds for incentivizing, 193
Mondale, Walter, 256
Moomaw, Ben, 47
Moore, Arch, 248
Moore, Bennie, 190
Moore, Frank, 257
Moral Majority, 242
Morris, John L., 47
Morrison, Douglas E. "Froggy," 99–100
mortgages: late payments on, 179–80; poor and working-class Americans locked into untenable, 1, 118, 119. *See also* Federal Housing Administration (FHA) mortgages; redlining
Moton, Robert R., 64
Moyers, Bill, 159
Moynihan, Daniel Patrick, 152–53, 174, 263, 264
municipal bonds: in Cleveland, 85, 86, 126, 139, 140, 162, 230, 235, 236, 301–2, 326; costs of municipal borrowing, 139; defaults during Great Depression, 60; as inducement for private investment, 17; markets, 17, 86, 214, 217, 219, 312, 335; Merriam and Chicago fiscal crisis, 76; nationally voters reject, 86; New Dealers on more expansive use of, 70; preferred to property tax burdens, 68; railroad expansion underwritten

by, 60; Shaker Heights, Ohio, default, 56; supply-side state builders employ, 13; tax-exempt, 217, 312; voters reject referenda for, 220, 221

municipal debt, 216–20; becomes unsustainable, 238; business elites and, 216, 220; in Cleveland, 20, 59–60, 61, 82, 84–86, 126, 140, 165, 215, 229, 234, 297, 300, 341; commercial banks hold, 239; cost of servicing, 172; crises of 1970s, 214–15, 240; federal government's role in subsidizing, 70; increasing, 21, 126; in northern industrial cities, 361n4; racial inequality underwritten by, 219; reactions to inflationary impact of, 20; short-term borrowing, 218–19, 234, 236, 239, 300; tax rates tied to, 242

municipal government. *See* city (municipal) government

Muskie, Edmund, 256

Myrdal, Gunnar, 124

NAACP (National Association for the Advancement of Colored People): on African American employment on federal projects, 8–9, 22; on ARA and race, 109; Businessmen's Interracial Committee on Community Affairs and, 144; in Cleveland, 64, 65, 135; on Cleveland Economic Opportunities Council, 157; on Housing Act's failure, 136; on racial discrimination in Cleveland, 82, 83; in Rome, Georgia, 32, 341; Wilkins' role in, 101

Nader, Ralph, 213, 237

NAM. *See* National Association of Manufacturers (NAM)

NAREB (National Association of Real Estate Boards), 123, 124

Nathan, Richard, 262

National Advisory Commission on Rural Poverty, 187

National Advisory Council on Economic Opportunity, 160–61

National Association for the Advancement of Colored People. *See* NAACP (National Association for the Advancement of Colored People)

National Association of Manufacturers (NAM): ARC opposed by, 113; business associations quit, 221; on business's alleged social responsibility, 223; Cleveland business elites in, 58, 361n7; Douglas's depressed areas bill opposed by, 104; federal programs opposed by, 221; in Greater Cleveland Growth Association workshops, 233; on industrial policy, 279; New Deal's pace debated by, 73; supply-side state builders partner with, 12

National Association of Real Estate Boards (NAREB), 123, 124

National Conference on Balanced Growth and Economic Development (1978), 259–60, 263–64

National Emergency Council, 35, 43

National Industrial Recovery Act (NIRA) of 1933, 15, 69–71

Nationalities Movement of Cuyahoga County, 165

National Labor Relations Act (Wagner Act), 43, 104, 152, 253

National League of Cities, 158, 220, 312, 321

National Negro Business League, 64

National Partnership for Reinventing Government, 14

National People's Action (NPA), 180, 304–5

National People's Platform, 231

National Planning Agency, 254

National Recovery Administration, 35, 39

National Resources Planning Board (NRPB): Coosa Valley APDC and, 97, 336; development commissions inspired by, 92; economic planning and, 75–76, 79, 102; elimination of, 15, 86, 88, 92; Georgia's Agricultural and Industrial Development Board compared with, 52; Hansen as consultant to, 42; industrial development efforts of, 93; in market restructuring, 15; Merriam and, 65, 76; new personal rights proposed by, 86; regionalism of, 79, 102; Roosevelt on, 88; supply-side liberal commitments in, 4

National Urban League, 146, 253

National Youth Administration, 46

neighborhood groups: business elites face, 221; in Cleveland, 177, 179, 231, 233, 306, 315; Kucinich and, 231–34; managing, 304; national movement of, 177; 1970s as "decade of the neighborhood," 232; in Ohio Public Interest Campaign, 230; urban fiscal crises and demands of, 214

neighborhood service centers, 156
Neighborhood Youth Corps, 207
neoliberalism: business producerism in emergence of, 238; credit rating agencies as quintessential institution of, 216; democracy in, 20, 183; on human capital, 291; local businesspeople in emergence of, 181; New Democrats and, 13, 20–21, 269, 276, 332; Nixon and, 153, 174; participation and, 20, 299, 328; emergence of, 13–14; supply-side liberalism and intractability of, 5; withdrawal of hope and opportunities in emergence of, 300
Neoliberals, The (Rothenberg), 279, 284
Ness, Eliot, 81
New Deal: anti-New Deal coalition among national elites, 36; Arnall and, 51, 52; boosters greet early, 34–39; "breadwinner" liberalism of, 7; bureaucratic inefficiencies of, 50–51; business producerism ratified by, 28; capital benefited by, 73; Carter's elite-led localism echoes, 184; Cleveland elites and, 57, 58; Cold War's international development and modernization programs' roots in, 7; compromises with racist and undemocratic elements, 8, 10, 40; decentralism and, 7, 26, 35, 43, 45, 241, 268; deficit spending by, 86; Democrats, 140; "the end of reform," 15; expectations for government raised by, 264; fault lines between local business interests and national lobbying associations exposed by, 36; federalism, 19, 51, 73, 153, 173, 263, 273, 276; federal-local "growth coalitions" have their roots in, 16; fiscal conservatism of early, 71; fiscal federalism of, 171; Ford administration calls for replacement of, 2–3; ideological opposition to, 87–88; industrial development efforts of, 93; on inequalities in local government, 10; Jim Crow built into developments of, 45–46; Keynesianism adopted by, 15, 71; liberalism, 9, 106, 239, 330; loss of faith in private sector, 284; market-making potential of programs of, 6–7; Moynihan on, 263; naturalizing subsidies of, 70–75; New Democrats compared with, 268, 269; planning programs, 18, 66, 75–81, 86, 253, 255; public authority and, 9, 14–15, 243;

public-private partnerships in, 3, 7, 73; racial inequality not addressed by, 43, 44–46; Reagan's attempt to overturn, 273, 274, 298; regional bases of coalition of, 242; in remaking of markets, 14–15; risk-abatement measures of, 282; Rose's history of Cleveland on, 87; in rural South, 189; supply-side liberalism born in late, 4; U.S. Chamber of Commerce on, 50; as watershed moment, 10–11; works through RFC, 57. *See also* New Deal works programs; *and other programs by name*
New Deal works programs: business and, 25–55; Cleveland African Americans and, 9, 14–15; Cleveland Chamber of Commerce leaders warm to, 67; indirect subsidies offered by, 68; as inducement for private investment, 17; Johnson on, 159; local elites empowered by, 3, 34–36, 45, 54, 58; RFC methods continued by, 68–69; school improvements in, 45–46; Urban Land Institute in programs of, 123; urban renewal and, 16. *See also* Works Progress Administration (WPA) *and other programs by name*
New Democrats: antipolitical legacy of, 334; Carter and, 241; Bill Clinton as, 20; Democratic Party remade by, 295; depoliticized government, 268, 269, 270, 332; on economic growth, 268, 282, 285, 332; on entitlements, 21, 269, 270, 332; on entrepreneurialism, 268–70, 276, 282, 284, 291–93, 296, 298, 309, 311; faith in capitalism of, 269; government spending as seen by, 21; on high tech, 21, 248, 268, 284; idea of the state of, 329–42; on innovation, 268; on insulating programs from democratic contestation, 7; on interest groups, 21, 267, 268, 269m 270; legitimation crisis of 1970s as context for, 20; the market as seen by, 21, 291, 296; market-oriented policies of, 21, 269–70, 300, 328; neoliberalism and, 13, 20–21, 232, 269, 276; on postindustrial policy, 268, 280; on private sector, 277, 285; *Rebuilding the Road to Opportunity* report, 276–77, 279–80, 294; on redistribution, 268, 291, 293; skepticism of programs and policies, 267, 331, 333; on social spending, 21,

291, 330; southern variant of, 248; special interests and, 20, 21, 267, 270, 272, 276, 284–85, 293, 294; supply-side liberalism and, 20–21, 284, 331–32, 334; on urban pathologies, 325; Wall Street financiers and, 268, 329–30; on welfare, 276, 292, 299; as white and male, 270; white suburban voters flattered by, 293. *See also* Democratic Leadership Council (DLC)

New Federalism, 171–75; aims of, 172; block grants in, 169, 173; builds on efforts to suppress "maximum feasible participation" principle, 153; Carter's policies compared with, 184, 203, 206, 252; central theme of, 171; deregulatory thrust of, 174, 175; enables cities to direct funds to downtown business interests, 177; expectations for government raised by, 264; formulas for funding allocation, 262; Housing and Community Development Act of 1974 as centerpiece of, 153; massive federal subsidies live on in, 181; new funding ensures passage of, 256; participatory ethos remains in, 20; private-sector elites in, 5; Reagan's New, 273–76; supply-side state builders support, 221; War on Poverty and urban renewal brought to an end by, 19, 151

New Left, 155

New Majority, 334

"New Orleans Declaration" (Democratic Leadership Council), 294

New South: business moderates in, 97, 110, 248; Carter and, 184, 197, 272; Democratic Party in, 202, 204, 272, 273; emergence of, 91; Republican Party in, 115; Roosevelt on a progressive, 28

new urbanism, 227, 228

New York City: bond bid rejected in, 219; Community Action Program in, 157; consultants in, 303; fiscal crisis of 1975, 214–15, 234, 236; Municipal Assistance Corporation, 301; profits from developing outer boroughs, 128; slum clearance in, 80; southern governors on avoiding fate of, 248; welfare state attributed to, 215, 220

New York State: AFDC growth in, 271; allocation formula for Carter public works program, 261; Syracuse, 157. *See also* New York City

Nichols, Roy, 96

NIRA (National Industrial Recovery Act) of 1933, 15, 69–71

Nixon, Richard: antigovernment governance of, 203, 209; Carter compared with, 252; Comprehensive Employment and Training Act of, 308; deregulation in administration of, 175; Housing and Community Development Act of 1974 of, 153; localism of, 153, 172–74, 209; majoritarianism of, 209, 242; New Federalism of, 5, 19, 151, 153, 169, 171, 172, 184, 203, 206, 221, 254, 256, 273–75; Perk and administration of, 168; plans to eliminate OEO, 206–7; on private sectors' leadership in federal programs, 153; on public-private partnerships, 19, 153, 173–74; on revenue sharing, 172–73, 218; Rural Development Act of 1972 of, 244–45; "silent majority" of, 171, 172, 175, 209; white ethnic strategy of, 167

Northeast-Midwest Congressional Coalition, 260–61

NPA (National People's Action), 180, 304–5

NRPB. *See* National Resources Planning Board (NRPB)

Nunn, Sam, 272–73; Citizens Committee for Reorganization run by, 203–4; at Cleveland Democratic Leadership Council convention, 294; on Democratic Leadership Council, 283; "Get Tough in Washington" slogan of, 272–73, 291; in new generation of Democrats, 249, 270; Reagan and, 274, 277; as southern New Democrat, 278; on special interests, 272

O'Connor, Alice, 155

Odum, Howard, 43, 51

OEO. *See* Office of Economic Opportunity (OEO)

Office of Economic Opportunity (OEO): accused of subsidizing riots, 200; Carter's Community Action program approved by, 182; Coosa Valley APDC reports on, 186; Johnson administration's commitment to reforming, 161; "maximum feasible public relations" campaign of, 156; in New York City, 157; under Nixon, 168, 206–7; Operation Mainstream, 206, 207; Stokes funded by, 163; U.S. Conference of Mayors on, 158

Office of Price Administration (OPA), 85
Ohio: Brook Park, 121, 128; Columbus, 323–24; Development Financing Commission, 313; local governments restricted from creating new forms of taxes, 59; Parma, 121, 128; RFC loans to companies in, 74; Shaker Heights, 56, 63; Thomas Edison program, 320. *See also* Cleveland; Cuyahoga County (Ohio)
Ohio Homeowners and Taxpayer Revolt, Inc., 140
Ohio Public Interest Campaign (OPIC), 230, 231
Ohlin, Lloyd, 155
Oldham, Harry, 97
Oldham, Lucian, 341
"one person, one vote," 94
Operation Mainstream, 206, 207
OPIC (Ohio Public Interest Campaign), 230, 231
opportunity, economic. *See* economic opportunity
opportunity theory, 155
Orlando (Florida), 222
Osborne, David, 269, 285–86, 292, 332

Pace, Stanley, 303
Parma (Ohio), 121, 128
participation: Carter on, 201; democratic, 17, 19, 228, 270, 299, 300; New Democrats on, 270; participatory democracy, 155; participatory ethos of 1970s, 228; Turner on hollowed out and managed forms of, 20; Watson and issues of, 257. *See also* community (citizen) participation
paternalism: of business elites, 12, 33, 60; of federal officials, 129; Johnson on Community Action Programs', 158; racial, 144, 184; southern, 34, 39; white, 12, 159
Payne, Mather, 186
Pei, I. M., and Associates, 137, 141, *142*
Pension Reserves Investment Board, 280–81
Perk, Ralph, 165; CDBGs and, 176–78, 323; on citizen participation in Model Cities, 168, 169; Cleveland's business elites' criticism of, 226; Davis and, 227, 229; economic planning commission of, 227, 230; federal assistance and, 167, 226; in financial crisis of 1975, 229; mayoral campaign of 1971, 165–66; on Model Cities audit, 170; Nationalities Movement of Cuyahoga County of, 165; New Federalism and, 173; political legitimacy collapses, 230; on property taxes, 140, 165–67; as Republican, 140, 165–67; tax abatements of, 229, 230, 232, 242; Twenty Point Action Program of, 229; Weir on, 234; white ethnics and, 165, 166, 226, 229
Personal Responsibility and Work Opportunity Reconciliation Act of 1996, 332
Pertz, Barbara, 178
Philadelphia: credit rating agencies and, 300; Democratic Party in, 213; Rizzo, 172; second-wave industrialization in, 58; slum clearance in, 80; southern governors on avoiding fate of, 248; WPA programs to benefit white-collar workers in, 71–72
Pittsburgh: Allegheny Conference, 120; federal-local "growth coalition" in, 16; labor campaigns in, 65; slum clearance in, 80; total assessed value decline in 1930s, 66
Plain Dealer (newspaper): on business elite in city government reorganization, 301; on "Civic Vision" plan, 318–19; on Cleveland paying more taxes than are returned, 261; on Cleveland Roundtable leadership changes, 337; on Cleveland's "Rubesville" image, 228; on elites in urban renewal, 138; on Evans, 120; on FHA, 129–30, 133; on Forbes, 317; on Greater Cleveland Growth Association, 220–21; on NRPB, 86–87; on proposal for WPA program for white-collar workers, 72; won't deliver to certain neighborhoods, 325; on WPA rules, 74
planning: centralized, 99, 113, 255, 310; federal standards for, 98; Humphrey-Hawkins bill on local councils for, 253; increasingly professionalized planners, 98; New Deal, 18, 66, 75–81, 86, 254, 255; Reagan policies and, 266. *See also* city planning; economic planning; National Resources Planning Board (NRPB); planning commissions; regional planning; urban planning
planning commissions: Carter's West Central Georgia APDC, 103, 110, 182; Cleveland City Planning Commission, 85; Cleveland Roundtable and

Cleveland Tomorrow, 303–4; Coosa Valley APDC works with local, 100; in eastern Kentucky, 108; Regional Association of Cleveland as, 79; in Rome, Georgia, 96, 101–2; Roosevelt on local, 88; 701 planning grant program funding of, 97–98. *See also* Area Planning and Development Commissions (APDC)

Planning Enabling Act of 1957, 16, 97–98

pluralism: democratic, 152, 156; liberals on, 284

Pogue, Richard, 236, 303

political power: African American, 152, 164, 213, 314–15; asymmetries of, 241; of banks, 236; business alliances augur new forms of regional, 27–28; cities' political autonomy wanes, 123; city governments in national balance of, 14; Community Action Program for remaking structures of, 152; CORE forges new strategies for developing, 145–46; Georgia's electoral system for controlling, 93; markets shaped by, 328; minorities' increases, 314; modern liberalism's wariness of, 10; Osborne on battles over, 332; Powell on business elites pursuing, 224; public authority in narratives of organizing, 330; supply-side liberalism and available forms of, 240; Talmadge on centralizing in Washington, 38; War on Poverty seen as direct assault on existing, 158; white racism becomes more explicit as blacks gain, 152; Wright on local elites and, 54

politics: anticommunism in American, 330; antiestablishment, 334, 335; of antigovernment governance, 203, 209; booster, 17; business's antigovernment, 223–24; calls for authentic forms of, 278; class-blind, 249; Cleveland's business elites' control over city, 58, 121; Clinton depoliticizes welfare, 332–33; constituency, 293; county courthouse, 18, 27, 28, 47, 98, 204; of defensive localism, 20; development, 112, 189, 334; economic development and, 30; of economic progress, 94; emerging class of businessperson with political clout, 99; emerging political-fiscal environment, 219; of fiscal federalism, 115; "good government," 93; growth, 270, 334; interest-group, 21, 269, 270, 284; Kennedy makes economic growth a political project, 89; "law and order," 201, 243; local interests shape national, 276; machine, 147, 299; majoritarian, 20, 201, 209, 242; Merriam on economics and, 77; midcentury bipartisan, 331; neoliberalism on, 13; New Democrats depoliticize government, 268–70, 332; outsider candidates, 205; "post-racial," 185, 197, 202–9, 248; postwar challenges to elites' hold on local, 88; pro-business, 82; public authority and zero-sum, 242–46; quality of life, 241, 248–49; of racial resentment, 199, 200, 204; racist, 164–65, 200; range of options narrows, 239; redistributionary, 232; white anger politicized by Carter, 201; white homeowner, 9, 20; women in formal, 340. *See also* political power

"Politics of Evasion, The" (Galston and Kamarck), 293

Polk, Franklin, 165

populism: of Carter, 200, 203, 204; in Cleveland, 225; of Kucinich, 213, 232, 238; liberals versus, 231; producerism and, 12; racial, 213; small-propertied, 140, 166, 213; white ethnic, 213

Porter, Albert, 146

Porter, Michael E., 290

postindustrial policy: biomedical, 297, 298; for Cleveland, 318–19; Clinton on national, 334, 335–36; entrepreneurial, 320; geared to white suburbanites, 304; in Georgia, 247, 339; Magaziner on, 279; New Democrats on, 268, 280; southern Democrats on, 283

postindustrial society: cities as hubs of health care and research, 137; managing transition from smokestack chasing to postindustrial economies, 247–48; New Democrat initiatives on, 21; public-private partnerships of, 268; in the South, 247–51; Southern Growth Policies Board and, 241; urban renewal as policy for, 138

"post-racial" society: Carter on, 185, 197, 202, 208, 251; Georgia as, 203; politics of, 185, 197, 202–9; in the South, 183–84, 197, 241, 247–51

poverty: African American, 28, 108, 287; Appalachian, 91, 107, 111, 112; ARC's approach to, 91; Arnall on, 51–53; Carter's state government reorganization

poverty (*continued*)
and, 206; in Cleveland, 60, 300, 327; Clinton on reducing, 288, 295; "community action" approach to, 155; Community Action Program organizes the poor, 157; Coosa Valley APDC and, 114; cultures of, 155; Democratic Leadership Council accused of neglecting, 285; development agendas framed in terms of, 184, 190; directly empowering, 340, 341; diverting federal subsidies for the poor, 17, 223; Douglas's depressed areas bill on, 104; economic development seen as solution to, 7, 43, 44, 91, 209, 221; eliminating by razing poor neighborhoods, 195; elite abandonment of the poor, 21, 302, 318, 324, 325; entrenched, 28, 90, 153, 191, 295, 328, 341; entrepreneurial poor people, 292; entrepreneurial solutions for, 294, 296; federal aid legitimized in terms of fighting, 241; FHA on financial viability of housing near poor neighborhoods, 119; fighting in Cold War context, 154–55; as fig leaf for supply-side state builders' growth agenda, 262; as funding and modernization opportunity, 194; illusory nature of supply-side liberal solutions for, 4; indexes of, 184, 187; individualist solutions to, 222; islands of, 107, 288; Jim Crow as cause of, 28; Johnson on attacking root causes of, 159; Kennedy and, 89, 107–14, 155; Keyserling on, 104; leveraging, 297–328; liberal economic policies and elimination of, 90; liberalism on uplifting the poorest, 341; making it pay, 182–209; Moynihan on poor's ability to wield power, 153; National Advisory Commission on Rural Poverty, 187; Osborne on, 292; pathologies seen as perpetuating, 152; the poor as special interest, 257; the poor in Busbee's Federal Powers triangle, 265; the poor in Carter's West Central Georgia APDC, 182; poor people's movements, 11; racialized, 43, 91, 110, 152, 153, 187, 191, 192, 287, 328; Reagan on enterprise zones and, 310, 311; reimagining, 287–94; rhetoric about attached to public-private partnerships, 88; rhetorical commitment to community participation in, 181; rural, 12, 110, 111, 189, 249, 289; Rural Development Act of 1972 on, 245; segregation of impoverished citizens, 324; silencing voices of the poor, 208; southern, 28, 39–40, 43, 44, 46, 262–63; structuralist critique of growth and, 19; Temporary Assistance to Needy Families for, 333; urban, 175, 249, 307; white, 91, 107, 108, 112; white Georgians on elevation of the poor, 198; working poor, 292–93. *See also* antipoverty programs; War on Poverty

Powell, Jody, 205
Powell, Lewis, 215, 224–25
power, political. *See* political power
PPI (Progressive Policy Institute), 283, 292–95, 332
President's Appalachian Regional Commission (PARC), 110
President's Commission on Juvenile Delinquency (PCJD), 155, 156
price controls, wartime, 85
Primus Venture Fund, 319
private investment: ARC and encouragement of, 112; Cleveland attempts to stimulate, 323; Clinton on, 289; Coosa Valley APDC leads to, 99; entrepreneurial investment, 281, 282, 293–94, 309; federal aid and, 46, 306; Georgia's venture capital fund akin to, 282; Hansen on, 17, 41, 42, 57, 77, 80, 105, 128; inflation restricts, 268; infrastructure spending seen as stimulating, 28; Kennedy on tax cuts and, 106; Keynesianism seen as insufficient to create, 40–41; leveraging, 299, 308, 309; Magaziner and Reich on, 279; New Democrats and, 268; public insurance of, 280; in Rome, Georgia, 47, 53; slum clearance provides opportunities for, 81, 123; supply-side fiscalism on, 310; supply-side liberalism's emphasis on, 7, 16; in UDAG requirements, 309; urban renewal for stimulating, 117, 138; urban triage for attracting, 298, 299
private sector: in administration of liberal initiatives, 3, 11; in affordable housing, 12, 66, 117, 136; in amelioration of poverty, 91; ARC and growth in, 112; Carter and, 257; Cleveland Lexington Village project and, 318; Clinton redirects subsidies to, 333; in Community Action Programs, 160; enterprise zones

criticized in, 311; in FHA practices, 118; Ford administration on role of, 181; "Good Government is Good Business in Georgia" ad, 53; government subsidies while maintaining authority of, 67; innovation by, 277, 339; Johnson and Nixon on its leadership in federal programs, 153, 173; Keynesianism seen as insufficient to create innovation by, 40; in legitimacy of publicly funded economic planning, 100; liberal progress redistributes resources to, 8; NETWORK cultivates, 283; New Dealers' loss of faith in, 284; New Democrats on, 277, 285; in public housing, 69; public resources invested in developments of, 21; and public sector as complementary, 3; public sector depends on profits of, 236; Reagan task force on, 309; Republicans on public-private partnerships and, 174; Rural Development Act of 1972 on, 245; seen as barrier to state building, 15; in slum clearance, 69; solutions for affordable housing, 117, 178; solutions for social progress, 112; in supply-side liberalism, 214; support for public investment by, 280; U.S. Chamber of Commerce on public sector versus, 50; in Voinovich's modernization of city government, 300–301; in War on Poverty, 5; Weir on accountability of officials in, 237; WPA hires officials from, 26. *See also* business

producerism: liberals' social priorities expands elites' sense of, 187; of supply-side state builders, 12, 129; War on Poverty and, 159, 162. *See also* business producerism

progress, social. *See* social progress

Progressive Era, 14, 25–26, 57, 297

Progressive Policy Institute (PPI), 283, 292–95, 332

progressives: business, 8, 197; on decommodifying social goods, 8, 332; elite efforts to bring them to heel, 240; Georgia as progressive, 53; Kucinich's election and, 214; liberals versus, 231; Merriam as, 76; New Democrats as, 276; public housing advocated by, 119; racial progressivism, 184; Roosevelt on a progressive New South, 28; southern governors as, 247; southern supply-side state builders see themselves as, 185; supply-side liberalism challenged by, 8–9

Project Afro, 305

property taxes: anti-property-tax sentiment, 275; bankruptcy as alternative to raising, 260; based on inflated land values, 59; in Cleveland, 82, 86, 140, 165, 166, 215, 229, 301; Cleveland Clinic pays no, 340; in Floyd County, Georgia, 335; Great Depression and, 59–60, 66; grievances about, 264; New Federalism and, 172; as percentage of locally raised revenue, 122–23; Perk on, 140, 165–67; and public services in the South, 40; redistribution of, 140; revenue bonds preferred to straining, 68; seen as overburdened, 217; seen as unfair, 172; Sunbelt suburbanization preserves, 121; as threat to homeownership, 140; white ethnic Clevelanders concerned with, 81; in white homeowner politics, 20

property values: in Cleveland, 143, 166, 229; decline in cities in 1970s, 214, 220; FHA in preserving, 119; fiscal imperative to boost, 16; local government revenues depend on, 81; in Rome, Georgia, 32; Roosevelt on southern, 40, 43; slum clearance and, 80, 129; urban, 122; urban renewal and increases in, 137

Proxmire, William, 273, 274

Public and Private Government (Merriam), 21–22

public goods: affordable housing seen as, 136; Lewis delivers, 340; New Deal democratizes, 11; private actors for carrying out, 268; privatization of, 232. *See also* social goods

public housing: Advisory Committee on Housing Policies and Programs on, 126; in Cleveland, 67–70, 79, 80, 125, 132, 136, 167, 315; economic and moral arguments for, 80–81; focus on failures of, 117; Housing Act of 1949 on, 118, 124–126; Housing Act of 1954 on, 118, 119, 127; liberals adopt decentralized approach to, 15; National Association of Real Estate Boards opposes, 124; postwar experiments with, 125; private solutions for, 69; progressives call for massive programs of, 8; Truman on, 124; urban renewal obviating need for, 117; for whites in Atlanta, 45

450   Index

public investment: Arnall calls for, 52; Cleveland Chamber of Commerce calls for, 85; Coosa Valley APDC leads to, 99; Galbraith on, 42; Georgia boosters seek, 27; Greater Cleveland Growth Association tries to leverage, 227; Hansen on, 42, 44, 46, 47, 51, 57, 77–78, 80, 249; as means to economic growth, 92; midcentury liberals on, 330; NRPB's 1942 report on, 87; private-sector and, 280, 339; social Keynesians on, 104; for structural interventions, 227; in supply-side liberalism, 4; targeted, 4, 28, 90, 105, 108, 123; in UDAG requirements, 309

public pension funds, 13, 320

public-private partnerships: activists challenge, 225; Allegheny Conference as, 120; bipartisan vogue for in 1990s, 14; Carter and, 103, 184, 207; as check on liberal state, 3, 19, 153; in Cleveland, 19, 67, 131, 134, 162–64, 296, 297; Clinton on, 21, 288, 333; Coosa Valley APDC as, 101; as crumbling, 337; differences between local, 19; elite-led, 2, 174, 337; Ford and, 2–3, 174; Forward Atlanta as, 227; in Georgia's Agricultural and Industrial Development Board, 53; Hansen on, 51, 77; in housing, 118; as ideologically up for grabs, 116; inequalities exacerbated by, 5; Job Corps as, 160; Kennedy and, 4; in legitimation crisis of 1970s, 20; liberals employ, 3, 5, 330; Merriam on, 21–22, 57, 66, 76, 77; for mortgage guarantees, 126; multicounty regional public-private planning and development organizations in Georgia, 88, 91, 92; nationalization of urban forms of, 14; in New Deal, 3, 7, 73; Nixon on, 19, 153, 173–74; Osborne and Gaebler on, 286; *Plain Dealer* editorial on, 87; postindustrial, 268; Powell on, 224; public authority flows to, 246; regional development commissions, 108; for relief, 60; Roosevelt on, 26, 35–36; Rural Development Act of 1972 and, 245; Selznick on dilemma of, 22; of Starr, 95–97; in supply-side liberalism, 140, 225, 231, 239, 331; UDAGs for, 309; unequally shared burdens of, 20; in War on Poverty programs, 156

public resources: accessing by the poor, 157; boundary-setting role of, 269; business producerism authorizes extraction of, 340; elites capture greater share of, 298; fighting poverty seen as waste of, 171; invested in private-sector developments, 21; local business elites' influence over, 221, 222; in market-oriented solutions, 298; redistribution in New Democrat policies, 268; resentful voters on control of, 242, 243; scarcity in the South, 30; Southern Growth Policies Board employs, 241; welfare seen as drain on, 292. *See also* public investment

public sector: Arnall on stimulus from, 52; consultants in, 303; crises of 1970s, 214; depends on private profits, 236; New Democrats on risk-taking by, 277; Osborne and Gaebler on transforming, 285–86; and private sector as complementary, 3; U.S. Chamber of Commerce on, 50; wages in, 217, 218; Weir on accountability of officials in, 237. *See also* government

public spending: businesspeople and, 225, 298; interest groups demand, 240; Keyserling on, 254; liberal policies associated with, 172; liberals on limiting, 256; Perk and, 226; private initiative and, 50; Rome, Georgia, businessmen educate voters on, 92; voter resistance to, 85. *See also* federal spending; social spending

Public Works Administration (PWA), 45, 49, 57, 69, 70, 71

PWA (Public Works Administration), 45, 49, 57, 69, 70, 71

race: AFDC as racialized issue, 270; Arnall on, 51–53; in battles over distribution, 240; biased policing, 315; chambers of commerce on racial inclusion, 222; in claims of special interests exercising public authority, 20; Cleveland Roundtable on race relations, 303, 307; Cleveland's racial tolerance, 58, 63; Davis on prospect of race war, 164; discrimination based on, 63, 82, 202; exclusions in liberal state, 11; federal spending associated with racial unrest, 199–200; FHA's racially conservative practices,

18; fiscal disciple as race discipline, 273; formal racial enfranchisement, 331; as funding and modernization opportunity, 194; in grievances over welfare, 7, 240, 264, 267; interracial dialogue, 144, 177, 190; interracial solidarity, 166; in legitimacy of publicly funded economic planning, 100; liberalism as multiracial political coalition, 9; Nixon administration on, 174; politics of racial resentment, 199, 200, 204; preferences in hiring based on, 166; racial conservatism, 131, 272; racial grievance, 166, 197, 203, 209; racialized battles over welfare, 7; racialized poverty, 43, 91, 110, 152, 153, 187, 191, 192, 287, 328; racial liberalism, 124; racially restricted democracy, 101; racial majoritarianism, 200, 243; racial paternalism, 144, 184; racial populism, 213; racial privilege, 331; racial progress, 119, 139, 140, 185; racial progressivism, 184; racial violence, 33, 119, 185, 196, 208, 209, 247, 248; southern racial exceptionalism, 40, 191; tokenism, 17, 157, 196, 222; Turner on racial progress under liberalism, 139; white anger over pace of racial change, 197, 198; white liberal obliviousness regarding, 250–51; white racial innocence, 197, 209; white racial majorities, 171. *See also* African Americans; "post-racial" society; racial inequality; racism

racial inequality: Carter's policies exacerbate, 203; imagining alternatives to, 342; municipal debt underwrites, 219; New Dealers as disinclined to address, 43–46; Nixon administration on, 174; "post-racial" politics and, 208; in urban renewal, 138–39, 142, 144, 146, 219

racism: acrimony over *Brown v. Board of Education*, 99; attributed to Carter, 206; becomes more explicit as blacks gain political power, 152, 164; Carter's calls to transcend, 184; in Cleveland, 64–65; Du Bois on, 55; of FHA, 18, 119, 131; in Georgia, 27, 91, 208; in housing market, 135; Ku Klux Klan, 33, 101; in local government, 11; of local welfare administrators, 157; New Deal's compromise with, 8, 10; New South Democrats reject overt, 272; in perceptions of fighting poverty, 171; in Perk's mayoral campaign, 165; racist politics, 164–65, 200; in Rome, Georgia, 54–55, 198; southern leaders declare end of, 248; Talmadge's racial demagoguery, 37–38; of white ethnic Clevelanders, 147; white supremacy, 38, 51

Rains, Albert, 132
Rampley, C. D., 266
Randolph, A. Philip, Institute, 146
Range, Athalie, 249–50
Ratner, Albert, 322, 342
Reagan, Ronald: AFDC and, 269, 271, 272, 274–76, 308; attempt to overturn New Deal, 273, 274, 298; austerity under, 7, 13, 239, 270, 298, 305, 307, 313–14, 321; battles over welfare under, 7, 270–72, 276; CDBGs and, 274, 307–8, 323; devolution under, 7, 13, 275, 298, 309; effects of election of, 266; on enterprise zones, 298, 310–12; federal aid cut by, 266, 305, 310; federal spending cuts of, 274–76, 312, 323; on markets, 291, 298, 309–11; New Federalism of, 273–76; Nunn and, 273; program "swap" with states, 275; Reagan Democrats, 326; reelection of, 282; Reich on, 279; social safety net attacked by, 269, 291; tax cuts by, 273–74, 277, 308, 311; UDAGs and, 307, 309; urban policy of, 307, 309, 310, 312; Volcker retained by, 277; on welfare state, 273

Reavis, Jack, 144–45
Rebuilding the Road to Opportunity (report), 276–77, 279–80, 294
recession: under Carter, 207, 242, 253; Clinton spends during, 288; Hansen on public debt and, 77; of late 1950s, 104; of 1914–15, 60; of 1952–54, 122; under Reagan, 274; "Roosevelt recession" of 1937, 40, 47
Reconstruction Finance Corporation (RFC): Cleveland banks bailed out by, 57; Cleveland public housing financed by, 67–69; Cuyahoga County, Ohio, applies for funds from, 62; Foster seeks loan from, 34; local elites partner with, 68–69; localism of, 68; model of federal debt-financing, 69; Ohio companies' loans from, 74; Polk's opposition to, 165; PWA bond purchases financed by, 70; Roosevelt on, 25, 34, 57

redistribution: alcohol and cigarette taxes as, 326, 327; in Cleveland, 299; Clinton's anti-politics of ending, 332; Democratic Leadership Council on, 294; Democrats on wealth, 285; economic growth emphasized over, 331; income, 271; Kennedy on, 107; Kucinich and, 232; midcentury liberals on, 330; New Democrats and, 268, 291, 293; of property taxes, 140; supply-side liberalism favors development over, 7, 90; in worthwhile infrastructure projects, 71
redlining: capital kept out of blighted areas by, 128; creating affordable housing in shadow of, 136; FHA and, 118, 131, 178; Housing Act of 1954 and, 127; insurgencies against, 232; mortgage options limited by, 179; neighborhood groups fight, 177
Reed, Bruce, 294
Regional Association of Cleveland, 79
regional development: Carter's West Central Georgia APDC in, 182; eastern Kentucky commission for, 108; federal subsidies for, 48–49, 250; in Georgia, 48, 52, 92, 96–98, 240; Franklin D. Roosevelt, Jr., on, 110
regionalism: as Achilles heel for larger cities, 79; business alliances augur new forms of regional political power, 27–28; Georgia businessmen's embrace of, 99; Moynihan accused of, 264; naturalizing and regionalizing federal aid, 46–51; pro-growth, 95; of supply-side state builders, 15, 51. *See also* regional development; regional planning
regional planning: boosters turn to, 47–50; business elites as resistant to, 18; Carter and, 200, 255, 257–58; in Cleveland, 55, 58, 79–80; Congress amplifies capacity for, 193; Coosa Valley APDC conference on comprehensive, 186–87; in federal urban programs, 16; in Georgia, 16, 18, 52, 88, 91, 92, 98, 103, 110; Keyserling on, 254, 255; liberals tap into existing machinery for, 15; Merriam on, 78; as mode of political-economic planning, 16–18; NRPB as model for, 79, 102; in post-racial, postindustrial South, 247–51; for rationalizing economic development, 75; around Rome, Georgia, 16; Roosevelt on, 52; Section 701 planning grant program fosters a model for, 98; Southern Growth Policies Board in, 241, 247–50; Starr and Harper on, 96, 97; suburbanites oppose, 58, 79, 80; Vandiver commissions industrial development plan, 95–96

rehabilitation (renovation) subsidies, 178–79
Reich, Robert, 278–79; on Clinton's concern with deficits, 329, 330; on human capital, 291, 329; *Minding America's Business,* 279; *The Next American Frontier,* 292; *Rebuilding the Road to Opportunity* report and, 276; on social justice and growth, 291–92; on supply-side investment, 329; as supply-side liberal, 6
Reidy, William, 301
reindustrialization, 193, 279
Reinventing Government (Osborne and Gaebler), 285–86
relief riots, 65, 72, 145, 165
relocation assistance, 143, 156
renovation (rehabilitation) subsidies, 178–79
rental housing: discriminatory rents, 64, 122; FHA and, 118, 134; private developers avoid, 133; rising rents in 1960s, 143; substandard for African Americans, 250
rent strikes, 143, 157
Report on Economic Conditions of the South, 43, 46
Republican Party: on AFDC, 272; CDBGs privilege, 175; Clinton's national postindustrial policy and, 336; Commerce Department opposed by, 336; on constitutional limits on spending, 273; Contract with America, 334, 335; "emerging Republican majority," 242; fundraising skews toward, 284; Heritage Groups Council of, 167; House majority won in 1994, 335; on market-based solutions, 300; New Democrats and, 267; in New South, 115; Perk and, 140, 165–67; in the South, 199; "trickle down" theory of, 277; voter mobilization by, 293; white majoritarian politics in, 20
research and development (R&D): business seeks it from government, 280; in Cleveland, 320; Clinton moves funding to, 336; Coosa Valley APDC on, 97; at

Georgia Tech, 95, 102, 336; Hodges on, 247; Rostow on, 249; short-term profits preferred to, 277
Research Triangle Institute, 247, 281
Resident Board of Trustees, 168
Revenue Act of 1913, 312
Revenue Act of 1964, 107
revenue sharing: Carter on, 174; Cleveland rejects, 121; expiry of, 276; Heller on, 173; National Association of Manufacturers opposes, 221; Nixon on general, 172–73, 218; Perk seeks, 167; Reagan considers cutting, 307; reauthorization of, 229, 275; Rural Development Act of 1972 compared with, 245; support for, 274–75; targeting versus, 257
RFC. *See* Reconstruction Finance Corporation (RFC)
Rich, Richard, 339
Richmond (Virginia), 224, 248
Rigas, Anne, 334, 335
rights, social and economic: conservatives oppose new federal, 83; Marshall on new, 284–85; Merriam on public-private cooperation and, 21–22; NRPB rights-oriented initiatives, 86; "trickle down" view and guarantees of, 8; welfare rights, 4, 157, 252, 271–72. *See also* civil rights
right-to-work laws, 91, 109
Rivers, E. D., 94
Rizzo, Frank, 172
Roanoke (Virginia), 47
Robb, Charles, 283, 285
Robinette, R. B., 61
Robinson, Graham, 32
Rock and Roll Hall of Fame, 326, *327*
Rockefeller, Nelson, 271
Rohaytn, Felix, 301
Rome (Georgia)
 city agencies and government: Community Action Committee, 186; Community Action Council, 194; Urban Renewal Board, 192, 195, 196
 demographics: growth, 31, 90; working-class whites, 33, 34, 45. *See also* African American Romans
 development and renewal: Altoview Terrace, 45; Area Planning and Development Commissions make fact-finding trips to, 103; DeSoto Homes, 45; East First Street project, *31,* 194; Etowah River dam project, 49, 53; Georgia Tech Industrial Development Board branch in, 101–2, 249, 336; Georgia Tech report, 92; levees built, 38–39, 47, 53; road improvement initiative rejected, 30–31; slum clearance, 45, 192–93; urban renewal, *31,* 191–97
 economy: industrial base, 29; as undercapitalized, 59; unions, 34
 events: Agricultural and Industrial Development Board district meeting, 53; Goldwater visits, 114; Labor Day festivities of 1931, 33
 federal programs: ARC projects, 113; Civil Works Administration program, 36–37; Foster on New Deal discrimination against, 26, 36–37; RFC loans as risky for, 34; TVA, 90; WPA projects, 6, 39, 47
 geographic constraints, 27, 31–32
 location, 28–29
 planning: Harper in, 96; planning commission, 96, 101–2; regional planning, 16, 92; Wagner in, 96
 politics and activism: growth politics, 334; small taxpayer frustration, 243; on Herman Talmadge, 94
 racial issues: Jim Crow, 32–33, 54–55; racial violence, 54–55, 185, 196, 208, 209; racism, 54–55, 198; segregation, 32, 33, 45, 185, 341; sit-in movement, 185
 social characteristics: blighted areas, 192, 195; Clevelanders compared with Romans, 56; homogenization of urban environments, 16; voluntarism, 60
 See also Rome Chamber of Commerce; *Rome News-Tribune* (newspaper); *and officials by name*
Rome Chamber of Commerce, 29; African Americans excluded from, 32; development groups in building of, 102; on government making venture capital available, 280; interracial meetings led by, 196; Labor Day festivities funded by, 33–34; McDonough's role in, 48; members on city levee committee, 38; producerist self-conception of, 209; on Rome's growth, 90; sit-in of 1963 and, 185; on three classes of residents, 209; Wagner's *Blueprint* and, 96
Rome Housing Authority, 194–96

454 Index

Rome News Tribune (newspaper): on ARC, 112; complaints about Rome Housing Authority in, 194; on Coosa Valley APDC, 99, 186; on Filipino development officer's visit, 114; on Floyd County Hospital, 39; Goldwater endorsed by, 199; on Goldwater on Coosa Valley APDC, 115; letter on possibility of violence in, 196; letter on the bright side of urban renewal in, 195; on local business elites serving the nation, 49–50; on OEO summer school affair, 200; publisher of, 48; racist fearmongering in, 198; on town hall meeting's demands, 244
Romney, George, 169
Roosevelt, Eleanor, 83
Roosevelt, Franklin D. (FDR): administration reaches out to local governments, chambers of commerce, and civic organizations, 35, 36; black Clevelanders appeal to, 83; Cleveland Chamber of Commerce members' grievances about, 72–73; on competitive localism, 51; economic bill of rights of, 86; on Etowah River dam project, 48; on "forgotten man," 25, 34, 225; "Four Freedoms" of, 76; idealized image of local democracy of, 25; incremental, growth-based vision of reform, 43–44, 51; Kennedy on critics of, 89; on national system of regional planning councils, 52; new public works spending of 1938, 47; on planning, 75, 87–88; on public-private cooperation, 26, 35–36, 49; public wealth rationale of, 40, 44, 81; on RFC, 25, 34, 57; "Roosevelt recession" of 1937, 40, 47; Second Bill of Rights of, 88; on social conditions as dependent on economic conditions, 44, 46; on the South, 10, 28, 39–40, 43–44; as supply-side liberal, 6; supply-side state builders commended by, 49; Talmadge on, 38; U.S. Chamber of Commerce on his attacks on big business, 50; in Warm Springs, Georgia, 39; WPA established by, 37. *See also* New Deal
Roosevelt, Franklin D., Jr., 110, 111
Rose, William Ganson, 87
Rosenfeld, Stuart, 278, 291
Rostenkowski, Dan, 313

Rostow, Walt Whitman, 105–6, 249, 263–64
Rothenberg, Randall, 279, 284, 285, 294
Rubin, Robert, 329
Rural Development Act of 1972, 244–45
Rural Electrification Administration, 36
Russell, Richard B., 34
Rustin, Bayard, 146

St. Germain, Fernand, 218–19
Saltzman, Maurice, 236
Samuelson, Paul, 103
Sanders, Beulah, 157
Sanders, Carl, 112, 197, 201
Sanford, Bill, 320
Sanford, Terry, 247, 248
San Francisco, 157, 179, 219, 220
schools. *See* education
Schumer, Charles, 270
Schumpeter, Joseph, 42
SCSA (Southern Commercial Secretaries Association), 29, 30, 47, 51
Section 8 vouchers, 307
Section 701 planning grant program, 16, 97–99, 103, 109, 193
sectionalism, 260–64
segregation: in Cleveland, 18, 64, 70, 82, 121, 122, 138; FHA Section 235 program for formerly segregated neighborhoods, 178; Forbes on Cleveland Clinic proposal as, 321; Housing Act of 1949 and residential, 125; of impoverished citizens, 324; national systems of, 124; in Rome, Georgia, 32, 33, 45, 185, 341; seen as surface manifestation in New South, 110; segregation academies, 201–2, 208; as visible surface of structural inequalities, 185; Wallace and, 244; white southerners continue to support, 198. *See also* desegregation; Jim Crow
self-help: in ARA, 108; in community development, 152; Conway employs, 156; Georgia Planning Enabling Act of 1957 and, 98; Goldwater on, 115; of organizations in War on Poverty, 4
self-liquidating projects: as difficult in states such as Georgia, 37; federal subsidies require, 14, 34; Hansen on, 77; RFC funding for, 68, 69; "worthwhile" defined in terms of, 71
Selznick, Philip, 22, 342

Senate Banking Committee on Neighborhood Preservation, 179
SGPB. *See* Southern Growth Policies Board (SGPB)
Shaker Heights (Ohio), 56, 63
shareholder value movement, 277, 337–38
Shatten, Richard, 303, 320
ShoreBank, 289, 290
Shriver, Sargent, 156, 159–61, 188
"silent majority": Carter's, 184, 197, 200, 203, 204, 209; conservatives claim, 242; Nixon's, 171, 172, 175, 209
Simon, William, 277
sit-in movement, 185
Skelton, Mrs. W. T., 195
Slash Pine APDC, 189
Slayton, William, 137–38, 141
Sloan, Edward W., Jr., 138
slum clearance: in Atlanta, 45; CDBGs for, 174–75; in Cleveland, 58, 66, 67, 69, 75, 79, 80, 120, 169; supply-side liberalism and, 81; FHA policies drive up scale of, 119; Housing Act of 1949 on, 124, 125; Jim Crow-style, 18; Keyserling and, 254; private solutions for, 69; property taxes redistributed for, 140; property values and, 80, 129; in Rome, Georgia, 45, 192–93. *See also* urban renewal
Small Business Administration, 109
Small Home and Land Owners Association, 62
Smith, Dan J., 311
Smith, Horace, 47
"smokestack chasing," 241, 245, 247, 278, 313
social democracy, 215, 253, 332, 347n7
social goods: "American way" for delivering, 15; Clinton on delivery of, 333; Hansen on cities and, 123; market-based solutions for, 13, 21, 216, 238; New Deal on expanding, 3; New Democrats on, 269; New York City's financing of, 215; progressives on decommodifying, 8, 332; Reagan on, 310. *See also* public goods
socialism: creeping, 89, 100; Merriam on, 76, 77; *Plain Dealer* editorial on public-private partnerships and, 87; Rose's history of Cleveland on, 87; of TVA, 36, 89
socially responsible investing, 280
social progress: business elites see themselves as advocates of, 147–48, 222;
economic preconditions of, 28, 44, 46, 53, 90, 103, 106, 107, 124, 154, 254; federal spending and southern, 46; incremental, elite-brokered, 185; liberals on the state and, 310; New Democrats on, 291; private-sector solutions for, 112; racial, 119, 139, 140, 185
Social Science Research Council, 78
Social Security, 274
social services: block grants for, 265; Bohn on Cleveland, 80, 122, 162, 168; in Community Action Program, 156; demand versus cities' ability to provide, 220; elites shear off costs of, 298; in Georgia, 256; Gray Areas program on, 155; poor people's energy channeled into provision of, 290; in War on Poverty, 4
social spending: on education, 292; Keyserling on economic value of, 254; liberals' commitment to, 231; New Democrats on, 21, 291, 330; Reagan on Great Society's, 310; rural voters' anger at, 246; slowdown in growth of federal, 309–10
social welfare: Merriam and, 76; New Democrats on, 270, 291; organizations in public-private partnerships, 156; race and discrediting, 267; Reagan and, 275, 276; state, 7, 13, 215. *See also* welfare; *and programs by name*
South, the: AFDC growth in, 272; antipoverty programs in rural, 189, 190; as capital-starved, 17, 19, 27, 81, 229; Carter's Commission on the Future of the South, 249–50; county courthouse politics in, 18; Democrats in, 8, 40, 43, 161, 189, 197–99, 244, 248, 272, 282–83; elites of, 39, 55, 181, 185–86, 189, 191; federal grants for, 46; federal spending in exceeds federal taxes from, 54, 260; foreign investment in, 207; industrial development bonds in, 313; New Deal and, 8, 242; in New Federalism formulas for funding allocation, 262; Odum on, 42–43; the "other" South, 288; paternalism in, 34; postindustrial policy in, 247–51; "post-racial," 183–84, 197, 241, 247–51; poverty in, 28, 39–40, 43, 44, 46, 262–63; pro-business politics emerge in, 82; racial exceptionalism in, 40, 191; Republican Party in, 199; right-to-work laws in, 91, 109;

South, the (*continued*)
  Roosevelt on, 10, 28, 39–40, 43–44; rural-metropolitan divide in, 250; in sectional competition over federal aid, 260–64; sit-in movement in, 185; suburbanization and urbanization in postwar, 97; supply-side state builders in, 91, 181, 183–85, 190; tax abatements in, 229; underdevelopment as "Nation's No. 1 economic problem," 28, 44, 46; urban renewal in, 16, 190–97. *See also* Arkansas; Georgia; New South; Sunbelt
Southern Commercial Secretaries Association (SCSA), 29, 30, 47, 51
Southern Growth Policies Board (SGPB), 241; in battle over federal funding formula, 261, 262; Carter and, 241, 249, 252; Clinton as head of, 288; Commission on the Future of the South, 288–89; on development and social investing, 291; on entrepreneurs, 277–78; *Halfway Home and a Long Way to Go* report, 288, 292; Keyserling and, 254; for managing transition from smokestack chasing to postindustrial economy, 247–48, 261; the North emulates model of, 260; as planning and research agency, 249–50; on the poor as underutilized human resource, 287–88; on federal funding for regional development, 250; on southern poverty, 262–63; Southern Technology Council of, 289
Southern Manifesto, 199
Southern Regional Council, 185
Southern Regions of the United States (Odum), 43
Southern Technology Council (STC), 289
Southland Academy (Americus, Georgia), 202, 208
Sparenga, John, 62–63
special interests: Carter and, 204, *204,* 257; Democrats and, 280; government seen as beholden to, 264; Knowles on, 335; John D. Lewis on, 22; negative attention to, 241; New Democrats and, 20, 21, 267, 270, 272, 276, 284–85, 293, 294; Porter on, 290; racialized battles over, 7, 20. *See also* interest groups
stagnation: Hansen on, 17, 41, 42, 77; Kennedy on, 107; marketized government avoids, 286; National Conference on Balanced Growth and Economic Development of 1978 on, 259; secular, 17, 41, 42
Starr, Fred F., 94–98, 100, 110, 200
state, the: American anti-statism, 342; liberals urged to democratize, 22; markets and, 282, 330, 331; Merriam on, 76, 77; mythically weak American, 331; New Deal legitimizes new forms of state capacity, 35; New Democrats' idea of, 329–42; private sector as model for remaking, 239. *See also* administrative state; government; liberal state; state building; supply-side state; welfare state
State and Local Governments Conference on Inflation, 214
state building: anticommunism and social-democratic opportunities for, 347n7; European-style, 67, 68; financialized forms of, 119; liberal antipoverty-oriented supply-side, 18; nationalization of urban public-private forms of, 14; New Deal and wartime, 27; urban governance as site of decentralized, 17. *See also* supply-side state builders
state pension funds, 291
states' rights, 54, 110, 199, 252
Steiner, Oscar, 133, 135
Steris, 320, 337, 340
Stillman, Saul, 168
Stokes, Carl: African American Clevelanders and, 146–47, 162, 163, 327–28; business elite and, 146, 162, 163–64; Citizens Participation Association of, 168; Cleveland: Now! program of, 162–64, 166, 232; Forbes and, 314; "Keep It Cool for Carl" strategy of, 163; mayoral campaign of, 146–47; on Model Cities, 168; Perk on, 166; public housing planned by, 167; reelection of, 164; as symbol of black political power, 213; on urban renewal, 144, 146; at U.S. Commission on Civil Rights hearings, 144–45; wins Cleveland's mayoralty, 148, 152
Stokes, Louis, 261, 314
Stuckey, William S., 188
Student Nonviolent Coordinating Committee, 146
Students for a Democratic Society, 155
subsidies, federal. *See* federal aid (subsidies)
suburbanization: in Atlanta, 93; bonded indebtedness in cities undergoing,

361n4; class-blind politics associated with, 249; in Cleveland, 80, 88, 121, 122; costs of, 79; need for social services due to, 220; northern industrial cities challenged by, 121, 214; in the South, 97; in Sunbelt cities, 121

suburbs: annexation of, 121; borrowing for school construction in, 216; business elites reside in, 18; CDBGs privilege, 175; cities as destinations for suburban recreation, 300, 302, 322; Cleveland attempts to draw suburbanites, 227, 228, 318, 322; Cleveland's business elites as suburbanites, 58, 80, 121, 138, 140, 146, 151, 166, 301; Democrat losses in midterms of 1966 in, 199; developers maximize profits in, 128; in "Dual Hub Corridor" plan for Cleveland, 318; equity planning and, 232; FHA focus on white, suburban housing, 118, 127, 133; individualism of suburbanites, 222; Kucinich recall funding from, 234; labor force growing in, 166; New Democrats flatter white suburban voters, 293; in New Federalism formulas for funding allocation, 262; Nixon's policies benefit, 153, 174; postindustrial policy geared to white, 304; "quality of life" politics in, 248; regional planning opposed by, 58, 79, 80; Republicans tap into anger in, 334; self-interest of, 79; share of federal aid increases, 226; regional resource sharing and, 81; in "silent majority," 171; small taxpayer frustration in, 244; Southern Growth Policies Board and, 241; suburbanites as disaffected members of New Deal coalition, 19; tax revolts in suburbanized states, 242; urban economic structuring focuses on, 137; War on Poverty funds sought to disrupt suburban elite control of city politics, 19; whites in, 146, 228, 334; White's suburban-oriented development plans, 326. *See also* suburbanization

Sumter County (Georgia), 208

Sunbelt: boom in, 227, 330; CDBGs privilege, 175; conservatism, 91; economic downturn in, 243; factors in divergence from Rustbelt, 18–19; Greater Cleveland Growth Association workshops of April 1978 and, 233; managed administrative participation in, 306; municipal debt becomes unsustainable in, 238; Nixon's policies benefit, 153, 174; poverty and unemployment in, 287; public-private planning institutions in, 304; Reagan policies and, 274; in sectional competition for federal aid, 260; suburbanization in, 121

"Supply Side, The" (Klein), 279

supply-side liberalism: African Americans challenge, 8–9, 22; American anti-statism entrenches, 342; bond markets relied on by, 335; building, 23–148; business elites and, 4, 5, 284, 311–12; businesslike reforms as inversion of, 298; Carter's state government reorganization and, 207; Cleveland elites and, 55; Clinton and, 6, 289; congressional appropriations of 1960s and priorities of, 112; contradictions and tensions in, 231; contrasting modes of political-economic planning, 16; converging interests between local officials and, 193; decentralism in, 5, 8, 101, 139, 140, 331; defined, 3–4; defining characteristic of, 10; economic growth emphasized by, 183; economists in emergence of, 40; elite, white male consensus undergirding, 116; as entrepreneurial, 268; fiscal frugality of, 119, 183; globalization threatens, 337; government spending as seen by, 21; of Hansen, 6, 216; at high tide, 103–14; in housing, 118–19, 125–28; as ideologically malleable, 202; inequitable outcomes from, 21–22, 119, 164; on innovation, 16, 106; insights on political economy of, 5–6; Jim Crow as not a concern for, 55; Kennedy administration as maturation of, 91; Kucinich's election as rejection of, 214; legitimacy of planning and development initiatives of, 101; liberals' social and racial imaginations limited by, 7–8; limits of, 149–209; localism of, 19, 183, 342; as naturalized, 284, 336; New Democrats and, 20–21, 284, 331–32, 334; new generation of Democrats reinvent, 266; in Personal Responsibility and Work Opportunity Reconciliation Act of 1996, 332; planning in, 75; political power and, 240; profitable conflicts of

supply-side liberalism (*continued*)
  interest in, 299; progressive challenges to, 8–9; public-private partnerships in, 140, 225, 231, 239, 331; reinventing, 276–82; Rothenberg on, 279; soft power of, 231; southern and rural businessmen as integral to, 114; structural subtleties of, 140; Sunbelt conservatism underwritten by, 91; supply-side fiscalism, 310; threats to in 1970s, 213; two sides of, 166; UDAGs as, 309; on War on Poverty as essential rupture, 173
supply-side state builders: alternatives to federal aid sought by, 13–14; anger at business domination of development missed by, 339; authority of, 19, 153; from banking sector, 338; broader range of constituencies sought by, 223; on bureaucracy, 50–51; Carter and, 182, 184; in Cleveland, 58, 85, 117, 209, 299, 326; coherence lacking in, 51; congressional appropriations of 1960s and priorities of, 112; federal subsidies and, 13, 129, 205; free enterprise championed by, 13; in Georgia, 188; on Housing Act of 1954, 125; Housing and Community Development Act of 1974 re-empowers, 175; Jim Crow and, 28; on Job Corps, 160; Kucinich takes on, 236; lobby for amendments to Housing Act, 133; in local and regional industrial policy, 15; local business elites as, 6; "maximum feasible participation" principle and, 152; in New South, 91; partnerships with the state, 12–13; poverty as fig leaf for growth agenda of, 262; press demands up the federal system, 241; producerism of, 12; Reagan and, 298, 307; Roosevelt commends, 49; small-city and rural, 48, 91; southern, 91, 181, 183–85, 190; on their pursuit of federal aid, 129; on TVA, 90; on urban renewal for revitalizing urban resources, 137; War on Poverty and, 162, 209
supply-side stimulus, 39, 77, 108, 254, 288
Sydnor, Eugene B., Jr., 224–25
Symington, Stuart, 105

Taft, Seth, 147
Talmadge, Eugene, 34, 37–38, 52, 93–94, 98
Talmadge, Herman, 94, 116, 244–45, 273
TANF. *See* Temporary Assistance to Needy Families (TANF)
Tankersley, G. J., 161, 162
"Target City Cleveland" program, 146
Tarver, Malcolm, 48, 49
tax abatements: budgets rendered precarious by, 13; in Cleveland, 162, 229–32, 242, 298, 304, 319, 321–22, 327, 340, 341; for saving struggling cities, 21; taxpayer discontent over, 242
tax anticipation notes, 218
tax base: decline in Cleveland, 302; declines during Great Depression, 59; Erieview project and, 143; prosperous economy for bolstering, 225; redevelopment for shoring up, 81; in the South, 40, 43; supply-side liberalism on creation of, 7, 14; supply-side state builders on remaking Cleveland's housing and, 117; urban renewal for revitalizing, 137
taxes: corporate, 166, 230, 238, 242; cuts in, 91, 105–7, 273–74, 277, 279, 308, 310, 311; Earned Income Tax Credit, 293, 295; income, 107, 122, 172, 229, 274, 293, 301, 302, 340; legal strategies to avoid, 279; raising to meet entitlements, 285; Republicans on confiscatory, 334; revolts over, 220, 240, 242, 264, 286; sales, 121, 172, 218, 335; tax-exempt municipal borrowing, 217, 312, 313; tax incentives, 278, 311; tax inversion trend, 340; user fees for replacing, 286; widespread anti-tax sentiment, 275. *See also* property taxes; tax abatements; tax base
Tax Reform Act of 1986, 312–13
tax sharing, regional, 79
Taylor, Keeanga-Yamahtta, 299
Taylor, L. W., Jr., 189
"technical assistance" programs, 102
technology: Advanced Technology Program, 336; transfer, 95, 278, 280, 281, 320. *See also* high tech
Temporary Assistance to Needy Families (TANF), 332, 333
Tennessee Valley Authority (TVA): grassroots participation in, 22; Harrington calls for TVA-style program, 261; Kennedy on, 89; Lilienthal's letter on economic development, 35; local, elite administration of, 36; as model for urban redevelopment, 123; Rome, Georgia, and, 90; "socialism" of, 36, 89; Southern Technology Council funding by, 289

Terriberry, Oliver, 187–88
Texas: Dallas, 179, 247; Houston, 121, 223, 227; Mercedes and Welasco, 6; San Antonio, 219, 222
Thomas, Sidney F., 96, 98–99
Thompson, M. E., 94
Thurmond, Strom, 145
Thurow, Lester, 240, 276, 285
tokenism, 17, 157, 196, 222, 299, 319
Toward Full Employment in Three Years (Keyserling), 254
triage, urban. *See* urban triage
Truman, Harry, 54, 124
Tsongas, Paul, 270
Turner, Ruth: on Cleveland as citadel of tokenism, 157; on Cleveland Democratic machine, 146; on community participation, 151; on liberalism, 139; organizes resistance to Housing Authority, 138; on urban renewal, 119–20; at U.S. Commission on Civil Rights hearings, 144
Turner, Sarah: federal-local public-private practices used against, 3; in HUD protests of 1976, 1, 2, *2,* 20, 180, 304; on more democratic community development, 22; at Neighborhoods Conference of 1978, 233; in political activism of 1970s, 213; as relegated to the margins, 5
TVA. *See* Tennessee Valley Authority (TVA)

UDAG. *See* Urban Development Action Grants (UDAG)
Unemployed Councils (UC), 11, 63
unemployment: among African Americans, 63, 253, 287; ARA on, 108; ARC's approach to fighting, 91; chronic, 162, 253, 311; in Cleveland, 60, 61, 63, 65–67, 162; Clinton on reducing, 288; Coosa Valley APDC conference on training the unemployed, 186–87; in Georgia, 287; Heller on German postwar, 105; Keynes on unemployment equilibrium, 41; Keyserling on, 254; long-term, 160; Merriam on freedom from, 86; pockets of, 107; PWA's impact on, 71; racialized, 110; Reagan on enterprise zones and, 310; in Rome, Georgia, 37; Roosevelt on federal spending and, 44; during "Roosevelt recession" of 1937, 40; Talmadge on alleviating, 116; urban redevelopment for reducing, 66; Volcker Shock and, 287; WPA for fighting, 27, 71
unions: African Americans and, 65; Coosa Valley APDC's wage gains for, 114; in northwest Georgia, 99; push for full employment, 241; in Rome, Georgia, 34, 39. *See also* labor movement
Union Trust (bank), 57
urban development: designed as short bursts, 14; enterprise zones in, 298; FHA Section 220 for recruiting capital for risky, 228; of rural areas, 184; slums seen as natural aspect of, 130. *See also* urban redevelopment
Urban Development Action Grants (UDAG): for Cleveland, 308, 322–23, 342; design of, 309; continuity across liberal development initiatives, 6; defunding of, 309; hotels use, 286; leveraging by, 298; Reagan and, 307, 309; supply-side liberalism infuses, 309
urban government. *See* city (municipal) government
Urban Land Institute, 123
Urban League, 64, 136, 146, 157, 253
urban planning: business associations in, 17; in Cleveland, 16, 17, 81, 82, 85, 162, 228; equity planning, 232; as mode of political-economic planning, 16; in smaller and rural communities, 184. *See also* city planning
urban policy: elements of 1980s, 324; New Deal works programs set pattern for twentieth-century, 14; Reagan's, 307, 309, 310, 312. *See also* urban development; urban renewal
urban redevelopment: Bohn on, 79; in Cleveland, 75, 165, 215, 227–29; federal investments become expectations, 88; in first- and second-wave industrial cities, 66; Hansen on government borrowing for, 77; Housing Act of 1949 on, 124, 125; New Dealers encourage, 80; in the South, 191; supply-side liberal agenda for, 119; Truman on, 124; Walker on benefits of, 123
urban renewal, 117–48; in Atlanta, 45; as big business, 128; borrowing for, 216, 219; in Cleveland, 129, 131–33, *132,* 135–36, 140–45, 162, 163, 165, 169, 178, 215, 319; end of federal, 19, 143, 151, 184, 194; FHA policies in failure of, 119; Housing Act of 1954 on, 97; Johnson

urban renewal (*continued*)
ignores, 154; local elites in, 144, 190, 191, 195; market-making potential of, 6; multiple actors in programs for, 15–16; origins as housing program, 193; pathology rationale for, 191–92; private investment leveraged by, 117, 138; racial inequities in, 138–39, 143–44, 146, 219; in Rome, Georgia, *31,* 191–97; as small-city program, 193, 194; in southern cities, 16, 184, 190–97; Stokes on, 144, 146; UDAGs contrasted with, 308; U.S. Commission on Civil Rights hearings on, 144–45; white-collar sectors focused on, 137, 138; white ethnics blame victims of renewal for its effects, 140, 144; "workable program" reports for, 193–94. *See also* slum clearance

Urban Renewal Administration (URA), 137, 191

Urban South, The: Northern Mistakes in a Southern Setting? (conference), 247

urban triage, 21, 179, 292, 298–99, 308, 323

U.S. Chamber of Commerce: Agnew partners with, 175; ARC opposed by, 113; on business guidance of poverty programs, 160, 222; on business's role as nation's producers, 225; Cleveland elite in, 18, 55, 58; Douglas's depressed areas bill opposed by, 104; on federal spending, 50, 51, 61; in Greater Cleveland Growth Association workshops of April 1978, 233; on Humphrey-Hawkins bill, 255; Johnson pitches War on Poverty to, 159; on Model Cities program, 223; among national business networks, 29; *Nation's Business,* 214; on NRPB's rights initiatives, 86; number of local chambers in 1929, 11–12; partnerships with the state, 12; on revenue sharing, 274–75; on Elias "Chino" Valdes, 222; on War on Poverty, 185

U.S. Commission on Civil Rights (CCR), 144–45, 151

U.S. Conference of Mayors, 158, 220, 308

user fees, 286, 302

Vail, Thomas, 228
Valdes, Elias "Chino," 222
Vandiver, Ernest, 95, 96, 98, 108
Van Sweringen, Otis and Mantis, 56–57, 60, 68, 322

Vaughn, Pamela, 206
Vindasius, Julia, 290
Voinovich, George: CDBGs as used by, 323; Cleveland Clinic plan of, 319; in Cleveland's comeback, 297; commission on neighborhoods of, 306, 307; consultants hired by, 303; on "Dual Hub Corridor" plan, 318, 321; on federal aid for local services, 305–6; Lexington Village project and, 317, 318; managed administrative participation by, 306–7; mayoral campaign of 1979, 237–38; Operations Improvement Task Force of, 301; Reagan urban policies criticized by, 312; reforms to reenter bond markets of, 300–302; tax abatements reactivated by, 304

Volcker, Paul, 277, 287
Voting Rights Act, 185, 198

Wagner, Kenneth, 95–98, 100–103
Wagner, Robert, 104
Wagner, Thomas, 301
Wagner Act (National Labor Relations Act), 43, 104, 152, 253
Walden, Omi, 190
Walker, Mabel, 81, 123
Walker, W. O., 83, 143
Wallace, George, 243, 244, 248, 273
War on Poverty, 151–81; activists emboldened by, 213; business elites and, 148, 221–22; Carter and, 182, 203; in Cleveland, 19, 164–71; enterprise zones contrasted with, 310; funds sought to disrupt suburban elite control of city politics, 19; Helms on, 200; Johnson makes case for, 154, 159, 172; local elites on, 158; "maximum feasible participation" mandate of, 4–5, 17, 115–16, 151–52, 154, 175, 177, 180, 183; Zell Miller on, 199; most durable and unexpected development of, 209; Moynihan on, 174; New Federalism brings to an end, 19, 151; Nixon and Ford and, 181, 203, 205; promise of, 147; seen as essential rupture, 173; seen as manpower development, 186; seen as war on business, 157, *158*; as short window, 340; Shriver and, 156; in smaller and rural communities, 184; structuralist critique of growth in, 19; supply-side state builders and, 162, 209; UDAGs contrasted with, 308; urban

renewal compared with, 194–95; U.S. Chamber of Commerce on, 185; white elites exposed by, 159; whites' caricatured versions of, 198; whites' criticism of, 115–16
Warren, Wilbur, 168
Washington, Booker T., 64
Washington, Harold, 300
Washington, D.C., 157, 301
Watson, Jack, 257, 260
Watts, Georgiana, 177
Waycross (Georgia), 92, 189
WCGAPDC. *See* West Central Georgia Area Planning and Development Commission (WCGAPDC)
Weir, Brock, 234–37, 319–20
Weissman, Sherwood "Bob," 166
welfare: activists seek to expand, 241; Clinton depoliticizes, 332–33; Clinton ends welfare as we know it, 21, 295, 329; Community Action Programs expand access to, 156; democratizing administration of, 213; economic development seen as replacement for, 7; FHA seen as expanding welfare state, 118; fraud, 271, 272; Georgia voters on, 200; impediments to access to, 271; Johnson on reducing the rolls, 159; liberal economic policies for sustained economic growth without, 90; New Democrats on, 276, 292, 299; new levy for welfare spending proposed in Cuyahoga County, Ohio, 62; Nunn on reforming, 273; racialized battles over, 7, 240, 264, 267; Reagan and, 7, 270–72, 276; reform, 292–94; rights, 4, 157, 252, 271–72; rural voters' anger at, 246; seen as disempowering women, 290. *See also* entitlements; social welfare; welfare state; *and programs by name*
welfare state: Colean on FHA and, 118; grievances over, 240; market and tax-base creation seen as component of, 7; Merriam and, 76; in New York City, 215, 220; Reagan on, 273, 276
Welfare to Work Partnership, 333
West, John, 248
West Central Georgia Area Planning and Development Commission (WCGAPDC): Carter and, 103, 250; in Community Action Program, 182–83, 187, 240; in Georgia planning commission expansion, 111; members ca. 1965, *183*; modeled on Rome's example, 186
Wheelis, Thomas, 198
White, George, 146
White, Michael R., 324–26, *327*
White, Walter, 9, 82
white-collar work: cities as destinations for, 300; in Georgia, 99; individualism of white-collar workers, 222; new generation of businesspeople in, 27; Southern Growth Policies Board pursues, 241; southern New Democrats on, 248, 249; unemployment in, 6, 72; urban renewal focuses on, 137, 138; in WPA, 6, 72, 79
white ethnic Clevelanders: on balanced budgets and low taxes, 86; Buckeye Boys, 164; Chamber of Commerce blames riots on, 145; Democrats supported by, 81, 165; eviction riots of, 62–63; homeowner politics of, 20; Lausche and, 81, 82, 84; leave Buckeye, 179; localist and racist fears, 147; Locher and, 146; mobilization of, 58, 88, 148; move to Parma, Ohio, 121; Perk and, 165, 166, 226, 229; populism among, 213; rehabilitation loans for, 179; in Rose's *Cleveland: The Making of a City,* 87; in slum areas, 69; Stokes opposed by, 147; Ukrainian Cultural Garden, 74; victims of renewal blamed for its effects by, 140, 144; voluntarism and, 60; Yugoslav Cultural Garden, 74
white ethnics: embrace racial antagonism over class loyalty, 147; in homeowner politics, 20; municipalities incorporate, 8; Nixon outreach to, 167; Rizzo in Philadelphia, 172; victims of renewal blamed for its effects by, 140, 144. *See also* white ethnic Clevelanders
Whitehouse, Alton, 304
white supremacy, 38, 51
white working-class. *See* working-class whites
Wicker, Tom, 198
Wigmore, Barrie, 283
Wilkins, Roy, 55, 101, 146
Williams, Napoleon, 182
Willingham, Osgood P., 45
Willkie, Wendell, 36
Wills, J. Walter, 64, 82
Winter, William, 288
Wirth, Timothy, 270, 276

Wirtz, Willard, 198
women: businesspersons with political clout claim to represent, 99; Carter on inclusion of, 184, 197; demands for empowerment by, 239; equal pay for, 285; feminists, 271, 290; microlending to, 289; minimum wage excludes many jobs held by, 40; single minority mothers, 290–91; wage work for, 271; War on Poverty empowers, 340
worker retraining, 280, 329
working-class whites: Alma, Georgia, Model Cities program and, 188–89; businesspersons with political clout claim to represent, 99; business producerism undercuts claims of, 209; Carter on segregation academies and, 201; in Cleveland, 20, 60, 88, 299; embrace racial antagonism over class loyalty, 147; growing alienation from liberal state, 139; in homeowner politics in Cleveland, 20; municipalities incorporate, 8; 1970s as "decade of the neighborhood," 232; as Reagan Democrats, 326; in Rome, Georgia, 33, 34, 45; in "silent majority," 171; supply-side liberal urban redevelopment agenda and, 119; at "town hall meetings," 244

Works Progress Administration (WPA): business elites use of, 71–72; Cleveland Chamber of Commerce members administer regional projects, 71–72; Cleveland projects, 72, 74–75, 79, 82, 87; Cuyahoga County, Ohio, projects, 74; establishment of, 37; Federal Writers Project, 87; Gainesville, Georgia, projects, 49; Georgia projects of, 6, 39, 47, 49; local enthusiasm for, 26–27; National Youth Administration, 46; Rome, Georgia, projects, 6, 39, 47; Rose's history of Cleveland on, 87; supply-side liberal commitments in, 4; takes over PWA's agenda, 71; white-collar workers hired by, 6, 72, 79
WPA. *See* Works Progress Administration (WPA)
Wright, E. L., 54
Wright, Gardner, Jr., 199

Yambor, Diane, 233
Yeilding, James, 129
Young, Whitney, 146
Younger, Paul, 151
Yunus, Muhammad, 289–90

Zeckendorf, William, 137
zoning, 98, 102, 193, 315

ACKNOWLEDGMENTS

I hope this book is worthy of the support I have received from so many people and institutions. For their patient assistance and indispensable guidance in the archives, I am especially grateful to Ann Sindelar, Vicki Catozza, and George Cooper at the Western Reserve Historical Society; Pat Millican at the Rome-Floyd County Library; Ray Wilson at the Ronald Reagan Presidential Library; Albert Nason at the Jimmy Carter Presidential Library; and, at Penn's Van Pelt Library, Girmaye Misigna and Nick Okrent. For sharing personal papers, stories about Rome, northwest Georgia, and the Coosa Valley, and for welcoming me into their home, I am eternally grateful to George and Irene Harper. In numerous interviews and conversations, many others also gave generously of their time and memories, and I am particularly grateful to Bill Gaskill, Wayne Hodges, Richard Hollington, Richard Pogue, Anne Rigas, and Taras Szmagala.

This project received generous financial support from a number of institutions, including the University of Virginia's Bankard Fund for Political Economy, Corcoran Department of History, Institute of Humanities and Global Change, and the Miller Center; the Gerald R. Ford Presidential Library; the Eisenhower Institute; the John Anson Kittredge Educational Fund; the Hagley Museum and Library; the Hoover Institution Library and Archives; the American Academy of Arts and Sciences; the Andrew W. Mellon Foundation; and, at the University of Pennsylvania, the Department of History, the Humanities+Urbanism+Design Initiative, and the Center for Undergraduate Research and Fellowships, which underwrote the fantastic research assistance of William Daniels.

I am grateful to the editors and interlocutors of a number of online forums and publications where I shared early research findings and refined a number of this book's key arguments and conceptual framings, including *American Panorama*, *The Atlantic's CityLab*, *Boston Review*, *Bunk*, and the *Washington Post's Made by History*. I published early portions of Chapter 3 and of Chapters

8 and 9 and the Epilogue in, respectively, "'They Were the Moving Spirits': Business and Supply-Side Liberalism in the Postwar South," in Richard R. John and Kimberly Phillips-Fein, eds., *Capital Gains: Business and Politics in the Twentieth Century* (Philadelphia: University of Pennsylvania Press, 2016); and "Supply-Side Liberalism: Fiscal Crisis, Post-Industrial Policy, and the Rise of the New Democrats," *Modern American History* 2:2 (July 2019), 139–164.

I have had the great good fortune of learning from many generous mentors and friends. At Hamilton College, my undergraduate mentor Maurice Isserman brought me into the field of historical scholarship, patiently overseeing my first research projects. Shelley Haley, Peter Rabinowitz, and, the late Damien Ellens, my dear friend, kindled my love of intellectual discovery. At the University of Virginia, I was fortunate to learn from and with so many, including the late Julian Bond, Michael Holt, Peter Onuf, Edmund Russell, Vesla Weaver, and Olivier Zunz. Beyond the history department, my outlooks and insights were immeasurably sharpened by the intellectual communities of the Institute for Advanced Studies in Culture and the Miller Center. My dissertation committee, Joe Crespino, Grace Hale, Claudrena Harold, and Guian McKee, deserve special thanks not only for their incisive criticism but also for the different ways they have all lifted me up at critical moments.

To Brian Balogh, I offer my deepest gratitude. He has been and continues to be a matchless mentor and model. I treasure our friendship and look forward to every visit, email, and phone call.

An upshot of academic itinerancy is the joy of discovering new intellectual communities. From Charlottesville to Brooklyn to Somerville to Richmond to Charlotte to Philadelphia, I have drawn from a deep well of generous scholars and friends. I am grateful to colleagues at the American Academy of Arts and Sciences, the University of Richmond, and the exceptionally collegial history department at the University of North Carolina, Charlotte. I have benefited from the support, camaraderie, and friendship of so many wonderful scholars: Jaime Allison, Nir and Miri Avissar, Ed Ayers, Megan Brown, Katie Brownell, Margot Canaday, Chris Capozzola, Merlin Chowkwanyun, Nathan Connolly, Bartow Jerome Elmore, David Freund, Dylan Gottlieb, Mimi Hanaoka and Shahan Mufti, Niki Hemmer, Ben Holtzman, Jenny LeZotte, Justin Madron, Andrew McGee, Sarah Milov, Rob Nelson, Laura Phillips-Sawyer, Emily Remus, Nicole Sackley and Eric Yellin, Robin Scheffler, Bruce Schulman, Mark Wilson, Leah Wright-Rigueur, Sunny Chen Yang, Joshua Yates, and Jonathan Zimmerman—thank you all. A number of friends and family members gave generously of their homes and couches, which made possible extended research trips and long commutes. My thanks to Justin Bain, Brooks Batcheller, Eleanor and John Billington, Julie and Scott Cebul, Eimear Goggin and Mr. Grey, Sasha Koehn, Annie and Dan Seidman, Fabrizio Verga, and Rae-Lynn and Steve Ziegler. I wish I had the space to name the many, many others whose friendship has kept me smiling over the years—but you know who you are. Thank you.

At all times but especially in the midst of a worldwide pandemic, I want to thank all of our wonderful teachers and childcare professionals, especially those at St. Mary's, the Parent Infant Center, and Penn Alexander School who managed to bring my children joy and a sense of normalcy in times that have been anything but. I am also eternally grateful to our 2020 parenting pod, Cecily Harwitt, Abe Tabor, Gideon, and (later!) Freddie Lou, our extended West Philly family.

The University of Pennsylvania has been a wonderful intellectual home to complete this project. The Design, Urban Studies, and Price Lab communities as well as the economic and legal history groups have been welcoming and inspiring. My colleagues in the history department have been steadfastly supportive. I especially want to thank Kathy Peiss and Ben Nathans for their mentorship; Sarah Gronningsater and Oscar Aguirre-Mandujano for their comradeship; Amy Offner and Karen Tani for their intellectual engagement and friendship even before we became colleagues; and department chairs Beth Wenger and Antonio Feros for their stewardship and generous support.

I was fortunate to workshop the ideas and material that became this book at many conferences and symposia. For their feedback in these and other venues I am grateful to Angus Burgin, Lizabeth Cohen, Gareth Davies, Louis Hyman, Suleiman Osman, Julia Ott, Keeanga-Yamahtta Taylor, Ben Waterhouse, and Sandy Zipp. A number of friends and colleagues have offered especially close readings and incisive criticism on the chapters that now compose this book. My deepest thanks to Michael Brenes, Jennifer Burns, Michael Glass, Ben Holtzman, Destin Jenkins, Richard John, Margaret O'Mara, Mark Rose, Bryant Simon, Jim Sparrow, and LaDale Winling.

Tom Sugrue went out of his way to help me prepare the early manuscript in order to secure an advanced book contract. At Penn Press, Bob Lockhart has been much more than a dream editor—he is, as one colleague put it, the hardest working man in the business. But he's still more than that. Bob also offered patience, counsel, good humor, and understanding as I white-knuckled an academic career. Noreen O'Connor-Abel and Jennifer Shenk delivered marvelous copy edits—any remaining errors are my own.

Kim Phillips-Fein offered a razor-sharp reading of the entire manuscript and helped clarify the project's biggest stakes. Matt Lassiter has read multiple versions of the entire manuscript, including, over a decade ago, a very rough research paper on Jimmy Carter that helped launched the whole thing. Matt's generosity, support, and repeated ability to zero in on what I'm really trying to say continues to inspire awe and gratitude.

This work also bears the imprint of three intellectual partners and dear friends whose insights, close readings, conversation, and debates over many years have continually sustained and replenished me: Stephen Macekura's brilliance is matched only by his gentle spirit and constancy; and Lily Geismer and Mason Williams, whose willingness to take seriously a naive email asking them to help me better define liberalism blossomed into numerous projects and, most important, great friendships. Thank you.

My greatest source of sustenance has been my family, whose belief in me, an often-bewildering source of grace, has seen me through doubts, fears, and failures. To Nancy and David Hooker; the Treppendahls; my wonderful and sadly departed grandparents, Cheer and Bob and Alice and Ray; all the Smiths and Cebuls; Kerry, Leila, and Rami; and, my parents, Mary-Scott and Randy, to whom this book is dedicated: I am profoundly humbled by your love and support. Thank you. My greatest debt is to Katherine Treppendahl whose love and patience, such patience, has kept me afloat, and who, through many moves, stresses, and pandemic lockdowns, continues to maintain our sense of true north. Words fail to describe how grateful I am to share this life with you and our wonderful daughters, Lucinda and Margot.